RELIGIOUS INTERACTIONS IN MUGHAL INDIA

Zoë High
2/2015

RELIGIOUS INTERACTIONS IN MUGHAL INDIA

EDITED BY

Vasudha Dalmia

Munis D. Faruqui

OXFORD
UNIVERSITY PRESS

OXFORD
UNIVERSITY PRESS

Oxford University Press is a department of the University of Oxford.
It furthers the University's objective of excellence in research, scholarship,
and education by publishing worldwide. Oxford is a registered trademark of
Oxford University Press in the UK and in certain other countries

Published in India by
Oxford University Press
YMCA Library Building, 1 Jai Singh Road, New Delhi 110 001, India

First Edition published in 2014

ISBN-13: 978-0-19-808167-8
ISBN-10: 0-19-808167-7

Typeset in Adobe Garamond Pro 10.5/13
by MAP Systems, Bengaluru 560 082, India
Printed in India at G.H. Prints Pvt. Ltd, New Delhi 110 020

Contents

Acknowledgments vii

Introduction ix
VASUDHA DALMIA and MUNIS D. FARUQUI

I Of Intersections

1. Ideology and State-Building 3
Humāyūn's Search for Legitimacy in a Hindu–Muslim Environment
EVA ORTHMANN

2. Dara Shukoh, Vedanta, and Imperial Succession in Mughal India 30
MUNIS D. FARUQUI

3. The Prince and the *Muvaḥḥid* 65
Dārā Shikoh and Mughal Engagements with Vedānta
SUPRIYA GANDHI

4. Learned Brahmins and the Mughal Court 102
The Jyotiṣas
CHRISTOPHER MINKOWSKI

5. Drowned in the Sea of Mercy 135
The Textual Identification of Hindu Persian Poets from Shi'i Lucknow in the Taẕkira *of Bhagwān Dās "Hindī"*
STEFANO PELLÒ

6. Faith and Allegiance in the Mughal Era — 159
Perspectives from Rajasthan
RAMYA SREENIVASAN

II Of Proximity and Distance

7. Inflected *Katha*s — 195
Sufis and Krishna Bhaktas in Awadh
FRANCESCA ORSINI

8. Sant and Sufi in Sundardās's Poetry — 233
MONIKA HORSTMANN

9. Hagiography and the "Other" in the Vallabha *Sampradaya* — 264
VASUDHA DALMIA

10. Diatribes against *Śākta*s in Banarasi Bazaars and Rural Rajasthan — 290
Kabīr and His Rāmānandī Hagiographers
HEIDI PAUWELS

11. Muslims as Devotees and Outsiders — 319
Attitudes toward Muslims in the Vārtā *Literature of the Vallabha Sampradāya*
SHANDIP SAHA

12. Mahamat Prannath and the Pranami Movement — 342
Hinduism and Islam in a Seventeenth-Century Mercantile Sect
BRENDAN LAROCQUE

About the Editors and Contributors — 379
Index — 380

Acknowledgments

This volume has been a long time in the making. As is to be expected, many institutions and individuals have made significant contributions along the way. The 2008 conference that forms the basis of this volume would have never come to pass without the generous administrative and financial support of the Institute of South Asia Studies, the Department of South and Southeast Studies (SSEAS), and the SSEAS Magistretti Chair, all at the University of California (UC)-Berkeley. We are particularly grateful to Raka Ray, Sanchita Saxena, Puneeta Kala, and Sudev Sheth at the Institute and Alexander von Rospatt and Gary Spears in the Department for their unstinting encouragement and willingness to help us overcome all obstacles. At the conference itself, the participants, most of whom have articles in this volume, engaged in discussions that were erudite and insightful, and always also cooperative and respectful. To our minds, however, no one stood out more than our discussants, David Gilmartin and Jack S. Hawley, whose gift for getting to the heart of an issue demonstrated their brilliance as well as deep familiarity with the Muslim or Hindu experience in South Asia.

Immediately following the 2008 conference, and from the time of our first steps toward putting this book together to the present, Francesca Orsini and Clare Talwalker have consistently and uncomplainingly offered us emotional support, intellectual guidance, and editorial help. Francesca Orsini, in particular, went beyond the call of personal friendship and scholarly camaraderie in assisting with the translation of Italian materials into English. Such kindness was matched by the patience, meticulousness and hard work of a number of graduate students: Aleksandra Gordeeva (at Yale University), Isaac

Murchie (at UC-Berkeley), and Nicolas Roth (at Harvard University). Without their various rounds of copyediting (in particular helping us check Sanskrit, Persian, and Braj diacritics) this volume would have been much the poorer. They, along with a remarkable group of graduate students—Catherine Dalton, Ali Hassan, Emma Kalb, Shraddha Navalli, Maria Packman, and Asif Sheikh—who participated in a jointly taught graduate seminar on religion in medieval India at UC-Berkeley in spring 2012, remind us of how graduate students enrich and shape the academic experience for all of us. Our gratitude for the final round of copyediting goes to Rimli Borooah who took on the task at very short notice and with very little fuss. She was a model of efficiency and good judgment. Ultimately, this book is dedicated to our children: Aynaz, Damini, Sivan, and Taru. May their mixed backgrounds always be a source of compassion, pride, and strength for them.

Introduction

Vasudha Dalmia
Munis D. Faruqui

The idea of bringing together a small group of people to talk about a period in subcontinental history during which religion experienced a dramatic resurgence came up in conversations, at first tentative but then increasingly intense, which we, the editors of this volume, began having soon after Munis Faruqui was hired as the first historian of South Asian Islam at UC-Berkeley's Department of South and Southeast Asian Studies in 2005. Over the next couple of years our discussions became deeper and more specific as we contemplated our individual areas of expertise as well as the respective gaps in our knowledge. There was great excitement in learning from each other; at the same time, we began to see that our conversations would and should be further enriched by the work of other scholars of late medieval India. And so it was that we began to plan toward a wider forum. This forum turned out to be a conference—titled "*Hunood wa Musalman*: Religion in Mughal India"—held in the Department in October 2008. The essays in this volume are based on that conference.

Guiding our 2008 conference was an appreciation of previous notable attempts to wrestle with the history of Hindus and Muslims in this period of Indian history. Among the most significant was a conference held in 1995 at Duke University. It resulted in an edited volume titled *Beyond Turk and Hindu: Rethinking Religious Identities in Islamicate South Asia* (University of Florida Press, 2000). This volume considers a vast span of Indian history, from the thirteenth to the nineteenth centuries; it aspires to cover the entire subcontinent, and it seeks to historicize diverse Indo-Islamicate identities. Indeed, its broad time span, geographical reach, and almost exclusive focus on issues pertaining to Islamicate identity are the great strength of this remarkable and innovative volume. Subsequent to our own conference in 2008, another conference, with a similar theme, was held at Oxford University in the summer of 2009. Many of our participants took part in this conference as well, feeding one into the other, so to speak. The proceedings were published soon thereafter, affording us the opportunity to glean yet more insights from the many excellent essays published there.[1] As we see it, however, the balance tends to tip in one or the other direction in both volumes. If there are more essays on Islamic formations in *Beyond Turk and Hindu*, there is more discussion of Hindu formations in *Religious Cultures in Early Modern India*.

We have tried to retain some balance between the two while maintaining a sharp focus on the nature of religious interactions, the theme of our 2008 conference.[2] In this volume then, we explore the dynamics of religious and social contacts, less in terms of "Hunood" and "Musalman" as two mutually exclusive entities, more in that of the groups which have now come to be classified under these two heads, as they reacted to and interacted with each other, while at the same time being acted upon, and responding to, a range of political, economic, and social forces. Our focus is on north India and primarily the first two centuries of Mughal rule, with all awareness that the boundaries in time and space that are thus drawn can only be arbitrary.

As the discussions at our 2008 conference so clearly highlighted, the changing nature of Mughal–Rajput–Jat–Maratha relations and their power equations greatly impacted Muslim–Hindu relationships as well as their understandings of each other. Crucially, memories changed with changing power relations. Thus, we pay careful attention to questions not only of memory but also to the nature of the sources we are drawing upon. Other questions that have variously guided us as we

[1] Initially as special issue of the journal South Asian History and Culture, followed by the book *Religious Cultures in Early Modern India: New Perspectives*, ed. Rosalind O'Hanlon and David Washbrook (London, New York, New Delhi: Routledge, 2011).

[2] We would have liked to include Jains and Sikhs in our discussion; this was not possible for various reasons.

worked on our respective articles included: How did political power and legitimacy relate to knowledge and knowledge communities, Islamic and Brahminical? What were the various communities of (religious) authority? To what extent were they textual? From what arenas did they emerge? How did the development of independent networks—economic, urban/merchant, ascetic/monastic—not wholly controlled or controllable by the state, play into religious configurations and their formation? How did cogitations at the top reverberate, if at all, at the regional and local levels? Did they circulate or linger (for instance, Dara Shukoh's religious interventions) even after they had ceased to figure at the top? Significantly, as the answers to some of these questions have come into sharper focus they have allowed us to more clearly appreciate: (*a*) the centrality of pre-existing and deeply sedimented historiographies in posing obstacles to new kinds of enquiries, and (*b*) the role of pan-Indian political, social, and economic developments in shaping religious trajectories.

Two examples speak to the first point. Any scholarship on the Mughal state's relationship to non-Muslim populations in South Asia must contend with a centuries-old historiography. In its most unsophisticated forms—more widely disseminated than ever thanks to the internet—this state is seen in one of two ways: an instrument of violence, oppression, and general mistreatment of its non-Muslim subjects, or a tolerant and inclusive entity, particularly during the reign of Akbar. The refusal by some historians to be drawn into what effectively was/is a religiously tinged polemic has allowed for a third orthodoxy to take shape: that religion played little role in conditioning the actions of the Mughal state which was a secular enterprise, whose only real concern was the extraction of wealth and the accrual of power. According to this narrative, religious invocations merely masked material concerns. Taken together these competing historiographical assessments have left little room for nuance. And yet, as some of the articles in this volume have noted, the actions of the Mughal state toward non-Muslims were varied—oscillating between cordiality, indifference, and hostility. There is wide agreement that understanding the Mughal state's interactions with non-Muslim communities demands more careful considerations of time, place, as well as the actors involved. Furthermore, the primary materials that address these interactions must be allowed to speak in their own languages if we are to ever adequately recover often-unpredictable relationships.

A second example of the challenges posed by entrenched historiographical traditions is how "bhakti" is generally talked about in relation to Islam during the medieval period. It bears noting that the period framing this book—the sixteenth and seventeenth centuries—was a time of major consolidation for a number of bhakti traditions in northern India. In fact, the Mughal period can be seen as the golden age of bhakti literature in the many vernacular traditions of the subcontinent. And yet, how often are bhakti and Muslim religious formations considered together, let alone as acting positively upon each other in contemporary scholarship? How often, for that matter, is Mughal imperial and sub-imperial patronage credited as significant for bhakti's rise in popularity or the vibrancy of its literature (especially hagiographical traditions)? Rarely. To explain this lacuna, we must consider the important role played by scholars like the venerable Ramchandra Shukla (1884–1941) who, although increasingly challenged by some contemporary scholars, is still widely considered authoritative. In his time, Shukla performed an enormous feat: he harnessed material still largely free-floating into the first systematic historical survey of Hindi literature. However, he and his fellow scholars—who derived some of their bias from Orientalist scholarship with its mistrust of Islam—saw the emergence of the bhakti movement (in the singular) as a direct reaction to the alien Muslim presence on the subcontinent and the sense of despair and inwardness (*udasi*) that Muslim political dominance occasioned in Hindus at large. Further, they consigned the more erotic aspects of Krishna bhakti to Muslim and, more specifically, Sufi influences.[3] Unfortunately these ideas continue to resonate in academic as much as popular discourses. Thus the continuing urgency of this volume and others like it toward complicating our understanding of Hindu and Muslim interactions in the late medieval period.

Speaking to the second point, that is, the broader political, social, and economic contexts shaping religious developments in Mughal India, we have been particularly struck by the significance of three powerful and

[3] Ramchandra Shukla, *Hindi Sahitya ka Itihas* (Kashi: Nagari Pracharini Sabha [1928–29], 1947), 63, 159. We need to recall that in the wake of missionary critiques and an infamous court case, the pastoral frolics of Krishna had come to be seen as suspect by the late nineteenth century.

interconnected phenomena—all beginning in the mid-to-late 1400s and picking up pace in the 1500s. The first relates to the gradual absorption of northern India's post-1398 regional kingdoms within a single imperial state. Although the political consolidation of northern India began with the Lodi dynasty (founded in 1451), it was the Mughals who completed the process. By 1600, the Mughal realm extended from Kabul to Bengal, from Kashmir to the northern Deccan. Even regions like Rajasthan that had previously only fleetingly accepted the power of north India's prior Muslim rulers were largely brought to heel. The consolidation of Mughal authority, it is clear, created a subcontinent-wide political context that no ambitious religious group could ignore. And yet, responses were rarely predictable. Where some groups willingly cozied up to Mughal authority, others chose to define themselves in opposition to Mughal power. Importantly, Mughal responses—whether to co-opt or attempt to crush groups—were conditioned by complex and never static assessments about the political strengths or weaknesses of individual religious networks. Because the story of shifting Mughal relations to, say, the 'ulama, the sant lineages, or Brahminical networks remain to be told, the significant intersection of political and religious developments remains underappreciated.

The second major trend from the late fifteenth century was improving communications and mobility. The rise of dominant imperial states in northern India played a central role in this dynamic. As well as engaging in conquests that slowly linked the disparate regions of northern India, the Lodis, Suris, and then the Mughals all worked to remove obstructive local toll barriers, build facilities (such as caravan-sarais and step-wells) along the major arteries of the empire, and engage in clearing and leveling projects that extended India's network of roads. A similar uptick in mobility in the lands and seas around the Indian subcontinent occurred from the late 1400s onwards. The emergence of powerful states in Iran and Central Asia, the Portuguese arrival after 1498, improvements in geographic knowledge and shipping technologies, as well as the rise of new or the strengthening of older regional and global networks, combined to expedite the trans-regional movement of people and ideas. Although recent, post-2008, works by Sanjay Subrahmanyam, Azfar Moin, Kumkum Chatterjee, and Nile Green have respectively offered us important insights into the transmission and rise of millenarianism and messianism in South Asia, the spread of Rajput cultural practices and Vaishnavism to Bengal, and the growth of north Indian-centric Sufi lineages in the Deccan, important areas of inquiry yet remain barely studied. For instance, relatively little is known about the massive transmission of Islamic scholars and religious knowledge between the Hejaz and Mughal India, the movement of Vedantic scholarship from the Deccan to northern India from the fifteenth century onwards, or the impact of dueling Maratha and Rajput religious patronage in centers like eighteenth-century Banaras. And yet understanding these and other lines of inquiry are crucial toward comprehending not only the development of individual Hindu and Muslim communities but also their interactions with one another.

Linked to the first two processes but also contributing to them was a third identifiable trend: the growing wealth of India from the late 1400s onwards. At the heart of this phenomenon was the simple fact that India was largely economically self-sufficient vis-à-vis the rest of the world. With the exception of horses and precious metals, India's import demands were few. In contrast, its capacity to export everything from cotton and silk textiles, to spices, to manufactured goods, to cut stones, to agricultural products was almost limitless. Over the course of the sixteenth and seventeenth centuries the volume of the world's gold and silver pouring into India steadily increased, fueling monetization and reinforcing economic growth. This wealth not only enhanced the military and administrative capacities of the Mughal Empire, its impact on the religious life of northern India also becomes evident in everything from widespread temple and mosque construction, the expansion of old pilgrimage sites, rising numbers of Hindu and Muslim pilgrims, as well as increasing religiously oriented textual production. Equally significant was the expansion of paper production and falling paper prices across India thanks to increasing demand for paper on the part of the Mughal administrative apparatus. To offer some insight into the complex interplay of these forces, consider the tremendous surge in both bhakti and Sufi textual production in the sixteenth and seventeenth centuries. These works clearly benefited from the patronage of a growing class of affluent patrons who were directly or indirectly linked to the Mughal state. Political consolidation, improved communications and mobility, and increasing wealth thus suggest powerful backdrops to the religious history of northern India between the fifteenth and eighteenth centuries.

***

One of the key themes to emerge from the essays comprising this volume is the intensity with which Hindus and Muslims interacted with ideas and knowledge systems associated with the "Other" and sought to accommodate them within their own vocabularies and worldviews. Crucially, these processes occurred in both courtly and non-courtly contexts. Eva Orthmann's article explores the Mughal emperor Humayun's (r. 1530–40, 1555–56) efforts to place Mughal dynastic rule on firmer ideological foundations by fashioning a new and ambitious imperial ideology that drew on pre-Islamic Iranian, Islamic (specifically Sufi), and Indic traditions as well as concepts linked to natural science and philosophy. It is clear that Humayun actively sought signs, markers, and/or traditions that echoed across different audiences. His wide-ranging efforts to associate his person and reign with solar symbolism offer one such example. Whereas the promulgation of solar-based Nawruz celebrations at the Mughal court would have resonated among certain India-based Iranian and Central Asian communities, Humayun's willingness to engage in imperial *darshan* (viewing) at sunrise would have placed him squarely within Indic politico-religious traditions. Other experiments—including enthronement rituals linked to the course of the sun and attempts to spatially organize the court to represent a cosmic order—simultaneously drew on pre-Islamic Iranian and Indic notions of kingship as well as mainstream Islamic astrological knowledge. Although Humayun has been traditionally dismissed as a secondary, even failed, Mughal emperor, his intellectual eclecticism seems to have set the stage for the even more dramatic and better known attempts by his son and successor Akbar to fashion an inclusive Mughal imperial ideology that amalgamated Islamic and Indic elements.

The articles by Munis Faruqui, Supriya Gandhi, Christopher Minkowski, and Stefano Pellò highlight the deepening exchanges between Hindu and Muslim over the course of the sixteenth and eighteenth centuries. Although Faruqui's article gestures to a centuries-long history of Muslim intellectual curiosity about Hinduism, its focus is on what arguably is the high-water mark in the middle of the seventeenth century. Under the direct patronage of Dara Shukoh (1615–59), eldest son of the Emperor Shah Jahan (r. 1628–58), inquiries about Hinduism increasingly took a breathtaking turn. Not only did Dara Shukoh and his acolytes claim that Hinduism had monotheistic origins, they also argued that certain scriptures like the Upanishads could offer insights on the Quran and, by extension, Islamic beliefs. Paradoxically, these assertions—largely derived from an incomplete understanding of Vedantic Hinduism—challenged deeply held Muslim beliefs that Islam was perfectly self-contained even as they sought to strengthen certain core Islamic beliefs. As with Orthmann's attempts to highlight a mix of personal and political motives informing Humayun's ritual experiments, Faruqui's piece offers a similarly mixed context for Dara Shukoh's religious inquiries. Ultimately, however, Orthmann and Faruqui depart over the place of the Hindu in the political imagination of Humayun and Dara Shukoh respectively. Where Orthmann sees an emperor trying to find ways to reach out to the majority of his subjects, Faruqui sees a prince for whom Hindus—if not Hinduism—were ultimately marginal to his larger political ambition to succeed his father, the Emperor Shah Jahan, to the Mughal throne.

Although Supriya Gandhi's article also spotlights Dara Shukoh's interest in Hindu beliefs, its central engagement is with a body of Persian texts that explored Hindu religious and philosophical topics. In some cases, these were translations of the *Yogavashistha*, in others, renditions of the supposed dialogues between Dara Shukoh and the Hindu renunciant Baba La'l. Given Gandhi's interest in the processes undergirding the production of these texts, the ways in which they interacted with one another, and their circulatory patterns, the reader is offered an invaluable history of Mughal engagement with Indic religions that extends beyond a narrower focus on individual patrons like Akbar and Dara Shukoh. Significantly, this methodological move enables two key lines of inquiry: (*a*) into the nature of Mughal religious cultures beyond the imperial courts, and (*b*) into the ways in which courtly and non-courtly contexts simultaneously influenced and were shaped by one another. This article's most important contribution, however, lies in drawing our attention to Persian's growing importance (between the sixteenth and eighteenth centuries) in shaping and then further popularizing particular threads—especially Vedanta and Nath Yoga—within Indic thought. Modern Hinduism was built on this critical but rarely acknowledged foundational work.

Christopher Minkowski's article focuses on learned Hindus, in particular clusters of Brahmin *jyotishas* (a category that included astronomers, astrologers, and diviners), during the high Mughal period. Some served Muslim patrons and engaged with Persian and Arabic scientific texts, others continued to compose works in Sanskrit. Crucially, Minkowski's piece highlights the ambivalence that often accompanied Brahminical engagements with Muslim rulers, culture, and intellectual traditions. Thus, even as some Brahmin scholars lauded Muslim patrons for their largesse and appreciated Islamic scientific achievements for their capacity to complement as well as occasionally correct Sanskrit-based knowledge, the Muslim patron was often also viewed as a direct threat to the physical and spiritual purity of the Brahmin as well as the capacity of the Brahmin to offer spiritual guidance to the world. Against this backdrop, Minkowski's article makes three important observations. First, theological differences with Islam—as opposed to the physical or political effects of contact with Muslims—do not appear to have played a significant role in fueling Brahmin disquiet. Second, the willingness of individuals or families to engage with Islamic knowledge systems did not necessarily correlate with physical proximity to or patronage from the Mughal court. Finally, Brahmin–Mughal interactions remained tenuous. Without interested patrons among the Mughal elite they were liable to extinction.

Although the collapse of the Mughal Empire in the early eighteenth century brought immense political and economic changes, the Mughal and post-Mughal periods were nonetheless marked by important continuities. This was especially true in the cultural realm. Persian's continued vibrancy as a vehicle for literary achievement as well as the joint participation of Hindus and Muslims in both courtly and non-courtly literary circles offer outstanding examples of this phenomenon. Stefano Pellò's article brings both elements into sharp relief. Focusing on the literary depictions of Hindu literary and intellectual figures (many of whom were Kayasthas or Khatris and from scribal families with former service links to the Mughals) in an early nineteenth century anthology by Bhagwan Das "Hindi," *Safīna-yi hindī*, Pellò points to the substantial ways in which Hindus—working in Persian—drew on both Islamic and Hindu cultural and textual referents to carve out a distinct poetic space within the context of Shia-dominated Awadh. As Pellò's article highlights, Muslim audiences and, more crucially, Muslim patrons understood and appreciated efforts by these figures to integrate Hindu cultural or religious symbols within a Persian literary frame. The religious affiliations of poets did not trump appreciation of the quality of their poetry, their educational attainments, and social rank. Men like Bhagwan Das "Hindi" (and most likely many of the Hindu subjects of

Safina-yi hindī as well) were cautious advocates for a religiously inclusive and tolerant environment.

If Pellò's article offers a positive perspective on intensifying Hindu–Muslim interactions, Ramya Sreenivasan's contribution—echoing threads in both Faruqui's and Minkowski's pieces—suggests an important counter-perspective. Sreenivasan's focus is on the tensions and anxieties that marked both Mughal and Rajput sources on the question of elite Rajput conversion to Islam. In Persian-language Mughal sources, for example, rather than celebrating conversions to Islam, there is a marked tendency to question their value. This is especially true when conversion is seen as linked to the promise of financial or political gain. Such conversions, it was widely believed, did not affect a lasting reorientation in one's religious worldview and, most crucially, political loyalties; they were thus of little worth. Another and more important source of Mughal unease, however, derived from the fear that conversion might negatively affect a subject's standing in existing Rajput socio-political hierarchies. Were this to happen, even if the individual Rajput's conversion to Islam was sincere, his political value to the Mughals would be compromised. Importantly, this was an outcome that the Mughals were loath to encourage. Concerns about standing and continued acceptance among the ranks of the Rajput elite are similarly etched into Rajput sources, both in Brajbhasha and Marwari. Such findings not only highlight the degree to which Rajput and religious identities were not only being continuously negotiated in the Mughal period but also configured within webs of power relations. In this world, being or becoming Muslim brought no visible advantage unless it was also accompanied by social acceptance and an acknowledgment of pre-eminence by non-Muslim Rajputs as well.

***

If the articles discussed above offer us different vantages on intensifying Hindu and Muslim interactions between the sixteenth and eighteenth centuries, other essays point to a second key theme of this volume. Simply put, it has to do with "fuzzy" boundaries—in Sudipta Kaviraj's apt phrasing—between and within the two communities.[4] Although

[4] Sudipta Kaviraj, "The Imaginary Institution of India," in *Subaltern Studies VII*, ed. Partha Chatterjee and Gyanendra Pandey (Delhi: Oxford University Press, 1992), 20–21.

scholars like David Lorenzen, Andrew Nicholson, and others have recently offered us examples of medieval Hindu communities who imagined themselves part of a pan-Indian Hindu community that sought to maintain its distance from Muslims/Islam, we would argue that this sentiment was the exception rather than the norm. The evidentiary record seems to support us on this point: it is much easier to find ideas, texts, tropes, tales, and even gods shared across what may appear today to be mutually antagonistic religious communities, Hindu, Muslim or Jain, than invocations of hostility or attempts at separation. A more interesting exercise therefore might be to explore the complicated forms that this sharing took and to consider the ends to which it was undertaken. The selective use of widely understood idioms (the Krishna narrative in a Sufi frame, for instance) often signals a level of accommodation that allowed for divergent readings while simultaneously addressing multiple communities. Importantly, it usually is one set of beliefs, already firmly in place, which frames the use of shared idioms and makes possible the absorption of contiguous traditions. The articles by Francesca Orsini and Monika Horstmann pay particular attention to this question.

In their readings of works from sixteenth-century Awadh and seventeenth-century Rajasthan respectively, Orsini and Horstmann both highlight the shared religio-cultural idioms made possible by the common linguistic base of much of north India, understood by most in its spoken form. From our vantage point, this common language is best regarded as a continuum with regional shades rather than under the fixed rubrics we use today. Although there were several "high" canonical languages (Persian, Arabic, Sanskrit), the non-standardized speech of the times—variously referred to as Hindi/Hindvi in the Persianate context and Bhakha/Bhasha in the Sanskritic, and written in various scripts including Kaithi, Nagari, and Perso-Arabic—enabled a degree of comprehensibility that worked across wide stretches of north India. The music, commentaries, stories, and tales produced by any given religious formation could then circulate freely across traditions, carried by itinerant singers and preachers.

So dynamic was what Alan Entwistle has called "the emotional variety of devotion to Krishna"[5] that swept through northern India from

[5] Alan W. Entwistle, *Braj, Centre of Krishna Pilgrimage* (Groningen: Egbert Forsten, 1987), 136.

the late fifteenth century on, that neither the eastern nor the western part of north India remained untouched by it. Even Awadh, astir in this period with a new kind of Rama devotion, in addition to its long tradition of Sufi practice, succumbed to and absorbed the Krishna tale into its own Sufi romances, with their dynamic fusion of regional and trans-regional literary and theological frames—of which Aditya Behl, Thomas de Bruijn, and Ramya Sreenivasan have written so eloquently. Francesca Orsini's essay on Malik Muhammad Jayasi's *Kanhavat* (1540) shows how the Krishna narrative could be so skillfully molded to fit into this Sufi frame that it could be read in both bhakti and Sufi registers. Orsini argues convincingly for a reading of this particular work as spiritual experience for all and as designed for performance in "an open arena of entertainment and exchange," in the *chaupal* or village square in a non-sectarian frame. This phenomenon was not restricted to eastern India. Christopher Shackle, Denis Matringe, and Jeevan Deol amongst others have similarly written about the fusion of regional love ballads and Sufi theology that surfaced powerfully in eighteenth-century Punjab, persisting until well into the colonial era, as Farina Mir's work has shown.

But this shared idiom was not restricted to the Sufi-Persianate adoption of Indic tales, landscapes, and metrical patterns. Other social and geographic contexts offered a different range of possibilities as we see in Monika Horstmann's analysis of a set of verses composed by the Dadupanthi sant Sundardas (1596–1689) in eastern Rajasthan. Nath Yogi and Nizari Ismaili traditions had long flourished here, and the language was familiar to the audiences most immediately addressed. The patronage similarly would be mixed: Sundardas enjoyed the favor of Hindu Marwaris for a member of their own community but also that of the local Qaimkhani chiefs, Rajputs who had converted to Islam two centuries ago but retained many Hindu customs. In the verses analyzed in this essay, which later tradition has seen fit to suppress, Sundardas integrates Sufi concepts within the *nirguna* frame of reference of his particular tradition, while also absorbing selective aspects of Vaishnava bhakti, and yogic practice. However, for all the mixing of idioms, Sundardas remains firmly rooted in his own ground, even as he reaches out to a variegated audience. This mixed idiom indicates, then, a level of accommodation possible at a particular historical and geographical juncture, even if undertaken for a specific end.

In contexts of widespread sharing, who, then, was generally considered the most reprehensible "Other"? Who provoked the greatest anxiety among adherents of a particular tradition? And how might the boundaries between self and Other be drawn? Vasudha Dalmia and Heidi Pauwels directly address these questions in their articles. They draw our attention to some of the deepest, if now mostly forgotten, fault lines dividing culturally and theologically aligned traditions. Instead of focusing on religious proximity offering comfort and succor, these papers highlight how intimate rival groups often worked extremely hard to emphasize differences rather than similarities. Inasmuch as this behavior seems to have been partially driven by real theological differences, competition for patronage and followers, as well as control of key pilgrimage sites and temples seem to have been important, if rarely acknowledged, factors. What is remarkable in these cases is that heightened hostility is mostly reserved less for the radically "Other" and much more for the broadly "similar." Thus, until well into the eighteenth century, we find that religious antagonism is more often expressed in terms of one *sampradaya* or *panth* against another and far less in terms of Hunood versus Musalman. The anti-Shiite polemics of Shaikh Ahmad Sirhindi (1564–1624) or the anti-Sunni polemics of Qazi Nurullah Shustari (1542–1610) recall the widespread prevalence of similar kinds of intra-community tensions among Muslims as well. Indeed, the large number of tracts denouncing the "false" beliefs of either Sunnis or Shiites compared to those directed against Hindus offer powerful corroborating evidence that Muslim elites in the sixteenth and seventeenth centuries were as obsessed as their Hindu counterparts about policing internal boundaries versus defining themselves against Hindus or Hinduism at large.

Vasudha Dalmia's essay provides a close reading of one case of "othering" undertaken in the seventeenth-century hagiographical compendium of the Vallabha *sampradaya*, the first of its kind in this particular community, comprising tales that were in circulation by the late sixteenth century. The compendium addresses a wide cross-section of devotees, of middling as well as lower castes. The demarcations that follow are directed at both high and low traditions: Brahminical authority and life styles as prescribed by the Dharma Shastras are derided with the same vehemence as folk practices. But the bitterest diatribe is reserved for the closely aligned Vaishnavas who often drew on the same repertoire of idioms, musical modes, and concepts. Material concerns are likely to have played a key role in making the Vaishnavas more dangerous than Muslims, who also figure here but not as the prime "Other."

This kind of antagonism toward traditions functioning in the immediate vicinity can be found in earlier periods as well. Heidi Pauwel's essay turns to the earliest songs of Kabir, that most famous of all medieval sants, to look for the othering peculiar to him. Contrary to the popular image, Kabir's vitriol is reserved not only for pandit and mullah, but also for Shaktas, often low caste and antinomian. Their pervasive presence in the low-caste milieu from which Kabir himself originated, makes them the most immediate "Other," although diatribes are also directed against Shaktas of Brahmin origin. Other hagiographical accounts of the life and works of Kabir, the late sixteenth-century Ramanandi *parchai*s, go on to address lower castes more explicitly; conversion by Ramananda counters the stigma that automatically attaches itself to low-caste religious practice, whether Nath Yogi or Shakta. The hostility toward Naths crystallizes yet more clearly in Kabirpanthi literature, ostensibly driven by competition for patronage as much as for a following.

***

The powerful centrifugal trends of the various bhakti *sampradaya*s in the period were, as always, countered by centripetal moves, undertaken by newly reinforced communities of Brahmins in Benares but also elsewhere under court patronage. Their focus on various shades of Advaita Vedanta as the unifying heart of what we know as Hinduism today seems almost to prefigure the developments of the colonial period.[6] The subsequent Hindu–Muslim polarization can perhaps be regarded as an inevitable corollary to this process of consolidation. The explicitly centrifugal practice of the premodern period would disappear increasingly with the advent of modernity, particularly as the fervor of the great reform movements of the nineteenth century abated. In the earlier period that we dwell upon in this volume, however, the pragmatics of coexistence and

[6] See the essays by Rosalind O'Hanlon, Monika Horstmann, and Christopher Minkowski in the O'Hanlon and Washbrook volume cited above, as also Andrew Nicholson's *Unifying Hinduism: Philosophy and Identity in Indian Intellectual History* (New York: Columbia University Press, 2010).

of the need for patronage and support would make for a flexibility that is increasingly difficult to imagine today.

The essays by Shandip Saha and Brendan LaRocque trace the beginnings of hardening attitudes toward Muslims in Bhasha hagiographies. Saha's essay focuses once again on the Vallabha *sampradaya*. Although the earlier hagiographical compendia of the Vallabhans treat Muslims as one of their many "Others," they also record the lives of individual Muslim devotees of the Acharyas, the most famous amongst them being Raskhan. As elsewhere in the Sanskrit and Bhasha literature of the period, they refrain from engaging with Islamicate belief systems, using ethnic terms such as "Turk" and "Pathan" for Muslims, but they also cater to the need for various caste groups to interact with Muslims; thus the Brahmin leaders of the *sampradaya* are depicted as readily accepting land grants from the Mughal emperors, and merchants in Muslim-dominated regions as freely entering into trading relationships with Muslims. Later hagiographies and tracts, however, become more explicit in their condemnation, particularly after the chief icon of the *sampradaya* moves from the Braj region and is installed in Nathdwara near Udaipur in the late seventeenth century. By the early eighteenth century, as Mewar once again reasserts its political autonomy vis-à-vis Delhi, the Mughals of the tract describing the move to Nathdwara are equated with Islam at large and their *mleccha* followers depicted as a serious threat to Vaishnavism and its practitioners.

The polarization that sets in during the eighteenth century ultimately has a similar impact on textual traditions of the Prannami sect, the focus of LaRocque's article. Rather than highlighting the efforts of the seventeenth-century sant Prannath to transcend established religious identities through an eclectic engagement with Vaishnava beliefs, Sufi mysticism, and Nizari Ismaili messianic and prophetic traditions, efforts are undertaken to obfuscate this mixed religious history. And yet, as LaRocque shows, Prannath founded a community that followed both Hindu and Muslim ritual practice and evolved a richly layered theology with radically different speech registers. Furthermore, only in this period of close interaction and more fluid religious identities could a liminal figure like Prannath win the kind of state support he so vigorously sought and finally found with the Bundela chief, Chhatrasal of Orcha. Crucially, Prannath's willingness to ally with Chhatrasal against Aurangzeb and the Mughals was never conceived as a Hindu reaction against an imperial oppressor driven by Islamic imperatives, but rather as an effort to fight an unjust sovereign who had violated the codes of conduct inherent in the holy books of all subjects of the Mughal Empire. In the hardening attitudes of the eighteenth and nineteenth centuries, however, Prannath's message was gradually absorbed within an anti-Muslim rhetoric and molded to fit into a narrative of historic Hindu resistance to Islam.

Such hardening attitudes among "Hindus" were matched by parallel trends within the Muslim community. Whether these might be traced to Aurangzeb or members of the old Mughal, urban-based 'ulama like Shah Waliullah (1703–62), the eighteenth century marked an important transitional process between the high Mughal period that preceded it and the British colonial period that followed. Although Pellò's article in this volume does point to significant continuities that persisted until well into the twentieth century, an increasing corpus of work by, among others, Muzaffar Alam, Sanjay Subrahmanyam, C.A. Bayly, Vasudha Dalmia, Heidi Pauwels, Najaf Haider, Abhishek Kaicker, and Vasudha Paramsivan does nonetheless suggest a world in which Hindu–Muslim interactions were increasingly in flux. It is our hope that a future edited volume exclusively focused on the eighteenth century will help clarify the context and outlines of these precolonial changes. The essays in our volume show conclusively, however, that the later religio-social polarizations cannot be projected without further question into the much more flexible societal weave of Mughal north India.

BIBLIOGRAPHY

Entwistle, Alan W. *Braj, Centre of Krishna Pilgrimage*. Groningen: Egbert Forsten, 1987.

Kaviraj, Sudipta. "The Imaginary Institution of India." In *Subaltern Studies VII*, edited by Partha Chatterjee and Gyanendra Pandey, 1–39. Delhi: Oxford University Press, 1992.

O'Hanlon, Rosalind and David Washbrook, eds. *Religious Cultures in Early Modern India: New Perspectives*. London, New York, New Delhi: Routledge, 2011.

Nicholson, Andrew J. *Unifying Hinduism: Philosophy and Identity in Indian Intellectual History*. New York: Columbia University Press, 2010.

Shukla, Ramchandra. *Hindi Sahitya ka Itihas*. Kashi: Nagari Pracharini Sabha [1928/1929], 1947.

I

Of Intersections

1 Ideology and State-Building

*Humāyūn's Search for Legitimacy in a Hindu–Muslim Environment**

Eva Orthmann

In a fairly recent article on the early Mughal Empire, Humāyūn's reign has been described as marking a transitional stage between a war band and a bureaucratic–absolutist state. According to this argument, Humāyūn was no longer a warrior king, as his father had been. Instead, he attempted to dissociate himself from his nobles and followers by establishing different norms for himself and them.[1] But what norms did Humāyūn establish, and what kind of bureaucratic structures did he seek to create? How did he legitimize his rule, and to what extent did his ideology anticipate later imperial endeavors?

In the following article, I attempt to answer some of these questions by reconstructing the religious and ideological basis for Humāyūn's state-building activities. Due to biased treatment in most of the source material, however, our understanding of Humāyūn is somewhat like a mosaic image in which most of the pieces are missing. I therefore begin my investigation with a short overview of the source material. I then turn to the three major

* The research for this piece was completed in 2011.

[1] Ali Anooshahr, "The King Who would be Man: The Gender Roles of the Warrior King in Early Mughal History," *Journal of the Royal Asiatic Society* 3, no. 18 (2008): 340.

pieces feeding Humāyūn's self-fashioning: pre-Islamic Iranian notions of kingship, natural science and philosophy, and Ṣūfism. Finally, this article will also query the importance of each of these components for the Indian environment and their compatibility with Indian ideas and concepts.

THE SOURCE MATERIAL

Humāyūn, the second ruler of the Mughal Empire, has been rather ill served by generations of historians.[2] This is partly explained by the fact that he never wrote an autobiography, unlike his father Bābur, nor did he commission any official histories of his reign, as several of his successors did. Most of the sources on Humāyūn were thus not written during his lifetime but in the time of his son and successor Akbar.[3] Consequently, it was Akbar's historiographers, especially his chief propagandist Abū'l-Fażl, who delineated Humāyūn's place in history.[4]

[2] For studies on Humāyūn, see Abraham Eraly, *The Mughal Throne: The Saga of India's Great Emperors* (London: Weidenfeld & Nicolson, 2003); Raj Kumar, *The Coming of the Mughals*, vol. 4 of *Survey of Medieval India*, ed. Raj Kumar (New Delhi: Anmol Publications, 1999); Ravinder Nath, *History of Mughal Architecture* (New Delhi: Abhinav Publication, 1982–1985); Shiri Ram Bakshi and Sri Kant Sharma, "Humayun (1530–56)," in *Humayun: The Great Moghul*, ed. Shiri Ram Bakshi and Sri Kant Sharma (New Delhi: Deep & Deep Publications, 2000), 1–76; Shyam Singh Shashi, "Humayun: Struggle and Success," in *Encyclopaedia Indica*, vol. 48 (Delhi: Anmol Publications, 1999); R.S. Avashty, *The Mughal Emperor Humayun* (Allahabad: Leader Press, 1967); Ram Prasad Tripathi, *The Rise and Fall of the Mughal Empire* (Allahabad: Central Book Depot, reprint, 1956), esp. 108–12, has a more favorable view on Humāyūn; and Douglas E. Streusand, *The Formation of the Mughal Empire* (New Delhi: Oxford University Press, 1989), 36–37, points to the importance of Humāyūn's administrative reforms. For a discussion of the sources on Humāyūn, see also Eva Orthmann, "Sonne, Mond und Sterne: Kosmologie und Astrologie in der Inszenierung von Herrschaft unter Humāyūn," in *Die Grenzen der Welt: Arabica et Iranica ad honorem Heinz Gaube*, ed. Lorenz Korn, Florian Schwarz, and Eva Orthmann (Wiesbaden: Reichert, 2008), 297–98.

[3] This is the case with the *Humāyūn-nāma* of Gulbadan Bīgam, the *Taẕkira-yi humāyūn wa akbar* of Bāyazīd Bayāt, and the *Taẕkirat al-wāqi'āt* of Jawhar Āftābchī.

[4] Nadir Purnaqchéband, *Strategien der Kontingenzbewältigung: Der Moghulherrscher Humāyūn (r. 1530–1540 und 1555–1556) dargestellt in der "Taẕkirat al-Wāqi'āt" seines Leibdieners Jauhar Āftābčī* (Schenefeld: EB, 2007), 31.

Against this backdrop, Humāyūn's rule is largely reduced to that of an inferior precursor to his highly regarded son Akbar.[5] Humāyūn's portrayal as a feeble and even immature king has also to be related, however, to his entourage's failure to appreciate the ideological and bureaucratic changes he sought to effect during his reign.[6]

To get a better idea of Humāyūn's intentions, one should turn to source material from his own times and thus uncontaminated by Abū'l-Fażl's interpretations. The only historiographical source written by order of the emperor is the *Qānūn-i humāyūnī* of Khwāndamīr. Completed in 1534, it describes Humāyūn's commissioning of various buildings and festivities, as also his many ritual innovations. Significantly, there are no descriptions of battles or conquests. It also offers little chronological data. Modern historians have generally dismissed the *Qānūn-i humāyūnī* as being of little value. It is therefore rarely used.[7] Its significance, in my view, however, lies in the fact that it offers critical insights into Humāyūn's mindset as well as how he wanted his imperial achievements to be recorded. In other words, Humāyūn did not neglect to cultivate his image.[8] Rather the image he cultivated was not that of a warrior-king, but of an innovator. Accordingly, we should turn to his innovations to better understand the transformations that took place during his reign. By analyzing their symbolic meaning, we can gain invaluable insight into the emperor's attempts to fashion a new ideological foundation for himself and, by extension, Mughal rule in India.

Any discussion of Humāyūn era sources must include two other sources: the *Ta'rīkh-i humāyūnī* of Ibrāhīm b. Jarīr[9] and the *Jawāhir*

[5] See, for example, Abū'l-Fażl ʿAllāmī, *Akbarnāmah*, ed. Āghā Aḥmad ʿAlī and ʿAbd al- Raḥīm (Calcutta: Baptist Mishan Press, 1877–1886), I, 13–16, 42–43; Abū'l-Fażl ʿAllāmī, *The Akbarnama of Abu'l Fazl: History of the Reign of Akbar including an Account of his Predecessors*, 3 vols, trans. Henry Beveridge (Calcutta: Asiatic Society of Bengal, 1897–1921), I, 40–48, 122–24. See also Harbans Mukhia, *The Mughals of India* (Malden, Mass.: Blackwell Publishing, 2004), 42.

[6] Anooshahr, "The King Who Would Be Man," 328–29, 340.

[7] Anooshahr is a good example for this rather derogatory attitude toward the *Qānūn-i humāyūnī*. "The King Who Would Be Man," 328, also fn. 7.

[8] Such neglect is postulated by Anooshahr, "The King Who Would Be Man," 328.

[9] The book is also called *Tārīkh-i ibrāhīmī* and was written around 957/1550–51. Charles A. Storey, *Persian Literature: A Bio-Biographical Survey*, vol. 1, part 1 (London: Luzac & Co., 2006), 113.

al-ʿulūm of Qāżī Muḥammad Fāżil Samarqandī.[10] Both were produced in Humāyūn's lifetime. The *Taʾrīkh-i humāyūnī* is a historiographical work that ends in 956/1550. It is interesting insofar as it provides some details about Humāyūn's flight to Iran.[11] While it does not contain much information about the emperor's ideological orientation, we learn of imperial visits to the shrines of Bāyazīd Bisṭāmī (d. ca. 874)[12] and Imām Riżā (d. 818).[13] This is significant insofar as it might point to the emperor's persistent interest in the Shaṭṭārī Ṣūfī order as well as his inclination toward Shīʿism.

Unlike the *Taʾrīkh-i humāyūnī*, the *Jawāhir al-ʿulūm-i humāyūnī* is a huge encyclopedia of science that contains only some historiographical parts.[14] Although the *Jawāhir al-ʿulūm* was dedicated to Humāyūn,[15] the history of the emperor's reign goes unmentioned. Nevertheless, the appreciation of science in the *Jawāhīr al-ʿulūm* and its emphasis on astronomy and magic give insight into the esteem in which these branches of knowledge were held during Humāyūn's time. Information about normative understandings of kingship and society can also be gathered from this text. Most interesting, however, is the chapter dedicated to *taskhīr al-kawākib*, the subjugation of the planets, testifying to the interest in magical practices back then.

Since Humāyūn was an initiate of the Shaṭṭārī Ṣūfī branch, the writings of the Shaṭṭāriyya also provide some source material for his

10 The *Jawāhir al-ʿulūm* was written in 936 or 937/ca. 1530, the year of Humāyūn's accession. Muḥammad Ḥusayn Tasbīḥī, "Jawāhir ul-ʿulūm-i humāyūnī," *Waḥīd* 211/212 (1356/1977): 34–35.

11 I consulted the manuscript in the Bodleian Library, MS Ouseley 84 (= vol. II), 296a. Since this manuscript is incomplete, with at least one folio missing between 294b and 295a, and an incomplete conclusion, there might be some more information about Humāyūn in one of the other extant copies available elsewhere.

12 An important Ṣūfī shaikh, to whom the Shaṭṭāriyya Ṣūfī order traced its origin; see below.

13 Mūsā ar-Riżā is the eighth Imām of the Twelver Shīʿa.

14 In this article, I quote from the manuscript of the Ganjbakhsh Library in Islamabad, No. 301 (Persian). The text has not yet been edited.

15 Khuda Bakhsh Library, Persian Catalogue, vol. 9, 144–45, http://kblibrary.bih.nic.in/, accessed August 19, 2011; Tasbīḥī, "Jawāhir ul-ʿulūm-i humāyūnī," 34–35.

reign. In the biographies of his Shaṭṭārī advisors, especially those of Muḥammad Ghawṣ Gwāliyārī, the emperor is mentioned, and some of their correspondence has been preserved as well.[16] Significant information might be contained in the *Manāqib-i ghawṣiyya*, a biography of Muḥammad Ghawṣ.[17] Sources on the Shaṭṭārī doctrine but especially Muḥammad Ghawṣ's own writings such as *Awrād-i ghawṣiyya* as well as his translation of the *Amṛtakuṇḍa* need also to be taken into account.

In an attempt to bypass Abū'l-Fażl's powerful efforts to mold Humāyūn's image, this article's insights are gleaned from the aforementioned sources rather than from material written in Akbar's time.

SOLAR SYMBOLISM AND THE TRADITIONS OF IRAN AND INDIA

One of the most striking features in Humāyūn's imperial staging were his efforts to represent himself as a sun king. His identification with the sun had a temporal as well as a spatial dimension.

The temporal dimension comprised the emperor's imitation of the daily and annual course of the sun.[18] The annual course of the sun was traditionally structured by the spring equinox, the day on which the sun enters Aries. On that day, the New Year begins, celebrated in Iran by the festival of Nawrūz. Humāyūn introduced the celebration of Nawrūz early in his reign and acted as the sun's simile on that occasion. According to Khwāndamīr: "The Emperor, protector of the world, like the shining sun, which by the light of its own presence provides to the sign of Aries the happy tidings of eternal exaltation, took on that day

[16] Muḥammad Ghawṣī Mandawī Shaṭṭārī, *Gulzār-i abrār: Tażkira-yi ṣūfiyā wa ulamā'*, ed. Muḥammad Dhakī (Patna: Khudabakhsh Oriental Public Library, 2001), 268–69.

[17] Carl W. Ernst, "Persecution and Circumspection in Shaṭṭāri Sufism," in *Islamic Mysticism Contested: Thirteen Centuries of Controversies and Polemics*, ed. F. de Jong and B. Radtke (Leiden [et al.]: Brill, 1999), 417, fn. 4; Scott A. Kugle, "Heaven's Witness: The Uses and Abuses of Muhammad Ghawth's Mystical Ascension," *Journal of Islamic Studies* 14 (2003): 4, also fn. 6.

[18] For a similar imitation of the sun's course in the time of Akbar, see Heike Franke, *Akbar und Ǧahāngīr: Untersuchungen zur politischen und religiösen Legitimation in Text und Bild* (Schenefeld: EBV, 2005), 224–31.

his seat in the tent of the twelve zodiacal signs and raised to the seventh heaven the ranks of a number of the court, the nest of imperial dignity, by the award of robes of honour and suitable appointments."[19]

However, one important detail of the traditional celebration was changed: Humāyūn shifted the date from the first of Farwardīn—the sun's entering of Aries—to the date of the sun's *sharaf* or exaltation,[20] which usually takes place on the 19th of Farwardīn. According to the *Qānūn-i humāyūnī*, this shift was motivated by the wish to avoid condemnation by religious scholars: "In the same way, the wisdom acquiring king celebrates a festival on the date on which the sun reaches its exaltation. He has dispensed with the ancient Nawrūz, as the latter day was observed by the Magi kings, and the followers of the orthodox faith have condemned the reactivation of their observances."[21] There might have been another reason for choosing the day of the sun's exaltation. As we know from more or less all sources on Humāyūn, the emperor was very interested in astrology. From an astrological point of view, however, the sun reaches its utmost strength not at the beginning of Aries but on the day of its exaltation, when it is "like a king on his throne."[22] For a king who wanted to imitate the sun, ascending the throne on the day of its exaltation was of very powerful symbolic import.

As well as marking the sun's yearly movement through Nawrūz celebrations, Humāyūn also imitated its daily course by showing himself every morning at sunrise to his people (= *darśana*):

19 Ghiyāṣ al-Dīn Muḥammad Khwāndamīr, *Qānūn-i humāyūnī, nīz musammā bah humāyūnnāmah*, ed. Muḥammad Hidāyat Ḥusayn (Calcutta: Rāyil Eshiyāt'ik Sosā'it'ī, 1940), 95–96; Ghiyāṣal-Dīn Muḥammad Khwāndamīr, *Qānūn-i Humāyūnī (also known as Humāyūn-nāma) of Khwāndamīr (died A.H. 942, A.D. 1535): A Work on the Rules and Ordinances Established by the Emperor Humāyūn and on Some Buildings Erected by His Order*, trans. B. Prashad (Calcutta: Royal Asiatic Society of Bengal, 1940), 70.

20 The sun's exaltation is at Aries 19°.

21 Khwāndamīr, *Qānūn-i humāyūnī*, 95; Khwāndamīr, *Qānūn-i Humāyūnī (also known as Humāyūn-nāma)*, 69.

22 Abū'l-Rayḥān Muḥammad b. Aḥmad al-Bīrūnī, *The Book of Instructions in the Elements of the Art of Astrology*, written in Ghaznah 1029 A.D., reproduced from British Museum MS, OR 8349, trans. R. Ramsay Wright (London: Luzac, 1934), 258 (§ 443).

> Every morning when the Jamshīd-like sun raised its head out of the garment of the heavens and put on the habit of blue satin of the sky, and the heavenly sky wore the golden crown of the sun, which adorns the world, on its head, and showed its shining face (*jabīn-i mubīn*) to the inhabitants of the earth, the king adorned his person in a robe of such a color as was appropriate to the day, and dressed in a new suit, he placed on his head a crown of the same color … and showed the face of the sun of joy (*ṭalʿat-i khurshīd-i bahjat rā*) to the people …[23]

By blending the metaphorical language for king and sun—the sun has a head, while the king rises like a planet[24]—the identification of king and sun is further amplified in this passage.

The spatial dimension of the sun's imitation is most obvious in the description of the so-called carpet of mirth, upon which the imperial court held some of its sessions. This huge round carpet represented the entire cosmos with all its spheres in concentric circles. The outer circle was the Atlas sphere, followed by the sphere of the fixed stars, Saturn, Jupiter, Mars, the Sun, Venus, Mercury, and the Moon. The sublunar elements—fire, air, water, and earth—were combined in two subsequent spheres in the center, with water and earth midmost. Each courtier was placed in a cosmic sphere appropriate to his occupation and standing. To himself, Humāyūn assigned the golden sphere of the sun. Sources indicate that he used to sit there "similar to the sun in lustre, light and pureness."[25]

The carpet was complemented by a two-layered tent which consisted of a dark inner cover with small holes in it and a white outer cover. The inner cover was divided into twelve segments representing the twelve

[23] Khwāndamīr, *Qānūn-i humāyūnī*, 72; Khwāndamīr, *Qānūn-i Humāyūnī (also known as Humāyūn-nāma)*, 51.

[24] *Ṭalʿat* usually means "ascendant," and is mostly used in the context of astrology.

[25] Khwāndamīr, *Qānūn-i humāyūnī*, 110–12. See also Abū'l-Fażl ʿAllāmī, *Akbar-nāma*, I, 361; Abū'l-Fażl ʿAllāmī, *The Akbarnama of Abu'l Fazl*, 649–50. For a detailed discussion of this carpet, see Orthmann, "Sonne, Mond und Sterne," 299–303; and Eva Orthmann, "Court Culture and Cosmology in the Mughal Empire: Humāyūn and the Foundations of the Dīn-i ilāhī," in *Muslim Court Culture: 7th–19th Centuries*, ed. Albrecht Fuess and Jan-Peter Hartung (London/New York: Routledge, 2011), 203–06.

zodiacal signs, and the small holes through which the white outer cover was seen followed the arrangement of the fixed stars.[26] Together with the carpet, the tent formed a three-dimensional mobile cosmos. This is the place where Humāyūn celebrated Nawrūz. It probably also served as the model for Akbar's later *dawlatkhāna-i khāṣṣ* in Fatehpur Sikri.[27]

Another quite remarkable instance of self-aggrandizement was the annual celebration of Humāyūn's accession to the throne that was called the "Talisman feast."[28] On that day, the throne was placed in the so-called *dawlatkhāna-i ṭilasm* (Talisman house) and the emperor sat on it from sunrise to sunset.[29] Since *ṭilasm* is the word used for amulets that are usually related to the planets and their magic potency,[30] and since we do not know about any (other) talisman or planetary image in the description of the feast, we may wonder about the role of the sun-like emperor in that context: was he himself the talisman, the representative of the sun and its magic potency? According to Khwāndamīr, Humāyūn also followed the movement of the sun, in effect, while sitting in other places in his palaces. Unfortunately, the staging is less evident in these cases.[31]

This solar symbolism had its roots in Iranian as well as Indian traditions. In the Iranian tradition, the identification of the king with the sun

26 Ishwari Prasad erroneously translates *burj* as "tower" in his description of Humāyūn's inventions. *The Life and Times of Humayun* (Bombay: Orient Longmans, 1956), 54.

27 There are, in fact, striking similarities between the concept of this tent and the building with the pillar in Fateḥpūr Sikrī. Orthmann, "Court Culture and Cosmology," 210–12.

28 Khwāndamīr, *Qānūn-i humāyūnī*, 86–95; Gulbadan Bīgam, *Humāyūn-nāma: The History of Humayun*, trans. and reprod. in the Persian by Annette S. Beveridge (London: Royal Asiatic Society, 1902), 30–35, trans. 117–26. While the name of this feast in the *Qānūn-i humāyūnī* is "accession day" (*rūz-i julūs*), it is called Talisman feast (*tū-yi ṭilasm*) in the *Humāyūn-nāma* of Gulbadan Bīgam. From the location and the timing, however, we can understand that it is the same feast.

29 Khwāndamīr, *Qānūn-i Humāyūnī*, 90.

30 Julius Ruska and Bernard Carra da Vaux, "Ṭilasm," in *Encyclopaedia of Islam*, New Edition, vol. 10, ed. P.J. Bearman, Th. Bianquis, C.E. Bosworth, E. van Donzel, and W.P. Heinrichs (Leiden: Brill, 2000), 500–02.

31 Cf. Khwāndamīr, *Qānūn-i humāyūnī*, 19, 29, 53.

probably goes back to the Avesta.[32] It certainly played a role in Sassanid royal ideology[33] and was later emphasized in the *Shāh-nāma*, the Persian book of kings. According to that book, the legendary king Jamshīd was the first to celebrate Nawrūz, sitting down on his throne at the moment of the sun's entering Aries, "similar to the shining sun in heaven."[34] The *Shāh-nāma* and its description of Nawrūz as well as the description of a huge round cosmic carpet might well have been a direct source of inspiration for Humāyūn.[35] It is not only the most famous and most popular Persian epic, but we also know that at least one manuscript of the *Shāh-nāma* was taken by Bābur to India and later was in the possession of Humāyūn.[36]

Given Humāyūn's interest in incorporating elements of solar symbolism into his courtly rituals the concerns of Islamic religious scholars regarding the introduction of Nawrūz were not baseless. As other evidence suggests, Humāyūn's interest in pre-Islamic Iranian and even Zoroastrian traditions exceeded the mere celebration of a feast and was closely related to his claims to legitimacy. His staging of himself as a sun king, however, points not only to pre-Islamic Iranian notions of kingship but also to the possible influence of Indian concepts. Such influence becomes especially manifest in traditions like the *darśana* which were unknown in Iran or the Arab world.

[32] Fritz Wolff, *Avesta: Die Heiligen Bücher der Parsen. Übersetzt auf der Grundlage von Chr. Bartholomae's altiranischen Wörterbuch* (Strasbourg: K.J. Trübner, 1910), 31 (= Yasna 9, 4); William W. Malandra, *An Introduction to Ancient Iranian Religion: Readings from the Avesta and Achaemenid Inscriptions* (Minneapolis: University of Minnesota Press, 1983), 152.

[33] Geo Widengren, *Die Religionen Irans*, vol. 14 of *Die Religionen der Menschheit* (Stuttgart: Kohlhammer, 1965), 314–15.

[34] Abū l-Qāsim Firdawsī, *Shāhnāma-yi firdawsī: Matn-i intiqādī*, ed. Evgenij Éduardoviè Bertel's (Moscow: Izdatel'stvo vostoènoj literature/Nauka, 1966), I, 41f (= "Jamshīd", verses 48–53). For the celebration of Nawrūz in the Sassanid Empire, see Arthur Christensen, *L'Iran sous les Sassanides* (Copenhagen: Levin & Munksgaard, 1936), 166–67.

[35] Firdawsī, *Shāh-nāma-yi firdawsī*, IX, 225, 3596–609.

[36] Eleanor Sims, "The Illustrated Manuscripts of Firdausī's 'Shāhnāma' Commissioned by Princes of the House of Tīmūr," *Ars Orientalis* 22 (1992): 48; for manuscripts of the *Shāh-nāma* in Indian libraries see also "Shahnama Project," http://shahnama.caret.cam.ac.uk/new/jnama/index/collection/fecountry: India, accessed August 21, 2011.

In ancient India, the king was regarded as a deva, a mighty being with supernatural powers, related equally to the sun and moon, and sometimes worshipped like the sun.[37] As Ronald Inden has shown, this connection persisted through early medieval times.[38] At the advent of Mughal rule in the 1520s, the kings of the Sīsodiyā dynasty still claimed direct descent from the sun. They also practiced the ancient tradition of the *darśana* ritual by showing themselves in the morning to their subjects.[39] Humāyūn may have been inspired by their practice, if he did not follow a prior Indo-Muslim rulers' custom.

The annual celebration of the day of enthronement was also a well-known festival in India.[40] The symbolism of the throne as the seat of the sun—important for the celebration of Nawrūz as well as for the celebration of the enthronement day—was deeply rooted in the Indian tradition and perhaps even more elaborated than in Iran. We thus read that the throne was not only identified with the seat on which Aditya, the sun, was anointed,[41] but was also put on a golden pillar which was raised every day until noon and then brought down again, imitating the movement of the sun.[42] Humāyūn's efforts to imitate the sun's course were therefore not alien to his Indian subjects, but well understood in their own tradition.

One further ceremonial with no background in the Iranian tradition should be taken into consideration here, namely the so-called *tulā puruṣa*

[37] Jan Gonda, "The Sacred Character of Ancient Indian Kingship," in *La Regalita Sacra: Contributi al tema dell' VIII Congresso Internat. Di Storia delle Religioni (Roma, Aprile 1955) = The Sacral Kingship* (Leiden: Brill, 1959), 172–73; Jan Gonda, "Ancient Indian Kingship from the Religious Point of View," *Numen* 4, fasc. 1 (1957): 32.

[38] Ronald Inden, "Ritual, Authority, and Cyclic Time in Hindu Kingship," in *Kingship and Authority in South Asia*, ed. J.F. Richards (New Delhi [et al.]: Oxford University Press, reprint, 1998), 46, 50.

[39] Franke, *Akbar und Ǧahāngīr*, 231; Gonda, "Ancient Indian Kingship," 30; Inden, "Ritual, Authority and Cyclic Time," 74. For the importance of *darśana* in India, see Diana L. Eck, *Darshan: Seeing the Divine Image in India* (New York: Columbia University Press, 1998), esp. 3–10.

[40] Inden, "Ritual, Authority and Cyclic Time," 56.

[41] Gonda, "The Sacred Character," 178.

[42] Jeannine Auboyer, "Le caractère royal et divin du trône dans l'Inde Ancienne," in *La Regalita Sacra*, 183.

or weighing ceremonial, which was again related to the sun. For this ceremonial the king was put on a huge scale and weighed in gold. Afterwards, the gold was handed over to the Brahmins who distributed it among the deserving poor. The *tulā puruṣa* was one of the great gifts, or *mahādāna*, of Hindu kings. The ritual was meant to establish their imperial sovereignty.[43] According to the *Matsya Mahāpurāṇa*, one of the ancient Purāṇas of the Indian tradition where this ritual has been described,[44] the kings held the image of the sun in their hands while sitting on the scales; they were expected to become "illustrious like the sun" by the performance of this ritual.[45] We find evidence of Humāyūn performing this very ritual on his birthday.[46] Given the solar symbolism of the ritual, its adoption is in line with the emperor's general imperial staging; it is not known if its Hindu origins were of any significance.

PHILOSOPHY AND COSMOLOGY

Ancient symbols of royalty derived from Iranian, Hindu, or Indo-Muslim traditions were not the only source of inspiration for Humāyūn. All sources agree that he was very well versed in natural science and philosophy as well. They emphasize his interest in astronomy, astrology, and cosmology.[47] This interest is strikingly reflected in the administrative

[43] Inden, "Ritual, Authority, and Cyclic Time," 55; K.L. Joshi, ed., *Matsya Mahāpurāṇa: An Exhaustive Introduction, Sanskrit Text, English Translation, Scholarly Notes and Index of Verses*, no. 93 of *Parimal Sanskrit Series* (Delhi: Parimal Publications, 2007), II, 431–37 (= chapter 274).

[44] The *Matsya Mahāpurāṇa* is the sixteenth Purāṇa of the Hindu tradition, earning its title to the fish incarnation of Vishnu. Joshi, *Matsya Mahāpurāṇa*, I, "Introduction," xv, xxix.

[45] Joshi, *Matsya Mahāpurāṇa*, II, 437. According to Shanti Lal Nagar, other hints at a solar cult are also found in the *Matsya Mahāpurāṇa*. Joshi, *Matsya Mahāpurāṇa*, I, "Introduction," xxxi–xxxiii.

[46] Khwāndamīr, *Qānūn-i humāyūnī*, 105.

[47] ʿAllāmī, *Akbar-nāma*, I, 363–64; ʿAllāmī, *The Akbarnama of Abu'l Fazl*, I, 656–57; Muhammad Qāsim Firishta, *Tarikh-i-Firishta: Or History of the Rise of the Mahomedan Power in India till the year A.D. 1612*, ed. John Briggs (Bombay: Government College Press, 1831), 397; Muhammad Qāsim Firishta, *History of the Rise of the Mahomedan Power in India till the year A.D. 1612*, trans. J. Briggs (New Delhi: Low Price Publications, 1990, repr. from 1829), II, 44;

classifications elaborated by the king. Thanks to the details provided by Khwāndamīr, it is possible to reconstruct two different classification systems that were somehow interwoven. Both systems can ultimately be traced back to Aristotle, even as they have Indian echoes.

The first classification is a comprehensive attempt to divide all people into three categories. According to the *Qānūn-i humāyūnī*, Humāyūn once decided on his way from Kabul to Qandahar to consider the names of the next three people he met as omens. Afterwards, he took their names as the basis for ordering all people living in his realm into three broad groups: the *ahl-i sa'ādat* (people of happiness), the *ahl-i dawlat* (people of governance), and the *ahl-i murād* (people of desire). To the *ahl-i dawlat* belonged his brothers and relatives, the ministers, the military leaders, and the cavalry. The *ahl-i sa'ādat* consisted of religious scholars, judges, wise men, Sayyids, and other respected persons. Musicians and painters were among the *ahl-i murād*.[48]

The importance Humāyūn attached to this classification scheme is suggested by his decision to dedicate two days per week to each of them: Saturday and Thursday to the *ahl-i sa'ādat*, Sunday and Tuesday to the *ahl-i dawlat*, and Monday and Wednesday to the *ahl-i murād*. On these days, the respective groups were granted audiences at court, and activities related to their responsibilities were carried out.[49] But the system also permeated the order of buildings and encampments: in the above mentioned Talisman house, a specifically equipped room was dedicated to each of these three divisions, and distinct tents were likewise erected for them.[50] At festivals and audiences as well as at the distribution of presents, the three groups are always mentioned as separate entities.[51]

Sayyidī 'Alī Ra'īs, *The Travels and Adventures of the Turkish Admiral Sidi Ali Reïs in India, Afghanistan, Central Asia and Persia during the Years 1553–1556*, ed. and trans. Á. Vambéry (London: Luzac, 1899), 48–49; Avashty, *The Mughal Emperor Humayun*, 23–24; Bakshi and Sharma, *Humayun*, 32.

48 Khwāndamīr, *Qānūn-i humāyūnī*, 31–36; 'Allāmī, *Akbarnāmah*, I, 357–59.

49 Khwāndamīr, *Qānūn-i humāyūnī*, 36–38.

50 Cf. Khwāndamīr, *Qānūn-i humāyūnī*, 58–59, 103; Gulbadan Bīgam, *Humāyūn-nāma*, 33–34, trans. 124.

51 Khwāndamīr, *Qānūn-i humāyūnī*, 95, 104; Gulbadan Bīgam, *Humāyūn-nāma*, 34; trans. 124–25.

Their respective principals received golden arrows symbolizing the three astrological lots: *sahm-i saʿādat, sahm-i dawla*, and *sahm-i murād*.[52]

While this classification may seem somewhat odd at first glance,[53] it was not "invented" by Humāyūn, as Khwāndamīr wants us to believe, but had earlier roots. Thus we find a similar tripartite classification in Aristotle's *Nicomachean Ethics*. Accordingly, the three groups are those who identify the Good with pleasure, who are content with a life of enjoyment; those who believe that the Good consists of honor and virtue, who strive for a life of politics; and those living a life of contemplation.[54] While the Aristotelian terminology for the first two groups is quite similar to Humāyūn's *ahl-i murād* and *ahl-i dawlat*, the designation of the third group is different. However, since—according to Aristotle—people belonging to the third group achieve complete happiness, which is the ultimate aim of humanity, it makes sense to see congruence with the *ahl-i saʿādat*. Humāyūn's classifications as well as his terminology are therefore in line with the Aristotelian model. Since the *Nicomachean Ethics* had been translated into Arabic at an early date,[55] and since its influence can be traced in Islamic philosophy,[56] Humāyūn probably was aware of Aristotle's threefold division and likely was inspired by it. This idea is reinforced by the fact that no previous Muslim ruler is noted for subdividing society along the very same lines.

The idea of subdividing all people into different classes or castes is of course deeply rooted in the Indian tradition. The primary caste system is, however, a fourfold system consisting of four varnas, and it is not

[52] Khwāndamīr, *Qānūn-i humāyūnī*, 39–40; Abū'l-Rayḥān Muḥammad b. Aḥmad al-Bīrūnī, *al-Tafhīm lī-avāʾil ṣināʿat al-tanjīm*, ed. Jalāl al-Dīn Humāʾī (Tehran: Wizārat-i farhang, 1316–18 hijri shamsi), 476.

[53] See, for example, Anooshahr, "The King Who would be Man," 328.

[54] Aristotle, *The Nicomachean Ethics*, trans. David Ross, rev. J.L. Ackrill and J.O. Urmson (Oxford: Oxford University Press, 1980), I, 5; Anna A. Akasoy and Alexander Fidora, eds, *The Arabic Version of the Nicomachean Ethics*, trans. Douglas M. Dunlop (Leiden: Brill, 2005), 120–23.

[55] Douglas M. Dunlop, "The Nicomachean Ethics in Arabic, Books I–VI," *Oriens* 15 (1962): 18; Douglas M. Dunlop, "Introduction," in Akasoy and Fidora, *The Arabic Version of the Nicomachean Ethics*, 6–11; Majid Fakhry, *Ethical Theories in Islam* (Leiden: Brill, 1994), 65.

[56] Fakhry, *Ethical Theories*, esp. 65–66, 78–92; Dunlop, "Introduction," 11–55.

possible to correlate the *ahl-i saʿādat, ahl-i dawlat*, and *ahl-i murād* to them. The same is true of the four canonical aims of human life, the *puruṣārthas* (*kāma, artha, dharma*, and *mokṣa*).[57] Therefore, only the general idea of subdivision fits into the Indian context. The actual division, however, does not correlate with any Indian model.

Compared to the first system of classification Humāyūn's second one was less broad, referring only to people related to the court and the government. It was based on Aristotelian cosmology. According to that model, which was taken over by Islamic natural philosophy, the entire cosmos is composed of concentric spheres. The innermost spheres consist of the four elementary spheres, that is, earth, water, air, and fire. These are followed by the planetary spheres, the sphere of the fixed stars, and the so-called Atlas sphere.

This spherical model was imitated in the composition of Humāyūn's administration by assigning specific groups to each of the spheres. We thus find (*a*) "elementary" people, who are related to earth, water, air, or fire, (*b*) "planetary" people, who are related to one of the seven planets, and (*c*) "zodiacal" people, who were related to the twelve zodiacal signs of the sphere of the fixed stars. Only the Atlas sphere was left out, maybe because it is beyond the observable realm.[58] All people fulfilled specific duties related to their element or planet. People connected with water, for example, were responsible for the wine cellar and the digging of canals.[59] The zodiacal classification was materialized in the *majlis*, when all attendants were seated on the cosmic carpet, each group in its respective sphere. It was on these occasions that the emperor sat in the sphere of the sun.[60]

Unlike the first classification, with its likely origins in the *Nicomachean Ethics*, this second classification has at least partially been described in Islamic works on ethics and statecraft before Humāyūn. In his *Akhlāq-i nāṣirī*, Ṭūsī thus proposed to assign certain groups of people to the four

[57] Axel Michaels, *Hinduismus: Geschichte und Gegenwart* (München: Beck, 1998), 108, table 8.

[58] Orthmann, "Court Culture and Cosmology," 205–06.

[59] Khwāndamīr, *Qānūn-i humāyūnī*, 48–50; ʿAllāmī, *Akbarnāmah*, I, 359–60.

[60] Khwāndamīr, *Qānūn-i humāyūnī*, 110–12; see also ʿAllāmī, *Akbarnāmah*, I, 361; Beveridge, trans., *The Akbarnama of Abu'l Fazl*, I, 649–50.

elements—earth, water, air, and fire.[61] The *Akhlāq-i nāṣirī* had been well known in the Timurid realm and had also been appreciated by Bābur for whom an abridged version was provided.[62] Later, the reading of the *Akhlāq* was highly recommended to Mughal officials.[63] In all probability, Humāyūn too was well aware of Ṭūsī's writings. The concept of a correlation between the elements and various groups of people therefore probably traces back to Ṭūsī, even if the actual correlations differ.[64]

The idea of such a classification might, however, have also been inspired by Humāyūn's interest in astrology. The allocation of specific professions and groups of people to the seven planets and the zodiacal signs was a very common phenomenon in astrology. Lists of correlations exist in many major astrological treatises, for example in the *Tafhīm* of al-Bīrūnī[65] or the *Rawżat al-munajjimīn*.[66] The twelfth-century Persian poet Niẓāmī can also be seen working through these notions in his epic poem *Haft Paykar*, where, upon the advice of a wise man and astrologer, the king Bahrām builds a palace with seven domes, each dedicated to one planet and built according to its nature. He then spends each day in the dome assigned to the respective dominant planet: on Saturday, for example, he sits in the dome of Saturn.[67] Humāyūn might very well have been inspired by this epic, since he not only chose astral criteria to classify his attendants but also built a similar palace with seven domes. Quite analogously to Bahrām in Niẓāmī's epic, he ran his affairs each

[61] Nāṣir ad-Dīn Ṭūsī, *Akhlāq-i nāṣirī*, ed. Mujtaba'ī Mīnuvī (Tehran: Shirkat-i Sihāmī-i Intishārāt-i Khwārazmī, 1369), 305.

[62] Muzaffar Alam, *The Languages of Political Islam: India 1200–1800* (Chicago: University of Chicago Press, 2004), 50–53.

[63] Alam, *The Languages of Political Islam*, 61.

[64] It would be interesting to examine this correlation in the *Akhlāq-i humāyūnī*, the abridged version of the *Akhlāq-i nāṣirī* provided for Bābur too. This text has not been consulted.

[65] al-Bīrūnī, *Tafhīm*, 362–64, 431–32, 435.

[66] Shahmardān b. Abī l-Khair Rāżī, *Rawżat al-munajjimīn*, ed. Khalīl Ikhwān Zanjānī (Tehran: Ṣafā, 1990), 57–63.

[67] Niẓāmī Ganjawī, *Haft Paykār: Ein romantisches Epos des Niẓāmī Genǧe'ī*, ed. H. Ritter and J. Rypka (Prague/Leipzig: Harrassowitz, 1934), 112–20 (= chapters 30–31).

day in the dome dedicated to that weekday's planet, attended to by the corresponding courtiers.[68]

Although Humāyūn's attempts to classify his courtiers along cosmological lines were new and original, they had roots in the intellectual and philosophical traditions of Iran. Thus this practice, as well as other actions including holding the *majlis* on the celestial carpet or building a palace of seven domes, was easy to understand for everybody familiar with these traditions.

The power of such cosmological symbolism, however, derived not only from its ability to plumb Islamic and Iranian natural philosophical ideas but also Indian conceptions of the cosmos—at least as they were understood by Muslim translators of Indian religious and scientific treatises. While the original Indian cosmology had been very different from the Aristotelian spherical model, with the earth imagined as a horizontal disk in the center of a vertical universe, and with Mount Meru in its center,[69] Indian astronomers adopted a spherical system during the fifth century CE.[70] In spite of having been inspired by Greek astronomy, the Indian spherical system was not entirely congruent with the Aristotelian model. However, these differences were ignored by Muslim interlocutors (like al-Bīrūnī) who fitted Indian cosmology into the Aristotelian concept of terrestrial and celestial spheres.[71] The design of Humāyūn's carpet thus corresponded not only with Islamic cosmology, but also with Indian cosmology as perceived by Muslim interlocutors.

In the field of astrology, the analogies between Indian and Islamic concepts are even more striking. In Varāhamihira's *Bṛhat Saṁhitā*, a major treatise on astrology, we find lists of correlations between zodiacal

68 Firishta, *Tarikh-i-firishta*, 397; Firishta, *History of the Rise*, tr. J. Briggs, II, 44–45.

69 David Pingree, "The Purāṇas and Jyotiḥśāstra: Astronomy," *Journal of the American Oriental Society* 110 (1990): 274–75; see also Konrad Klaus, *Die altindische Kosmologie, nach den Brāhmanas dargestellt* (Bonn: Indica-et-Tibetica, 1986), passim.

70 Pingree, "The Purāṇas," 277–78; David Pingree, *Jyotiḥśāstra: Astral and Mathematical Literature* (Wiesbaden: Harrassowitz, 1981), 12.

71 David Pingree, "Brahmagupta, Balabhadra, Pṛthūdaka and Al-Bīrūnī," *Journal of the American Oriental Society* 103 (1983): 356–60.

signs, planets, and professions very similar to what we know from Islamic astrology.[72] This similarity had already been observed by al-Bīrūnī. In his book on India, he depicts tables of astrological correspondences quite comparable to the tables he gives in his major book on Islamic astrology, the *Tafhīm*.[73]

By classifying his attendants according to astrological criteria, and by creating "planetary" and "zodiacal" divisions, Humāyūn hence used a system intelligible to both Hindus and Muslims. He might have chosen this cosmological symbolism to create a common language between his Hindu and Muslim subjects. It is, however, again not possible to decide whether Humāyūn was indeed searching for such a common language, or if the choice of philosophical and cosmological concepts was rather due to his personal interest in philosophy and science, and thus whether their accord with Indian concepts is merely coincidental.

ṢŪFĪS AND YOGIS

Any analysis of Humāyūn's ideological self-fashioning is incomplete without considering his Ṣūfī inclinations. Close relationships between rulers and Ṣūfī shaikhs were no exception in Indian Islam. During the Delhi Sultanate, we find many examples of such symbiotic connections,[74] and the close contact between Akbar and Shaikh Salīm ad-Dīn Chishtī is all too well known.[75]

72 Varāhamihira, *Bṛhat Saṁhitā: With English Translation, Exhaustive Notes, and Literary Comments* (Delhi [et al.]: Motilal Banarsidass, 1986–1987), I, 185–204 (= chapters XV, XVI).

73 Abū'l-Rayḥān Muḥammad b. Aḥmad al-Bīrūnī, *Kitāb al- taḥqīq mā lil-hind min maqūla maqbūla fī l-ʿaql ʿan marẕūla*, ed. Edward Sachau (London: Trübner, 1887), 515–24; Abū'l-Rayḥān Muḥammad b. Aḥmad al-Bīrūnī, *Alberuni's India: An Account of the Religion, Philosophy, Literature, Chronology, Astronomy, Customs, Laws and Astrology of India about A.D. 1030*, ed. Edward Sachau (London: Trübner, 1888), II, 211–22.

74 See, for example, Carl W. Ernst, *The Eternal Garden: Mysticism, History, and Politics at a South Asian Sufi Center* (Albany: Suny, 1992), 59–61; Franke, *Akbar und Ǧahāngīr*, 55–61; Jamal Malik, *Islam in South Asia: A Short History* (Leiden [et al.]: Brill, 2008), 77–84.

75 Cf. Franke, *Akbar und Ǧahāngīr*, 62–73.

Humāyūn was an initiate of the Shaṭṭāriyya Ṣūfī order and established a close relationship with two of its shaikhs, Shaikh Phūl or Bahlūl and his brother Muḥammad Ghawṣ Gwāliyārī. The Shaṭṭāriyya trace their origins back to Bāyazid Bisṭāmī and came to India via Central Asia toward the end of the fifteenth century.[76] Muḥammad Ghawṣ Gwāliyārī, who had been living in Gwalior, won the favor of Bābur by facilitating the conquest of this town.[77] Once the relationship with the Mughals was established, Humāyūn became an adept of Muḥammad's elder brother Shaikh Phūl who was well known for his interest in astrology and magic, and often accompanied Humāyūn on his travels. He served as both a spiritual mentor and political advisor. His importance is attested by the fact that in 1528, Humāyūn sent the shaikh to dissuade his half-brother Mirzā Hindāl from rebelling against Humāyūn. Instead of complying with this advice, Mirzā Hindāl ordered that the shaikh be put to death. The execution marked a final break with Humāyūn and highlights the extent of the shaikh's former power.[78]

[76] Fużail Aḥmad Qadri, "Mughal Relations with the Shaṭṭârî Sufis: Abu'l-Faḍl's Treatment of Shaikh Muḥammad Ghauth Gwâliorî," *Islamic Culture* 73 (1999): 63–65; Fużail Aḥmad Qadri, "Abū Yazīd Bisṭāmī and Shaṭṭârî Sufi Thought," *Islamic Culture* 75 (2001): 79–83; Saiyid Athar Abbas Rizvi, *A History of Sufism in India* (New Delhi: Munshiram Manoharlal Publication, 1978–1983), II, 151–53; Marc Gaborieau, "La Chattāriyya," in *Les voies d'Allah: Les ordres mystiques dans l'islam des origins à aujourd'hui*, ed. Alexandre Popovic and Gilles Veinstein (Paris: Fayard, 1996), 497.

[77] Ẓāhir ad-Dīn Muḥammad Bābur, *The Babur-nama in English (Memoirs of Babur)*, trans. Annette S. Beveridge (London: Luzac, 1922), 539–40, 690; Ernst, "Persecution and Circumspection," 418; Kugle, "Heaven's Witness," 29; Qadri, "Mughal Relations," 67.

[78] ʿAllāmī, *Akbar-nāma*, I, 154–56; ʿAllāmī, *The Akbarnama of Abu'l Fazl*, 337–39; ʿAbd al-Qādir Badāʾūnī, *Muntakhab at-tawārīkh*, ed. Mowlawī Aḥmad ʿAlī (Calcutta: College Press, 1868–69), I, 350, III, 4; Mīrzā Muḥammad Ḥaidar Dughlāt, *A History of the Moghuls of Central Asia, being the Tarikh-i-Rashidi of Mirza Muhammad Haidar, Dughlát*, ed. N. Elias, trans. E. Denison Ross (London: Curzon Press, 1972), 470; Gulbadan Bīgam, *Humāyūn-nāma*, 42; trans. 137; Ghawthī Mandawī Shaṭṭārī, *Gulzār-i abrār*, 212; Rizvi, *A History of Sufism*, II, 155, 156–57; Gaborieau, "La Chattāriyya," 498; Ernst, "Persecution and Circumspection," 418–19; Qadri, "Mughal Relations," 67.

After 1538, Humāyūn turned to Muḥammad Ghawṣ for succor. Their relationship continued even following the emperor's defeat by Sher Shāh Sūr in 1540. This is attested in a consolation letter written by Muḥammad Ghawṣ following Humāyūn's flight to Iran.[79] Even as other Shaṭṭārī shaikhs struggled to establish good relations with Sher Shāh and the ascendant Sūr dynasty during Humāyūn's exile,[80] Muḥammad Ghawṣ chose exile in Gujarat instead. There, however, he faced charges of heresy because of his treatise on ascension, the *Awrād-i ghawṣiyya*, in which he had described in detail his own ascension experience.[81] His claims of spiritual ecstasy generated so much opposition that he had to renounce the report of his bodily ascension. Muḥammad Ghawṣ's notion of cosmic emanation also displeased his opponents.[82] Following Humāyūn's return to India in 1555, Muḥammad Ghawṣ settled in Gwalior.[83] Humāyūn's unexpected death in 1556 deprived the Shaṭṭārī of an important opportunity to become India's pre-eminent Ṣūfī order. Akbar showed little interest in the order or its ideas even if he did visit Muḥammad Ghawṣ on at least one occasion.

Since Shaikh Phūl and Muḥammad Ghawṣ Gwāliyārī were both famous for their interest in magic, Humāyūn's sympathies for the Shaṭṭāriyya may have revolved around a shared inclination toward the occult sciences.[84] Muḥammad Ghawṣ was known for taking into consideration astrological criteria while praying to God. Using a technique that he called *taskhīr al-kawākib*, he claimed to subjugate the planets.[85]

[79] Ghawṣī Mandawī Shaṭṭārī, *Gulzār-i abrār*, 268–69; Qadri, "Mughal Relations," 67; Rizvi, *A History of Sufism*, II, 158.

[80] Simon Weightman, "Symbolism and Symmetry: Shaykh Manjhan's Madhumālatī Revisited," in *The Heritage of Sufism, Vol. III: Late Classical Persianate Sufism (1501–1750)*, ed. L. Lewisohn and D. Morgan (Oxford: Oneworld Publication, 1999), 465–66.

[81] Ernst, *Persecution and Circumspection*, 419; Kugle, "Heaven's Witness," 2–4, 12–26.

[82] Ghawṣī Mandawī Shaṭṭārī, *Gulzār-i abrār*, 273; Ernst, "Persecution and Circumspection," 419–26, 432–34; Fużail Aḥmad Qadri, "Abū Yazīd Bisṭāmī," 84–85; Rizvi, *A History of Sufism*, II, 157–58; Kugle, "Heaven's Witness," 31–34.

[83] Ghawṣī Mandawī Shaṭṭārī, *Gulzār-i abrār*, 273; Badā'ūnī, *Muntakhab at-tawārīkh*, III, 5; Ernst, "Persecution and Circumspection," 423.

[84] Qadri, "Mughal Relations," 66; Rizvi, *A History of Sufism*, II, 160–61.

[85] Kugle, "Heaven's Witness," 26–27. This technique is described in his *Jawāhir al-khams*. Muḥammad b. Khaṭīr ad-Dīn Ghawṣ al-Hindī, *Al-Jawāhir*

This rather unusual concept has also been dealt with in the *Jawāhir al-ʿulūm*, the encyclopedia dedicated to Humāyūn.[86]

Although available sources do not indicate whether Humāyūn was familiar with *taskhīr al-kawākib*, it is not unlikely that it informed the emperor's efforts to symbolically enact the movement of astral bodies in Mughal court ritual. His astrological calculations, his adjusting of his daily and yearly routine to the movements of the sun, and his planetary categorizations might well have been linked to the notion of *taskhīr* and the desire to influence fate. Humāyūn's Talisman house may have also been built to correspond to Shaṭṭārī-influenced ideas. Shaikh Phūl and especially Muḥammad Ghawṣ were not only famous for their interest in magic, however, but also for their approach to yogic teachings embodied in the translation of the *Amṛtakuṇḍa*.[87]

The *Amṛtakuṇḍa* is a yogic text about the teachings of *Haṭha Yoga*. This text was translated from Sanskrit into Arabic at the beginning of the fifteenth century,[88] probably by somebody well trained in the school of Illuminationism.[89] Muḥammad Ghawṣ supposedly used this text in his teachings.[90] Around 1550, he not only finally translated the Arabic version into Persian but also enlarged it, adding many details he presumably learnt from encounters with local yogis in Gujarat.[91] The Persian translation of the *Amṛtakuṇḍa* is interesting for the study of possible yogic influences on Ṣūfī practices. It also gives valuable insight

---

al-khams, ed. Aḥmad b. al-ʿAbbās (Cairo: Muḥammad Rifʿat ʿĀmir, 1973–1975), I, 187–98.

86 Qāḍī Muḥammad Fāżil Samarqandī, *Jawāhir al-ʿulūm* (Ganjbakhsh Library, Islamabad), fol. 498b–99a.

87 Qadri, "Mughal Relations," 68–72.

88 Carl W. Ernst, "The Islamization of Yoga," *Journal of the Royal Asiatic Society* 3, no. 17 (2003): 203–06.

89 Carl W. Ernst, "Sufism and Yoga According to Muhammad Ghawth," *Sufi* 29 (1996): 9. Ernst does not give reasons for that assumption in the article and refers to his forthcoming edition of the Arabic text of the *Amṛtakuṇḍa*. Illuminationism, that is the school of Suhrawardī, goes back to Shahāb ad-Dīn Suhrawardī (d. 1191) and is characterized by a correlation of existence and light.

90 Ernst, "The Islamization of Yoga," 205; Ernst, "Sufism and Yoga," 10.

91 Ernst, "Sufism and Yoga," 10; Ghawṣ al-Hindī, *Baḥr al-ḥayāt*, microfilm nr. 3760 (University of Tehran), 2a–2b.

into the rendering of yogic terminology and concepts into Persian.[92] The translator not only equated Ṣūfī and yogic practices, and tried to reconcile their doctrines, but also offered concurrences between yogic teaching and Hellenistic philosophy.[93] The translator frequently mentions the spheres and the elements, thereby implying an identity between the Hindu and the Muslim cosmology.[94] Most remarkable, however, are the practices described in Chapter VII, dealing with the subjugation of the planets (*taskhīr*) and their magical use. Here, we find concepts very similar to those in the *Jawāhir al-khams* and the *Jawāhir al-ʿulūm*.[95] This similarity is not accidental, according to Muḥammad Ghaws̱: "Most of the friends of God have discovered these influences and have explained them, and the Indian monks who are called yogis have discovered them in the same way. Although their language is different, their explanations are the same."[96]

As already noted, the concept of *taskhīr* fitted very well with Humāyūn's own cosmological symbolism. It is difficult to decide, however, if the emperor knew anything about its assumed similarity with yogic concepts. On the one hand, the Persian translation of the *Amṛtakuṇḍa* dates from 1550, that is, long after the introduction of Humāyūn's symbolic ceremonial in the early 1530s. On the other hand, the Arabic translation was already available in northern India, and Muḥammad Ghawṣ̱ is supposed to have used it in his teachings. He or his brother might well have explained the *Amṛtakuṇḍa* to Humāyūn long before the Persian translation was undertaken. We are thus again in a situation in which the emperor used concepts harmonizing with his Indian environment, or at least with what some of his close advisors regarded as ideas shared with the yogis, but we cannot decide whether Humāyūn deliberately chose those concepts because he wanted to create a common language and a symbolic enactment of power comprehensible to all, or whether

[92] Ernst, "Sufism and Yoga," 11.
[93] Ernst, "Sufism and Yoga," 10–12.
[94] Muḥammad b. Khaṭīr ad-Dīn Ghawṣ̱ al-Hindī, *Baḥr al-ḥayāt* (Persian translation of the *Amṛtakuṇḍa*), microfilm nr. 3760 (University of Tehran), chapter 3 (12b–13b).
[95] Ernst, "The Islamization of Yoga," 207–08.
[96] Ghawṣ̱ al-Hindī, *Baḥr al-ḥayāt*, fol. 26b, lines 5–8.

this approach was an unintentional by-product of his own cosmological speculations.

***

Solar symbolism, (natural) philosophy, and Ṣūfism together played a very important part in Humāyūn's ideology. In his attempt to create correspondences between the upper and lower worlds, the emperor shaped the design of his bureaucratic structure with regard to cosmology and presented himself as the sun's simile on earth. While the outlines of imperial bureaucracy designed by Humāyūn were changed and reshaped under his successors, many other elements of his ideology were eventually taken up by Akbar and enhanced. This is especially true of his reliance on pre-Islamic Iranian royal symbolism as well as the close association between the sun and the king. Humāyūn's rule was thus a transitional stage, anticipating much more of the ideological orientation under his successors than has been conceded to him so far.

BIBLIOGRAPHY

Akasoy, Anna A. and Alexander Fidora, ed. *The Arabic Version of the Nicomachean Ethics*. With an Introduction and Annotated Translation by Douglas M. Dunlop. Leiden: Brill, 2005.

Alam, Muzaffar. *The Languages of Political Islam: India 1200–1800*. Chicago: University of Chicago Press, 2004.

'Alī Ra'īs, Sayyidī. *The Travels and Adventures of the Turkish Admiral Sidi Ali Reïs in India, Afghanistan, Central Asia and Persia during the Years 1553–1556*. Edited and translated by Á. Vambéry. London: Luzac, 1899.

'Allāmī, Abū'l-Fażl. *The Aín-i-Akbarí: A Gazeteer and Administrative Manual of Akbar's Empire and Part History of India*. 3 volumes. Translated by H. Blochmann and H.S. Jarrett. Calcutta: The Asiatic Society of Bengal, 1868–1894.

_____. *Ā'īn-i Akbarī*. 2 volumes. Edited by H. Blochmann. Calcutta: Baptist Mishan Press, 1872–1877.

_____. *Akbarnāmah*. 3 volumes. Edited by Āghā Aḥmad 'Alī and 'Abd al-Raḥīm. Calcutta: Baptist Mishan Press, 1877–1886.

_____. *The Akbarnama of Abu'l Fazl: History of the Reign of Akbar including an Account of his Predecessors*. 3 volumes. Translated by H. Beveridge. Calcutta: The Asiatic Society of Bengal, 1897–1921.

Anooshahr, Ali. "The King Who would be Man: The Gender Roles of the Warrior King in Early Mughal History." *Journal of the Royal Asiatic Society* 18, Series 3 (2008): 327–40.

Aristotle. *The Nicomachean Ethics*. Translated by David Ross, revised by J.L. Ackrill and J.O. Urmson. Oxford: Oxford University Press, 1980.

Auboyer, Jeannine. "Le caractère royal et divin du trône dans l'Inde Ancienne." In *La Regalita Sacra: Contributi al tema dell' VIII Congresso Internat. Di Storia delle Religioni (Roma, Aprile 1955) = The Sacral Kingship*, 181–88. Leiden: Brill: 1959.

Avashty, R.S. *The Mughal Emperor Humayun*. Allahabad: The Leader Press, 1967.

Bābur, Ẓāhir ad-Dīn Muḥammad. *Bābur-nāma*. Edited by Annette S. Beveridge. London: Gibb Trust, 1905.

_____. *The Babur-nama in English (Memoirs of Babur)*. Translated by Annette S. Beveridge. London: Luzac, 1922.

Badā'ūnī, 'Abd al-Qādir. *Muntakhab at-tawārīkh*. 3 volumes. Edited by Mowlawī Aḥmad 'Alī. Calcutta: College Press, 1868–1869.

Bakshi, Shiri Ram and Sri Kant Sharma. "Humayun (1530–56)." In *Humayun: The Great Moghul*, edited by Shiri Ram Bakshi and Sri Kant Sharma, 1–76. New Delhi: Deep & Deep Publications, 2000.

Bayāt, Bāyazīd. *Tazkira-yi humāyūn va akbar*. Edited by M.H. Ḥusain. Calcutta: Royal Asiatic Society, 1941.

Bīgam, Gulbadan. *Humāyūn-nāma: The History of Humayun*. Translated and reprod. in the Persian by Annette S. Beveridge. London: Royal Asiatic Society, 1902.

al-Bīrūnī, Abū'l-Rayḥān Muḥammad b. Aḥmad. *al-Tafhīm lī-avā'il ṣinā'at al-tanjīm*. Edited by Jalāl al-Dīn Humā'ī. Tehran: Wizārat-i farhang, 1316–18 hijri shamsi.

_____. *Alberuni's India: An Account of the Religion, Philosophy, Literature, Chronology, Astronomy, Customs, Laws and Astrology of India about A.D. 1030*. Edited in English by Edward Sachau. London: Trübner [et al.], 1887.

_____. *Kitāb al-taḥqīq mā lil-hind min maqūla maqbūla fi l-'aql 'an marẕūla*. Edited in English by Edward Sachau. London: Trübner [et al.], 1887.

_____. *The Book of Instructions in the Elements of the Art of Astrology*. Written in Ghaznah 1029 A.D. Reproduced from British Museum MS, OR 8349. Translated by R. Ramsay Wright. London: Luzac, 1934.

Blochmann, H. and H.S. Jarrett, trans. *The Aín-i-Akbarí: A Gazetteer and Administrative Manual of Akbar's Empire and Part History of India*. 3 volumes. Calcutta: The Asiatic Society of Bengal, 1868–1894.

Christensen, Arthur. *L'Iran sous les Sassanides*. Copenhagen: Levin & Munksgaard, 1936.

Dughlāt, Mīrzā Muḥammad Ḥaidar. *A History of the Moghuls of Central Asia, being the Tarikh-i-Rashidi of Mirza Muhammad Haidar, Dughlát*. Edited by N. Elias, translated by E. Denison Ross. London: Curzon Press, 1972.

Dunlop, Douglas M. "The Nicomachean Ethics in Arabic, Books I–VI." *Oriens* 15 (1962): 18–34.

———. "Introduction." In *The Arabic Version of the Nicomachean Ethics*, edited by Anna A. Akasoy and Alexander Fidora, 1–109. Leiden/Boston: Brill: 2005.

Eck, Diana. L. *Darshan: Seeing the Divine Image in India*. New York: Columbia University Press, 1998.

Eraly, Abraham. *The Mughal Throne: The Saga of India's Great Emperors*. London: Weidenfeld & Nicolson, 2003.

Ernst, Carl W. *The Eternal Garden: Mysticism, History, and Politics at a South Asian Sufi Center*. Albany: State University of New York Press, 1992.

———. "Sufism and Yoga According to Muhammad Ghawth." *Sufi* 29 (1996): 9–13.

———. "Taṣawwuf wa yūgā." *Sufi* 30 (1996): 24–31.

———. "Persecution and Circumspection in Shaṭṭāri Sufism." In *Islamic Mysticism Contested: Thirteen Centuries of Controversies and Polemics*, edited by F. de Jong and B. Radtke, 416–35. Leiden [et al.]: Brill, 1999.

———. "The Islamization of Yoga." *Journal of the Royal Asiatic Society* 3, no. 17 (2003): 199–226.

Fakhry, Majid. *Ethical Theories in Islam*. Leiden: Brill, 1994.

Firdawsī, Abū'l-Qāsim. *Shāhnāma-yi firdawsī: Matn-i intiqādī*. 9 volumes. Edited by Evgenij Éduardoviè Bertel's. Moscow: Izdatel'stvo vostoènoj literature/Nauka, 1966.

Firishta, Muḥammad Qāsim. *History of the Rise of the Mahomedan Power in India till the Year A.D. 1612*. 2 volumes. Translated by J. Briggs. New Delhi: Low Price Publications, 1990, reprinted from 1829.

———. *Tarikh-i-Firishta: Or History of the Rise of the Mahomedan Power in India till the year A.D. 1612*. Edited by John Briggs. Bombay: Government College Press, 1831.

Franke, Heike. *Akbar und Ǧahāngīr: Untersuchungen zur politischen und religiösen Legitimation in Text und Bild*. Schenefeld: EBV, 2005.

Gaborieau, Marc. "La Chattâriyya." In *Les voies d'Allah: Les ordres mystiques dans l'islam des origines à aujourd'hui*. Edited by Alexandre Popovic and Gilles Veinstein, 497–99. Paris: Fayard, 1996.

Ganjawī, Niẓāmī. *Haft Paykār: Ein romantisches Epos des Niẓāmī Genǧe'ī*. Edited by H. Ritter and J. Rypka. Prague/Leipzig: Harrassowitz, 1934.

Ghawṣ al-Hindī, Muḥammad b. Khaṭīr ad-Dīn. *Al-jawāhir al-khams*. 2 volumes. Edited by Aḥmad b. al-ʿAbbās. Cairo: Muḥammad Rifʿat ʿĀmir, 1973–1975.

———. *Baḥr al-ḥayāt*. (Persian translation of the *Amṛtakuṇḍa*.) Microfilm nr. 3760 (University of Tehran).

Ghawṣī Mandawī Shaṭṭārī, Muḥammad. *Gulzār-i abrār: Tazkira-yi ṣūfiyā wa ulamā'*. Edited by Muḥammad Dhakī. Patna: Khudabakhsh Oriental Public Library, 2001.

Gonda, Jan. "Ancient Indian Kingship from the Religious Point of View." *Numen* 3, fasc. 1 (1956), 36–71; 3, fasc. 2 (1956), 122–55; 4, fasc. 1 (1957), 24–58; 4, fasc. 2 (1957), 127–64.

_____. "The Sacred Character of Ancient Indian Kingship." In *La Regalità Sacra: Contributi al tema dell' VIII Congresso Internat. Di Storia delle Religioni (Roma, Aprile 1955) = The Sacral Kingship*, 172–80. Leiden: Brill, 1959.

Ibrāhīm b. Jarīr: *Ta'rīkh-i humāyūnī*. MS Oxford, Bodleian Library, Ouseley 83 and 84.

Inden, Ronald. "Ritual, Authority, and Cyclic Time in Hindu Kingship." In *Kingship and Authority in South Asia*, edited by J.F. Richards, 41–91. New Delhi [et al.]: Oxford University Press, reprint, 1998.

Joshi, K.L., ed. *Matsya Mahāpurāṇa : An Exhaustive Introduction, Sanskrit Text, English Translation, Scholarly Notes and Index of Verses*. Number 93 of *Parimal Sanskrit Series*. Translated by a board of scholars. Delhi: Parimal Publications, 2007.

Khwāndamīr, Ghiyāṣ al-Dīn Muḥammad. *Qānūn-i humāyūnī, nīz musammā bah humāyūnnāmah*. Edited by Muḥammad Hidāyat Ḥusayn. Calcutta: Rāyil Eshiyātik Sosā'itī, 1940.

_____. *Qānūn-i Humāyūnī (also known as Humāyūn-nāma) of Khwāndamīr (died A.H. 942, A.D. 1535): A Work on the Rules and Ordinances Established by the Emperor Humāyūn and on Some Buildings Erected by His Order*. Translated by B. Prashad. Calcutta: Royal Asiatic Society of Bengal, 1940.

Klaus, Konrad. *Die altindische Kosmologie nach den Brāhmanas dargestellt*. Bonn: Indica-et-Tibetica, 1986.

Kugle, Scott A. "Heaven's Witness: The Uses and Abuses of Muhammad Ghawth's Mystical Ascension." *Journal of Islamic Studies* 14 (2003): 1–36.

Kumar, Raj. *The Coming of the Mughals*. Volume 4 of *Survey of Medieval India*. New Delhi: Anmol Publications, 1999.

Malandra, William W. *An Introduction to Ancient Iranian Religion: Readings from the Avesta and Achaemenid Inscriptions*. Minneapolis: University of Minnesota Press, 1983.

Malik, Jamal. *Islam in South Asia: A Short History*. Leiden [et al.]: Brill, 2008.

Michaels, Axel. *Der Hinduismus: Geschichte und Gegenwart*. München: C.H. Beck, 1998.

Mukhia, Harbans. *The Mughals of India*. Malden, Mass.: Blackwell Publishing, 2004.

Nath, Ravinder. *History of Mughal Architecture*. New Delhi: Abhinav Publication, 1982–1985.

Orthmann, Eva. "Sonne, Mond und Sterne: Kosmologie und Astrologie in der Inszenierung von Herrschaft unter Humāyūn." In *Die Grenzen der Welt: Arabica et Iranica ad honorem Heinz Gaube*, edited by Lorenz Korn, Florian Schwarz, and Eva Orthmann, 297–306. Wiesbaden: Reichert, 2008.

———. "Court Culture and Cosmology in the Mughal Empire: Humāyūn and the Foundations of the Dīn-i ilāhī." In *Muslim Court Culture: 7th–19th Centuries*, edited by Albrecht Fuess and Jan-Peter Hartung, 202–20. London/New York: Routledge, 2011.

Pingree, David. *Jyotiḥśāstra: Astral and Mathematical Literature.* Wiesbaden: Harrassowitz, 1981.

———. "Brahmagupta, Balabhadra, Pṛthūdaka and Al-Bīrūnī." *Journal of the American Oriental Society* 103 (1983): 353–60.

———. "The Purāṇas and Jyotiḥśāstra. Astronomy." *Journal of the American Oriental Society* 110 (1990): 274–80.

Prasad, Ishwari. *The Life and Times of Humayun.* Bombay: Orient Longmans, 1956.

Purnaqchéband, Nadir. *Strategien der Kontingenzbewältigung: Der Mogulherrscher Humāyūn (r. 1530–1540 und 1555–1556) dargestellt in der "Taẕkirat al-Wāqiʿ āt" seines Leibdieners Jauhar Āftābčī.* Schenefeld: EB, 2007.

Qadri, Fużail Aḥmad. "Mughal Relations with the Shaṭṭârî Sufis: Abu'l-Faḍl's Treatment of Shaikh Muḥammad Ghauth Gwâliorî." *Islamic Culture* 73 (1999): 63–77.

———. "Abû Yazîd Bisṭâmî and Shaṭṭârî Sufi Thought." *Islamic Culture* 75 (2001): 79–95.

Rizvi, Saiyid Athar Abbas. *A History of Sufism in India.* 2 volumes. New Delhi: Munishiram Manoharlal Publishers, 1978–1983.

Ruska, Julius and Bernard Carra da Vaux. "Ṭilasm." In *Encyclopaedia of Islam*, New Edition, volume 10, edited by P.J. Bearman, Th. Bianquis, C.E. Bosworth, E. van Donzel, and W.P. Heinrichs, 500–502. Leiden: Brill, 2000.

Samarqandī, Qāżī Muḥammad Fāżil Samarqandī. *Jawāhir ul-ʿulūm.* MS. 301. Ganjbakhsh Library, Islamabad.

Shahmardān b. Abī l-Khair Rāżī. *Rawżat al-munajjimīn.* Edited by Khalīl Ikhwān Zanjānī. Tehran: Ṣafā, 1990.

Shashi, Shyam Singh. "Humayun: Struggle and Success." In *Encyclopaedia Indica*, volume 48. Delhi: Anmol Publications, 1999.

Sims, Eleanor. "The Illustrated Manuscripts of Firdausī's 'Shāhnāma' Commissioned by Princes of the House of Tīmūr." *Ars Orientalis* 22 (1992): 43–68.

Storey, Charles A. *Persian Literature: A Bio-Biographical Survey.* Volume 1, part 1. London: Luzac & Co., 2006 (= 1927–1939).

Streusand, Douglas E. *The Formation of the Mughal Empire.* New Delhi: Oxford University Press, 1989.

Tasbīḥī, Muḥammad Ḥusayn. "Jawāhir ul-ʿulūm-i humāyūnī." *Waḥīd* 211/212 (1356/1977): 34–43.

Tripathi, Ram Prasat. *The Rise and Fall of the Mughal Empire*. Reprint of 3rd edition. Allahabad: Central Book Depot, 1956.

Ṭūsī, Nāṣir ad-Dīn. *Akhlāq-i nāṣirī*. Edited by Mujtaba'ī Mīnuvī. Tehran: Shirkat-i Sihāmī-i Intishārāt-i Khwārazmī, 1369.

Varāhamihira. *Bṛhat Saṁhitā: With English Translation, Exhaustive Notes and Literary Comments*. 2 volumes. Delhi [et al.]: Motilal Banarsidass, 1986–1987.

Weightman, Simon. "Symbolism and Symmetry: Shaykh Manjhan's Madhumālatī Revisited." In *The Heritage of Sufism, Vol. III: Late Classical Persianate Sufism (1501–1750)*, edited by L. Lewisohn and D. Morgan, 464–92. Oxford: Oneworld Publication, 1999.

Widengren, Geo. "The Sacral Kingship of Iran." In *La Regalita Sacra: Contributi al tema dell' VIII Congresso Internat. Di Storia delle Religioni (Roma, Aprile 1955) = The Sacral Kingship*, 242–57. Volume 4 of *Studies in the History of Religions*. Leiden: Brill, 1959.

_____. *Die Religionen Irans*. Volume 14 of *Die Religionen der Menschheit*. Stuttgart: Kohlhammer, 1965.

Wolff, Fritz. *Avesta: Die Heiligen Bücher der Parsen. Übersetzt auf der Grundlage von Chr. Bartholomae's altiranischen Wörterbuch*. Strasbourg: K.J. Trübner, 1910.

2 Dara Shukoh, Vedanta, and Imperial Succession in Mughal India*

Munis D. Faruqui

A large gathering of Sanskrit scholars met in Banaras at the end of 1656, urgently summoned by Prince Dara Shukoh, the eldest and favorite son of Emperor Shah Jahan. Dara Shukoh required a Persian translation of the sacred Hindu "text," the Upanishads.[1] Working at a furious pace, they completed their task in six months, in the first week of July 1657. When Dara Shukoh wrote his introduction to the completed translation, his tone was excited, even frenzied. He called the translation *Sirr-i akbar*, "The Great Secret," proclaiming that he had discovered the Upanishads to be the textual source of monotheism (*tawhid*) itself.[2]

* My special thanks to Clare Talwalker, Vasudha Dalmia, Bob Goldman, and the participants in the 2008 "Hunood wa Musalman" conference at UC-Berkeley for their insights and help in improving this essay. Any mistakes, however, are mine alone.

[1] I refer to the Upanishads as a text throughout this essay. I do so with an awareness of Valerie Roebuck's warning that "in the context of Hindu sacred texts, the words 'text' and 'literature' are not restricted to something written down." "Upanisads," in *Encyclopedia of Hinduism*, ed. Denise Cush, Catherine Robinson, and Michael York (New York: Routledge, 2008), 894.

[2] Although there is no exact Islamic equivalent for the English term "monotheism," *tawhid* is commonly used to refer to the "act of believing and affirming

Within months of its completion, however, the prince found himself unexpectedly embroiled in a war of succession with his brothers. Two years later, in 1659, following his defeat and capture by his younger brother and the new Mughal emperor Aurangzeb, Dara Shukoh was executed. The central charges against him were heresy and apostasy from Islam. It was the claims he made in his introduction to *Sirr-i akbar* that formed a key component of the indictments.

Over the centuries, opinions about Dara Shukoh have become fairly polarized. At one end, his fiercest detractors have charged him with heresy and suggested that his intellectual endeavors were entirely misguided and, moreover, that those efforts posed an existential threat to Islam. This view is perhaps best summed up in the *'Alamgirnama* (c. 1680s)—the near-contemporary and court-sponsored account of the first ten years of Aurangzeb's reign (r. 1658–1707). It notes:

> Dara Shukoh in his later years did not restrict himself to free thinking and heretical notions, which he had adopted in the name of *tasawwuf* (or Sufism), but showed an inclination for the religion of the Hindus … He was constantly in the society of *Brahmans*, *Jogis*, and *sannyasis*, and he used to regard these worthless teachers of delusions as learned and true masters of wisdom … Thanks to these perverted opinions, he had given up prayers, fasting, and other obligations imposed by the law … It became clear that if he should obtain the throne, and establish his power, the foundations of the (Islamic) faith would be in danger and the precepts of Islam would be changed for the absurdity of infidelity.[3]

---

that God is one and unique (*wahid*), in a word monotheism." Interestingly, the word *tawhid* is not derived from the Quran (where it is never used), even if the idea that God is a single divinity is repeatedly affirmed across the text. D. Gimaret, "Tawhid," *Encyclopaedia of Islam, Second Edition*, ed. P. Bearman, Th. Bianquis, C.E. Bosworth, E. van Donzel, and W.P. Heinrichs (Leiden: Brill, 2011), http://www.brillonline.nl/subscriber/entry?entry=islam_SIM-7454, accessed April 2, 2012. Unless otherwise indicated, all translations are my own.

[3] Muhammad Kazim, "Alamgirnama," in *History of India as Told by Its Own Historians: Muhammadan Period*, vol. 7 of *History of India as Told by Its Own Historians*, ed. Henry Elliot and John Dowson (London: Trübner and Co., 1867–77), 179. See also Muhammad Kazim, *'Alamgirnama*, ed. Khadim Husain and Abd al-Hayy (Calcutta: College Press, 1868), 34–35.

Milder twentieth-century versions of the same can also be found in the writings of Shibli Nomani, Zahiruddin Faruki, I.H. Qureshi, S. Moinul Haq, Aziz Ahmad, and others.[4] At the other end, his strongest supporters see in him a tragic figure who embodied the failed promise of greater Hindu and Muslim understanding. In the nationalist myth-making of Jawaharlal Nehru, first prime minister of India, Dara Shukoh thus becomes an example of "the genius of the nation," a leader who aimed at "a common nationality and synthesis of the various elements of the country."[5] Indian secular-nationalist historians have often expressed similar sentiments.[6] In a recent study, Rajeev Kinra calls for recognizing more shades of opinion on Dara Shukoh. Drawing on a number of late seventeenth- and eighteenth-century accounts, Kinra points to a third

[4] Shibli Nomani, *Alamgir* (Delhi: Idarah-i Adabiyat-i Delli, reprint, 1982); Zahiruddin Faruki, *Aurangzeb and His Times* (Delhi: D.B. Taraporevala Sons & Co., 1935); I.H. Qureshi, *The Muslim Community of the Indo-Pakistan Sub-continent, 610–1947: A Brief Historical Analysis* (The Hague: Mouton, 1962); S. Moinul Haq, *Prince Awrangzib* (Karachi: Pakistan Historical Society, 1962); Aziz Ahmad, *Studies in Islamic Culture in an Indian Environment* (Delhi: Oxford University Press, reprint, 1999). See also Sadiq Ali, *A Vindication of Aurangzeb* (Calcutta: R. Rahman, 1918); S.M. Jaffer, *The Mughal Empire: From Babar to Aurangzeb* (Peshawar: S. Muhammad Sadiq Khan, 1936); Iftikhar H. Ghauri, *War of Succession between the Sons of Shah Jahan, 1657–1658* (Lahore: Publishers United, 1964).

[5] Jawaharlal Nehru, *The Discovery of India* (New York: The John Day Company, 1946), 219.

[6] A. Eraly, *The Last Spring: The Life and Times of the Great Mughals* (Delhi: Viking, 1997); Rekha Joshi, *Aurangzeb* (Delhi: Munshiram Manoharlal, 1979); V.D. Mahajan, *Muslim Rule in India* (Delhi: S. Chand, 1962); R.C. Majumdar, H.C. Raychaudhuri, and Kalikinkar Datta, *Advanced History of India* (Delhi: Macmillan, 1967); Jaswant Mehta, *Advanced Study of History of Medieval India* (Delhi: Sterling, 1979–1981); R. Mukherjee, *History of Indian Civilisation*, vol. 1 (Bombay: Hind Kitabs, 1958); A.B. Pandey, *Later Medieval India* (Allahabad: Central Book Depot, 1963); Ishwari Prasad, *Mughal Empire* (Allahabad: Chugh Publications, 1974); K.R. Qanungo, *Dara Shukoh* (Calcutta: S.C. Sarkar, 1952); Jadunath Sarkar, *A Short History of Aurangzib, 1618–1707* (Calcutta: M.C. Sarkar, 1930); K.A. Nilakanta Sastri, ed., *A Comprehensive History of India* (Bombay: Orient Longmans, 1957), II; R.P. Tripathi, *Rise and Fall of the Mughal Empire* (Allahabad: Central Book Depot, 1956).

set of opinions besides linking the prince's failure to either his "liberal" or "heretical" religious views. Those holding alternative views "disliked him for entirely non-sectarian reasons, sometimes having to do with a belief that Dara Shukoh's narcissistic arrogance made him unfit for the throne, and sometimes out of pure personal enmity."[7] Over the centuries, according to Kinra, such views have been drowned out by the "good Muslim/bad Muslim" polemics surrounding Dara Shukoh.

The present essay focuses on this controversial Mughal prince's spiritual quest and demonstrates that the stories told of him necessitate further nuance and consideration. It considers closely Dara Shukoh's engagement with the Upanishads toward the end of his life, detailing his extended efforts to understand the nature of *tawhid* and exploring what he understood as its many appearances across different religious traditions. Ultimately, regarding this final stage of his lifetime, it argues that both his fiercest supporters and detractors get him wrong. In *Sirr-i akbar*, his most intimate encounter with Hinduism, he was not as much of a town crier for tolerant syncretism as supporters believe and not as much of a threat to Islam as detractors have thought. Dara Shukoh fervently believed he had found proof that elements within Hinduism were in fact more Islamic than anyone had previously credited them. His foray into Hindu texts thus served, paradoxically, to solidify and secure his essentially Quranic worldview.

The following discussion proceeds in four parts. The first lays out a historical context for the study of other religious traditions by Muslims. Dara Shukoh's scholarly inquiries are read against this centuries-long intellectual engagement. The second section considers why the prince chose to rely specifically on the Upanishadic commentaries of Shankaracharya, the ninth-century Advaita Vedantin. The third section closely analyzes Dara Shukoh's introduction in the *Sirr-i akbar* to understand his highly charged argument that the Upanishads embody humanity's first revelation about Divine Unity and a commentary on all subsequent revelations. And finally I evaluate the possibility that Dara Shukoh's political and spiritual interests intersected in ways hitherto unrecognized. I argue that the prince's introduction to the *Sirr-i akbar* may be read as simultaneously working on two levels: explicit/

[7] Rajeev Kinra, "Infantilizing Baba Dara: The Cultural Memory of Dara Shekuh and the Mughal Public Sphere," *Journal of Persianate Studies*, no. 2 (2009): 168.

theological and implicit/political. Explicitly, it is a straightforward celebration of the discovery of a "monotheistic" ur-text. Politics has no place in this narrative. Implicitly, however, it is possible to discern Dara Shukoh's intention to fashion a very particular princely self-portrait highlighting his personal qualities—including intelligence, discernment, and spiritual enlightenment. Nor could he have been entirely unconscious or uncaring of his destiny as a Mughal prince: his self-portrait hints at the kind of Islamic thought and practice he envisioned as appropriate for his projected ascension to the Mughal throne.[8]

I

In a process that began in the first centuries following Islam's revelation, Muslim intellectuals read and commented on a large body of Greco-Hellenistic, Zoroastrian, Buddhist, and Hindu philosophical texts. Most did so through translations from Greek, Pahlavi, or Sanskrit into Arabic. Consideration of what many viewed as a diverse and massive, yet non-revealed or non-Abrahamic corpus led many Muslim intellectuals to experience skepticism and doubt about what constituted religious truth. It was against this backdrop, which scholar of religion Paul Heck describes as an accompanying "crisis of knowledge,"[9] that some tenth- and eleventh-century Middle East-based Muslim intellectuals concluded that all people, monotheists and non-monotheists alike, had some access to divine truth and revelation.

This conclusion, in certain extreme cases, led either to rejecting the existence of any true knowledge or disavowal of the possibility of ever fully comprehending it. More common, however, were guarded responses such as that of Ibn al-'Arabi (d. 1148), the influential Andalusian jurist and mystic. Although al-'Arabi argued that all religions were manifestations of the Divine, he noted that not all were of equal value, and he posited a hierarchy with Islam occupying the topmost rung. Evocatively, he characterized Islam as sunlight and all other religions as

[8] See Supriya Gandhi's essay in this volume for another exploration of Dara Shukoh's complex engagement with Vedanta, one that calls particular attention to the wider cultural and political contexts in which these efforts evolved.

[9] Paul Heck, "The Crisis of Knowledge in Islam (I): The Case of al-'Amiri," *Philosophy East and West* 56, no. 1 (2006): 106.

stars that were outshone when the light of Islam appeared.[10] Al-'Arabi's views would be powerfully echoed by later intellectuals and mystics. None, perhaps, is more famous than the Anatolian-based Jalal al-Din Rumi (d. 1273), one of the foremost poets of mystical Islam. Rumi joyfully concedes that there are many paths to the Divine, just as there are many paths to get to the Ka'ba. Yet, he too suggests that God has offered many signs pointing to Islam's superiority over all other routes.[11] Such ideas, in which other religious systems were accorded a lawful, if lesser, place in the hierarchy of religions, would be powerfully echoed in Islam's dealings with Hinduism.

One of the first Muslim scholars to engage in an in-depth study of Hinduism, the eleventh-century Ghaznavid scholar al-Biruni (d. 1050), asserted that Hinduism was not unlike Judaism and Christianity. Like these, he claimed, Hinduism used idols and icons to represent abstract ideas to the uneducated masses. At the same time, al-Biruni asserted that Brahmin elites themselves worshipped a single God on account of their superior religious training and education. Other scholars from the same period, including the Persian geographer and historian al-Gardezi (d. 1060) and the Andalusian philosopher and jurist Ibn Hazm (d. 1064), further explained that although Brahmins did not speak of prophetic revelation, their belief in a single God was apparent from their acceptance of the idea of God as creator of the world. Roughly a century later, in thinking through Hinduism's apparent lack of prophets, the Persian scholar al-Shahrastani (d. 1151) homed in on the lack or loss of written accounts. He argued that both Shiva and Vishnu were in fact messengers from God; they took human forms in order to reveal divine laws to Indians. Their prophetic missions were forgotten, however, because they failed to leave a written record of their revelations. Such ideas would broadly resonate with men like the India-based poet and mystic Amir Khusrau (d. 1325). Thus, even as Amir Khusrau condemned Brahmins for engaging in idol worship, he noted that they believed in the existence of a single God. They worshipped a series of objects and things,

[10] William Chittick, *Imaginal Worlds: Ibn Arabi and the Problem of Religious Diversity* (Albany: State University of New York Press, 1994), 125.

[11] Carl A. Keller, "Perceptions of Other Religions in Sufism," in *Muslim Perceptions of Other Religions: A Historical Survey*, ed. Jacques Waardenburg (New York: Oxford University Press, 1999), 186–87.

he explained, because they viewed everything as God's creation. Amir Khusrau was clear, however, that Brahmins did not in fact mistake these concrete manifestations for the divine itself. For all these early attempts to render Hinduism comprehensible to a Muslim audience, none of these scholars questioned the essential Quranic dictum: "The true religion with God is Islam."[12] The possibility of spiritual parity between Islam and another faith tradition—let alone a non-Abrahamic one like Hinduism—was never publicly countenanced.[13]

By the sixteenth century, and with the establishment of Mughal rule in India, we can point to deeply ingrained views in certain Muslim intellectual circles that Hinduism had core beliefs that resonated with Islam. Foremost among them was the acknowledgment of God's Oneness. Shaikh Abu'l Fazl (d. 1602), the closest friend and political counselor to Emperor Akbar (r. 1556–1605), therefore scoffed at continuing claims by certain conservative Muslims that Hindus did not "believe in the unity of God." To the contrary, he asserted, all of them (*hamangi mardum*) harbored this belief. Repeating an old argument, Abu'l Fazl proclaimed idol worship to be nothing more than an aid to focus the mind on a single God.[14] Abu'l Fazl's debt to the skeptical tradition within Islam—one which recognized that universal principles of truth were common to all peoples—also led him to contest assertions that Islam was the only true religion.[15] Although the focus of this article, Akbar's great-grandson Dara Shukoh, rarely refers to either Akbar or

[12] *Sura al-'imran* ("The House of 'Imran," 3: 19). A.J. Arberry, trans., *The Koran Interpreted* (New York: Macmillan, 1955), 75.

[13] This paragraph is based on a distillation of the following writings: Carl Ernst, "Muslim Studies of Hinduism? A Reconsideration of Persian and Arabic Translations from Sanskrit," *Iranian Studies* 36, no. 2 (2003): 173–87; Yohanan Friedmann, "Islamic Thought in Relation to the Indian Context," in *India's Islamic Traditions, 711–1750*, ed. Richard M. Eaton (Delhi: Oxford University Press, 2003), 50–63; Bruce Lawrence, "Shahrastani on Indian Idol Worship," *Studia Islamica* 38 (1973): 61–73; Keller, "Perceptions of Other Religions in Sufism," 181–94; Sarah Stroumsa, "The *Barahima* in Early Kalam," *Jerusalem Studies in Arabic and Islam* 6 (1985): 229–41; S.H. Nasr, *Sufi Essays* (Albany: State University of New York Press, 1991), 139–42, 173–87.

[14] Shaikh Abu'l Fazl, *A'in-i akbari*, ed. H. Blochmann (Calcutta: Asiatic Society of Bengal, 1877), III, 2, 5.

[15] Friedmann, "Islamic Thought in Relation to the Indian Context," 55–56.

Shaikh Abu'l Fazl in his own writing, he too was no doubt shaped by these same legacies of skeptical thinking.

To understand Dara Shukoh's writings, however, we need to consider another strand of Islamic thinking about Hinduism. That thought, characterized by scholars like the Baghdad-born al-Jili (d. 1428), explicitly placed Hinduism and Islam within the same line of revelation stretching back to the Prophet Abraham, who is viewed as humanity's first prophet to assert God's unique and single character. Al-Jili made the case for the existence of linguistic traces of this shared legacy. For instance, he suggested, it was no coincidence that the word *barahimah* (a term used to describe upper-caste Hindu Brahmins) sounded like "Abraham." He viewed such etymological links as buttressed by philosophical similarities that suggested Hinduism was a primordial Abrahamic faith. Thus Hindu metaphysical tenets were tied with the Islamic concept of Oneness of Being (*wahdat al-wujud*). According to al-Jili such linguistic and metaphysical resonances corroborated what the Brahmins themselves said of their own beliefs: "… [*barahimah*] claim that they belong to the religion of Abraham and that they are his progeny and possess special acts of worship … Their worship of the Truth is like that of the prophets before their prophetic mission. They claim to be the children of Abraham—Peace be upon Him…"[16] The vast majority of Muslim scholars, however—even those willing to see similarities between certain specific Muslim and Hindu beliefs—found such claims preposterous. They pointed out that since Hindus themselves were opposed to any notion of prophets how could they share any link whatsoever to Abraham or their faith be seen as akin to Abrahamic faiths?[17]

By the 1650s, however, Dara Shukoh became increasingly convinced that Vedantic Hinduism and Islam were distinct in name only. On account of their greater provenance, he declared, certain Hindu texts

[16] Quoted in Nasr, *Sufi Essays*, 139–40.

[17] Even al-Shahrastani—the twelfth-century scholar who equated Vishnu and Shiva with *ruhaniyat* (a cross between a prophet and an angel)—decried "those among the people who believe they [the Hindus] are called *Barahimah* because of their affiliation to Abraham—upon whom be peace. But this is wrong, for they are a people especially known to have denied prophecy completely and totally." Nasr, *Sufi Essays*, 140.

could in fact help clarify Islam and provide unique insights into the "boundless ocean" that is Divine Oneness.

Dara Shukoh's scholarly career can be divided into two periods; the first spanned the mid-1630s to the late 1640s, and the second culminated in the publication of the *Sirr-i akbar* in 1657. During the first period, Dara Shukoh focused his enquiries almost exclusively on the nature of mystical Islam under the guidance of two Qadiri Sufi masters, Miyan Mir (d. 1635) and Mulla Shah Badakhshi (d. 1661).[18] What emerged was a highly idiosyncratic understanding of Qadiri spirituality that the prince laid out in his 1642 tract *Sakinat al-awliya'*. He wrote of his own unique spiritual visions and of having been singled out by God for greatness, [19] and denounced all emphasis on simple clothing and affect, physically demanding disciplinary exercises, or the performance of miracles as part of the spiritual quest.[20] Dara Shukoh's grandiose claims met with only muted dissent within the Qadiri *tariqah*; people likely feared offending this powerful Mughal prince. This is evident in the cautious epistolary exchanges between Dara Shukoh and Shaikh Muhibullah Allahabadi (d. 1648), one of the seventeenth century's greatest Qadiri pirs.[21]

Starting in the late 1640s, however, Dara Shukoh's study and writing underwent a further shift. He wrote of his mastery of Sufism's "secrets and subtleties" (*ramuz wa daqa'iq*) and his consequent restlessness, his sense that there remained questions that an exclusive focus on Islamic texts

[18] The Qadiri *tariqah* (order) traced its spiritual lineage back to the Baghdad-based saint, Sayyid 'Abd al-Qadir Gilani (d. 1166). Following its arrival in India in the late fifteenth century, the *tariqah*'s popularity grew rapidly. By the seventeenth century, the Qadiris had eclipsed most other *tariqah*s in terms of both wealth and influence. Fatima Z. Bilgrami, *History of the Qadiri Order in India: 16th–18th Century* (Delhi: Idarah-i Adabiyat-i Delli, 2005); Arthur Buehler, "The Indo-Pakistani Qadiriyya," *Journal of the History of Sufism: Special Issue: The Qadiriyya Order*, 1–2 (2000): 339–60.

[19] Dara Shukoh, *Sakinat al-awliya'*, ed. Tara Chand and Sayyid Muhammad Reza Jalali Naini (Tehran: Mu'assasah-i Matbu'ati 'Ilmi, 1965), 5–6. See also Dara Shukoh, *Risala-i haqnuma*, Zakariya Coll. Mss. 177, National Library of India, ff. 7b–8a.

[20] Shukoh, *Sakinat al-awliya'*, 5, 6, 105.

[21] S.A.A. Rizvi, *History of Sufism in India* (Delhi: Munshiram Manoharlal, 1978–1983), II, 139–42.

left unanswered.[22] In many ways his *Tariqat al-haqiqat* (written around 1648–49) is crucial in pointing to changes in the prince's interests and thinking. In it Dara Shukoh points to his growing conviction that Islam and Hinduism both speak of the same ultimate truth. Although the text is primarily a description of the stages a devotee must travel in his quest for self-realization, it powerfully affirms the idea that God is everywhere and in everything. Thus Dara Shukoh credits God for being the spirit behind not only the religiously inspired chiming of prayer bells in Hindu temples but also of Muslim prayers at the Ka'ba.[23] It is the prince's belief in the omnipresence and omniscience of God that increasingly informs his view that Vedantic Hinduism and Islam are both part of and echo the same divine scheme.

Over the next six years, Dara Shukoh's growing interest in Vedantic philosophical and mystical ideas manifested itself in a number of ways. He directly commissioned or encouraged Persian translations of a number of important Vedantic texts. As Supriya Gandhi's essay in this volume highlights, one of the most important was the *Yogavasishtha*, which centrally focuses on the Hindu God Rama's quest to attain spiritual liberation (*jivanamukta*) while carrying on with his worldly duties. Members of Dara Shukoh's princely household also undertook translations of a number of other texts including *Prabodhachandrodaya*, the *Atmavilasa*, and Shankara's *Brahmasutrabhasya*.[24] Furthermore, the prince sought out the company of Hindu theists like the Punjab-based Baba Lal Das in the early 1650s. Such endeavors, building on earlier insights, seem to have convinced him that Hinduism had a *tawhid*-ic

[22] Dara Shukoh, *Majma' al-bahrayn*, Ashburner Coll. Mss. CXXVII, British Library, fol. 2a. Also, Dara Shukoh, *Majma'-ul-Bahrain*, ed. and trans. M. Mahfuz-ul-Haq (Calcutta: Bibliotheca Indica, 1929), 80.

[23] B.J. Hasrat, *Dara Shikuh: Life and Works* (Delhi: Munshiram Manoharlal, reprint, 1982), 114.

[24] Ernst, "Muslim Studies of Hinduism?," 183–84; Fathullah Mujtabai, *Aspects of Hindu–Muslim Cultural Relations* (Delhi: National Book Bureau, 1978), 60–91. The broad-ranging nature of these texts can be gauged by the fact that the *Prabhodachandrodaya* is an eleventh-century dramatic rendition of a Vedantic theological allegory. *Atmavilasa* is a mystical text attributed to the Vedantic sage Shankaracharya, and the *Brahmasutrabhasya* is Shankaracharya's commentary on the *Brahmasutras*.

core, that the worship of idols was merely intended to help the worshipper focus and concentrate on God, and that mere semantic differences separated the tenets of Hindu monotheists (whom he referred to as *muvahhidan-i Hind*[25]) from those of Muslims. It is precisely his attempt to uncover these spiritual and lexicographical affinities that marks his second-to-last major work, *Majma' al-bahrayn*, completed in 1655–56.

As noted above, Dara Shukoh's arguments about Hindu–Muslim resonances were not entirely unprecedented or novel in the Indian context. Very similar arguments had already been made by other scholars including Saiyid 'Abdul Quddus Gangohi (d. 1537), Saiyid Muhammad Ghaus Gwaliori (d. 1563), and Mir 'Abdul Wahid Bilgrami (d. 1608).[26] Bilgrami, for example, in his book *Haqa'iq-i hindi* explains that many Vaishnava symbols, terms, and ideas have equivalents in Islam. What sets *Majma' al-bahrayn* apart from these earlier efforts, however, is both its ambition as also the royal identity of its author. Over the course of twenty-two chapters—which include discourses on everything from the elements, the senses, devotional exercises, the attributes of God, the soul, the Divine Sound, light, visions of God, the names of God to resurrection and salvation—Dara Shukoh tries to "prove" that there are no differences "except verbal" ones (*ikhtalaf-i lafzi*) in the way that both groups (*fariqain*) comprehend the Truth.[27] The scholar-prince then goes on to assert that his findings will make special sense to those who are "just" and "perceptive." By contrast, those of "dull intellect" (*kund fahm*) will receive no benefits.[28] He ends his introduction by citing the authority of Khwaja Ahrar—an esteemed fifteenth-century Naqshbandi master: "If I know that an unbeliever immersed in sin is

[25] The word "*wahid*" (unique or sole) is repeatedly used in the Quran in discussions about God's character. Dara Shukoh's use of the term "*muvahiddan*" thus refers to "those who believe in the uniqueness of God."

[26] Muzaffar Alam, *The Languages of Political Islam in India 1200–1800* (Delhi: Permanent Black, 2004), 92–93; K.A. Nizami, *State and Culture in Medieval India* (New Delhi: Adam Publishers & Distributors, 1985), 238; S.A.A. Rizvi, *Muslim Revivalist Movements in Northern India in the Sixteenth and Seventeenth Centuries* (New Delhi: Munshiram Manoharlal, reprint, 1993), 60–62.

[27] Shukoh, *Majma' al-bahrayn*, fol. 2a.

[28] Shukoh, *Majma' al-bahrayn*, fol. 2a–b.

in a way chanting the note of Divine Unity, I learn, and I am grateful to him."[29] This ending recapitulates an idea expressed right at the beginning of the introduction where, quoting the Persian poet Sana'i (d. 1131?), he provocatively claims that unbelief and submission (to God) "are both galloping on the same path toward Him."[30]

Majma' al-bahrayn's tone—at once mocking and patronizing—must have raised hackles among both Hindu and Muslim scholars when the text was first made public. Furthermore, this work hints—without directly saying so—that elements within Hinduism stood to supplement Islamic wisdom or that scholars of Islam might learn from certain Hindu insights. Of course, such claims flew in the face of centuries of dogma that proclaimed Islam as a self-contained and perfect revelation.

The introduction to *Majma' al-bahrayn* seems to anticipate public controversy. In it, the prince sharply demarcates his intended audience: this research work (*tahqiq*), he writes, is only intended for the benefit of his family and has nothing to do with "the masses of either community" (*'awam har do qaum kari nist*).[31] On the one hand, this could be read as elitist—not surprising, since most learned men of the period viewed the average individual as lacking the tools to comprehend esoteric knowledge. On the other hand, it might also be read as an early defense of the book against critics who might emerge in wider audiences. But on this very point Dara Shukoh wavers, for he also puts out a call to all just, perceptive, and intelligent men to read his book and become enlightened.[32] Although it is impossible to gauge how many copies of the text were in circulation between 1656 and 1657, considering Dara Shukoh's massive princely household, his powerful networks of supporters across the empire, and the publicity that necessarily came from his position as a favored Mughal prince, *Majma' al-bahrayn* likely was quickly circulated among interested Mughal political and religious circles.

It is a sign of Dara Shukoh's growing confidence in his own achievements, and the seeming inability of his opponents to hurt him, that the prince shifted tactics yet again with what turned out to be his final book, *Sirr-i akbar*. While echoing *Majma' al-bahrayn*'s refrain that this work

[29] Shukoh, *Majma' al-bahrayn*, fol. 2b.
[30] Shukoh, *Majma' al-bahrayn*, fol. 1b.
[31] Shukoh, *Majma' al-bahrayn*, fol. 2b.
[32] Shukoh, *Majma' al-bahrayn*, fol. 2a–b

was primarily intended for his own edification and that of his family (*awlad-i khud*) and friends (*dostan-i khud*), the prince now specifically proclaimed that devout Muslims (*mominin*) also would be beneficiaries of his work.[33] He makes no effort to soothe the anxieties of people who disagreed with his religious views. Instead, he forthrightly announces what he sees as his duty to reveal to the world that deep within Hinduism exists knowledge that not only clarifies the innermost secrets of Islam but the entire monotheistic tradition as well. Having first asserted the presence of divinely inspired elements in Hinduism in the late 1640s, then highlighted important overlaps between Hinduism and Islam in the mid-1650s, with *Sirr-i akbar*, Dara Shukoh marks the final leg of a long and winding intellectual quest that would—according to his critics—irrevocably place him beyond the Islamic pale. Even if the short time between *Sirr-i akbar*'s completion in the summer of 1657 and the prince's execution means that few people could have read the text by the time of his death in 1659, Dara Shukoh's political opponents nonetheless successfully deployed it to justify his execution on grounds of heresy.

II

When Dara Shukoh decided to translate the Upanishads into Persian with the help of invited Brahmin scholars in Banaras, there were a number of distinct commentarial traditions to choose from.[34] Among the major ones were the then vibrant and popular schools of Visishtadvaita ("qualified non-dual," part dualist, part non-dualist) and Dvaita (dualist). These emerged in the eleventh and thirteenth centuries respectively, and both stipulated that the individual was distinct from a singular divinity.[35] In light of the prince's efforts to uncover what he believed was

[33] Dara Shukoh, *Sirr-i akbar*, Ethe 1980, British Library, fol. 3b.

[34] Edeltraud Harzer, "Vedanta," in *Encyclopedia of Hinduism*, ed. Cush, Robinson, and York, 950–51. See also Roebuck, "Upanisads," 894–902; Roma Chaudhuri, *A Critical Study of Dara Shikuh's 'Samudra-sangama'*, vol. 2 of *Comparative Religion and Philosophy Series* (Calcutta: Government of West Bengal, Sanskrita Siksa, 1954), I, 42–43.

[35] The main figure of the Visishtadvaita school of Vedanta was the theologian Ramanuja (d. ca. 1137). Visishtadvaita arose in reaction to the strict non-dualistic (reality as one) ideas of Advaita Vedanta. It specifically sought

Hinduism's monotheistic core, either offered a good starting point from which to undertake his inquiries.[36] Instead, he chose the commentaries of Shankaracharya (d. 820?), the greatest exponent of the Advaita Vedanta school and a scholar who argued, among other things, that there was no divinity outside the individual soul.[37] This section considers why Shankaracharya resonated so powerfully with Dara Shukoh.

Depending on the manuscript in question, the *Sirr-i akbar* offers between fifty and fifty-two Upanishads from just over a hundred that were in circulation in the 1650s. Of these anywhere between ten and twelve are considered core compositions (*mukhya*).[38] They are the oldest and are generally accepted by Hindus as having divine origins

---

to accommodate the theistic bhakti devotionalism that was extremely popular in southern India at the time. While agreeing with Shankaracharya that Brahman is a unity or non-dual (*a-dvaita*), Ramanuja posited that Brahman is also qualified (*visishta*) by its attributes. Ramanuja analogized that "just as a soul possesses a body and at the same time is not identical with it is the same way that Brahman exists independently while at the same possessing its attributes. In the same way that a body cannot live separately from a soul and is dependent on the soul for its existence, all individual souls and the inanimate world are dependent on Brahman for their existence and at the same time are essentially different from each other." According to Visishtadvaita, Brahman is a personal deity manifested in the form of *avataras* (descents) of Vishnu. Robert Goodding, "Visishtadvaita," in *Encyclopedia of Hinduism*, ed. Cush, Robinson, and York, 961–63. The Dvaita (dualist) school of Vedanta draws its lineage back to Madhva (d. 1317). Like Visishtadvaita it too is considered theistic. It differs from Visishtadvaita, however, in viewing God (associated with the god Vishnu) as supreme to and "independent" (*svatantra*) from everything in the universe. Such strict "dualism" is reinforced by the belief that all individuals and objects exist independently of one another (as well as God), even if they are completely dependent on the latter. Robert Goodding, "Dvaita," in *Encyclopedia of Hinduism*, ed. Cush, Robinson, and York, 215–17.

36 This insight was shared in person by Professor Robert Goldman (Department of South and Southeast Asian Studies, UC-Berkeley). September 2008.

37 Hasrat, *Dara Shikuh: Life and Works*, 275.

38 W. Winternitz, *A History of Sanskrit Literature*, trans. S. Ketkar and H. Kohn (Calcutta: University of Calcutta, 1927), I, 239, cited in B.J. Hasrat, *Dara Shikuh: Life and Works*, 270.

(*shruti*). The remaining numbers were probably composed some time between the first century CE and the early 1000s. Scholars like B.J. Hasrat have called our attention to two important facts about Dara Shukoh's translation. First, it has no organizational markers. This marks a significant departure from the original Sanskrit versions likely used by the prince. They would have had *adhyaya*s (parts), *kanda*s (sections), and *pada*s (subsections). Second, Hasrat also noticed how metrical and non-metrical portions of the Sanskrit original are all untidily mixed together.[39] We can thus gather that Dara Shukoh took great liberties, often disregarding Hindu commentarial traditions, and impressing upon his Brahmin interlocutors his desire to insert commentarial texts (*Upanishadbhasyas*) wherever he pleased alongside the original narratives. Against this backdrop, a reader of *Sirr-i akbar* often faces a big challenge of distinguishing between commentary and text. For anyone conversant with the original Sanskrit version(s), Dara Shukoh's Persian rendition can be highly confusing.[40]

The commentarial part of the *Sirr-i akbar* extensively uses the work of Advaita Vedantin Shankaracharya, as noted above. Important parts of the Persian texts of at least nine Upanishads—*Brhadaranyaka*, *Chandogya*, *Aitareya*, *Isha*, *Prashna*, *Mundaka*, *Katha*, *Kena*, and *Mandukya*—are especially reliant on this scholar's interpretations.[41] And yet, as a number of noted Vedanta scholars have already pointed out, the doctrines of Advaita Vedanta (non-dual, hence *a-dvaita*) cannot be characterized as monotheistic at all.[42] In fact, Shankaracharya's interpretations of *nirguna*

[39] Hasrat, *Dara Shikuh: Life and Works*, 270–73, 275–76.

[40] Hasrat, *Dara Shikuh: Life and Works*, 270–73, 275.

[41] Hasrat, *Dara Shikuh: Life and Works*, 270. Regarding *Taittiriya*, it does not seem to be consistently included in those Persian manuscripts of the *Sirr-i akbar* that only have fifty Upanishads. Thus it is missing from the primary manuscript consulted by Hasrat. *Dara Shikuh: Life and Works*, 271–73. It is also missing from the Persian edition prepared by Tara Chand and Sayyid Muhammad Reza Jalali Naini (Tehran: Intisharat-i 'Ilmi, reprint, 1989).

[42] Eliot Deutsch, *Advaita Vedanta: A Philosophical Reconstruction* (Honolulu: East-West Center Press, 1969), 13; Surendranath Dasgupta, *A History of Indian Philosophy* (Delhi: Motilal Banarsidass, reprint, 1975), I, 437–42. See also Patrick Olivelle, *Upanisads* (New York: Oxford University Press, 1996); Richard King, *Indian Philosophy: An Introduction to Hindu and Buddhist Thought* (Washington, D.C.: Georgetown University Press, 1999); Hajime Nakamura,

Brahman (Brahman without attributes) and *saguna* Brahman (Brahman with attributes) offer an understanding of God that sets him apart from later theistic exponents of Vedanta whose writings are arguably more compatible with monotheistic views.[43] Therefore, Shankaracharya's *bhasya*s (commentaries) are in a distinctly awkward relationship with the remaining Upanishads selected for inclusion in the *Sirr-i akbar*.

To begin with, Shankaracharya did not subscribe to a view of God/ Universal Soul/Ultimate Principle/Brahman as such. For him, as Deutsch suggests, Brahman in fact is neither a "He" nor an "It" but rather a "state of being."[44] Furthermore, this "state of being" incorporated individuals and all other beings and aspects of reality; it did not exist, as a monotheist would have it, as separate from the individual. Writes Edeltraud Harzer, "According to Shankara there is nothing either real or non-real apart from Brahman. Thus the individual self (*atman*) must be understood as identical with Brahman."[45] By no means was this Brahman of Shankaracharya's "a personal deity who responds to prayer, bestows grace, or enters into history."[46] For someone like Dara Shukoh, searching as he was for Hinduism's monotheistic core, Shankaracharya's ideas therefore offer little support. It is possible that Dara Shukoh either misread Shankaracharya or was misled by his Brahmin interlocutors into believing that he was a theist.[47] What really transpired on this score is

---

A History of Early Vedanta Philosophy, trans. Trevor Leggett (Delhi: Motilal Banarsidass, 1985), I; T.M.P. Mahadevan, *The Philosophy of Advaita* (Tisbury, England: Compton Russell, 1977); Harzer, "Vedanta," 950–51. Deutsch in fact argues that Shankaracharya's ideas should not even be confused with monism since they reject "any position that views reality as a single order of objective being." In Advaita, unity or oneness "does not require variety or multiplicity, as in the case with most monistic views, in order to be affirmed." *Advaita Vedanta*, fn. 2, 3.

43 Gavin Flood, *Introduction to Hinduism* (Cambridge: Cambridge University Press, 1996), 243–46.

44 Deutsch, *Advaita Vedanta*, 9.

45 Harzer, "Vedanta," 951. See also Flood, *Introduction to Hinduism*, 242.

46 Deutsch, *Advaita Vedanta*, 9, 13.

47 In an essay detailing medieval efforts (and the political impulses driving them) to vest Shankaracharya with the authority of a *jagadguru* (world teacher), Angelika Malinar highlights one important textual endeavor, namely the *Shankara-digvijaya* ("Shankar's Conquering of the Direction," ascribed to the

beside the point, however, since Shankaracharya's attractiveness to Dara Shukoh seems to have lain elsewhere.

The ultimate goal of Shankaracharya's Advaita Vedanta is the attainment of freedom, liberty—moksha (or *mukti*)—with Brahman (*Brahmajnana*).[48] Such a state of mental purity (*citta shuddhi*) can only be attained, however, through the mental-spiritual discipline of *jnana* yoga (the discipline/path of knowledge). For instructional purposes, Shankaracharya lays down four qualifications that must be fulfilled and three stages that must be overcome.[49] Discipline is absolutely central to the pursuit of this path if the person is to finally attain the status of a *jivanamukta* or someone totally liberated from living experience while

---

fourteenth-century *mahant* Madhavacharya/Vidyaranyamuni of the Shankara monastery in Shringeri), in which the Advaita Vedantin's monistic doctrines acquire a *saguna* or theistic hue. This reinterpretation of Shankaracharya's ideas seems to have gained considerable currency in the Deccan (thanks especially to the important role of the Shankara *matha* in legitimizing the nascent Vijayanagara Empire). "Sankara as Jagadguru According to Sankara-Digvijaya," in *The Oxford India Hinduism Reader*, ed. Vasudha Dalmia and Heinrich von Steitencron (New Delhi: Oxford University Press, 2007), 129–50. According to Vasudha Dalmia, it is highly likely that this gloss or some variant of it traveled to the main centers of Hinduism in northern India, becoming, by the seventeenth century, the received wisdom on Shankaracharya. Personal communication, June 2011.

[48] Deutsch, *Advaita Vedanta*, 104.

[49] The four qualifications include: (*a*) an ability to distinguish (*viveka*) between what is real (*nitya*) and unreal (*anitya*); (*b*) non-attachment (*vairagya*) to all enjoyment and desire; (*c*) acquisition of mental ontrol (*sama*), control over sense organs and organs of action (*dama*), withdrawal (*uparati*), endurance (*titiksa*), single-mindedness (*samadhana*), and faith (*sraddha*) in valid knowledge and the teacher who shares it; (*d*) complete concentration upon the attainment of freedom and wisdom (*mumuksutva*). The three stages include: (*a*) "listening" (*sravana*) to the masters (gurus) and studying the Vedantic texts; (*b*) "thinking" (*manana*) and therefore appropriating not only outwardly but also inwardly all the lessons of Advaita; (*c*) "contemplation" (*nididhyasana*). Deutsch, *Advaita Vedanta*, 105–10; Anantanand Rambachan, *Accomplishing the Accomplished: The Vedas as a Source of Valid Knowledge in Sankara* (Honolulu: University of Hawaii Press, 1991), 88–92, 97–113. See also Roger Marcaurelle, *Freedom through Inner Renunciation: Sankara's Philosophy in a New Light* (Albany: State University of New York Press, 2000).

still alive, someone who recognizes no difference between the world and Brahman. According to the tenets of Advaita Vedanta, this liberation only comes with the recognition that life is a magical illusion (maya) superimposed on a reality that is without distinction or plurality.[50] It bears noting that neither of the other most famous schools of Vedanta, namely Visishtadvaita or Dvaita, recognize the possibility of *jivanamukti* (liberation in life).[51] Significantly, by the last decade of Dara Shukoh's life, he and his followers were claiming that the prince had achieved a status akin to a *jivanamukta*, namely that of a Muslim *insan-i kamil*, or Perfect Man. They described this as an individual liberated from all fault and in a state of direct consciousness of God, while still possessing human form.[52]

The Islamic concept of the Perfect Man can be traced back to the writings of al-'Arabi. Although subsequent Islamic thinkers—including al-Qunawi (d. 1274) and al-Jili, among others—added their individual glosses to al-'Arabi's original insights, there was essential agreement that, quoting the Islamicist R.W.J. Austin, "the Perfect Man is that human individual who has perfectly realized the full spiritual potential of the human state, who has realized in himself and his experience the Oneness

[50] Martin Ovens, "Jivanamukta," in *Encyclopedia of Hinduism*, ed. Cush, Robinson, and York, 391–92; Richard King, "Advaita," in *Encyclopedia of Hinduism*, ed. Cush, Robinson, and York, 5–6. See also Karl H. Potter, ed., *Advaita Vedanta up to Samkara and His Pupils*, vol. 3 of *Encyclopedia of Indian Philosophies* (Delhi: Motilal Banarsidass, 1998), 34–35.

[51] Goodding, "Dvaita," 217.

[52] Dara Shukoh, *Diwan-i dara shikoh*, ed. Ahmad Nabi Khan (Lahore: Research Society of Pakistan, 1969), 168–69. See also Hasrat, *Dara Shikuh: Life and Works*, 143; Qanungo, *Dara Shukoh*, 89. For the *insan-i kamil* as with the *jivanamukta*, "the body continues" just as "the potter's wheel spins for a period of time after the potter's hand has been withdrawn." Final release only comes with death. Ovens, "Jivanamukta," 392. Although the two concepts do not correspond exactly—most significantly, even if the Perfect Man is a manifestation of God, he is not God but rather remains in the subordinate position of a worshipper unlike the *jivanamukta* who is Brahman—there is enough resonance that an outsider like Dara Shukoh might easily fail to comprehend such key distinctions. For a critical discussion of the ways in which Dara Shukoh may have fundamentally misinterpreted the idea of the *jivanamukta*, see Chaudhuri, *A Critical Study of Dara Shikuh's 'Samudra-sangama'*, I, 115–16.

of Being that underlines all the apparent multiplicity of existence."[53] Dara Shukoh wrote of attaining a similar kind of perfection in his devotional texts *Risala-i haqnuma* and *Tariqat al-haqiqat*.[54] By Dara Shukoh's own reckoning these manuals showed a devotee the way to realize unity with the Divine even as they testified to the fact that the prince had already attained such realization himself.[55] Although we cannot be sure that Dara Shukoh viewed his own claim to *insan-i kamil* status as corresponding to Shankaracharya's ideas about *jivanamukta* (or whether he mistakenly equated the two as suggested by Roma Chaudhuri[56]), this much is certain: Dara Shukoh was inspired by his engagement with Shankaracharya to advance the extraordinary claim that the Upanishads were God's original revelation about Divine Unity. Given his earlier declarations of his own exalted spiritual attainments, it is not hard to imagine the attraction Shankaracharya's ideas of *jivanamukta* held for the prince, to the point that he could even brush aside Shankaracharya's decided lack of monotheist leanings.

Besides the attractive idea of *jivanamukta*, Dara Shukoh was also clearly beguiled by talk of secret and esoteric knowledge in Shankaracharya's writings. Shankaracharya argued that the Upanishads were "the secret doctrine of all the Vedas" and "the highest [secret doctrine] even for the gods." By way of warning, Shankaracharya added: "This secret and supreme knowledge should not be given to [a student] who is not tranquil."[57] Shankaracharya proclaimed that the word

[53] R.W.J. Austin, trans., *Ibn al-'Arabi: The Bezels of Wisdom* (New York: Paulist Press, 1980), 37, quoted in Alexander Knysh, *Ibn 'Arabi in the Later Islamic Tradition: The Making of a Polemical Image in Medieval Islam* (Albany: State University of New York Press, 1998), 15. See also R. Arnaldez, "al-Insan al-Kamil," in *Encyclopaedia of Islam, Second Edition*, ed. Bearman, Bianquis, Bosworth, van Donzel, and Heinrichs.

[54] Shukoh, *Risala-i haqnuma*, fol. 35a. See also Hasrat, *Dara Shikuh: Life and Works*, 114–15.

[55] Shukoh, *Risala-i haqnuma*, fol. 6b.

[56] Chaudhuri, *A Critical Study of Dara Shikuh's 'Samudra-sangama'*, I, 114–16.

[57] *Sankara's Upadesasahasri*, ed. and trans. Sengaku Mayeda (Delhi: Motilal Banarsidass, reprint, 2006), II, 168. References in the Upanishads point to hidden or secret knowledge. Hence in the *Kena* Upanishad (IV, 7) a student and his teacher converse about "the hidden connection (*upanisad*)." In the *Katha*

"Upanishad" gestured to a very particular knowledge that had the near (*upa*) certainty (*ni*) of destroying (*sad*) those who were unqualified to possess it.[58] His gloss of the term was distinct from the more common alternative: the verb *sad* (to sit), preceded by the preverbs *upa-* (near) and *ni-* (down), here referring to a session consisting of pupils, assembled around their teacher's feet.[59] Shankaracharya, however, believed the Upanishads to embody such powerful knowledge that it could only be entrusted to the most spiritually advanced. Indeed, in Shankaracharya's commentaries, such terms as *rahasyam* (secret), *paramam guhyam* (the greatest/supreme secret), or *guhyatamam* (the highest secret) often serve as stand-ins or accompaniments for the term "Upanishad."[60]

The following section highlights how Dara Shukoh accommodated Shankaracharya's insights. Thus, although it is hard to confuse Shankaracharya as a monotheist (in the tradition of the erstwhile *muvahhidan-i Hind*), and likely Dara Shukoh himself did not do so either, the prince nonetheless drew on the scholar's insights to advance his claim in the *Sirr-i akbar* that the Upanishads were the spring/source (*sar-i chashma*) of all expressions of *tawhid*.[61] The strength of this claim was, in turn, important to Dara Shukoh's political aspirations.

Upanishad (I, iii, 17), the text says: "If a man, pure and devout, proclaims this great secret/in a gathering of Brahmins,/or during a meal for the dead,/it will lead him to eternal life." Patrick Olivelle, ed. and trans., *The Early Upanishads* (Oxford: Oxford University Press, 1998), 371, 391.

58 F. Max Müller, trans., *The Upanishads*, vol 1. of *Sacred Books of the East*, ed. F. Max Müller (Oxford: Clarendon Press, 1879), lxxxiii; Signe Cohen, *Text and Authority in the Older Upanisads* (Leiden: Brill, 2008), 3–5; Swami Gambhirananda, trans., *Eight Upanishads: With the Commentary of Sankaracarya* (Calcutta: Advaita Ashrama, 1957–58), I, 93–94.

59 Müller, *The Upanishads*, lxxxii; Cohen, *Text and Authority*, 3. See also Roebuck, "Upanisads," 894; Olivelle, *Upanisads*, lii; J.G. Suthren Hirst, *Samkara's Advaita Vendanta: A Way of Teaching* (London: RoutledgeCurzon, 2005), 69.

60 Paul Deussen, *The Philosophy of the Upanishads*, trans. A.S. Geden (Edinburgh: T. & T. Clark, 1906), 10, 12. For further discussion about the Upanishads as a secret text embodying esoteric knowledge, see Cohen, *Text and Authority*, 9–13.

61 Hasrat, *Dara Shikuh: Life and Works*, 267.

III

Dara Shukoh's introduction to *Sirr-i akbar* is extremely succinct. The British Library manuscript version consulted for this essay, written in a clean *nasta'liq* script, only spans four folio sides. It pronounces the Upanishads a "treasure of Divine Oneness" (*ganj-i tawhid*) and a crucial commentary on the Quran, even as it claims the text for Islam.[62] As such, it speaks to Dara Shukoh's interest in pushing the boundaries of religious inquiry as well as to his religious eclecticism. At the same time, his treatment of the Upanishads as "Islamic" scripture suggests the possibility of denying some parts of Hinduism an independent religious basis outside an Islamic theological framework. Thus this final text of Dara Shukoh can also be read as a call to all Indian "believers in the unity of God" (*muvahhidan*) and "realizers of the truth" (*muhaqqiqan*) to accept their rightful place within the Islamic fold.

Following an invocation of God's greatness, the introduction begins by addressing two additional pillars of Islamic dogma: the abrogative supremacy of the Quran, and the beatific qualities of the Prophet Muhammad, his family, and his companions. An autobiographical snippet follows next. Here the prince takes pains to establish three points. First, he proclaims the greatness of his own spiritual preceptor, Mulla Shah Badakhshi, whom he describes as "the most perfect of the perfects, the flower of the gnostics (*arifan*), the master of the masters, the pir of the pirs, the guide of the guides, the believer in the unity of God accomplished in the Truth (*muvahhid-i haqa'iq agah*)."[63] Second, the prince emphasizes the length of his association with Badakhshi—seventeen years. Third, and most crucially, he relates the manner in which his intellectual journey has unfolded.

As Dara Shukoh explains, despite extensive research and writing aimed at explicating the secrets of God's Oneness, he remained filled with doubt. Finally, the prince says, he realized that he needed to turn to "God's word" (*kalam-i ilahi*) itself to overcome his distress. Naturally, he first turned to the Quran.[64] Unfortunately, doing so did not offer him the succor he sought because the Quran was—by his own account—filled with subtleties/enigmas (*marmuz*). The prince turned next to the

[62] Shukoh, *Sirr-i akbar*, fol. 3a.

[63] Shukoh, *Sirr-i akbar*, fol. 2a.

[64] Shukoh, *Sirr-i akbar*, fol. 2b.

other standard monotheistic texts; he specifically mentions the Old and New Testaments. As he explains, he clearly hoped that they might offer answers. Again, however, the prince found little comfort or satisfaction; these texts too were enigmatic and their translations so poor as to render them unintelligible (*matlub ma'lum nagirdid*).[65] Up to this juncture there is nothing particularly unique about Dara Shukoh's investigations. His frustration with the enigmas of the Quran and even biblical texts echoes the quiet grouses of generations of Muslim scholars before him. It is the next step that will push him toward the outer edges of permissible inquiry among Muslims.

Dara Shukoh wonders why discussions of monotheism were so widespread in India (*az che juhat dar Hindustan … guftagu-yi tawhid bisyar ast*).[66] He seems to have been particularly struck by the idea that scholars and mystics of the "old school" neither objected to "ideas about the oneness [of God]" nor spoke against monotheists (*taifa-yi qadim-i Hind ra bar wahdat inkari wa bar muvahhidan guftari nist*).[67] His curiosity piqued, the prince says, he began to examine the "heavenly books" (*kutb-i asmani*) of this "ancient nation" (*qaum-i qadim*).[68] What followed was a startling discovery: the Vedas were in fact revealed to the Hindus' greatest prophet, Brahma, who—Dara Shukoh asserts—is none other than the Prophet Adam by another name.[69]

As mentioned above, Dara Shukoh was not the first Muslim scholar to wonder whether the Vedas might be viewed as the Quran or Bible of the ancient Hindus. It is the prince's association of Brahma with Adam, however, that signaled his rejection of two other longstanding, if controversial, ideas: the first associating Brahma with God/Allah, and the second connecting Brahma with the Prophet Abraham. In fact, only two years earlier, in 1655–56, the prince had himself argued that Brahma was none other than the Angel Gabriel—in other words, an important figure but nothing like the law-giving prophet of a monotheistic faith.[70]

[65] Shukoh, *Sirr-i akbar*, fol. 2b.
[66] Shukoh, *Sirr-i akbar*, fol. 2b.
[67] Shukoh, *Sirr-i akbar*, fol. 2b.
[68] Shukoh, *Sirr-i akbar*, fol. 2b.
[69] Shukoh, *Sirr-i akbar*, fol. 3a.
[70] Shukoh, *Majma' al-bahrayn*, ff. 6a–b. Indeed, in the hierarchy of beings, angels occupy a lower rung than humans. It was the refusal of Satan/Iblis to accept this fact that resulted in his banishment from God's presence.

While other scholars like the Iran-based Mir 'Abul Qasim Findiriski (d. 1640)—who translated the *Yogavasishta* into Persian—did go so far as to proclaim a secondary spiritual importance for that text, Dara Shukoh seemed to go further in claiming parity in the monotheistic status, at any rate, of the Vedas and the Quran. He seemed to suggest that the Upanishads represented an earlier source for monotheism, just as the Bible was earlier than the Quran. He also seemed to suggest something no other Muslim scholar had ever publicly breathed: that certain Hindu texts might serve as a commentary (*tafsir*) on all monotheistic religious texts, not only the Quran. Thus the Vedas had not been entirely superseded by later more inspired texts; rather, they retained some original insights that were lost in the later texts. It was these radical claims that earned Dara Shukoh great infamy.

Having asserted a connection between the Vedas and Prophet Adam, Dara Shukoh claims that the Upanishads offer a synthesis (*khulasa*) of all the secret shlokas and contemplations of *tawhid* found across the first four Vedas (namely the *Rig*, *Yajur*, *Sama*, and *Atharva*). Without ever mentioning Shankaracharya by name, the prince claims that he had access to "commentaries" (*tafsir*) by prophets of Sanskrit (*anbiya-yi zaban*) that are considered to be "the best interpretations" (*behtarin ibarat*). It was these same commentaries, he asserts, that helped him uncover this "great secret" about the Upanishads. Following the assertions of Shankaracharya, the prince claims that the term "Upanishads" means "secrets to be concealed" (*asrar-i poshidni*).[71]

Dara Shukoh attached great significance to his discovery of the Upanishads' "monotheistic" character. Besides arguing that he had uncovered a deliberate plot, spanning centuries, to "conceal and hide" (*poshida wa pinhan*) the Upanishads from Muslims (*ahl-i Islam*), Dara Shukoh also claimed that he had finally found answers to all the questions that had forced him to look beyond the Quran and biblical texts in the first place.[72] Dara Shukoh is wholly convinced that these "first heavenly books" (*awwalin kutb-i samawi*) are not only "the spring/source of the inquiry as well as the ocean of Divine Oneness" (*sar-i chashma-yi tahqiq wa bahr-i tawhid*) but, more crucially, that they conform with

[71] Shukoh, *Sirr-i akbar*, fol. 3a.
[72] Shukoh, *Sirr-i akbar*, fol. 3a.

and provide commentary for the Quran (*mutabiq-i Quran Majeed balkih tafsir-i an ast*).[73] With this judgment—one that raises serious doubts about the Quran's perfection and Islam's complete self-sufficiency in relation to all preceding religions—Dara Shukoh conclusively overstepped the bounds of accepted Islamic dogma.[74]

Clearly anticipating attack as a heretic or an apostate, Dara Shukoh's introduction offers a scattered but vigorous three-part defense of his claims directed almost exclusively at the Muslim community. Importantly, only the opinion of fellow Muslims appears to have mattered to him.

The first element in this defense is a blistering attack on the Muslim *'ulama*. Mocking the *'ulama*'s claims to knowledge and learning, Dara Shukoh characterizes these men as the "uninformed of this age" (*jahlai in waqt*). By using the plural form of "*jahil*" (ignorant/barbarian/unbeliever) Dara Shukoh deliberately equates the *'ulama* to the pre-Islamic Arabs who are derided in Muslim historical and religious accounts as living in the lowest state of civilization. Like the *jahils* of yore, the *'ulama* are also engaged in unbelief (*kufr*) by virtue of their willful rejection (*inkar*) of non-Islamic Indian monotheists (*muvahhidan*) who are "knowers of God" (*khuda ashnasan*) and "congregation of Divine Oneness" (*jam'-i sukhanan-i tawhid*).[75] The implications of this line of argument are clear: given the *'ulama*'s lack of religious credibility, how can they sit in judgment over Dara Shukoh's religious inquiries?

An attempt to clarify his interpretative reasoning forms the second part of Dara Shukoh's self-defense. The prince explains that his inspiration to take a serious look at the Upanishads came from no less a source than the Quran itself. He cites *Sura al-fatir*'s proclamation that every community everywhere and throughout history had, at one point or another, received divine guidance (*wa az Quran Majeed niz ma'lum mishud keh hich qaumi nist keh bi-kitab wa payghumbar bashad*) to put it

[73] Shukoh, *Sirr-i akbar*, ff. 3a–b.

[74] For further insight about why Dara Shukoh's analysis was considered heretical by most Muslims, see Irfan Omar, "Where the Two Oceans Meet: An Attempt at Hindu–Muslim Rapprochement in the Thought of Dara Shikuh," *Journal of Ecumenical Studies* 44, no. 2 (2009): 303–14.

[75] Shukoh, *Sirr-i akbar*, fol. 2b.

on the right track.[76] The prince remarks that the Quran makes this point elsewhere as well. *Sura al-isra* ("The Night Journey," 17: 15), for instance, explicitly states, "We never chastise, until We send forth a Messenger."[77] After studying the Upanishads, Dara Shukoh notes, he had no doubt that they were one of the prior "exercises in Divine Oneness" (*ashghal-i tawhid*) referred to in both *Sura al-fatir* and *Sura al-isra.*[78]

Dara Shukoh offers additional citation from the Quran—specifically *Sura al-waqi'ah* ("The Occurrence," 56: 77–80)[79]—to support his more conspiratorial claim that the Upanishads are not only God's first monotheistic text but in fact the spring from which all subsequent discussions about Divine Oneness flow. He notes *Sura al-waqi'ah*'s reference to a "hidden/protected book" (*kitab maknun*) that has already been revealed by God. Dismissing the possibility that this "hidden book" might be a reference to any of the commonly known monotheistic texts—the Torah, the Psalms, or the New Testament—Dara Shukoh also rejects any connection with the *Lawh-i mahfuz* (the "Safely Preserved" tablet widely regarded by Muslims as the original copy of the Quran and the source of all revelation). After all, *Sura al-waqi'ah*, Dara Shukoh writes, refers to an existing revelation (*tanazzul*) unlike the *Lawh-i mahfuz*, which, he claims, remains unrevealed.[80] From this, he infers, the "hidden book" can be no other than the Upanishads. He offers three proofs to cement this argument.

One, the very essence (*asal*) of the Upanishads is to conceal secrets, precisely as might be expected of a "hidden book."[81] Two, he claims (although without corroboration) that actual verses (*ayat*s) in the Quran

[76] Shukoh, *Sirr-i akbar*, fol. 3a. *Sura al-fatir* ("The Originator," 35: 24) states: "Verily We have sent thee in truth, as a bearer of glad tidings, and as a warner: and there never was a people, without a warner having lived among them (in the past)." Abdullah Yusuf Ali, trans., *The Meaning of the Holy Quran* (Beltsville, Maryland: Amana Publications, 1989), 1102.

[77] Arberry, trans., *The Koran Interpreted*, 303.

[78] Shukoh, *Sirr-i akbar*, fol. 3a.

[79] "It is surely a noble Quran in a hidden book (*fi kitab maknun*). None but the purified shall touch, a sending down from the Lord of all Being." Arberry, trans., *The Koran Interpreted*, 256.

[80] Shukoh, *Sirr-i akbar*, fol. 3b.

[81] Shukoh, *Sirr-i akbar*, fol. 3b.

are also found in this "ancient book" (*kitab-i qadim*).[82] And, finally, the divine and originary character of the Upanishads is confirmed by the fact that Dara Shukoh himself experienced enlightenment through reading it: "Unknown things became known and incomprehensible things became comprehensible to this devotee [i.e., Dara Shukoh]" (*nadanastha danasta wa nafahmidaha fahmida*).[83] After all, "the words of God are their own commentary" (*kalam-i ilahi tafsir-i khud ast*).[84]

The final defense Dara Shukoh offers to support his claims in *Sirr-i akbar* is based on the notion of service to Islam. The prince argues that he is serving his fellow Muslims by revealing to them the secrets of a divine text that had been deliberately concealed from them. Thanks to his efforts, the prince implies, he has enabled Muslims to claim ownership of humanity's first historical witness to *tawhid*. By extension, his work vindicates the universality of the Quranic worldview by demonstrating how its monotheism is traceable back to classical Brahminical and philosophical texts. Lest any doubts arise whether God approves of his enterprise, Dara Shukoh refers to a divination he received from *Sura al-'araf* in the Quran when he first commenced his translation of the Upanishads: "A Book revealed unto thee—so let thy heart be oppressed no more by any difficulty on that account—that with it thou mightest warn (the erring) and teach the Believers."[85] Although this Quranic verse refers to the Prophet Muhammad and the Quran, the implied connection to Dara Shukoh's own "revelation" and his appointment by God to lead humanity to salvation, a Perfect Man, is noteworthy.

Most Muslims of the time rejected Dara Shukoh's conclusions. Religious scholars especially would have found his claims to religious authority to be unacceptable. After all, to be considered a qualified exegete (*mufassir*) in the Islamic tradition requires years of training, the development of widely acknowledged scholarly credentials, and the demonstration of one's mastery of customary Quranic exegesis (*tafsir*). Dara Shukoh was lacking on all these scores. His years spent in the company of Mulla Shah Badakhshi counted for little given the

82 Shukoh, *Sirr-i akbar*, fol. 3b.

83 Shukoh, *Sirr-i akbar*, fol. 3b.

84 Shukoh, *Sirr-i akbar*, fol. 2b.

85 Shukoh, *Sirr-i akbar*, fol. 3b. See *Sura al-'araf* ("The Elevated Places," 7: 2). Ali, trans., *The Meaning of the Holy Quran*, 345.

latter's contested status within Miyan Mir's own circle of disciples, never mind the widespread dislike of him across the larger Qadiri order. The prince's claims to scholarly authority were also undermined by his seeming failure to follow established rules of Quranic exegesis. None was more important than the principle that obvious meaning or explanation takes precedence over esoteric meaning or explanation. Thus as long as Dara Shukoh seemed to derive his argument that the Upanishads be considered a revelation by basing his reasoning on multiple sources within the Quran, he did not necessarily run afoul of his critics. His failure, however, to offer anything similar to buttress either his (*a*) explicit claim that the Upanishads were monotheism's very source or (*b*) implicit claim that the Quran's logic of supersession had been overridden landed him in deep trouble. From the perspective of his detractors, Dara Shukoh seemed to be both deliberately misreading *Sura al-waqi'ah* and relying on *ta'wil*—an interpretative but controversial subset of *tafsir* that uses dreams and/or other esoteric signs—to directly contradict a well-established understanding of the Quran. This was unacceptable. Although Dara Shukoh's introduction to the Upanishads stands as a creative Islamicizing of a non-monotheistic text and might provide a route for certain communities of Hindus to take their place within the Islamic fold, the prince was eventually put to death by his brother, the new emperor Aurangzeb, on the charge of having forsaken Islam.

How might Dara Shukoh's quest for spiritual greatness have been entangled with his other major ambition: to follow his father as the next Mughal emperor? This question is especially pertinent since *Sirr-i akbar* was written against the backdrop of a brewing war of succession.

IV

The Mughal dynasty never evolved clearly articulated rules of dynastic succession. In theory, every son of a reigning emperor had an equal claim to succeeding his father to the imperial throne. In the seventeenth century, these rights came to be worked out through often-vicious wars of succession. Knowing that their lives depended on their achievements and their ability to outmaneuver their brothers, generations of Mughal princes placed great stock in constructing powerful princely households and creating expansive networks of political alliances. These efforts invariably proceeded in tandem with the princes' appointments as imperial governors or military commanders. Competition was intense as each prince tried to outdo the other for maximum political advantage. Such competition kept the Mughal system coursing with political energy.[86] Dara Shukoh was not oblivious to his own importance nor, judging from writings of contemporary historians or foreign visitors to Mughal India, was he a reluctant political player. So how do we evaluate the relationship between his equally significant political and religious personas—both as he understood them and as we might perceive them today in hindsight?

In a 2001 entry on Dara Shukoh in the second edition of the *Encyclopedia of Islam*, the eminent medieval Indian historian Satish Chandra discounted the possibility that political considerations motivated the prince's religious inquiries.[87] There is indeed little textual evidence to indicate the prince's conscious pursuit of his spiritual quest as an argument for his political advancement, for asserting why he, as opposed to his younger brothers, deserved the Mughal throne. On another level, however, once we move beyond the prince's literal words, can we not discern in Dara Shukoh's written corpus an effort to not only fashion a self-image but also hint at the qualities that equipped him to be the next emperor? The prince's introduction to *Sirr-i akbar* is especially illuminating in this regard. Before examining the text, however, let us briefly evaluate Dara Shukoh's unusual trajectory as a Mughal prince.

Dara Shukoh was in fact unique among sixteenth- and seventeenth-century Mughal princes. He never served in one of the Mughal *suba*s (provinces) as a governor, and aside from one terribly mismanaged campaign in 1653 against the Safavid-held fortress of Qandahar, he also never commanded a major military undertaking. Instead, he spent most of his adult life cocooned in the relative safety and comfort of the Mughal court. Where Dara Shukoh's rivals could lay claim to administrative or military experience, Shah Jahan's favorite son had little of either. This was not an insignificant fact. The fight for the Mughal throne was always

[86] These ideas are comprehensively explored in my book, *Princes of the Mughal Empire* (Cambridge: Cambridge University Press, 2012).

[87] Satish Chandra, "Dara Shukoh," in *Encyclopaedia of Islam, Second Edition*, ed. Bearman, Bianquis, Bosworth, van Donzel, and Heinrichs. This idea is also echoed by the Islamicist Irfan Omar, "Where the Two Oceans Meet."

a popularity contest of sorts. Non-princely players in the Mughal system had to be wooed to join one side or another. Even a favored prince like Dara Shukoh had to find some way to impress the most powerful nodes in Mughal society with a sense of who he was and why they should support him against his brothers.

Indisputably, Dara Shukoh's most significant play was to consistently point to the sheer inevitability of his own accession. Not only did he have his father's unalloyed favor but, by the 1650s—at least on paper—he also enjoyed access to military and financial resources equal to those of his three brothers combined.[88] Dara Shukoh's accumulation of power did not go unnoticed. In a 1657 letter to his older sister Jahan Ara, his third brother Aurangzeb angrily queried why "despite twenty years of service and loyalty, [I am] not considered worthy of the same level of confidence as [even] my brother's [Dara Shukoh's] son (Sulaiman Shukoh)?"[89] At the heart of Aurangzeb's complaint was the perception that the imperial deck was being rapidly and unfairly stacked in favor of the older prince and his own sons. But Dara Shukoh may have made another subtler case for his own candidacy over and above its inevitability.

The introduction to the *Sirr-i akbar* offers no explicit references to Dara Shukoh's political interests, but a potent princely self-portrait nevertheless emerges from its pages. In broad terms, the reader feels carefully nudged to consider Dara Shukoh as a man of rare intelligence, wisdom, discernment, courage, tenacity, and conviction. He is also divinely blessed in the tradition of an *insan-i kamil*. Such assertions of the prince's character and qualities afford a clear, if highly partisan, sense of what he might bring to the table as king. So, even if bereft of military or administrative genius, Dara Shukoh might be expected to provide the spiritual wisdom and gravitas—in the vein perhaps of the first three Rightly Guided Caliphs of Islam (Abu Bakr, 'Umar, and 'Usman) who also did not have the distinction of leading their own armies—to allow the Mughal Empire to continue to flourish.

[88] By 1657, the last full year of Shah Jahan's reign, Dara Shukoh had been elevated to the extraordinary standing of 50000/40000 within the Mughal *mansab* system. This is compared to a combined rank of 55000/42000 for Shujā', Aurangzeb, and Murad all together.

[89] Aurangzeb, *Adab-i 'alamgiri*, ed. Abdul Ghafur Chaudhuri (Lahore: Idarat-i Tahqiqat-i Pakistan, 1971), II, 829.

We also see Dara Shukoh directly clarifying his relationship to Islam, to perhaps allay potential discomfort within the Muslim nobility. Here, again, the message is a reassuring one. Dara Shukoh takes great pains to highlight how, far from forsaking Islam, as his critics were quietly charging, his ability to uncover monotheism's greatest secret (*sirr-i akbar*) fundamentally depended on an intense engagement with the Quran. Furthermore, he goes to some lengths to highlight his essential belief that Islam is the best religion of all and that it, with the help of inputs from the Upanishads, will emerge clarified and theologically stronger than ever in the future (during his reign?).[90]

As we know, Dara Shukoh failed to win the argument. Perhaps Emperor Shah Jahan's sudden and premature sickness, coming close on the heels of the completion of *Sirr-i akbar*, cut short any possibility of the prince advertising or clarifying what he had achieved. Perhaps *Sirr-i akbar*, with its explicit disregard for the norms of Quranic exegesis, to say nothing of its controversial ideas, could not but irrevocably antagonize Muslim political and religious opinion. Perhaps it did not matter what Dara Shukoh said or did in the 1650s since, as Kinra highlights, he may have already alienated all but his most devoted followers years before.[91] Regardless, Dara Shukoh's ideas and insights largely died with him. And, over the centuries that followed, his life's story became encrusted in all sorts of myths. These need to be reconsidered, however, if we are to finally more beyond simplistic understandings of Dara Shukoh as the "good" or "bad" Muslim.

[90] Crucially, there is no evidence in Dara Shukoh's writings to suggest that his desire to award the Upanishads a special status was in any way linked to currying favor with politically or militarily powerful communities of Hindus, such as the Rajputs. This echoes M. Athar Ali's findings that there is "no proof in either the actions of any [princely] contenders or in the behaviour of any section of the nobility, that the War of Succession was regarded as a war between faiths." *Mughal India: Studies in Polity, Ideas, Society, and Culture* (Delhi: Oxford University Press, 2006), 245. While certain Hindu religious groups may have eventually favorably received Dara Shukoh's message, this reception and engagement only occurred in the decades following his execution (as copies or translations of *Sirr-i akbar* slowly became available).

[91] Kinra, "Infantilizing Baba Dara."

BIBLIOGRAPHY

Abu'l Fazl, Shaikh. *A'in-i akbari*. 3 volumes. Edited by H. Blochmann. Calcutta: Asiatic Society of Bengal, 1877.

Ahmad, Aziz. *Studies in Islamic Culture in an Indian Environment*. Delhi: Oxford University Press, reprint, 1999.

Alam, Muzaffar. *The Languages of Political Islam in India 1200–1800*. Delhi: Permanent Black, 2004.

Ali, Abdullah Yusuf, trans. *The Meaning of the Holy Quran*. Beltsville, Maryland: Amana Publications, 1989.

Ali, M. Athar. *Mughal India: Studies in Polity, Ideas, Society, and Culture*. Delhi: Oxford University Press, 2006.

Ali, Sadiq. *A Vindication of Aurangzeb*. Calcutta: R. Rahman, 1918.

Arberry, A.J., trans. *The Koran Interpreted*. New York: Macmillan, 1955.

Arnaldez, R. "al-Insanal-Kamil." In *Encyclopaedia of Islam, Second Edition*, edited by P. Bearman, Th. Bianquis, C.E. Bosworth, E. van Donzel, and W.P. Heinrichs. Leiden: Brill, 2011. http://www.brillonline.nl/subscriber/entry?entry=islam_COM-0375. Accessed April 2, 2012.

Aurangzeb. *Adab-i 'alamgiri*. Edited by Abdul Ghafur Chaudhuri. 2 volumes. Lahore: Idarah-i Tahqiqat-i Pakistan, 1971.

Austin, R.W.J., trans. *Ibn al-'Arabi: The Bezels of Wisdom*. New York: Paulist Press, 1980.

Bilgrami, Fatima Z. *History of the Qadiri Order in India: 16th–18th Century*. Delhi: Idarah-i Adabiyat-i Delli, 2005.

Buehler, Arthur. "The Indo-Pakistani Qadiriyya." *Journal of the History of Sufism: Special Issue: The Qadiriyya Order* 1–2 (2000): 339–60.

Chandra, Satish. "Dara Shukoh." In *Encyclopaedia of Islam, Second Edition*, edited by P. Bearman, Th. Bianquis, C.E. Bosworth, E. van Donzel, and W.P. Heinrichs. Leiden: Brill, 2011. http://www.brillonline.nl/subscriber/entry?entry=islam_SIM-1711. Accessed April 2, 2012.

Chaudhuri, Roma. *A Critical Study of Dara Shikuh's 'Samudra-sangama'*. 2 volumes. Volume 2 of *Comparative Religion and Philosophy Series*. Calcutta: Government of West Bengal, Sanskrita Siksa, 1954.

Chittick, William. *Imaginal Worlds: Ibn Arabi and the Problem of Religious Diversity*. Albany: State University of New York Press, 1994.

Cohen, Signe. *Text and Authority in the Older Upanisads*. Leiden: Brill, 2008.

Dasgupta, Surendranath. *A History of Indian Philosophy*. 5 volumes. Delhi: Motilal Banarsidass, reprint, 1975.

Deussen, Paul. *The Philosophy of the Upanishads*. Translated by A.S. Geden. Edinburgh: T. & T. Clark, 1906.

Deutsch, Eliot. *Advaita Vedanta: A Philosophical Reconstruction*. Honolulu: East-West Center Press, 1969.

Eraly, A. *The Last Spring: The Life and Times of the Great Mughals*. Delhi: Viking, 1997.

Ernst, Carl. "Muslim Studies of Hinduism? A Reconsideration of Persian and Arabic Translations from Sanskrit." *Iranian Studies* 36, no. 2 (2003): 173–95.

Faruki, Zahiruddin. *Aurangzeb and His Times*. Bombay: D.B. Taraporevala Sons & Co., 1935.

Faruqui, Munis D. *The Princes of the Mughal Empire, 1504–1719*. Cambridge: Cambridge University Press, 2012.

Flood, Gavin. *Introduction to Hinduism*. Cambridge: Cambridge University Press, 1996.

Friedmann, Yohanan. "Islamic Thought in Relation to the Indian Context." In *India's Islamic Traditions, 711–1750*, edited by Richard M. Eaton, 50–63. Delhi: Oxford University Press, 2003.

Gambhirananda, Swami, trans. *Eight Upanishads: With the Commentary of Sankaracarya*. 2 volumes. Calcutta: Advaita Ashrama, 1957–58.

Ghauri, Iftikhar H. *War of Succession between the Sons of Shah Jahan, 1657–1658*. Lahore: Publishers United, 1964.

Gimaret, D. "Tawhid." In *Encyclopaedia of Islam, Second Edition*, edited by P. Bearman, Th. Bianquis, C.E. Bosworth, E. van Donzel, and W.P. Heinrichs. Leiden: Brill, 2011. http://www.brillonline.nl/subscriber/entry?entry=islam_SIM-7454. Accessed April 2, 2012.

Goodding, Robert. "Dvaita." In *Encyclopedia of Hinduism*, edited by Denise Cush, Catherine Robinson, and Michael York, 215–17. New York: Routledge, 2008.

_____. "Visishtadvaita." In *Encyclopedia of Hinduism*, edited by Denise Cush, Catherine Robinson, and Michael York, 961–63. New York: Routledge, 2008.

Haq, S. Moinul. *Prince Awrangzib*. Karachi: Pakistan Historical Society, 1962.

Harzer, Edeltraud. "Vedanta." In *Encyclopedia of Hinduism*, edited by Denise Cush, Catherine Robinson, and Michael York, 950–51. New York: Routledge, 2008.

Hasrat, B.J. *Dara Shikuh: Life and Works*. Delhi: Munshiram Manoharlal, reprint, 1982.

Heck, Paul. "The Crisis of Knowledge in Islam (I): The Case of al-'Amiri." *Philosophy East and West* 56, no. 1 (2006): 106–35.

Jaffer, S.M. *The Mughal Empire: From Babar to Aurangzeb*. Peshawar: S. Muhammad Sadiq Khan, 1936.

Joshi, Rekha. *Aurangzeb*. Delhi: Munshiram Manoharlal, 1979.

Kazim, Muhammad. *'Alamgirnama*. Edited by Khadim Husain and Abd al-Hayy. Calcutta: College Press, 1868.

_____. "Alamgirnama." In *History of India, as Told by Its Own Historians: The Muhammadan Period*. Volume 7 of *History of India, as Told by Its Own*

Historians, edited by Henry Elliot and John Dowson, 174–80. London: Trübner and Co., 1877.

Keller, Carl A. "Perceptions of Other Religions in Sufism." In *Muslim Perceptions of Other Religions: A Historical Survey*, edited by Jacques Waardenburg, 181–94. New York: Oxford University Press, 1999.

King, Richard. *Indian Philosophy: An Introduction to Hindu and Buddhist Thought*. Washington, D.C.: Georgetown University Press, 1999.

———. "Advaita." In *Encyclopedia of Hinduism*, edited by Denise Cush, Catherine Robinson, and Michael York, 5–7. New York: Routledge, 2008.

Kinra, Rajeev. "Infantilizing Baba Dara: The Cultural Memory of Dara Shekuh and the Mughal Public Sphere." *Journal of Persianate Studies*, no. 2 (2009): 165–93.

Knysh, Alexander. *Ibn 'Arabi in the Later Islamic Tradition: The Making of a Polemical Image in Medieval Islam*. Albany: State University of New York Press, 1998.

Lawrence, Bruce. "Shahrastani on Indian Idol Worship." *Studia Islamica* 38 (1973): 61–73.

Mahadevan, T.M.P. *The Philosophy of Advaita*. Tisbury, England: Compton Russell, 1977.

Mahajan, V.D. *Muslim Rule in India*. Delhi: S. Chand, 1962.

Majumdar, R.C., H.C. Raychaudhuri, and Kalikinkar Datta. *An Advanced History of India*. Delhi: Macmillan, 1967.

Malinar, Angelika. "Sankara as Jagadguru According to Sankara-Digvijaya." In *The Oxford India Hinduism Reader*, edited by Vasudha Dalmia and Heinrich von Steitencron, 129–50. New Delhi: Oxford University Press, 2007.

Marcaurelle, Roger. *Freedom through Inner Renunciation: Sankara's Philosophy in a New Light*. Albany: State University of New York Press, 2000.

Mehta, Jaswant. *Advanced Study of History of Medieval India*. 3 volumes. Delhi: Sterling, 1979–1981.

Mujtabai, Fathullah. *Aspects of Hindu–Muslim Cultural Relations*. Delhi: National Book Bureau, 1978.

Mukherjee, R. *History of Indian Civilization*. Volume 1. Bombay: Hind Kitabs, 1958.

Müller, F. Max, trans. *The Upanishads*. Volume 1 of *Sacred Books of the East*, edited by F. Max Müller. Oxford: Clarendon Press, 1879.

Nakamura, Hajime. *A History of Early Vedanta Philosophy*. 2 volumes. Translated by Trevor Leggett. Delhi: Motilal Banarsidass, 1983–2004.

Nasr, S.H. *Sufi Essays*. Albany: State University of New York Press, 1991.

Nehru, Jawaharlal. *The Discovery of India*. New York: The John Day Company, 1946.

Nizami, K.A. *State and Culture in Medieval India*. New Delhi: Adam Publishers & Distributors, 1985.

Nomani, Shibli. *Alamgir*. Delhi: Idarah-i Adabiyat-i Delli, reprint, 1982.

Olivelle, Patrick, ed. and trans. *Upanisads*. Oxford, New York: Oxford University Press, 1996.

———, ed. and trans. *The Early Upanisads*. Oxford: Oxford University Press, 1998.

Omar, Irfan. "Where the Two Oceans Meet: An Attempt at Hindu–Muslim Rapprochement in the Thought of Dara Shikuh." *Journal of Ecumenical Studies* 44, no. 2 (2009): 303–14.

Ovens, Martin. "Jivanamukta." In *Encyclopedia of Hinduism*, edited by Denise Cush, Catherine Robinson, and Michael York, 391–92. New York: Routledge, 2008.

Pandey, A.B. *Later Medieval India*. Allahabad: Central Book Depot, 1963.

Potter, Karl H., ed. *Advaita Vedanta up to Samkara and His Pupils*. Volume 3 of *Encyclopedia of Indian Philosophies*. Delhi: Motilal Banarsidass, 1998.

Prasad, Ishwari. *Mughal Empire*. Allahabad: Chugh Publications, 1974.

Qanungo, K.R. *Dara Shukoh*. Calcutta: S.C. Sarkar, 1952.

Qureshi, I.H. *The Muslim Community of the Indo-Pakistan Subcontinent, 610–1947: A Brief Historical Analysis*. The Hague: Mouton, 1962.

Rambachan, Anantanand. *Accomplishing the Accomplished: The Vedas as a Source of Valid Knowledge in Sankara*. Honolulu: University of Hawaii Press, 1991.

Rizvi, S.A.A. *History of Sufism in India*. 2 volumes. New Delhi: Munshiram Manoharlal, 1978–1983.

———. *Muslim Revivalist Movements in Northern India in the Sixteenth and Seventeenth Centuries*. New Delhi: Munshiram Manoharlal, reprint, 1993.

Roebuck, Valerie. "Upanisads." In *Encyclopedia of Hinduism*, edited by Denise Cush, Catherine Robinson, and Michael York, 894–902. New York: Routledge, 2008.

Sarkar, Jadunath. *A Short History of Aurangzib, 1618–1707*. Calcutta: M.C. Sarkar, 1930.

Sastri, K.A. Nilakanta, ed. *A Comprehensive History of India*. 11 volumes. Bombay: Orient Longmans, 1957–2008.

Shankara. *Sankara's Upadesasahasri*. 2 volumes. Edited and translated by Sengaku Mayeda. Delhi: Motilal Banarsidass, reprint, 2006.

Shukoh, Dara. *Diwan-i dara shikoh*. Edited by Ahmad Nabi Khan. Lahore: Research Society of Pakistan, 1969.

———. *Majma' al-bahrayn*, Ashburner Coll. Mss. CXXVII, British Library.

———. *Majma'-ul-Bahrain, or the mingling of the two oceans*. Edited and translated by M. Mahfuz-ul-Haq. Calcutta: Bibliotheca Indica, 1929.

———. *Risala-i haqnuma*, Zakariya Coll. Mss. 177, National Library of India.

———. *Sakinat al-awliya'*. Edited by Tara Chand and Sayyid Muhammad Reza Jalali Naini. Tehran: Mu'assasah-i Matbu'ati 'Ilmi, 1965.

Shukoh, Dara. *Sirr-i akbar,* Ethe 1980, British Library.

_____. *Sirr-i akbar.* Edited by Tara Chand and Sayyid Muhammad Reza Jalali Naini. Tehran: Intisharat-i 'Ilmi, reprint, 1989.

Stroumsa, Sarah. "The *Barahima* in Early Kalam." *Jerusalem Studies in Arabic and Islam* 6 (1985): 229–41.

Suthren Hirst, J.G. *Samkara's Advaita Vedanta: A Way of Teaching.* London: RoutledgeCurzon, 2005.

Tripathi, R.P. *Rise and Fall of the Mughal Empire.* Allahabad: Central Book Depot, 1956.

Winternitz, W. *A History of Sanskrit Literature.* 2 volumes. Translated by S. Ketkar and H. Kohn. Calcutta: University of Calcutta, 1927–1933.

3 The Prince and the *Muvaḥḥid*

*Dārā Shikoh and Mughal Engagements with Vedānta**

Supriya Gandhi

A painting, attributed to the seventeenth-century artist Govardhan, provides an emblematic vision of the Mughal prince Dārā Shikoh (1615–1659), chiefly remembered today for his engagements with Hindu thought.[1] Here, a youthful Dārā sits beside a saffron-clad renunciant

* This essay draws on a part of my doctoral dissertation, "Mughal Self-Fashioning, Indic Self-Realization: Dārā Shikoh and Persian Textual Cultures in Early Modern South Asia," Harvard University, 2011. I thank Wheeler Thackston and James Mallinson for commenting on aspects of this essay. I also thank Vasudha Dalmia and Munis Faruqui for their editorial comments.

[1] I am grateful to the late Stuart Cary Welch and Ryo Kawaguchi for providing me with an image of this painting, which is housed in a private collection. While the painting is unsigned, Cary Welch ascribes it to Govardhan through a stylistic analysis. Stuart Cary Welch, personal communication, April 26, 2008. We have few accounts of the ateliers and the painters who worked in them, beyond what can be gleaned from the inscriptions and signatures on their paintings. Govardhan, a *khānāzād* painter, whose father Bhavānidāsa had also been in imperial service under Akbar, joined the ateliers toward the end of Akbar's reign, and was active through the Shāh Jahān era. See Som Prakash Verma, *Mughal Painters and their Work* (Aligarh and Delhi: Oxford University Press, 1994), 160.

in a verdant, terraced garden. On either side of the ascetic are Muslim scholars, their religious affiliation reflected in their beards and the knotting of their robes (*jāmās*) on the right-hand side. A musician playing the santūr sets the atmosphere for a discussion of esoteric matters, while a supplicant in a patched cloak bows down before the ascetic, whose outward, distant gaze suggests his detachment from the material world.[2] Reminiscent of earlier Mughal cultural productions, such as Nar Singh's depiction of Akbar (r. 1556–1605) convening a discussion between representatives of different religions,[3] this painting portrays Dārā Shikoh as the quintessential sage-prince, seeking to comprehend Indic spiritual concepts and practices. Furthermore, the ascetic here resembles religious figures who feature in two of Govardhan's other paintings.[4] The painting, rather than mirroring the reality of Dārā's life and his activities, projects an idealized visual idiom shaped by a set of conventions and stock characters.

Imagining Dārā Shikoh and debating his significance forms a powerful strand in modern historiographical discourses about the Mughals. One of the central tropes revolves around Dārā Shikoh's relationship with Indic ascetics. This site of interest, expressed both visually and textually, has shaped how Dārā Shikoh has been memorialized, but also condemned.

[2] For an insightful analysis of the outward gaze in Mughal painting, see Gregory Minissale, "Seeing Eye-to-Eye with Mughal Miniatures: Some Observations on the Outward Gazing Figure in Mughal Art," *Marg* 58, no. 3 (2007): 41–49.

[3] Nar Singh, "*ʿIbādatkhāna*," folio from *Akbarnāma*, ca. 1605, Chester Beatty Library MS 3, fol. 263b. Nar Singh's painting of Akbar in his *ʿibādatkhāna* in turn recalls depictions of Alexander with Greek sages, such as Bihzād's "Iskandar and Seven Sages," folio from *Khamsa-i Niẓāmī*, ca. 1494–95, British Library MS, OR 6810, fol. 214a.

[4] In "Prince and Ascetics: Leaf from the Late Shāh Jahān Album," Cleveland Museum of Art, 1971.9, attributed to Govardhan, a youthful prince who sits pensively between a Sufi recluse and a musician playing a tānpura resembles the figure depicted in the painting with Dārā. Another painting by Govardhan, "Visit to Holy Man," Paris, Musée national des Arts asiatiques-Guimet, of a Muslim holy man and his attendants in a hermitage, features a figure with similar facial characteristics. Seated at the side, bent over, he is dressed in a "Muslim" *jāmā*. He thus appears to be a stock character in Govardhan's paintings of religious men, his appearance altered to suit different contexts.

A source often cited in modern scholarship is a record of the charges laid against him preserved in the *Ālamgīrnāma*, an official chronicle of Aurangzeb's reign. Authored in 1688, three decades after Dārā Shikoh's death, by Mīrzā Muḥammad Kāẓim, private munshī or secretary to Aurangzeb, this work vividly describes Dārā's "heresies." Here, the motif of Dārā in conversation with a Hindu renunciant, finds a condemnatory echo:

> ... not content with displaying the degrees of permissiveness (*ibāḥat*) and heresy (*ilḥād*) that were fixed in his nature, which he named *taṣavvuf*, he developed an inclination for the religion of the Hindus (*dīn-i Hinduvān*), and the traditions and institutions of those people of bad faith (*badkīshān*). He always had affection for Brahmins, Jogīs and Sanyāsīs, and considered that straying, misleading and false group to be perfect spiritual guides and gnostics united with the truth. He thought that their books, which they call "Bed,"[5] were the word of God revealed in heaven, and he called them "eternal codex," (*muṣḥaf-i qadīm*) and "noble book" (*kitāb-i karīm*).[6]

[5] That is, the "Vedas." The shift from 'v' to 'b' was a characteristic of some north Indian forms of Hindavī. This form was commonly used in Indic words transliterated in the Perso-Arabic script, suggesting the role of Hindavī in mediating the translation of Sanskrit learning into Persian. Muḥammad Kāẓim's reference to the Vedas most likely refers to Dārā Shikoh's translation of roughly fifty Upaniṣads, conflated here with the Vedas. A similar misidentification is found in the manuscript tradition of the Upaniṣad translations. For instance, three manuscripts that I have seen in the Andhra Pradesh Government Oriental Manuscripts Library purport to be translations of the *Ṛg Veda*, *Sāma Veda*, and *Atharva Veda* respectively; however, upon inspection, they appear to be compilations of Persian Upaniṣad translations, rearranged according to their associated Vedas.

[6] Mīrzā Muḥammad Kāẓim further remarks that had Dārā Shikoh succeeded to the throne, "Islam" would have most definitely been turned into "infidelity." He notes the additional charges put forth against Dārā, that the prince wore a ring inscribed with Prabhu which he explains was the Hindu name for God, and that he neglected the essentials of religion such as fasting and prayer. Muḥammad Kāẓim, *Ālamgīrnāma* (Calcutta: Asiatic Society of Bengal, 1868), 34–35. The translation is my own as are all others in this essay unless otherwise mentioned. A translation of this passage is also quoted in Louis Massignon, "An Experiment in Hindu–Muslim Unity: Dārā Shikoh," in *On Becoming an Indian Muslim: French Essays on Aspects of Syncretism*, trans. and ed. M. Waseem (Delhi: Oxford University Press, 2003), 96.

This retrospective characterization of Dārā's Shikoh's relationship with Indic religious figures serves to legitimize Aurangzeb's role in the fratricidal struggle for succession. Yet even during Aurangzeb's reign, we find a perpetuation and further proliferation of Persian renditions of Indic texts, often structured around the motif of a Dārā-like ruler in conversation with an Indic ascetic. Modern scholarship has tended to focus on the personalities of the imperial patrons, such as Dārā Shikoh, who commissioned several such writings, often attributing these projects to the tolerance and pluralistic outlook of their Mughal sponsors.[7] This essay approaches the translation of Indic texts into Persian in terms of broader cultural processes that began well before Dārā, rather than associating them primarily with the agency of a few Mughal royals. By turning to the texts associated with Dārā Shikoh, their interactions with other texts, and the processes of meaning-making created through their dissemination, we can gain further insight into the broader topography of Mughal engagements with Indic religions. The numerous extant copies of Dārā's writings and those that he commissioned speak not only to the wide circulation of his project, but also to the enduring importance of Persian as a vehicle for encoding and disseminating Indic thought.[8]

The narrative frame of dialogue between prince and spiritual preceptor structures several early modern Persian texts that present Vedāntic ideas as part of a discourse seeking to excavate a monotheistic core common to Islamic and Indic mystical traditions. I discuss here two textual clusters in which the pairing of prince and ascetic appears prominently. The first is a group of Mughal translations of the abridged *Yogavāsiṣṭha* into Persian, including one commissioned by Dārā Shikoh. The second comprises the dialogues between Prince Dārā and the renunciant Bābā La'l Dās,

[7] For examples of this approach see K.R. Qanungo, *Dara Shukoh* (Calcutta: S.C. Sarkar, 1952), and Bikrama Jit Hasrat, *Dara Shikuh: Life and Works* (Calcutta: Visvabharati, 1953).

[8] A partial list of manuscripts of Dārā Shikoh's writings can be found in D.N. Marshall, *Mughals in India: A Bibliographic Survey* (London: Mansell, 1967), 126–28. Copies of the prince's writings are to be found in several Euro-American repositories, as well as in the majority of Persian manuscript repositories in South Asia. Most of the latter, however, do not have published catalogues, or catalogues that document their entire collections. Marshall's list thus serves merely to provide an indication of the wide reach and circulation of Dārā Shikoh's writings.

rendered in Persian prose. There is a tendency in modern scholarship to treat the latter as a documentary record of the encounters between the prince and Bābā La'l. However, the literary qualities of the dialogues point to their discursive interconnectedness with an established body of texts and tropes, as articulated in the Persian translations of *Yogavāsiṣṭha* abridgments and several early modern Persian Vedāntic works which are similarly framed by a dialogue between a ruler and an ascetic. In this article, I use the term "dialogue genre" to identify and denote this group of Persian texts treating Indic religious and philosophical topics through the narrative frame of a dialogue.

The patterns of manuscript survival in South Asia entail that our access to seventeenth-century cultural products is often refracted through their iterations in eighteenth- and nineteenth-century manuscripts. To view the reception history of the works written and commissioned by Dārā Shikoh as a stable reflection of their seventeenth-century forms invariably strips away the significance of their subsequent diachronic circulation. While the Persian texts on Indic thought produced within Dārā Shikoh's circles engage with Mughal notions of kingship, the surviving manuscripts and lithograph records of these texts are also inseparably connected to their Hindu and Sufi copyists and readers, beyond the arena of the court.

The multiple textual iterations of Dārā Shikoh's dialogues with Bābā La'l Dās reference both Persianate and Indic literary traditions. As a polysemous metaphor in Persianate writings, the trope of kingship, which runs through these works on asceticism, carries a range of discursive meanings, from sublime temporal and spiritual dominion to material attachment. Thus we may read these dialogues through the prism of Mughal royal self-fashioning, where the figure of the royal interlocutor as a stylized trope is grounded in a specific set of courtly ideals. Furthermore, this topos of the encounter between prince and ascetic reflects the wide prevalence of the dialogue or *saṃvāda* genre in Sanskrit and other Indic literatures. *Saṃvāda*, literally meaning "speech together," has multiple connotations ranging from dialectical dispute to harmonious accord. The *saṃvāda*, which appears as early as the *Ṛg Veda* but spans Brahminical, Buddhist, Jain, and Nāth texts, among others, tends to have a varied cast of protagonists including rulers, sages, and gods.[9] The numerous Indo-

[9] While *saṃvāda*, unlike *kāvya*, as a genre has traditionally not been the subject of literary criticism, Laurie Patton suggests that it be considered

Persian works in the dialogue genre are largely renditions of Vedāntic or Nāth yogic works, thus speaking to the religious climate of early modern north India, while themselves also contributing to a particular construction of Indic religions.

MUGHAL CONSTRUCTIONS OF INDIC RELIGIONS AND THE *MUVAḤḤIDĀN-I HIND*

The writings on Indic religions that Dārā Shikoh composed or commissioned formed part of a broad process within Mughal intellectual history of classifying and selectively privileging aspects of Indic religious thought. A central hermeneutic key to this process is Dārā's idea of the *muvaḥḥidān-i Hind* (the monotheists of India), a term used to identify and privilege a class of Indic saints as superior to other Hindus, akin to Sufis in their mystical insight and commitment to affirming divine unity. Dārā Shikoh's own writings highlight the monistic or monotheistic strains of Indic thought rather than drawing upon a wider range of religious expression. In general, his work reveals a pronounced commitment to the external forms of Islamic orthodoxy and piety, positioned as the dominant religious framework through which he integrates and ultimately subsumes his construction of Indic monotheism.

In his introduction to the *Majma' al-baḥrayn* ("Meeting Place of the Two Oceans"), his famous work, composed in 1656, which compares Vedāntic and Sufi metaphysical concepts, Dārā makes clear that, having grasped the subtleties of Islamic mysticism, his project is to elucidate the thought of a specific group, namely "the monotheists of India (*muvaḥḥidān-i Hind*) and the affirmers of truth (*muḥaqqiqān*) of this ancient people," adding: "[I] have had repeated encounters and carried out dialogues with some among them, who have attained perfection, who have achieved the extremities of ascetic practice, comprehension and understanding, and the utmost levels of mystical experience, God-seeking and gravity."[10]

---

an "indigenous genre." Laurie L. Patton, "Samvada: A Literary Resource for Conflict Negotiation in Classical India," *Evam: Forum on Indian Representations* 3, nos. 1–2 (2004): 177–90.

[10] Muḥammad Dārā Shikoh, *Majma' al-baḥrayn*, ed. Muḥammad Riżā Jalālī Nā'inī (Tehran: Nashr-i Nuqra, 2001), 2.

While Dārā's early writings focus primarily on Sufi masters, in his later works he expands his notion of spiritual authorities to include figures outside the fold of Islam and institutional Sufism. In his 1642 hagiographic tribute to his Qādirī preceptors, the *Sakīnat al-awliyā'* ("The Tranquility of Saints"), Dārā defines the *muvaḥḥidān* as Sufis of the highest rank. However, his *Ḥasanāt al-'ārifīn* ("Fine Words of the Gnostics"), composed in 1652, which arranges a collection of *shaṭḥiyyāt*, or ecstatic expressions, according to the respective saints who uttered them, includes sections on the non-Muslim saints Kabīr (ca. 1398–1448) and Bābā La'l Dās, who he mentions had a shaved head (*mundiya*), and was one of the most perfect gnostics.[11] According to Dārā, Bābā La'l told him that every religious community (*qawm*) had a spiritually perfected person, through whose blessings the community was saved by God.[12] This inclusive attitude toward non-Muslim saints is not, however, reflected in Dārā's comments about ordinary Hindus, to whom he casually refers as *kāfir*s throughout his writings.[13] In the course of the *Majma' al-baḥrayn*, Dārā makes more than a dozen references to the *muvaḥḥidān*, naming specifically his contemporary Bābā La'l, as well as the legendary Bāsisht (Vasiṣṭha) and Byās (Vyāsa).[14]

By Dārā's time, associations between kings or princes and renunciants had become a constitutive element of Mughal political relations, their encounters memorialized in paintings and literary works. The visual and textual motif of a king or prince in dialogue with an ascetic spoke to the expectation for Indo-Muslim rulers that they balance, in the phrasing of the fourteenth-century historian Baranī, kingship (*jamshīdī*) with renunciation (*darvīshī*).[15]

[11] Muḥammad Dārā Shikoh, *Ḥasanāt-i 'ārifīn*, ed. Makhdūm Rahīn (Tehran: Mu'assasa-i Taḥqīqāt va Intishārāt-i Vīsman, 1973), 49.

[12] Dārā Shikoh, *Ḥasanāt-i 'ārifīn*, 49.

[13] Dārā Shikoh, *Ḥasanāt-i 'ārifīn*, 53.

[14] The sparse scholarly literature that exists on Dārā's relationship with Indic ascetics and scholars attempts, in a positivist fashion, solely to identify these "*muvaḥḥidān*" with specific figures who may have influenced Dārā. For example, see Norbert Hintersteiner, "Dara Shukuh's Search for Muvahhidan-i-hind: Liminal Religious Identity and Inter-Religious Translation," in *On the Edge of Many Worlds*, ed. F.L. Bakker and J.S. Aritonang (Zoetermeer: Meinema, 2006), 263–75.

[15] Ḍiyā' al-Dīn Baranī, *Fatāvā-yi jahāndārī*, ed. Afsar Salīm Khān (Lahore: Intishārāt-i Idāra-yi Taḥqīqāt-i Pākistān, 1972), XXV, 140.

Furthermore, an ongoing process of the equation of Sufism and select aspects of Indic thought had been taking place both within and beyond the Mughal court circles. Within the imperial context, Jahāngīr (r. 1605–27) describes in his memoirs a trip to meet with the ascetic Jadrūp (d. ca 1637–38), whose company he enjoyed greatly, being much impressed by his austerity and learning. In passing, he mentions that Jadrūp had "excellently mastered the science of Bedānt (Vedānta), which is the science of *taṣavvuf*."[16] However, Jahāngīr mentions with contempt in his memoirs a "Hindu" known as Arjun, who gathered disciples from among the foolish and simple-minded of both Hindu and Muslim communities, who called him "Guru."[17] Here the emperor is referring to the fifth guru (b.1563–d.1606) of the Sikh tradition; his description suggests that at the time Sikhs were not universally recognized as a distinct religious group. Eventually, after the guru blessed Jahāngīr's rebel son Khusraw with an auspicious mark, the emperor ordered his execution.[18] Unlike Guru Arjun, *muvaḥḥidān* such as Jadrūp, who tended to be renunciants, appear not to have posed a threat to the Mughal social and political order.

THE INDIC DIALOGUE GENRE AND MUGHAL KINGSHIP

By the seventeenth century, the abridged *Yogavāsiṣṭha* had come to play an important role in the elaboration of Mughal conceptions of imperial authority, as well as the development of a Sufi-inflected Persian idiom for conveying Indic religious and philosophical notions. In this work, the Persianate literary motif of a prince on a spiritual quest, seeking the guidance of an ascetic, finds a parallel in the narrative frame, which

[16] Jahāngīr, *Jahāngīr-nāma: Tuzuk-i Jahāngīrī*, ed. Muḥammad Hāshim (Tehrān: Bunyād-i Farhang Press nd.), 203. Shireen Moosvi argues that this notion of equivalence between these two traditions was starting to take root in Mughal circles, highlighted by a version of this statement recorded by Jahāngīr's historian, Muʿtamad Khān, which reads, "the science of Bedānt, which, today (imrūz) is taken to mean taṣavvuf." Quoted in Shireen Moosvi, "The Mughal Encounter with Vedanta: Recovering the Biography of Jadrup," *Social Scientist* 30 (2002): 16.

[17] Jahāngīr, *Jahāngīr-nāma*, 42.

[18] John F. Richards, *The Mughal Empire* (Cambridge: Cambridge University Press, 1993), 97.

consists of a series of dialogues between the young Rāma and his tutor Vasiṣṭha.[19] Tradition attributes the *Yogavāsiṣṭha* to Vālmīki, author of the Sanskrit epic the Rāmāyaṇa, which was composed between the third or fourth century BCE and the third century CE. Modern scholars, however, estimate the *Yogavāsiṣṭha*'s date of composition as falling between the ninth and twelfth centuries CE.[20]

An abridgment of the *Yogavāsiṣṭha*, known as the *Laghu* (concise) *yogavāsiṣṭha*, prepared in the ninth or tenth century by the Kashmiri Abhinanda Paṇḍita, formed the basis for the Mughal translations produced at the court. However, the Mughal engagements with *Yogavāsiṣṭha* recensions did not generally distinguish between the multiple versions of this text, all of which tend to be referred to as *Jog Bāsisht*, this term reflecting the vernacular as opposed to the Sanskrit form of *Yogavāsiṣṭha*. Henceforth, I use *Jog Bāsisht* to distinguish the Mughal Persian iterations of the *Yogavāsiṣṭha* from the various Sanskrit *Mokṣopāya* and *Yogavāsiṣṭha* redactions.

In both the long and abridged versions of the *Yogavāsiṣṭha*, Rāma, the semi-divine prince, later king, of Vālmīki's epic, is portrayed as a troubled youth experiencing *vairāgya* (detachment) with regard to the world, and therefore in search of answers to core philosophical and theological questions. The *Yogavāsiṣṭha*'s doctrine of salvation is presented here in the form of dialogues between Rāma, cast as a disciple, and his guru Vasiṣṭha. Rāma's guru Vasiṣṭha expounds philosophical concepts that are key to the tradition of Advaita Vedānta, through the medium of an interlocking continuum of stories. Gradually, Rāma moves from his state of discontent to deeper understanding, until finally, in the sixth and last chapter, he experiences liberation. The driving theme throughout this work is the notion of *jīvanmukti*, or the spiritual liberation from attachment while carrying out worldly duties. External renunciation of the world is thereby

[19] A monistic work known as the *Mokṣopāya* ("Means of Liberation") in its early recensions, it later acquired layers of Advaitic thought, Rāma devotion, and a narrative frame holding the various tales, and came to be known as the *Yogavāsiṣṭha Mahārāmāyaṇa*. See Jürgen Hanneder's discussion of the text, in *The Mokṣopaya, Yogavāsiṣṭha and Related Texts*, ed. Jürgen Hanneder (Aachen: Shaker Verlag, 2005), 9–21.

[20] Hanneder considers 950 CE as the likely date. Hanneder, ed., *The Mokṣopāya*, 14.

deemed unnecessary, making this vision of spiritual self-realization particularly relevant to rulers, for whom kingship constrains the quest for liberation from this world. The Mughals were not the first dynasty to engage with this textual tradition; for instance, the Kashmiri rulers Zayn al-ʿĀbidīn (r. 1423–70) and Ḥaydar Shāh (r. 1470–72) reportedly listened to recitations of the *Mokṣopāya* by the Sanskrit litterateur Śrīvara.[21]

Niẓām Pānipatī, a scholar in Akbar's court, is credited with producing an early translation of the *Laghu yogavāsiṣṭha*, with the assistance of two paṇḍits including the famous Sanskrit litterateur, Jagannātha Miśra. Although the original imperial manuscript does not appear to be extant, there exist multiple copies from the text's later manuscript tradition.[22] In his introduction, the translator cites the story of how the young prince Salīm (who later became the emperor Jahāngīr) requested the translation of this work. He praises the precocious prince, who, in the prime of his youth tamed his natural carnal inclinations, and was "inclined to keep company with the zealous God-knowers, and listen to the speech of Sufism (*taṣavvuf*), and the expression of verities (*ḥaqāʾiq*)."[23] Here too Vedānta and *taṣavvuf* are implicitly equated with each other.

A manuscript held at the Chester Beatty Library of another Persian translation of this text, produced in 1602, is the earliest extant manuscript of the *Yogavāsiṣṭha* in any language, according to Wendy Doniger.[24] Lavishly illustrated with forty-one miniatures and replete with visual

[21] See verse 1:5:80 of Śrīvara's chronicle, the *Rājataraṅgiṇī*, in *Śrīvara's Zaina Rājataraṅgiṇī*, trans. Kashi Nath Dhar (Delhi: Indian Council for Historical Research and People's Publishing House, 1994), 215, and "Rājataranginī," in J.C. Dutt, *Medieval Kashmir*, ed. S.L. Sadhu (Delhi: Atlantic, 1990), 125. I thank Luther Obrock for bringing to my notice Śrīvara's references to the *Mokṣopāya*.

[22] Copies, many of which are uncatalogued, are to be found in several Indian manuscript repositories. A partial list of manuscripts is included in Heike Franke, "Die persischen Übersetzungen des *Laghuyogavāsiṣṭha*," in Hanneder, ed., *The Mokṣopāya*, 126–27.

[23] Niẓām Panipatī, *Jūg Bāsisht*, ed. Muḥammad Riżā Jalālī Nāʾīnī and M.S. Shukla (Tehran: Iqbal, 1981), 2.

[24] Wendy Doniger, *Dreams, Illusions and Other Realities* (Chicago: University of Chicago Press, 1984), Plate 1. Doniger, however, does not distinguish between the *Laghu yogavāsiṣṭha*, of which this is a translation, and the longer, earlier version of the work.

depictions of the encounter between hermit and ruler, the manuscript bears the seal and inscription of Shāh Jahān in the year of his accession, suggesting that it was a prized item in the royal library.[25] An inscription by Jahāngīr on the manuscript describes the work as stories from the ancients (*ḥikāyāt-i mutaqaddimīn*), mentioning that he had brought it about from "Hindī," and adding, "It is a most excellent book, if one were to listen to it with an alert mind (*hūsh ravā*)."[26] A note from the translator, Farmulī, self-deprecatingly states that he was the lowliest disciple of Kabīr, and that he translated this work by imperial order so that those Persophones (*fārsī zabān*) who did not know Sanskrit could benefit from it.[27] However, Heike Franke has recently pointed out that this manuscript had actually been prepared for Akbar himself, as is evident from the encomia to the emperor presented in the preface. It is likely, as Franke surmises, that Jahāngīr mistook this manuscript for the *Jog Bāsisht* that actually was produced for him.[28]

In view of the several existing versions of the *Laghu yogavāsiṣṭha* in Persian, the translation that Dārā commissioned in the early 1650s served a purpose beyond merely rendering the text accessible to himself or other Persian readers. As with Niẓām Pānipatī's translation, our access to this text is mediated through its later manuscript tradition. The anonymous translator[29] states that his patron Dārā commissioned this translation partly because he felt that the previous ones "did not convey any benefit

[25] Shāh Jahān's seal is dated 1037/1627–28, roughly corresponding to the period after his accession. See J.V.S. Wilkinson, "A Note on an Illustrated Manuscript of the Jog Bashisht," *Bulletin of the School of Oriental and African Studies* 12 (1948): 692.

[26] Jahāngīr's undated inscription on the manuscript has in modern times given rise to the impression that he had commissioned the work. See Linda York Leach, *Mughal and Other Indian Paintings from the Chester Beatty Library* (London: Scorpion, 1995), I, 155. I have adapted the translation provided here.

[27] Leach, *Mughal and Other Indian Paintings*, I, 155.

[28] Franke, "Akbar's *Yogavāsiṣṭha* at the Chester Beatty Library," paper prepared for presentation at the Annual Conference on South Asia, Madison, October 2010. I am grateful to Heike Franke for sharing this paper with me.

[29] The text contains several Hindavī verses attributed to a certain Valī. The editors, Muḥammad Rižā Jalālī Nā'īnī and Tārā Chand, have therefore surmised that the translator could have been Banvālidās "Valī," who composed Persian mystical verse and translated the allegorical Sanskrit play *Prabodhacandrodaya*

to the seekers of truth (*haqīqat*)."[30] By commissioning a new translation Dārā Shikoh was very likely claiming the work for himself. Dārā's stamp on the text is evident in its opening which narrates a dream in which he sees Rām (Rāma) and Bāsisht (Vasiṣṭha). The trope of a dream as legitimizing an author's project is well established throughout Islamicate literature.[31] The translator relates that Dārā had this dream after reading selections from the *Jog Bāsisht* attributed to a certain Shaikh Ṣūfī. In the dream, he is drawn to Bāsisht, and makes obeisance to him: "Bāsisht said, 'O Rāmachandra! This is a disciple who is absolutely sincere; please embrace him.' With the utmost affection, Rām took me into his arms. Thereafter, Bāsisht gave Rāmachandra sweets to feed me. I ate the sweets. After having this vision, the desire to make a new translation grew stronger."[32]

The story of Rāma, who in Vālmīki's telling was the ideal king for all times, had been previously appropriated into the Mughal court through a translation commissioned by Akbar.[33] The *Jog Bāsisht* image of Rāma,

---

into Persian around 1672–73. See Banvālidās Valī (attributed), *Gulzār-i hāl yā tulū'-yi qamar-i ma'rifat*, ed. Tara Chand and Amir Hasan Abidi (Aligarh: Aligarh Muslim University, 1967). Later *taẕkira* identify Banvālidās as Dārā Shikoh's Hindu secretary, although there does not appear to be any contemporary literature confirming this. His own poetry, however, speaks to his affiliation with Mullā Shāh Badakhshī, Dārā's spiritual preceptor. See *Dīvān-i Valī Rām*, Asiatic Society of Bengal, MS II 240.

30 Tara Chand and S.A.H. Abidi, eds, *Jūg Bāsisht* (Aligarh: Aligarh Muslim University, 1978), 3.

31 For an overview of the importance of dreams in Islamic traditions see Nile Green, "The Religious and Cultural Role of Dreams and Visions in Islam," *Journal of the Royal Asiatic Society* 3 (2003): 287–313. For a discussion of the role of dream narratives in Arabo-Islamic literary traditions, see Dwight Reynolds, ed., *Interpreting the Self: Autobiography in the Arabic Literary Tradition* (Berkeley: University of California Press, 2001), 88–93.

32 Chand and Abidi, eds, *Jūg Bāsisht*, 4.

33 The lavishly illustrated manuscript of this work, completed in 1588, is preserved in the Maharaja Sawai Man Singh II City Palace Museum in Jaipur; however, of late it has been out of the reach of scholars. For a description of the manuscript and reproductions of some of its images see Ashok Kumar Das, "An Introductory Note on the Emperor Akbar's Ramayana and its Miniatures," in *Facets of Indian Art*, ed. Robert Skelton (London: Heritage Publishers, 1987), 94–104.

in which he appears in the position of disciple, rather than a semi-divine king, serves to legitimize a prince's spiritual pursuits. The translation that Dārā commissioned establishes a link with the figure of Rāma as a seeker addressing the balancing act between rulership and world-renouncing asceticism, which for Dārā had been a persistent concern. For instance, in his *Sakīnat al-awliyā'*, he repeatedly invokes the trope of conflict between the spiritual and temporal realms, to highlight that he alone among Mughal dynasts had been divinely chosen for a special spiritual role.[34]

Behind Dārā's fleeting mention of Shaikh Ṣūfī's translation lies a web of crisscrossing engagements with the various recensions and abridgments of the *Jog Bāsisht* in seventeenth-century Mughal India, existing outside, or on the margins of, the realm of court patronage. It is hard to reconstruct the details of Shaikh Ṣūfī's life and oeuvre, given the scanty references to him in other texts. However, the availability of several works attributed to him, all drawing on Indic texts in the genre of dialogue between master and disciple, and engaging with the theme of liberation from the material world, attests to the wide circulation of his writings.

One brief reference to a Persian translation of a *Yogavāsiṣṭha* abridgment is to be found in the *Dabistān-i maẕāhib* ("School of Religions"), a mid-seventeenth century ethnographic classification of various religious groups and figures. According to this work, an abridged version of the *Jog Bāsisht* made by a Kashmiri Brahmin was translated into Persian by a certain Mullā Muḥammad Ṣūfī. While the abridgment mentioned in the *Dabistān* is likely the *Laghu yogavāsiṣṭha* of the Kashmiri Abhinanda, its author, "Mullā Muḥammad Ṣūfī," might well refer to the same Shaikh Ṣūfī with whom Dārā was familiar.[35]

[34] Muḥammad Dārā Shikoh, *Sakīnat al-awliyā'*, ed. Tara Chand and Muḥammad Riḍā Jalālī Nā'inī (Tehran: Mu'assasa-yi Matbū'at-i 'Ilmī, 1965), 5.

[35] *Dabistān-i maẕāhib*, ed. Kaykhusraw Isfandiyār and Raḥīm Riżā-zāda Malik (Tehran: Kitābkhāna-i Ṭahūrī, 1983), I, 128. For further details on the *Dabistān* and debates surrounding its authorship, see M. Athar Ali, "Pursuing an Elusive Seeker of Universal Truth—the Identity and Environment of the Author of the Dabistan-i Mazahib," *Journal of the Royal Asiatic Society* 9, no. 3 (1999): 365–75, and Aditya Behl, "An Ethnographer in Disguise: Comparing Self and Other in Mughal India," in *Notes on a Mandala: Essays in Honor of Wendy Doniger*, ed. Laurie Patton and David Haberman (Newark: University of Delaware Press, 2010), 113–48.

Shaikh Ṣūfī's work, most commonly known as *Aṭvār fi ḥall al-asrār* ("Stages in the Unraveling of Secrets") in its surviving manuscripts, is not, however, a translation of Abhinanda's *Laghu yogavāsiṣṭha*. It delineates ten stages (*ṭawr*) to liberation, and eliminates the stories to present an abbreviated series of Bāsisht's exhortations to Rām. This format closely parallels that of the *Yogavāsiṣṭhasāra*,[36] a further abridgment of the *Yogavāsiṣṭha* by an unknown author, comprising 230-odd verses and, judging from the numerous extant copies, a work that enjoyed a wide circulation.[37] As Persianate writers of the seventeenth century tended not to explicitly distinguish between the various recensions and abridgments of the *Yogavāsiṣṭha*, it is quite possible that the author of the *Dabistān* did indeed have Shaikh Ṣūfī's *Aṭvār fi ḥall al-asrār* in mind.

Dārā Shikoh's contemporary, the Ṣābirī Chishtī 'Abd al-Raḥmān (d. 1683) also mentions Shaikh Ṣūfī's work on the *Yogavāsiṣṭha* in the introduction to his *Mir'āt al-ḥaqā'iq* ("Mirror of Truths"), an imaginative rendition of the *Bhagavad Gītā* into Persian. Here he suggests parallels between the *Gītā* and the *Yogavāsiṣṭha*, seeing them as embodying similar truths. He likens his own rendition of the *Gītā* to Shaikh Ṣūfī's translation:

> All the learned Hindus agree that Kṛṣṇa has taken the secrets of the knowledge of God (*asrār-i ma'rifat-i ḥaqq*)—may he be praised and exalted—from the four Vedas [i.e., Books] and has revealed this explanation. So, just as the enlightened Shaikh Ṣufi Qubjahānī once wrote a commentary on the *Kashf al-kunūz*, also known as *Jog Bāsisht*, now for the sake of a few friends, who are as a flaming torch seeking after the sublime goal, the above-mentioned translation has been written out in Persian.[38]

'Abd al-Raḥmān's view that the Vedas are the repositories of gnostic secrets accords with the aforementioned Mughal construction of these texts as embodying the monotheistic strands of Indic religions. It is remarkably similar to Dārā Shikoh's characterization of the Upaniṣads

36 S.N. Dasgupta, *History of Indian Philosophy* (Cambridge: Cambridge University Press, 1922), II, 232.

37 Peter Thomi, "The Yogavāsiṣṭha in Its Longer and Shorter Version," *Journal of Indian Philosophy* 11 (1983): 107.

38 The translation is adapted from the one provided in Roderic Vassie, "Persian Interpretations of the Bhagavad Gītā in the Mughal Period" (PhD diss., School of Oriental and African Studies, University of London, 1989)," 191. It corresponds to *Mir'āt al-ḥaqā'iq*, British Library MS, OR 1883: 259a.

as holding the secret key to the "hidden book" (*kitāb maknūn*) of the Qur'ān, in his *Sirr-i akbar* ("The Greatest Secret"), composed in 1657. Furthermore, the fleeting mentions of Shaikh Ṣūfī by both Dārā Shikoh and 'Abd al-Raḥmān serve as an explicit clue to the textual world that all three share.

Another work by 'Abd al-Raḥmān, the *Mir'āt al-makhlūqāt* ("Mirror of Creation"), explicitly engages both with the dialogue genre as well as the figure of Bāsisht/Vasiṣṭha. Based on a loosely structured dialogue between the deities, Pārvatī and Mahādev, the work incorporates storytelling, cosmology, and a series of equivalences between Indic and Islamic religious figures and concepts, subsuming the Indic material within Islamic narratives. It claims to be a translation from a Sanskrit book authored by Bāsisht, who is described as a "prophet" (*rasūl*), or "sage" ("*mun*," i.e., *muṇi*), from the community of jinns (*qawm-i jinnāt*).[39] While this work lacks the soteriological focus of the *Jog Bāsisht* translations, its invocation of Bāsisht's authority speaks to the canonization of select personages from Indic traditions in the growing body of Persian writings dealing with Indic religions.

In contrast to the *Mir'āt al-makhlūqāt*, the works attributed to Shaikh Ṣūfī tend to be brief and didactic, eschewing the creative acts of establishing equivalence between Indic and Islamic concepts and figures or the colorful appropriation of Indic texts into an Islamic narrative framework that are so prominent in 'Abd al-Raḥmān's writings. Among the extant manuscripts attributed to Shaikh Ṣūfī, those of the *Aṭvār* (sometimes bearing different names) are by far the most numerous. At the outset of this work, he introduces himself as Ṣūfī Sharīf, after the customary praises to God and the Prophet. The author does not specify the name of the Indic text which he draws upon, but rather mentions that he has provided an account of the words of Rām and Bāsisht, which he, while on the mystical path, has brought to light and translated into Persian. He dedicates the work to Jahāngīr, referring to the emperor by such fulsome epithets as "God's caliph" (*khalīfa-yi jahānbānī*), "aware of (mystical) verities and knowledge" (*ḥaqā'iq va ma'ārif āgāh*), "knower of God's secrets" (*'ārif va vāqif-i asrār-i Allāh*), and "refuge of the Muslims, especially the scholars, mystics, and the poor" (*maljā'-i muslimīn va*

[39] 'Abd al-Raḥmān Chishtī, *Mir'āt al-makhlūqāt*, British Library MS, OR 1883: 239b.

khuṣūṣan fuẓalā' va 'urafā' va masākīn).[40] While such praise of the current ruler was not uncommon, it could suggest that Ṣūfī Sharīf was hoping for royal favor through this dedication. The text does not reveal more about the context of its production; we do not know if a copy ever entered Jahāngīr's library thence making its way to Dārā. If so, Jahāngīr did not consider it noteworthy enough to include in his memoir.

The *Yogavāsiṣṭhasāra* serves as a recognizable source for the *Aṭvār*, which follows all its ten chapters (*prakaraṇas*) on the stages of self-realization, substituting for these stages the terminology of Persianate Sufism. Unlike the *Laghu yogavāsiṣṭha* translations sponsored by Akbar and Dārā, the *Aṭvār* does not retain any of the Sanskrit/Hindavī terminology. Instead, it directly provides the author's Persian equivalents. While Shaikh Ṣūfī follows quite faithfully the order of the *Yogavāsiṣṭhasāra*'s Sanskrit verses, he weaves into his translation a commentary that expands on and explains certain verses, sometimes interspersed with Sufi sayings in Arabic. The opening verse of his work provides a good example of such textual appropriation and interpretation:

> *Sajda-yi man va ta'ẓīm az dil-i ṣamīn barā-yi nūr-i āramīda kih dā'iman ba-rang va qarār va ārām ast va bī-qararī bar-ū rāh na-yāfta pāk ast az aṭrāf va javānib va az amkana va ānkih na-tavān guft dar ḥaqq va agar sharqī ast yā gharbī junūbī ast yā shumālī fawqānī ast yā taḥtānī zamānī ast yā makānī na-ū rāst ibtidā' va na intihā' 'ayn-i 'ilm-i ma'rifat ast va rāh-i yāft-i ū juz ba-ma'rifat-i nafs-i khud ast man 'arafa nafsahu fa-qad 'arafa rabbahu ishārat barīn-ma'nā ast.*[41]

> My obeisance and salutation from the depth of my heart to that calm light, which is always in repose, and tranquility, to which restlessness has no path, and (which is) purified of environs, directionality, and space. It cannot be said about Truth, that it is eastern, or western, northern or southern, underground or high above, spatial or temporal. It has neither beginning nor end, it is just as the science of gnosis, and the road to it is only through knowledge of the self. "He who knows his soul, knows his Lord," points to this very meaning.

Compare the *Aṭvār*'s rendition with the Sanskrit verse below:

40 Ṣūfī Sharīf, *Aṭvār fī ḥall al-asrār*, British Library MS, OR 1883: 272a.

41 Ṣūfī Sharīf, *Aṭvār*, 272b.

dikkālādyanavacchinnānantacinmātramūrtaye
svānubhūtyekamānāya namaḥ śāntāya tejase.

Salutations to that pure consciousness whose image, infinite, is unbounded by space, time and all else, the calm, luminous being apprehended through self-realization (*svānubhūti*) alone.[42]

This verse in the *Yogavāsiṣṭhasāra* appears to have been drawn from the *Nītiśataka*, attributed to Bhartṛhari, a prince of the first century BCE, who is said to have renounced his throne in favor of his younger brother, Vikramāditya.[43] Shaikh Ṣūfī's rendition amplifies the Sanskrit, while adding the famous *ḥadīth qudsī*, or the Prophet Muḥammad's report of God's words to him, "he who knows his soul, knows his Lord" (*man 'arafa nafsahu fa-qad 'arafa rabbahu*),[44] a saying that circulated extensively in Islamic mystical writings.

While the source text for Shaikh Ṣūfī's translation remains unclear, a Hindavī translation of the *Yogavāsiṣṭhasāra* is attributed to Kavīndrācārya Sarasvatī, a Sanskrit litterateur of Maharashtrian origin, who also composed Brajbhāṣā poetry dedicated to Shāh Jahān and Dārā Shikoh, including the *Kavīndrakalpalatā* ("Wish-fulfilling Vine of Kavīndra").[45] A manuscript of the Sanskrit *Yogavāsiṣṭhasāra* with interlinear Hindavī translation dates the text to ca. 1656–57, close to the time when Dārā was preparing his translation of fifty-odd Upaniṣads in collaboration with a group of paṇḍits.[46] A festschrift dedicated to Kavīndrācārya, the

[42] Compare Peter Thomi's German translation of this verse in Peter Thomi, ed., *Yogavasisthasara: Die Quintessenz des Yogavasistha* (Wichtrach: Institut für Indologie, 1999), teil II, 15, and the translation of the same verse in Bhartṛhari, *The Nītiśataka, Śriṅgāraśataka and Vairāgyaśataka*, ed. and trans. Purohit Gopinath (Bombay: Shri Venkateshwar Press, 1896), 59.

[43] Peter Thomi attributes it to Bhartṛharī's *Vairāgyaśataka*. *Yogavasisthasara*, teil II, 15.

[44] Ṣūfī Sharīf, *Aṭvār*, 272b. This *ḥadīth* is quoted again, for instance on 273b.

[45] Allison Busch, "Hidden in Plain View: Brajbhasha Poets at the Mughal Court," *Modern Asian Studies* 44, no. 2 (2010): 289.

[46] The work is sometimes entitled the *Jñānasāra*, an alternative name for the *Yogavāsiṣṭha*. The manuscript, when at one point in the possession of a certain Shastri Krishnaji Hari Patankar of Rajapur, was used as the basis of V.G. Rahurkar's edition of the work. See V.G. Rahurkar, "The Bhasa-Yogavasisthasara

Kavīndracandrodaya, refers to his instruction of Dārā Shikoh in Indic philosophy.[47] Whether or not Dārā Shikoh was aware of this vernacular translation of the *Yogavāsiṣṭhasāra*, its composition speaks to the growing seventeenth-century production of Vedāntic works outside of the Sanskrit arena, in the cosmopolitan languages of Hindavī (Brajbhāṣā) and Persian. Interestingly, at least one eighteenth-century text links this vernacular *Yogavāsiṣṭhasāra* to Dārā Shikoh's oeuvre. The *Rāfi' al-khilāf*, authored in 1181 AH/1767 CE by one Sītā Rām Kāyasth Saksena of Lucknow, compares the *dohās* of Kavīndrācārya's vernacular *Yogavāsiṣṭhasāra* to Persian mystical poetry, Qurānic verses, and *ḥadīth*, with the explicit aim of clarifying and furthering Dārā Shikoh's project in the *Majma' al-baḥrayn*.[48]

Other Persian renditions of Indic texts are ascribed to Shaikh Ṣūfī; these too are organized around the narrative frame of a dialogue between a seeker and a spiritual master. The *Navādir al-sulūk*, which states that the author had translated the text from "Hindi" (*zabān-i Hindī*), bringing it to light from darkness (*ẓulamāt*), is a dialogue between Nārad (Nārada), the legendary sage who appears frequently in Purāṇic literature, especially those texts with a Vaiṣṇava leaning, and Parbat (Parvata), the father of Śiva's consort Pārvatī.[49] In the course of answering Parbat's questions on the means of liberation from the lower self and material world, Nārada provides a discourse on *haṭha* yoga. Unlike the *Aṭvār*, the text retains the relevant Indic terms such as the names of the āsanas, the bodily postures

of Kavindracarya Sarasvati," *Proceedings of the All-India Oriental Conference* 18 (1955): 471–82.

47 V. Raghavan, "Kavindracarya Sarasvati," in *Indian Culture, D.R. Bhandarkar Volume* (Calcutta: Indian Research Institute, 1940), 161. This is also cited in Busch, "Hidden in Plain View," 292.

48 Tara Chand, "Rafi' al-Khilaf of Sita Ram Kayastha Saksena," *The Journal of the Ganganatha Jha Research Institute* 11 (1944): 7–12. Unfortunately, according to Kazuyo Sakaki, this manuscript can no longer be traced at the Ganganath Jha Kendriya Sanskrit Vidyapeeth, where it should be housed. See Kazuyo Sakaki, "Yogavāsiṣṭha and the Medieval Islamic Intellectuals in India," in *Yogavāsiṣṭha Mahārāmāyaṇa: A Perspective*, ed. Manjula Sahdev (Patiala: Punjabi University, 2003), 286, fn. 1.

49 Ṣūfī Sharīf, *Navādir al-sulūk*, Bodleian Library MS, Ouseley Add 69: 128a–30b.

of *haṭha* yoga, or the concepts of *iḍā* and *piṅgalā*, the left and right-hand subtle channels (*nāḍīs*) of the body.

Ṣūfī Sharīf is also credited with the translation of a dialogue between Kṛṣṇa and Mahādeva. Among the manuscript copies of this work, one, entitled *Gharā'ib al-aṭvār fī kashf al-anvār* ("Marvelous Stages in the Revelation of Lights"), is held at the Khudā Bakhsh Library in Patna, bound together with a copy of the *Aṭvār fī ḥall al-asrār*, both in the same hand.[50] The *Aṭvār* has a colophon stating that it was copied in Akbarābād in the seventeenth year of Ālamgīr's reign, or ca. 1674. An inscription below identifies the scribe as "Faqīr Dūst Muḥammad, servant of the (Sufi) renunciants" (*khādim al-fuqarā'*), and describes the text copied as presenting mystical truths in a "new fashion" (*naw bāf*). The evidence of this manuscript, together with 'Abd al-Raḥmān Chishtī's and Dārā's familiarity with the shaikh's writings, suggests that, in the seventeenth century at least, such works included Sufis among their readership.

THE BĀBĀ LA'L DIALOGUES

In their emphasis on the role of the spiritual guide in initiating the royal disciple into Vedāntic metaphysics and ascetic practices, Dārā's dialogues with Bābā La'l are on a similar discursive plane as the Mughal *Jog Bāsisht* translations. Our access to Dārā's own encounters with Bābā La'l are filtered through layers of manuscript recensions, and the memorialization of these dialogues in later cultural productions. The scholarly edition by Louis Massignon and Charles Huart treats the dialogues between the prince and the saint as a documentary record of their encounter, glossing over the literary qualities of the text. A mistranslation of the introductory line is a case in point. The Bodleian Library manuscript used as the base for this edition begins with the following line, which serves to describe the work's contents and indicate the spiritual rewards that would accrue to the reader:

> *Javāb su'āl-i Dārā Shikoh, har kih ba-khvānad ḥaqā'iq-i dunyā ma'lūm gardad, bā faqīr ṣāḥib-i ḥāl dar bayān-i taḥqīq-i ba'ẓī maṭālib-i ḥaqīqat āyandī.*

50 Ṣūfī Sharīf, *Gharā'ib al-aṭvār fī kashf al-anvār* and *Aṭvār fī ḥall al-asrār*, Khudā Bakhsh Library MS 2081 HL.

> The questions and answers of Dārā Shikoh, to whomsoever reads them the truths (*ḥaqā'iq*) of the world will be made known, with the faqīr, master of the mystical state [Bābā La'l], on the realization (*taḥqīq*) of some matters of reality.[51]

In Huart and Massignon's rendering, however, this line reads (translated from the French), "The prince in search of knowledge about the universe, wants to understand what is reality, with the help of an inspired ascetic."[52] The term for reality, *ḥaqīqa*, and its plural, *ḥaqā'iq*, which in a Sufi context refer to esoteric mystical truths, by the seventeenth century have come to connote the monistic traditions of Indic knowledge, filtered through a Persian idiom drenched in Sufi vocabulary. In effacing this *phalaśruti*, that is, the traditional mention of the "fruits" of reading or reciting a text in Indic literatures, this trace of the text's interaction with its intended audience is lost.

While other contemporary works, such as historical chronicles or Dārā's own writings, provide no further information about these dialogues, a manuscript held at the Bodleian Library is one of many that attribute their compilation to Shāh Jahān's Brahmin secretary and noted Persian litterateur, Chandarbhān.

> *Gosht-i Srī Bābā Lāl va shāhzāda Dārā Shikoh kih dar miyān-i har dū 'azīzān mazkūr shuda ast va ān rā ahl-i farāsat dānishvar Chandarbhān az zabān-i Hindavī ba lisān-i Fārsī taṣnīf namūda.*
>
> The discussion (*gosth*, Sans., *goṣṭha*) of Srī Bābā La'l and the prince Dārā Shikoh, which took place between both of these illustrious ones. The sagacious scholar Chandarbhān translated this from the Hindavī tongue into the Persian language.[53]

51 Bodleian Library MS, Ouseley Pers Add 69: 145b–51b.

52 The English translation is from M. Waseem, ed. and trans., *On Becoming an Indian Muslim: French Essays on Aspects of Syncretism* (New Delhi: Oxford University Press, 2003), 107. The original reads "Le prince étudiant pour savoir les vérités relatives á l'univers se propose de chercher á comprendre, avec un ascéte inspiré, quelques problémes concernant la réalité …" C. Huart and L. Massignon, "Les Entretiens de Lahore (entre le Prince imperial Dārā Shikoh et l'ascete Hindou Baba La'l Das)," *Journal Asiatique* 209 (October–December, 1926): 314.

53 Bodleian Library MS, Fraser 268: 1a.

The word *gosth*, of Sanskrit origin, meaning discussion, appears in Huart and Massignon's edition as well; here, *Gosth-i Bābā La'l* (the discussion of Bābā La'l) is rendered by scribal or editorial error as *Gosha Bābā La'l*. Huart and Massignon translate this as "L'ascete Bābā La'l," understanding *gosha* here as a short form of the Persian *gosha nashīn*, literally "dwelling in a corner," a common term to designate a recluse. That the aforementioned Bodleian manuscript begins, in Perso-Arabic script, with *Niranjan Dev Antarjāmī*, an invocation to the "indwelling God" in the Hindavī idiom of the *nirguṇa* bhakti or proto-Sikh communities, further speaks to the context of its production and its intended audience. Dārā Shikoh's dialogues with Bābā La'l are here re-contextualized for a community of non-Muslim readers.

Other manuscripts provide further details; in the absence of extant seventeenth-century manuscripts of the work, it is hard to trace their stemmata; we cannot be certain whether the details multiplied incrementally with time. Thus, an apparently undated manuscript discovered in Lucknow by Vladimir Ivanow, who made it available to Huart and Massignon, adds to its prologue that the dialogues took place at Niyula, in two sessions, continuing for nine days, upon Dārā Shikoh's return from his Qandahar expedition. Furthermore, the prologue states that a certain Rāu Jādav Dās transcribed the dialogues in Hindavī as they occurred, before Rāu Chandarbhān Brahman rendered them into Persian.[54] The mention in the manuscript tradition of the original dialogues taking place in Hindavī, although eminently plausible, also speaks to a broader trope in Persian writings on Indic religions: that the Hindavi or Sanskrit idiom of their Indic sources underscores the authenticity of the knowledge they convey.

Chandarbhān is known for his mastery of Persian, seen in his ornate accounts of life at court and his poetry. Besides producing a vast epistolary and poetic corpus, Chandarbhān composed the prose work entitled *Chahār chaman* ("Four Meadows").[55] This is an elaborately crafted, didactic series of anecdotes and letters on topics such as the ideal characteristics of a munshī, filial devotion to parents, hard work, study of the Persian classics, life in court, descriptions of places in Hindustan, in which,

54 Huart and Massignon do not mention a date. "Les Entretiens," 128.

55 Chandarbhān Brahman, *Chahār chaman*, ed. Yunus Jaffery (New Delhi: Iran Culture House, 2004).

nevertheless, the terminology of *waḥdat al-wujūd* has a strong presence. Apart from the association of Chandarbhān with the Bābā La'l dialogues in the manuscript tradition, as well as in later historiography, there does not appear to be strong contemporary evidence linking him with the text, nor do Chandarbhān's writings mention Dārā as his patron.[56]

Like Salīm in Panipatī's introduction to the *Jog Bāsisht*, the dialogues cast Dārā as a novice seeking truths (*ḥaqā'iq*) about the universe. In this text, Dārā is referred to as 'Azīz (the Illustrious), a term also connoting the beloved of his spiritual master, while the ascetic is referred to as Kāmil (the Perfected One). The work represents Dārā as an earnest and persistent student, asking thoughtful questions, some of which reveal a very specific knowledge of Indic terms and concepts, while others deal more generally with asceticism (*riyāżat*), and the ideal relationship between a spiritual preceptor and his disciple.

Dārā's questions, and Bābā La'l's replies, comprise, but are not limited to, several identifiable categories. For one, he inquires about the definitions of certain Indic terms that are related to metaphysics and ascetic practice. His first question pertains to the difference between *nād* (the creative word) and *Bed* (the Vedas), to which Bābā La'l's reply, emphasizing the primacy of the Logos, gives the analogy of a king (*nād*) and his order.[57] Later on in the dialogues, Dārā asks how *dhyāna* (meditation) and *samādhi* (complete absorption) are defined. In keeping with the crafted, literary form of these dialogues, Bābā La'l's response uses a very Persianate simile, comparing the heart to a gazelle captured in a desert. Its initial condition of captivity is comparable to *dhyāna*, while its restful sleep after having come to terms with its captivity is like *samādhi*, the state of releasing the divine embrace in which the heart had been arrested in its prior state of *dhyāna*.[58] The Indic terms discussed, Dārā's questions, and Bābā La'l's replies all reflect the text's bent toward Vedāntic thought of the Advaitic, or non-dualist, kind; thus, in reply to a question about the distinction between ātman (soul) and *paramātman* (supreme soul), Bābā La'l states that there is no difference.[59] There are also several ques-

[56] Rajeev Kinra corroborates this point. Rajeev Kinra, "Infantalizing Baba Dara: The Cultural Memory of Dara Shekuh and the Mughal Public Sphere," *Journal of Persianate Studies* 2 (2009): 179.

[57] Huart and Massignon, "Les Entretiens," 289.

[58] Huart and Massignon, "Les Entretiens," 303.

[59] Huart and Massignon, "Les Entretiens," 303.

tions about the stages of waking, dreaming, and deep sleep, with which Advaitic philosophical traditions are deeply preoccupied, these states serving to explain the different levels of reality and illusion.

The questions also engage with certain Indic beliefs and practices that are at odds with Islamic orthopraxy. Among these are questions about Hindu idol worship, as well as the basis of the theory of avatārs, referring to what the prince had read in "Hindu books."[60] Bābā La'l answers them in such a way as would be acceptable to a mystically oriented Muslim. For example, he explains the significance of Indian "idol worship" as a technique "to strengthen the heart," likening the practice to the way in which unmarried girls play with dolls and give up the game after marriage.[61]

By far the strongest theme emerging from Dārā's questions, however, pertains to liberation through renouncing the material world and through ascetic practice. Several of these questions have to do with the relationship between a renunciant and his spiritual master. Other questions reflect more directly an important concern present in Dārā's writings, that is, the compatibility of rulership with renunciation. For instance, Dārā interrogates the conundrum of a *jogishāra* (*yogīśvara*): "It is clear that the king remains a yogī even when dressed up for his royal function (*rāj*), but how can it be guaranteed that he does not start acting with worldly appearance." Bābā La'l replies, in keeping with the notion of *jīvanmukti* propounded in the *Yogavāsiṣṭha*, "The yogī is inside the king even in his relations with the people of the world."[62]

Recorded also in these dialogues is Bābā La'l's refusal to answer some of Dārā's questions. We are told that for a few days he gave ready answers to this barrage of questions but then fell silent. Explaining his response, Bābā La'l expresses his frustration with these detailed questions referring to abstruse book-knowledge. Bābā La'l adds, "But our interview aims at the heart. If it reposes there, we will be satisfied with it and the truth thus discovered becomes very valuable to us."[63]

[60] Huart and Massignon, "Les Entretiens," 295.

[61] Huart and Massignon, "Les Entretiens," 290–91. Compare Louis Massignon and C. Huart, "Dārā Shikoh's Interview with Baba La'l Das at Lahore," in Waseem, ed. and trans., *On Becoming an Indian Muslim*, 109.

[62] Huart and Massignon, "Les Entretiens," 298; Waseem, ed. and trans., *On Becoming an Indian Muslim*, 115.

[63] Huart and Massignon, "Les Entretiens," 299; Waseem, ed. and trans., *On Becoming an Indian Muslim*, 116.

On another occasion, when Dārā asks what the faqīr's attitude to the world should be, Bābā La'l remains silent. When pressed again, he again gives no response. According to a gloss in the answer section, added by Chandarbhān, or the initial transcriber, this silence suggests "that the questioner was an initiate (*maḥram*) to the secret of the language of the glance (*ḥālat-i nigāh*)." Even when Dārā presses, for the third time, asking for an explanation of what this glance has said, there is silence.[64] In a striking parallel, the unabridged *Yogavāsiṣṭha* also depicts Vasiṣṭha's silence during certain moments. For instance, in a scene toward the latter part of the work, in the section on liberation, Vasiṣṭha instructs Rāma in self-realization, telling him that he will ultimately arrive at a state of consciousness in which there is no duality. Thereupon Rāma poses the question, "If such be the truth concerning the ego-sense, O sage, how do you appear here being called Vasiṣṭha?" Vasiṣṭha's response is to remain silent; when Rāma presses him again he explains that he was silent because silence was the only answer to the question.[65] The Bābā La'l dialogues thus implicitly reference the role of silence in the apophatic rhetoric of both Persianate Sufism and Advaita Vedānta.

The crafted, literary quality of these dialogues is also evident in the quotations of Persian poetry, which, in keeping with the conventions of Persian prose, supplement and embellish some responses. The verse below, which explicates the state of being "present" (*ḥāżir*) with God, bears the imprint of a courtier conversant in Persian rather than a Hindavī-speaking ascetic:

Gar dar yamanī ba manī pīsh-i manī
Dar pīsh-i manī bī manī dar yamanī
If you are in Yemen with me, you are in my presence,
If you are in my presence, without me you are in Yemen.[66]

The base text of Huart and Massignon's edition, however, represents only one version of the dialogues as they were circulated and rewritten. Another manuscript, copied in 1758, draws on a completely different

[64] Huart and Massignon, "Les Entretiens," 303; Waseem, ed. and trans., *On Becoming an Indian Muslim*, 101.

[65] Swami Venkatesananda, trans., *Vasistha's Yoga* (Albany: State University of New York Press, 1993), 512.

[66] Huart and Massignon, "Les Entretiens," 308.

recension, in which the dialogues are divided into seven sessions (*majālis*), each indicating its exact location in the environs of Lahore.[67] The dialogues themselves are brief and highly stylized, taking the form of rapid-fire questions and answers regarding asceticism and the attributes of a faqīr. While Huart and Massignon consider this manuscript to be the initial rough notes transcribed during Dārā's meetings with Bābā La'l,[68] the text's aphoristic, alliterative crafting suggests, rather, its construction as a literary work. This recension, examples of which are provided below, is preserved in a number of nineteenth-century lithographed editions:

Guftam kih bādshāhī-yi faqīr chīst?
Guftā kih bī-parvāyī va khud āgāhī jahān panāhī ast.
...
Guftam kih mawjūdāt-i takīyā-gāh-i faqīr chist?
Guft al-muflis fī amān Allāh.
I asked, "What is rulership (*bādshāhī*) for a faqīr?"
He replied, "Being self-aware, without a care, is kingship [lit., being refuge of the world]."
...
I asked, "What is the nature of the faqīr's pillow rest?"
He replied, "The penniless one is in Allah's protection."[69]

At times the dialogues touch upon topics that would not sit well with the earlier recension. For instance, in a series of exchanges the disciple, that is, Dārā, asks the faqīr, that is, Bābā La'l, about the permissibility of using drugs in order to arrive at a mystical state of intoxication.

Guftam kih bang?
Guftā kih naqṣ-i nāmūs va nang.
Guftam kih kūknār?
Guftā kih nā-hamvār.
Guftam kih āfyūn-i tariyāq?
Guftam ba-bīdāran-i dargāh-i ḥaqq va 'āshiqān va khalvatiyān shāqq.
...
Guftam kih ma'jūn?

67 British Library MS, Add 18, 404, 248–59. The rest of the manuscript consists of Dārā Shikoh's *Sirr-i akbar* and his *Majma' al-baḥrayn*.

68 Huart and Massignon, "Les Entretiens," 288; Waseem, ed. and trans., *On Becoming an Indian Muslim*, 108.

69 Chiranji Lal, ed., *Risāla-i su'āl va javāb*, lithograph (Delhi, 1885), 12.

> *Guftā kih agar bī-bang va bī āfyūn bāshad ahl-i dunyā rā dilpaẓīr va man' bar faqīr ast.*
> I asked, "(What about) cannabis?"
> He replied, "Damages good name and character."
> I asked, "Poppy-head infusion?"
> He replied, "Unworthy."
> I asked, "Opium?"
> He replied, "Repellent for the wakeful of the threshold of Divine Truth, lovers and recluses."
> ...
> I asked, "Hemp-opium sweetmeat?"
> He replied, "If it were free of cannabis and opium, it would be agreeable for worldly people and forbidden for the faqīr."[70]

While opium and alcohol often serve as tropes in Persian literature to highlight esoteric, spiritual states, the above conversation playfully veers back and forth between the disciple's eager curiosity about such substances, and the faqīr's condemnation of them.

Before the publication of these lithographs, the orientalist Horace Hayman Wilson appears to have had access to a related recension of the Bābā La'l dialogues, entitled *Nādir al-nikāt*, excerpts from which he quotes in his *Sketches of the Religious Sects of the Hindus* (1832).[71] Sections of this are similarly crafted, with terse, formulaic questions and answers that also incorporate quotations from Hāfiẓ and Rūmī, while others seem to be more detailed versions of the dialogues in the aforementioned recension. For instance, the question about the faqīr's pillowrest (*takīyā*) is also included here, the answer, however, being further amplified.[72] Through these varied tellings of their legendary dialogues, Dārā Shikoh and Bābā La'l are emplotted within the generic

70 Chiranji Lal, *Risāla-i su'āl va javāb*, 5. Another edition published in Lahore, under the title *Rumūz-i taṣavvuf*, together with an Urdū translation, is similar, but more abbreviated, and smooths over the section on the permissibility of drugs and intoxicants for a faqīr. See Muḥammad Dārā Shikoh (attributed), *Rumūz-i taṣavvuf* (Lahore: Mashhūr-i 'ālam Press, 1923), 6.

71 H.H. Wilson, *Religious Sects of the Hindus* (Calcutta: Sushil Gupta, 1958). Wilson, as he himself clarifies in the introduction, relied extensively on Persian texts for the preparation of this work, two of which were prepared specifically for colonial patrons.

72 Wilson, *Religious Sects of the Hindus*, 195.

conventions of an evolving Indo-Persian literary genre that draws on Sufi as well as Indic ascetic and soteriological traditions. The divergent recensions of the dialogues thus speak as much to the literary forms and tropes circulating in the early modern period, as they do to the prince's actual exchanges with the ascetic.

Dārā's conversations with the saint are also appropriated as a poetic motif in the idiosyncratic *Maṣnavī-yi kajkulāh.* This work, composed in 1794 by the poet Ānandaghana, who went by the *takhallus̤* "Khwash," comprises two volumes that have some overlap, and is dedicated to the figure of the *kajkulāh*, literally meaning "one whose cap is askew," a stock image symbolizing the beloved in Persian poetry.[73] For Ānandaghana the *kajkulāh* appears to be closer to a divine rather than an earthly beloved; the poet expresses reverential gratitude toward him at the end of each section, for enabling its completion.[74] Each volume contains as its frontispiece a painting of Kṛṣṇa resplendent in his peacock crown, with a scribe sitting reverentially at his feet. This image suggests an unspoken resonance with the figure of the *kajkulāh*, for the producers of the manuscript at least, if not the author. At the outset of his work, Ānandaghana expresses his belief in the underlying unity of religions:

Bed dar hindī va dar ʿarabī Qurʾān,
Gasht chūn tūrāt bā Mūsā ʿayān,
Gasht kutub-i injīl bā ʿĪsā ʿaṭā,
Dar zabān-i har yak amr dāda khudā
The Veda in Hindi and in Arabic the Qur'ān
Came to be like the Torah revealed to Moses.
The books of the Bible were bestowed upon Jesus,
In the language of each one did God give his command.[75]

Detailing these different forms of divine revelation, the poet also decries intolerance (*taʿaṣṣub*). This pluralistic vision, though, is grounded

[73] The basis for this image is to be found in a prophetic *ḥadīth* stating: "I saw my Lord in the form of a young man with his cap awry." See Annemarie Schimmel, *Islam in the Indian Subcontinent* (Leiden: E.J. Brill, 1980), 29.

[74] The *kajkulāh* is thanked, with the following line repeated after each section: "*Az tafżīl-i kajkulāh īn shud tamām / mīkunam bar pāy-i ān sajda va salām.*"

[75] Ānandaghana, *Maṣnavī-yi kajkulāh*, British Library MS, Ethe 1725: 2a. This catalogue number corresponds to the second volume of the *Maṣnavī-yi kajkulāh.*

in an Islamic framework, its emphasis on multiple revelations recalling the Qur'ānic verse, "For each We have appointed a divine law and a traced-out way. Had Allah willed He could have made you one community. But that He may try you by that which He has given you (He has made you as you are)."[76]

The *masnavī* itself comprises a range of narratives, several of which, however, are variations on the theme of a renunciant meeting a person rooted in the material world. It is in this context that the story of Dārā meeting Bābā La'l appears, amongst tales of encounters including those of Emperor Hārūn with 'Ayn al-Quẓāt, Żiyā' al-Ḥaqq with Farrukh Shāh, a childless king of Hindustan with an ascetic, Mubārak Shāh with a *darvīsh*, Nānak Shāh *darvīsh* with an emperor, Mūsā with Khiẓr, and a devotee (*'ābid*) with a grain merchant. While such meetings between bearers of spiritual and temporal authority do not form the sole theme of the *masnavī*, they do make up a prominent and distinctive strand of the work.

Dārā Shikoh, here introduced as an emperor rather than the prince that he was, does not come across in a particularly flattering light, in a work that tends to celebrate the renunciant's power over that of the ruler. In the first volume of the *masnavī*, he seeks counsel from Bābā La'l on controlling his lust, incurring reprimands in reply.[77] Rajeev Kinra, analyzing these passages, argues that such a portrayal reflects a "larger cultural memory of Dārā's immaturity."[78] Ānandaghana chooses to incorporate the characters of Dārā and Bābā La'l in the second volume of his *masnavī* as well; here Dāra's questions pertain to Bābā La'l's prayer beads (*taṣbīḥ*) and his lack of a robe (*jāma*) and turban (*dastār*). Here too Bābā La'l's reply highlights the superiority of the ascetic over the ruler:

Mā faqīrān rā hama jubba o kulāh,
Jāma o dastār bā tū, bādshāh.
...
Gharq tū dā'im ba-fikr-i dunyavī,
Ay kujā dar dil-i tū fikr-i ma'navī?

[76] *Qur'ān* 5:48, adapted from the Pickthall translation.

[77] Ānandaghana, *Masnavī-yi kajkulāh*, British Library MS, Ethe 2905. This catalogue number corresponds to the first volume of the *Masnavī-yi kajkulāh*.

[78] Kinra, "Infantalizing Baba Dara," 184.

We faqīrs have our cloaks and hats,
The robe and the turban is for you, emperor.
...
You are constantly immersed in material thought,
O, where in your heart is spiritual thought?[79]

Whether or not these verses reflect contemporaneous views about Dārā Shikoh in particular, they represent the appropriation of the prince's meetings with Bābā La'l into a stock literary motif, divested of much of the relevant historical details. In the *Maṣnavī-yi kajkulāh*, the story of Dārā and Bābā La'l forms one component of a larger tapestry of kings and rulers who are often humbled by the wise ascetics from whom they take instruction.

We may conclude our discussion of the Bābā La'l dialogues by considering also their multilingual dissemination in the early modern era. Christopher Minkowski has recently identified an undated Sanskrit translation of these dialogues in the Jamnottarī Mahal collection of the Jaipur royal family, housed in the City Palace Museum.[80] Entitled the *Praśnottarāvalī* ("Series of Questions and Answers"), its longer title states these questions and answers took place between Bābā Lāl Dayālu and Dārā Śikoh, son of the *yavana* emperor (*dhipendra*), Śāh Jahān. Minkowski notes that the manuscript's gold lettering, coupled with a formulaic statement in its preface, indicate that it was prepared for one of the rulers of Jaipur. This work thus epitomizes a broader pattern of the circulation of cultural products that took place between the Mughal and Rājpūt courts.

In the Sanskrit rendering, the Bābā La'l dialogues have acquired a new shape. The *Praśnottarāvalī* is shorter than the text of Huart and Massignon's edition, yet, going by Minkowski's description, it does not seem to correspond to the other, much briefer and stylized recensions. The order of its twenty-nine questions and answers differs from that of Huart and Massignon's Persian text, as does the correspondence between questions and answers. Minkowski also observes that two additional questions are not mentioned in the Persian recensions, one asking why the "family of Muḥammad" was without shadow, and another question pertaining to

[79] Ānandaghana, *Masnavī-yi kajkulāh*, British Library MS, Ethe 1725: 43 a.

[80] I thank Christopher Minkowski for sharing with me his unpublished paper, "Dara Shikuh's 'Praśnottarāvalī'," which was delivered at the annual meeting of the American Oriental Society in 1998.

impediments on the mystical path, despite the seeker's good intentions. This Sanskrit version of a Mughal prince's philosophical dialogues with an Indic renunciant is testament to the currency of its central motif amongst early modern rulers beyond the Mughal court.

Another instance of the ways in which Dārā Shikoh's conversations with Bābā La'l traveled can be seen in its incorporation into the Sikh tradition of dialogues between Guru Nānak (b. 1469–d. 1538) and various other religious personages. These dialogues, which showcase Nānak as the true spiritual authority, arise both within and outside of the genre of *janamsākhīs*, or accounts of the life of Nānak consisting of hagiographic anecdotes.[81] Those dialogues that are not strictly part of *janamsākhī* narratives include debates between Nānak and Arabian authorities in Mecca and Madīna, Nānak and Sufi notables such as 'Abd al-Qādir Jīlānī and Shams al-Dīn Tabrīzī, as well as Nānak and various Nāth yogīs.[82] Among these is a brief text, which, like the other dialogues, is composed in Punjābī, of the dialogue between Bābā Nānak and Bābā Lāl (*Gośṭ Bābe Lāl Nāl*).[83] This dialogue is based closely on the briefer recension of the Dārā–Bābā La'l exchanges on the characteristics of the faqīr, except that here, the roles are reversed—Nānak is the preceptor and Bābā Lā'l the student and seeker. Needless to say, there is an anachronism in Nānak's meetings with Bābā Lā'l; they lived at least a century apart from one another. This also holds true of the other aforementioned examples in this genre; their main purpose is to juxtapose the ideas of Guru Nānak against those of other spiritual figures who would have had a following in Punjāb.

THE LATER RECEPTION OF THE BĀBĀ LA'L DIALOGUES AND THE *JOG BĀSISHT*

The diachronic reception of the Bābā La'l dialogues as well as the *Jog Bāsisht* renditions further suggest that they were viewed as interlinked by genre. These dialogues find their way into the Persian compendium

[81] W.H. McLeod, *Early Sikh Tradition: A Study of the Janam-Sākhīs* (Oxford: Clarendon Press, 1980), 12.

[82] McLeod, *Early Sikh Tradition*, 102–03.

[83] I am grateful to Harpreet Singh for drawing my attention to this text, and sharing with me his copy of it. "Gośṭ Bābe Lāl Nāl" in *Purātan punjabi Vartak*, ed. Surinder Singh Kohli (Chandigarh: Panjab University, 1988), 97–100.

of Indic knowledge, *Khulāṣat al-khulāṣa* ("The Quintessence of the Quintessence"), which introduces itself as a translation of the Indic work *Sārtat* ("The Quintessence"), prepared in 1673, sixteen years after Aurangzeb's accession, by one Debī Dās ibn Bāl Chand Sandilvī. The author concludes with an autobiographical sketch in which he describes how, as a youth, he sought the company of pure Brahmins (*ṣuḥbat-i Barahmanān-i ṣāfī*) and acquainted himself with the various branches of knowledge (*ma'rifat*) including the Purāṇas, Vedas, *Smṛti*, and Śāstras,[84] finally achieving *jīvanmukti* under the guidance of Svāmī Nand La'l Jīu, a perfect spiritual master (*murshid-i kāmil*).[85]

While the text covers an encyclopedic range of topics, from cosmology, medicine, and archery to a timeline of the rulers of Hindustan, it also contains several works in the dialogue genre. These include a translation of the *Gyān Mālā*, described as the *dharm* that Srī Krishan Jīu conveyed to Arjun, and the first two sections of the *Jog Bāsisht*, dealing with detachment (*vairāgya*) and origination (*utpatti*). They are followed by the aforementioned dialogue between Krishan and Mahādev credited to Shaikh Ṣūfī, here entitled *Harīhar Sanbādh* (*Harīhara Saṃvāda*), as well as a discussion between Mahādev and Pārbatī on '*jog*' (yoga). Dārā Shikoh's conversations with Bābā La'l, identified here as a *bayragī*, follows these, in a recension similar to the base text of Huart and Massignon's edition. This dialogue links almost seamlessly with a discourse between Gorakh and other unidentified spiritually elect personages (*ṣāfī nihādān*), the appellations 'Azīz and Kāmil here carrying over from the Bābā La'l dialogue. The compilation culminates in a meditation on *Bedānt* (Vedānta) and the gnosis of Brahman, and an extract from Krishan Jīu's teachings to Arjun, from the *Mahābhārat* (Mahābhārata). This grouping of the Dārā Shikoh-Bābā La'l dialogues with an assemblage of Indic texts that draw on Vedānta and Nāth yoga, among other traditions, reflects their appropriation within the "Hindu" knowledge that Sandilvī seeks to showcase in his compilation.

The later reception of the *Jog Bāsisht* similarly highlights its inclusion within the dialogue genre of Indic texts rendered in Persian. Later manuscript compendia continue to group the *Aṭvār* together with other

[84] Debī Dās ibn Bāl Chand Sandilvī, *Khulāsat al-khulāṣa*, Aligarh University MS, Ḥabībganj 24/3: 565a.

[85] Sandilvī, *Khulāsat al-khulāṣa*, 565b.

Indic texts on liberation that are structured around a dialogue. A manuscript produced in Lahore, in 1882, contains five such works: the *Aṭvār*, referred to as *Mokhopāya* (*Mokṣopāya*) or *Jog Bāsisht*, the *Aṣṭāvakra Gītā*, the *Gyān Mālā* (*Jñāna Mālā*), an excerpt from an abbreviated *Bhagavad Gītā* translation, and the Kṛṣṇa–Mahādeva dialogue, here entitled the *Hari Harisnabad*.[86] The lavish gold illumination, the detailed illustrations of lovers that form the title pages to each dialogue, and the quality of the calligraphy suggest a wealthy patron. In each case, only the dialogues are provided, with Sanskrit-derived Hindavī rather than Persian titles, while the introductions to each text are omitted. This move of effacing details about the authors or translators of these works and the Islamicate contexts of their production serves to in effect create a new text, in which these five works form a pious continuum, linked by the genre of the dialogue. That in the second half of the nineteenth century, many of these works, in their Urdu or Hindustani incarnations, were also widely disseminated in lithograph editions, speaks both to their influence at that time as well as the persistence of manuscript cultures in the age of print.

Of the works in this compendium, the *Aṣṭāvakra Gītā* recalls the dialogues between Dārā and Bābā La'l in its usage of the terms 'Azīz and Kāmil respectively to refer to King Janaka and Aṣṭāvakra, the sage from whom the king receives emancipatory instruction. Another manuscript of the *Aṣṭāvakra Gītā* in Persian, held in the Osmania University Library, Hyderabad, attributes its authorship to a certain Jadūn Dās Dārā Shikohī, thereby suggesting that he was in the prince's retinue, while a third, in the Berlin Staatsbibliothek, like the British Library copy, remains anonymous.[87] Whether or not anyone in Dārā Shikoh's immediate circles translated the *Aṣṭāvakra Gītā*, the work has been received as being associated with him; moreover, it resembles other Persian Vedāntic writings on liberation.

We have sought to illustrate that the broader context of Dārā Shikoh's encounters with the *muvaḥḥidān-i Hind*, chief among them Bābā La'l Dās, must be navigated through cultural products that memorialize such encounters rather than provide a documentary record of them. The details of Dārā's meetings with Bābā La'l cannot be extricated from

[86] British Library MS, OR 13743. "*Hari Harisnabad,*" however, is probably a scribal error in transcribing from *Harihara Saṃvāda*.

[87] *Aṣṭāvakra Gītā*, Staatsbibliothek, Berlin MS, Sprenger 1661.

the various literary renditions of their dialogues, which are governed by certain generic conventions. Identifying and delineating the dialogue genre as a distinct type in the broader field of Persian writings on Indic religious thought serves, then, as a step toward contextualizing the Bābā La'l dialogues as part of a constantly evolving literary form.

The dialogue genre, forming the narrative structure for many Vedāntic and Nāth texts that were translated into Persian and circulated amongst Sufis and Persophone Hindus, speaks to a specific process of articulating an Indic tradition. Through his spiritual activities and patronage, Dārā Shikoh played an important but not unique role in contributing to the development of this genre. The various works in the dialogue genre reveal a general trend toward privileging Vedānta and the *muvaḥḥidān*, who comprised a select few amongst Indic renunciants, as well as a preoccupation with soteriology. The circulation and proliferation of these writings provide an insight into Mughal religious cultures beyond the imperial courts. An exploration of the intertextual connections between Dārā's named and unnamed interlocutors, for instance Shaikh Ṣūfī and 'Abd al-Raḥmān Chishtī, shows that the production of knowledge in Persian about Indic religions was not solely driven by imperial patronage, nor were these imperial patrons the sole addressees. Furthermore, the development of a critical mass of Hindus literate in Persian ensured that they too took part in creating, circulating, and reading these Persian texts.

BIBLIOGRAPHY

Manuscripts

Akbarnāma, Chester Beatty Library MS 3.

Ānandaghana, *Masnavī-yi kajkulāh*, British Library MS, Ethe 1725.

Ānandaghana, *Masnavī-yi kajkulāh*, British Library MS, Ethe 2905.

'Abd al-Raḥmān Chishtī, *Mir'āt al-makhlūqāt*, British Library MS, OR 1883.

'Abd al-Raḥmān Chishtī, *Mir'āt al-ḥaqā'iq*, British Library MS, OR 1883.

Aṣṭāvakra Gītā, Staatsbibliothek, Berlin MS, Sprenger 1661.

Bodleian Library MS, Ouseley Pers Add 69.

Bodleian Library MS, Fraser 268.

British Library MS, Add 18,404

British Library MS, OR 13743

Debī Dās ibn Bāl Chand Sandilvi, *Khulasat al-khulāṣa*, Aligarh University MS, Ḥabībganj 24/3.

Dīvān-i Valī Rām, Asiatic Society of Bengal, MS, II 240.

Khamsa-i Niẓāmī, British Library MS, OR 6810.
Ṣūfī Sharīf, *Aṭvār fī ḥall al-asrār*, British Library MS, OR 1883.
Ṣūfī Sharīf, *Gharā'ib al-aṭvār fī kashf al-anvār* and *Aṭvār fī ḥall al-asrār*, Khudā Bakhsh Library MS, 2081 HL.
Ṣūfī Sharīf, *Navādir al-sulūk*, Bodleian Library MS, Ouseley Add 69.

Published Material

Athar Ali, M. "Pursuing an Elusive Seeker of Universal Truth—the Identity and Environment of the Author of the Dabistan-i Mazahib." *Journal of the Royal Asiatic Society* 9, no. 3 (1999): 365–75.
Banvālidās Valī (attributed). *Gulzār-i hāl yā tulū'-yi qamar-i ma'rifat*. Edited by Tara Chand and Amir Hasan Abidi. Aligarh: Aligarh Muslim University, 1967.
Baranī, Ḍiyā' al-Dīn. *Fatāvā-yi jahāndārī*. Edited by Afsar Salīm Khān. Lahore: Intishārāt-i Idāra-yi Taḥqīqāt-i Pākistān, 1972.
Behl, Aditya. "An Ethnographer in Disguise: Comparing Self and Other in Mughal India." In *Notes on a Mandala: Essays in the History of Indian Religions in Honor of Wendy Doniger*, edited by Laurie Patton and David Haberman, 113–48. Newark: University of Delaware Press, 2010.
Bhartṛhari. *The Nītiśataka, Śriṇgāraśataka and Vairāgyaśataka*. Edited and translated by Purohit Gopinath. Bombay: Shri Venkateshwar Press, 1896.
Brahman, Chandarbhān. *Chahār chaman*. Edited by Yunus Jaffery. New Delhi: Iran Culture House, 2004.
Busch, Allison. "Hidden in Plain View: Brajbhasha Poets at the Mughal Court." *Modern Asian Studies* 44 (2010): 267–309.
Chand, Tara. "Rafi' al-Khilaf of Sita Ram Kayastha Saksena." *The Journal of the Ganganatha Jha Research Institute* 11 (1944): 7–12.
Chand, Tara, and S.A.H. Abidi, eds. *Jūg Bāsisht*. Aligarh: Aligarh Muslim University, 1978.
Dabistān-i mazāhib. Edited by Kaykhusraw Isfandiyār and Raḥīm Rizāzāda Malik. Tehran: Kitābkhāna-i Ṭahūrī, 1983.
Dārā Shikoh, Muḥammad. *Ḥasanāt-i 'ārifīn*. Edited by Makhdūm Rahīn. Tehran: Mu'assasa-yi Taḥqīqat va Intishārat-i Visman, 1973.
———. *Majma' al-baḥrayn*. Edited by Muhammad Riza Jalali Naini. Tehran: Nashr-i Nuqra, 2001.
——— (attributed). *Rumūz-i tasavvuf*. Lahore: Mashhūr-i 'ālam Press, 1923.
———. *Sakīnat al-awliyā'*. Edited by Tara Chand and Muhammad Riza Jalali Naini. Tehran: Mu'assasa-yi Matbū'at-i 'Ilmī, 1965.
Das, Ashok Kumar. "An Introductory Note on the Emperor Akbar's Ramayana and its Miniatures." In *Facets of Indian Art*, edited by Robert Skelton, 94–104. London: Heritage Publishers, 1987.

Dasgupta, S.N. *History of Indian Philosophy*. Cambridge: Cambridge University Press, 1922.

Doniger, Wendy. *Dreams, Illusions and Other Realities*. Chicago: University of Chicago Press, 1984.

Franke, Heike. "Akbar's *Yogavāsiṣṭha* at the Chester Beatty Library." Paper presented at the Annual Conference on South Asia, Madison, October 2010.

_____. "Die persischen Übersetzungen des *Laghuyogavāsiṣṭha*." In *The Mokṣopaya, Yoga Vāsiṣṭha and Related Texts*, edited by Jürgen Hanneder, 113–30. Aachen: Shaker Verlag, 2005.

Green, Nile. "The Religious and Cultural Role of Dreams and Visions in Islam." *Journal of the Royal Asiatic Society* 3 (2003): 287–313.

Hanneder, Jürgen, ed. *The Mokṣopaya, Yogavāsiṣṭha and Related Texts*. Aachen: Shaker Verlag, 2005.

Hasrat, Bikrama Jit. *Dara Shikuh: Life and Works*. Calcutta: Visvabharati, 1953.

Hintersteiner, Norbert. "Dara Shukuh's Search for Muvahhidan-i-hind: Liminal Religious Identity and Inter-Religious Translation." In *On the Edge of Many Worlds*, edited by F.L. Bakker and J.S Aritonang, 263–78. Zoetermeer: Meinema, 2006.

Huart, C. and L. Massignon, 1926. "Les Entretiens de Lahore (entre le Prince imperial Dārā Shikoh et l'ascete Hindou Baba La'l Das)." *Journal Asiatique* 209 (October–December 1926): 285–334.

Jahāngīr. *Jahāngīr-nāma: Tuzuk-i jahāngīrī*. Edited by Muḥammad Hāshim. Tehran: Bunyād-i Farhang, n.d.

Kāẓim, Muḥammad. *Ālamgīrnāma*. Calcutta: Asiatic Society of Bengal, 1868.

Kinra, Rajeev. "Infantalizing Baba Dara: The Cultural Memory of Dara Shekuh and the Mughal Public Sphere." *Journal of Persianate Studies* 2 (2009): 165–93.

Kohli, Surinder Singh, ed. *Purātan punjābī vārtak*. Chandigarh: Panjab University, 1988.

Lal, Chiranji, ed. *Risala-i su'āl va javāb*. Lithograph. Delhi 1885.

Leach, Linda York. *Mughal and Other Indian Paintings from the Chester Beatty Library*. Volume 1. London: Scorpion, 1995.

Marshall, D.N. *Mughals in India: ABibliographic Survey*. London: Mansell, 1967.

Massignon, Louis. "An Experiment in Hindu–Muslim Unity: Dārā Shikoh." In *On Becoming an Indian Muslim: French Essays on Aspects of Syncretism*, edited and translated by M. Waseem, 95–105. Delhi: Oxford University Press, 2003.

Massignon, Louis and C. Huart. "Dārā Shikoh's Interview with Baba La'l Das at Lahore." In *On Becoming an Indian Muslim: French Essays on Aspects of Syncretism*, edited and translated by M. Waseem, 106–30 Delhi: Oxford University Press, 2003.

McLeod, W.H. *Early Sikh Tradition: A Study of the Janam-Sākhīs*. Oxford: Clarendon Press, 1980.

Minissale, Gregory. "Seeing Eye-to-Eye with Mughal Miniatures: Some Observations on the Outward Gazing Figure in Mughal Art." *Marg* 58, no. 3 (2007): 41–49.

Minkowski, Christopher. "Dara Shikuh's 'Praśnottarāvalī'." Paper presented at the annual meeting of the American Oriental Society, 1998.

Moosvi, Shireen. "The Mughal Encounter with Vedanta: Recovering the Biography of Jadrup." *Social Scientist* 30 (2002): 13–23.

Niẓām Panipatī. *Jūg Bāsisht*. Edited by Muhammad Riẓa Jalālī Nā'inī and N.S. Shukla. Tehran: Iqbal, 1981.

Patton, Laurie L. "Samvada: A Literary Resource for Conflict Negotiation in Classical India." *Evam: Forum on Indian Representations* 3, nos. 1–2 (2004): 177–90.

Qanungo, K.R. *Dara Shukoh*. Calcutta: S.C. Sarkar, 1952.

Raghavan, V. "Kavindracarya Sarasvati." In *Indian Culture, D.R. Bhandarkar Volume*, 159–65. Calcutta: Indian Research Institute, 1940.

Rahurkar, V.G. "The Bhasa-Yogavasisthasara of Kavindracarya Sarasvati." *Proceedings of the All-India Oriental Conference* 18 (1955): 471–82.

Reynolds, Dwight, ed. *Interpreting the Self: Autobiography in the Arabic Literary Tradition*. Berkeley: University of California Press, 2001.

Richards, John F. *The Mughal Empire*. Cambridge: Cambridge University Press, 1993.

Sakaki, Kazuyo. "Yogavāsiṣṭha and the Medieval Islamic Intellectuals in India." In *Yogavāsiṣṭha Mahārāmāyaṇa: A Perspective*, edited by Manjula Sahdev, 282–97. Patiala: Punjabi University, 2003.

Schimmel, Annemarie. *Islam in the Indian Subcontinent*. Leiden: Brill, 1980.

Śrīvara. *Śrīvara's Zaina Rājataraṅgiṇī*. Translated by Kashi Nath Dhar. Delhi: Indian Council for Historical Research and People's Publishing House, 1994.

———. "Rājatarangini." In *Medieval Kashmir*, translated by J.C. Dutt, edited by S.L. Sadhu. New Delhi: Atlantic, 1990.

Thomi, Peter, ed. *Yogavasisthasara: Die Quintessenz des Yogavasistha*. Teil I–II. Wichtrach: Institut für Indologie, 1999.

———. "The Yogavāsiṣṭha in its Longer and Shorter Version." *Journal of Indian Philosophy* 11 (1983): 107–16.

Vassie, Roderic. "Persian Interpretations of the Bhagavad Gītā in the Mughal Period." PhD diss., School of Oriental and African Studies, University of London, 1989.

Venkatesananda, Swami, trans. *Vasistha's Yoga*. Albany: State University of New York Press, 1993.

Verma, Som Prakash. *Mughal Painters and their Work*. Aligarh and Delhi: Oxford University Press, 1994.

Waseem, M., ed. and trans. *On Becoming an Indian Muslim: French Essays on Aspects of Syncretism*. New Delhi: Oxford University Press, 2003.

Wilkinson, J.V.S. "A Note on an Illustrated Manuscript of the Jog Bashisht." *Bulletin of the School of Oriental and African Studies* 12 (1948): 692–94.

Wilson, H.H. *Religious Sects of the Hindus*. Calcutta: Sushil Gupta, 1958.

4 Learned Brahmins and the Mughal Court

The Jyotiṣas

Christopher Minkowski*

Sanskrit sources offer much information on the social history of the interactions between Haindavas (Indians) and Pārasīkas (Persians), to use the parlance of the paṇḍits, during the sixteenth and seventeenth centuries. They also provide valuable insights into the service provided by learned Brahmins at the Mughal court. Here we shall focus especially on the archive available for the history of the *jyotiṣas*, or experts in the "astral sciences," as David Pingree called them, who not only produced astronomical, mathematical, calendrical, astrological, and divinatory texts, but also advised their clients on their plans for life and for action: ritual, military, and personal.[1] It is not so much the scientific content of the works that is relevant here, as what those works tell us about the connections that their authors had with the Mughal court. In a

* I thank the editors of this volume and the participants in the 2008 Berkeley conference for their useful comments, S.R. Sarma, Yigal Bronner, and Emma Mathiesen for assistance in compiling the materials included in this study, and Isaac Murchie for editorial assistance.

[1] See, for example, Hermann Hunger and David Pingree, *Astral Sciences in Mesopotamia* (Leiden: Brill, 1999).

more general way, the sources can also tell us something about attitudes toward the "westerners" (*yavanas*), or "strangers" (*mlecchas*), and the impact that their presence had on the world of learned Brahmins.

These Sanskrit sources are best understood in two contexts: a social one, of the history of Brahmins and other "literate service elites" during this period, and a textual one, of the discursive world of Sanskrit knowledge systems (śāstra), and of their formation in the early modern period. Therefore we shall briefly consider the sources of livelihood available to the Brahmins, ranging from those in worldly, or *laukika*, service to *yavana* rulers, to those who accepted patronage from no one. We shall also consider the distinctive shaping of Sanskrit texts produced in this setting, and their rhetorical style which—while stressing the importance of Brahmin families—gives some inkling of the rivalries that drove them to make their choices. The authors we will encounter here, especially those who were based in Banaras, were operating in a highly competitive intellectual context. The city had once again, in the sixteenth and seventeenth centuries, become the great subcontinental hub for Sanskrit scholarship, science, and collective authority. Works produced there reveal something of the way that the prestige and authority of a paṇḍit family was developed through its interaction with patrons and with the community of *śāstrins* around India. Past studies that have mined these texts for the extraction of factual nuggets about their authors and patrons have tended to underemphasize this rhetorical and social context.

Read in this way, the Sanskrit sources reveal several conflicting attitudes current among observant Brahmins, and thus a general ambivalence verging on resistance regarding the very idea of service to a patron, especially to the *yavanas*. The presence of the *yavana*-ruled kingdoms (Mughal and others) thus presented a problem for Brahmins in that the ruler was the source both of honor and of emolument for a Brahmin. The Mughal state, in particular, actively worked to fulfill this double role.

Astral scientists were particularly in demand in the courts of *yavana* rulers. Although the Mughals and their courtiers had astral scientists proficient in the Islamicate traditions, they also sought out the *jyotiṣas*, just as Rajputs and other Hindus sought experts in the *yavana* astral sciences.

This study proceeds, therefore, in three parts. In the first are collected some examples of Sanskrit discourse in this period that show the ambivalence in the attitudes of paṇḍits toward *yavana* rulers and culture. Then there is a summary of the general history of the relationship of the paṇḍit community in Banaras with the Mughal rulers and their courtiers. Finally, we turn in greater detail to the *jyotiṣa*s of the period, and consider their rhetoric of self-presentation, elaborating on the importance of their families, and of the honors and gifts they received from the Mughal emperor or his court.

THE *YAVANA* PROBLEM AND BRAHMIN AMBIVALENCE

Passages from Sanskrit works composed during this period show that, for at least some Brahmin authors, *yavana*s presented a problem, in at least two ways. Their presence could endanger the maintenance of the personal regimes of Brahminical bodily purity and refinement, and their political control could deprive the world of Brahminical guidance and clarity. At the same time, as we shall see later, *yavana* rulers were described as pious and dharmic kings, or as protectors of the *varṇāśrama* dharma; it was further said that the texts of the *yavana*s, even in their own language, could be valuable improvements or corrections to the Sanskrit-based tradition of astronomical principles or *siddhānta*s. One text, the *Viśvaguṇādarśacampū* ("The Poetic Mirror of All Qualities"), perfectly captures Brahmin ambivalence regarding *yavana*s.

VIŚVAGUṆĀDARŚACAMPŪ ON BANARAS

The *Viśvaguṇādarśacampū*, a sort of human geography and satire of manners of mid-seventeenth-century India, was composed by the south Indian author, Veṅkaṭādhvarin.[2] It depicts two semi-divine beings, *gandharva*s, flying southward over India and discussing what they see.

[2] For the text, Veṅkaṭādhvarin, *Viśvaguṇādarśacampūḥ*, ed. Surendranatha Śāstrin (Vārānasī: Chaukhambā Vidyābhavana, 1963), and for a French translation, Marie-Claude Porcher, *La Viśvaguṇādarśacampū de Veṅkaṭādhvarin* (Pondichéry: Institute Français d'Indologie, 1972). The work has been discussed a number of times in recent scholarship. See especially V. Narayana Rao, David Shulman, and Sanjay Subrahmanyam, *Symbols of Substance: Court and State in Nāyaka Period Tamilnadu* (Oxford: Oxford University Press, 1998), 1–12.

One of the *gandharvas* is a relentless optimist, the other a relentless cynic. Of interest to us here are their comments about Banaras.

They find that the Kali age has descended even over Kāśī. The chief problem consists in the dangers that the place presents for Brahmins. Aside from the unhealthy and somewhat impoverished condition of its inhabitants, it is especially the city's social mix and the close contact necessitated by passing through its streets to bathe in the river that constitute the threat. The cynical *gandharva* notes that Brahmins bathe without concern in water that has been brought to them in pails by Shudras, eat food that has been carried through the street where it has been looked at by dogs and vile *yavanas*, and eat their food with Brahmins who have fallen from caste through their misbehavior and ignorance of the Vedas.[3] Some Brahmins live a voluptuary existence, supported by wrong livelihoods, and even travel to distant places on business, or throw over Vedic practices for Tantric ones.[4] Thus the *yavanas* are only one of many sources of danger for Brahmins in the city.

The optimistic *gandharva* replies that, even in this Kali age, when strangers (*mlecchas*) cover India from its southern tip to the Himalayas, we should be grateful that there is one good Brahmin in a hundred, and that there are, in fact, many good and observant Brahmins in the city.[5] To defend their service to *yavana* rulers, the optimistic *gandharva* concedes that Kāyasthas, princes, and Brahmins bear arms and serve the "pitilessly arid" Turks/Mughals (*turuṣkas*). In doing so, however, they end up protecting the gods and the Brahmins. If they did not, good people would have to offer the funeral rites of Brahminhood itself.[6] Thus, even the optimistic *gandharva* is not enthusiastic about the presence of

[3] *nīcair duryavanaiḥ śunībhir api vā niḥśaṅkam ālokitaṃ, bhuṅkte paṅktividūṣakaiḥ saha narair ajñātavedākṣaraiḥ | madyāsvādanamattacittajanatāmohāya bhīhānitaḥ karmāṇy ārabhate śrutismṛtivacodūrāṇy asārāṇy aho || Viśvaguṇādarśacampū*, vs. 91. See also vs. 89 for bodily contact with *yavanas* of both high and low standing (*yavanair uccāvacaiḥ*), and the water brought to them by Shudras.

[4] *Viśvaguṇādarśacampū*, vss 83 and 91.

[5] *ākrāntāsu vasundharāsu yavanair āsetuhaimācalam | Viśvaguṇādarśacampū*, vs. 97a. On the rarity of learned observant Brahmins, vs. 94.

[6] *ye kāyasthajanāś ca ye nṛpasutā ye ca dvijāś śastriṇas, te yatnād anusṛtya nirdayatayā śuṣkāṃs turuṣkādhipān | devān bhūmisurāṃś ca pānti kṛtinas te*

yavanas in India, but claims that those Brahmins who offer them *laukika* service are somehow defending whatever can be saved of the ancient dharmas through these actions.

This problem of Brahmins serving *yavana* rulers is raised elsewhere in the *Viśvaguṇādarśacampū* as well. As the two *gandharvas* are flying over Maharashtra, the cynic claims that in this country the Brahmins don't follow their observances, and instead carry out farming and trade or serve as village accountants.[7] Rather than studying the Vedas, they are learning to read and write the script of the *yavanas* (*yavanānī-vācanā-abhyāsam*).[8] They sell their service to the Western rulers to fill their bellies.[9]

The optimist's response is much the same as his response in Banaras: there are nevertheless Brahmins who are pure and observant of their Brahminical duties. Furthermore, if some did not become rulers and generals, or learn the ways of the *yavana*, there would be no one to protect the livelihood of Brahmins. Then the world would be without Brahmins', and engulfed by *yavanas*.[10] Again, even the optimistic view holds Brahmins' service of *yavanas* to be the least objectionable option in a degraded period. What appears to be at stake is the support of the lives and livelihoods of observant and studious Brahmins.

Something like this attitude is found elsewhere in the literature of the period, although it is far from uniform. There were Brahmins willing to accept the support of *yavanas*, while continuing their pursuit of Sanskrit learned disciplines. Remaining for a moment in Maharashtra, we may refer to the example of Sābāji Pratāparāja, or as he is known in the Persian chronicles, Pratāp Rāy. Pratāparāja, a Brahmin of the Jāmadagnya *gotra*, was a prominent minister in the revenue department of the Ahmadnagar kingdom of Burhān Niẓām Shāh, in the middle of

---

ced gṛheṣv āsate, brāhmaṇyāya jalāñjaliḥ kila bhuvi prājñaiḥ pradeyo bhavet || *Viśvaguṇādarśacampū*, vs. 96.

7 *Viśvaguṇādarśacampū*, vs. 133.

8 *Viśvaguṇādarśacampū*, vs. 134.

9 *kukṣeḥ pūrtyai yavananṛpater bhṛtyakṛtyāni kartum, vikrīṇīte vapur api nijaṃ vetanair etad āstām* | *Viśvaguṇādarśacampū*, vs. 136ab.

10 *camūniyamena vā janapadādhikāreṇa vā, dvijavraja upavrajan prabhu-padaṃ mahārāṣṭrajaḥ* | *na vṛttim iha pālayed yadi dharāsurāṇāṃ tato, bhaved yavanaveṣṭitaṃ bhuvanam etad abrāhmaṇam* | *Viśvaguṇādarśacampū*, vs. 141.

the sixteenth century. He was also the author of a vast Dharmaśāstric treatise, the *Paraśurāmapratāpa*.[11] This text, which was dedicated to Burhān Niẓām Shāh, depicts the kingdom's capital, Ahmadnagar, as a rival to Indra's paradise, with its majestic buildings, happy citizens, leafy gardens, and throngs of learned Brahmins.[12]

A more ambivalent attitude regarding connections with the Niẓām Shāhī court is expressed in the chronicle of the Bhaṭṭas, whom we will encounter again in the next section of this study. Rāmeśvara Bhaṭṭa moved his family from the banks of the Godāvarī in the Ahmadnagar kingdom to Banaras at the beginning of the sixteenth century. His grandson, Śaṅkara Bhaṭṭa, wrote a history of the lineage, in which he devoted six of the work's nine chapters to the life of his grandfather. Rāmeśvara is credited in this account with acquiring, against his own wishes, a *yavana* follower, Ẓafar Malik, who was a state official. This was while Rāmeśvara was still living in Maharashtra. Ẓafar Malik described the wondrous powers of Rāmeśvara to the Niẓām Shāh himself, who duly invited him to court, but Rāmeśvara summarily refused.[13] Nevertheless Rāmeśvara was willing to accept the support of Ẓafar Malik, who paid for all of his meals over the course of a year. Then again, in a later episode, Rāmeśvara visited Vijayanagara, and refused the generosity of Kṛṣṇadevarāya.[14] Thus his reluctance to visit the court in Ahmadnagar may have had to do with Niẓām Shāh as a king, rather than as a *yavana*.

[11] Har Dutt Sharma, "*Paraśurāmapratāpa*: Its Authorship, Date and the Authorities Quoted in It," *The Poona Orientalist* (1942): 9–10. It is possible that this vast work was composed by another Brahmin, Pratāparāja's guru Karmasūri, and attributed to the patron. For the purposes of establishing that a learned Brahmin served at the Niẓām Shāhī court, that does not make a difference.

[12] *saudhair amba[ra]cumbiratnaśikharair ānandapūrṇair janair, udyānaiḥ kalakaṇṭhasaṅgavila[sa]tkalpadrumābhair drumaiḥ | śakrādhiṣṭhitapūr iveyam amalā brahmarṣisaṃsevitā, śrīmadrājanijāmaśāhanagarī saṃlakṣ<ya>te bhūmipaiḥ* || *Upodghāṭakāṇḍa*, *Paraśurāmapratāpa*, vs. 15, cited in Sharma, "*Paraśurāmapratāpa*," 7.

[13] James Benson, "Śaṃkarabhaṭṭa's Family Chronicle: The Gādhivaṃśavarṇana," in *The Pandit: Traditional Scholarship in India (Festschrift P. Aithal)*, ed. Axel Michaels, volume 38 of *Heidelberg South Asian Studies* (New Delhi: Manohar Publications, 2001), 109–10. The Niẓām Shāh in this period would have been Ahmad, the founder of the dynasty.

[14] Benson, "Śaṃkarabhaṭṭa," 111.

The traces of attitudes toward *yavanas* that we find in texts of the period reflect a variety, with only some of them exhibiting what we might call a sense of the *yavana* problem. The nature of the problem that the *yavanas* posed does not appear to be directly related to their religious doctrines or practices, but rather to the somatic and political effects on Brahmins of their physical presence.

THE CITY OF PAṆḌITS AND THE MUGHAL COURT

There is by now a considerable literature on the relationship between the learned Brahmins in Banaras and the Mughal court.[15] Here it will suffice to trace the arc of a period of about eighty-five years, from ca. 1585, when the Viśvanātha temple was rebuilt (probably by Ṭoḍar Mal, a Kāyastha Hindu minister of Akbar), until 1669, when that temple was demolished again under Aurangzeb. This period has long been remembered among learned Brahmins, and has provided a vocabulary for discussion of the "Hunūd–Musulmān question" in later times. It should be possible to give a sense of the arc of this history by way of mentioning three well-known figures. In chronological order, they are Nārāyaṇa Bhaṭṭa, Kavīndrācārya Sarasvatī, and Jagannātha Paṇḍitarāja.

[15] See, for example, Dineshchandra Bhattacharya, "Sanskrit Scholars in Akbar's Time," *Indian Historical Quarterly* 13 (1937): 31–36; M.M. Patkar, "Moghul Patronage to Sanskrit Learning," *The Poona Orientalist* 3 (1938): 164–75; P.K. Gode, "Bernier and Kavīndrācārya Sarasvatī at the Mughal Court," *Journal of S.V. Oriental Institute, Tirupati* 1, no. 4 (1941): 1–16; P.K. Gode, "The Identification of Gosvāmi Nṛsiṃhāśrama of Dara Shukoh's Sanskrit Letter with Brahmendra Sarasvatī of the Kavīndra-Candrodaya—Between AD 1628 and 1658," *Adyar Library Bulletin* 6 (1942): 172–77; Jatindra Bimal Chaudhuri, *Muslim Patronage to Sanskrit Learning*, part 1 (Delhi: Idarah-i Adabiyat-i Delli, 1942); P.K. Gode, "Samudrasaṃgama, a Philosophical Work by Dārā Shukoh, Son of Shāh Jahān, Composed in 1655 A.D.," *Bhāratīya Itihāsa Saṃśodhana Maṇḍal* 24 (1943): 75–88; Sri Ram Sarma, *A Bibliography of Mughal India (1526–1707 AD)* (Bombay: Karnatak Publishing House, 1964); Carl Ernst, "Muslim Studies of Hinduism? A Reconstruction of Arabic and Persian Translations from Indian Languages," *Iranian Studies* 36, no. 2 (2003): 173–95; Audrey Truschke, "Akbar as Shah or Raja? Reimaginings of Encounters with the Mughal Court in Jaina Sanskrit Literature" (unpublished paper presented at the 14th World Sanskrit Conference, Kyoto University, 2009).

Nārāyaṇa Bhaṭṭa, the Jagadguru

Nārāyaṇa Bhaṭṭa was the son of Rāmeśvara Bhaṭṭa, mentioned above, and a member of one of the most prominent Brahmin families in Banaras in the sixteenth and seventeenth centuries.[16] This family dominated the discourse of Dharmaśāstra and Mīmāṃsā in the city, and works by its members were widely circulated in India. Nārāyaṇa was the author of the *Tristhalīsetu*, the *Prayogaratna*, and many other works.

It was Nārāyaṇa Bhaṭṭa who elevated the family's standing in Banaras. He is remembered as having a connection to Rājā Ṭoḍar Mal, the chief revenue officer in Akbar's empire.[17] The family chronicle of the Bhaṭṭas that was composed by Nārāyaṇa's nephew, Śaṅkara, remembers Nārāyaṇa Bhaṭṭa as winning a debate with the paṇḍits of Bengal and Mithilā, at the home of Ṭoḍar Mal in Delhi.[18] Later family tradition has it that Nārāyaṇa Bhaṭṭa persuaded Akbar to rebuild the Viśvanātha temple in Banaras. Akbar also conferred on him the title of Jagadguru, or guru of the world.[19] The more commonly accepted history is that it was Ṭoḍar

[16] Haraprasad Shastri, "Dakshini Pandits at Benares," *The Indian Antiquary* 41 (1912): 7–12. For a family tree, and more on Nārāyaṇa, see Pandurang V. Kane, *History of Dharmaśāstra* (Poona: Bhandarkar Oriental Research Institute, 1975), I, part 2, 903ff.

[17] Richard Salomon, "Biographical Data on Nārāyaṇa Bhaṭṭa of Benares," in *Ācārya-vandanā*, ed. Samaresh Bandyopadhyay (Calcutta: University of Calcutta, 1984), 331–33.

[18] Shastri, "Dakshini Pandits," 9–10.

[19] See Salomon, "Biographical Data," 333–34. The *Bhaṭṭavaṃśakāvya*, composed by Kāntanātha Bhaṭṭa, a descendant of Rāmeśvara, and published in 1903, devotes its third chapter to an account of Nārāyaṇa's life. In this modern account, the world was oppressed by un-Aryan, violent *yavanas* who were badly behaved and hostile to the Veda (vs. 3). Śiva sent a drought (vs. 4). The *yavana* emperor, concerned by the drought, searched the kingdom and found Nārāyaṇa (vs. 5). He bowed before Nārāyaṇa in supplication, who thought of Śiva, and wished for rain. The rain came (vss 6–9). The emperor was so impressed that he showered wealth on Nārāyaṇa, and gave him the title Jagadguru (vs. 12). Nārāyaṇa then asked that the Viśvanātha temple be rebuilt, and the emperor ordered that it be so. Nārāyaṇa installed the image in the temple, and thenceforth the Bhaṭṭas got the right of first worship there (vss 15–18). Kāntanātha Bhaṭṭa, *Bhaṭṭavaṃśakāvyam* (Mirzapur: Anandakadambini, 1903).

Mal who did the building, perhaps at Nārāyaṇa's insistence. Nārāyaṇa's descendants remembered that Nārāyaṇa officiated at the installation of the *liṅgam* in the temple.[20] P.L. Vaidya maintained that Nārāyaṇa supervised the Ṭoḍarānanda, the compendious work of Dharmaśāstra commissioned by Ṭoḍar Mal.[21] The text was certainly produced by paṇḍits based in Banaras. Praise of Ṭoḍar Mal in the introductions to the sections of the work refer to him as the foremost official (*rājāgraṇī*) of the king of the Indians and Persians (*Haindava-pārasīka-dharaṇīśakra*).[22] He is also the one who retrieved the Vedas sunk in a sea of *mlecchas*, thereby making the deeds of the fish *avatāra* of Viṣṇu hold good again in the world.[23] Thus the Hindu courtier, Ṭoḍar Mal, mediated Nārāyaṇa's relationship to Akbar, and this mediation was remembered in Banaras for generations.

Kavīndra, the Sarvavidyānidhāna

The second figure was a learned *sannyāsin* in the city, an Advaitin philosopher and a poet, whose monastic name was probably Kṛṣṇānanda Sarasvatī.[24] He was and is better known by his titles: Kavīndra, the lord among poets, Sarvavidyānidhāna, the repository of all sciences,

[20] *śrīrāmeśvarasūrisunur abhavan nārāyaṇākhyo mahān | yenakāri avimuktake suvidhinā viśveśvarasthāpanā ||* Vs. 4ab of beginning of *Dānahārāvalī* of Divākara Bhaṭṭa, great-grandson of Nārāyaṇa Bhaṭṭa. Cited from Julius Eggeling, *Catalogue of the Sanskrit Manuscripts in the Library of the India Office*, part 3 (London: Secretary of the State for India, 1891), 547. See also the preceding footnote. The same text includes this verse at its conclusion: *śrirāmeśvaratas tataḥ samabhavac chrībhaṭṭanārāyaṇaḥ, śāstrāmnayaparāyaṇaḥ khalamatadhvāntaikavidrāvaṇaḥ | kāśyāṃ pātakividrutaṃ bhagavato viśveśvarasyācalaṃ, liṅgaṃ bhāgyavaśāt sukhāya jagatāṃ saṃsthāpayām āsa.* Cited from Pandurang V. Kane, *History of Dharmaśāstra*, I, part 2, 905.

[21] Salomon, "Biographical Data," 331–33.

[22] *śrīmān haindavapārasīkadharaṇīśakrasya rājāgraṇī, rājā ṭoḍaramallacaṇḍakiraṇas tīvrapratāpodayaḥ | Vyavahārasaukhya* section of *Ṭoḍarānanda*, P.L. Vaidya, ed., *Ṭoḍarānandam* (Bikaner: Anup Sanskrit Library, 1948), xxvi.

[23] *yena mlecchapayodhimagnanigamoddhārakriyā kāritā | kalpāntoditam ādimīnacaritaṃ lokeṣu satyāpitam || Varṣakṛtyasaukhya* section of *Ṭoḍarānanda*, Vaidya, *Ṭoḍarānandam*, xxvii.

[24] V. Raghavan, "Kavīndrācārya Sarasvatī," in *D.R. Bhandarkar Volume*, ed. B.C. Law (Calcutta: Indian Research Institute, 1940), 160.

and Acharya. A Brahmin born in a Ṛgvedin family from the Godāvarī region of the Deccan, he moved to the city in his youth.

Kavīndra was a leader of *śāstrins* and *sannyāsins*, and an opinion maker. He is best remembered for interceding directly with Shāh Jahān and Dārā Shukoh to have a tax on Hindu pilgrims to Banaras and Allahabad suspended. It was also at his behest that Shāh Jahān arranged for money to be distributed to pilgrims.[25] So well received was this accomplishment that the paṇḍits of Banaras produced a felicitation volume, the *Kavīndracandrodaya*, in his honor.[26] It comprises some 350 honorific verses and addresses, composed by about seventy different luminaries of the city. From this text it is possible to reconstruct something of his relationship with Shāh Jahān and Dārā, couched though the volume is in florid poetic effusions about Kavīndra's glories.

We learn, for instance, that he received the title of Kavīndra from Shāh Jahān. Shāh Jahān, we are told, was acting only as the mouthpiece of the goddess whom Kavīndra worshipped.[27] It was the Banarsi *sannyāsins* and *śāstrins* who gave him the titles Sarvavidyānidhāna and Acharya.[28] Kavīndra frequented the court of the emperor, and expounded aspects of Hindu literature, religion, and philosophy to him—among other things the commentary (*bhāṣya*) of Śaṅkarācārya, the Advaitin.[29] The compendium suggests that Dārā Shukoh was present for Kavīndra's visits and lectures.[30] The *Kavīndracandrodaya* also suggests that Kavīndra was first offered other gifts by the Mughaḷ emperor, but insisted on the lifting of

[25] Some sources state that this annual pension amounted to two thousand rupees, an enormous sum. R.B. Athavale, *Kavīndrakalpadruma of Kavīndrācārya Sarasvatī* (Calcutta: Asiatic Society, 1981), xxii.

[26] Har Dutt Sharma and M.M. Patkar, *Kavīndracandrodaya* (Poona: Oriental Book Agency, 1939).

[27] *kāmākṣī prathamaprayāṇasamaye vidyānidhānaprabhor, indratvam tava mastake kṛtavatī śrīsāhijāhāmukhāt* | *Kavīndracandrodaya*, vs. 118ab, by Pūrṇānanda Brahmacārin. See Raghavan, "Kavīndrācārya," 160–61.

[28] *vijitamahītala (sic) tasmai dattaṃ vidyānidhānapadam asmai | ācāryāhvayasahitaṃ yatibuddhavṛndair mahītalam mahitam ||* *Kavīndracandrodaya*, vs. 8.

[29] Raghavan, "Kavīndrācārya," 161–62.

[30] *yena śrīsāhijahāṃ narapatitilakaḥ svaysa vaśyaḥ kṛto 'bhūt, kiṃ cāvaśyaṃ prapannaḥ punar api vihitaḥ śāhidārāśakohaḥ* | *Kavīndracandrodaya*, by Hīrārāma Kavi, vs. 169ab.

the tax. The court itself is described as an appropriately cosmopolitan one, with Portuguese, Iraqis, Afghans, Balkhis, Arabs, Turks, and Ethiopians in attendance, all of whom praised Kavīndra.[31]

A composition by Kavīndra in Sanskrit and Brajbhāṣā and dedicated to Shāh Jahān survives. In it Kavīndra praises the ruler's many ideal qualities and goes on to praise Dārā Shukoh even more fulsomely, describing him as no less than representing the knowledge of Brahman (*brahmajñāna*).[32] Similarly flattering comments are made about Dārā in an anthology of Kavīndra's short poems, addresses, and messages of blessing.[33]

Despite the admiration expressed by the assembled paṇḍits of this glittering court, the Brahminical ambivalence about *yavanas* comes through even in this collective document. A good number of the addresses and verses by the luminaries of Banaras describe the situation in the world as one in which the earth is submerged in a sea of *yavana* taxation and in need of rescue, just as the earth needed to be rescued by the boar incarnation of Nārāyaṇa in the ancient legend.[34] The ruler at Delhi (*dillīśvara*) is mostly referred to as the source of the tax, and therefore of fear among the populace.[35] He does not receive credit in *Candrodaya* for eventually suspending it.

Jagannātha, the Paṇḍit Rāy

Jagannātha was a celebrated Sanskrit poet who is known to have received patronage from four different rulers: Jahāngīr, Shāh Jahān,

[31] *kāśmīrair ākakāraskaradaradakhurāsānahabśānajātā, baṅgārabbāḥ phiraṅgās turukaśakavadakśānamultānavalkāḥ | khāndhārāḥ kābilendrā api dharaṇibhṛtas te magnā rūṃmaśāmāḥ śrīmacchrīsāhijāhānarapatisadasi tvām kavīndra stuvanti* || *Kavīndracandrodaya*, by Hīrārāma Kavi, vs. 170.

[32] V. Raghavan, "The Kavīndrakalpalatikā of Kavīndrācārya Sarasvatī," in *Indica: the Indian Historical Research Institute Silver Jubilee Commemoration Volume* (Bombay: St. Xavier's College, 1953), 337–38.

[33] Athavale, *Kavīndrakalpadruma*, vss 352–57. Jahāngīr is also mentioned at vs. 324.

[34] *yavanakaragrahaṇābdhau magnā yenoddhṛtā pṛthivī* || Vs. 7cd, and *mlecchāmbhonidhi-magnahaindavavṛṣoddharāya nārāyaṇaḥ, sākṣād eṣa samastalokakṛpayā pūrṇo 'vatīrṇo bhuvi* || *Kavīndracandrodaya*, vs. 83cd.

[35] *Kavīndracandrodaya*, vs. 24.

Jagat Singh (Udaipur), and Prāṇa Nārāyaṇa (Assam).[36] Pollock has referred to Jagannātha as the "last Sanskrit poet," possessing a "very new sensibility."[37] Jagannātha appears to have been particularly favored by Āṣaf Khān, for whom he composed a prose-poetic *ākhyāyikā*, the *Āṣafavilāsa*.[38] Āṣaf Khān was closely linked to both Jahāngīr and Shāh Jahān, as we shall see below. At the end of the *Āṣafavilāsa*, Jagannātha notes that he has been given the title Paṇḍit Rāy, or king among paṇḍits, by Shāh Jahān.[39] Later legend has it that Jagannātha had an affair with a *yavanī* (a "Western girl") and that for this he was criticized by some paṇḍits in Banaras.[40] Kavīndrācārya composed several verses that refer in an oblique but deprecatory way to this affair, and to the associated wine drinking.[41] It thus appears that Jagannātha, the Paṇḍit Rāy, was perceived as having taken things too far.

Despite some uneasiness, the learned Brahmins in Banaras recognized the Mughal court as a source of patronage and of honors of which they could be proud. Contacts with this court tended to proceed through an officer or courtier, either Muslim or Hindu, these officers usually having their own circles and salons. There were, unsurprisingly, differing degrees of involvement on the part of paṇḍits, with Nārāyaṇa Bhaṭṭa, the first of our three examples, appearing to be the most standoffish, and Jagannātha, the last, the least.

ASTRAL SCIENTISTS AND THE MUGHAL COURT

Let us now turn to the specific example of the *jyotiṣa*s, and how their connection to the Mughal court was presented in their own texts and remembered in the texts of their successors. Although many of

[36] Chaudhuri, *Muslim Patronage*, 46–71.

[37] Sheldon Pollock, "The Death of Sanskrit," *Comparative Studies in History and Society* 43 (2001): 404–12.

[38] For the text, see Chaudhuri, *Muslim Patronage*, 112–16. The text as represented there appears to have been severely truncated, as Chaudhuri notices.

[39] *śrīsārvabhauma-sāhijahāna-prasādādhigata-paṇḍitarāya-padavīvirājitena … paṇḍita-jagannāthenāsaphavilāsākhyeyam ākhyāyikā niramīyata*. Chaudhuri, *Muslim Patronage*, 116.

[40] Chaudhuri, *Muslim Patronage*, 47–49.

[41] Athavale, *Kavīndrakalpadruma*, vss 348–49, and probably also 350.

the relevant Sanskrit works remain unpublished, it is still possible to assemble a substantial dossier of material, thanks to the work of David Pingree, especially his *Census of the Exact Sciences in Sanskrit.*[42]

The *jyotiṣas* occupied a somewhat anomalous position in the history of connections between the *śāstrins* and the Mughals. They appear to have had more to do both with *yavana* rulers and with *yavana* science itself than their colleagues in other Sanskrit disciplines. In fact, the *jyotiṣas* had been connected with extra-Sanskritic knowledge systems over a much longer period. The disciplines of the *jyotiṣas* and their Arabic-Persian counterparts had long been related through a continent-wide, Eurasian history of science. They were therefore more mutually accessible.[43]

Evidence from contemporary Persian chronicles makes it clear that the Mughal rulers employed Hindu astrologers, giving them the title of Jotik Rāy, or in Sanskrit, Jyotiṣarāja, king among *jyotiṣas*. This was an innovation that was subsequently followed by some Rajput rulers, who gave their court astrologers the same title.[44] Some evidence suggests that the Jotik Rāy would travel with the emperor during military expeditions. It was the Jotik Rāy's job to cast the birth chart of members of the royal family according to the *jyotiṣa* system, to answer questions according to *praśna*, the *jyotiṣa* version of catarchic astrology, in which a chart is cast for the moment that the question was asked, and to choose favorable moments to undertake activities, according to the *jyotiṣa* system of *muhūrta*.[45] *Muhūrta* was a specialty of *jyotiṣa* astrology, and did

[42] David Pingree, *Census of the Exact Sciences in Sanskrit*, series A, 5 vols (Philadelphia: American Philosophical Society, 1970–1994). Henceforth CESS. See also Sudhākara Dvivedi, *Gaṇakataraṅgiṇī* (Benares: B.K. Shastri, 1933); Sankar Balkrishna Dikshit, *History of Indian Astronomy*, trans. R.V. Vaidya, 2 vols. (Delhi: Directory General of Observatories, 1969); and Patkar, "Moghul Patronage."

[43] See Christopher Minkowski, "The Study of Jyotiḥśāstra and the Uses of Philosophy of Science," *Journal of Indian Philosophy* 36 (2008): 587–97.

[44] David Pingree, *From Astral Omens to Astrology; From Babylon to Bikaner* (Roma: Instituto Italiano per L'Africa e L'Oriente, 1997), 92–93.

[45] Sri Ram Sarma, "Persian-Sanskrit Lexica and the Dissemination of Islamic Astronomy and Astrology in India," in *KAYD: Studies in History of Mathematics, Astronomy and Astrology in Memory of David Pingree*, ed. Gherardo Gnoli and Antonio Panaino (Rome: Instituto Italiano per l'Africa e l'Oriente, 2009), 133.

not have an exact counterpart in the astral sciences of the *yavana*s, which assumed a less deterministic conception of astrological causation than that of birth charts. A flurry of *muhūrta* texts were written in this period, many by authors associated with the Mughal court, as we shall see. The Jotik Rāy may also have used the *tājika* system of astrology, more about which below.

A Jotik Rāy in service to Humāyūn cast the astrological chart of Akbar at the time of his birth in 1542. Akbar employed a Jotik Rāy whom the Persian chronicles do not name but who was probably Nīlakaṇṭha. Jahāngīr's Jotik Rāy was Keśava. Shāh Jahān may have had two: Paramānanda and then Mālajit/Śrīmālajī, although the latter had a different title, Vedāṅga Rāy. Aurangzeb is not believed to have had a Jotik Rāy, but his brother, Shāh Shujā' employed the *jyotiṣa* Balabhadra at his court for the long period during which he was governor of Bengal, and would probably have made him Jotik Rāy had he, Shujā', won the civil war with his brothers.[46]

We will look at six family groupings of astral scientists, and then consider three *jyotiṣa*s whose careers were more autonomous. Families of learned Brahmins were particularly important to the constitution of *śāstric* knowledge in this period. With some exceptions, prominent figures in the world of learning in early modern Banaras were members of extended families of accomplished, 'published' *śāstrin*s. This was the case not just among the *jyotiṣa*s but also among *śāstrin*s more generally. As we have seen in the case of the Bhaṭṭa family, more often than not these families came from the Deccan, and retained family links there, and patronage connections elsewhere on the subcontinent.[47]

Such statements constituted a sort of business card, if you like, in which the lineage and contemporary connections of the author were displayed. Self-descriptions of Sanskrit authors by way of an account of their family heritage were not new, but they became unusually detailed and lengthy in this period, their difference in extent becoming a difference in degree.

[46] Pingree, *Astral Omens*, 92–93; S.R. Sarma, "Astronomical Instruments in Mughal Miniatures," *Studien zur Indologie und Iranistik* 16–17 (1992): 256–60.

[47] Rosalind O'Hanlon and Christopher Minkowski, "What Makes People Who They Are? Pandit Networks and the Problem of Livelihoods in Early Modern Western India," *Indian Economic and Social History Review* 45, no. 3 (2008): 381–416.

This is one reason why we have more information about authors of this period in comparison with earlier periods. These chronicles are much more emphatically family-directed in their self-presentation. But descriptions of authors' families are found not just in lineage histories, such as the Bhaṭṭa family chronicle discussed above; they are also found in the opening and closing statements (*ādivākya* and *puṣpikā*) of *śāstric* works.

The rhetorical style of these statements shows what Brahmins of the period thought would make them desirable as experts. The statements tend to emphasize the piety or observant behavior of the earlier generations of the family, especially the founder, and thereby suggest the unusual, extra-rational powers that the author had inherited by virtue of his descent. The ancestors' proficiency in knowing and following the teachings of the Vedas was often balanced by their interest in "higher subjects," that is, in Vedānta and theology. Sometimes the predecessors were also noted for their devotion to particular deities. While prominence in the study and practice of *jyotiḥśāstra* was emphasized, there was often a grandfather in these histories who was praised for the breadth of his learning, or his accomplishments as a poet.

The themes that will reappear as we consider these families are, first of all, their location, in Kāśī, Delhi, or elsewhere. The presence of a *jyotiṣa* at a particular court appears in some cases to have been rather notional. The Banarsī paṇḍits, in particular, received gifts, honors, or patronage simultaneously from several courts, large and small. Other themes are the nature of the relationship and rivalries between the large, powerful families of *jyotiṣas*, as opposed to single outliers; whether the nature of the connection to the Mughal court was direct or via a courtier; whether the works were commissioned or simply offered in hope of reward; and the extent to which honors or pensions proffered by the Mughal rulers drove the intellectual agenda of the scientists who received them.

Four Generations of the Gārgyas[48]

A family of *jyotiṣas* belonging to the Gārgya *gotra* moved to Banaras from a town on the River Godāvarī. Earlier generations of the family had lived there in a village, probably a land-grant village, called Dharmapura.

[48] See table 15 in David Pingree, *Jyotiḥśāstra: Astral and Mathematical Literature* (Wiesbaden: Otto Harrassowitz, 1981), 127.

We know the names of Cintāmaṇi, and his son Ananta, who wrote several astrological works.[49] Ananta's two sons moved north, and were successful at the Mughal court. One son was Rāma, who wrote a handbook for calculation (*karaṇa*) and a set of tables generated by that handbook (*koṣṭhaka*), both called *Rāmavinoda*. Rāma did this, he says, at the command of a Rajput prince, Rāmadāsa, who is described as the prime minister (*paramāmātya*) of Akbar.[50] Rāma also wrote a text of horary astrology (*muhūrta*), completed in Banaras in 1600.[51]

Rāma's elder brother, Nīlakaṇṭha, wrote the *Jyotiṣasaukhya* for Ṭoḍar Mal. That is, he wrote the *jyotiṣa* sections of the *Ṭoḍarānanda*, the compendious text mentioned above. This work was completed by 1572.[52] Nīlakaṇṭha also wrote an extremely popular work of *tājika* astrology, one popular even today, the *Tājikanīlakaṇṭhī*, completed in 1587.[53] "*Tājika*" is specifically Persianate astrology in Sanskrit, including "exotic" Persian technical terms for features not found in *siddhāntic* astrology.[54] Nīlakaṇṭha too was based in Banaras, although in a contemporary miniature, a figure that is probably Nīlakaṇṭha is depicted as present at the birth in 1569 of Salīm, who would assume the title Jahāngīr upon ascending the throne.[55]

Nīlakaṇṭha's son, Govinda, born in 1569, wrote commentaries both on his father's *Tājikanīlakaṇṭhī* and on his uncle's *Muhūrtacintāmaṇi*. He is of particular interest to us here because his commentary on the *Muhūrtacintāmaṇi*, the *Pīyūṣadhārā*, includes several accounts of earlier

49 Ananta was the author of the *Kāmadhenuṭīkā* and the *Janipaddhati*. CESS I, 40–41.

50 The colophon of the karaṇa includes the phrase: *śrīmadakkabaraśāha-paramāmātya-dhurya-śrīmahārājādhirāja-śrīrāmadāsakārite*. CESS V, 427.

51 The last verse of the ending: *giriśanagare vare bhujabhujeṣucandrair mite, śake viniramād imaṃ khalu muhūrtacintāmaṇim*. CESS V, 443.

52 *yatkīrtyā vijito bhujaṅgamapatiḥ pātālam adhyāsta yad-vāṇīnaipuṇamādhurīṣu vijito vācām patiḥ svargataḥ | dagdhārivrajayatpratāpaśikhino dhūmasya lekhāṃ vyadhād, indau lakṣmaṇaṭoḍaro vijayate sāṃrājyalakṣmīṃ śritaḥ* || Nīlakaṇṭha at beginning of *Jyotiṣasaukhya*, CESS III, 178. He also composed the *Vivāha-*, *Vāstu-*, *Vyavahāra-*, *Saṃskāra-*, and *Samaya-saukhya* sections of the *Ṭoḍarānanda*.

53 CESS III, 180–89.

54 Pingree, "Tājika: Persian Astrology in Sanskrit," in *From Astral Omens to Astrology*, 79–90.

55 Sarma, "Astronomical Instruments," 254–58.

generations of the family. It also records the relationship of the family to the Mughal court. The *Pīyūṣadhārā* was widely circulated with the *Muhūrtacintāmaṇi*, and thus provided an amplification of the merits of that work's author. Govinda asserts that Rāma and Nīlakaṇṭha were not "just" *jyotiṣas*. Nīlakaṇṭha was, rather, learned in Mīmāṃsā, Nyāya, and Vyākaraṇa as well. He was the leader of the paṇḍits, the shining adornment of the incomparable assembly hall of Akbar, the emperor.[56] As a result of his devotion to Gaṇeśa, Rāma acquired a clear understanding of many sciences, he says. Govinda describes himself as active in Banaras, and confirms as well that his uncle wrote his work in Banaras.[57] Govinda's son, Cintāmaṇi, describes himself as a leader in the meetings of astronomers and astrologers in Jahāngīr's court.[58] Cintāmaṇi wrote a commentary not on the *Muhūrtacintāmaṇi* of his uncle, Rāma, but rather on the *muhūrta* work of a close friend (*atimitra*), Raghunātha, who had studied under Rāma along with Cintāmaṇi.[59] We thus move to another family of *jyotiṣas* who are linked to the Gārgyas.

RAGHUNĀTHA "KAVIKAṆṬHĪRAVA" (1660)

Cintāmaṇi's friend, Raghunātha, composed a work on horary astrology, the *Muhūrtamālā*. His father, Nṛsiṃha, was a Citpavan Brahmin from the Konkan coast who had moved to Banaras. In the account of his family, Raghunātha records proudly that Akbar, the emperor

[56] *sīmā mīmāṃsakānāṃ kṛtasukṛtyacayaḥ karkaśas tarkaśāstre, jyotiḥśāstre ca gargaḥ phaṇipatibhaṇitivyākṛtau śeṣanāgaḥ* | *pṛthvīśākabbarasya sphurad atulasabhāmaṇḍanaṃ paṇḍitendraḥ, sākṣāc chrīnīlakaṇṭhaḥ samajani jagatīmaṇḍale nīlakaṇṭhaḥ* || Vs. 8 of beginning of *Pīyūṣadhārā*, CESS II, 140–41.

[57] CESS II, 140, see concluding verses 4—*rāmo 'nujas tasya babhūva kāśyāṃ*— and 6—*kāśyāṃ... govindo vidhividvaro 'tivimalām pīyūṣadhārāṃ vyadhāt.*

[58] *sa nīlakaṇṭhāc chitikaṇṭhapuryāṃ govindaśarmājani dharmakarmā* | *yaḥ śrījahāṅgīrasabhāsu dhuryaḥ śauryaś ca mauhūrtikatārakāsu* || Vs. 6 at the conclusion of Cintāmaṇi's *Saṃmatacintāmaṇi*, CESS III, 50. Pingree, following the ASB catalogue No. 2746, reads some missing syllables here—XX *mādhurya*— but the extant words provide a regular *upajāti* verse. Note again that Govinda is said to have been born in Banaras (*śitikaṇṭha-purī*).

[59] *rāmāṅghri-sannidhi-sahādhyayanātimitra-daivajñavarya-raghunātha-kavipraṇītām* | *govindaśarmatanayo 'tra muhūrtamālāṃ cintāmaṇir guṇimaṇir*

in glorious Delhi (*dillī-matallī-īśvara*) gave his father the sobriquet of Jyotirvit Sarasa (roughly: "the most appealing of *jyotiṣas*").[60] Raghunātha composed the *Muhūrtamālā* in Banaras (*purāri-puryāṃ*), soon after the civil war between the sons of Shāh Jahān, which resulted in Alamgīr/Aurangzeb ascending the throne. Raghunātha refers to these events as a way of dating his text, but makes no mention of support or recognition from Aurangzeb.[61] Raghunātha styles himself the Kavikaṇṭhīrava, the "lion among poets."[62] He does not make clear from whom he received this title, nor the poetry for which he was thus honored.[63]

Īśvaradāsa (1663) and Keśava Śarma, Jotik Rāy

To Raghunātha we may compare another author active in the same field and in the same period, Īśvaradāsa, the author of the *Muhūrtaratna*, completed in 1663. In this text Īśvaradāsa too dates the completion of the work by reference to the reign of Aurangzeb, although he says that he is writing in Delhi.[64] Thus he appears not to have been based in Banaras. His family were not Deccanīs, but rather Kanauji Brahmins from Bundelkhand, another difference from the other Brahmins

---

viśadīkaroti || Final verse of Cintāmaṇi's commentary on Raghunātha's work, the *Muhūrtamālā*, CESS III, 50.

60 *śāhākabbarasārvabhaumatilakād dillīmatallīśvarāj | jyotirvitsarasatvam āpa padavīm āseridurgagrahe* || Vs. 4 at the close of the *Muhūrtamālā*, CESS V, 376. *Aseridurga* refers to the Asīrgarh fort, in Khandesh, which Akbar's forces conquered in 1600. If he was given the title there, then one might infer that he was traveling with the emperor. Raghunātha also refers to his father by this title, as *sarasa-daivavit*, in the second verse of the opening of the work, and in the colophon. Thus he was absolutely proud of it.

61 *jitvā dārāśāhaṃ sūjāśāhaṃ murādaśāhaṃ ca | avaraṅgajevaśāhe śāsaty avanīṃ mamāyaṃ udyogaḥ* || *Muhūrtamālā*, concluding verses, CESS V, 376.

62 The colophon of the *Muhūrtamālā* begins: *iti śrī-cittapāvana-jñātīya-śāṇḍilyakula-maṇḍana-jyotirvitsarasātmaja-raghunātha-kavikaṇṭhīrava-viracitāyāṃ*. CESS V, 376.

63 Raghunātha was the author of "Gaṅgāmṛtataraṅginī," published in Ramapada Chakravarty, *Gaṅgājñānamahodadhi* (Banaras: Raghava Prakashan, 2001), 350–66.

64 *sampūrṇam āsīt tu muhūrtaratnaṃ prasthe maghonas tv avaraṅgarājye* | Final verse of 27th and final chapter of *Muhūrtaratna*, CESS I, 56.

we have considered. Īśvaradāsa's father was Keśava Śarma.[65] Like Raghunātha, Īśvaradāsa was proud of his father's connection with the Mughal court, and records in his final chapter that his father, who had been honored by rulers in Bundelkhand with gifts of horses, elephants, chariots, and villages, was given the title of Jyotiṣarāya by the emperor Jahāngīr. Eventually he gave away the "innumerable riches" he had received from rulers including Jahāngīr.[66]

Kavīndrācārya Sarasvatī wrote a verse in praise of an astral scientist, whom he referred to as the *jyotirvidvat-pradhāna*, chief among the *jyotiṣa*s. This appears to be a Sanskritic variant of the title, Jotik Rāy, and probably refers to Keśava. Kavīndra describes him as a source of joy to others, generously giving away untold amounts every day, radiating knowledge, and foretelling the future.[67]

[65] It is unclear whether Keśava Śarma wrote anything. There is a *Muhūrtadīpaka* by a Keśava Śarma listed in CESS II, 65, which could be his work. *Muhūrta*, or horary astrology, would certainly be an appropriate topic for a *jyotiṣarāya* to write about.

[66] *tasmāt keśavaśarmābhūt khyātas triskandhavigramaḥ | gajāśvaratha-saṃgrāmairyo 'rcitaḥ syān nṛpottamaiḥ || so 'yaṃ jyotiṣarāyākhyo jahāṅgīrāvanīpateḥ | svagūḍhapraśnasaṃvādair lebhe praśnavidāṃ varaḥ || tulāpramukhadāneṣu yas tv asaṃkhyavasūni vai | viprasātkṛtavān kāle nārāyaṇaparāyaṇaḥ || Muhūrtaratna* 27, vss 2–4. This version is corrected from that cited in CESS I, 56, by reference to Shastri's description of ASB 2724. Note that in M.M. Patkar, "Muhūrtaratna: A Religio-Astrological Treatise Composed in the Reign of Aurangzeb," *The Poona Orientalist* 3 (1938): 85, and following him, in Sarma, "Instruments," 256–57, vs. 4 is translated to mean that Jahāṅgīr gave Keśava his weight in gold and other gifts, but the subject of the relative clause has to be Keśava, as he is also described as a devotee of Nārāyaṇa.

[67] *ānandālipradāna pratidinavihitānekasaṃkhyākadāna, sphūrjanmānapratāna prakaṭitavilasatkīrtipīyūṣapāna | āmodāghāna viṣṇusphuṭakamalapadadhyāna vijñānabhāna, jyotirvidvatpradhāna śritabhuvanasamādhāna bhavyābhidhāna || Kavīndrakalpadruma*, vs. 338. The following two verses 339–40 are possibly also about Keśava, and were probably all composed together. Keśava's name appears in 340, along with Kavīndra's signature. Keśava is, incidentally, described in these verses too as generous, subsisting on very little, and very pious. This would be in keeping with Īśvaradāsa's description, as discussed in the preceding footnote.

Īśvaradāsa's *Muhūrtaratna* includes an entire chapter that recounts the lineage of Aurangzeb. Aurangzeb is depicted rather less favorably by comparison to his father and grandfather, but is nevertheless honored. It is mostly his deeds in the civil war that are remembered. Although pious (*dharmya*), this lord, born as king, imposed a tax on the entire country he captured, and while he released some of his captured foes, he mercilessly (*adayam*) executed most, wherever he encountered them.[68]

Mālajit the Vedāṅga Rāy (1643) and Nandikeśvara (ca. 1640)

Based in Śrīsthala in Gujarat, Mālajit, or Śrīmālajī, was a *jyotiṣa* who created a text for the use of astronomers by working back and forth between the Sanskritic and Persianate astronomical systems, the *Pārasīprakāśa* or *Saṃskṛta-pārasīka-racanā-bheda-kautuka*.[69] This work included methods for date conversions and a glossary of terms. Mālajit says at the outset of this work that he wrote it to please Shāh Jahān.[70]

Mālajit went by the title Vedāṅga Rāy, or Vedāṅgarāya, king of the supporting disciplines of the Veda, which include astronomy. He says at the end of another work, the *Giridharānanda*, that he received the title from the ruler in Delhi, presumably Shāh Jahān. The *Giridharānanda* was composed for the Rajput ruler of Ajmer, Giridhara Dāsa.[71] It is

68 I have only the brief excerpt provided by Patkar, which by contrast describes Jahāngīr and Shāh Jahān as equally adept at loving the women in their harems as they were at fighting on the borders of their kingdom. Patkar, "Muhūrtaratna," 83. Īśvaradāsa does concede that Aurangzeb's imposition of tax was lawful (*vidhivat*).

69 Sarma, "Lexica," 134–35.

70 *natvā śrībhuvaneśvarīṃ hariharau lambodaraṃ ca dvijān, śrīmacchāhajahān-mahendra-parama-prīti-prasādāptaye* | *brūte saṃskṛta-pārasīka-racanā-bheda-pradaṃ kautukaṃ, jyotiḥśāstrapadopayogi saralaṃ vedāṅgarāyaḥ sudhīḥ* || First verse of *Pārasīprakāśa*. Cited from CESS IV, 421. See Patkar, Moghul Patronage," 173.

71 Vs. 74cd at the end of the *Giridharānanda*, cited from CESS IV, 422: *yaṃ dillīnāyako 'yaṃ vyaracata vibudhoddāmavedāṅgarāyaṃ, so 'yaṃ gauḍendra-bhūpapravara-giridharasyājñayāmuṃ cakāra* || For Mālajit's self-identification using the title, see the previous footnote.

probable that Mālajit's connection to the Mughal court was mediated by his relationship with this Rajput ruler.[72]

His son Nandikeśvara, in his own astronomical treatise, the *Gaṇakamaṇḍana*, commemorated Mālajit's status in the Mughal court.[73] Nandikeśvara, like his father, provided an account of the lustre of the family's attainments at the close of his work. He emphasized, as Mālajit did, that their ancestors were *vaidika* Brahmins who were learned in other disciplines. In fact, Mālajit made no mention of his father and grandfather as *jyotiṣas*, describing instead his father's attainments in poetry, Mīmāṃsā, and Vedic ritual, and his grandfather's attainments as a *vaidika*, a *smārta*, and a Vedāntin.[74] It was Nandikeśvara who insisted more on the hereditary nature of their craft as *jyotiṣas*.[75]

Two Rival Families: Devarātas and Bhāradvājas

There were two large, rival families of *jyotiṣas* in Banaras, who belonged to the Devarāta and Bhāradvāja *gotras* respectively. Both families moved to Banaras from the Deccan and both spent most of the sixteenth and seventeenth centuries there. Many members of these families were authors of *jyotiṣa* works.[76] The rivalry between the two families concerned, among other things, the incorporation of features of *yavana* astronomy into *jyotiṣa* theory and practice. Polemical works attacking members of the other family by name were produced.

It was Ballāla of the Devarāta *gotra* who moved his family from the banks of the River Payoṣṇī or Peṅgaṅgā in Berar to Banaras in the late sixteenth century. Ballāla had five sons, of whom two, Kṛṣṇa and Raṅganātha,

[72] Sarma, "Lexica," 135.

[73] The last verses of the *Gaṇakamaṇḍana* include this description of Mālajit, cited from CESS III, 131: *tatputro mālajit-saṃjño vedavedāṅgapāragaḥ, yena vedāṅgarāyeti prāptaṃ dillīśvarāt padam.*

[74] *Giridharānanda*, vss 72 and 73, CESS IV, 422. The grandfather is *śrauta-smārta-vicāra-sāra-catura* and *vedānta-akhila-śāstra-vāsara-maṇi*, while the father is *kavitā-latā-sura-taru* and *śrī-yajña-vidyā-yuta*.

[75] The last verses of the *Gaṇakamaṇḍana* include this description of Mālajit's grandfather, cited from CESS III, 131: *tatrāsīj jyotiḥśāstrajño ratnabhaṭṭāhvayo dvijaḥ.*

[76] See Tables 11 and 13 in Pingree, *Jyotiḥśāstra*, 125–26.

were authors of *jyotiṣa* texts. Raṅganātha's son, Munīśvara and two other grandsons of Ballāla, Gadādhara and Nārāyaṇa, were also authors.[77]

Kṛṣṇa, Ballāla's son, studied not only with his own family, but also with an expert in the innovative Gaṇeśapakṣa, founded by the sixteenth-century *jyotiṣa*, Gaṇeśa of Gujarat.[78] Kṛṣṇa wrote several astronomical works, including a commentary on the *Bījagaṇita* of Bhāskara. Of the greatest interest, however, is a commentary he produced on one of the standard astrological works on "nativities" or birth charts, the *Jātakapaddhati* of Śrīpati. In this commentary, the *Jātakapaddhaty-udāharaṇa*, Kṛṣṇa took for his practical example the birth date of a prominent courtier of Akbar, Abdur Rahīm Khān-i Khānān, an accomplished litterateur in several languages.[79] In this work, Kṛṣṇa lavished praise both on Akbar and on Khān-i Khānān, calling Akbar, among other things, the one whose lovely lotus feet were caged by rays from the gems flashing in the crowns of all the rulers bowing down to him.[80] He described Khān-i Khānān as skilled in every regional language and in the fine writing of every script, and delighting in every perfectly delightful science that the goddess Sarasvatī teaches.[81]

[77] Among their works we may mention: Kṛṣṇa, *Bījāṅkura* (1601) and *Jātakapaddhatyudāharaṇa*; Raṅganātha, *Gūḍhārthaprakāśikā* commentary on *Siddhāntaśiromaṇi* (1603); Munīśvara (b. 1603) *Marīci*, *Siddhāntasārvabhauma* (1646), and many more; Gadādhara, *Lohagolasamarthana*; Nārāyaṇa, *Grahalāghavodāhṛti* and on *Jātakakaustubha* (1678).

[78] The school is best known for its labor-saving approach to calculation. Kṛṣṇa describes his teacher, Viṣṇu, as the pupil of Gaṇeśa's nephew, Nṛsiṃha. He apparently studied with him in Gujarat. For Kṛṣṇa's own statement in the *Bījāṅkura*, see CESS II, 56.

[79] See Jatindra Bimal Chaudhuri, *Khān Khānān Abdur Rahīm and Contemporary Sanskrit Learning* (Calcutta: J.B. Chaudhuri, 1952); C.R. Naik, *'Abdur-Raḥim Khan-i-Khanan and His Literary Circle* (Ahmedabad: Gujarat University Press, 1966).

[80] *nikhilabhūpāla-maulimālāmilan-mukuṭataṭanaṭan-maṇimarīci-mañjarīpuñjapiñjaritamañju-pādāravindasya … śrīmaj-jallāladīnasyākavara-pātiśāhamahāpratāpasya.* Jatindra Bimal Chaudhuri, *Jātaka-padhaty-udāharaṇa by Kṛṣṇa Daivajña* (Calcutta: J.B. Chaudhuri, 1955), 4.

[81] *nikhilalipiśilpadeśabhāṣāviśāradaḥ śāradopadiśyamānasarvānavadyahṛdya-vidyāvinodamānamānasaḥ … śrīkhānikhānāparanāmadheyaḥ pradhānapuruṣaḥ.* Chaudhuri, *Jātaka-padhaty*, 4–5.

From this we can judge that Kṛṣṇa was a personality of some interest to a favored courtier of Akbar. That he subsequently received the confidence of Jahāngīr, and honor and emoluments from him, was a matter of some pride for his family.[82] This fact was commemorated by his younger brother Raṅganātha both at the beginning and end of his commentary on the *Siddhāntaśiromaṇi*.[83] Three of his nephews, Munīśvara, Gadādhara, and Nārāyaṇa, each the son of a different brother of Kṛṣṇa, all mentioned this relationship to Jahāngīr in their works as well, and celebrated the range of his learning. Munīśvara referred to the emperor by his title Nūr-ud-Dīn.[84] Munīśvara appears to have received the patronage of Shāh Jahān. He used the horoscope of the moment of the emperor's accession as an example of a particular astrological practice in his *Siddhāntasārvabhauma*, in a manner that is reminiscent of his uncle Kṛṣṇa's use of Āṣaf Khān's birth date.[85]

The rivals of the Devarātas were a family of Brahmins who came from a village on the banks of the Godāvarī in the kingdom of Ahmadnagar. This family, of the Bhāradvāja *gotra*, was even more prolific in producing works on *jyotiṣa* topics. Its eight authors, active in three generations, all made a point of recounting the family tree and the literary attainments of its members. It was Divākara who moved the family to Banaras, the later generations tell us. Divākara had gone to Nandigrāma in Gujarat to study directly with Gaṇeśa, the founder of his own school of thought, the Gaṇeśapakṣa, mentioned above. Divākara's sons wrote commentaries

[82] As far as I have been able to detect, Kṛṣṇa himself nowhere mentions this.

[83] *sārvabhaumajahāṅgīraviśvāsāspadabhāṣaṇam | yasya taṃ bhrātaraṃ kṛṣṇaṃ budhaṃ vande jagadgurum* || Raṅganātha, *Gūḍhārthaprakāśikā*, vs. 3. CESS V, 389. See also the third verse of the conclusion, CESS V, 389.

[84] Munīśvara referred to the emperor by his title Nūr-ud-dīn: *śrīnūradīnaparamapraṇayaikapātraṃ | kṛṣṇo babhūva janipaddhativṛttikāraḥ* || Munīśvara, vs. 8cd, at the end of the *Marīci* commentary on *Siddhāntaśiromaṇi*, CESS IV, 438; *yena … jyotiḥśāstramahārṇavasya culukenāgastyavat prāśanaṃ | prāptā yāvana-sārvabhaumavaśato bhūtis tathā gauravam* || Nārāyaṇa, vs. 5 at the end of the *Jātakakaustubha*, CESS III, 166; *śrīsārvabhaumajahāṅgīrakṛpaikapātraṃ bījāṅkurasya janako 'khilaśāstravettā | śrīpaty-apūrvajanipaddhativṛttikāraḥ kṛṣṇo 'bhavad bhuvi sadeśvaranāmasaktaḥ* || Gadādhara, vs. 84, at the end of the *Lohagolasamarthana*, CESS II, 115.

[85] Dvivedi, *Gaṇakataraṅgiṇī*, 62.

on Gaṇeśa's works, and it was through these commentaries, which were disseminated from Banaras, the central hub of a continent-wide system of textual circulation, that Gaṇeśa's work attained the prominence it did.[86]

Divākara's son, Viśvanātha, wrote commentaries on two *jyotiṣa* works by the two brothers, Rāma and Nīlakaṇṭha, mentioned in the first section above.[87] Viśvanātha was the most prolific author in the family, producing at least sixteen different works, but it was the authors in the fourth generation who were the most innovative. Kamalākara, son of Nṛsiṃha, and great-grandson of Divākara, wrote a *siddhānta* of his own, the *Siddhāntatattvaviveka* (completed 1658). This interesting work drew not only from the *siddhāntic* astronomical tradition, but also from the astronomy that was current among the *yavana* scientists. At Ulugh Beg's court in Samarkand in the fifteenth century there had been an active astronomical program supported by the ruler. Among other things, Aristotelian physics, Euclidean geometry, and Ptolemaic astronomy, as adapted into Arabic, were employed in creating the state almanac, the *Zīj-i Ulugh Beg*. It appears that some elements of these Hellenistic sciences were adopted by Kamalākara based on knowledge of Ulugh Beg's *Zīj*, which had been circulated in India in a Sanskrit translation, probably through the mediation of the Mughal court.[88]

Kamalākara appears to have produced his *Siddhāntatattvaviveka* in response to a *siddhānta* composed by Munīśvara, a member of the rival Devarāta family. Munīśvara's *Siddhāntasārvabhauma* was by its title the "emperor of *siddhānta*s," using a term (*sārvabhauma*) that in the period seems to have referred usually to the Mughal ruler, but was a title that Munīśvara also took for himself, as emperor among *jyotiṣa*s. In

[86] Gaṇeśa's works are most commonly published today with the commentaries of members of this family. A partial list includes Viśvanātha, son of Divākara, *Tithicintāmaṇiṭīkā*; Mallāri, son of Divākara, *Grahalāghavaṭīkā*; Nṛsiṃha, grandson of Divākara, *Bṛhaccintāmaṇiṭīkā*; Divākara II, son of Nṛsiṃha, *Pātasāraṇīṭīkā*. Lastly we should mention Viṣṇu, son of Divākara I, *Bṛhaccintāmaṇiṭīkā*. This Viṣṇu may have been the Viṣṇu with whom Kṛṣṇa, the Devatrāta, studied the Gaṇeśapakṣa.

[87] *Rāmavinodadīpikā* (1614), *Tājikanīlakaṇṭhīprakāśikā* (1629).

[88] CESS II, 21. Kamalākara refers by name to "*mīrjolugabega*" in *Siddhāntatattvaviveka* 2, vs. 89.

the *Siddhāntasārvabhauma* Munīśvara accepted the usefulness of *yavana* trigonometry, but he was otherwise unenthusiastic about the *yavana* scientific techniques with which he had become familiar. In particular, he was vehemently opposed to the theory of precession as used by the *yavanas* to establish a tropical rather than sidereal system of astronomical reference points.[89] In opposition to this, Kamalākara argued in his *Siddhāntatattvaviveka* for the acceptance of precession with its implications, and for accepting other features of *yavana* astronomy. He also criticized Munīśvara for his strong attachment to the work of Bhāskara II, the medieval astronomer.[90]

It was Kamalākara's brother, Raṅganātha, however, who entered into the spirit of the polemical argument with the Devarāta family. He published a work criticizing Munīśvara's cosmological proposal that the outermost sphere, surrounding the cosmos as a whole, was made of iron.[91] Munīśvara, who included this idea in his *Siddhāntasārvabhauma*, attributed it to the *siddhāntic* tradition, in opposition to the view of the crystalline spheres that was propounded by the *yavanas*. Munīśvara had also proposed a calculatory technique that he called the winding method or *bhaṅgī*. Raṅganātha criticized this method as well, in an independent treatise called the *Bhaṅgīvibhaṅgīkaraṇa*, promising at the outset to "shatter the face" of Munīśvara.[92] Then Munīśvara's cousin, Gadādhara, responded to Raṅganātha, promising in his introduction to "cut back Nṛsiṃha's boy, the inhibitor of Munīśvara."[93] At the end of this work, Gadādhara said that he wrote it in order to please Jagannātha.[94] Pingree has speculated that this Jagannātha was Jagannātha Paṇḍit Rāy discussed above, himself no stranger to conflicts in Banaras.[95]

[89] David Pingree, "Islamic Astronomy in Sanskrit," *Journal for the History of Arabic Science* 2 (1978): 321–22.

[90] Pingree, "Islamic Astronomy," 322–23.

[91] *kṛtam avara-munīśvarena golaṃ tam aham apākaravāṇi lohajātam. Lohagolakhaṇḍana*, vs. lcd, CESS V, 391.

[92] *munīśvarasyānanabhañjanārthaṃ, bhaṇgīvibhaṅgīkaraṇodyato 'smi* || Raṇganātha, vs. 1cd of *Bhaṅgīvibhaṅgīkaraṇa*, CESS V, 390.

[93] *dhyānāsaktamunīśvarasya niyamaṃ chettum nṛsiṃhārbhakaṃ*. Gadādhara, vs. 1a of the *Lohagolasamarthana*, CESS II, 115.

[94] *gurūn natvā praharāhvaṃ lohagolasamarthanam | akarod gaṇitagranthaṃ jagannāthasya tuṣṭaye* || *Lohagolasamarthana*, vs. 87, CESS II, 115.

[95] CESS II, 115. In this place in the text, however, it is just as possible that jagannātha refers to Nārāyaṇa, the lord of the world.

Even among prominent scholarly families based in Banaras in those days, Divākara's family is notable for the consistency with which its members provided an account of the family's accomplishments and literary attainments. Despite all of their literary and scientific activity, however, no member of the family ever mentioned a courtly connection, be it with a *yavana* ruler or otherwise. We thus confront something of a paradox here, in the disconnection between social and intellectual unorthodoxy. While one of the two rival families was consistently proud of the connection of one of its members with Jahāngīr, and regularly emphasized this honor, and another member of the same family enjoyed some sort of connection to Shāh Jahān, the other family did not mention patronage of any kind in its formal accounts of the family heritage.

It was this latter family, however, the Bhāradvājas, those with no connection to the court, who were more interested in the possibility of "intercultural" scientific exchange with the *yavana* scientists. Kamalākara, a member of this family, had brought in elements of Hellenistic and Arabo-Persian science, and his cousin, Raṅganātha, had argued strenuously for that stance. Their great uncle, Viśvanātha, meanwhile, had commented on the *tājika* work of Nīlakaṇṭha and on the astronomical table of Rāma, both composed in the environment of Akbar's court.

Paramānanda, Nityānanda, and Balabhadra

We conclude with three *jyotiṣa*s who were successful at the Mughal court, but who were neither Deccanī Brahmins nor based in Banaras. They are arranged here more or less chronologically. The latter two are notable for their interest in and explicit arguments for engagement with the astral sciences of the *yavana*s.

PARAMĀNANDA, JOTIK RĀY (1614)

Jahāngīr had another Jyotiṣarāya, probably before Keśava, who should be mentioned here. This was Paramānanda Śarma, son of Vāsudeva. Paramānanda composed a *karaṇa* or astronomical handbook called the *Jahāngiravinodaratnākara* ("Ocean of Amusement for Jahāngīr").[96] The introduction of this work includes seven verses (2–8) that extol the lineage of Jahāngīr, who is also called *nūradīna* (Nūr-ud-Dīn), from

[96] CESS V, 211.

Babur through Humāyūn and Akbar, who is also called *jalāladīna* (Jalāl-ud-Dīn). The text also mentions Jahāngīr's trusted minister, 'Itibār Khān, who is identified as a descendant of the Candela Rajput clan. It was 'Itibār Khān who commissioned Paramānanda's work, to please Jahāngīr. In this same passage Paramānanda says that he, the brightest gem in the array of paṇḍits attending on Jahāngīr, was given the title Jotik Rāy for his labors.[97] The text sets its epochal year, that is, the year from which astronomical calculations of the motions of the planets are made, as 1614.[98] We have no information about a connection between Paramānanda and Banaras, or with the other families of *jyotiṣas*.

NITYĀNANDA (1628, 1639)

Nityānanda was an astronomer based in Delhi with a connection to the Mughal court. In the introduction to one of his works he describes Delhi as a city shining with *vaidika* and *dhārmika* Brahmins.[99] He also describes the four preceding generations of his family as *jyotiṣas*, all living in Delhi and all learned in various disciplines.

Nityānanda composed two works that are of interest to us here. The first, completed in 1628, was the *Siddhāntasindhu*. This was a reworking in Sanskrit of the *Zīj-i Shāh Jahānī*, the imperial almanac and astronomical gazetteer composed in the reign of Shāh Jahān. Nityānanda was commissioned to produce the *Siddhāntasindhu* by Āṣaf Khān, one of the principal figures at the Mughal court, the brother-in-law of Jahāngīr and the father-in-law of Shāh Jahān. At the beginning of the work, Nityānanda provides an elaborate poetic account of the lineage of Shāh Jahān, beginning with Timur, and passing through all of the male

97 *candelānvayacandramā samabhavat khānetivārah kṣitau, tena śrīmadakavvarātmajajahāṅgīrasya santuṣṭaye | granthaḥ paṇḍitamaṇḍalādṛta-jahāṅgīrādyaratnākaro, vidvajjyotiṣarāyaśarmaparamānandena nirmāpitaḥ ||* *Jahāngiravinodaratnākara*, vs. 10, CESS V, 211.

98 This may be the date of composition, for it is not the year of accession of Jahāngīr, nor of any other major event of his reign.

99 *Siddhāntasarvarāja*, first verse of conclusion. Cited from Peter Peterson, *Catalogue of the Sanskrit Manuscripts in the Library of His Highness the Maharaja of Ulwar* (Bombay: Maharaja of Ulwar, 1892), 228.

ancestors in the line down to Jahāngīr.[100] There are then eleven verses in praise of Shāh Jahān, and three in praise of Āṣaf Khān, who is extolled for his protection of the *varṇāśrama dharma*.[101] Nityānanda goes on to state at the beginning of the *Siddhāntasindhu* that this work will present a system of astronomy that coincides with direct observation of the planetary positions, according to the rationale developed by the *yavana*s.[102]

Although the tables in the *Siddhāntasindhu* did circulate among *siddhāntic* astronomers, it appears that this work and its "intercultural" significance did not attract their interest, for eleven years later in 1639 Nityānanda completed another *siddhāntic* treatise, the *Siddhāntasarvarāja*.[103] This later work, although organized more recognizably as an astronomical *siddhānta*, offered more of an argument for the appropriation of the astronomy of the *yavana*s. It freely incorporated elements of their astronomical system, using, for example, the tropical year length preferred by the *yavana*s as the basis for calculations, rather than the sidereal year length preferred in *jyotiḥśāstra*.[104]

100 It begins in the fifth verse of the introduction: *āsīt taimūranāmā caturudadhidharādhīśvaro yaś ca gantā, mīrāsāhābhidhānas tad anu sutanayas tasya rājādhirājaḥ | tajjaḥ sullāmahaṃmakṣitipatitilako 'syātmajo 'būsayīdo, bhūbhṛn nakṣatracandro ripukuladalanoddāmadhāmaikamallaḥ* || *Siddhāntasindhu*, vs. 5, Peterson, *Catalogue*, 230.

101 For example, on Shāh Jahān: *yo dṛpyadvaravāhinīpatir api prāyāt svato vīryavān, yo 'pīndūdayavarddhamānamahasā velām nijāṃ nojjhati | duṣprāpo 'pi ca matsyakacchapagaṇo yo ratnadātā satāṃ, sa śrīśāhajahā samudravad asau vavartti ḍhillīpatiḥ* || *Siddhāntasindhu*, vs. 17; and on Āṣaf Khān: *yo rājyāhvayamaṇḍapasya sudṛḍhaḥ staṃbhaḥ sthito niścalaḥ, saṃsārārṇavadharmapotatarane yaḥ karṇadhāraḥ kṛtī | yaḥ pṛthvīpatiratnayojyakanakaṃ bhūpārthaśabdo 'thavā, so 'yaṃ vāsaphakhāṃ vibhāti sakalān varṇāśramān pālayan* || *Siddhāntasindhu*, vs. 23, Peterson, *Catalogue*, 231.

102 *apārasaṃsāragaṃbhīranīradhau, svatantraratnāni kiyanti santi na | tathāpi dikpratyayakārakhecaram tanomi tantraṃ yavanoktiyuktibhiḥ* || *Siddhāntasindhu*, vs. 26, Peterson, *Catalogue*, 231.

103 See David Pingree, "The *Sarvasiddhāntarāja* of Nityānanda," in *The Enterprise of Science in Islam*, eds. Jan P. Hogendijk and Abdelhamid I. Sabra (Cambridge, MA: MIT Press, 2003), 269–84.

104 For more on the conceptual features of Nityānanda's two works, see below.

BALABHADRA (1629, 1654)

Balabhadra was a pupil of Rāma, the author of the *Rāmavinoda* mentioned above. He too was in the service of the Mughals. Balabhadra was the third generation of learned *jyotiṣa*s in a family of Kanauji Brahmins.[105] Some of his uncles wrote commentaries on astronomical texts, but nothing written by members of the family came close to the success of Balabhadra's *Hāyanaratna*.[106] This was a compendious work about *tājika* astrology. Balabhadra composed it, he says, for the sake of Shāh Shujā' in 1629, when the prince would have been thirteen years old. Balabhadra went with Shāh Shujā' to Rājmahal when the prince was made governor of the province of Bengal.[107] The other work that he wrote for Shāh Shujā' while in Rājmahal was a species of *muhūrta* text, the *Horāratna*, completed in 1654.[108]

***

Balabhadra begins his *Hāyanaratna* with a meditation on the *yavana* problem, in its intellectual form. He acknowledges the objections of other Brahmins to the study of *yavana* sciences. They cite a verse of Dharmaśāstra to the effect that one should not speak the language of the *yavana*s even if one's life depends on it.[109] This includes the Sanskrit reworkings of *yavana* science. Balabhadra replies, however, that the *śāstric* verse did not apply to the astral sciences, which are exceptional in this regard. For, as Balabhadra, Nityānanda, and others argue, *Jyotiḥśāstra* had long recognized the value of scientific works produced by the *yavana*s. After all, there was a Sanskrit astrological work called the *Yavanajātaka*, available and in use since the third century. Varāhamihira himself cited Romaka and Pauliśa as legitimate

105 CESS IV, 234–37.

106 Pingree, *Astral Omens*, 85.

107 *pṛthivīpate mahāvīra śrīmatsāhisujātike | śrīrājamahalasthena mayā grantho vinirmitaḥ ||* Penultimate verse of *Hāyanaratna*, CESS IV, 236.

108 … *pṛthvīpatiḥ śāhaśujādhināthaḥ || tadantikasthena kṛtaṃ mayaitat* … From the final two verses of *Horāratna*, CESS IV, 237.

109 *na vaded yāvanīṃ bhāṣāṃ prāṇaiḥ kaṇṭhagatair api.* Balabhadra, *Hāyanaratna* (Bombay: Veṅkateśvara Steam Press, 1904), 2r, line 3. Balabhadra does not identify his source.

authorities on astronomy, and the "*yavana* guru" is counted among the canonical list of sages in the *jyotiṣa* tradition.[110] There is, furthermore, a story that the god Sūrya, the legendary promulgator of most of the traditions of *jyotiṣa*, was cursed to be born as a *yavana*, and that in that incarnation, using the *yavana* language, he taught a system of astronomy that was both divinely inspired and unusually accurate.[111]

This sort of "domestication" of *yavana* science found a counterpart in the Jotik Rāys' domestication of their Mughal patrons into the world of Sanskritic discourse of the generous ruler. As we have seen, *jyotiṣa*s composed verses of praise of the *pādshāh* (emperor) and his lineage in the style of Sanskrit royal eulogy. Other prominent paṇḍits like Kavīndra and Jagannātha did so as well. Akbar thus became the protector of cows and Brahmins, Āṣaf Khān the maintainer of the fourfold order of the Varnas. Jahāngīr was as celebrated for his erotic conquests as for his military ones. Shāh Jahān and Dārā Shukoh were deemed wise and deeply learned, and even Aurangzeb was called pious and lawful. This sort of incorporation of *yavana* rulers into the political discourse of Sanskrit was for the most part a development of the Mughal period.[112]

Some of this history is still difficult to disentangle because of the historiography produced in the nineteenth and twentieth centuries, both in Sanskrit and in English, in which a later understanding of enmities between discrete communities has been read into the earlier situation. For example, Athavale in his detailed study of Kavīndra is aware of the evidence that Kavīndra received his title Sarvavidyānidhāna from Shāh Jahān, but endorses instead the view that he did not, because of the argument that "Shāh Jahān was at heart a fanatic Muslim and hated the Hindus."[113] Patkar considered it doubtful whether the two *jyotiṣa*s, Īśvaradāsa and Raghunātha, could have received patronage from

[110] Balabhadra, *Hāyanaratna*, 2r–2v; Pingree, *Astral Omens*, 86–87.

[111] Pingree, *Astral Omens*, 86–87; Pingree, "Indian Reception of Muslim Versions of Ptolemaic Astronomy," in *Tradition, Transmission, Translation: Proceedings of Two Conferences on Pre-modern Science held at the University of Oklahoma*, ed. F.J. and S.P. Ragep (Leiden: E.J. Brill, 1996), 477–80.

[112] An interesting forerunner can be found in Gujarat in the fifteenth century. See Aparna Kapadia, "The Last Cakravartin?: The Gujarat Sultan as 'Universal King' in Fifteenth Century Sanskrit Poetry," *Medieval History Journal* 16, no. 1 (2013): 63–88.

[113] Athavale, *Kavīndrakalpadruma*, xxvi.

Aurangzeb, even though the former devoted some space to recounting Aurangzeb's lineage, and the latter dated his work by reference to Aurangzeb's reign, because "Aurangzeb's hostile attitude toward Hindus is well known."[114]

It would be a mistake, in an attempt to correct for these sorts of judgments, to coat the history of the relationship of learned Brahmins and the Mughals in sugar. Nevertheless, a careful reading of the sources does suggest that we would be right to bring into question some of their guiding assumptions.

BIBLIOGRAPHY

Athavale, R.B. *Kavīndrakalpadruma of Kavīndrācarya Sarasvatī*. Calcutta: Asiatic Society, 1981.

Balabhadra. *Hāyanaratna*. Bombay: Veṅkateśvara Steam Press, 1904.

Benson, James. "Śaṃkarabhaṭṭa's Family Chronicle: The Gādhivaṃśavarṇana." In *The Pandit: Traditional Scholarship in India (Festschrift P. Aithal)*, edited by Axel Michaels. Volume 38 of *Heidelberg South Asian Studies*, 105–18. New Delhi: Manohar Publications, 2001.

Bhaṭṭa, Kāntanātha. *Bhaṭṭavaṃśakāvyam*. Mirzapur: Anandakadambini, 1903. [Republished, edited by Sivasankar Tripathi. Allahabad: Bharatiya Manisa Sutram, 1983.]

Bhattacharya, Dineshchandra. "Sanskrit Scholars in Akbar's Time." *Indian Historical Quarterly* 13 (1937): 31–36.

Chakravarty, Ramapada, ed. *Gaṅgājñānamahodadhi*. Varanasi: Raghav Prakashan, 2001.

Chaudhuri, Jatindra Bimal. *Muslim Patronage to Sanskrit Learning*. Part 1. Delhi: Idarah-i Adabiyat-i Delli, 1942.

———. *Khān Khānān Abdur Rahīm and Contemporary Sanskrit Learning*. Calcutta: J.B. Chaudhuri, 1952.

———, ed. *Jātaka-padhaty-udāharaṇa by Kṛṣṇa Daivajña*. Calcutta: J.B. Chaudhuri, 1955.

Dikshit, Sankar Balkrishna. *History of Indian Astronomy*. 2 volumes. Translated by R.V. Vaidya. Delhi: Director General of Observatories, 1969.

Dvivedi, Sudhākara. *Gaṇakataraṇgiṇī*. Benares: B.K. Shastri, 1933.

Eggeling, Julius. *Catalogue of the Sanskrit Manuscripts in the Library of the India Office*. Part 3. London: Secretary of State for India, 1891.

114 Patkar, "Muhūrtaratna," 83. He says, furthermore, that "the author was under the subjection of the Moghul emperor and hence he must have mentioned Aurangzeb only in a laudatory style."

Ernst, Carl. "Muslim Studies of Hinduism? A Reconstruction of Arabic and Persian Translations from Indian Languages." *Iranian Studies* 36, no. 2 (2003): 173–95.

Gode, P.K. "Bernier and Kavīndrācārya Sarasvatī at the Mughal Court." *Journal of S.V. Oriental Institute, Tirupati* 1, no. 4 (1941): 1–16.

———. "The Identification of Gosvāmi Nṛsiṁhāśrama of Dara Shukoh's Sanskrit Letter with Brahmendra Sarasvatī of the Kavīndra-Candrodaya—Between AD 1628 and 1658." *Adyar Library Bulletin* 6 (1942): 172–77.

———. "Samudrasaṃgama, a Philosophical Work by Dārā Shukoh, Son of Shāh Jahān, Composed in 1655 A.D." *Bhāratīya Itihāsa Saṃśodhana Maṇḍal Quarterly* 24 (1943): 75–88.

Hunger, Hermann and David Pingree. *Astral Sciences in Mesopotamia*. Leiden: Brill, 1999.

Kane, Pandurang V. *History of Dharmaśāstra*. Volume 1, part 2. Poona: Bhandarkar Oriental Research Institute, 1975.

Kapadia, Aparna. "The Last Cakravartin?: The Gujarat Sultan as 'Universal King' in Fifteenth Century Sanskrit Poetry," *Medieval History Journal* 16, no. 1 (2013): 63–88.

Minkowski, Christopher. "The Study of Jyotiḥśāstra and the Uses of Philosophy of Science." *Journal of Indian Philosophy* 36 (2008): 587–97.

Naik, C.R. *'Abdur-Raḥim Khan-i-Khanan and His Literary Circle*. Ahmedabad: Gujarat University Press, 1966.

O'Hanlon, Rosalind and Christopher Minkowski. "What Makes People Who They Are? Pandit Networks and the Problem of Livelihoods in Early Modern Western India." *Indian Economic and Social History Review* 45, no. 3 (2008): 381–416.

Patkar, M.M. "Moghul Patronage to Sanskrit Learning." *The Poona Orientalist* 3 (1938): 164–75.

———. "Muhūrtaratna: A Religio-Astrological Treatise Composed in the Reign of Aurangzeb." *The Poona Orientalist* 3 (1938): 82–85.

Peterson, Peter. *Catalogue of the Sanskrit Manuscripts in the Library of His Highness the Maharaja of Ulwar.* Bombay: Maharaja of Ulwar, 1892.

Pingree, David. *Census of the Exact Sciences in Sanskrit*. Series A. 5 volumes. Philadelphia: American Philosophical Society, 1970–1994.

———. "Islamic Astronomy in Sanskrit." *Journal for the History of Arabic Science* 2 (1978): 315–30.

———. *Jyotiḥśāstra: Astral and Mathematical Literature*. Wiesbaden: Otto Harrassowitz, 1981.

———. "Indian Reception of Muslim Versions of Ptolemaic Astronomy." In *Tradition, Transmission, Translation*, edited by F.J. and S.P. Ragep, 471–85. Leiden: E.J. Brill, 1996.

———. *From Astral Omens to Astrology; From Babylon to Bikaner*. Roma: Istituto Italiano per L'Africa e L'Oriente, 1997.

Pingree, David. "Tājika: Persian Astrology in Sanskrit." In *From Astral Omens to Astrology: From Babylon to Bikaner*, 79–90. Roma: Istituto Italiano per L'Africa e L'Oriente, 1997.

———. "The *Sarvasiddhāntarāja* of Nityānanda." In *The Enterprise of Science in Islam*, edited by Jan P. Hogendijk and Abdelhamid I. Sabra, 269–84. Cambridge MA: MIT Press, 2003.

Pollock, Sheldon. "The Death of Sanskrit." *Comparative Studies in History and Society* 43 (2001): 392–426.

Porcher, Marie-Claude. *La Viśvaguṇādarśacampū de Veṅkaṭādhvarin*. Pondichéry: Institut Français d'Indologie, 1972.

Raghavan, V. "Kavīndrācārya Sarasvatī." In *D.R. Bhandarkar Volume*, edited by B.C. Law, 159–65. Calcutta: Indian Research Institute, 1940.

———. "The Kavīndrakalpalatikā of Kavīndrācārya Sarasvatī." In *Indica: the Indian Historical Research Institute Silver Jubilee Commemoration Volume*, 335–41. Bombay: St. Xavier's College, 1953.

Rao, V. Narayana, David Shulman, and Sanjay Subrahmanyam. *Symbols of Substance: Court and State in Nāyaka Period Tamilnadu*. Oxford: Oxford University Press, 1998.

Salomon, Richard. "Biographical Data on Nārāyaṇa Bhaṭṭa of Benares." In *Ācārya-vandanā*, edited by Samaresh Bandyopadhyay, 326–36. Calcutta, University of Calcutta, 1984.

Sarma, Sri Ram. *A Bibliography of Mughal India (1526–1707 AD)*. Bombay: Karnatak Publishing House, 1964.

———. "Astronomical Instruments in Mughal Miniatures." *Studien zur Indologie und Iranistik* 16–17 (1992): 235–76.

———. "Persian-Sanskrit Lexica and the Dissemination of Islamic Astronomy and Astrology in India." In *KAYD: Studies in History of Mathematics, Astronomy and Astrology in Memory of David Pingree*, edited by Gherardo Gnoli and Antonio Panaino, 129–50. Rome: Instituto Italiano per l'Africa e l'Oriente, 2009.

Sharma, Har Dutt. "Paraśurāmapratāpa: Its Authorship, Date and the Authorities Quoted in It." *Poona Orientalist* 7 (1942): 13–26.

Sharma, Har Dutt and M.M. Patkar, eds. *Kavīndracandrodaya*. Poona: Oriental Book Agency, 1939.

Shastri, Haraprasad. "Dakshini Pandits at Benares." *The Indian Antiquary* 41 (1912): 7–12.

Truschke, Audrey. "Akbar as Shah or Raja? Reimaginings of Encounters with the Mughal Court in Jaina Sanskrit Literature." Unpublished paper presented at the 14th World Sanskrit Conference, Kyoto University, 2009.

Vaidya, P.L., ed. *Ṭoḍarānandam*. Bikaner: Anup Sanskrit Library, 1948.

Veṅkaṭādhvarin. *Viśvaguṇādarśacampūḥ*. Edited by Surendranatha Śāstrin. Vārāṇasī: Chaukhambā Vidyābhavana, 1963.

5 Drowned in the Sea of Mercy

The Textual Identification of Hindu Persian Poets from Shi'i Lucknow in the Tazkira *of Bhagwān Dās "Hindī"**

Stefano Pellò

Several observers and scholars have remarked upon the fertile dynamics of social and cultural communication between the composite religious landscape of Awadh and the Shi'i minority that ruled there from the second half of the eighteenth to the mid-nineteenth centuries. Mostly the focus has been on ritual and cultic aspects.[1] Biancamaria Scarcia Amoretti even raised the question whether one could speak of a peculiar "Shi'i way" of interaction with Indic traditions, on the basis precisely

* I am particularly Thankful to Francesca Orsini for her willingness to discuss the English translation of the original Italian materials.

[1] For an analytical survey, in the context of a discussion of popular Shi'ism in Awadh, see Juan Ricardo Cole, *Roots of North Indian Shi'ism in Iran and Iraq: Religion and State in Awadh, 1722–1859* (Berkeley: University of California Press, 1988), 92–119 and ff., who also provides a rich bibliography; see also Juan R.I. Cole, "Shi'ite Noblewomen and Religious Innovation in Awadh," in *Lucknow: Memories of a City*, ed. Violette Graff (Delhi: Oxford University Press, 1997), 83–90; and Mushirul Hasan, "Traditional Rites and Contested Meanings: Sectarian Strife in Colonial Lucknow," in *Lucknow: Memories of a City*, ed. Violette Graff (Delhi: Oxford University Press, 1997), 19.

of the example of Awadh, beside the more familiar interaction through Sufism.[2] The question remains unanswered, nor does this essay attempt to resolve it in a comprehensive manner. What it seeks to do is provide material that will help illuminate one of the lesser-known aspects of the relationship between the multiple socio-religious commonalities, identifications, and self-identifications[3] in Shi'i Lucknow. The significant presence of poets who define themselves (or are defined by contemporary Persian-writing literary critics) as "Hindus" (*hindū*)[4] in the Persian poetic circles of the capital of Awadh allows us to analyze the literary

2 "It is still to be resolved whether the transposition of Hindu elements into one's own cultural makeup without necessarily the mediation of Sufism, whose role in such a process is well-known, was in India a constant feature of Shi'i regimes (minoritarian vis-à-vis both Hindus and Sunnis)." Biancamaria Scarcia Amoretti, *Sciiti nel mondo* (Roma: Jouvence, 1994), 221. On the debates between *taṣawwuf* and Shi'as in Awadh, see Cole, *Roots of North Indian Shi'ism*, 146–48.

3 I use, here and elsewhere in this paper, the terms "commonality," "identification," and "self-identification" in an attempt to avoid the slippery category of "identity" (even when understood specifically, as in this article, as a "semiotic identity"), following quite closely the critical analysis by Rogers Brubaker and Frederick Cooper, "Beyond 'Identity'," *Theory and Society* 29 (2000): 1–47.

4 As I have already noticed elsewhere, the term *hindū* has been extensively employed in Persian literature to describe non-Muslim Indians, identified especially with the Vaishnava traditions. The word *hindū* has a long history in the Persian poetic space, being commonly used from the Ghaznavid period onward, originally indicating simply the "native of India," by definition dark and idolater. See J.T.P. de Bruijn, "Hindu," in *Encyclopædia Iranica* (New York: Encyclopædia Iranica Foundation, 2012), http://www.iranicaonline.org/articles/hindu-persian-poets, accessed April 7, 2012. The image of the *hindū* (as well as that, equally old, of the *barahman*, the "Brahmin") and a composite set of related canonical tropes connected to "idolatry" are often used by non-Muslim Indian writers of the Mughal period as metaphors for self-descriptions, thus creating an interesting interplay between supposed "real" and "literary" individualities. See Stefano Pellò, "Persian as a 'Passe-partout': The Case of Mīrzā 'Abd al-Qādir Bīdil and His Hindu Disciples," in *Culture and Circulation*, ed. Allison Busch and Thomas de Bruijn (Leiden: Brill, 2014, 21–46), and Stefano Pellò, "Poeti hindu e circoli intellettuali persiani tra Delhi e Lucknow: un caso di interazione letteraria" (PhD diss., Università degli Studi di Roma "La Sapienza," Roma, 2006), passim, especially 27–63 and 161–93.

dimensions of this cultural dynamic.[5] Given the cosmopolitan features of Persian as a literary culture during pre- and early-modern times and its pivotal aesthetic and ideological relationship with the Arabic-Islamic textual world, and recognizing that this linguistic and literary code acquires in Shi'i Awadh additional layers because of a peculiar political and cultural connection with an almost "nationalized" Iran, it becomes useful to ask how socio-religious and linguistic-literary identifications can be mapped onto each other. This was, after all, an environment in which the *imāmbāra* took the place of the Sufi majlis as a privileged space for poetic interaction, and where a devotional genre like the *marṣiya* for the Imām acquired a crucial public value.[6] Contemporary *taẕkiras* provide an excellent vantage point to observe these dynamics. *Taẕkiras* were literary self-histories that allow us to investigate from the inside the system of relationships (often more "imagined" rather than historically "objective") that was typical of that poetic culture. More especially, by filtering reality through a system of expressive codes that were well established but never too rigid, *taẕkiras* allow us to analyze how a social space was translated on a textual plane, which can also be understood as providing an interpretative mirror. In this essay I will focus on a single *taẕkira*, the *Safīna-yi hindī*, completed in 1804 in Lucknow by Bhagwān

[5] On the basis of a study of fourteen *taẕkiras* composed between 1768 and 1883, I have so far identified more than seventy non-Muslim poets active in Lucknow during Nawāb rule; see Pellò, "Poeti hindu," 127–28.

[6] For the inclusive social importance of the *imāmbāra* and *ta'ziyakhāna* as institutions in eighteenth–nineteenth century Awadh, and in the Gangetic region in general, noted by both European and Iranian travelers, see Cole, *Roots of North Indian Shi'ism*, 313–36, 331. What is particularly significant for our purposes is that the cultural centrality of the *imāmbāra* appears directly reflected in the Persian poetic language of this period, as in this verse by the Shi'a convert Mīrzā Ḥasan 'Qatīl' (d. 1817): "The spectacle of your face will be my support there: for me the *imāmbāra* is better than the house of God" (*shawad naẓẓāra-yi rūy-i tu rūzīy-am ānjā/ imāmbāra bih az khāna-yi khudā-st ma-rā*). Mīrzā Ḥasan Qatīl (Ms.), *Dīwān* (Rampur: Rampur Raza Library, 30196M), f. 7a. (All translations are mine unless indicated otherwise.) For a monograph on the *marṣiya*, a hugely popular and cultivated genre among non-Muslim poets in Lucknow, especially in Urdu, see S.A. Husayn, *Ghayr muslim marṣiyanigār* (Lucknow: n.p., 1995); see also G.S. Srīvāstavā, *Urdū shā'irī ke irtiqā mẽ hindū shu'arā kā ḥiṣṣa* (Allahabad: n.p., 1969), 456–59.

Dās "Hindī" (1750–?).[7] I will select the biographies he wrote of Persian Hindu poets of Shi'i Awadh and analyze how their social and religious identifications are semiotically constructed in relation to a dominant Islamicate expressive ideology; I will also refer to other important texts of the period in my analysis. This choice is not random: the author himself was a Vaishnava poet of Persian who lived in Lucknow and had a direct interest in representing the literary community he moved in, and his collection of biographies is among those that give most space to non-Muslim authors.

Of the 335 biographical notes in the *Safīna-yi hindī*, a work which dealt exclusively with Indian authors who lived between the second half of the seventeenth and eighteenth centuries, forty-three deal with non-Muslim poets (including a former Vaishnava converted to Islam), that is, 12.8 percent of the total number. This is the highest percentage of all Indo-Persian *tazkiras*, if we exclude the third volume of the *Gul-i ra'nā* of Lachhmī Narāyan "Shafīq," which declaredly deals exclusively with Hindu Persian poets ("the sagacious authors of the idolaters," *nuktapardāzān-i aṣnāmiyān*, as the Vaishnava author introduces them), and the *Anīs al-aḥibbā* of Mohan La'l "Anīs," where Hindu writers are also presented in separate sections.[8] In the *Safīna-yi hindī*, twenty-three, that is, more than half, of the Hindu authors included are connected to poetic circles in the Awadh capital:

1. Mohan La'l "Anīs"(16–17)[9]
2. Lāla Baijnāth "Anīs"(22)
3. Medī La'l "Bīmār"(29–30)
4. Jūgal Kishor "Sarwat"(46–47)
5. Rāy Sarab Sukh "Dīwāna"(72–74)

[7] Bhagwān Dās "Hindī," *Safīna-yi hindī: Tazkira-yi shu'arā'-yi fārsī*, ed. Sayyid Shāh Muḥammad 'Aṭā al-Raḥmān 'Aṭā Kākwī (Patna: The Institute of Post-Graduate Studies and Research in Arabic & Persian, 1958).

[8] See Lachhmī Narāyan Shafīq, *Tazkira-yi gul-i ra'nā* (Hyderabad: 'Ahd-i Afarin Barqi Press, n.d.), and Mohan La'l Anīs, *Anīs al-aḥibbā: Tazkira-yi shu'arā'-yi fārsī*, 2nd ed., ed. Anwār Aḥmad (Patna: Khuda Bakhsh Oriental Public Library, 1999), in whose work the proportion of Hindu authors reaches almost 33 percent.

[9] The name in brackets is the poetic nom de plume, while the numbers in brackets refer to the pages in the printed edition (Hindī, *Safīna-yi hindī*).

6. Rāy Dawlat Rām "Dawlat"(74)
7. Rāy Khem Narāyan "Rind"(88)
8. Makhan Lāl "Rāy"(95–97)
9. Rawshan Lāl "Rawshan"(97–98)
10. Lāla Shitāb Rāy "Zār"(100–01)
11. Debī Parshād "Shād"(116–17)
12. Shabāb Rāy "Azīz"(133)
13. Khushḥāl Chand Barahman "Irfān"(135)
14. Kishan Chand "Qarīb"(167–68)
15. Mīrzā Ḥasan "Qatīl" (formerly Dīwālī Singh; 172–73)
16. Sītal Dās "Mukhtār"(193–94)
17. Malhār Singh "Miskīn"(196)
18. Rāy Maykū La'l "Mastāna"(203–05)
19. Rāy Sakhī Mal "Ma'nī"(205)
20. Lāla Rām Bakhsh "Muṭi"(206–08)
21. Miṭhan La'l "Mā'il"(212)
22. Rāy Panjāb Rāy "Walī"(238–39)
23. Bhagwān Dās "Hindī"(241–59)

Most of these authors, who are often mentioned in other *taẕkiras* from the same or slightly later period, were employed in the Awadh administration by the nawabs or else came from the late-Mughal administrative class in Delhi.[10] They were typical representatives of the well-known Mughal intellectual figure of the Hindu munshī (very often Kayastha or Khatri), a person whose intellectual education was indistinguishable from that of Persianate Muslim intellectuals of the same period, and whose textual and contextual referents he shared.[11]

[10] For example, Dīwāna's biography appears in at least seven other *taẕkiras*; see Pellò, "Poeti hindu," 129.

[11] For a discussion of the social and cultural referents of an eighteenth-century Kayastha scribe and secretary, see Muzaffar Alam and Sanjay Subrahmanyam, "The Making of a Munshi," *Comparative Studies in South Asia, Africa and the Middle East* 24, no. 2 (2004): 61–72. A more recent survey of the contribution of Hindu writers to Persian literary culture is Stefano Pellò, "Hindu Persian Poets," in *Encyclopædia Iranica* (New York: Encyclopædia Iranica Foundation, 2008), http://www.iranicaonline.org/articles/hindu-persian-poets, accessed April 7, 2012, where further bibliography is given.

Following the common pattern of Indo-Persian *tazkiras*, it was one's poetic education and relations with masters and peers, apart from, of course, one's social rank and the aesthetic judgments on the quality and quantity of one's verses, that provided the semantic axis around which most biographies of Persian poets by Bhagwān Dās "Hindī" revolve. Hindī himself was a disciple of the poet of Iranian descent Mīrzā Fākhir Makīn (d. 1806). As an example, we can quote the first part of the biographical note on the Khatri Sarab Sukh "Dīwāna" (d. 1789), one of the chief Persian poets in Lucknow and undoubtedly the most influential Hindu Persian poet there:

> He was the son of the daughter of that refuge of royalty, Rāja Mahānārāyan Mahindar Bahādur, who belonged to the chancellery of the late Shujā' al-Dawla Bahādur. He was born in Shāhjahānābād and grew up there. When the time came for him to enter that office, he came to Lucknow. He found a placement appropriate to his rank and spent his time in this city, honored and respected. The gatherings of *faqīrs* and meetings of poets took mostly place in his house, and his behavior towards guests was exemplary. Some people of sensitive nature became his disciples in the composition of poetry in Hindi, and he himself composed a *dīwān* in that language, too; then he decided that he would apply himself exclusively to composing poetry in Persian. At first he got correction from that noble master [Mīrzā Fākhir Makīn] but he did not continue that relationship for very long and began to compose poetry in his own way. His creative power was so intense that he would practice writing two or three ghazals a day, and his total output almost reached one hundred thousand verses. He left four *dīwāns*, the first two named respectively *dardīya* and *'ishqīya*. He called his third *dīwān sharafiya*, since the poems it contains follow the rhyme and *radīf* of Sharaf Jahān Qazwīnī's compositions. His fourth *dīwān* consists of poems written in response to Shaikh Muḥammad 'Alī Ḥazīn's. He intended to work on a fifth *dīwān* but he died before he could begin to work on it. None of his contemporaries can be compared to him in terms of copiousness of output. This writer received great favours from him.[12]

This full integration of a Vaishnava intellectual into the Persianate socio-textual world of Lucknow is *encoded* equally clearly in the biographical note dedicated to Hindī's fellow disciple Mohan La'l "Anīs."

[12] Hindī, *Safīna-yi hindī*, 72–73.

Hindī's *tazkira* here becomes a sort of literary meta-memory, since it mentions another *tazkira* that was dedicated to the same circle Bhagwān Dās belonged to, and that included Hindī's own biography in a reciprocal gesture: "He learnt the subtleties of poetry from that lofty guide (*janāb irshādma'āb*) [Mīrzā Fākhir Makīn] and studied the sciences of rhetorics, metrics, and *qāfiya* from him. The *tazkira* entitled *Anīs al-aḥibbā*, which contains biographical information about that great master and his disciples, is admirably written. Anīs also wrote a *dīwān*, and his poetry is full of fresh ideas and polished contents."[13]

Within this system of literary relationships, Hindī also described himself, not only as a disciple of Makīn in a dedicated note to himself, as we shall see, or by praising his master in the terms we just saw, but also in notes dedicated to other poets, whom he indicated as being his own disciples.[14] Through a kind of "extended autobiography" the author presents himself as a full-fledged master, and the fact that many of his disciples were actually only occasional poets hardly matters. Representing himself as a disciple and a master authorizes him as a full member of the poetic school.[15]

Within these perfectly integrated expressive strategies, we note in Hindī's *tazkira*, as in other similar works composed by Vaishnava writers (just like in the above-mentioned works by Anīs and Shafiq, but also, for instance, in Bindrabān Dās Khwushgū's *Safīna*),[16] a particular attention paid to non-Muslim authors. In some cases this involves conveying

[13] Hindī, *Safīna-yi hindī*, 17.

[14] According to the *Safīna-yi hindī*, the poets who were part of Hindī's circle included Lālā Baijnāth "Anīs," Rāy Dawlat Rām "Dawlat," Malhār Singh "Miskīn," Rawshan Lāl "Rawshan," Rāy Khem Narāyan "Rind," and Debī Parshād "Shād."

[15] The structural value of the idea of a "poetic school" is underscored by Bhagwān Dās in the Introduction to the *Safīna-yi hindī* when he writes: "You must know that the expression *janāb irshādma'āb* refers here to the celebrated name of that pride of these times and places, Mīrzā Muḥammad Fākhir Makīn, may God the Defender protect him." Hindī, *Safīna-yi hindī*, 1. Also noteworthy is the fact that Hindī establishes his own literary *silsilā* by referring explicitly also to his master's master, the Iranian poet and painter Mīrzā 'Aẓīmā "Iksīr." See Hindī, *Safīna-yi hindī*, 3–5.

[16] See Pellò, "Persian as a 'passe-partout'."

simple information, as in the case of Malhār Singh "Miskīn," another member of Hindī's poetic circle; the way his belonging to the Sikh community is mentioned is typical: "He is the son of the Khatri Kulwant Rāy, who was put in charge of the administration of Bareilli district. He was born in Lucknow, and after his father's death he was appointed to the same post. Every time he composed verses, thanks to his sensitive nature, he had it checked by this writer. Both father and son were disciples of Guru Nānak, and he had with me a special relationship. He was lively, upright."[17]

In other instances, the relationship between the Persian textual frame of a poetic *tazkira* and the extra-textual individuality of Hindu authors is more composite and revealing. Exploiting the possibilities offered by the Persian linguistic code, elements related to Hindu traditions are at times transposed onto a Persian poetic plane by bending familiar metaphors and using a technique of juxtaposition and assimilation at the same time. We can see these dynamics at work, for example, in the section dedicated to the death of Sarab Sukh"Dīwāna:"

> When he was ailing in Lucknow I went to see him. Animated by a profound feeling of compassion (*shafaqat*), he said: "After my death one must remember Gayā."[18] Then he went to the Ganges, and once he reached there, the next day he rose to the highest paradise (*ba'd-i yak rūz ba bihisht-i barīn shitāft*). His body was cremated and his ashes dispersed in the river, and this is the meaning of the expression "drowned in the sea of mercy" (*gharīq-i baḥr-i raḥmat*) ... He was a person who was very attentive toward his friends, of generous and tranquil disposition, and with very kind manners; in accordance with his will, this writer made sure that his wife could go to Gayā in order to fulfill his testament.[19]

[17] Hindī, *Safīna-yi hindī*, 196.

[18] It must be noted that in the same years as the events described, the holy city of Gayā directly entered Persian literature thanks to a work dedicated to it by the poet Anandghan Khwush, called *Gayā māhātmya*; see A.B.M. Habibullah, "Medieval Indo-Persian Literature Relating to Hindu Science and Philosophy, 1000–1800 AD," *Indian Historical Quarterly* 14 (1938): 173.

[19] Hindī, *Safīna-yi hindī*, 73–74. A similar tendency toward adaptation can also be found in some *tazkiras* composed by Muslim authors. In the *tazkira Natā'ij al-afkār* (completed in 1842), for example, the death of Chandra Bhān "Barahman" is described using the image of the burning harvest, an image that belongs to the canon of classical Persian poetry but can also fittingly describe

The holy city of Gayā and the Ganges, "Hindu" textual objects, are immediately balanced by the evocation of the "highest paradise" (*bihisht-i barīn*), a canonical image both from the point of view of Islamic vocabulary and of Persian poetic language. Thus in this *tazkira* Dīwāna dies like a Hindu but goes to heaven like a Muslim.[20] In a similar fashion, the next characteristically "idolatrous" image of the body burnt to ashes and dispersed in the river is immediately re-codified by being transferred onto a symbolic plane that belongs to the Perso-Islamic register, thanks to the evocation of the "sea of mercy." In the last section of this passage, it is interesting to note how Hindī divests himself of his poetic persona to discreetly suggest that he helped the family of his late co-religionist in fulfilling in the sacred city of Gayā an unspecified religious ritual (*kār*), probably the *śrāddha*.[21] These are brief mentions, short parenthetical notes—that I systematically read as "hints" (*indizi*) in the methodological way described by Carlo Ginzburg[22]—that lead back more or less accidentally (but never casually) to the extra-textual world. The use of the same topos of the Ganges as the Islamic *baḥr-i raḥmat* in another

---

the Hindu rite of cremation: "In the year 1073 the lightning of death burnt the harvest of his life (*dar sana-yi 1073 barq-i ajal kharman-i ḥayāt-ash-rā sūkht*)." Muḥammad Qudratallāh Gopāmawī, *Kitāb-i tazkira-yi natā'ij.al-afkār* (Bombay: Khaze Book-Seller, 1957), 107. In an analogous fashion, the even later *tazkira Sham'-i anjuman* describes Chandra Bhān's death and cremation using another typical literary image of fire, that of the Zoroastrian "temple of fire" (*ātashkada*), here linked metaphorically to the equally typical mystical annihilation (*fanā*): "In 1073 he became ashes in the fire-temple of annihilation (*dar 1073 dar ātashkada-yi fanā khākistar gardīd*)." Sayyid Ṣiddīq Ḥasan Khān Nawāb, *Sham'-i anjuman* (Bhopal: Matba'-i Shahjahani, 1878), 92.

20 This is not the case of the death of another Hindu poet, Mithū Lāl "Mużtar," narrated in the *tazkira Anīs al-aḥibbā* by Mohan La'l Anīs. Here the protagonist is described as a devotee of Vishnu (Anīs uses the Hindī/Urdu expression *bishan bhagat*) and finds rest in one of the paradises (*loka*) of Brahminical tradition. Anīs, *Anīs al-aḥibbā*, 206.

21 Gayā is famous as a site for performing *piṇḍa dāna*, the religious offerings given to the dead. See Vijay Nath, "Puranic *Tīrthas*: A Study of their Indigenous Origins and Transformation (Based Mainly on the Skanda Purāṇa," *Indian Historical Review* 34 (January 2007): 1–46.

22 See Carlo Ginzburg, "Spie. Radici di un paradigma indiziario," in *Crisi della ragione*, ed. Aldo Gargani (Turin: Einaudi, 1979).

passage of the *Safīna-yi hindī* describing the funeral rites of Rāy Maykū La'l "Mastāna" signals the structural semiotic value of these expressive choices: "His body was taken to the Ganges, burnt with sandalwood, and consigned to the waters. This is the meaning of 'drowned in the sea of mercy' (*gharīq-i baḥr-i raḥmat*)."[23]

Similar strategies were used not only to textualize within the textual system of Persian aesthetic referents cultural and religious elements that were specifically Hindu, but also to integrate Hindu individuals themselves in this system as recognizable characters. I refer here in particular to the widely spread motif of the "beautiful idolater," which allowed the literary sign to be projected onto the biographical reality of these poets, thus harmonizing (or overlapping or confusing, which in this case amount to the same thing) their different social and textual locations. We can find one example at the beginning of the note that Hindī devoted to his fellow disciple, Mohan La'l "Anīs:" "He began studying Persian books under the guidance of a poet called Rawnaq and quickly devoted himself to poetic composition. Initially he chose the *takhalluṣ* Khasta, but after falling in love with a Hindu boy (*hindūpisar*) called Shitāb Rāy, he changed his poetic name to Bītāb, and then again to Anīs."[24]

The story of a poet whose falling in love with a Hindu boy had direct consequences for his literary activity (and, in parallel, in a Persian context, for his spiritual development) is not new in Indo-Persian *tazkiras*. We can find a model, based on the story of Aṭṭār's Ṣan'ān, in the biography of the Vaishnava ascetic and Persian poet Bhopat Rāy "Bīgham" Bayrāgī (d. 1719) as told in another *tazkira*, *Hamīsha bahār*, by a Vaishnava author, Kishan Chand "Ikhlāṣ," which was completed in 1723–24:[25]

[23] Hindī, *Safīna-yi hindī*, 205.

[24] Hindī, *Safīna-yi hindī*, 17.

[25] This motif was reinterpreted in different contexts within Mughal literary culture: see, e.g., the story of the *hindavi* poet Muḥammad Afżal who fell in love with a Hindu woman as told in Wālih Dāghistānī's *tazkira*. 'Alī Qulī Khān Wālih, *Riyāż al-shu'arā*, ed. Sharīf Ḥusain Qāsimī (Rampur: Kitabkhana-yi Raza, 2001), 64–67. See Shantanu Phukan's analysis in "The Rustic Beloved: Ecology of Hindi in a Persianate World," *The Annual of Urdu Studies* 15 (2000), 25–29. Another example is the apparently mirror narrative about the Sanskrit Mughal poet Jagannātha Paṇḍitarāja, where the object of love is a Muslim woman.

At first in order to earn a living he worked as a servant and scribe for the governors of his land. Then the desire to live free and without ties became too strong in his heart and he chose the path of spiritual poverty (*ṭarīq-i darwīshī ikhtiyār numūd*). Fate destined that he should come to Delhi and fall into the trap laid by the beautiful face of a Hindu boy, Narāyan Chand. For him he translated and versified the *Prabodhacandronāyak*[26] and wrote several treatises on Sufism.[27]

Here the name of the Hindu boy directly reflects the title of the work Bayrāgī chooses to translate. Several other "Hindu boys" are mentioned in the *Safina-yi hindī*. Although they are always described in purely literary terms as recognized "idolaters," a precise socio-historical typology is still allowed to emerge. We can read the note that Bhagwān Dās dedicated to Shaikh Muḥammad Qāyim "Qāyim:"

He was most excellent among the teachers (*mu'allimān*) in our city of Lucknow, and he knew all the most important Persian books in great detail, and he spent his time teaching. His school (*maktab-ash*), attended by fairy-faced and silver-chested [youths] (*parīrūyān-i sīmbar*), was the envy of the fairy houses of China (*parīkhāna-yi chīn*), and the earthly place where he held court was begrudged by the heavenly wheel (*charkh-i barīn*), and among those who attended his lessons were mostly Hindu boys with pleasant and handsome faces and appearance (*hindūpisarān-i zībāṭal'at-i nīkūmanẓar*).[28]

Here Hindī is directly conveying a historical reality: *hindūpisarān* are the non-Muslim boys who attended the schools of great masters in Lucknow and Awadh and learnt Persian there,[29] here transposed on a poetic plane

---

Sheldon Pollock. "The Death of Sanskrit," *Comparative Studies in Society and History* 43, no. 2 (2001): 409.

26 This is most probably the *Prabodhacandrodaya* (or *Prabodhacan drodayanāṭaka*), a Vedantic allegorical play written in Sanskrit by Krishna Mishra in the eleventh century and translated into several Indian vernaculars. The title given in the *tazkira* appears corrupt.

27 Kishan Chand Ikhlāṣ, *Hamīsha bahār: Tazkira-yi shu'arā-yi fārsī*, ed. Waḥīd Qurayshī (Karachi: Anjuman Taraqqi-yi Urdu Pakistan, 1973), 37–38.

28 Hindī, *Safina-yi hindī*, 171.

29 According to Francis Buchanan, as reported in Umar, especially in early-nineteenth-century Bihar and Bengal, Persian schools were "nearly as much frequented by Hindus as by Muhammadans, for the Persian language is considered

and aesthetically "naturalized" through well-honed lexical and rhetorical instruments such as the metaphor and comparison with China, traditionally a land of pagan beauties. Hindī inserts within this typology also the Hindu Shabāb Rāy "Azīz," only an occasional writer of Persian verses who was born and lived in Lucknow. In order to describe his beauty, the *tazkira* employs the famous image of Joseph in the slave market—a slave everyone wanted to purchase—evoking Jāmī's classic Persian poetic reworking of the Quranic story in sura XII in his *Yūsuf u zulaykhā*: "This *'azīz*, because of his handsome appearance, was as famous as Joseph in the market of the world, and whole crowds wanted to have him as their companion (*khalq-ī khwāstgārī-yi ū mīkardand*)."[30] We may note that Shabāb Rāy's *takhalluṣ* makes it possible for Hindī to paradoxically identify Shabāb Rāy through an oxymoron, with the poetic model represented by Joseph: in that story the "'*azīz* of Egypt" is in fact Zulaykhā's husband, while Zulaykhā desperately and passionately loves Joseph.

Equally noteworthy, as far as the interplay between social and poetic realities are concerned, are the various cases of "poetic" conversion to Islam that *tazkiras*, including the *Safīna-yi hindī*, record. Bhagwān Dās's narrative of the conversion to Muslim religious practice of the handsome *rastogi* Medī La'l "Bīmār"—a student of Dīwāna—is an exemplary case. In Hindī's interpretation, Persian language and literature in fact play a fundamental role in this conversion (which remains implicit in the telling). It is the study of Rūmī's mystical *Masnawī* that brings the conversion about, and the terms used to describe it are essentially aesthetic, as in the very classical reference to the Central Asian ethnonym "Chigil," a (initially pagan) Turkic people renowned in Persian poetry for their beauty, who had already been textualized as a metaphorical referent at least from the tenth century:

---

as a necessary accomplishment for every gentleman, and it is absolutely necessary for those who wish to acquire fortune in the courts of law." Muhammad Umar, *Islam in Northern India during the Eighteenth Century* (New Delhi: Munshiram Manoharlal [for the Centre of Advanced Study in History, Aligarh Muslim University], 1993), 397, n. 41. According to slightly earlier evidence relating to only a few districts of Bengal, the number of Hindu students of Persian was one-and-a-half that of Muslim students (2096 vs. 1558; the figures are taken from Umar, Islam in Northern India).

30 Hindī, *Safīna-yi hindī*, 133.

He belonged to the caste of the Rastogis (*rastogiyān*) of Lucknow. He was extraordinarily handsome in his youth and had a burning, sensitive, and sorrowful heart. He spent most of his time in the company of loving ascetics (*gushanishīnān-i ahl-i dil*) and sweethearts who were the envy of the beauties of the Chigils, and he was always engaged in the study of various Sufi treatises and in reading Mawlawī's *Mas̱nawī*, and he read the verses of the *Mas̱nawī* suffering intensively. I saw him myself once or twice while he was reciting poetry with tears streaming down his cheeks. In the end, in 1182 [= 1768–69] he severed all ties and went to Ajmer. They say that he remained there a while, and that he later went on pilgrimage to the holy places of Islam, God knows more about it. In any case he was a very special person and his soul was full of ardor. His verses are numerous, and for some time he received instruction in this art by Rāy Sarab Sukh"Dīwāna."[31]

It is fair to ask at this point, in this complex system of relations between literary and historical realities, and faced with these narrative reflections of a conversion that seems to have taken place through the canonical medium of Sufism, where the "identitarian" Shiʿism of Lucknow that I referred to at the outset is to be found. We may turn first of all to another case of "literary" conversion to Islam mentioned by our *taẕkira*, that is, the famous one of the Khatri Dīwālī Singh, who at a young age decided to become a Twelver Shiʿa under the name of Mīrzā Ḥasan and to accept the poetic *takhalluṣ* of "Qatīl" (i.e., slain), thus making direct reference to the fundamental Shiʿi concept of martyrdom in his poetic self-identification of choice.[32] But if we look into the *Safīna-yi hindī* we find no direct reference to Shiʿism in the biographical note on him:

[31] Hindī, *Safīna-yi hindī*, 29–30.

[32] This is how Ghulām Hamadānī Muṣḥafī describes Dīwālī Singh's conversion in his own *taẕkira*: "When, in accordance to fate's decree, his parents moved to Fayẓābād, he accrued honor by converting to Islam thanks to Mīrzā Muḥammad Bāqir Shahīd Iṣfahānī, at the age of eighteen. Then, giving free rein to the delicate and harmonious temperament that had been characteristic of him since childhood, he also began to write poetry and to take lessons from that great master. And since at that time, the time of the late Nawāb Wazīr, there were many more Iranians than now, he chose that religion [= Shiʿism] and his master gave him the *takhalluṣ* Qatīl: his master was called Shahīd [martyr], and thus the disciple should be known as Qatīl [slain]." Ghulām Hamadānī

> His father belonged to the Khatri caste from Paṭiala, near Lahore, and was related to Siyalkoṭī Mal. He was born in Shāhjahānābād, and when he was still young he chose the honor to be converted to Islam. He studied Persian and Arabic sciences and began to compose poetry, an art in which he displays great skills, writing multi-colored verses on the page of Time. Despite his free and emancipated nature he is always a prisoner of love. The notables of these parts show him respect and honor.[33]

It is likely that the superficiality of this note that Hindī dedicated to Qatīl was because Qatīl was extraneous to the circle of Hindī's own master, Mīrzā Fākhir Makīn. Nevertheless, Hindī's brief notes point the way to some further observations. As in the case of Bīmār, Hindī describes Qatīl's conversion to Islam without any fanfare, as a consequential and natural fact: it is perhaps not accidental that he does not even mention Mīrzā Ḥasan's name before the conversion (unlike Muṣḥafī[34]), just as he did not in the case of Medī La'l "Bīmār," the neo-Muslim who went on pilgrimage to Mecca. On a textual level as codified in Hindī's *tazkiras*, then, the different religious affiliations of the various members of the Indo-Persian literary community of Lucknow seem to exist on a level plane: they are distinct but can be superimposed one on the other along a continuum. They are not treated differently, whether it is the case of the Ganges as the "sea of mercy" for poetically idolatrous ashes or of a conversion to Islam that brings honor (as did, implicitly, the vow that took Dīwāna to Gayā). Unlike other narratives, they are not marked by contrasting images of "idolatry" versus "truefaith."[35]

Muṣḥafī, *'Iqd-i ṡurayyā: (tazkira-yi fārsīgūyān)*, ed. Mawlawī 'Abdulḥaq (Delhi: Jami' Barqi Press, 1934), 46.

[33] Hindī, *Safīna-yi hindī*, 172.

[34] Muṣḥafī, *'Iqd-i ṡurayyā*, 46

[35] See by contrast the words Abū Ṭālib Iṣfahānī uses for Qatīl's conversion in his *tazkira Khulāṣat al-afkār* (completed in 1792–93): "Through the intercession of the grace of well-leading companions, a ray of eternal benevolence shone in his noble heart and took him to the door/threshold of Islam, and this is why he dedicated himself body and soul to Muhammad's faith, thus saving himself from the fire of polytheism." Abū Ṭālib Muḥammad Iṣfahānī (Ms.), *Khulāṣat al-afkār* (London: Indian Office Library, I.O. Islamic 2692), f. 360a. Just as interesting is the passage devoted to the pro-Shi'a tendency of Ulfat Rāy 'Ulfat' in the late *tazkira Ṣubḥ-i gulshan* (completed in 1878): "As the saying goes, people follow the religion of their rulers: despite his idolatry, he displayed an

What is even more interesting here is that Hindī does not specify which kind of Islam Qatīl converted to. This does not necessarily mean that Hindī was inattentive toward Shiʿism. On the contrary, we can argue that writing in a context where Shiʿa Islam was the "state religion" despite being that of a small minority in demographic terms, an intellectual well connected with the Awadh political elite like Hindī would denote by "Islam" primarily "Shiʿa Islam," that is, the form of Islam that he considered more legitimate in that context. This matches the tendency just noted above of a political de-stressing of the semiotic value of the various religious spaces: if the boundaries between devotional spaces are resolved in *tazkira*s, as we have seen, through nuances of expression and the layering of aesthetic ideas, it is all the more likely that the preference would be to dilute the contrast between Sunni and Shiʿa Islam—using the latter as the common denominator. If we move away for a moment from individual biographies and observe the *Safīna-yi hindī* as a whole—and consider it an extended autobiographical memoir of its author Bhagwān Dās—we can actually find a series of pro-Shiʿa or pro-Alid references that support this hypothesis. First, Hindī mentions more than once the Twelver Shiʿa holy sites in Iraq and Iran with eulogistic formulas that are easily recognized: *Karbalā-yi muʿallā* ("Exalted Karbala," twice[36]), *Najaf-i ashraf* ("Noble Najaf"[37]), *Mashhad-i muqaddas* ("Holy Mashhad"[38]). The only exception is Qum, which although mentioned four times in the text, is never accompanied by any qualifier.[39] Visits to these holy places are described in terms full of praise. In the note about Mīr Awlād ʿAlī "Zāyir," for example, we read that: "He accrued honor by visiting the holy places of Iraq … and after acquiring additional honor with the pilgrimage to Imām Riżā's Mashhad—peace be upon him—he returned to India."[40] A similar Shiʿi

---

inclination towards Shiʿism and took part in the gatherings for the commemoration of the lord of martyrs—blessings and praise be upon him" (*bā wujūd-i ṣanamparastī mayl ba mazhab-i tashayyuʿ wa ihtimām dar taʿziyadārī wa tartīb-i majālis-i ʿazā-yi janāb sayyid al-shuhadā ʿalayhi al-tahiyat wa al-sanā*). ʿAlī Ḥasan Khān, *Ṣubḥ-i gulshan*, Bhopal: Matbaʿ-i Shahjahani, 1878), 32.

[36] Hindī, *Safīna-yi hindī*, 80, 153.
[37] Hindī, *Safīna-yi hindī*, 220.
[38] Hindī, *Safīna-yi hindī*, 56.
[39] Hindī, *Safīna-yi hindī*, 8, 110, 112, 114.
[40] *ba ziyārat-i ʿatabāt-i ʿāliyāt-i ʿIrāq musharraf shuda* [...] *ba mashhad-i imām Riżā ʿalayhi 'l-salām musharrafandūz gashta bāz ba hindūstān murājaʿat numūda*. Hindī, *Safīna-yi hindī*, 99.

mimetic touch at the level of expression is the completely "Iranian" reference to the *rawża-yi rażawiya* ("Riżā's garden," that is, the mausoleum of the eighth Imām in Mashhad), in which Sayyid Muḥammad "Hasrat" was among the hereditary "servants."[41] When discussing Shaikh Muḥammad "Āshiq," the *Safīna-yi hindī* works into its structure not only Shi'i geographical and cultic markers but even concepts, such as the fundamental ideas of love for the Prophet's family and descendants and the complementarity between *nubuwwat* and *wilāya*: "His nature was extremely passionate because of his love and solidarity for the family of prophecy and tutelage."[42]

Two more episodes narrated in the *tażkira* further support the Shi'i attitude Bhagwān Dās takes on in the text. The first episode, told with pietistic overtones in the note on the Iranian Shi'a writer Muḥammad "Ja'far," is about the dream seen by "a *sayyid*, a servant of the holy garden of his excellence Imām 'Alī Mūsā Riżā," in which the Imām himself stated that he wanted Ja'far to be near him—a premonition that was fulfilled, Hindī informs us, when Ja'far died three days later.[43] The second episode is more political and concerns the murder of the Naqshbandi master and Persian poet of Delhi Mīrzā Maẓhar Jān-i Jānān at the hands of some Shi'as during Muharram in 1195 (between December 1780 and January 1781). That this incident is mentioned at all in the *tażkira* is worthy of note as somewhat of an exception to the ecumenism of its agenda. But it is in fact only somewhat of an exception: Jān-i Jānān's murder is expressly linked to an alleged absence of ecumenic feelings in him: "He used to say that he gave no importance to divergence in religious views and claimed to be an innovator, but in real fact he was a fanatical Sunni (*dar mażhab-i sunnat u jamā'at ghuluww dāsht*), and for this reason some Shi'as made him a martyr (*shahīd sākhtand*) during the days of Ashura in the year 1195."[44] The murder is thus somewhat justified, and Bhagwān Dās's use of the verb *shahīd sākhtan* might even be read as an ironical touch. What is more significant, though, is that

41 *dar silk-i khadma-yi rawża-yi rażawiya 'alayhi 'l-salām arsan munsalik būd.* Hindī, *Safīna-yi hindī*, 56.

42 *ṭab'-ash ba muḥabbat u walā-yi khāndān-i nubuwwat u wilāyat 'alayhimal-salām wa 'l-taḥiya kamāl-i mashghūf-ast.* Hindī, *Safīna-yi hindī*, 144.

43 Hindī, *Safīna-yi hindī*, 48.

44 Hindī, *Safīna-yi hindī*, 188.

here the Hindu "integrated" intellectual seems to express quite openly, in the context of a process of semiotic transfer, his support for religious inclusivity, which we have seen is one of the *aesthetic* characteristics of the *Safīna*.[45]

To go back to Dīwālī Singh/Mīrzā Ḥasan "Qatīl," it is therefore not necessary for Hindī to specify which kind of Islam Qatīl converted to, since Shiʿi Islam is already pre-codified as a dominant semantic framework relating to the contextual space. In the same way, it is not necessary to spell out that the Hindu poets whose literary persona interacts with that framework are close to, and well-versed in, Shiʿi pietism. In the biography of "Mukhtār" by Sītal Dās, for example, there is no mention of his personal pro-Shiʿi beliefs and devotional practices—which contemporary sources do mention[46]—but the verses Bhagwān Dās selects in the note dedicated to him have clear overtones:

yā shāh-i najaf ba khāk-i pāy-i ḥasanayn
bāshad dil u jān-i mā fadā-yi ḥasanayn
az jawr-i falak sakht ba jān āmada-īm
mā-rā binawāz az barāy-i ḥasanayn

You reign in Najaf, the land Ḥasan and Ḥusayn walked on,
We proffer our hearts and mind to Ḥasan and Ḥusayn.
The violent sky led us to almost leave our life:
In the name of Ḥasan and Ḥusayn grant us sweet caresses.[47]

[45] In an eloquent passage on this issue, Hindī speaks with fulsome praise of the "indeterminate" spiritual eclecticism of the Delhi Sufi Mīrzā Girāmī "Girāmī," who "looked like a Sufi master but at times lived like Indian wandering mystics" and "had warm and friendly relations with people of all confessions;" he became a "firm reference point for people" because of his "ability" and his "generosity of heart." Hindī, *Safīna-yi hindī*, 175.

[46] In Anīs's *taẕkira*, for example, we read that "he became so devoted to the Lion of God, his excellence ʿAlī, son of Abū Ṭālib, that he gave up many of the customs of his religion." Anīs, *Anīs al-aḥibbā*, 178. In the context of the representation of the contrast between Islam and idolatry mentioned above, the comment on the religious views of this poet in the *taẕkira Ṣubḥ-i gulshan* is worth noting: "Rāy Sītal Dās 'Mukhtār' was a Kayastha who lived in Lucknow and belonged to the retinue of Nawāb Āṣaf al-Dawla Bahādur. He did not really believe in idolatry but inclined toward the path of Shiʿism." Khān, *Ṣubh-i gulshan*, 391.

[47] Hindī, *Safīna-yi hindī*, 193–94.

It is therefore clear that, according to the logic of the *Safīna-yi hindī*, a Shi'i sensibility forms an integral part of the poetic character (both as a writing subject and as an object of description) of a Hindu author from Awadh, and this is presented as something not at all extraordinary. The following episode about a poet who did not live in Lucknow but which has a general iconic value highlights how biography and poetry mix and overlap perfectly in the text within the framework of this sensibility. It projects on a generic canonical level the narrative fact that the Vaishnava poet Rām Narāyan (a disciple of the Iranian emigre intellectual 'Alī Ḥazīn, d. 1766) "recited" the agony of Ḥusayn dying of thirst in Karbalā and commented on his own death with an elegiac verse for the Imām:

> When his killers were about to hit him they asked him if he had one last wish. He replied: "A mouthful of water." They brought him a full glass, but that noble rāja refused it and threw it on the ground while reciting this verse:
>
> *maḥrūm rafta az tu lab-i tishna-yi ḥusayn*
> *ay āb khāk shaw ki tu-rā ābrū namānd.*
>
> You denied yourself to Ḥusayn's thirsty lips:
> oh water, become dust, since there is no fresh honor for you![48]

For Hindī, the *marsiya*'s poetic convention and the rituals of Ashura determine the poet's figure more than anything else. Thus in his note on Rām Narāyan—just like the one on Mukhtār—he makes no reference to an actual conversion. To go back to my observations on Qatīl's devotional shift, it is clear that there is no substantial contrast on the level of expression between this "Shi'i" death and the "Hindu" deaths of Dīwāna and Mastāna described above: they all belong to a system of self-representation that strives toward creating harmony.

Such mimetic processes can be found in the *Safīna* also in the autobiographical note that Hindī reserved for himself, with which I conclude this essay. If, as I have suggested above, we can consider the *tazkira* (at least those texts whose authors deal specifically with their contemporaries) a kind of extended autobiographical memoir, we can also read the Kayastha Bhagwān Dās's representation of himself in the text in more general terms. I here translate it in full:

[48] Hindī, *Safīna-yi hindī*, 85.

Bhagwān Dās Hindī, the author of these pages, is the son of Dalpat Dās, son of Harbans Rāy, of the caste of *kāyastha srībāstam dūsrā*. The original home of my ancestors was Kalpi, and their residence was in Sundha. During the reign of Nawāb Burhān al-Mulk, my father, after an invitation from his uncle Bulāqī Dās, who was then in charge of the army in the northern region, moved from there to Lucknow together with my grandfather. Since he moved together with the father of Karīm Dād Khān, who had administrative duties (and has been mentioned elsewhere), my father became one of the favorites at the court of Burhān al-Mulk and then of Nawāb Āṣaf al-Dawla. He was always immersed in thinking about the Lord of servants (*rabb al-ʿibād*) and wrote many Indian (*hindī*)[49] poems in praise of the Creator in the language of Braj. The writer of these pages was born in Ṣaydpūr in the house of his maternal grandfather Lāla Rām Ghulām,[50] the *qanungo* of that place, and the chronogram of his birth is *ṣabī-yi jawānbakht* "fortunate boy" [=1153H, i.e., 1740–41]. Aged two I moved to my father in Lucknow, and as soon as I reached the appropriate age I began studying grammar, the main Persian books, and other scientific texts. I showed an inclination toward the study of the *dīwān*s of the masters, of history books, and of *taẕkira*s, and also started to compose poetry, initially choosing the *takhalluṣ* Bismil. I was instructed in this art by the great master [Mīrzā Fākhir Makīn], and I wrote three *masnawī*s: the *Silsilat al-muḥabbat*, according to the meter of the *Silsilat al-ẕahab*; the *Maẓhar al-anwār*, in the meter of the *Makhzan al-asrār*; and the *Bhāgawat* entitled *Mihr-i żiyā*, according to the meter of *Yūsuf u zulaykhā*. I also wrote two *dīwān*s, one entitled *shawqīya* and one *ẕawqīya*, which contained *qaṣīda*s, *tarjīʿ band*s, and various other kinds of poems. Later I worked on a *taẕkira* entitled *Ḥadīqa-yi hindī*, which contains information relating to ancient and contemporary poets born in that paradise that is India, from the beginning of Islam to the year 1200 [1785–86]; that *taẕkira* is both a *taẕkira* and a history book. According to the noble Sayyid Khayrat ʿAlī's wishes I also composed a text entitled

49 I choose here to translate *hindī* as "Indian" (i.e., "of Indian argument" or "in the Indian manner") instead of as Hindī (i.e., "in the Hindī language") due to the presence of the specific reference to Brajbhasha in the same sentence.

50 Note the composite Hindi-Arabic name Rām Ghulām ("servant of Rām"), whose structure evokes both names common among Vaishnavas, such as its synonym Rām Dās, and among Shiʿas, such as Ghulām ʿAlī ("servant of ʿAlī"). This seems to be a common trend in the Persianate Indian milieu: the name of Hindī himself, Bhagwān Dās, can after all be easily read as a calque of the diffused Muslim name ʿAbd Allāh ("servant of God").

> *Sawāniḥ al-nubuwwat* that includes and summarizes the stories of the prophets and of the twelve imāms. Now that it is the year 1219 [1804] I have concluded these pages. At the onset of youth I had, among others, the job of harbor master in the district of Ilahabad at the order of Nawāb Mukhtār al-Dawla Bahādur. Then I entered the administration of Āṣaf al-Dawla Bahādur as secretary to Mīrzā Rāja Nidhi (?) Singh, who was put in charge of Khayrābād and Selak, and eventually I became directly responsible for five hundred *sawārs*. After the death of that rāja, I was taken into the circle of Rāja Paṛchand Bahādur, among those intimates blessed with the luminous presence of the nawāb. When Rāja Paṛchand also died, I was accepted into the circle of the *adirāja* [*adhirāja*] *mahārāja* Ṭīkait Rāy, Āṣaf al-Dawla's secretary. From then on the gracious, powerful, generous, intelligent glance of Rāy Jay Singh Rāy rests upon me and has increased my power, so that the princes and notables of these lands show me their support. I have preliminarily explained all these things in the dedicatory *qaṣīda* of the *Ḥadīqa-yi hindī*, since there is no space for them in this short text.[51]

To confirm the centrality of the "Shi'i mirror" in Hindī's construction of his own literary figure it is interesting to note that the work dedicated to the Prophet and the Imāms that Bhagwān Dās mentions finds echo, in the anthology of verses that follows the aubiographical entry, in a *qaṣīda* of fifty-four verses dedicated to Muḥammad, Fāṭima, and the twelve Imāms, as well as in other *bayt*s dedicated to Ẕū'l-fiqār, 'Alī's sword.[52] Yet this is a mirror that includes and reflects, within its frame, many other things as well. It is quite evident from the beginning that Bhagwān Dās sought, and managed to find, a balance between his literary figure and his extra-literary determinations, as shown by the emphasis placed on his own caste—including his sub-caste—and kin relations, and the words he uses to describe his father. His father was arguably the author of devotional poetry in Brajbhasha, yet Hindī's description is completely assimilative: the specific religious marker becomes a simple linguistic-geographical marker (he wrote culturally "Indian," but also linguistically "Hindī" poems, as shown by the subsequent reference to "the language of Braj"), and the expression used to describe the object of his father's piety is an Arabic one with a clear Islamic connotation

51 Hindī, *Safīna-yi hindī*, 241–43.

52 See Hindī, *Safīna-yi hindī*, 241–43.

(*rabb al-'ibād*, "the Lord of servants"). At the same time, following the expressive strategy that I have already highlighted, Hindī leaves out any definition that would point to an exclusive religious affiliation. We could make a similar argument about Hindī's literary activities and place his poetic devotion to the symbolic figures of Shi'i piety side by side with the aesthetic attention he devotes to the Krishnaite universe, following a common trend in later Indo-Persian literature. Here too the logic of assimilation is evident in the declared choice of a wholly canonical work such as Jāmī's *Yūsuf u zulaykhā,* itself based on a Qur'anic story, as the metrical model for Hindī's own version of the *Bhāgavata Purāṇa*[53] (a work which Hindī himself mentions elsewhere among the "voluminous Indian/Hindī books," *kutub-i mabsūṭ-i hindī*[54]) and in the very title given to it (*Mihr-i żiyā*, "The Sun of the Lights," an expression that takes one directly back to Neoplatonic ideas[55]). Equally significant is

[53] We know from Mohan La'l "Anīs," a fellow disciple of Hindī's and always well informed, that this rendering was only of the tenth book of the *Bhāgavata Purāṇa*. Anīs, *Anīs al-aḥibbā*, 194.

[54] Beside the *Bhāgavata Purāṇa*, the *Rāmāyaṇa* is also mentioned in this passage. Hindī, *Safīna-yi hindī*, 22.

[55] This is, again, a common trend in later Indo-Persian poetry. Compare, for instance, the use of the expression *Jilwa-yi ẕāt* ("The Epiphany of the Essence," a Sufi-Neoplatonic expression already used, for instance, in a ghazal by the hyper-canonical Ḥāfiẓ) as the title for the Persian rewriting of the tenth *skandha* of the tenth skanha of the *Bhāgavata Purāṇa* by Amānat Rāy, a Vaishnava member of the very influential school of Mīrzā Bīdil (1744–1721) in Delhi. On this point, and on the general diffusion of themes related to Krishna within Bīdil's very influential poetic circle, see Pellò, "Persian as a 'passe-partout.'" For the general currency of Krishnaite themes and genres in the Indo-Persian world, see also the sixteenth-century Sufi work by Mīr 'Abd al-Waḥīd Bilgrāmī, the *Haqā'iq-i hindī*. See Sayid Athar Abbas Rizvi, *A History of Sufism in India* (New Delhi: Munshiram Manoharlal, 1978–1983), I, 359–62; Muzaffar Alam, "The Culture and Politics of Persian in Precolonial Hindustan," in *Literary Cultures in History: Reconstructions from South Asia*, ed. Sheldon Pollock (Berkeley: University of California Press, 2003), 181; Francesca Orsini, "'Krishna is the Truth of Man': Mir 'Abdul Wahid Bilgrami's *Haqā'iq-i Hindī* (Indian Truths)," in *Culture and Circulation*: Literature in Motion in Early Modern India ed. Allison Busch and Thomas de Bruijn (Leiden: Brill, 2014: 226–46); and Francesca Orsini and Stefano Pellò, "Bhakti in Persian," unpublished paper.

Hindī's decision to mention the *Mihr-i żiyā* as part of a series of three *masnawīs* that ideally form a sort of trio, which immediately recalls the canonical *khamsa*, "Quintet," by Niẓāmī (1141–1209), and other prestigious regroupments of *masnawīs* by the great master-poets of the past; in fact the metrical models indicated by Hindī for his other two *masnawīs* (*Silsilat al-muḥabbat* and *Maẓhar al-anwār*) are, respectively, classical mystical works by Jāmī (*Silsilat al-ẕahab*) and Niẓāmī himself (*Makhzān al-asrār*).

Aside from the specific value attributed to single instances, Bhagwān Dās "Hindī" therefore places himself and other Hindu poets of Persian from Lucknow in an "open" and "extended" framework of belonging, where one can move between Gayā and Karbalā without having to cross any boundary. Hindī's verses in praise of the twelve Imāms and those celebrating Krishna can be placed side by side because they adhere to a single code with a shared system of aesthetic references, which we find also in Sarab Sukh "Dīwāna" "burning" on the Ganges and Rāja Rām Narāyan's identification with Ḥusayn at the moment of his death. The fact of being part of the same literary community and of sharing the same canonical system, here overdetermined by a Shi'i political and cultural framework marked by inclusivity and cosmopolitanism, works powerfully to defuse the importance given to the fact that these authors were related to different religious groups. In Hindī's *taẕkira*, religious affiliation never creates fault lines, unlike in other contemporary *taẕkiras* by non-Muslim authors such as *Gul-i ra'nā* and *Anīs al-aḥibbā*, where the Hindu–Muslim dichotomy plays a structural role. In the *Safīna-yi hindī*, by contrast, religious identifications appear to be sub-identifications: they are not denied but present as secondary expressive possibilities within a system that is perceived as one.

BIBLIOGRAPHY

Alam, Muzaffar. "The Culture and Politics of Persian in Precolonial Hindustan." In *Literary Cultures in History: Reconstructions from South Asia*, edited by Sheldon Pollock, 131–98. Berkeley: University of California Press, 2003.

Alam, Muzaffar and Sanjay Subrahmanyam. "The Making of a Munshi." *Comparative Studies of South Asia, Africa and the Middle East* 24, no. 2 (2004): 61–72.

Anīs, Mohan La'l. *Anīs al-aḥibbā: Taẕkira-yi shu'arā-yi fārsī*. 2nd edition. Edited by Anwār Aḥmad. Patna: Khuda Bakhsh Oriental Public Library, 1999.

Brubaker, Rogers and Frederick Cooper. "Beyond 'Identity'." *Theory and Society* 29 (2000): 1–47.

Cole, Juan Ricardo. *Roots of North Indian Shi'ism in Iran and Iraq: Religion and State in Awadh, 1722–1859*. Berkeley: University of California Press, 1988.

Cole, Juan R.I. "Shi'ite Noble women and Religious Innovation in Awadh." In *Lucknow: Memories of a City*, edited by Violette Graff, 83–90. Delhi: Oxford University Press, 1997.

de Bruijn, Johann T.P. "Hindu." In *Encyclopædia Iranica* (New York: Encyclopædia Iranica Foundation, 2012). http://www.iranicaonline.org/articles/hindu. Accessed April 7, 2012.

Ginzburg, Carlo. "Spie. Radici di un paradigma indiziario." In *Crisi della ragione*, edited by Aldo Gargani, 57–106. Turin: Einaudi, 1979. [English translation by Anna Davin in Carlo Ginzburg, "Morelli, Freud and Sherlock Holmes: Clues and Scientific Method," *History Workshop Journal* 9, no. 1 (Spring 1980): 5–36.]

Gopāmawī, Muḥammad Qudratallāh. *Kitā-i tazkira-yi natā'ij al-afkār*. Bombay: Khaze Book-Seller, 1957.

Habibullah, A.B.M. "Medieval Indo-Persian Literature Relating to Hindu Science and Philosophy, 1000–1800 AD." *Indian Historical Quarterly* 14 (1938): 167–81.

Hasan, Mushirul. "Traditional Rites and Contested Meanings: Sectarian Strife in Colonial Lucknow." In *Lucknow: Memories of a City*, edited by Violette Graff, 114–35. Delhi: Oxford University Press, 1997.

Hindī, Bhagwān Dās. *Safīna-yi hindī: Tazkira-yi shu'arā-yi fārsī*. Edited by Sayyid Shāh Muḥammad 'Aṭā al-Raḥmān 'Aṭā Kākwī. Patna: Institute of Post-Graduate Studies and Research in Arabic & Persian, 1958.

Ḥusayn, S.A. *Ghayr muslim marṣiyanigār*. Lucknow: n.p., 1995.

Ikhlāṣ, Kishan Chand. *Hamīsha bahār: Tazkira-yi shu'arā-yi fārsī*. Edited by Waḥīd Qurayshī. Karachi: Anjuman Taraqqi-yi Urdu Pakistan, 1973.

Iṣfahānī, Abū Ṭālib ibn Muḥammad (Ms.). *Khulāṣat al-afkār*. London: India Office Library: I.O. Islamic 2692.

Khān, 'Alī Ḥasan. *Ṣubḥ-i gulshan*, Bhopal: Matba'-i Shahjahani, 1878 [1295].

Muṣḥafī, Ghulām Hamadānī. *'Iqd-i ṡurayyā: (tazkirah-yi fārsīgūyān)*. Edited by Mawlawī 'Abdulḥaq. Delhi: Jami' Barqi Press, 1934.

Nath, Vijay. "Puranic *Tīrthas*: A Study of Their Indigenous Origins and Transformation (Based Mainly on the Skanda Purāṇa)." *Indian Historical Review* 34 (January 2007): 1–46.

Nawāb, Sayyid Ṣiddīq Ḥasan Khān. *Sham'-i anjuman*. Bhopal: Matba'-i Shahjahani, 1878.

Orsini, Francesca. "'Krishna is the Truth of Man': Mir 'Abdul Wahid Bilgrami's *Haqā'iq-i Hindī* (*Indian Truths*)." In *Culture and Circulation: Literature in*

Motion in Early Modern India, edited by Allison Busch and Thomas de Bruijn. Leiden: Brill, 2014: 222–46.

Orsini, Francesca and Stefano Pellò. "Bhakti in Persian." Unpublished paper.

Pellò, Stefano. "Poeti hindu e circoli intellettuali persiani tra Delhi e Lucknow: un caso di interazione letteraria." PhD diss., Università degli Studi di Roma "La Sapienza," Roma, 2006.

———. "Hindu Persian Poets." In *Encyclopædia Iranica* (New York: Encyclopædia Iranica Foundation, 2008). http://www.iranicaonline.org/articles/hindu-persian-poets. Accessed April 7, 2012.

———. "Persian as a 'Passe-partout': The Case of Mīrzā 'Abd al-Qādir Bīdil and His Hindu Disciples." In *Culture and Circulation: Literature in Motion in Early Modern India*, edited by Allison Busch and Thomas de Bruijn. Leiden: Brill, 2014: 222–46.

Phukan, Shantanu. "The Rustic Beloved: Ecology of Hindi in a Persianate World." *The Annual of Urdu Studies* 15 (2000): 3–30.

Pollock, Sheldon. "The Death of Sanskrit." *Comparative Studies in Society and History* 43, no. 2 (2001): 392–426.

Qatīl, Mīrzā Ḥasan (Ms.). *Dīwān*. Rampur: Rampur Raza Library, 30196M.

Rizvi, Sayid Athar Abbas. *A History of Sufism in India*. 2 volumes. New Delhi: Munshiram Manoharlal, 1978–1983.

Scarcia Amoretti, Biancamaria. *Sciiti nel mondo*. Roma: Jouvence, 1994.

Shafīq, Lachhmī Narāyan. *Taẕkira-yi gul-i ra'nā*. Hyderabad: 'Ahd-i Afarin Barqi Press, n.d.

Srīvāstavā, G.S. *Urdū sha'irī ke irtiqā mẽ hindū shu'arā kā ḥiṣṣa*, Allahabad: n.p., 1969.

Umar, Muhammad. *Islam in Northern India during the Eighteenth Century*. New Delhi: Munshiram Manoharlal [for the Centre of Advanced Study in History, Aligarh Muslim University], 1993.

Wālih, 'Alī Qulī Khān. *Riyāż al-shu'arā*. Edited by Sharīf Ḥusayn Qāsimī. Rampur: Kitabkhana-yi Raza, 2001.

6 Faith and Allegiance in the Mughal Era

*Perspectives from Rajasthan**

Ramya Sreenivasan

Sixteenth- and seventeenth-century accounts from northern India contain numerous references to Rajputs becoming Muslim. The sources often recount instances of individual conversions as accompanying political submission to a Muslim overlord. A particular memory of forced conversions at the point of the sword circulates widely in the public domain today, and for Hindu nationalists it has come to symbolize the inherently coercive nature of Muslim rule over Hindu subjects between the thirteenth and eighteenth centuries. Today, most historians of South Asia broadly agree that this majoritarian-nationalist interpretation is based on reading the available sources selectively and misinterpreting them.[1] In this essay, I hope to show that Mughal-era literati—and, by implication, their patrons—intensely debated the nature of elite conversions such as the ones

* I am grateful to Indrani Chatterjee, Richard Eaton, Jamal J. Elias, Sumit Guha, and to the editors of this volume, Munis Faruqui and Vasudha Dalmia, for their close reading of this essay. Their constructive criticisms have helped to strengthen and refine the argument.

[1] Peter Hardy, "Modern European and Muslim Explanations of Conversion to Islam in South Asia: A Preliminary Survey of the Literature," in *Conversion to Islam*, ed. Nehemia Levtzion (New York: Holmes and Meier, 1979), 68–99;

I describe below. They pondered the motives behind such conversions, and whether they resulted in immediate transformations or in a more gradual transformation of affiliations and practices. I thus hope to show that such polemics about religious conversion are not a peculiarly colonial and modern phenomenon, but that they were already prevalent in the Mughal Empire during the late sixteenth and seventeenth centuries.[2] A careful reading of Mughal-era accounts also shows us how *all* identities and affiliations—Hindu, Muslim, Rajput—should be comprehended only within particular contexts. Such contexts could range from the normative relations between overlords and newly subjugated vassals, to the place of marriage, to sexual access to a community's women. In that sense, this essay outlines a series of such contextualized discussions of affiliation during the Mughal era, rather than discussing instances of conversion in terms of their consequences for belief and ritual practice.[3]

Richard M. Eaton, *The Rise of Islam and the Bengal Frontier, 1204–1760* (Delhi: Oxford University Press, 1997), 113–19; and Carl Ernst, "The Indian Environment and the Question of Conversion," in *Eternal Garden: Mysticism, History, and Politics at a South Asian Sufi Center* (Delhi: Oxford University Press, 2004), 155–68. For a critique of the historiography of Muslim conquest in South Asia and an attempt to write an alternative account, see Shahid Amin, "On Retelling the Muslim Conquest of South Asia," in *History and the Present*, ed. Partha Chatterjee and Anjan Ghosh (New Delhi: Permanent Black, 2002), 19–32.

[2] For debates about conversion to Christianity in eighteenth-century western India, see Ines G. Zupanov, "Conversion Historiography in South Asia: Alternative Indian Christian Counter-histories in Eighteenth Century Goa," *The Medieval History Journal* 12, no. 2 (2009): 303–25; for discussions of conversion in southern India in the same period, see Susan Bayly, *Saints, Goddesses and Kings: Muslims and Christians in South Indian Society, 1700–1900* (Cambridge: Cambridge University Press, 1989).

[3] Devin DeWeese has similarly shown how in Turkic and Inner Asian contexts, narratives of conversion to Islam routinely speak of entry into a community and submission to its norms. In this sense, they speak of a change of status rather than a change of heart, hoping and expecting that the latter will occur over time. See *Islamization and Native Religion in the Golden Horde: Baba Tukles and Conversion to Islam in Historical and Epic Tradition* (University Park: Pennsylvania State University Press), 1994, esp. 17–27. I am grateful to Jamal J. Elias for this citation.

Academic interest in the subject was initially focused on the material incentives offered by conversion to Islam. Aligarh "school" historians of Sultanate and Mughal India—based primarily at Aligarh Muslim University in India—thus emphasized the fact that Islamic doctrine ostensibly offered lower-caste groups greater equality than Brahminical Hinduism.[4] Richard Eaton's critique of this older historiography is well known: that the regions with the most instances of mass conversion, in the far west and east of the subcontinent, were regions where Brahminical Hinduism with its elaborate social hierarchies had never been very strong. Eaton's own work on the ecological and political frontier zone of Bengal points to the role of recipients of land grants—who extended the agrarian frontier through wet rice cultivation—in gradually transforming the eastern parts of the Ganges–Brahmaputra delta into a Muslim majority region. Pious Muslims in East Bengal later construed some of these early modern grantees as "Sufis," in seeking to explain their origins.[5] Equally, in the instance of one lineage in the far west of the subcontinent, the Siyals of Punjab, Eaton has shown how accommodation within Sufi patronage networks led to a gradual transition to visibly Muslim names between the fourteenth and early nineteenth centuries.[6] Eaton's work has thus helped to explain long-term processes of mass Islamization in South Asia, driven by individuals who were as much agrarian settler landlords as they were wielders of the charismatic

[4] See, for instance, Mohammad Habib, "Introduction to Elliot and Dowson's *History of India*, Vol. II," in *Politics and Society during the Early Medieval Period: Collected Works of Professor Mohammad Habib*, ed. K.A. Nizami (New Delhi: People's Publishing House, 1974), I, 72–73; and K.A. Nizami, "Hind: v. Islam," in *Encyclopedia of Islam, Second Edition*, ed. P. Bearman, Th. Bianquis, C.E. Bosworth, E. van Donzel, and W.P. Heinrichs (Leiden: Brill, 2012), http://www.brillonline.nl/subscriber/entry?entry=islam_COM-0290, accessed April 16, 2012.

[5] For a useful summary of the argument in *The Rise of Islam and the Bengal Frontier*, see Richard M. Eaton, "Who Are the Bengal Muslims? Conversion and Islamization in Bengal," in *Essays on Islam and Indian History* (Delhi: Oxford University Press, 2000), 249–75.

[6] Richard M. Eaton, "The Political and Religious Authority of the Shrine of Baba Farid," in *Moral Conduct and Authority: The Place of* Adab *in South Asian Islam*, ed. Barbara Daly Metcalf (Berkeley: University of California Press, 1984), 333–56.

authority associated with the shrines of Sufi pirs. In parallel, biographical memoirs (*tazkirat*) of Sufi lineages and the recorded conversations of prominent Sufi pirs (*malfuzat*) also conventionally described contests between Sufi pirs and Hindu yogis, in which the Sufi usually triumphed. Suitably inspired, the yogi, and sometimes onlookers as well, converted to Islam. Given that such hagiographic traditions were concerned about exalting particular Sufi lineages and their most prominent charismatic figures, they tell us more about the "strategies of prestige" that resonated with Sufi communities than they do about the nature of the conversion and its consequences for the convert and his kin.[7]

The inscriptional evidence from Rajasthan suggests that processes akin to the ones described by Eaton for western Punjab and eastern Bengal were at work here too. By the fourteenth century, we start to find segments of artisanal groups who had clearly become Muslim. Thus a baker (*khabbaz*) Raja Ramadan built a mosque in Didwana (Nagaur district) in 1377–1378 CE. Evidence from the sixteenth and seventeenth centuries is more widespread, as we see weavers, stonecutters, washermen, oil crushers, shoemakers, barbers, and blacksmiths building or repairing mosques in towns like Bari Khatu, Didwana, and Merta.[8] The inscriptional evidence also offers tantalizing suggestions of the social affiliations of some of these groups. Thus we learn of Muhammad, son of Usman Chauhan, who built a mosque in village Dinjawas (Nagaur district) in 1655. We learn of other Chauhans who had become Muslim in Bari Khatu town (also in Nagaur district). Nahir Chauhan or Nahir Shah, son of Miyan Shah, built a mosque in 1639 at the dargah of Samman Shah in the town; we know from one of the inscriptions at the mosque that Miyan Shah and his son were stonecutters. Jamal Shah, son of Adam, son of Jumishah of the Chauhan community, built another mosque in the same

[7] Simon Digby, "To Ride a Tiger or a Wall? Strategies of Prestige in Indian Sufi Legend," in *According to Tradition: Hagiographical Writing in India*, ed. Winand M. Callewaert and Rupert Snell (Wiesbaden: Harrassowitz Verlag, 1994), 99–130. For an example of a text in which such "strategies of prestige" are deployed, see Bruce B. Lawrence, trans., *Nizam ad-din Awliya: Morals for the Heart: Conversations of Shaykh Nizam ad-din Awliya Recorded by Amir Hasan Sijzi* (New York: Paulist Press, 1992).

[8] Z.A. Desai, *Published Muslim Inscriptions of Rajasthan* (Jaipur: The Directorate of Archaeology and Museums, 1971), 40, 59, 62, 65, 108, 110.

place in 1641.[9] The inscriptional and narrative evidence, however, offers us little additional information about these individuals and groups, or the processes by which they became Muslim.

In contrast to the rich historiography of mass conversions to Islam and the role of Sufis in such processes,[10] less attention has been paid to those members of elite groups—military and landed—who converted to Islam under political pressure, or in the expectation of political gain from a Muslim overlord or patron.[11] While scholars have acknowledged the role of "political patronage" as an incentive for conversion, they have not focused on the consequences for the convert and his kin. In this essay I explore how observers in the late sixteenth and seventeenth centuries actually comprehended instances of elite conversion. Such observers included Persian literati and administrators at the courts of sultans and Mughal emperors, as well as poets, administrators, and chroniclers at the courts of Rajput chiefs who were incorporated into the Mughal Empire as vassals. Regardless of their location and their particular target audiences, all of the writers discussed here were functioning within the political context of the Mughal Empire at its peak, in the late sixteenth and seventeenth centuries.

Mughal-era observers of elite conversions to Islam shared two concerns: they were preoccupied with the impact of conversion upon the affiliations of the new convert, and with his status within existing socio-political hierarchies. Authors patronized by the Mughal overlord were thus often uncertain about the political loyalties of new converts as vas-

[9] Desai, *Published Muslim Inscriptions*, 22, 33.

[10] Richard M. Eaton, "Sufi Folk Literature and the Expansion of Indian Islam," *History of Religions* 14, no. 2 (November 1974): 117-27; Bruce B. Lawrence, "Early Indo-Muslim Saints and Conversion," in *Islam in Asia, vol. 1: South Asia*, ed. Yohanan Friedmann (Jerusalem: Max Schloessinger Memorial Foundation, 1984), 109–45; Raziuddin Aquil, "Sufi Cults, Politics and Conversion: The Chishtis of the Sultanate Period," *Indian Historical Review* 22 (1995-96): 190-97; Raziuddin Aquil, "Conversion in Chishti Sufi Literature (13th-14th Centuries)," *Indian Historical Review* 24 (1997–98): 70-94; and Ernst, *Eternal Garden*.

[11] For an exception, see S.A.A. Rizvi, "Islamic Proselytization: Seventh to Sixteenth Centuries," in *Sufism and Society in Medieval India*, ed. Raziuddin Aquil (New Delhi: Oxford University Press, 2010), 52-69.

sals. In contrast, a seventeenth-century Brajbhasha narrative of a Muslim Rajput lineage celebrated its clan's steadfast loyalty to a succession of Muslim overlords precisely because of shared religious affiliation. At the same time, this clan chronicle was deeply concerned with demonstrating the continuing membership of its author's lineage within the Rajput elite. For their part, authors patronized by the Rajput lineages from which some of these converts were recruited wrote in Marwari and were more concerned with defining the basis of Rajput-hood, and with the basis for membership in the upper ranks of the Rajput elite.

This essay has two objectives: one, to put these sources in conversation with each other, something that has hitherto been rare in the historiography;[12] and second, to comprehend how conversion to Islam among political elites was actually understood by early modern observers. Thus all of the Mughal-era accounts discussed in this essay—in Persian, Marwari, and Brajbhasha—explored the extent to which the motives for conversion expressed the web of power relationships around the convert. All of them were also concerned with the convert's position in relation to other Rajputs (including his kinsmen who had not converted), as well as to his Muslim overlord. That observers as well as converts from the sixteenth and seventeenth centuries could not resolve such questions as neatly as they might have liked suggests how contested the interpretations of Rajput conversions to Islam were during this period. In the modern period, when Rajputs are broadly comprehended in the nationalist imagination as proto-patriots for an immanent nation who resisted invaders, the politics of elite Rajput conversions to Islam in the past remain as contested, although for different reasons that are beyond the scope of this essay.

[12] S. Inayat, A. Zaidi, and Sunita Zaidi describe the Persian and Marwari evidence without exploring their relation to each other. See their "Conversion to Islam and Formation of Castes in Medieval Rajasthan," in *Art and Culture: Felicitation Volume in Honour of Professor S. Nurul Hasan*, eds. Ahsan Jan Qaisar and Som Prakash Verma (Jaipur: Publication Scheme, 1993), 27–42. Heidi Pauwels has recently compared Persian and Braj materials about the Bundela Rajputs in "The Saint, the Warlord, and the Emperor: Discourses of Braj Bhakti and Bundela Loyalty," *Journal of the Economic and Social History of the Orient* 52 (2009): 187–228.

RAJPUTS AND MUSLIM OVERLORDS

In the mid-fifteenth century, the Sisodiyas of Mewar were perhaps the most prominent among the Rajput lineages of western India. Rana Kumbha of Mewar embarked on repeated campaigns against the rival sultans of Gujarat and Malwa, and expanded Mewar's territories at the expense of his Rajput neighbors as well. While Kumbha's successors were forced to give up many of these gains, his grandson Rana Sanga successfully mobilized a significant coalition against the Mughal Babur in the 1520s. The triangular rivalry between Mewar and the Malwa and Gujarat Sultanates that persisted between the mid-fifteenth century and the 1520s offered opportunities for advancement to enterprising warlords such as the Purabiya Rajput Silhadi.

Born in the hinterland of Gwalior (less than two hundred miles south of Delhi), Silhadi rose to prominence as an associate of Medini Rai, the Rajput warlord who, in 1514, had been appointed wazir (minister) at the court of Mahmud Khalji II in Malwa. By 1520, Rana Sanga of Mewar had married his daughter to the increasingly prominent Silhadi. By 1529, Silhadi had antagonized the Malwa sultan and fled to the court of Bahadur Shah in Gujarat. In 1531 he aided his new overlord against the old one in Malwa. In return, he was given the *sarkar*s of Ujjain and Sarangpur in *iqta* (transferable revenue assignments), along with control of the strategic fort of Raisen. However, his control over his home territories as well as his rank among the amirs at the Gujarat court remained contentious issues in his negotiations with his new overlord. In January 1532 Bahadur Shah laid siege to Raisen. This was the context in which Silhadi offered to surrender, accept Bahadur Shah's terms, and convert to Islam. In the accounts that have come down to us, Bahadur Shah does not initially insist upon Silhadi's conversion as a precondition to his surrender.[13]

By the 1570s, the Mughal Emperor Akbar had successfully marginalized most potential rivals in northern India through his military campaigns.

[13] This account of Silhadi is based on Upendra Nath Day, *Medieval Malwa: A Political and Cultural History 1401–1562* (Delhi: Munshiram Manoharlal, 1965), 280–319; and Dirk Kolff, *Naukar, Rajput and Sepoy: The Ethnohistory of the Military Labour Market in Hindustan, 1450–1850* (Cambridge: Cambridge University Press, 1990), 85–110.

Against this backdrop, imperial service offered the pre-eminent avenue for advancement for ambitious Rajputs. Over the next century, Rajput chiefs and their troops played a significant role in expanding and preserving Mughal conquests across the Indian subcontinent. The importance of the Rajputs is best gauged by the fact that, through the first half of the seventeenth century, roughly one in every six or seven *mansabdars* in the Mughal aristocratic order was a Rajput chief.[14] It was especially at the middle and lower rungs of the Mughal hierarchy that some Rajputs converted to Islam.[15]

Members of some older Muslim Rajput lineages also rose to prominence in Mughal imperial service. Taj Khan Khatriya, in all likelihood Taj Khan Chauhan, the Kyamkhani[16] chief from Fatehpur, is listed as holding a rank of 200 *zat* in Abul Fazl's *Ain-i Akbari*. His grandson Nyamat Khan, better remembered as Jan Kavi, composed the Brajbhasha verse chronicle commemorating his lineage, the *Kyamkhan Rasa*, between 1630 and 1655. As Cynthia Talbot has pointed out, Jan Kavi's chronicle provides us with an invaluable window into the worldview and concerns of a prominent Muslim Rajput lineage in the mid-seventeenth century.[17] Those concerns were articulated in a discursive context in which others—overlords and their chroniclers, as well as rival Rajput chiefs and their chroniclers—were all expressing a range of attitudes toward such

[14] Between 1575 and 1595, there were 27 Rajput chiefs and Hindu officials among a total of 184 *mansabdars* with a rank of 500 *zat* and above. See Iqtidar Alam Khan, "The Nobility under Akbar and the Development of his Religious Policy, 1560–1580," *Journal of the Royal Asiatic Society of Great Britain and Ireland* 1–2 (April 1968): 36. In 1647–68, during Shah Jahan's reign, there were 73 Rajputs among a total of 443 *mansabdars*. John F. Richards, *The Mughal Empire*, vol. I.5 of *The New Cambridge History of India* (Cambridge: Cambridge University Press, 1995), 145.

[15] For instances, see S. Inayat, A. Zaidi and Sunita Zaidi, "Conversion to Islam."

[16] Since Jan Kavi used Brajbhasha to narrate his lineage's history, my transliterations follow the Brajbhasha throughout in referring to the Kyamkhani Chauhan chiefs.

[17] Cynthia Talbot, "Becoming Turk the Rajput Way: Conversion and Identity in an Indian Warrior Narrative," *Modern Asian Studies* 43, no. 1 (2009): 211–43.

Rajputs who were already Muslim, or who were converting to Islam in the present.

PERSIAN CHRONICLERS AND THEIR PERSPECTIVES

Chroniclers and their patrons at the Mughal court expressed unease about the loyalties of Rajput converts to Islam. As I show below, Persian-language chroniclers were articulating attitudes validated by Islamic doctrine and confirmed by political realities in early modern north India. Such attitudes are apparent when we consider two Persian-language accounts of Silhadi Purabiya's "conversion." The first appears in Nizam al-Din Ahmad's *Tabaqat-i Akbari*, completed in 1594 (some sixty years after Silhadi's death). Ahmad had served as Akbar's *bakhshi* for the Mughal province of Gujarat in 1585 and for the entire empire in 1593. The second major account appears in Sikandar Manjhu's *Mirat-i Sikandari*, completed in 1613. Manjhu was a mid-level official in the Mughal province of Gujarat; he supervised the administration of the *jagir* of the Bukhari Saiyids of Betwa and Dholka, who belonged to a powerful faction at the court of the Gujarat sultans. In 1610, Manjhu joined the Mughal administration.[18]

In the *Tabaqat-i Akbari*, Silhadi expresses his desire to convert to Islam when besieged at Raisen by Bahadur Shah: "This slave (*banda*) wishes to be dignified with the nobility of Islam (*beh sharf-i Islam musharraf gardad*); and after that if he gets leave, he would go above, and after evacuating the fort, make it over to the representative of the Bahadur Shahi government."[19] Akbar's chronicler Nizam al-Din Ahmad ascribes Silhadi's

[18] S.C. Misra has pointed out how Manjhu's rootedness in Gujarat, his nostalgia for its former sultans, and his loyalty to his Bukhari Saiyid patrons colored his perspective. At the same time, the *Mirat* was clearly intended to be read as local knowledge by a Mughal audience, as apparent from Emperor Jahangir's appreciation for its author's grasp of Gujarati history and politics. Misra, introduction to *The Mirat-i-Sikandari: A History of Gujarat from the Inception of the Dynasty of the Sultans of Gujarat to the Conquest of Gujarat by Akbar, of Shaikh Sikandar ibn Muhammad urf Manjhu ibn Akbar*, ed. S.C. Misra and M.L. Rahman (Baroda: Maharaja Sayaji Rao University, 1961), 42–51.

[19] *The Tabaqat-i Akbari of Khwajah Nizamuddin Ahmad (A History of India from the Early Musalman Invasions to the Thirty-Eighth Year of the Reign of Akbar)*,

impulse to convert to his recognition of "the weakness of the Purabias, and the great strength of the enemy (*quwwat-i khasam*)." Whatever the Rajput's motives, Ahmad represents Bahadur Shah as delighted upon hearing this news: "The Sultan repeated to him the words expressing the unity of God (*kalma-i tawhid*). When Silhadi accepted the faith (*iman award*), the Sultan gave him a special robe of honour (*khil'at-i khas*); and sent him various kinds of food from the (royal) kitchen."[20]

In Sikandar Manjhu's *Mirat-i Sikandari* as well, Silhadi expresses an intent to become a Muslim (*man musalman mishawam*)[21] when the fort of Raisen, still under his control, is being bombarded by Bahadur Shah's artillery. Manjhu's account adds a further detail, however, to the story of the pressure on Silhadi. In the *Mirat-i Sikandari*, when Silhadi first arrived at Bahadur Shah Gujarati's court in 1529, the sultan honored Silhadi with a gift of 700 robes of gold and 70 horses, and then with an additional gift of 30 elephants and 1,500 robes.[22] As negotiations continued over Silhadi's appropriate rank at the Gujarat court, Bahadur Shah sent Malik Amin Nas to persuade the Purabiya chief to present himself at court. Silhadi was reluctant to do so. The chronicler Sikandar Manjhu has Malik Amin, clearly hostile to Silhadi, aver: "this accursed one in fact deserved death (*wajib-ul-qatl*) since he had seized (*tasarruf*) Muslim women (*'aurat-i muslimat*) from their husbands and kept them in his house as concubines (*tasallut*)." Manjhu represents the sultan's reaction with approval: "This wretch (*badbakht*) keeps Muhammadan women in his house, and by the Holy Law of the Prophet (*bar hukm-i shari'-i sharif*)

trans. B. De, rev. and ed. Baini Prashad (Calcutta: Asiatic Society of Bengal, 1996), III, 360; Persian text ed. B. De and M. Hidayat Hosain (Calcutta: Asiatic Society of Bengal, 1935), III, 221. I have provided the Persian text in parentheses and retained the original spelling of Brajendranath De's English translation.

[20] *Tabaqat-i Akbari*, trans. B. De, III, 360; Persian text, III, 221.

[21] Sikandar, *Mirat-i Sikandari or The Mirror of Sikandar, by Sikandar, the Son of Muhammad, Alias Manjhu, Gujarati*, trans. Fazlullah Lutfullah Faridi (Gurgaon: Vintage Books, 1990), 172; Persian text, Sikandar, *Mirat-i Sikandari*, ed. Misra and Rahman, 284. I have provided the Persian text in parentheses and retained the original spelling of Faridi's English translation.

[22] *Mirat-i Sikandari*, trans. Faridi, 165; Persian text, 275.

he deserves death (*wajib-ul-qatl*). I will never let him go alive unless he becomes a Musalman (*magar an keh musalman shawad*)."[23]

The taking of female captives from the households of political rivals had long been a practice confirming the victor's sovereignty.[24] What is significant in Sikandar Manjhu's account is that in order to justify their military campaign against Silhadi, both Bahadur Shah himself and his emissary invoke the particular charge of Silhadi having Muslim women in his household. Furthermore, in Sikandar's account, the charge of holding captured Muslim women becomes legitimate ground for the killing of Silhadi unless he converts to Islam. This is the context for the siege of Raisen, and this is the context in which Silhadi expresses an intent to become a Muslim (*man musalman mishawam*).

Sikandar Manjhu, however, adds a further discussion of Silhadi's religious conversion, one that he says was known among "reliable people" in Gujarat. The account is striking and worth quoting in full:

> When Silahdi was imprisoned and asked to accept Islam, he would on no account agree (*beh hich wajh qabul nemikard*), and it was with great difficulty (*bas'ai-yi bisyar wa kushish beshumar*) that he did himself the honour of entering Islam, and was named Salah-ud-din (righteous of religion). It was ordered that Malik Burhan-ul-mulk Bunyani, who was unequalled in probity and religious devotion, should attend to the religious instruction of the man and should inculcate in him the principles of the Sacred Law (*talaqin-i ahkam-i shara'*). It is said that when Silahdi first observed the fasts of the month of Ramzan, he was much pleased and said he had never found food and water taste so exquisitely delicious as they did after a fast. He used to say that while yet a Hindu he had once asked a Brahman whether there was a way to forgiveness for the innumerable sins and shortcomings of which he was guilty. The Brahman said there was none. He then asked a Musalman Mulla the same question, and the Mulla said there certainly was hope of forgiveness for the worst of sinners, but the Mulla said he was afraid to say by what

23 *Mirat-i Sikandari*, trans. Faridi, 170; Persian text, 281–82.

24 Daud Ali, "War, Servitude, and the Imperial Household: A Study of Palace Women in the Chola Empire," in *Slavery and South Asian History*, ed. Indrani Chatterjee and Richard M. Eaton (Bloomington: Indiana University Press, 2006), 44–62; Ramya Sreenivasan, "Drudges, Dancing Girls, Concubines: Female Slaves in Rajput Polity, 1500–1850," *Slavery and South Asian History*, ed. Chatterjee and Eaton, 136–61.

way he could get salvation. Silahdi said that when he assured the Mulla of his safety, he said that if a sinner entered Islam with a truly penitent heart he would become as pure as a babe newborn (*agar musalman shawad chunan pak migardad ki goya az shikam-i madar bar amadeh*). He said he was really inclined towards Islam in the fullest sense of the term (*mail beh din-i Islam budam*) from that day.[25]

For the chronicler Sikandar, Silhadi's conversion is seen as a process following upon his initial, political decision to convert. Following his religious instruction under a devout nobleman at Bahadur Shah's court, he fasts during the month of Ramzan, thereby observing one of the central pillars of the Islamic faith. He is then educated by a "Mulla" about the greater possibility of redemption that Islam offers to all sinners who truly repent. Whether or not Silhadi actually experienced this transformation, the chronicler lays out for us familiar milestones along the journey that conversion is understood to entail in Islamic thought.[26] These include the invocation of the key trope of repentance (*tawba*), signaling Silhadi's recognition of the superior grace of Islam. Also implicit in Manjhu's account is a broader Muslim critique: namely that Hindu notions of karma and rebirth do not allow for the possibility of repentance wiping the slate clean, as it were, and enabling an individual to start afresh without sin. Manjhu contrasts such Muslim interpretations of karma with Islamic teachings that emphasize how nobody is held responsible for their ancestors' deeds and how sincere repentance can indeed pave the way for new beginnings.[27]

The accounts of Nizam al-Din Ahmad and Sikandar Manjhu, produced six to eight decades after Silhadi's death, are not necessarily to be taken as indicating the Purabiya Rajput's actual motives. These Mughal-era accounts do, however, tell us how Mughal chroniclers interpreted such acts in terms of their consequences. In the *Tabaqat-i Akbari*,

25 *Mirat-i Sikandari*, trans. Faridi, 175–76; Persian text, 287–88.

26 William M. Brinner and Devin J. Stewart, "Conversion," in *The Oxford Encyclopedia of the Islamic World*, *Oxford Islamic Studies Online*, http://www.oxfordislamicstudies.com/article/opr/t236/e0165, accessed April 16, 2012; L. Gardet, "Īmān," in *Encyclopaedia of Islam*, ed. Bearman, Bianquis, Bosworth, van Donzel, and Heinrichs.

27 I am grateful to Jamal J. Elias for pointing out the resonance of Manjhu's account with systemic Muslim critiques of Hindu doctrine.

Silhadi's brother Lakhman argues that Bahadur Shah and his court will read Silhadi's conversion as proof of his transformed loyalties. He thus declares that the conversion has saved Silhadi's life: "Now it is not right, according to their religion, to shed your blood (*khun rikhtan-i tu beh mazhab-i ishan jayez nist*)." Silhadi similarly expects political gains from becoming a member of his new overlord's group (*zumrat*). Ahmad reports Silhadi telling his brother Lakhman, "As I am now included in the community of Musalmans (*Islamiyan*), Sultan Bahadur will, either on account of a feeling of communal favour (*beh jihat-i ri' ayat*), or on account of his noble spirit (*'ulu-yi himmat*), raise me to a high rank (*maratib-i 'ala*)." However, the Mughal chronicler also represents Silhadi as transcending mere opportunism; at this point he fully intends to be loyal to his new overlord: "It is fit that after surrendering the fort to the adherents of the Sultan, I should bind the girdle of service strongly (*kamar-i khidmat ra mustahkam bastah*) and continue to render him service."[28]

And yet, Nizam al-Din Ahmad remains uneasy about the new convert's brother who had not converted to Islam. In the *Tabaqat-i Akbari*, Silhadi's brother Lakhman sees his conversion as a stratagem to buy them time, so that Silhadi's son Bhupat may bring his father-in-law, Rana Sanga of Mewar, to their rescue with 40,000 men. When Silhadi brings word of the sultan's offer to grant the *qasba* of Baroda to him, his queen, Durgawati, and brother Lakhman demur. They state: "Still for many generations (*'amreha ast*) this country has been in our possession (*saltanat-i in diyar beh ma moyassar ast*), in reality (*dar m'ani*) if not in name like an empire ... The right way of bravery (*tariq-i mardanagi*) is this, that we should perform *jauhar* of our women and children, and should ourselves fight and be slain; and there should be no further longing left in our hearts." Silhadi is inspired by their example and joins them, rejecting his new overlord's offer: "If we are killed with our women and children, what honour and glory (*'izz wa sharf*)!" In his death, then, Silhadi reasserts his solidarity with his fellow Rajputs, and is dispatched to hell (*beh jahannum*) with them, according to the author of the *Tabaqat-i Akbari*.[29]

Nizam al-Din Ahmad's account reveals his own uncertainties. At one level, he expects that conversion to Islam should result in the new convert

28 *Tabaqat-i Akbari*, trans. B. De, III, 360–61; Persian text, III, 221.

29 *Tabaqat-i Akbari*, trans. B. De, III, 366–67; Persian text, III, 225–26.

changing his political loyalties to align with those of his new, Muslim overlord. Such expectations were intrinsic to the Islamic understanding of conversion, in which a convert was taken to be rejecting his old community and entering a new one, thereby permanently realigning his loyalties.[30] The *Tabaqat-i Akbari* thus depicts Silhadi as determined to serve his new overlord loyally, if only in pursuit of high rank.

On the other hand, Nizam al-Din Ahmad is skeptical as to whether the conversion will turn Silhadi decisively against his fellow Rajputs.[31] Silhadi's final decision only confirms his suspicions. It is worth remembering that Nizam al-Din Ahmad had been the Mughal emperor's *bakhshi*—paymaster for the Mughal army—in Gujarat. His account of Silhadi can thus be read as pointing to his awareness of the mutability of alliances and loyalties on the ground, especially the loyalty owed by newly subjugated vassals to imperial overlords. In the turbulent sixteenth century that had seen several aggressive attempts at building conquest empires, Ahmad would have been well aware of the routine deviations from such norms. It is no surprise, therefore, that the Mughal chronicler sees a tension between Silhadi's loyalties as a new Muslim and his loyalties as a Rajput. As his old loyalties to his Rajput brethren reassert themselves, the nature and extent of his conversion to Islam are tacitly called into question.

As in the *Tabaqat-i Akbari*, so in the *Mirat-i Sikandari* as well, all the relevant actors interpret Silhadi's expressed desire to convert to mean that he will accept Bahadur Shah as overlord and surrender the Raisen fort to the Sultan. As Sikandar Manjhu spells out the nature of Silhadi's acceptance of the Muslim faith, he also expects that Salah al-Din would

[30] Gardet, "Īmān." Such expectations were not uncommon as seen in other historical contexts in which widespread conversions to Islam occurred. For the seventeenth-century Ottoman Empire, see Marc David Baer, *Honored by the Glory of Islam: Conversion and Conquest in Ottoman Europe* (New York: Oxford University Press, 2008), 23–24, passim. I am grateful to Jamal J. Elias for this citation.

[31] In an earlier period, the prominent Chishti Nizam al-Din Awliya had expressed comparable skepticism about forced conversions, and emphasized how hearts could only be transformed gradually through the company of pious people. See Raziuddin Aquil's discussion, "Conversion in Chishti Sufi Literature," 85.

be more loyal to his new overlord, Sultan Bahadur Shah, than Silhadi Rajput would have been. And yet, such hopes are revealed as naive in the *Mirat-i Sikandari*. Thus, as in the *Tabaqat-i Akbari*, in Manjhu's account too, Silhadi and his Rajput brother Lakhman Sen expect that becoming a Muslim will bring Silhadi tangible political benefits—at least he will not be suspected by the sultan and his advisors.

As Dirk Kolff points out, Bahadur Shah offers the Purabiya warlord the *sarkar* of Baroda, far from Raisen and its hinterland where he would typically recruit the soldiers who made him such a formidable military presence in the Malwa region. It is far clearer to Silhadi's wife Durgawati and to his followers that he has run out of options. They prefer to die with their honor intact, the men in battle and the women in *jauhar* (mass immolation). In death, then, Silhadi has returned to being one of the *hinduwan*.[32] It is significant that while the chronicler Sikandar had earlier recounted Silhadi's transformation as marked by a genuine affinity toward Islam, he reads the latter's final decision to return to his fellow Rajputs and join them in battle against Bahadur Shah as a return to the *hinduwan*. And in Sikandar's account, this final apostasy, as much as his holding of Muslim women in his harem, legitimizes Bahadur Shah's final assault on the Raisen fort in which the Purabiya chief is killed.

Thus Nizam al-Din Ahmad and Sikandar Manjhu, both writing chronicles that would circulate in Persian-literate circles at the Mughal court, concur in their ultimate assessment of Silhadi's conversion to Islam. Both chroniclers recount intense political pressure as the context in which Silhadi considered becoming a Muslim. Both concur in regarding his conversion as driven by his own calculations of political gain from sharing the religion of his new overlord. Both chroniclers also hope that the conversion to Islam will transform Silhadi's political loyalties; and both see Silhadi's conversion as ultimately failing to do so. Furthermore, both chroniclers see Silhadi's new overlord, Sultan Bahadur Shah of Gujarat, as being aware of this possibility; the Purabiya warlord remains under close scrutiny and continues to be distrusted by the sultan and his close associates. Ultimately, nobody in either Mughal account seems surprised at Silhadi's quick return to solidarity with his Rajput kinsmen and kinswomen. What is noteworthy is that in both accounts of a

32 *Mirat-i Sikandari*, trans. Faridi, 174–75; Persian text, 286–87.

Rajput warlord's conversion to Islam in a politically volatile environment, politics—as opposed to any consideration of spiritual or ritual transformations—remains the primary ground on which the nature and extent of the conversion are evaluated.

A MUSLIM RAJPUT'S PERSPECTIVE

As we have just seen, Mughal chroniclers hoped, somewhat futilely, that Silhadi Purabiya's conversion to Islam would confirm his loyalty to his new Muslim overlord and therefore turn him away from his Rajput brethren who had not converted. In contrast to that perspective of an imperial chronicler, the heroic narrative of a Muslim Rajput lineage of aspiring imperial vassals from the mid-seventeenth century suggests a very different relationship between being Rajput and being Muslim. Nyamat Khan or Jan Kavi's *Kyamkhan Rasa* was composed in northeastern Rajasthan between 1630 and 1655. A heroic verse chronicle written in Brajbhasha, it recounts the glorious deeds of the Kyamkhani clan, known after their founder Kyam Khan, or Qawam Khan Chauhan, of Hisar in modern Haryana (a hundred miles west of Delhi). The Kyamkhanis controlled the environs of Fatehpur and Jhunjhunu in northeastern Rajasthan during the sixteenth and much of the seventeenth centuries.[33]

We see their emergence in the local arena in northern Rajasthan by the early sixteenth century. Contemporary chroniclers mention their defeat by the Bikaner ruler Rao Lunkaran in 1512.[34] In 1552, Nawab Daulat Khan constructed a palace in Fatehpur and had a Persian inscription engraved on it.[35] By the end of the sixteenth century the Kyamkhani Rajputs had attracted Mughal attention for their military resources. Abu'l Fazl mentions the Kyamkhanis as controlling the towns of Narhar, Fatehpur, and Jhunjhunu. He estimated that Fatehpur and Narhar could each muster

[33] For a history of the clan based mainly on the *Kyamkhan Rasa*, see Sunita Budhwar Zaidi, "The Qayamkhani Shaikhzada Family of Fatehpur-Jhunjhunu," *Proceedings of the Indian History Congress* 39 (1978): 412–25.

[34] Richard D. Saran and Norman P. Ziegler, trans., *The Mertiyo Rathors of Rajasthan: Select Translations Bearing on the History of a Rajput Family, 1462–1660* (Ann Arbor: Centers for South and Southeast Asian Studies, University of Michigan, 2001), II, 194.

[35] Z.A. Desai, *Published Muslim Inscriptions*, 72.

500 horsemen and 2,000 foot soldiers; while Jhunjhunu was estimated to be able to muster 2,000 cavalry and 3,000 infantry.[36] By 1595–96, Taj Khan "Khatriya" had been awarded a Mughal *mansab* of 200.[37] As Talbot notes, this was the lowest rank of *mansab* listed by Abu'l Fazl; however, Taj Khan was one of a total of only 283 men recognized as *mansabdar*s who were expected to provide cavalry for the Mughal army, in a period *prior* to the steady inflation of *mansab* ranks under Akbar's successors in the seventeenth century.[38] Taj Khan's son Alif Khan rose to the more substantial *mansab* rank of 2000/1500 by the end of his life, and was appointed Mughal commander of the strategic fort of Kangra in 1622–23.[39] Alif Khan's son Daulat Khan also attained the rank of 1500/1000 in the 1640s.[40] It was Daulat Khan's brother, Nyamat Khan or Jan Kavi, who composed the clan's heroic genealogy between 1630 and 1655.

The *Kyamkhan Rasa* begins with the explicit assertion that *haindu* and *musalman* share the same ancestor (*pind*) Adam, and therefore the same blood; they ended up having different names because of their different deeds (*pai karani nahina milai, tatein nyare nam*).[41] Furthermore, Chauhan and Pathan, Uzbek and Hindi, were all sons of the same patriarch Noah.[42] As Talbot points out, Jan Kavi insistently affirms the Chauhan identity of the Kyamkhanis, the term Chauhan figuring at least 136 times in the *Kyamkhan Rasa*.[43] In Jan Kavi's account, his progenitor

36 Abu al-Fazl ibn Mubarak, *'Ain-i Akbari*, trans. H.S. Jarrett (Calcutta: Asiatic Society of Bengal, 1891), II, 194, 277. See also Talbot, "Becoming Turk the Rajput Way," 212–13.

37 M. Athar Ali, *The Apparatus of Empire: Awards of Ranks, Offices and Titles to the Mughal Nobility (1574–1658)* (Delhi: Oxford University Press, 1985), 27 [# A740].

38 Talbot, "Becoming Turk the Rajput Way," 227–28, esp. fn. 48.

39 Ali, *Apparatus of Empire*, 84 [#J1365].

40 Ali, *Apparatus of Empire*, 194 [#S3935], 216 [#S3194].

41 Dasharath Sharma, Agarchand Nahta, and Bhanwarlal Nahta, eds *Kavi Jan krt Kyamkhan Rasa*, trans. Ratanlal Mishra, 3rd ed. (Jodhpur: Rajasthan Prachyavidya Pratishthan, 1996), vss 14–15.

42 Sharma, Nahta, and Nahta, *Kavi Jan kit Kyamkhan Rasa*, vss 32–34.

43 Talbot, "Becoming Turk the Rajput Way," 234; for her suggestive analysis of this genealogy, see 234–37.

Karamchand, son of Moterao Chauhan, the chief of Dadreva, was made *turak* and given the name of Kyamkhan by the emperor (*patisah*).

In stark contrast to the Persian-language accounts by Nizam al-Din Ahmad and Sikandar Manjhu discussed above—of a Rajput converting to Islam under intense political pressure—Jan Kavi's account of the conversion recounts the charisma (*karamat*) of the sleeping boy Karamchand, the recognition of this charisma by the great man Saiyid Nasr and his patron the Sultan of Delhi,[44] the latter's "loving embrace" of the boy and his offer of respect and honor (*adara*, *mana*), and the boy's education with Saiyid Nasr.[45] The boy Karamchand's anxious father Moterao goes to the emperor's court at Hisar and is greeted with great cordiality (*pyar*) by the *patisah*.[46] The sultan reassures the father that he has not made Karamchand a *turak*, he will treat him as a son, and will award him the rank of 5000[47]—a clearly anachronistic reference to the Mughal *mansab* ranks that were so familiar by the mid-seventeenth century when the *Kyamkhan Rasa* was composed. The father, duly honored, returns to his home—he has not been expected to convert to Islam himself and is confident of his son's prospects. His teacher and mentor Saiyid Nasr next invites Karamchand to do namaz and enter the faith following the completion of his education.[48] Jan Kavi recounts how his forefather's mind was already turned toward the faith, presumably because of the affection and the education he had received. However, in the *Kyamkhan Rasa*, the young man Kyamkhan is anxious that if he does formally convert to Islam, none of his peers will marry their daughters to him.[49] His mentor Saiyid Nasr assuages this anxiety by prophesying that the biggest rulers of the age will wish to marry their daughters to Kyamkhan.[50] Significantly, the term used to describe such rulers, Karamchand's assumed peers even after he becomes Kyamkhan, is *rai*—clearly referring to Rajputs rather than Muslim sultans. Jan Kavi clearly assumes that while his forefather

[44] Sharma, Nahta, and Nahta, *Kavi Jan krt Kyamkhan Rasa*, vss 129–31.
[45] Sharma, Nahta, and Nahta, *Kavi Jan krt Kyamkhan Rasa*, vs. 133.
[46] Sharma, Nahta, and Nahta, *Kavi Jan krt Kyamkhan Rasa*, vs. 139.
[47] Sharma, Nahta, and Nahta, *Kavi Jan krt Kyamkhan Rasa*, vs. 140.
[48] Sharma, Nahta, and Nahta, *Kavi Jan krt Kyamkhan Rasa*, vs. 148.
[49] Sharma, Nahta, and Nahta, *Kavi Jan krt Kyamkhan Rasa*, vs. 149.
[50] Sharma, Nahta, and Nahta, *Kavi Jan krt Kyamkhan Rasa*, vs. 151.

Kyamkhan entered the faith and was an unquestioned Muslim, he was still definitively a Rajput.

The warrior Kyamkhan serves Sultan Firuz Shah with great distinction, defeating the Mughals and sending all the loot to the emperor without keeping anything for himself. At his home in Hisar, all the lineages with customary rights on the land (*bhomia*) come to serve under him—Kachhwaha, Bhati, Tonwar, Ghori, Jatu, Khokhar, and Chandel, from Dunpur, Bhatner, Kalpi, Etawah, Ujjain, and Dhar, and all the Mewasis in between. This is a region extending from parts of modern west Punjab and Sind in the west to the western parts of Madhya Pradesh and Uttar Pradesh in the east. While such territorial and political claims are clearly inflated, they nevertheless reveal the Kyamkhani Chauhans' sense of who their strongest rivals were at the time of *Kyamkhan Rasa*'s composition—the Kachhwahas of Amber (controlling the hinterlands to the south of Kyamkhani domains), and the Rathors of Marwar and Bikaner (to the west). Thus Kyamkhan's son Akhan Khan (Ikhtiyar Khan) subjugates the *bhomia*s of Amber and Amarsar.[51] His brother Mauna Chauhan is the enemy of the Kurmas (Kachhwahas) and defeats their chief Kuntal.[52]

In Jan Kavi's account, the other rival of the Kyamkhanis, the Rathor chief Jodha, is compelled to seek peace with the Chauhan Fatan Khan by seeking a matrimonial alliance with him. In a gesture suggesting Jan Kavi's interpretation of their respective political ranks in the *Kyamkhan Rasa*, it is Jodha who sends the ceremonial coconut offering his daughter in marriage. But Fatan Khan refuses the alliance; he is still angry at Jodha's brother Kandhal for killing his warrior Bahugun.[53] So Jodha, still seeking an alliance with the Kyamkhanis, sends a coconut to another Kyamkhani, Samas Khan, at Jhunjhunu instead, and the alliance is accepted there. Jan Kavi's account loses no opportunity to assert the superior rank of the Kyamkhanis in these negotiations. Samas Khan of Jhunjhunu accepts the offer from Rao Jodha, but then refuses to travel to Jodhpur for the wedding. Instead, he sends his sword, and the Rathor chief sends his daughter back with the sword in a palanquin (*dola*)[54]—the equivalent of acknowledging Samas Khan as his overlord.

[51] Sharma, Nahta, and Nahta, *Kavi Jan krt Kyamkhan Rasa*, vs. 326.

[52] Sharma, Nahta, and Nahta, *Kavi Jan krt Kyamkhan Rasa*, vs. 329.

[53] Sharma, Nahta, and Nahta, *Kavi Jan krt Kyamkhan Rasa*, vss 432–33.

[54] Sharma, Nahta, and Nahta, *Kavi Jan krt Kyamkhan Rasa*, vss 434–36.

It is worth noting here that in the 1640s Daulat Khan Chauhan rose to a maximum *mansab* rank of 1,500/1,000 as the *faujdar* (commandant) of Kangra fort. In the same years, Jaswant Singh Rathor of Marwar had a *mansab* rank of 5,000/5,000.[55] As is well known in the scholarship, *mansab* rank in the Mughal hierarchy indicated both imperial estimates of the military resources of the chief involved, as well as imperial perceptions of their importance to the empire. In describing Rao Jodha's matrimonial proposals, Jan Kavi was therefore clearly asserting the pre-eminence of his forefathers for a target audience of rival Rajput chiefs, even though at the present moment those rivals far outstripped his own kinsmen in entitlements and resources. The preoccupation with marriage alliances as indicating the Kyamkhanis' pre-eminence among their peers continues through the *Kyamkhan Rasa*. Samas Khan's son Fateh Khan of Jhunjhunu marries the daughter of the Delhi Sultan Bahlul Lodi;[56] the Bikavat Rathors marry the daughter of their chief, Rao Lunkaran of Bikaner, to Nahar Khan of Fatehpur, thereby accepting his overlordship. Even Emperor Akbar is seen expressing his desire for a marriage alliance; he eventually marries Fadan Khan's daughter.[57]

Jan Kavi also suggests that there were advantages to being Muslim *mansabdar*s in the Mughal Empire. In the *Kyamkhan Rasa*, the emperor does not trust his (Rajput) *bhomia*s as they tend to become wayward and rebellious (*gumaraha*). He wants some assurance of their continued loyalty, so he urges Fadan Khan Chauhan to stand surety for the other *bhomias*. In Jan Kavi's account, this was how Fadan Khan became *zamin* (guarantor) for the *bhomias*.[58] It is not clear if the episode ever occurred; nevertheless, it suggests how the Kyamkhani Chauhans perceived their dual affiliations as Muslim and as Rajput. The first gave them greater reliability and legitimacy as allies and trusted vassals of the Mughal Emperor, at least in their own eyes; and the second allowed them to act as trusted mediators between other Rajput chiefs and the Mughal emperor, again, in their own opinion. Thus, in Jan Kavi's account, it is Fadan Khan of Fatehpur who first helps to induct Raisal Shekhawat (better known in the

55 Ali, *Apparatus of Empire*, 166 [#S2275], 204 [#S3569].

56 Sharma, Nahta, and Nahta, *Kavi Jan krt Kyamkhan Rasa*, vs. 464.

57 Sharma, Nahta, and Nahta, *Kavi Jan krt Kyamkhan Rasa*, vs. 638.

58 Sharma, Nahta, and Nahta, *Kavi Jan krt Kyamkhan Rasa*, vss 640–41.

Mughal chronicles as Raisal Darbari) into Mughal service by presenting him at the imperial court and having a *mansab* rank awarded to him.[59]

In strenuously asserting the Kyamkhanis' position in the upper echelons of the Rajput hierarchy, Jan Kavi narrates how the other prominent Rajput lineages acknowledged this pre-eminence repeatedly, in every generation as it were. Thus Dalpat Rathor of Bikaner, defeated by Fadan Khan's grandson Alif Khan, once again hails the latter as the preserver of all the *bhomias*' honor.[60] For his part, the Mughal emperor continues to depute the Kyamkhani chiefs against their wayward fellow Rajputs. Daulat Khan Chauhan is thus sent out to subjugate the Kurmas (Kachhwahas) of Pataudhi and Rasulpur, who have been thieving and killing livestock, and is given the rights to collect revenue from those two Shekhawat Kachhwaha domains.[61] For his part, Alif Khan Chauhan achieves the pinnacle of Rajput glory by dying in the battle to conquer the Kangra fort for his Mughal overlord. So great are his exploits on the battlefield that he is praised not only by the traditional Dhadhi, Bhat, and Charan poets who sing of the martial exploits of Rajput warriors, but even by the emperor himself.[62] In his death, then, as in his life, Alif Khan Chauhan, like his Kyamkhani forebears, successfully reasserts his dual affiliations, heritage, and politics—as Muslim and as Rajput.

OTHER RAJPUT PERSPECTIVES

How does one assess the value of Jan Kavi's claims for his contemporaries in the middle and later decades of the seventeenth century? In order to get a sense of that contemporary reception, we must consider the implications of the *Kyamkhan Rasa* being composed in Brajbhasha rather than in Persian. We must also consider how Jan Kavi's contemporaries among other major Rajput lineages may have perceived the Kyamkhanis and other Muslim Rajputs. When we see that these other Rajput perceptions are largely confirmed by Mughal imperial assessments of status

59 Sharma, Nahta, and Nahta, *Kavi Jan krt Kyamkhan Rasa*, vs. 642.

60 Sharma, Nahta, and Nahta, *Kavi Jan krt Kyamkhan Rasa*, vss 713–16.

61 Sharma, Nahta, and Nahta, *Kavi Jan krt Kyamkhan Rasa*, vss 756–63.

62 Sharma, Nahta, and Nahta, *Kavi Jan krt Kyamkhan Rasa*, vs. 895. The *Kyamkhan Rasa* does not identify the Mughal emperor by name here but Kangra was conquered in 1622 during the reign of Jahangir.

hierarchies among the Rajput lineages, the exaltation of the Kyamkhanis in the *Kyamkhan Rasa* takes on a different hue.

This essay has so far outlined how Persian-language chroniclers at the courts of Muslim rulers were ambivalent about the effect of conversion to Islam upon a Rajput's relationship with his Muslim overlord, especially when his Rajput kinsmen and associates did not convert as well. Where the Persian-language chroniclers thus saw a tension between the politics of being Rajput and being Muslim among new converts in particular, the chronicle of a Muslim Rajput lineage from the mid-seventeenth century offered the opposite perspective—it asserted that the Kyamkhani Chauhans were both Rajput and Muslim, and that they were respected and honored by both other Rajput lineages and Muslim overlords.

In the context of such claims, it is significant that Nyamat Khan Chauhan or Jan Kavi chose to compose his narrative in Brajbhasha, a language that was firmly identified with devotional bhakti traditions—both Vaishnava and *nirgun*—by the sixteenth and seventeenth centuries. I have referred earlier in this essay to the Persian-language inscription from 1552 at the palace in Fatehpur that one of Jan Kavi's forebears had commissioned. That inscription clearly indicates that the Kyamkhanis were aware of the resources that Persian offered for assertions of lordship throughout this period. By comparison, Brajbhasha was a newer literary language, initially associated with the poetic compositions of devotional communities in northern India. At least one of the leaders of one such community, Sundardas of the Dadupanth, may have been more directly associated with the Kyamkhani nawabs of Fatehpur.[63] From the late sixteenth century onward, however, Brajbhasha also found a hospitable reception at Rajput and Mughal courts, with rulers and prominent courtiers offering patronage to Brajbhasha poets. A prominent Mughal aristocrat such as Abdur Rahim Khan-i Khanan and a Rajput ruler such as Jaswant Singh Rathor of Marwar also went on to compose Braj poetry and a treatise on Braj poetics respectively. As Allison Busch has shown recently, by the early

[63] Monika Thiel-Horstmann, *Crossing the Ocean of Existence: Braj Bhasa Religious Poetry from Rajasthan* (Wiesbaden: Otto Harrassowitz, 1983), 3–14; Dasharath Sharma, "Kyamkhan Rasa ke Kartta Kavivar Jan aur unke granth," in Sharma, Nahta, and Nahta, *Kavi Jan krt Kyamkhan Rasa*, 11–12; Talbot, "Becoming Turk the Rajput Way," 231.

seventeenth century Braj aesthetics were linked with (and shaped by) "the politics and court culture of Mughal India."[64]

And yet, as Busch acknowledges, Persian remained the dominant literary language at the Mughal court, while the Rajput courts emerged as the most significant locations for the composition and circulation of Brajbhasha poetry in the seventeenth century. Jan Kavi's choice of Brajbhasha while composing the *Kyamkhan Rasa* may therefore suggest his desire to align the Kyamkhani ethos with that of fellow Rajput lineages in the mid-seventeenth century. Moreover, Jan Kavi is reputed to have composed several dozen other narratives as well, all in Brajbhasha and none in Persian, and drawing on both Persianate and Indic romance themes.[65] While it is difficult to say more in the absence of further evidence, Jan Kavi's poetic oeuvre actually confirms that he was as deeply immersed in the linguistic and cultural repertoire of Brajbhasha as many other members of the contemporary Rajput elite.

As Talbot argues, the *Kyamkhan Rasa* thus demonstrates how Jan Kavi and other Kyamkhani Chauhans inhabited multiple cultural realms. In some of its cultural referents, the narrative displays a familiarity with stock Islamic tropes such as a genealogy tracing Kyamkhani origins back to Adam through Noah. At the same time, the particular expressive resources that Brajbhasha offered to Jan Kavi are displayed most brilliantly in the description of the narrative's climax: the death in battle of Alif Khan Chauhan, the poet's father. As Jan Kavi narrates it, the Diwan (Alif Khan) died by the sword, and his Rajput honor (*raja*) was demonstrated for the entire world.[66] So fierce was the battle that the ash-smeared Shiva, his trident, skull bowl, and shield in hand, came to the battlefield and danced.[67] The yoginis too could be seen drinking

[64] Allison Busch, *Poetry of Kings: The Classical Hindi Literature of Mughal India* (New York: Oxford University Press, 2011), 244. For Abdul Rahim Khan-i Khanan, see Busch, *Poetry of Kings*, 138–40; for Jaswant Singh Rathor's *Bhashabhushan* on Braj aesthetics, see Busch, *Poetry of Kings*, 176–78.

[65] Sharma, Nahta, and Nahta, "Kyamkhan Rasa ke Kartta," 5–10; Vina Lahoti et al., eds *Jan Granthavali Bhag 3: Premakhyan Sangraha* (Jodhpur: Rajasthan Prachyavidya Pratishthan, 2004); Vandana Singhvi et al., eds *Jan Granthavali Bhag 4: Premakhyan Sangraha* (Jodhpur: Rajasthan Prachyavidya Pratishthan, 2005).

[66] Sharma, Nahta, and Nahta, *Kavi Jan krt Kyamkhan Rasa*, vss 879–81.

[67] Sharma, Nahta, and Nahta, *Kavi Jan krt Kyamkhan Rasa*, vs. 897.

from the oceans of blood on the battlefield, and eating the flesh of the dead warriors.[68] A reader familiar with other instances of the *raso*, the heroic chronicle form associated with Rajput contexts in northern and western India, will recognize the stock tropes of that genre here. Thus the great rajas, *raos*, *ranas*, *umrao*, and kings wish they could die in the same fashion.[69] Appropriately, Alif Khan reaches Amarapura after his death, having become immortal (*amara*). That is, he goes to Vaikuntha in the year 1683 (Samvat).[70] In this striking description of a Muslim Rajput warrior attaining a distinctly Hindu heaven through the manner of his heroic, appropriately Rajput, death on the battlefield, Jan Kavi shows his intimate familiarity with the poetic resources of Brajbhasha and with their precise cultural valence.

More remarkably, the poet then infuses Persianate Islamic vocabulary into this description, so that the significance of Alif Khan's death is dramatically enlarged. Thus the warriors who die with Alif Khan on the battlefield are *mujahid* (engaged in a war seen as holy);[71] and he himself has, in addition to dying like a true Rajput, also achieved martyrdom (*sahadat*).[72] Miracles then became manifest, and the world did pilgrimage, yearning to worship at his tomb shrine:

> *Karamata*$_{P}$ *paragata*$_{I}$ *bhayi, jyarata*$_{P}$ *karata jahana*$_{P}$
> *Dekhata daragaha*$_{P}$ *kau, pujata*$_{I}$ *icchhya*$_{I}$ *prana*$_{I}$*...*[73]

> Seeing the light at the dargah, one's sorrows are banished; the childless obtain sons, the pauper wealth; the heedless finds wisdom, such miracles occur by the grace of God. Alif Khan Chauhan was not greedy for his life, he had obtained the rewards of remaining loyal to his overlord. The dargah is full of blessings, full of *jahur*; seeing the light at the dargah, one's sorrows are removed.

[68] Sharma, Nahta, and Nahta, *Kavi Jan krt Kyamkhan Rasa*, vss 904, 908.

[69] Sharma, Nahta, and Nahta, *Kavi Jan krt Kyamkhan Rasa*, vs. 929.

[70] Sharma, Nahta, and Nahta, *Kavi Jan krt Kyamkhan Rasa*, vss 930, 933.

[71] Sharma, Nahta, and Nahta, *Kavi Jan krt Kyamkhan Rasa*, vs. 914.

[72] Sharma, Nahta, and Nahta, *Kavi Jan krt Kyamkhan Rasa*, vs. 929. Transliterated from the Brajbhasha variant of the Persian term.

[73] Sharma, Nahta, and Nahta, *Kavi Jan krt Kyamkhan Rasa*, vs. 934. The subscript markers help identify terms of Persianate (P) and Indic (I) origins in Jan Kavi's verses here.

Hota dukha$_{I}$ *dura dekhain nura*$_{P}$ *daragahakau*$_{P}$
Niradhana$_{I}$ *pavai bitu*$_{I}$ *nirasuta*$_{I}$ *pavai suta*$_{I}$
Aisi adbhuta$_{I}$ *bata karama*$_{I}$ *ilahakau*$_{P}$ ...
Alifakhan chahuvana lobha$_{I}$ *nahin kinau prana*$_{I}$
Payo phala$_{I}$ *rakhyau svamadharma*$_{I}$ *paisahakau*
Nyamata sampura$_{I}$ *hai jahura*$_{P}$ *hajira*$_{P}$ *hajura*$_{P}$
Hota dukha$_{I}$ *dura dekhen nura*$_{P}$ *daragahakau*$_{P}$ ...[74]

We may be tempted to infer a melding of Hindu and Islamic practices from this seamless merging of Sanskritic and Persianate vocabularies, as, for instance, in the desire to offer puja at a dargah to which one has made *ziyarat* (pilgrimage). Fragmentary ethnographic evidence from the late nineteenth century suggests just such a melding of practices among the Kyamkhanis.[75] However, further evidence would be needed to explore whether Jan Kavi's description of his father's death and of the subsequent worship at his tomb constitutes a brilliant poetic blending of distinct cultural vocabularies and their semiotics, or whether it gestures to a more pervasive blending of Hindu and Muslim beliefs and practices, particularly those pertaining to death and the afterlife, among the Kyamkhani Rajputs.

And how did Jan Kavi's Rajput peers receive his claims about the Kyamkhanis being both favored Muslim vassals of the Mughal overlord and pre-eminent among the Rajput lineages? As discussed above, the *Kyamkhan Rasa* reveals a deep anxiety about whether the Kyamkhanis' Rajput peers will continue to marry into their clan once they convert to Islam. Whether or not such anxieties were current in the fourteenth century when Karamchand Chauhan is said to have converted and become Kyam Khan, marriages certainly were a key arena for negotiating status hierarchies among the Rajput lineages by the seventeenth century when the *Kyamkhan Rasa* was composed.

Jan Kavi lists the multiple marriages between the Kyamkhani chiefs over the generations and the daughters of other prominent Rajput lineages. What is more, in each instance it is the head of the peer lineage

[74] Sharma, Nahta, and Nahta, *Kavi Jan krt Kyamkhan Rasa*, vs. 936.

[75] "The Bhati Musalmans ... and the Chohans ... Kaimkhanis ... scarcely differ in their customs and manners from the Hindu Rajputs." Munshi Hardyal Singh, *The Castes of Marwar: Being (Census Report of 1891)*, 2nd ed. (Jodhpur: Books Treasure, 1991), 18.

who seeks the marriage alliance with the Kyamkhani chief in question—a maneuver clearly suggesting the superior status of the Kyamkhanis. Among the Rajput chiefs who seek such alliances in the *Kyamkhan Rasa* are some of the most prominent figures of the period. As I argue above, the issue is a significant enough indicator of status for Jan Kavi that he has his progenitor hold off on turning toward Islam until his Sufi mentor reassures him that he will not lose rank in the matrimonial arena. And Jan Kavi returns to the issue again when he sees the alliance with Rao Jodha as fulfilling the Sufi prophecy about the Kyamkhanis' exalted rank ratified through their marriage alliances.

In contrast to these claims, the evidence of matrimonial alliances recovered from Bhat genealogies of other Rajput lineages suggests that while the Kyamkhanis did enter into marriage alliances with other Rajput lineages such as Chauhan, Tanwar, and even Rathor, these were with the daughters of chiefs who controlled far more modest resources—sometimes a single village.[76] Furthermore, when we look for corroborative evidence in seventeenth-century Rathor genealogies, we find no references to the major marriage alliances with the Rathors mentioned in the *Kyamkhan Rasa*. Even assuming that genealogies were progressively rewritten such that alliances that had lost some of their status value could be marginalized in later redactions of such lineage maps, it is significant that Muhata Nainsi's chronicle of the Rajput lineages, compiled shortly after the *Kyamkhan Rasa* was composed, mentions not a single Kyamkhani marriage. It is important not to read this absence of evidence in the Rathor genealogies and chronicles as evidence of absence—that is to say, that there had never been marriage alliances between the Kyamkhanis and the Rathors before the mid-seventeenth century. What does emerge clearly, however, is that by the time Nainsi compiled his encyclopedic *Khyat*, he and his Rathor patrons had clearly removed the Kyamkhanis from any list of peer Rajput lineages with whom the Rathors could enter into marriage alliances.

By way of comparison, it is revealing that Nainsi does record elsewhere that (in the mid-sixteenth century) Rao Maldeo's daughter Kanakavati

[76] Ratanlal Mishra, *Kyamkhani Vansh ka Itihas evam Sanskriti* (Jodhpur: Rajasthani Granthagar, 2002), 164–69. I have been unable to locate the unnamed Bhat genealogies cited by Mishra.

married the Gujarat Sultan Mahmud, and another daughter Ratanavati was married to Haji Khan Pathan,[77] the Afghan lieutenant of Sher Shah Sur who controlled Ajmer and Nagaur briefly in the 1550s. Similarly, the eighteenth-century chronicler Bankidas records how Rao Maldeo married his daughter, Bai Kankan, to Sultan Mahmud of Gujarat, another daughter, Jasodabai, to the Khan of Nagaur, and a third daughter, Lalbai, to Sher Shah Sur after being defeated by him at the Battle of Samel.[78] Thus not all Rajput–Muslim marriages were erased from seventeenth- and eighteenth-century Rathor genealogies.

Nainsi also derides the Kyamkhanis' status as lowly, in contrast to his descriptions of other Rajputs who had become Muslim. He recounts without any editorializing how Bhuhad Solanki became a *turak* (*turak huva*) in Sind, and his son Rujha Solanki became a *turak* in Thatta.[79] Similarly, one segment of the Bhatis near Jaisalmer, the Mangariyas, "were *hindu* earlier, now for some reason they have become *musalman*."[80] Nainsi's hostility to the Kyamkhanis in particular might then well reflect his affiliation with the Rathor court in Jodhpur, as Talbot argues; the Rathors, while clearly superior in might and status to the Kyamkhanis, might still have regarded them as rivals, although lesser ones. And yet, the terms of his derision are suggestive.

According to the *Khyat*, when Saiyid Nasir of Hisar, governor for the sultan of Delhi, attacked Darera, its Chauhan inhabitants fled, leaving behind two boys, one Chauhan and the other Jat. Saiyid Nasir took both boys back to his wife, who raised them. When the two boys were ten and twelve, they were handed over to the local Sufi shaikh who brought them up. After Saiyid Nasir's death, his son took these two boys to the court of Bahlul Lodi in Delhi, and gifted them to the sultan. The sultan did not notice Saiyid Nasir's son, but did notice the Chauhan boy and gifted him

77 Muhata Nainsi, *Muhata Nainsi ri Likhi Marwar ra Parganan ri Vigat*, ed. Narayan Singh Bhati (Jodhpur: Rajasthan Prachyavidya Pratishthan, 1968–1974), I, 52.

78 Narottam Das Swami, ed., *Bankidas ri Khyat* (Jodhpur: Rajasthan Prachyavidya Pratishthan, 1989), 20.

79 Muhata Nainsi, *Muhata Nainsi virachit Muhata Nainsi ri Khyat*, ed. Badariprasad Sakariya (Jodhpur: Rajasthan Prachyavidya Pratishthan, 1960–1967), I, 80.

80 Nainsi, *Muhata Nainsi ri Khyat*, II, 31.

with Saiyid Nasir's *mansab*, and made him the faujdar of Hisar. Later, the sultan also granted him Jhunjhunu in *jagir*. Nainsi appends an epigrammatic verse to the end of this brief account:

> First they were *hindu*, then they became *turakka*
> So first they became slaves (*golai*), then in adulthood, menial (*tukka*).

In contrast to Jan Kavi's elaborate representation of his progenitor Karamchand Chauhan's entirely *voluntary* conversion to Islam, Nainsi depicts the conversion as following upon the Chauhan boy being raised at the Lodi court, where he had been given to the sultan. Nainsi spells out the implications of such a transfer of the Chauhan boy to the Lodi sultan: it had resulted in the boy becoming a *golai*, a slave and a menial.

Nainsi's *Khyat* clearly ranks the various Rajput lineages in order of prominence—we see this in the amount of space given to the different lineages. Where the Rathors of Jodhpur and Bikaner, the Sisodias of Udaipur, and the Kachhwahas of Amber take up most of the space in the four volumes of the modern critical edition of the *Khyat*, the Kyamkhani Chauhans of Fatehpur-Jhunjhunu take up three pages. The Purabiya Rajputs are similarly given a cursory three pages. One indication of hierarchy was material: how many horses and soldiers a given lineage could muster, and the lineage's relationship with the regional and/or imperial overlord. However, Nainsi's compilation of his *Khyat*, and his account of the Kyamkhanis within it, also suggest how, by the mid-seventeenth century, the elite Rajput lineages had begun to articulate the grounds for a sharper hierarchy among themselves. In this period, they began to commission the systematic production and preservation of manuscript genealogies, thereby streamlining, reorganizing, and controlling more tightly their remembered record of ancestors and alliances.

Furthermore, starting in Akbar's reign, the size of *jagir* grants and *mansab* ranks functioned as an index parallel to the internal ranking mechanisms evolving among the Rajput clans. In this context, it is worth reiterating that for all their martial exploits, the Kyamkhani Chauhans never rose beyond the middle levels of Mughal *mansabdar* ranks. Alif Khan, Jan Kavi's father, achieved the most success in these terms, as he was rewarded with the rank of 2000/1500 in 1621–22 for his loyal military service. Neither his predecessors nor his successors attained that rank. The available evidence thus suggests that Muslim Rajputs within the cohort of Mughal *mansabdars* did not fare dramatically better than their Hindu Rajput peers. If anything, they seem to have fared somewhat worse. While this is likely to have been because of the superior military resources that the latter commanded, it is still noteworthy that being Muslim brought no visible advantages to the Kyamkhani Chauhans in ascending the Mughal hierarchy during the late sixteenth and seventeenth centuries. When reviewed in the light of evidence such as Nainsi's account emerging from a pre-eminent contemporary Rajput court, and the sparse references in Mughal sources, Jan Kavi's celebration of his Kyamkhani forebears starts to look a little less exultant and a little more anxious.

***

This essay has outlined varying perspectives from Mughal, Rajput, and Muslim Rajput courts, in the high Mughal era, about Rajput elites who converted to Islam. Mughal chroniclers displayed much unease about the loyalties of Rajputs who were compelled to convert under political pressure. They seem to have been concerned not so much with the ethics of such conversion as with its efficacy in procuring the desired consequence—of the Rajput confirming his allegiance to his new overlord through entering the community of Islam. Neither of the two chroniclers whose accounts of one such conversion—by Silhadi Purabiya—we have explored in this essay is particularly surprised when Silhadi ultimately returns to the Rajput fold in the arena that mattered most, of loyalty. In this sense, the Mughal chroniclers seem to have concurred, Silhadi remained Rajput, and by implication his conversion to Islam remained incomplete.

While the instance of Silhadi raises the issue of converts to Islam from among the upper echelons of the Rajput hierarchy and the tussle between their old and new loyalties, the *Kyamkhan Rasa* provides the perspective of a Muslim Rajput lineage, which, at least at the cultural level, effortlessly tapped into the resources of both a martial Rajput ethos as well of a lived Islam, Sufi in its orientation. Jan Kavi repeatedly asserts how his lineage is foremost among the Rajputs by virtue of being Chauhan. He also avers that his clansmen are trusted to a greater degree by the Mughal overlord because of the greater familiarity and trust that came from a shared Muslim identity. In Jan Kavi's world, then, Shiva danced at Alif Khan Chauhan's death on the battlefield, paving the way for his tomb to become a dargah where pilgrims have their every wish granted because Alif Khan died a true Rajput, loyal to the Mughal emperor.

When we consider the Kyamkhani Chauhans' fortunes in the seventeenth century, as well as opinions of them in rival Rajput courts, their successes seem more modest. It is debatable whether being Muslim brought them any special favor from the Mughal emperor in terms of entitlements or privileges. And it seems that being Muslim and aspiring to be seen as pre-eminent among the Rajput lineages actually brought upon them some ire from the Jain chronicler of another, Hindu Rajput lineage that was in fact significantly higher on the *mansabdari* "totem pole." In Nainsi's epigrammatic formulation, *turakka* is made to rhyme with *tukka* (lowly, menial); whether or not such hostility was motivated by political rivalries on the ground, it was articulated in terms denigrating the status of an ambitious Muslim Rajput lineage. Across Persian, Marwari, and Brajbhasha accounts, then, there was no easy consensus either on the significance of members of the Rajput elite converting to Islam, or on the impact of such conversion upon their status within a more sharply drawn Rajput hierarchy by the seventeenth century. The political benefits of being a Muslim Rajput or becoming one during the Mughal period remained contested.

BIBLIOGRAPHY

Abu al-Fazl ibn Mubarak. *'Ain-i Akbari*. Translated by H.S. Jarrett. 2 volumes. Calcutta: Asiatic Society of Bengal, 1891.

Ahmad, Khwajah Nizamuddin. *Tabaqat-i Akbari*. Edited by B. De and M. Hidayat Hosain. 3 volumes. Calcutta: Asiatic Society of Bengal, 1935.

———. *The Tabaqat-i Akbari of Khwajah Nizamuddin Ahmad (A History of India from the Early Musalman Invasions to the Thirty-Eighth Year of the Reign of Akbar)*. 3 volumes. Translated by B. De, revised and edited by Baini Prashad. Calcutta: Asiatic Society of Bengal, 1996.

Ali, Daud. "War, Servitude, and the Imperial Household: A Study of Palace Women in the Chola Empire." In *Slavery and South Asian History*, edited by Indrani Chatterjee and Richard M. Eaton, 44–62. Bloomington: Indiana University Press, 2006.

Ali, M. Athar. *The Apparatus of Empire: Awards of Ranks, Offices and Titles to the Mughal Nobility (1574–1658)*. Delhi: Oxford University Press, 1985.

Amin, Shahid. "On Retelling the Muslim Conquest of South Asia." In *History and the Present*, edited by Partha Chatterjee and Anjan Ghosh, 19–32. New Delhi: Permanent Black, 2002.

Aquil, Raziuddin. "Conversion in Chishti Sufi Literature (13th–14th Centuries)." *Indian Historical Review* 24 (1997–98): 70–94.

Aquil, Raziuddin. "Sufi Cults, Politics and Conversion: The Chishtis of the Sultanate Period." *Indian Historical Review* 22 (1995–96): 190–97.

Baer, Marc David. *Honored by the Glory of Islam: Conversion and Conquest in Ottoman Europe*. New York: Oxford University Press, 2008.

Bayly, Susan. *Saints, Goddesses and Kings: Muslims and Christians in South Indian Society, 1700–1900*. Cambridge: Cambridge University Press, 1989.

Brinner, William M. and Devin J. Stewart. "Conversion." In *The Oxford Encyclopedia of the Islamic World. Oxford Islamic Studies Online*. http://www.oxfordislamicstudies.com/article/opr/t236/e0165. Accessed April 16, 2012.

Busch, Allison. *Poetry of Kings: The Classical Hindi Literature of Mughal India*. New York: Oxford University Press, 2011.

Day, Upendra Nath. *Medieval Malwa: A Political and Cultural History 1401-1562*. Delhi: Munshiram Manoharlal, 1965.

Desai, Z.A. *Published Muslim Inscriptions of Rajasthan*. Jaipur: The Directorate of Archaeology and Museums, 1971.

DeWeese, Devin. *Islamization and Native Religion in the Golden Horde: Baba Tukles and Conversion to Islam in Historical and Epic Tradition*. University Park: Pennsylvania State University Press, 1994.

Digby, Simon. "To Ride a Tiger or a Wall? Strategies of Prestige in Indian Sufi Legend." In *According to Tradition: Hagiographical Writing in India*, edited by Winand M. Callewaert and Rupert Snell, 99–130. Wiesbaden: Harrassowitz Verlag, 1994.

Eaton, Richard M. "Sufi Folk Literature and the Expansion of Indian Islam." *History of Religions* 14, no. 2 (November 1974): 117–27.

_____. "The Political and Religious Authority of the Shrine of Baba Farid." In *Moral Conduct and Authority: The Place of* Adab *in South Asian Islam*, edited by Barbara Daly Metcalf, 333–56. Berkeley: University of California Press, 1984.

_____. "Who Are the Bengal Muslims? Conversion and Islamization in Bengal." In *Essays on Islam and Indian History*, by Richard M. Eaton, 249–75. Delhi: Oxford University Press, 2000.

_____. *The Rise of Islam and the Bengal Frontier, 1204–1760*. Delhi: Oxford University Press, 1997.

Ernst, Carl. *Eternal Garden: Mysticism, History, and Politics at a South Asian Sufi Center*. Delhi: Oxford University Press, 2004.

Gardet, L. "Īmān." In *Encyclopaedia of Islam, Second Edition*. Edited by P. Bearman, Th. Bianquis, C.E. Bosworth, E. van Donzel, and W.P. Heinrichs. Leiden: Brill, 2011. http://www.brillonline.nl/subscriber/entry?entry=islam_COM-0370. Accessed April 16, 2012.

Habib, Mohammad. "Introduction to Elliot and Dowson's *History of India*, Vol. II." In *Politics and Society during the Early Medieval Period: Collected Works of Professor Mohammad Habib*, edited by K.A. Nizami, I, 33–110. New Delhi: People's Publishing House, 1974.

Hardy, Peter. "Modern European and Muslim Explanations of Conversion to Islam in South Asia: A Preliminary Survey of the Literature." In *Conversion to Islam*, edited by Nehemia Levtzion, 68–99. New York: Holmes and Meier, 1979.

Inayat, S., A. Zaidi, and Sunita Zaidi. "Conversion to Islam and Formation of Castes in Medieval Rajasthan." In *Art and Culture: Felicitation Volume in Honour of Professor S. Nurul Hasan*, edited by Ahsan Jan Qaisar and Som Prakash Verma, 27–42. Jaipur: Publication Scheme, 1993.

Khan, Iqtidar Alam. "The Nobility under Akbar and the Development of his Religious Policy, 1560–1580."*Journal of the Royal Asiatic Society of Great Britain and Ireland* 1–2 (April 1968): 29–36.

Kolff, Dirk. *Naukar, Rajput and Sepoy: The Ethnohistory of the Military Labour Market in Hindustan, 1450–1850.* Cambridge: Cambridge University Press, 1990.

Lahoti, Vina et al., eds. *Jan Granthavali Bhag 3: Premakhyan Sangraha.* Jodhpur: Rajasthan Prachyavidya Pratishthan, 2004.

Lawrence, Bruce B. "Early Indo-Muslim Saints and Conversion." In *Islam in Asia, Vol. 1: South Asia*, edited by Yohanan Friedmann, 109–45. Jerusalem: Max Schloessinger Memorial Foundation, 1984.

——, trans. *Nizam ad-din Awliya: Morals for the Heart: Conversations of Shaykh Nizam ad-din Awliya Recorded by Amir Hasan Sijzi.* New York: Paulist Press, 1992.

Mishra, Ratanlal. *Kyamkhani Vansh ka Itihas evam Sanskriti.* Jodhpur: Rajasthani Granthagar, 2002.

Misra, S.C. Introduction to *The Mirat-i-Sikandari: A History of Gujarat from the Inception of the Dynasty of the Sultans of Gujarat to the Conquest of Gujarat by Akbar, of Shaikh Sikandar ibn Muhammad urf Manjhu ibn Akbar*, edited and introduction with notes by S.C. Misra and M.L. Rahman, 42–51. Baroda: Maharaja Sayaji Rao University, 1961.

Nainsi, Muhata. *Muhata Nainsi ri Likhi Marwar ra Parganan ri Vigat.* 3 volumes. Edited by Narayan Singh Bhati. Jodhpur: Rajasthan Prachyavidya Pratishthan, 1968–1974.

——. *Muhata Nainsi virachit Muhata Nainsi ri Khyat.* 4 volumes. Edited by Badariprasad Sakariya. Jodhpur: Rajasthan Prachyavidya Pratishthan, 1960–1967.

Nizami, K.A. "Hind: v. Islam." In *Encyclopedia of Islam, Second Edition.* Edited by P. Bearman, Th. Bianquis, C.E. Bosworth, E. van Donzel, and W.P. Heinrichs. Leiden: Brill, 2012. http://www.brillonline.nl/subscriber/entry?entry=islam_COM-0290. Accessed April 16, 2012.

Pauwels, Heidi. "The Saint, the Warlord, and the Emperor: Discourses of Braj Bhakti and Bundela Loyalty."*Journal of the Economic and Social History of the Orient* 52 (2009): 187–228.

Richards, John F. *The Mughal Empire*. Volume I.5 of *The New Cambridge History of India*. Cambridge: Cambridge University Press, 1995.

Rizvi, S.A.A. "Islamic Proselytization: Seventh to Sixteenth Centuries." In *Sufism and Society in Medieval India*, edited by Raziuddin Aquil, 52–69. New Delhi: Oxford University Press, 2010.

Saran, Richard D. and Norman P. Ziegler, trans. *The Mertiyo Rathors of Rajasthan: Select Translations Bearing on the History of a Rajput Family, 1462–1660*. 2 volumes. Ann Arbor: Centers for South and Southeast Asian Studies, University of Michigan, 2001.

Sharma, Dasharath, Agarchand Nahta, and Bhanwarlal Nahta, eds. *Kavi Jan krt Kyamkhan Rasa*. Translated by Ratanlal Mishra. 3rd edition. Jodhpur: Rajasthan Prachyavidya Pratishthan, 1996.

_____. "Kyamkhan Rasa ke Kartta Kavivar Jan aur unke granth." In *Kavi Jan krt Kyamkhan Rasa*, edited by Dasharath Sharma, Agarchand Nahta, and Bhanwarlal Nahta, translated by Ratanlal Mishra, 3rd edition, 5–13. Jodhpur: Rajasthan Prachyavidya Pratishthan, 1996.

Sikandar. *Mirat-i Sikandari or The Mirror of Sikandar, by Sikandar, the son of Muhammad, alias Manjhu, Gujarati*. Translated by Fazlullah Lutfullah Faridi. Gurgaon: Vintage Books, 1990.

_____. *Mirat-i Sikandari*. Edited by S.C. Misra and M.L. Rahman. Baroda: Maharaja Sayaji Rao University, 1961.

Singh, Munshi Hardyal. *The Castes of Marwar: being (Census Report of 1891)*. 2nd edition. Jodhpur: Books Treasure, 1991.

Singhvi, Vandana et al., eds. *Jan Granthavali Bhag 4: Premakhyan Sangraha*. Jodhpur: Rajasthan Prachyavidya Pratishthan, 2005.

Sreenivasan, Ramya. "Drudges, Dancing Girls, Concubines: Female Slaves in Rajput Polity, 1500–1850." In *Slavery and South Asian History*, edited by Indrani Chatterjee and Richard M. Eaton, 136–61. Bloomington: Indiana University Press, 2006.

Swami, Narottam Das, ed. *Bankidas ri Khyat*. Jodhpur: Rajasthan Prachyavidya Pratishthan, 1989.

Talbot, Cynthia. "Becoming Turk the Rajput Way: Conversion and Identity in an Indian Warrior Narrative." *Modern Asian Studies* 43, no. 1 (2009): 211–43.

Thiel-Horstmann, Monika. *Crossing the Ocean of Existence: Braj Bhasa Religious Poetry from Rajasthan*. Wiesbaden: Otto Harrassowitz, 1983.

Zaidi, Sunita Budhwar. "The Qayamkhani Shaikhzada Family of Fatehpur-Jhunjhunu." *Proceedings of the Indian History Congress* 39 (1978): 412–25.

Zupanov, Ines G. "Conversion Historiography in South Asia: Alternative Indian Christian Counter-histories in Eighteenth Century Goa." *The Medieval History Journal* 12, no. 2 (2009): 303–25.

II

Of Proximity and Distance

7 Inflected *Kathas*

Sufis and Krishna Bhaktas in Awadh

Francesca Orsini

> Once [Hazrat Shah Abdur Razzaq] Bansawi arrived at the home of Chait Ram and Paras Ram in Rampur village, 10 kilometers from Bansa. He found the *bhagatiyas* dancing; one of them played the role of Krishna and the other was dressed as a *gopi*. They sang Sant Kabir's *dohas*. Moved by their songs, the Hazrat fell into a trance. Meanwhile the singing reached a high-pitch note. That is when the Hazrat, now under the spell of the divine, opened his eyes. The audience—Hindu and Muslim zamindars, *bairagis* and *faqirs*—were moved to tears. All those present, rich and poor, were spellbound.[1]

Other essays in this volume lead us to imagine religious interchange as a face-to-face exchange between religious experts—Akbar's famous *'ibadat-khana* or the pandits' *shastrarthas*—or as the philosophical cogitation of keen individuals. The *Harikatha* or tale of Krishna's life that is at the center of this essay leads us instead to imagine oral and performative settings in towns, villages, and homes, courtyards, *chaupals*, or *ahatas* (covered

[1] Quoted in Muzaffar Alam, "Assimilation from a Distance: Confrontation and Sufi Accommodation in Awadh Society," in *Tradition, Dissent and Ideology: Essays in Honour of Romila Thapar*, ed. R. Champakalakshmi and S. Gopal (Delhi: Oxford University Press, 1996), 174. In order not to burden this essay with diacritics, I will limit them to titles and direct quotations. All translations are mine unless indicated otherwise.

assembly spaces and courtyards in the villages) where singers performed and storytellers (*kathavachaks*) recited and expounded in front of mixed audiences like the one described above. While the type of performance will have varied—with or without a book as a substantive source or as a symbolic token, in the language of the gods (= Sanskrit?) or that of men, as part of a ritual offering or as a free-standing performance—the fact that we find the same stories, stock characters, episodes, and religious vocabulary occurring in performative texts that for us belong to different religious traditions suggests that *katha*s (stories) were in fact part of a kind of public sphere (Samira Sheikh has used the suggestive term "religious marketplace").[2] In other words, whether *katha* texts choose to clearly place a particular theological stamp on a story or to work through double channels of exoteric/esoteric signification, and whether they explicitly acknowledge other participants and possible opponents or not, *we* can see them as reflections of debates that encompassed a whole range of actors and audiences.[3] So, for example, whereas we tend to see the *Harikatha* as "belonging" to Krishna bhakti groups and to be attentive only to debates and variations among these groups, in actual terms the range of *Harikatha*s in early modern India, the treatment and inflections of the characters and the story, and audience reactions like that of Shah Abdur Razzaq show that the *chaupal* (here used as a shorthand for open performative spaces) was one site where stories and faith were pooled together. Not in some harmonious fashion, with no distinctions made, but with a partly common idiom and vocabulary allowing poets, performers, and audiences to establish equivalences, not (necessarily) equations or mergings, as Malik Muhammad Jayasi's *Harikatha* will make amply clear.[4] While it would be foolish to generalize, it is

[2] Samira Sheikh, *Forging a Region: Sultans, Traders, and Pilgrims in Gujarat, 1200–1500* (New Delhi: Oxford University Press, 2010), especially chapter 4, "Religion, Politics, and Patronage in a Settling Society."

[3] Someone who clearly acknowledged rival participants in this debate was Tulsidas, who famously accused sants of wishing to "create discourses with *sakhi, sabadi* and *dohra*; the Bhagats of the Kali age explain Bhagati and pillow the Vedas and Puranas." Tulsidas, *Tulasī Granthāvalī, Dohāvalī*, ed. Ram Chandra Shukla (Varanasi: Nagari Pracarini Sabha, 1973–1977), II, 554.

[4] I would like to thank Vasudha Dalmia for help with this formulation, as well as her and Munis Faruqui for their more general comments on this essay.

nonetheless striking that observers at different points in time have noted how the tales represented a palimpsest that was continuously rewritten and reworked across the board.[5]

KRISHNA BHAKTI IN AWADH: A COMPARATIVE PERSPECTIVE

The first thing to say about Krishna bhakti in Awadh is that sectarian and scholarly accounts—skewed not only toward Braj and Puri but also Bengal, Gujarat, and Rajasthan—have hardly anything to say about it. Tradition claims that Vallabha studied and was married in Banaras and occasionally stopped there, but that is about it.[6] So it is actually Sufi sources that alert us to the important circulation and appeal of Krishna bhakti in this area, and it is only within a comparative perspective that we can begin to piece together the context of a *Harikatha* like Malik Muhammad Jayasi's *Kanhāvat* (1540).[7]

[5] See, for example, Father della Tomba's remark in the late eighteenth century that Kabir *panthi*s studied Tulsidas's *Ramcharitmanas*. Quoted in Purushottam Agrawal, *Akath Kahānī Prem kī: Kabīr kī Kavitā aur unkā Samay* (New Delhi: Rajkamal Prakashan, 2009), 143. Also the north Indian Muslim *qasbati* children in Intizar Hussain's narratives who are exposed to different creation stories from their grandparents and from itinerant storytellers; for example, Intizar Husain, *Basti*, trans. Frances W. Pritchett (New Delhi: Indus, 1995).

[6] According to the *Nijvārtā-gharuvārtā*, Vallabha and Vitthalnath traveled all over north India during their various tours. Quoted in Hariharnath Tandon, *Vārtā-sāhitya: Ek Bṛhat Adhyayan* (Aligarh: Bharat Prakashan Mandir, n.d.), 603. In drawing an extensive pilgrimage map, hagiographical texts like the *Caurāsī Baiṭhak* extend the Vallabhan geography of influence over religious sites connected to Ram in this area (e.g., Chitrakut, Ayodhya, Naimisharanya, Hanuman Ghat, Janakpur, etc.). Gokulnatha, *Chaurasi Baithak: Eighty-four Seats of Shri Vallabhacharya*, ed. Vrajesh Kumar, trans. Shyam Das, vol. 10 of *Śrī Vallabha Studies Series* (Delhi: Butala Publications, 1985), 39–45.

[7] Malik Muhammad Jayasi, whose *pem katha* (Awadhi Sufi romance) *Padmāvat* has long been recognized as a masterpiece of Hindi literature, was a Sufi poet who seems to have lived all his life in Jais (now Rae Bareilly district); for a review of the information we have on him, his milieu, and his Sufi pir, see Thomas de Bruijn, *The Ruby in the Dust: Poetry and History of the Indian Padmavat by the Sufi Poet Muhammad Jayasi* (Leiden: Leiden University Press,

Consider these dates and locations. After the "discovery" of Shrinathji in 1492 Vallabhacharya undertook several tours of India. According to the *Śrī Vallabhadigvijaya* he came to Arail, across the river from Prayag/Allahabad, after his son's Vitthalnath's birth in 1515 (VS1572), and returned there again in 1519.[8] It is here, according to the *Caurāsī Vaiṣṇavan kī Vārtā*, that he met Parmananddas (who would become one of the Ashta Chap poets whose songs are part of temple worship). The latter was a Kanaujiya Brahmin who had come and settled in Prayag and made his living as a famous poet-singer of kirtans. Known as Parmanand Svami, he attracted a regular audience and disciples: "a group of listeners always gathered around Paramānanda Svāmī at about eight o'clock at night," and on special occasions he would sing all night long.[9] The sectarian hagiography sets the encounter in the familiar trope of the poet-singer who "did not know how to sing the *lila* of union and sang only of *viraha*" until his meeting with the *acharya* and his sectarian initiation, and then spent the rest of his life singing for the *seva* at one of the sect's Krishna temples in Braj. But we can read this account against the grain and imagine Parmananddas—much like Surdas—as a flourishing and independent singer of Krishna bhakti, already active in one of the urban hearts of Awadh in the first decades of the sixteenth century, *before* a sect like Vallabha's took root.

It was also in Kannauj that the Sufi shaikh 'Abdul Wahid Bilgrami (1510–1608), from the nearby *qasba* of Bilgram, spent part of his life later in the century. He must have heard numerous Krishna songs (*bishnupad*), for he suggested a Sufi mystical interpretation of the terms found in *dhrupad* and *bishnupad* songs in a Persian text he called *Haqā'iq-i*

2012), and Ramya Sreenivasan, *The Many Lives of a Rajput Queen: Heroic Pasts in India c. 1500–1900* (New Delhi: Permanent Black, 2007); for the subsequent fortune of his *Padmāvat*, see Sreenivasan, *The Many Lives of a Rajput Queen*, and Shantanu Phukan, "Through a Persian Prism: Hindi and *Padmāvat* in the Mughal Imagination" (University of Chicago PhD thesis, 2000), 158, 160, who suggests that he interacted with the neighboring Raja of Amethi.

[8] After his trip from Jagadishvara; this is when the *svarupa* of Sri Dwarkanath also came to Arail and stayed with Damodardas Sambhalvale. Dindayalu Gupta, *Aṣṭachāp aur Vallabh-sampradāy* (Prayag: Hindi Sahitya Sammelan, 1970), I, 222n.

[9] Richard Barz, *The Bhakti Sect of Vallabhacharya* (Faridabad: Thomson Press, 1976), 144.

Hindī ("The Truths of India," 1566). This included a systematic treatment of terms related to the story of Krishna, and from the tenor of his explanation it is clear that while the songs greatly appealed to him aesthetically (and emotionally), the *theology* of Krishna bhakti did not interest him at all.[10]

In the case of Krishna songs, *bishnupad* and kirtan, we can imagine them circulating in Awadh through groups of singers, sometimes taught and managed by wandering *bairagi*s, resident *svami*s, and even Sufi shaikhs, and performed in urban centers, at fairs, at Sufi *sama'* gatherings, as well as for private *seva* and worship. In the case of the tale of Krishna's life, commonly known as *Harikatha* and based on the tenth book (*Dasam Skandha*) of the *Bhāgavata Purāṇa*, even the relatively abundant textual sources and references for this period probably obscure a much wider and more varied range of performance practices, this time at the borderline between Sanskrit and *bhasha* (lit., "language"), the general term used in Hindi for the vernacular. Sectarian traditions themselves point toward a wider circulation. Thus the *Caurāsī Vaiṣṇavan kī Vārtā* tells the story of another Brahmin of Kannauj, Padmanabhadas, who used to support his family by discoursing on the *Bhāgavata Purāṇa* and other texts. After he heard Shri Mahaprabhu (that is, Vallabha) "recite some lines from his treatise, the *Nibandha*, in which he explained that the *Bhāgavata Purāṇa* should not be used for one's income," he temporarily gave up his profession and later turned to reciting the *Mahābhārata* to a "local king."[11] We see here the sect trying to place its theological stamp on the story (several *varta*s feature disciples of other *svami*s being

[10] See my "'Krishna is the Truth of Man': Mir 'Abdul Wahid Bilgrami's *Haqā'iq-i Hindī* (*Indian Truths*) and the Circulation of *Dhrupad* and *Bishnupad*," in *Culture and Circulation*, ed. Allison Busch and Thomas de Bruijn (Leiden: Brill, 2014, 222–46). Muzaffar Alam has already considered the text within a paradigm of "assimilation from a distance" in which the Sufis of Awadh worked, out of their belief in the (inclusive) doctrine of *wahdat al-wujud*, but also out of political necessity in the face of continued threats and attacks from local Rajput zamindars. In *Haqā'iq-i Hindī*, according to Alam, Bilgrami "sought to *reconcile* Vaisnav symbols as well as the terms and ideas used in Hindu devotional songs with orthodox Muslim beliefs" within the "syncretistic religious milieu" of Awadh *qasba*s. Alam, "Assimilation from a Distance," 174, emphasis added.

[11] Gokulnatha, *Eighty-four Vaishnavas*, trans. Shyam Das (Delhi: Butala Publications, 1985), 31–37.

won over by Vallabha's commentary or oral discourse on it), but also on the practice itself by placing it outside the economics of religious performance. That Brahmin *kathavachaks* were not the only tellers of the story is proved by the first Hindi vernacular adaptation of the *Dasam Skandha*, the *Haricharit* in *chaupai doha* by Lalach Kavi, a Kayastha from "Hastigram" (present-day Hathgaon) near Rae Bareilly, concluded in 1530 (VS1587).[12] This is only ten years and forty miles away from where Jayasi saw it performed in Jais in 1540 and decided to retell the story "to all."[13] Lalach's *Harikatha* does not invoke any specific sectarian affiliation but generally praises bhakti, sants, and *satsang*, the gathering and singing of devotional songs, as we shall see. It circulated widely and for a long time; the text was completed by another poet a hundred years later and scores of manuscript copies of this text have been found as far afield as eastern UP and Bihar, Malwa and Gujarat, all in the *kaithi* script.[14]

Of course, we should also remember that Krishna tales and poems had circulated long before bhakti and Sufi poets took them up and molded

[12] For the date, see Theodore Pavie, *Krichna et sa doctrine* (Paris: B. Duprat, 1852), 3; Lalachdas, *Haricarit (Lālacdās kṛt Avadhī-kāvya)*, ed. Nalinimohan Sharma (Patna: Bihar Rashtrabhasha Parishad, 1963) (only the first twenty-three chapters, on the basis of five mss). It was partly translated into French by Pavie (*Krichna et sa doctrine*). According to R.S. McGregor, it was well known in the eighteenth century, *Hindi Literature from the Beginnings to the Nineteenth Century*, vol. 8, fasc. 6 of *History of Indian Literature*, ed. Jan Gonda (Wiesbaden: Harrassowitz, 1984), 96n. Lalach is also credited with a *Viṣṇupurāṇa* (Vi. 1585); see "Avadhī mẽ Kṛṣṇakāvya ke Praṇetā: Kavi Lālacdās," *Hindī Anuśīlan* 14, no. 3: 18, quoted in Murari Lal Sharma "Suras," *Avadhī Kṛṣṇa Kāvya aur unke Kavi* (Agra: Ranjan Prakashan, 1967), 40n.

[13] Elsewhere, as we shall see, he mentions the fact that he "read and heard" the story (*paṛheũ suneũ*) the story. This might well be an interpolation, since it is not present in the Berlin manuscript and is a very common devotional locution, as Imre Bangha has suggested. Personal communication, June 2009.

[14] A later adaptation, Ramdas Nema's *Haricharitra* (from Malwa, dated 1644 (VS1701)), acknowledges Lalach directly; Lalach's *Haricharit* was completed in 1614 (VS1671) by one Asanand, from a village near Rae Barelli; see Uday Shankar Dube, "Lālacdās kṛt *Haricarit Grantha* kī ek Prācīn Prati," private copy, *Maru-Bhāratī*, 1967?, 15; also, oral communication, August 2008. Almost all the manuscript copies date from the nineteenth century.

them to their own purposes, both in courtly and non-courtly milieus.[15] And the same is true of the Rama story as well, as has been so well documented. What a comparative and geographically sensitive perspective can offer is a more vivid sense of the various forms that existed and circulated at a particular time in a particular place. Within that particular field of possibilities, how did authors inflect their versions of that familiar tale? What did they hold up as important before their audiences? The written texts we have at our disposal clearly do not exhaust all available strands since they occasionally refer to oral performances of which we have no other trace—for example, Jayasi mentions, at the beginning of his work, the Ahirs singing the *Harikatha* at Divali, a festival we nowadays associate with Ram:

> It is nine hundred and forty-seven. At this time the poet speaks with words full of *rasa* [*sarasa bacana*];
> At Divali, which falls in the month of Karttik, the Ahirs sang clapping to the beat.
> So I said, I will sing this *khaṇḍ,* I will tell Kanha's story to all.[16]

What was the performance like? How much of Jayasi's version echoes theirs? Impossible to know.

KATHAS AS MERITORIOUS PASTIME

Harikathas were part of a much larger body of stories, which at this time were generally touted as a ritual that could substitute for other, more expensive and cumbersome duties, and was just as good as listening to

[15] Notably with Jayadeva in Orissa and Vidyapati in Mithila. For Krishna bhakti in Gujarat from the twelfth century onward, see Françoise Mallison, "Development of Early Krishnaism in Gujarāt: Viṣṇu, Raṇchoḍ, Kṛṣṇa," in *Bhakti in Current Research, 1979–1982*, ed. Monika Thiel-Horstmann (Berlin: Dietrich Reimer Verlag, 1983) and Françoise Mallison, "Early Kṛṣṇa Bhakti in Gujarat: The Evidence of Old Gujarati Texts Recently Brought to Light," in *Studies in South Asian Devotional Literature*, ed. Alan W. Entwistle and Françoise Mallison (New Delhi: Manohar, 1994); also Sheikh, *Forging a Region*,132ff.

[16] Jayasi, *Kanhāvat* (14.1–3), 140; Heidi Pauwels has noted that the word is spelt *āhira/āhara*, i.e., "day" (and not *ahīra*), but given the "Ahir touch," see below, and the need for a subject in the sentence, I would still go for Ahirs. Pauwels, "When a Sufi tells about Krishna's Doom: The Case of *Kanhāvat*

the "Vedas and Puranas." As this fifteenth-century story of a virtuous wife put it in its final stanza:

> Whoever listens intently (*mana lāī*) to the tale of Satyavati loses his great sins (*mahāpāpa*)
> Knowledge springs in the mind of the listener, as if he'd heard the Vedas and Puranas,
> As if he'd given gifts and money (*dravya dāna*) to the Brahmins, and dispatched them honorably;
> As if he'd performed ritual obligations (*nema, dharma, acārā*), and gained *darśan* of Deva Gopala;
> As if he'd bathed in all the *tīrthas*, been there and given gifts.
>
> Doha: The fruit of telling the story equals that of listening to the thousand names of God;
> Isar *kabi* sang and it was as if he'd traveled to scores of *tīrthas*.[17]

Phala shruti, the merit (*punya*) accrued by listening to a story, was tagged onto all kinds of tales, not only ones we would now recognize as "religious."[18] It could also of course be inserted by the storyteller in a performance context, as in the following stanza which is not found in

(1540?)," *The Journal of Hindu Studies* 6 (2013): 35; Gupta, *Aṣṭachāp aur Vallabh-sampradāy*, I, 140. References from the *Kanhāvat* in brackets, here and below, are to the stanza and verse numbers in Parameshvari Lal Gupta's printed edition (Varanasi: Annapurna Prakashan, 1981); occasional reference is made to Shiv Sahay Pathak's edition (Allahabad: Sahitya Bhavan, 1981). The only available manuscript at present, the MS OR 29 of Sprenger's collection held at the Staatsbibliothek in Berlin, is incomplete in the beginning and its folios have clearly been mixed up after stanza 96. I have followed Gupta's reconstruction since it seems to correspond more to the order of the story, unless otherwise specified.

[17] Ishvardas, *Īśvardās kṛt Satyāvatī Kathā tathā anya Kṛitiyā̃*, ed. Shivgopal Mishra (Gwalior: Vidyamandir Prakashan, 1958), 94.

[18] See, e.g., a martial tale from a Baghela milieu, Bhima Kavi's 1493 *Daṅgvai Kathā*; see *Bhīma Kavi kṛt Daṅgvai Kathā*, ed. Shivgopal Misra (Allahabad: Hindi Sahitya Sammelan, 1966), which has the line "by reading and listening to it your sins will be removed" (*paṛhe gune te pātakhu jāī* (2.4)). Although fitting a broad epic-Puranic genre and featuring Krishna as a "*baṛa sultāna*," it nonetheless calls itself a *Kṛṣṇa caritra*. Bhima Kavi, *Daṅgvai Kathā*, 82, 2 *doha*.

the oldest manuscript of the *Kanhāvat* and glosses the text as a devotional *katha*:

> Eternal is Hari and eternal Hari's story!
> The Vedas, *Bhāgavata*, and the sants all sing it.
> The *Viṣṇu, Padma, Śiva*, and *Agni Purāṇas*,
> The *[Mahā]bhārata* and the *Harivaṃśa* all tell his tale.
> I heard and read the *Bhāgavata Purāṇa*,
> I acquired the *sandhāna* of the path of love [*pem pantha*].
> Yoga, *bhoga, tapa*, and *śṛṅgāra*,
> *dharma, karma, sata*—all combined.
> ...
> I remember the feet of Ved Vyasa,
> Who told the story of Hari a thousand times.
> Kanha's *katha* is as numerous
> As the stars and asterisms in the sky.
> There is no other love story like it in the whole world,
> I have seen and checked in Turki, Arabic, and Farsi.[19]

Equivalence with the "Vedas and Puranas" is a familiar self-legitimizing strategy for religious texts that set themselves up as alternatives to the *smarta* religiosity for which the Vedas and Puranas were a shorthand. But here we can think of it also as a strategy to legitimize the *katha* as a genre which could and did actualize a religious/spiritual experience.[20] Jayasi's move in *Kanhāvat*, as we shall see, is a complex one: he never denies that

[19] *Kanhāvat*, ed. Pathak (14.1–4, 6–8 and *doha*), 12.

[20] Ken Bryant brilliantly showed how Surdas's *padas* in performance actualize the spiritual experience of longing, absence, and presence central to Krishna bhakti. Bryant, *Poems to the Child-God: Structures and Strategies in the Poetry of Sūrdās* (Berkeley: University of California Press, 1978). Aditya Behl showed that *pem kathas*, of which Jayasi's *Kanhāvat* can be rightfully considered an example, signaled and actualized the spiritual experience to the initiated seeker—but we could also say to the careful listener—through the careful repetition of code words and a denser texture of coded vocabulary and references (of flowers, gems, fruit, trees, as we shall see) at key moments of the story. Aditya Behl, "Love's Subtle Magic: An Indian Islamic Literary Tradition" (Series of four lectures delivered at the School of Oriental and African Studies, London, November 14, 20, 21, and 28, 2008). Behl's life work has now been published as Aditya Behl, *Love's Subtle Magic: An Indian Islamic Literary Tradition, 1379–1545*, ed. Wendy Doniger (New York: Oxford University Press, 2012).

Krishna is an *avatara* of Vishnu, that he can show his cosmic form to the *gopis*, etc. In other words, Jayasi does not disturb the overt theology of Krishna or the basic elements of his story. Yet, in his precise choice and use of terms, in the arrangement and coding of the story, and in skillfully directing the listener to what are for him the key moments, Jayasi also conveys a particular reading of the Krishna story as a Sufi tale, a kind of hidden, or *batin*, counterpart to the visible, or *zahir*, well-known story of Krishna. In making both readings and identifications possible at the same time, isn't Jayasi in effect offering the *katha* as a spiritual experience "for all"—not by transcending religion as Kabir did, but in a way that worked for several religious strands at the same time?[21] While we must posit the possibility that members of the audience responded and were moved and transported into a spiritual experience by listening to a discourse, a song, a poem, or a tale, and construed its religious message in tune with their own sensibility and beliefs—as in Bansawi's example quoted at the beginning—with Jayasi's *Kanhāvat* we have an author who consciously mobilized multiple religious audiences.

Finally, it is useful to think of *katha*s as a religious pastime because of the obvious "entertainment value" of certain scenes, like the fights between wrestlers, the colorful language Radha and Chandravali exchange during their quarrel, and the playful banter between Krishna and the *gopis*. To this must be added the pleasure of intertextuality, with especially Sufi romance authors keen to evoke other heroes and other stories.[22] In the *Kanhāvat* Krishna and Radha quote Rama and Sita at various stages with an eye to a good laugh. When the "supreme God" (*paramesura*), angered at Kamsa's pride, decides to "create" Vishnu in order to punish him, Vishnu initially pleads not to be sent back into the world:

[21] As Aditya Behl put it in his last public lecture at the School of Oriental and African Studies in November 2008, "I would like to propose that, in larger cultural historical terms, we adopt what it seems to me obvious that the cultural forms of the period indicate: that the historical agents who put these forms together thought in at least a 'both and' way. That is to say, they produced forms that signified in various ways, both Indic and Islamic and much more besides." Aditya Behl, "Love's Subtle Magic."

[22] See, e.g., Thomas de Bruijn, "Dialogism in a Medieval Genre: The Case of the Avadhi Epics," in *Before the Divide: Hindi and Urdu Literary Culture*, ed. Francesca Orsini (New Delhi: Orient BlackSwan, 2010).

I suffered a lot as Rama's *avatara*, now I won't descend into the world.
I spent that life in austerities, I knew but one wife, Sita,
And Ravana kidnapped her—never did the earth know such pain.[23]

But the supreme God reassures him that this time he will have a life of enjoyment (*rasa bhoga*), with 16,000 *gopitas* created expressly for that purpose, and all enemies will be disposed of speedily.[24] While *rasa bhoga* is the central concept of the poem, in this circumstance its humorous effect is undeniable.[25]

In the rest of the essay I will first compare our three available *Harikathas* from this period—Nanddas's incomplete translation of the *Dasam Skandha*, Haricarit's also incomplete version, and Jayasi's version—in terms of religious inflection. I will then concentrate on Jayasi's *Kanhāvat* and its reworking of the Krishna story and use of coded religious vocabulary in a way that resonates for both Krishna devotees and Sufi practitioners.

OPENINGS

In her work on the printing of Punjabi *qissas*, which also circulated in a mixed religious milieu, Farina Mir has noted how often it is the opening section, with its invocations, that reveals the religious inflection of a particular version of the story. This is a useful insight to bring to our *Harikathas*.[26] We may start by comparing the opening of Lalach's *Haricharit* with the *Dasam Skandha* (ca. 1570) by the Vallabhan poet Nanddas. Nanddas has a "friend" ask him to explain the *Bhāgavata*

[23] Jayasi, *Kanhāvat* (42.5–7), 156.

[24] Jayasi, *Kanhāvat* (43), 157.

[25] Heidi Pauwels has dedicated two essays to this text: "Whose Satire? Gorakhnāth confronts Krishna in *Kanhāvat*," in *Indian Satire in the Period of First Modernity*, ed. M. Horstmann and Heidi Pauwels, Wiesbaden: Harrassowitz, 2012, 35–64, and the aforementioned "When a Sufi tells about Krishna's Doom." Her argument is that the *Kanhāvat* is really a satire of Krishna by the Sufi poet Jayasi; while recognizing the undeniable humor—rather than satire—in parts of the narrative (a feature of many episodes of Krishna's life and indeed part of his personality), I would argue that Jayasi's project is rather one of reworking and speaking at multiple levels.

[26] Farina Mir, "Genre and Devotion in Punjabi Popular Narratives: Rethinking Cultural and Religious Syncretism," *Comparative Studies in Society and History* 48 (2006): 727–58.

Purāṇa in "easy language" (*sarala bhāṣā*) because "I cannot understand Sanskrit words." Nanddas at first recuses (*Aho mitra, etī mati kahā̃*)[27]—how can he succeed where "great poets have got stuck," and after the first commentator on the *Bhāgavata Purāṇa*, the great Shridhar Svami? But with the grace of one's guru "a dumb man can read the whole *piṅgal* and a lame man can climb mountains."[28] Nanddas then begins by explaining in great detail the exact meaning of the nine *lakṣa*s and tenth *lakṣaṇa*. In other words, Nanddas is keenly aware of the existing textual (*granthana*) and commentarial tradition, and also of the need to produce a doctrinal text, and his tone is at once more didactic and sectarian.[29] By contrast, Lalach's opening is more broadly devotional. Between the usual invocation to Ganesha and Sarasvati,[30] in the first stanza he turns to Gopala, whose praise he will sing in a *katha* full of *rasa*: it was thanks to Gopala that Brahma (*pitāmaha*) undertook creation, that Shiva became an ascetic and destroyed the world in the *pralaya*. "You are immanent in all beings" (*saraba bhūta ke antarjāmī, saba maha vyāpa rahe tuh sāmī*),[31] he says, and "remove the obstacles from the path of the sants" (*bighina harana santanha sukhadāī*).[32] It is for the sake of bhaktas (*bhagata hetu*) that Lalach invokes Sarasvati; he also asks for Murari's grace and that of "all the sants." No patron is mentioned, only the place of composition and date (Rae Barelli, 1587Vi, although the editor reads it as 1527)—this therefore seems to be an independent composition: it is for the sake of all the sants (*sakala santa*) here that he is attempting to sing this *kathā bisālā* in *bhasha*.[33] Lalach's theological introduction is limited to

[27] Nanddas, *Daśam Skandha*, in *Nanddās Granthāvalī*, ed. Brajratnadas (Varanasi: Nagari Pracharini Sabha 1949), ch. 1, I.3.

[28] Nanddas, *Daśam Skandha*, 1 *doha*.

[29] There is no invocation to other gods, and Shuka and Parikshit do not need to become bhaktas, they are already ones: "Parikshit is counted among the excellent listeners [*uttama śrotā*], drenched through with *rasa*. He forgets food and shelter, his only support is listening to the praises of Hari. In the same way, Shuka became an excellent expounder [*baktā*], drenched in the highest *rasa* of love." Nanddas, *Daśam Skandha*, 218.

[30] Lalachdas, *Haricharit* (Invocation, stanzas I–II), 13–14.

[31] Lalachdas, *Haricharit* (Invocation, I.7),12.

[32] Lalachdas, *Haricharit* (Invocation, I.8),12.

[33] Lalachdas, *Haricharit* (Invocation, III), 14–15. He also asks Sarasvati's grace to "gain the letters" (*ākhara pāvõ*) in order to sing Hari's praises, although he lacks intelligence. Lalachdas, *Haricharit* (ch. 1, II.6), 13.

describing Hari as the Highest Being (*paramahaṃsa*) who has no home, son, mother, or father, no shape, body, birth, or karma, no ears, mouth, or hands—he is the *parama purusha*.[34] Then Lalach brings us straight into the Puranic frame of the *Bhāgavata Purāṇa*—Narada obtained this *Harikatha* and retold it to Vyasa, Shukadeva overheard it ...

Karahu kripā saba Hari guna gāvo, Paramahaṃsa kaha bheda sunāvo.
Gṛha, suta, mātu, pitā nahı̃ jāke, rekha rūpa nahı̃ kachu tāke.
Sīsa na ākhi, badana nahi rasanā, janama, karama kachu āhi na racanā.
Sravana, bacana, kara-pallava nāhı̃, parama purāna purukha niju āhi.
Nābhi kavala te Brahmā upāne, niraguna ke prabhu ihai na jāne.
Divya purukha eka khojata āe, paramahaṃsa ko anta na pāe.
Haṃsa rūpa Hari āe dekhāvahi, caturabeda Brahmā samujhāvahi.
Uhe kathā Hari Nārada pāī, Vyāsadeva kaha āni sunāī.
Suni Sukhadeva sravana sukha lāgī, upajī bhagati, bhae anurāgī.
Uha to harıpada sadā viyogī, sabha taji bhae bihaṅgama jogī.

Doha: *Amrita kathā bhāgavanta, pragaṭita ehi saṃsāra.*
Carana sarana Jana Lalac, gāvahi guna bistāra.

Please sing all the qualities of Hari, tell us the secret of the Highest Being.
He has no home, son, mother, or father, nor any form or shape.
No head or eyes, no face or tongue, no birth or karma to leave behind.
No hearing, speech, or hands/touch, he is himself the most ancient *puruṣa*.
He created Brahma from his lotus navel, he [Brahma?] does not know the *nirguṇa* lord.
[If a divine *puruṣa* came to look for the [beginning or] end of the Highest Being, he would not find it.]
Hari came and showed his *haṃsa* form and taught the four Vedas to Brahma.
It was that *Harikathā* that Narada received, and went and told to Vyasadeva.
Sukhdeva heard it, and his ears were glad, bhakti arose in him and he became a passionate devotee.
He is always lost in the feet of Hari, and has left everything to become a wandering yogi.

Doha: The immortal tale of the lord was revealed to the world.
Jan Lalach, taking refuge in Hari's feet, sing the vastness of his qualities.[35]

[34] Brahma was born from his navel. Hari showed himself in the form of a *haṃsa* (goose) and explained the four Vedas to Brahma. Lalachdas, *Haricharit* (Invocation, IV) 15–16.

[35] Lalachdas, *Haricharit* (Invocation, IV), 15–16.

As for the rest of the story, Lalach's *Haricharit* follows quite closely the *Bhāgavata Purāṇa*, and the narrative moves swiftly, as in other *kathas* from this period. Only, instead of theological asides, Lalach inserts more direct intimations to pursue bhakti: those who forget the Lord have squandered their human birth like dogs[36] and there is a whole stanza inveighing against *pakhaṇḍa dharma* ("hypocritical *dharma*").[37] Lalach often uses *dohas* as refrain, where he uses stock expressions of thanks and invocations and praises for his Lord—in other words general expressions that are not specific to any tradition:

Doha: *Alakha, agocara ṭhākura, so bica Gokula āva*
Braja kula santa saṅga raha, Jana Lālac guna gāva.

The invisible and imperceptible Lord came into Gokula,
With the people of Braja and the sants Lalach the servant sang his praises.
Variant second line:
Nagara loga saba harakhīta...
With all the townspeople happily...[38]

The terms in the first line—*alakha* and *agocara*—are terms used by Naths and sants like Kabir to refer to the invisible Higher Being, but here they seem to be employed without a specific theological underpinning but rather to underscore Hari's movement from invisibility to manifestation in Gokul.

In line with other Awadhi Sufi romances, the opening of Jayasi's *Kanhāvat* consists of several elements, as follows. It begins with a statement on the impermanence of the world and of false pride, a coded reference to the core idea of the poem—Kamsa, and even Krishna, all die at the end, just as the world is created and will disappear. There follows a short *hamd*, an Islamic introduction in praise of God, the Prophet, his companions, the ruler of the time (Humayun *badshah*), and Jayasi's own spiritual masters (Sayyid Ashraf Jahangir Simnani and Shaikh Burhan).[39] God the Creator is beyond praise, and even though Sheshnaga—whose two tongues in his thousand hoods are often used in images of praise and

[36] Lalachdas, *Haricharit* (ch. 1, III.7), 25.

[37] Lalachdas, *Haricharit* (ch. 1, IV), 26–27.

[38] Lalachdas, *Haricharit* (Invocation, III *doha*), 15.

[39] For an extensive discussion of Jayasi's pirs, see Jayasi, *Kanhāvat*, ed. Pathak; de Bruijn, *The Ruby in the Dust*; and de Bruijn, "Dialogism in a Medieval Genre."

who features also in the story—praises him with all his tongues, this is still not praise enough. Thus, even in the *hamd* Jayasi introduces figures familiar from Puranic lore.

Next, Jayasi introduces a reference to what will become a recurrent feature of Indo-Persian historical writing (from Firishta onward)—that is, the history of India of pre-Islamic times; in this case Jais, "a *dharma asthānu* since the time of the Satya Yuga," an abode of rishis during the Treta, who abandoned it in the Kaliyuga, when it was resettled by "Turkan."[40] We may notice how Jayasi does not mention conquest but resettlement. He also directly affiliates his town with Puranic history and geography, using an idiom that everyone around him would have understood:

Kahaũ nagara bara āpuna ṭhāū̃, sadā sohāvā Jāyasa nāū̃.
Satajuga hutau dharama asthānū̃, tahiyā kahata nagara udiyānū̃.
Puni tretā gaeu, dvāpara [mukhī], Bhū̃jā rāja mahā rikhi rikhī̃.
Rahata rikhīsura sahasa aṭhāsī, ghanai [*ghanṭa*?] *pokhara caurāsī.*
Bā̃dhā ghāṭa ī̃ṭa gaṛhi lāe, au caurāsī kuvā̃ banāe.
Bica-bica bā̃dhe bhī̃ṭa sohāī̃, nisi bhae gāgana janahu tarā̃ī.
Ṭhāū̃-ṭhāū̃ para bana bahu bārī, tehi ūpara saba marhī sāvārī.

Doha: *Baiṭhi tapā tapa sādhe, sabai purukha autāra,*
Homa jāpa japa nisi-dina, karahī jagata asa pāra.

I'll tell you about my great town, the ever-beautiful Jais.
In the *satyayuga* it was a holy place, then it was called the "Town of Gardens."
Then the *treta* went, and when the *dvapara* came, there was a great rishi called Bhunjaraja.
88,000 rishis lived here then, and dense ... and eighty-four ponds.
They baked bricks to make solid ghats, and dug eight-four wells.
Here and there they built handsome forts, at night they looked like stars in the sky.
They also put up several orchards,[41] with temples on top.

Doha: They sat there doing *tapas*, all those human *avataras*.
They crossed this world doing *homa* and *japa* day and night.[42]

---

[40] I prefer Pathak's reading here (Gupta reads *baṛa āpuna* as *Bid[rā] ban ṭhāū̃*) since this is clearly about Jais; Jayasi, *Kanhāvat*, ed. Pathak (stanzas 7–8), 6–7.

[41] The meaning of *bārī* is unclear here.

[42] Jayasi, *Kanhāvat*, ed. Pathak (8), 7–8.

Puni kayajuga kīnhaū paisāru, gae jo rikhīsura taji saṃsārū.
[jiha ṭhāī] puni basagata rahā, bhā aravana Jaikarana kahā.
[āi] caṛhi tiha tatakhana dasā, bhā Turakāna puri bhari basā.
[saba] bhagavanta sarāhai jogū, pāna-phūla nau nidhi rasa bhogū.
[rāu] raṅka ghara ūca avāsā, agara candana ghana āvai bāsā.
Meru sugandha rahā bhari pūri, kumkuma parimala au kastūrī.

Doha: *Dekhaī nagara sohāvana, ḍhalai puhupa jasa bāsa.*
Jasa jasa niyare jāī, jānaū carḥai Kailāsa.

Then *kaliyuga* came, and the rishis left this world and disappeared.
This place became a bamboo thicket again, a forest called Jaykarana.
When it was in such condition, it was settled again by Turks.
Its lord is worthy of praise [?], and there is enjoyment of delicate things and nine kinds of *rasa*s.
Rich men and poor men live in high houses, and a rich scent of incense and sandalwood wafts through.
It is full of the scent of *meru*, *kumkum*, and *kasturi*.

Doha: When you see this beautiful town, with the scent of flowers,
And the closer you get, you feel you are climbing the Kailasa.[43]

The failure to mention a specific patron is not unusual in Jayasi and some of the other Awadhi Sufi poets. What is striking in this case, however, is the insistence on the town as an "open" setting for performance. I am not suggesting that we take this as a realistic description, only that by going into such detail concerning the economy of service, trade, and entertainment in a town Jayasi is perhaps signaling the way in which he would like us to frame the story. Thus both in his brief historical account of the town of Jais and in the more elaborate description of Kamsa's town of Mathura—which geographically reflects the site of Jais, with its fort and city on top of a hill and ponds lying all around—*katha*s feature prominently in the public life of the town.[44] In Jais, the local sultan has built a fort with twelve doors, but also markets with thriving trade. A minister and a pandit sit there with him, as well as horsemen.[45] Others sit reading the

[43] Jayasi, *Kanhāvat*, ed. Pathak (9), 8.

[44] "Dancing, prancing, and many tales are happening all around." Jayasi, *Kanhāvat* (10 *doha*), 138.

[45] "One minister and learned pandit(s), and armed men riding on their horses." Jayasi, *Kanhāvat* (12.4), 139.

Puranas, or read out and explain from a book (*kitab*, possibly the Quran). Attendants sing songs and play music full of *rasa*. There is a sense that the full talent of Malik Muhammad is *not* appreciated here, although it could refer to the spiritual knowledge (*marama*) he can infuse in his poetry:

Tahā̃ kabi Malik Muhammad, marama na janai koi,
Lahai so lākh karoran, jo koi gāhak hoi.
There the poet Malik Muhammad, no one knows his secret,
If someone becomes a customer, he will earn hundreds of thousands.[46]

The description of Mathura is not only longer, but also seems to suggest the pattern by which towns were settled. First the fort is built[47] and then a moat, after which the town is given a name. Then the king builds his palace, with a harem of ranis from other regions (the "seven climes"), and several courtyards (*akharas*) containing houses.[48] Then a city grows *around* the fort, with walled gardens and pavilions and tall dwellings for the rich and the poor. This is when the populace begins to grow. Public seating is arranged for people to sit and play games. Kings and chiefs from neighboring areas also come to the *rajasabha*. Good roads and water supply encourage traders to settle—possibly attracted by the wealth of these chiefs/soldiers or their ability to trade over long distances.[49] Once this healthy trade is established, sadhus and wrestlers wander into the city. Various kinds of actors and mime artistes also perform while pandits sit and expound the shastras (*bhāṇḍ, naṭ, naṭinī nācahĩ, paṇḍit baiṭhi sāstar bācahĩ*).[50] People sing, tell stories, it is a good way to pass the time. People from the fort relax and are happy to give a handsome reward:

Gīta nāda rasa kathā, bhala hoi bisarām,
Gaṛha kai log bhaeu sukhī, dān dehĩ bhala dām.[51]

[46] Jayasi, *Kanhāvat* (12 *doha*),139.

[47] With seven doors made of seven different precious metals, which Krishna will cross and defeat one by one; Kamsa's fort is clearly an extension of his false pride and his desire to conquer not just the whole world but also death; hence the precious metals of each door must resonate with esoteric meanings. Jayasi, *Kanhāvat* (19), 143.

[48] Jayasi, *Kanhāvat* (21), 144–45.

[49] Jayasi, *Kanhāvat* (24), 146

[50] Jayasi, *Kanhāvat* (24.7), 146.

[51] Jayasi, *Kanhāvat* (24 *doha*), 146.

Once again, I am not suggesting that we read this as a realistic description, since wealth and elegant buildings and a profusion of music and poetry are standard elements in the "description of cities" (*nagara varṇana*), but that it is striking that the setting for entertainment in the town is neither court nor Sufi *khanqah*—are these open spaces where he suggests we should frame his story?

THE AHIR TOUCH

Perhaps in the version of Krishna's story that Jayasi saw performed by the Ahirs in Jais certain traits were already emphasized in the representation of Nanda as the semi-independent chief of the cow herders of Braj. What in the *Bhāgavata Purāṇa* is a passing mention of customary tribute to the king[52] acquires a thicker social and political inflection in the *Kanhāvat*: Nanda and the cow herders go merrily into town for Karttik puja and Divali in order to offer obeisance (*johar*). They call out to be allowed to perform their dances and songs in order to receive a reward (*prasada*) from the king, who is also called *gosain*:

> We look forward to your cheerful offering (*dāna*), o king!
> We will all come again after twelve months.[53]

The king offers Nanda some betel nuts and makes him "sit before him" (*āgẽ baisāvā*) in a ritualized mutual recognition of loyalty. But isn't the performance also an occasion to recruit military manpower from among the Ahirs? This is suggested by Kamsa's words as he lures Nanda into bringing young Krishna to show off his fighting prowess against the court wrestlers (*malla*):

> I also want to see how he fights, and I will send him a robe of honor (*pahirāī paṭhāvõ*)
> To all the cow herders (*govār*) who come, I will give twice as much (*bisāī bisāha*)[54]
> To you I will give a Tukhara horse and will make you a cavalryman (*karihõ asavāra*)[55]

[52] *Bhāgavata Purāṇa*, XXXIX.11–12.

[53] Jayasi, *Kanhāvat* (164 *doha*), 224.

[54] This line is unclear: *bisār* is grain given on credit, for which 1/4 more is taken back.

[55] Jayasi, *Kanhāvat* (165.5–7), 225.

In the event, it is the Ahirs who easily overpower the royal wrestlers in a lively "action scene," and King Kamsa has to take refuge inside his fort. The point of marking out this inflection is to suggest an Ahir/"Bundela" martial tinge to Krishna bhakti in Awadh and Bundelkhand, and possibly an audience for Jayasi's story. (Among Bundelas, the rajas were usually Krishna devotees, while the ranis were devoted to Rama.)

THE *KANHĀVAT* ANALYZED

In the same year that he composed the *Kanhāvat*, during the paramountcy of Sher Shah Suri, Jayasi began to compose his most celebrated work, the *Padmāvat*, which we know traveled far and wide, from Arakan to the Deccan, and was eagerly copied and retold in Persian and other languages.[56] We can safely say that Jayasi's version of the Krishna story enjoyed less fame. Only three manuscript copies have been found so far, and the *only* one dated (1067H/1657) tells us that it was copied by a certain Sayyid Abdulrahim Husain, the son of a drug seller and resident of Masauli near Kannauj, for a local Kayastha, Rajaram Saksena of Qasimpur, also in Kannauj district. This is meager evidence but it does suggest that this Awadhi version of the Krishna story written by a Sufi poet did have some local circulation at least.

The story of Krishna in the *Kanhāvat* largely follows the blueprint of the *Bhāgavata Purāṇa* (and Lalach's *Haricharit*), although with less of a Puranic taste for the slaying of demons and less attention to Brahminical rituals.[57] Jayasi also draws upon some of the popular *lila*s, like the *phulvari lila* and the *dana lila*, when Krishna poses as a tax collector demanding a tax in kind from the *gopi*s who are going into town to sell their milk and curds, which were not part of the *Bhāgavata Purāṇa* but came to form a popular stock of situations for Braj poets. At the same time,

[56] For a list of translations and retellings of the *Padmāvat*, see de Bruijn, *The Ruby in the Dust*.

[57] Similar features include: Krishna's birth and the swapping with Yashoda's baby girl, an incarnation of Bhavani; Akrura sent by Kamsa to summon Krishna, although less fulsome in his *stuti* here than in the *Bhāgavata Purāṇa*; Krishna lifting Mount Govardhan on his left hand (rather than little finger), although not to protect the inhabitants of Gokul from Indra's wrath but his cows from the stones thrown by Kamsa's army; also Krishna's death and end of the Yadu clan are the same as in the *Bhāgavata Purāṇa*.

Jayasi rearranged the sequence of episodes and the cast of characters so as to make Krishna's story also work as an allegory for the Sufi Chishti path of love. Heeding Aditya Behl's warning, we should not try to find a one-to-one match between characters and episodes and mystical concepts and stages, but rather listen carefully to the text and what the episodes, situations, and code words suggest each time.[58] The rearrangement of episodes and cast of characters, the narrative "thickening" at important moments, and the profusion and repetition of code words guide us in this pursuit.

To begin with the rearrangement of episodes and characters, we may note that the episode in which the child Krishna dives into the river to fetch the ball he has lost and defeats the snake Kaliya is transformed into a descent to the nether world to fetch the thousand-petaled lotus from Shiva's garden, which is guarded by the snake Sheshnaga. Kamsa had asked Nanda to get the lotus, sure that Krishna would offer to undertake the task in his place and would be killed in the attempt. As Krishna descends the ladder that takes him to the "unpassable path, the *tirtha* of the Tirbeni (Triveni)," this is marked as the beginning of Krishna's journey (73.1). But lo and behold, all the rivers—Sona, Sharda, Gandaki, Narmada, Kalindi/Yamuna, Ganges, Gomti, and so on—come and pay their respects, and so does the sea (*samudra*).[59] Krishna stands unafraid in front of sleeping Sheshnaga, paying no heed to the warnings of the Naga's wife, Basuki, and reveals to the angry Sheshnaga who he really is (see below). While the terms belong to a familiar religious *langue*, they are rearranged to convey a specific *parole*; the idiom is a common one but the message is enigmatic.

Another major rearrangement concerns Krishna's love-making, here divided into three phases: the first involves the *gopi*s and Radha (also called Rukmini Devi after their wedding, coalescing the two distinct figures) and culminates in his forest wedding night and simultaneous dalliance with all the *gopi*s in a kind of round dance. Thereafter Krishna goes

[58] Aditya Behl, "Love's Subtle Magic."

[59] As usual, numbers suggest an esoteric meaning (here "18 x 4"); the key locus of love, the garden (*phulvari*), appears here for the first time. The water and *agama pantha* reappear at the moment of Kamsa's death, when he receives "seven mortal wounds" and is thrown into the Yamuna by Krishna. Jayasi, *Kanhāvat* (297), 289.

to fight Kamsa's wrestler Chanvara/Chanura (an episode that occurs later in the *Bhāgavata Purāṇa*) and returns to Gokul. Now a second extended love episode takes place with Chandravali, who becomes the second heroine; the usual fight between the two heroines ensues. The episode in which Kamsa sends Krishna's uncle Akrura to Gokul, where he is welcomed courteously, follows the *Bhāgavata Purāṇa*, as does Krishna's meeting with his old friend Sudama and curing of Kubja the hunchback, although in the *Kanhāvat* she becomes his third love interest. Krishna easily overcomes the seven gates of Kamsa's castle and defeats him, but here the story diverges again. After defeating Kamsa, Krishna spends his time in Mathura in pleasure with Kubja, while Radha, Chandravali, and the other *gopi*s pine away in Gokul, and the message they ask the wind to deliver to Krishna scorches everything on the way.[60] Krishna now takes pity on the *gopi*s and sends boats to fetch them: but only some *gopi*s manage to climb onto the boats, others fall into the river. Krishna helps them. They travel by boat and spend their time in pleasure with Krishna.[61]

In the *Kanhāvat*, then, Krishna does not rule or move to Dwarka. Rather he establishes a dharamshala in Mathura offering food and shelter to all itinerant ascetics (an oblique reference to Sufi *khanqah*s?). When he hears that the sage Durvasa lives on the other side of the Yamuna he asks the *gopi*s to take food to him; Krishna, however, orders the *gopi*s to tell the river that they have never been with Krishna. The *gopi*s do so, although they wonder why they are supposed to lie, and sure enough the river lets them pass. The sage eats their food, blesses them, and tells them to cross the river in a similar manner (that is, by telling a lie, that he did not eat anything).[62] The *gopi*s sulk until Krishna tells them what the mystery behind it is, and he once again opens his mouth to reveal to them his cosmic form and his secret (*bheda*).[63] One more episode is inserted before the curse that leads to Krishna's

[60] Jayasi, *Kanhāvat* (300–24), 290–304.

[61] Jayasi, *Kanhāvat* (324–28), 304–06.

[62] Jayasi, *Kanhāvat* (329–35), 307–10.

[63] Jayasi, *Kanhāvat* (336–41), 310–13. The episode reworks a famous story about a saint, his wife, and a *derwish* across the river told by the Sufi master Nizam al-Din Awliya; cited in Behl, *Love's Subtle Magic*, 9.

death and the end of the Yadus—a long dialogue with Gorakhnath on the respective merits of *bhoga* and *yoga*, on which more below.

CREATION, DESCENT, AND REVELATION

Krishna in the *Kanhāvat* retains the character of both *avatara* and supreme God. As he tells Basuki at the beginning of the poem:

> The creator who created the world has taken a human *avatara*.
> Neither was he ever born, nor did anyone beget him.
> Nobody has such a light-form (*joti sarūpā*), no one is of such lineage.
> He stands unblemished and untarred (*nihakalaṅka niramala*) amidst everything, you can glimpse him like light and shade,
> Life and death appear to all [or, he shows], yet he is without shape or form.[64]
> Such a Lord (*gosāī*), a king of kings, the world and men are his creation.
>
> Doha: Just like the drop and the sea, I am its/his particle (*aṃsa*);
> I descended as Kanha, I have come to kill Kamsa.[65]

Unlike the heroes of the other Sufi romances, Krishna needs to undergo no transformation in order to enter the spiritual path. Rather he *is* God who wants to make himself known and to love and be loved by his creatures. This is one way we can read all the various instances in the romance when Krishna reminds his interlocutor of his divine nature and the ten *avataras*, as well as the various instances in which he appears before Radha, Chandravali, and the *gopis* in disguise—first as a tax collector (*dani*),[66] then as a *bairagi* accusing them of stealing the forest flowers,[67] and a third

[64] The text reads *bihāī*, which could be taken as a "renunciant", since *bihānā* means "to renounce." Kalika Prasad, Rajvallabha Sahay, and Mukundilal Srivastava, eds., *Bṛhad Hindī Kośa* (Varanasi: Prakashak Jnanmandal, 1989), 815.

[65] Jayasi, *Kanhāvat* (80), 176. And yet to his brother Balabhadra who asks him how he got so dirty, he replies enigmatically: "The one who is unblemished and untarred, who created the world and played all the games (*khela saba khelā*), and who descended without blemish, acquired a blemish and his light dimmed" by descending into the nether world. Jayasi, *Kanhāvat* (86.2), 179.

[66] Jayasi, *Kanhāvat* (97), 185.

[67] Jayasi, *Kanhāvat* (130), 206–07.

time again as a *bairagi* in Chandravali's garden.[68] Each disguise, or doubt expressed by the *gopis*, is followed by a revelation.

Jayasi skillfully uses Vaishnava metaphysics in order to formulate the Sufi metaphysics of God's essence and manifestation and what Aditya Behl called the "circulation of desire:"[69] thus the world is manifested for the sake of God's play (*khela* = *lila*), the *avataras* are "created" by the "supreme God" (*paramesura*), and there is a secret identity between God and his creatures—as Krishna tells both Radha and Chandravali: I am you and you are me, a message that listeners of Surdas's *padas* would also have related to very well.[70] As Krishna himself puts it, "I don't know who is the bee and who the flower."[71] And again he tells Radha: "There is no difference between you and me, like a shadow inside a *piṇḍa*."[72] When Radha hesitates to follow him to his abode of love (Kabilasu = Kailasha) because she does not want a "bee husband" who will spend a moment with her and then flit away to some other flower, he replies that he is actually with all the *gopis* at the same time:

> You Radha, who are so smart, why do you pretend to be so unknowing/innocent?
> Like the sun in the sky is the *ādi sarūpa*, whose light shines forth over the whole world;
> And it pervades/lives in the whole world and its light shines over everything;
> In the same way I am *tapa* (?) with all the *gopis*, [*kāhu hutaĩ*] I am not hidden.
> ...
> I make love with them all the time, none of their beds ever remains empty.
> In a manner appropriate to each of them, I enjoy *bhogu* with all, night and day.[73]

68 Jayasi, *Kanhāvat* (208), 246.

69 Aditya Behl, "Love's Subtle Magic."

70 I am grateful to Vasudha Dalmia for suggesting this point to me.

71 Jayasi, *Kanhāvat* (111.4), 193.

72 Jayasi, *Kanhāvat* (140.1), 211; a *piṇḍa* is a round clod (or cake made as offering to the ancestors); here it could mean the shadow inside a solid round object.

73 Jayasi, *Kanhāvat* (142.1–4, 6–7), 212.

Krishna is often described in his beautiful form (*rupa anupa*), and yet he is also a *bahurupiya* who can take on many forms. When he enters Mathura to challenge Kamsa, everyone sees him in his own image:

> Krishna disguised himself (*bhesa apuna kīnhā*) so that each saw him according to his own hue (*barana*).
> A king saw him as a king, a young man as a marvelous young man,
> *Daityas* saw him as a *daitya*, and Kamsa saw in him his death.
> Khatri (Kshatriya) heroes said: "He's a hero," Ahirs said: "He's an Ahir,"
> Yogis said: "He's is a yogi," and Brahmins said: "He is a *jyotikhi*."
>
> Doha: He appeared so clearly (*darasana nirmala*) as if in a special mirror;
> Each saw his own face, Kanha [*agara nirekha*?][74]

This is God who wants to make himself visible as if through an unblemished mirror, a typical image of Sufi poetry. In the *Kanhāvat*, then, Jayasi sets side by side the typical Krishnaite metaphor for revelation—Krishna opening his mouth to reveal the whole cosmos within it—with a whole range of other metaphors, some more everyday (e.g., like ghee in the milk, like scent in the flower), and others more particularly of Sufi origin, like that of the mirror. Another metaphor for revelation is that of the opening of the *antarpata*, the inner door to the *guputa jagata*, the secret world. As he tells the *gopis* one final time:

> Krishna said, "Now look young women," and opened the inner door of his body;
> "I am/There is difference only for deceit, it is *gosāīn* who takes leasure [with] himself,
> And like Durvasa said, this happens in every body (*ghaṭa-ghaṭa māha*).
> He[75] himself takes pleasure, and the blame falls on someone else.
> He is the flower (*jagata phūla*) that blossoms, and he is the bee who loses itself in the *rasa* of its scent;
> He is the fruit and the gardener, and he is the one who tastes all *rasas*.[76]

And again:

> There is no one apart from the one, and the whole world is its shadow.

[74] Jayasi, *Kanhāvat* (287.2–7, *doha*), 284.

[75] Lit., "*apu*," which could stand for the indefinite pronoun as well as for "oneself" or the"self."

[76] Jayasi, *Kanhāvat* (339.1–3, 5–7), 312.

Wherever you look, it is all the artwork of *gosāīn.*[77]
He created the game as he wanted, and filled fourteen worlds.
There is colour, light and form in all of them, like the sun that shines over/pervades everything.
See the art of *pargaṭa guputa*, visible and hidden: he is in everything, everything is within him.
He dictates where every eye turns, no mouth can speak without him;
Just like life is inside the body, so he pervades the whole world.[78]

Durvasa, who here seems to stand for the enlightened seeker, has understood this secret, which is why he sees through and accepts Krishna's "lie" and replies with a similar statement: he has eaten the food that was brought to him, but since there is no duality, who has eaten what?[79] Thus, not only immanence but even the doctrine of *avatara* can be made to carry a Sufi connotation as God's creation of the visible world. The Vaishnava doctrine according to which Krishna is the only man and everyone else is a woman can similarly be reformulated in terms of God inhabiting all his creatures ("Sixteen thousand women, and one man in all of them").[80]

Rasa Bhoga, Kapata Gyan

Rasa bhoga, "the enjoyment of *rasa*," is the term with which Jayasi seeks to present the story of Krishna as equivalent to the mutual desire, longing, and union between God and man. This is the key for interpreting *bhoga* as a spiritual path—*bhoga bhagati* as it is called in the poem. We are used by now to the transformation of the hero into a yogi in Sufi romances and *qissas*,[81] but what is the relationship

[77] This is almost a literal translation of the Persian verse, for which 'Abdul Quddus Gangohi had already found a Hindavi equivalent.

[78] Jayasi, *Kanhāvat* (340.1–7), 312.

[79] See footnote 63.

[80] Jayasi, *Kanhāvat* (328 *doha*), 306.

[81] See Christopher S. Shackle, "Transition and Transformation in Varis Shah's Hir," in *The Indian Narrative*, ed. Christopher Shackle and Rupert Snell (Wiesbaden: Otto Harrassowitz, 1992); Jeevan S. Deol, "Love and Mysticism in the Punjabi Qissas of the Seventeenth and Eighteenth Centuries" (MPhil diss., School of Oriental and African Studies, University of London, 1996) for Sufi *qissas* in Punjabi; and of course Aditya Behl's work on Awadhi romances.

between yoga and *bhoga* in this poem (also rhyming, and to be contrasted, with Kamsa's pride-sickness, *garaba roga*)?

Twice, we have seen, Krishna appears to the *gopi*s and to Chandravali as a yogi, significantly both times in a garden or garden-like forest, a spiritually charged place, for the many trees, flowers, fruit, and scents listed are all code words for the awakening and circulation of desire, as Aditya Behl would put it. The second time the *gopi*s wonder, "How come he, a *bairagi* and a yogi, is staring at Chandravali, with *bhoga* in his heart?!"[82] This is the time when Krishna himself has fallen sick with love and has become despondent (*audāsī, nirāsī*), hidden love raging within him like a sickness.[83] Any medicine only increases the "pain of *biraha*," so much so that the people of Braj think he may have caught the evil eye.[84] Chandravali's nurse Agasta—not a character I have found in other tellings of the story—has come to visit him, and he begs her to be his guru and lead him to Chandravali.[85] Agasta reminds him of who he really is, and that his *tapa* will bring him the *bhoga* he desires; she advises him to go and hide in Chandravali's garden in the guise of a yogi. This seems at first sight only a disguise but it is also a preparation in order to attain Chandravali.[86] Krishna sits for fourteen nights in her garden, repeating (*japa*) her name—"the *bairagi* does *bhagati*," the

[82] Jayasi, *Kanhāvat* (214 *doha*), 249.

[83] This is when the phrase "The path of love is thin and harsh/hard, one crosses, the other is killed" is uttered a second time. Jayasi, *Kanhāvat* (196.7), 240.

[84] Jayasi, *Kanhāvat* (197), 241.

[85] "You can do whatever you wish, and get me wherever you want … Now you are my guru and I am your *chela*, if you say so I will get the game (*khela*) I have played. I will follow any path you set me, which will get me the happy *darasana* I ask for." Jayasi, *Kanhāvat* (203.4, 6–7), 244.

[86] Jayasi, *Kanhāvat* (196.3–7, *doha*), 240:

Nothing pleased him, everything saddened him: how can hope rise in a desperate man?
His body seethed, his heart scorched, nobody can spell out such pain.
Love cannot be revealed [not sure]; once it's revealed, it kills you.
Love revealed is a risky business: it's a player playing with his head.
Love's path is narrow and hard, one may be spared, the other is struck.
Its branding mark is hidden, not even the smoke shows.
The heart/mind (*man*) suffers and refines itself, nobody knows its secret.

text says[87]—and only then does Chandravali come. To her he appears a strange creature, a mixture of Vaishnava god and Shaiva yogi, a beautiful man with a *gada*, a *chakra*, and a conch shell, who counts the *rudraksha* beads and plays the flute—the sight of him is *bhagati* that makes her forget the world.[88] When she asks him why he is dressed like a beggar if he is the king that he says he is, he first reveals that he is actually not a yogi but Gopala, the *rasa bhogi* and *avatara* of Vishnu, and when questioned further he reveals his secret knowledge:

> Listen Gaura this is my knowledge, I am untouched by pleasure or pain.
> Nothing comes, nothing goes, I [one] sit quietly throughout.
> This is what you call a basic knower (*mūla gyānī*), one who does not smile at pleasure or weep in pain.
> This is the game of the creator, and I am it, like the shadow inside a *piṇḍa*.
> Outwardly I look (*pragaṭa rūpa)* like Gopala Gobinda, but the hidden knowledge (*kapaṭa gyāna*) is: neither Turk nor Hindu.
> Murari's *rūpa* comes in different shades: sometimes a king, sometimes a beggar.
> Sometimes a pandit, sometimes a fool, sometimes a woman, sometimes a man.
>
> Doha: So, for the sake of my *rasa*, it's all a game, after all.
> Many different shades/guises, the only one (*akelā*) takes pleasure in all.[89]

As we have seen already, at one level this declaration is perfectly in tune with the theology of Krishna bhakti: Krishna has created his beautiful form, in fact any form, for the sake of his *lila*, and he is at one time the ineffable Being *and* the *saguna* God. At another level, according to the Sufi theology of *wahdat al-wujud,* this is Allah, the only God, revealing that he is immanent in all people and that there is a hidden realm in which no outward difference matters; the enlightened seeker knows this and remains unmoved by appearances and events because he can see through them. A third possible way of looking at it is that Jayasi has used language, concepts, and metaphors in such a way that he has been able to speak to all and to suggest a kind of equivalence

87 Jayasi, *Kanhāvat* (211 *doha*), 248.
88 Jayasi, *Kanhāvat* (212), 248.
89 Jayasi, *Kanhāvat* (217), 250.

between different religious ideas. "Neither Turk nor Hindu" is, I suspect, not to be read in Kabir's terms—as a rejection of both institutionalized religions—but as the existence of a hidden realm of truth behind the world of appearances, although of course no one would have stopped the audience from giving it a different meaning.

That the yogi in this romance is not really a yogi, and that the path of *rasa bhoga* is different from, and superior to, the path of yoga is finally spelt out in the debate between Krishna and Gorakhnath at the end, a significant innovation by Jayasi to which I shall return shortly.[90]

In other Sufi *premakhyans* the married hero leaves his wife to go on a quest for the heroine, or he first meets the heroine but then, in the course of his quest for her, acquires another wife on the way. Within this scheme, the hero is the novice whose first experience of worldly love prepares him but also needs to be left behind, because he must undergo various trials before he can attain the divine essence (and light) represented by the second heroine.[91] Heroines, embodiments of divine essence, are also actively loving, just as God actively loves created beings.[92] Krishna's love exploits (*rati keli*) with Radha, Chandravali, the other *gopis*, and Kubja fit well within the theology of *rasa* as *shauq* (passion, desire) and of the mutual, active love between God and created beings, and Krishna plays with all of them the role of teacher as well as lover, as we have seen. Once again Jayasi takes up characters with a well-established personality and theology, and fits them within his scheme.

Radha (also called Rahi or Radhika, and Rukmini later) is a strong presence in the poem, with a well-defined character and identity, the daughter of Devchand Mahar. She is the first to meet Krishna in disguise in the *dana lila* episode and to tell him that she will not give in to his request for *bhoga bhagati* because she is a *tapasvini sati* and astrologers have told her that she will marry the one all gods bow to, to which

90 See also Pauwels, "Whose Satire?"

91 Ramya Sreenivasan has argued that the presence of the two wives and the tension between them can be traced back to the dual context of these narratives, that is, Sufi circles and elite lay courts, each with their own ethic: "The inexorable fact of elite polygyny seems to coexist uneasily with a Sufi monogamous ethic here." Sreenivasan, *The Many Lives of a Rajput Queen,* 55.

92 Aditya Behl, "Rasa and Romance: The Madhumālatī of Shaikh Mañjhan Shattari" (PhD diss., University of Chicago, 1995).

Krishna laughingly replies that he indeed is the one. Radha then asks him to show his real face and "tie the knot" (echoing God's covenant with his people in the *Qur'an*?): "You who are called a *bahurupai*, like sun and shade. Show yourself to me quickly in many new forms."[93] Krishna immediately shows his child and cosmic forms.[94] Radha then goes home pledging to return; her slow self-adorning in a long *nakha shikha* marks the awakening of desire and of the "game of love," with flowers, fruit, scents, and colors acting as code words for the forthcoming love union and arousing the senses of the listeners. As Aditya Behl put it, "The *sarapa* captures the moment of the arousal of desire (*shauq*) … and introduces the multiple resonances of longing and love: the relation between God and created beings, lover and beloved, and reader and text."[95] Music here acts as that which bewitches and makes one forget the world: whether it is the musical instruments that accompany Radha's *shringara* and that make the whole world and the earth forget themselves,[96] or the "ragas of *bairaga*" that Krishna plays on his flute while waiting for Chandravali, himself lost to the world[97] and of course bewitching everyone who hears him.

The love union with Radha is presented as a wedding, albeit a forest wedding, with all the gods, rishis, and the sun and the moon rejoicing. Brahma recites the Vedas, Shiva spreads the *mandapa*, and Parvati sings the wedding songs[98]—a scene found in other *katha*s of the time.[99] Their union is like the long-awaited meeting of the *chataka* bird and the *svati* asterism familiar from the poetic tradition, and the emphasis is on "new love, new wife, new husband."[100] We noted above the hidden meaning of this union as of the other erotic moments with the other heroines. That Radha and Chandravali and even Kubja are equivalent with respect to Krishna is hinted at through repeated references to Krishna

93 Jayasi, *Kanhāvat* (103 *doha*), 188.

94 Jayasi, *Kanhāvat* (104), 189.

95 Behl, "On Reintegration," the fourth lecture of Behl, "Love's Subtle Magic."

96 Jayasi, *Kanhāvat* (129), 205.

97 Jayasi, *Kanhāvat* (211), 247–48.

98 Jayasi, *Kanhāvat* (145), 213–14.

99 For example, Isvardas's 1501 *Satyāvatī kathā*.

100 Jayasi, *Kanhāvat* (147), 214–15.

as the sun and the heroines as the moon: Radha is the moon and the *gopis* are the stars; Chandravali of course *is* the moon and her beauty "shines by night and hides during the day,"[101] and after her transformation even Kubja is "four times more beautiful and unblemished than the moon."[102] However, metaphors of light abound more explicitly in the Chandravali episode, making her a more overt representative of the divine light that the seeker must turn to after being awakened to human love. It is perhaps for this reason that Krishna seeks Chandravali and is trapped by her in a way that he was not by Radha.[103] Krishna's union with Chandravali is like the conjunction of the sun with the moon (although Krishna playfully replies to a jealous Radha that this is indeed not possible: how can he and Chandravali dally when the sun and the moon can never be together?). Their erotic union is described once again as "*bhoga bhagati*," but Chandravali, who has learnt from the "pandits reading the Vedas and what is written in Puranas,"[104] reminds Krishna to go and fight Kamsa and asks him to show his royal form to her. The character of Chandravali is more developed in Gaudiya Krishna bhakti, where she is not just one of the *sakhis* but Radha's chief rival.[105] This rivalry is replayed here as the rivalry between the two wives, or rather the wife and the lover (although Radha addresses Chandravali derogatorily as *savati*, her co-wife,[106] while Chandravali scoffs haughtily at her for her rusticity). When both women and their 16,000 companions are on their way to offer puja to Mahendra and they start exchanging insults, Chandravali, resplendent in her beautiful *shringara*, asks Mahendra to have Krishna all for herself,[107] while Radha appears with wasted body and unkempt hair, like a *virahini*, and

[101] Jayasi, *Kanhāvat* (187.2), 236.

[102] Jayasi, *Kanhāvat* (280), 281.

[103] The poet dwells here on the metaphor of the heroine's eyebrows as a wounding bow, and the heroine as a hunter, well familiar in Persian (and later Urdu) love poetry. Jayasi, *Kanhāvat* (213–35), 248–59.

[104] Jayasi, *Kanhāvat* (228.2), 255.

[105] See, for example, Rupa Gosvami's Sanskrit play *Vidagdhamādhava*. Donna M. Wulff, *Drama as a Mode of Religious Realization: The* Vidagdhamādhava *of Rūpa Gosvāmi* (Chico: Scholars Press, 1984).

[106] Jayasi, *Kanhāvat* (245), 264.

[107] Jayasi, *Kanhāvat* (238–43), 260–63.

pleads with Mahendra to free her from the co-wife; she briefly speaks in Sita's voice, underscoring her virtue as a sati.[108] After their verbal and physical fight, Krishna not only separates the women but also teaches both that he is with each of them at the same time.

As for the episode with Kubja, its place within the overall structure of the poem is to provide a counterpart of *bhoga* (in Madhubana) to the *gopis*' *biyoga* in Gokul.[109] The *bhoga* with her, encapsulated in a "six-season" set piece, contains all the accompanying elements that we have found before—flowers, scents, fruit, and colorful clothes; if anything now they are all concentrated in the same person, and the final season leads to the communal enjoyment (*bhoga vilasa*) of dance and color at Holi, when "the heart's desire was fulfilled for all six seasons and twelve months."[110] Earlier Krishna had told Chandravali that he was a *bhogi* of "all the six *rasa*s," and the "six seasons" seem to correspond to that fullness. And while in the other Sufi romances the juxtaposition between *bhoga* and *viyoga/viraha* is represented by the contrast between the second heroine's "six seasons" and the plaintive "twelve months" of the first wife, here both Radha and Chandravali pine together with the other *gopi*s in the *barahmasa* that follows upon Krishna's love play with Kubja.[111] With another interesting twist, the *gopi*s are not left behind in Mathura to fulfill their bhakti of *biraha* but are brought along to enjoy *rasa bhoga* with Krishna, when they are further enlightened in the Durvasa episode mentioned above.

The meaning of *bhoga* is thus explained several times in the course of the story through Krishna's various encounters and exchanges with Radha, Chandravali, and the other *gopi*s. What the path of *bhoga* means in relation to other paths is explained at the end, through the encounter between Krishna and Gorakhnath.

[108] Jayasi, *Kanhāvat* (251), 267.

[109] Jayasi, *Kanhāvat* (307), 294–95.

[110] Jayasi, *Kanhāvat* (305 *doha*), 293.

[111] Jayasi, *Kanhāvat* (300–19), 290–301. For a comprehensive analysis of the "six seasons" and "twelve months" in Sufi romances, see chapter 8 of Aditya Behl's *Love Subtle Magic* ("The Seasons of Madhumālatī's Separation," 264–85), where he points out that the first wife's call for the hero to return is a signal to the Sufi seeker that the inner spiritual quest is necessary, but also a reintegration with the material world.

Gorakhnath (also called Matsyendranath in the text) appears in Mathura with an impressive retinue (*kaṭaka*) of yogis because the fame of Krishna bhakti has spread through the whole world and he has heard of Krishna as a famous and talented *gyani*. Now, however, he is disappointed to see him enveloped (*lipaṭāna*) in *bhoga*: he should take advantage of the time he has left to become a yogi, so as to acquire an immortal body and the powers that come with it. Krishna goes to meet Gorakh at the camp, partly in humble courtesy and partly holding his ground, and claims to be overjoyed by this *darasana*, but he goes with 20,000 bhaktas all shouting "Bhakti"![112] Krishna rejects Gorakhnath's offer on various grounds: (*a*) yoga is "outward knowledge and outward form" that is no good to him. (*b*) Beside, what do yogis know of *bhoga*? (*c*) "He is a true ascetic who remains detached at home (or in the body)." "Outwardly I live where everyone else lives, in secret I repeat[113] the name of *paramesur*."[114] (*d*) He is in a position to teach the 16,000 *gopis* who serve him with folded hands: as long as he is there, they will not sin. (*e*) And what is the point of taking human birth if one does not experience *bhoga*? This is why *avatara* took place, and why the *jiva* takes on a body and experiences emotions (*kāma krodha tiśanā mana māyā*). Death will come for all, whether *bhogi* or yogi.[115] After this debate, they decide to fight, but it is a brief and inconclusive fight with an accommodating ending: "Yoga is best for the yogi, and *bhoga* best for the *bhogi*."[116] Gorakh and his Naths return to Mount Sumeru, while Krishna's abode is a Kailasha-like Madhubana.

We are familiar with the Krishna bhakti juxtaposition between the "simple devotion" of the *gopis* vs formless knowledge as exemplified in the popular repartee between Uddhav and the *gopis* of the *bhramar git*,[117] but what should we make of this juxtaposition between Krishna

[112] Jayasi, *Kanhāvat* (344), 315.

[113] *Japaũ* an alternative reading is *jīvaũ*, "I live by God's name."

[114] Jayasi, *Kanhāvat* (346.6–7), 316.

[115] Jayasi, *Kanhāvat* (348), 317.

[116] Jayasi, *Kanhāvat* (350 *doha*), 318.

[117] In the *Kanhāvat*, Krishna is himself called Uddhav a couple of times briefly (e.g., Jayasi, *Kanhāvat*, (133, 300), 208, 290), possibly because he is the *gopis*' teacher, as well as Arjuna—and his brother Balarama is called Balabhadra—during the final fight with Kamsa (for example, Jayasi, *Kanhāvat* (291), 286).

and Gorakhnath, especially since Gorakhpanthi verses and techniques were familiar and popular among Awadh Sufis, and the prince-as-yogi in Jayasi's other romance, the *Padmāvat*, is clearly modeled on a Nath Yogi? We have seen that code words are not fixed and have multiple meanings. *Bhoga*, which in most of the poem stands for the erotic-theological union between God and his creatures, may also stand for appropriate enjoyment of a kingdom, as Krishna says in his short sermon to Kamsa's son when enthroning him.[118] While in the rest of the poem yoga stands for the intermediate stage when the lover has left the world and is preparing himself for *bhoga*, in the debate between Krishna and Gorakh yoga seems to stand for an outward form of religion (*pragaṭa bidyā, pragaṭa bhesū*, as Krishna calls it[119]) that is blind to the true, secret essence of things and an attitude that values spiritual exercises for the sake of personal benefits, in other words, for *shari'a* Islam. Once again, Jayasi brilliantly makes two religious statements at the same time—one about the superiority of Krishna bhakti over Nath Yoga, and the other about the superiority of the Sufi path to the *shari'a*.

***

There are several reasons why a comparative approach to *Harikatha* texts and performances, and the *Kanhāvat* in particular, is significant for a project that seeks to rethink religious interchange. Textual traditions from early modern India often speak in exclusive or else assimilative terms—by and large Sufi texts speak of Sufis, their faithful and Muslim rulers and officials; Persian courtly texts speak of rulers and courtiers; sant texts speak of sants, scheming Brahmins, and the occasional royal patron; Vaishnava texts speak of Vaishnava religious leaders and devotees, with non-Hindus making rare and formulaic appearances. The same is true of literary scholarship and its categories: thus we have Sufi literature, bhakti literature (divided according to religious and sectarian affiliation: Krishna bhakti, and Vallabhan poets, Haridasis, Radhavallabhas, etc.), courtly literature in Brajbhasha and in Persian. Once these categories occupy the theoretical centre stage, they engender

[118] "Today I am giving you the kingdom, do not be proud when enjoying the kingdom." Jayasi, *Kanhāvat* (299.3), 290.

[119] Jayasi, *Kanhāvat* (346.2), 316.

a whole vocabulary for describing literary activities: Hindus "contribute" to Persian and Muslims "contribute" to Hindi as if they were outsiders having to negotiate entry, and not part of a comprehensive/shared social world. Histories old and new (*tazkiras*, *vartas*, as well as the more recent scholarship since the nineteenth century) evolve intriguing stories in order to explain how a Hindu could write Persian verse or a Muslim write about Krishna.

By contrast, the proliferation and circulation of *Harikatha* texts and performances (such as Lalach's *Haricharit* and Jayasi's *Kanhāvat*), exhibiting a striking range of inflections and a high degree of inter-textuality, give us a very different picture of that world. *Kathas*, and the *Harikatha* in particular, offered a wide, non-sectarian pool of stories, characters, and performative and generic forms from which both the bhakti poets and Sufi poets like Jayasi drew. Both Lalach and Jayasi explicitly evoke performances and refer to other textual and performative sources in their texts. A comparative approach is both necessary and fruitful in this regard, for it highlights how each text was the outcome of precise choices and strategies within a wide range of possibilities. Unlike other texts, where language and genre suggest which audience is being addressed (clearly a sectarian work addresses an internal audience, but it may also be a dig at philosophical opponents), *kathas* were by nature open and circulated easily, and that made them particularly liable to becoming narrative sites of interchange and inflection.

Together with Samira Sheikh's idea of a "religious marketplace," the metaphor of the *bisat* may be useful for imagining the religious (and literary) world of this period—a kind of a chessboard on which players knew they were surrounded by other players and could be closer to or further from centers of power (of which there were many: local, imperial, religious, moneyed, landed). While religious history tends to be written from the perspective of the authorities and institutions that produced archives, hagiographies, and lineages, Lalach's *Harikatha*, with its clear devotional slant yet lack of sectarian drive (unlike Nandadas's), is significant because its centuries-long spread testifies to the popularity of this kind of non-sectarian Krishna devotion in central north India.

One consequence of this crowded *bisat* was that players often found themselves addressing multiple audiences (insiders and outsiders) and playing multiple games, as the *Kanhāvat* shows. In fact, Jayasi's *Kanhāvat* forces us to reflect on the reason why this provincial Sufi poet writing in the local language took on the Krishna story. Is it evidence of symbolic appropriation? In his analysis of another, almost contemporary, Awadhi Sufi tale, Manjhan's *Madhumālatī* (ca. 1545), Aditya Behl argued that we should read the Sufi poets' choice of idealized Indian locales and the romantic quest of Indian heroines in terms of "appropriation" within the context of the now "dominant" Islamic polities.[120] More recently, Ramya Sreenivasan has suggested that: "While the ethos of many regional courts in North India during the Sultanate and Mughal periods may have been broadly Islamicate, *local networks* for the circulation of such narratives were by no means exclusively Muslim. In fact, such taxonomies of religious affiliation may not even be useful in considering the lay patrons and audiences of such narratives."[121] This is true even of an explicitly religious story such as Krishna's.

First, as I have tried to show, if we take the local geography and local networks seriously, we are minded to understand power less in terms of sovereignty or domination (whether worldly or spiritual, the sultan's or the shaikh's) and more, as Muzaffar Alam has suggested, in terms of accommodation between local groups. In order to understand the *Kanhāvat* we need first of all to place it within the local geography of Krishna bhakti, in which Jayasi is one of many different actors—Kayastha and Brahmin storytellers and poets, Ahir performers, *sampradayas*, and Sufis.

Second, Sreenivasan highlights *circulation* as a stage in the literary cycle that goes beyond the putative origin of a text as its locus of identity. And while it is true that circulation always potentially exceeds the framework and intentions of the producer, this is all the more true within a multilingual and layered world like that of north India, whose exemplary figure is that of the palimpsest. So while Aditya Behl was unsurpassed in providing a Sufi reading of the Awadhi *premakhyans*, we remain aware that this would have been only one reading because—and the *Kanhāvat* itself is an example of this—circulation to a different audience meant a new "interpretive community." Neither only "Sufi" or "Krishnaite," the *Kanhāvat* plays multiple registers at the same time, and creates something new in the process. Here attention to genre, audience, and

120 Aditya Behl, "Rasa and Romance."

121 Sreenivasan, *The Many Lives of a Rajput Queen*, 45, emphasis added.

setting is crucial: for if both the *Kanhāvat* and 'Abdul Wahid Bilgrami's *Haqā'iq-i Hindī* are Sufi takes on Krishna motifs, whereas the *Haqā'iq-i Hindī* addresses an audience of Sufi disciples, the *Kanhāvat*, I have suggested, locates itself as a *katha* in the open arena of entertainment and exchange. Although it is clear that neither complete equivalence nor "syncretism" was Jayasi's aim, the cultural multilingualism of authors and audiences, and the presence of multiple aesthetics, pressed among some the desire to bring those aesthetic worlds together, and led others to realize that some religious ideas could be considered at least formally equivalent.

BIBLIOGRAPHY

Agrawal, Purushottam. *Akath Kahānī Prem kī: Kabīr kī Kavitā aur unkā Samay.* New Delhi: Rajkamal Prakashan, 2009.

Alam, Muzaffar. "Assimilation from a Distance: Confrontation and Sufi Accommodation in Awadh Society." In *Tradition, Dissent and Ideology: Essays in Honour of Romila Thapar,* edited by R. Champakalakshmi and S. Gopal, 164–91. Delhi: Oxford University Press, 1996.

"Avadhī mẽ Kṛṣṇakāvya ke Praṇetā: Kavi Lālacdās," *Hindī Anuśīlan* 14, no. 3.

Barz, Richard. *The Bhakti Sect of Vallabhācārya.* Faridabad: Thomson Press, 1976.

Behl, Aditya. "Rasa and Romance: The Madhumālatī of Shaikh Mañjhan Shattari." PhD diss., University of Chicago, 1995.

———. "Love's Subtle Magic: An Indian Islamic Literary Tradition." Series of four lectures delivered at the School of Oriental and African Studies, London, November 14, 20, 21 and 28, 2008.

———. *Love's Subtle Magic: An Indian Islamic Literary Tradition, 1379–1545.* Edited by Wendy Doniger. New York: Oxford University Press, 2012.

Bhima Kavi. *Bhīma Kavi kṛt Daṅgvai Kathā.* Edited by Shivgopal Misra. Allahabad: Hindi Sahitya Sammelan, 1966.

De Bruijn, Thomas. "Dialogism in a Medieval Genre: The Case of the Avadhi Epics." In *Before the Divide: Hindi and Urdu Literary Culture*, edited by Francesca Orsini, 121–41. New Delhi: Orient BlackSwan, 2010.

———. *The Ruby in the Dust: Poetry and History of the Indian Padmavat by the Sufi Poet Muhammad Jayasi.* Leiden: Leiden University Press, 2012.

Deol, Jeevan S. "Love and Mysticism in the Punjabi Qissas of the Seventeenth and Eighteenth Centuries." MPhil thesis, School of Oriental and African Studies, University of London, 1996.

Dube, Uday Shankar. "Lālacdās kṛt *Haricarit Grantha* kī ek Prācīn Prati." *Maru-Bhāratī*, private copy, 1967?

Gokulnatha. *Chaurasi Baithak = Eighty-four seats of Shri Vallabhacharya*. Edited by Vrajesh Kumar. Translated by Shyam Das. Volume 10 of *Śrī Vallabha Studies Series*. Delhi: Butala Publications, 1985.

———. *Eighty-four Vaishnavas*. Translated by Shyam Das. Delhi: Butala Publications, 1985.

Gupta, Dinadayalu. *Aṣṭachāp aur Vallabh-sampradāy*. Volume 1. Prayag: Hindi Sahitya Sammelan, 1970.

Husain, Intizar. *Basti*. Translated by Frances W. Pritchett. New Delhi: Indus, 1995.

Ishvardas. *Īśvardās kṛt Satyāvatī Kathā tathā anya Kṛitiyā̃*. Edited by Shivgopal Mishra. Gwalior: Vidyamandir Prakashan, 1958.

Jayasi, Malik Muhammad. *Kanhāvat*, MS OR 29, Sprenger's collection, Staatsbibliothek zu Berlin.

———. *Kanhāvat*. Edited by Parameshvari Lal Gupta. Varanasi: Annapurna Prakashan, 1981.

———. *Kanhāvat*. Edited by Shiv Sahay Pathak. Allahabad: Sahitya Bhavan, 1981.

Lalachdas. *Haricharit (Lālacdās kṛt Avadhī-kāvya)*. Edited by Nalinimohan Sharma. Patna: Bihar Rashtrabhasha Parishad, 1963.

Mallison, Françoise. "Development of Early Krishnaism in Gujarāt: Viṣṇu, Raṇchoḍ, Kṛṣṇa." In *Bhakti in Current Research, 1979–1982*, edited by Monika Thiel-Horstmann, 245–56. Berlin: Dietrich Reimer Verlag, 1983.

———. "Early Kṛṣṇa Bhakti in Gujarat: The Evidence of Old Gujarati Texts Recently Brought to Light." In *Studies in South Asian Devotional Literature*, edited by Alan W. Entwistle and Françoise Mallison, 51–64. New Delhi: Manohar, 1994.

McGregor, R.S. *Hindi Literature from the Beginnings to the Nineteenth Century*. Volume 8, fascicle 6 of *History of Indian Literature*, edited by Jan Gonda. Wiesbaden: Harrassowitz, 1984.

Mir, Farina. "Genre and Devotion in Punjabi Popular Narratives: Rethinking Cultural and Religious Syncretism." *Comparative Studies in Society and History* 48 (2006): 727–58.

Nanddas. *Daśam Skandha*. In *Nanddās Granthāvalī*, edited by Brajratnadas. Varanasi: Nagari Pracharini Sabha, 1949.

Orsini, Francesca. "'Krishna is the Truth of Man': Mir 'Abdul Wahid Bilgrami's *Haqā'iq-i Hindī* (Indian Truths) and the Circulation of *Dhrupad* and *Bishnupad*." In *Culture and Circulation*, edited by Allison Busch and Thomas De Bruijn. Leiden: Brill, 2014.

Pauwels, Heidi. "Whose Satire? Gorakhnāth Confronts Krishna in *Kanhāvat*." In *Indian Satire in the Period of First Modernity*, edited by M. Horstmann and Heidi Pauwels. Wiesbaden: Harrassowitz, 2012, 35–64.

Pauwels, Heidi. "When a Sufi Tells about Krishna's Doom: The Case of the *Kanhāvat* (1540?)." *The Journal of Hindu Studies* 6 (2013): 21–36.

Pavie, Theodore, trans. *Krichna et sa doctrine*. Paris: B. Duprat, 1852.

Phukan, Shantanu. "Through a Persian Prism: Hindi and *Padmāvat* in the Mughal Imagination." University of Chicago PhD thesis, 2000.

Prasad, Kalika, Rajvallabha Sahay, and Mukundilal Srivastava, eds. *Bṛhad Hindī Kośa*. 6th revised edition. Varanasi: Prakashak Jnanmandal, 1989.

Shackle, Christopher S. "Transition and Transformation in Varis Shah's Hir." In *The Indian Narrative*, edited by Christopher Shackle and Rupert Snell. Wiesbaden: Otto Harrassowitz, 1992, 241–63.

Sharma, Murari Lal "Suras." *Avadhī Kṛṣṇa Kāvya aur unke Kavi*. Agra: Ranjan Prakashan, 1967.

Sheikh, Samira. *Forging a Region: Sultans, Traders, and Pilgrims in Gujarat, 1200–1500*. New Delhi: Oxford University Press, 2010.

Sreenivasan, Ramya. *The Many Lives of a Rajput Queen: Heroic Pasts in India c. 1500–1900*. New Delhi: Permanent Black, 2007.

Tandon, Hariharnath. *Vārtā-sāhitya: Ek Bṛhat Adhyayan*. Aligarh: Bharat Prakashan Mandir, n.d.

Tulsidas. *Tulasī Granthāvalī*. 4 volumes. Edited by Ram Chandra Shukla. Varanasi: Nagari Pracarini Sabha, 1973–1977.

Wulff, Donna M. *Drama as a Mode of Religious Realization: The* Vidagdhamādhava *of Rūpa Gosvāmi*. Chico: Scholars Press, 1984.

8 Sant and Sufi in Sundardās's Poetry

Monika Horstmann

The religious and philosophical-didactic poetry of Sundardās (1596–1689[1]) holds an extremely prominent place within the sant tradition of Rajasthan. Sundardās's importance has been long recognized by modern scholars.[2] Coterminous as his life was with the "long" seventeenth

[1] The traditional date of Sundardās's birth is the Caitra, ś. 9, VS 1653. This corresponds to March 28, 1596. The date of his death is given on the commemorative slab made for him and another Dādūpanthī in Sanganer. It is Kārttika, ś. 8, VS 1746, Thursday. There is an incongruence here, for that day was a Friday. The same lunar day fell, however, on a Thursday in VS 1747. This would perhaps place Sundar's death on October 30, 1690. The slab was made many years after Sundar's demise. That Sundar died at or beyond the age of ninety-three is proven by a *sākhī* which he composed at this age, which is mentioned therein. Purohit Harinārāyaṇ Śarmā, *Sundar-granthāvalī* (Kolkata: Rajasthan Research Society, VS 1993), II, 1008, "*aṃt samay kī sākhī*," no. 5. For a discussion of the dates of his birth and death, see Śarmā, *Sundar-granthāvalī*, I, 1–3, 119–24 (pagination of the chapter "*Jīvan-caritra*"). That magisterial study and edition by Purohit Harinārāyaṇ Śarmā remains the unsurpassed treatment of Sundardās's works, obsolete only for some details.

[2] For Rāmcandra Śukla, "He was a sant alright, but he was also a poet (*sant to ye the hī, par kavi bhī the*)." *Hindī sāhitya kā itihās*, 18th ed. (Vārāṇasī: Nāgarīpracāriṇī Sabhā, VS 2035), 61. Śukla was notoriously reluctant to accept

century, it offers great insight into the historical and literary dynamics of the sant tradition in this period. For all the resemblances that tied various sant poets to one another, each was yet distinguished from the other, with specific local milieus fostering distinctive attitudes or styles.[3] This article's goal is to explore how Sundardās entered into the discourses of the different traditions which shared his habitat and horizon of experience.[4]

The first of this article's four sections locates Sundardās's place within the larger sant tradition as also within the geographic context of eastern Rajasthan—a region rich in Hindu and Islamicate traditions. The section also presents the argument that although the sants, including Sundardās, were extremely proud of having shown a "middle way" (*madhi mārg*) between Hinduism and Islam, this no longer features in the poetry of Sundardās as preserved today. Rather, most of his attention seems focused on carving a distinctive position for himself vis-à-vis

---

as poetry the vernacular compositions not following *śāstric* poetic rules. Here, to his great satisfaction, was an author who met his standards. Less idiosyncratic, but also expressive of a rather skeptical view of the quality of sant poetry in general, is McGregor's statement: "Sundardās brings to sant poetry a more explicit literary quality than it generally displays." Ronald Stuart McGregor, *Hindi Literature from Its Beginnings to the Nineteenth Century*, vol. 8, fasc. 6 of *A History of Indian Literature*, ed. Jan Gonda (Wiesbaden: Otto Harrassowitz Verlag, 1984), 137.

3 For the lineage formation among sants, see Daniel Gold, *The Lord as Guru: Hindi Sants in North Indian Tradition* (New York: Oxford University Press, 1987), 79–115. Gold discusses also "Sufi Style; Indic Interpretation" (202–07), which is a paragraph that is related to the present topic. However, whereas Gold studies "the closeness of the parallels between the *sants*' experience and that of the Sufis," the thrust of the present contribution is on the deliberate appropriation of a Sufi register of writing by a sant author.

4 When writing this article I was mindful of the fact that it is not, or at least not yet, possible to disengage the various chronological stages in Sundardās's work, except of course for the works that happen to be dated. It is unknown to what extent the sequence of texts established by the final redaction of his works, which Sundardās himself supervised, follows chronological criteria. To neglect the stages in the productivity of an author, especially one of such unusual longevity, is clearly a poor way to treat his work. And yet, this issue needs to be suspended for want of data.

the powerful orthodox *saguṇa* Vaiṣṇava sects of his time. This section concludes by investigating the background of Sundardās's patrons and the particular intellectual influences that shaped him. The second section explores the place of Islam and Muslims in the Śekhāvāṭī region of Rajasthan. It specifically focuses on the role of the Qāimkhānī lineage of Fatehpur as political and religious patrons of not just Muslims but Hindus as well.

The third section begins with an examination of the ways in which Sundardās positioned himself as an opponent of orthodox Hindu views, especially as they pertained to rituals. It offers examples of how Sundardās satirized his Hindu (and occasionally Jain) opponents. Importantly, orthodox Muslims do not feature as objects of ridicule. In answering this absence, this section argues that although Sundardās may have wished to include Muslims in his critique, the literary conventions and expectations of his audience may have asked for their exclusion. The final section looks at two little-known compositions by Sundardās to explore the ways in which he did engage in a deliberate artistic and theological effort to express his sant message in Sufi terms.

I

Sundardās was a Dādūpanthī monk, a yogī, a preacher, a scholar, and a poet.[5] As a poet he was a master of the Rajasthani type of western Hindi literature. However, he constantly played with the language as also vernacular idioms outside his own literary language. He was proficient in Sanskrit, which he adapted with great ease to the vernacular literary idiom. His work exhibits marked intertextuality, for he reworked his compositions several times and did so in various poetic genres. Sundardās's poetry catered to listeners and religious students, and a good part of it was supposed to be supplemented by narrative during live performance. It was not predominantly poetry for readers. The virtual duplication,

[5] The term "monk" used for Sundardās represents the Indian word *sādhu* (or *svāmī* in case of an especially venerable holy man, preferably one heading a monastic lineage or similar institution). It is used in contrast with the term "ascetic," for the early Dādūpanth, although encouraging yoga and contemplation, was not in favor of austerities pursued to bring about indifference to the world and, ultimately, liberation.

even redundancy, of themes, motifs, and phrases is thus a characteristic feature of his work, reflecting the practical use of his poetry in preaching to gatherings of devotees whose expectancy of certain elements of content and style was likely to have been satisfied in this fashion.

Sundardās represents the case of a seventeenth-century heterodox religious intellectual, someone who could use and differentiate style in language to great effect. As a heterodox intellectual, he was a harsh critic of the immoral mores of the representatives of Brahminical orthodoxy. Yet, he also drew on the orthodox tradition for his own purposes. In typical sant fashion and also as an intellectual, he relied on an authority founded on intellect—a superior, religiously authenticated intellect aroused and guided by the "True Guru," a figure representing a merger of his guru Dādū (d. 1603) with God. Claiming superior, religiously defined reason, he also militated against what he took to be the folly of superstition. This folly, as well as wickedness, in the guise of righteousness was thus his target. This is not surprising for a sant preacher, especially not for a disciple of Dādū, whose faith was "one God," and whose moral principle was "do as you preach."

As an inhabitant of Rajasthan and especially as a disciple of Dādū, Sundardās was educated in a milieu encompassing Hindus and Muslims. He spent most of his life in eastern Rajasthan and Śekhāvāṭī, notwithstanding the fact that he spent a good number of his formative years as a student in Banaras and traveled much, as would be in consonance with the peripatetic lifestyle of Dādūpanthī monks. This part of Rajasthan was particularly rich in both Hindu and Islamicate traditions, of both high and folk culture.

Sundar was born in Dausā.[6] By caste he was a Khaṇḍelvāl Mahājan (Bania) of the Būsar *gotra*. Apart from his accomplishments as a religious man, his Mahājan origin was likely to have prompted the patronage of merchant caste families that he received at a later stage in his life. Sundar became a member of Dādū's fold around 1601/02, when Dādū came to Dausā. Dādū recruited and initated the boy on the spot. He became one

[6] The hagiographical record according to which Sundar's birth was granted to his mother by a saint is still remembered at Sundardās's native place. A couple of years ago, I accompanied the Women Commissioner of Rajasthan on a tour to Dausā. She was received by the Superintendent of Police and welcomed by him "to the land of Sundardās."

of Dādū's last and youngest disciples. From early on, a merchant caste constituency had found an important niche in the Dādūpanth. One of its strongholds was—and has remained—Ḍīḍvānā, which would also play a significant role in Sundardās's life.[7]

Dādū himself had a Muslim background, a fact that started being tampered with and "upgraded" in a Hindu fashion, that is, Brahminized, from half a century after his death onward.[8] This is not to say that a self-conscious Hinduization of Dādū and the Dādūpanth wiped out the memory of Dādū's roots, but rather that it has continued to determine the discourse of major spokesmen of the sect, as also of certain sections of its patrons. The issue remains delicate to this day. The tendency to obscure Dādū's origin is, however, absent in Sundardās's writings.

By the time of Dādū's death in 1603, his sect was well established in a region of Rajasthan that bore the imprint of various religious communities. Among others these included orthodox and heterodox groups of Hindus (the Nāth Yogīs being especially important), Jains, and Muslims. Among the latter, Sufis and Nizārī Ismā'īlīs notably functioned as important cultural conduits to the sants.[9] The sants usually defined themselves by stressing the contrast precisely with the groups with which they shared their habitat. They usually did this in established literary genres—mainly short poetic utterances or, for longer forms, serial poems in which they treated the several groups one by one. The early sants had also done the same, as for example Kabīr, and Dādū himself. An enumeration of sants who did likewise would make for a lengthy list.[10] Sundardās followed suit.

[7] Winand M. Callewaert, ed. and trans., *The Hindī Biography of Dādū Dayāl* [*Jangopāl's* Dādū-janma-līlā] (Delhi: Motilal Banarsidass, 1988), 71–73. For merchant caste patrons, see chapters 12–13; for Ḍīḍvānā, chapter 13.1–3.

[8] Callewaert, *The Hindī Biography of Dādū Dayāl*, 17–21.

[9] For an overview of the various Indo-Muslim cultural layers, see Marc Gaborieau, "Typologie des spécialistes religieux chez les musulmans du sous-continent indien," *Archive de science sociales des religions* 55, no. 1 (1983): 29–51. For the Nizārīs, see Dominique-Sila Khan, *Conversions and Shifting Identities: Ramdev Pir and the Ismailis in Rajashtan* (New Delhi: Manohar and Centre de Science Humaines, 1997).

[10] For Jñānī's composition, see Monika Horstmann, "The Test of Words by Kabīr's Disciple Jñānī," in *Gurumālā: Papers in Honour of Shyam Manohar Pandey*, ed. Stefania Cavaliere, *Annali dell'Università degli Studi di Napoli 'L'Orientale'* 6, nos. 1–4 (2008), 2012: 159–73.

The place of the sants in Hindu religious tradition has been a central topic of research as well as of ideological dispute.[11] Worth remembering above all is the manner in which the sants defined themselves, amongst them also Dādū. They proudly claimed to follow a middle way (*madhi mārg*) between Hindu and Muslim. This implied faith in the unity of the soul with the supreme and an emphasis on moral action, challenging the hypocrisy of the representatives of the orthodoxy in their claim to be the sole models for all men. The quintessential hypocrites were the opinionated and unsophisticated pandit and the *qāżī* of the village or small town.[12] The middle way of the sants presupposed clear notions of what other groups were like or at least what was held to be characteristic of them. The option for the middle way was, however, not accompanied by philosophical or dogmatic debate. This was very different from what was going on within mainstream Hindu and Muslim traditions. What is documented for the sants is not debate but rather the instruction they themselves imparted, on the basis of superior spiritual and moral insight. In the early period, say up to 1600, the training of sants in philosophical reasoning as a prerequisite for debate was not yet encouraged, and the orthodox, for their part, could not carry out debates with people who did not share the prerequisites of philosophical debate as they understood them. There thus exists no instance of sustained debate between the heterodox tradition of the sant type and the orthodox tradition during the period under review. There prevailed a kind of intellectual impasse caused by different presuppositions. This does not mean, however, that the sants lacked intellectuals or men of letters.

Leading early Dādūpanthīs were well aware of this. Some of them had an orthodox background. Either to redress the silent unassailability of orthodox Hinduism or with the objective of drawing orthodox

[11] See especially Charlotte Vaudeville, "*Sant Mat*: Santism as the Universal Path to Sanctity," in *The Sants: Studies in a Devotional Tradition of India*, ed. Karine Schomer and W.H. McLeod (Berkeley and Delhi: Berkeley Religious Studies Series and Motilal Banarsidass, 1987), 21–40. For the ideological edge of such reflections and with special reference to Kabīr, see Pradeep Bandyopadhyay, "The Uses of Kabīr: Missionary Writings and Civilisational Differences," in *Images of Kabīr*, ed. Monika Horstmann (New Delhi: Manohar, 2002), 9–31.

[12] Gaborieau, "Typologie des spécialistes religieux."

principles into the sect or perhaps to beat the orthodox with their own weapons, they saw to it that capable young Dādūpanthīs were accordingly trained in the art of debating. Among the first generation of young Dādūpanthīs trained in this fashion, Sundardās became the most prominent. While remaining devoted to the teachings of Dādū, he moved intellectually toward an appropriation of issues and elements of the orthodox Sanskritic traditions, especially the current Vaiṣṇava debates, and their subsumption to sant principles.[13] His heterodox, monistic stance separated him from the orthodox *saguṇa* Vaiṣṇava sects of his day. This needs perhaps to be mentioned in view of his Khaṇḍelvāl Vaiṣṇava origin, which might be related to a conservative religious position.[14]

When Sundardās was eleven years old, he was sent to Banaras for further study.[15] Allegedly he was accompanied by Jagjīvandās and

[13] He takes stock of Vaiṣṇava concepts of emotion (*bhāva*) and complete surrender in the bhakti of love as they were especially propagated by the Gauḍīyas and reinterprets these in a sant fashion in his *Jñānsamudra*. See Monika Thiel-Horstmann, "The Bhakti Theology of the Dādūpanthī Sundardās," *Indologica Taurinensia* 12 (1984): 263–79.

[14] There are also Jain Khaṇḍelvāls, but there is no indication of Sundar having a Jain background. His case is thereby different from Māvo's. Māvo wrote in 1530 and also used the serial genre of moralistic poetry, and in so far resembles Sundardās. However, unlike Sundar, he affirmed Vaiṣṇava ritual practice and wrote in the spirit of Rāma worshippers rather than of the Rāmānandī type. That Jain monasticism informed both Vaiṣṇava and sant monastic norms is a different matter. For Māvo, see Amṛtlāl Mohanlāl Bhojak, "Kavi māvā-māvjī racit vaiṣṇavabhaktaprabodhacopāī," *Sambodhi* 6, nos. 3–4 (1977–1978): 1–5, and Françoise Mallison, "The Definition of a Vaiṣṇava According to Medieval Gujarātī Devotional Poetry," in *Bhakti in Current Research 1982–85: Proceedings of the Third International Conference on Devotional Literature in the New Indo-Aryan Languages, Noordwijkerhout 1985*, ed. M.K. Gautam and G.H. Schokker, vol. 10 of *Kern Institute Miscellanea* (Lucknow, Ghaziabad, Delhi: Indo-European Publications, 2000), 291–300. For Jain norms adopted by Dādūpanthīs in the same genre of texts as that used by Māvo and discussed by Mallison, see Monika Horstmann, "Treatises on Dādūpanthī Monastic Discipline," in *Pathways to Literature, Art and Archaeology: Pt. Gopal Narayan Bahura Felicitation Volume*, vol. 1, ed. C. Singh and N. Vasishtha (Jaipur: Publication Scheme, 1991), 95–113.

[15] Rāghavdās, *Bhaktamāl*, ed. Agaracanda Nāhatā, vol. 78 of *Rājasthān purātan granthamālā* (Jodhpur: Rājasthān Prācyvidyā Pratiṣṭhān, 1965), 199

Rajjab, two of the elder disciples of Dādū. This is not documented but it remains a persistent tradition, nevertheless. From a contemporary perspective, one might speculate if this persistence has to do with an anxiety in the Dādūpanth to project the cohesion of its Hindu and Muslim constituencies.[16] The earliest hagiographical reports testify at least to such an anxiety when they more often than not relate faithfully the social group to which a disciple of Dādū belonged. Jagjīvandās may have been a kind of spiritual warden for Sundardās. He had come to Rajasthan from Banaras, had become a follower of Dādū, and was the first incumbent of the Dādūpanthī seat of Ṭahalṛī, located on the hill of that name above Dausā. He was a learned man and also left some poetry. His seventeenth-century hagiographer Rāghavdās calls him a great pandit (*mahāpaṇḍita*).[17] He is usually identified as a Brahmin, but his caste is nowhere stated explicitly, although Rāghavdās emphasizes that he had renounced orthodox norms.[18] Rāghavdās mentions the recognition received by Jagjīvandās from the king of Āmer, Mānsingh (r. 1589–1614), who allegedly came to visit Jagjīvandās. There is no archival evidence preserved for this. However, there are documents from the year 1716 (VS 1773) which prove that the kings of Āmer/Jaipur did indeed pay visits to the incumbents of Ṭahalṛī.[19] That means that the *mahant* of Ṭahalṛī had come to figure in the perception of royalty as a religious person of some consequence.

(*manhar chand* 421). Rāghavdās completed his hagiography, the *Bhaktamāl*, in 1660, nine years prior to Sundar's death. He was from the lineage of the elder (!) Sundardās.

[16] Dādū's disciples came from various groups. It may well be that patronage granted to them more often than not followed particular group identities. In the case of Sundardās and some other merchant class disciples of Dādū this is obvious. This group-specific thrust may have been in tension with the principle that the fold should be open to all social groups.

[17] Rāghavdās, *Bhaktamāl*, 190 (*manhar chand* 391).

[18] "… *divasā maiṃ dila lāi prabhu, barṇāśrama kula bala tajyau*" (… In Dausā he had taken the Lord to his heart, he had renounced the constraints of *varṇāśrama* and family norms). Rāghavdās, *Bhaktamāl*, 190 (*manhar chand* 361).

[19] For VS 1773–1781, see *Dastūr komvār* (transcript of the *taujī*) records of the court protocol of Jaipur), (Bikaner: State Archives of Rajasthan, n.d.), vol. 31, 752–53; for VS 1823 and 1827, see *Dastūr komvār*, vol. 31, 563–64.

Rajjab, the Paṭhān, who also espoused the "middle way,"[20] was one of the most distinguished and prolific Dādūpanthī authors and compilers of the first generation. In all likelihood Sundardās became attached to Rajjab during the latter's lifetime. For he moved to Rajjab's seat at Sanganer when he was over ninety years old, to die there about three years later.

In addition to Rāghavdās and Rajjab, another man who was crucial for Sundardās's shaping as a religious personality and for his establishing himself in Fatehpur was Prāgdās (local form of Prayāgdās) Bihāṇī, a merchant caste disciple of Dādū's.[21] Prāgdās resided in Ḍīḍvāṇā, but moved to Fatehpur (Sīkar district) in 1606 (VS 1663). The young Sundardās had stayed for certain periods with Prāgdās and his disciples in Ḍīḍvānā. (In Fatehpur, Prāgdās's disciples caused a meditation cave to be constructed for him. In 1625 (VS 1681), five Agravāl families built a house for him.[22] To this were added further constructions in 1637 (VS 1694). Prāgdās had died by this time, in 1631 (VS 1688),[23] and had been succeeded by Santdās.[24]) In Ḍīḍvānā there had thus been continuous

[20] See his *Vāṇī*, chapter 57, entitled by the editor in modern Hindi as "*Madhya mārg nijsthān kā aṃg*," "One's own/authentic place on the middle way," that place being defined as located on the interior path. Rajjab, *Śrī rajjab vāṇī*, ed. and trans. by Svāmī Nārāyaṇdās (Ajmer: Nārāyaṇsiṃh Śekhāvat, 1967).

[21] Callewaert, *The Hindī Biography of Dādū Dayāl*, 12.22.

[22] These were the Poddārs, Khejṛīvāls, Mors, Cāṛiyās, and Budhiyās. The Poddārs and Cāṛiyās are to this day patrons of the Nāthyogīs of Fatehpur. See Véronique Bouillier, *Itinérances et vie monastique: Les ascètes Nāth Yogīs en Inde contemporaine* (Paris: Editions de la Maison des sciences de l'homme, 2008), 214.

[23] Inscription built into the wall of what came to be known as Sundar's *maṭh* in Fatehpur commemorating Prāgdās's death on Kārttika b. 8, VS 1688, Wednesday. Ratan Lal Mishra, *Epigraphical Studies of Rajasthan Inscriptions* (Delhi: B.R. Publishing Corporation, 1990), no. 74, 114. The date and the day of the week do not tally, for the eighth day of the dark half of the moon of that month was a Saturday. However, in VS 1689, that lunar day was a Wednesday.

[24] He died on Māgha b. 5, VS 1696, a Friday, as is commemorated in an inscription built into the wall of Sundar's *maṭh* in Fatehpur. Mishra, *Epigraphical Studies of Rajasthan Inscriptions*, no. 77, 115–16. This corresponds to January 13, 1643.

Marwari patronage for the Dādūpanthī sant yogī Prāgdās since 1606. It became manifest again after Sundardās's arrival in Fatehpur in 1625 (VS 1682). Sundardās's establishment was extended in 1632 (VS 1688) and then again in 1638 (VS 1695) by the same five Agravāl families who had patronized Prāgdās in 1625.[25] Thus there was sustained investment by the Agravāls of Fatehpur in monks from their own caste. This suggests that the caste of their religious reference person mattered considerably to the patrons. Whereas a monk could declare that he held caste distinctions in contempt, his own caste origin underpinned the social status of his householder patrons. This complementarity of values is noteworthy.

Not only did there prevail a complementarity of values, the religious practices of sants and others also partly converged. The documents discussed by Śarmā also show the particular religious practice followed by the Dādūpanthīs. For instance, meditation in a cave (*guphā*) was a standard feature of monastic orders—including, among others, the Nāth Yogīs.[26] In the case of the Dādūpanth, an example of this would be Dādū's second-earliest residence in Rajasthan, Āmer. Here an underground chamber has been made into a shrine. The Dādūpanthī headquarters in Narainā (Jaipur district) provide more examples of underground or basement cells and caves, inside and outside of the temple respectively. One extended complex of meditation cells is adjacent to the *samādhi*s of the successors of Dādū. Underground or basement meditation cells attached to or below *samādhi*s constitute a link between the sant and the Nāth Yogic tradition: all Nāth Yogic monasteries have such caves or cells.[27]

Rāghavdās reports that Sundardās went to Banaras to study when he was eleven years old, that is, around 1606 or 1607, and he is known to have settled in Fatehpur in 1625.[28] During the intervening years he is likely to have spent time in Rajasthan.[29] He studied philosophy and

[25] Śarmā, *Sundar-granthāvalī*, I, "*Jīvan-caritra*," 36.

[26] Śarmā, *Sundar-granthāvalī*, I, "*Jīvan-caritra*," 27.

[27] Bouillier, *Itinérances et vie monastique*, 204, n. 4; see also Bouillier, *Itinérances et vie monastique*, index s.v. *guphā*.

[28] Rāghavdās, *Bhaktamāl*, 199 (*manhar chand* 421); Śarmā, *Sundar-granthāvalī*, I, "*Jīvan-caritra*," 29–30.

[29] For the places he himself mentions having visited or stayed in, including Lahore, see his *Deśāṭan*. Śarmā, *Sundar-granthāvalī*, II, 1004–07; for a

literature, acquiring proficiency in the prevalent poetic styles and subsequently growing into a poet. He approached Dādū's legacy via the thinking and parlance of Sanskritic systemic philosophy and the categories of the Vaiṣṇava *sampradāya*s without compromising his master's message. Dādū's central concept of the unity of the soul and the supreme, his emphasis on morality rather than on dogma, his indebtedness to the Nāth Yogī doctrine and practice—all of this Sundar retained. While abiding by the middle way, he nonetheless did refer to other systems of thought in an explicit, systematic, and comprehensive way and accepted certain positions, such as the stages of bhakti elaborated by the Vaiṣṇavas.[30]

Two examples may illustrate the way in which Sundardās referred to other positions. One is his evaluation of the yogic practice suitable for his co-religionists. He takes the physical preparations for yogic practice, the purification of the channels of the body, for a given yoga, but he favors *rājayoga*, the yoga of contemplation, over all other forms of yoga. While he accepts yoga, he expresses contempt for certain practices which he thought bordered on charlatanry, or, as he would say, folly. Foremost among them was the production of miracles.[31]

The second example relates to his construction of his genealogy (the composition is named *Gurusampradāya*).[32] This genealogy lists only three historical figures: Dādū, Buḍḍhan (whose historicity is debated), and himself. All other figures in the genealogical chain are allegorical. The beginning and the end of the genealogy are formed by the *parabrahman*, the Supreme. It thus works forward and backward, because it is expres-

German translation, see Monika Horstmann, "Als Reiseführer unbrauchbar" (2009): 1–7, http://archiv.ub.uni-heidelberg.de/savifadok/volltexte/2009/331/, accessed April 6, 2012.

30 Thiel-Horstmann, "The Bhakti Theology."

31 Sundardās wrote two treatises of yoga, one of them contained in chapters 3 and 4 of his *Jñānasamudra*, the other called the *Sarvāṅgayogapradīpikā*. Śarmā, *Sundar-granthāvalī*, I, 31–69 and 87–115 respectively. It is ironical that Rāghavdās in his *Bhaktamāl* extols Sundardās for producing magical feats in order to prove his authenticity. This only goes to show what the popular notions of the proofs of saintliness were. Rāghavdās, *Bhaktamāl*, 199 (*manhar chand* 422).

32 Śarmā, *Sundar-granthāvalī*, I, 197–207.

sive of the indelible, primeval unity of the soul and the Supreme, which takes flesh in the sants during the period of their life. The text is likely to be more than a theological statement on monism, for it may also be a gently ironical piece of refutation of the northern Vaiṣṇavas of his time who made so much of genealogy. These orthodox Vaiṣṇavas projected their four *sampradāya*s as descending from largely mythological personalities and labored hard to legitimize themselves on those grounds.[33] The orthodox Vaiṣṇavas snubbed the heterodox sants, whose very existence was an irritant to them because of their anti-ritualistic stance. In the air was also the constitution of the Mādhva *sampradāya* of the new order, comprising the Gauḍīyas. The Mādhva *sampradāya* was also known as the Brahma *sampradāya*, because it claimed to have descended from the god Brahmā, while the other orthodox Vaiṣṇava sects claimed no less distinguished divine pedigree. Sundardās, however, in his genealogy used the term Parabrahma *sampradāya* (*sampradāya* of the supreme brahman) for his own sect, the Dādūpanth, and thereby claimed for his fold of believers the rank of a *sampradāya*, claiming parity with the Vaiṣṇava *sampradāya*s, although, of course, authenticated in a *nirguṇa* fashion. The name Parabrahma *sampradāya*, "line of tradition started by the eternal self," indicates superiority over the four orthodox Vaiṣṇava *sampradāyas*, to whom perishable divine forebears are attributed. This obliqueness is fairly typical of the "middle way debates": subversive arguments were more common than frontal attacks, which were reserved for castigating hypocrisy and folly. In the process of foregrounding the "middle way," doctrinal differences, subject as they were to dispute and disputations in the orthodox milieu, were dismissed as irrelevant.

II

Fatehpur lies in the Śekhāvāṭī region of Rajasthan. In the sixteenth century this region was the realm of the Qāimkhānīs. They were Cauhāns who had converted to Islam under Firūz Shāh Tughluq. Their ancestor

33 The four Vaiṣṇava *sampradāya*s, here followed by the names of their real or purported founders in brackets, are Śrī *sampradāya* (Rāmānuja, eleventh/twelfth century), Brahma *sampradāya* (Madhva, thirteenth/fourteenth century), Sanakādi *sampradāya* (Nimbārka, twelfth century?), and Rudra *sampradāya* (Viṣṇusvāmī, fourteenth century?).

Karamcand, renamed Qāimkhān, became *ṣubadār* (governor) of Hissar. He died around 1418.[34] A branch of his descendants, headed by Fateh Khān, founded an independent state with a new capital Fatehpur (D2), established in 1449. By the time of Sundardās, the rulers of Fatehpur had thus been Qāimkhānīs for nearly two hundred years, a dynasty as much Hindu as Muslim. (The last independent ruler of Fatehpur lost his kingdom to Rāo Śeosingh of Sīkar in 1731.[35] In 1780, the Qāimkhānī territory of Jhūṃjhunū also fell to the Śekhāvats.[36]) The way in which Muslim and Hindu cultures coexisted in Fatehpur is well illustrated by a 1522 inscription on the door of the Sītārām temple. It states that the *nija mandir*, the own or actual temple of the deity, was in the underground cell. That underground cell was connected to the ruler's fort by an underground passage so that the Rajput queens of the nawāb and their retinue could go there for worship.[37] The existence of underground passages, claimed or factual, connecting Hindu and Muslim places, is emblematic of the discourse about the relationship between the two groups in Śekhāvāṭī (as much as it is emblematic of the present-day situation that the access to those underground passages is usually declared to be blocked).[38]

At the time of Prāgdās's death in the early 1630s, the ruler of Fatehpur was Daulat Khān, one of the five sons of Alaf Khān.[39] Daulat Khān is

[34] See Daśaratha Śarmā, Agarcand Nāhṭā, and Bhaṃvarlāl Nāhṭā, *Kyāmkhāṃ rāsā*, 3rd ed., trans. Ratanlāl Miśra (Jodhpur: Rajasthan Oriental Research Institute, 1996), 46–47, which reproduces a family tree of the Qāimkhānīs where Qāimkhān's regnal period is given as VS 1441–1475/ca. 1384–1418.

[35] Rima Hooja, *A History of Rajasthan* (New Delhi: Rupa & Co., 2006), 412.

[36] Hooja, *A History of Rajasthan*, 412.

[37] Inscription of Phālguna ś. 4, VS 1578. Mishra, *Epigraphical Studies of Rajasthan Inscriptions*, no. 61, 106.

[38] Véronique Bouillier, "Samādhi et dargāh: hindouisme et islam dans la Shekhavati," in *De l'Arabie à l'Himalaya: chemins croisés en hommage à Marc Gaborieau*, ed. Véronique Bouillier and Catherine Servan-Schreiber (Paris: Maisonneuve & Larose, 2004), 255.

[39] According to the family tree reproduced in Śarmā, Nāhṭā, and Nāhṭā, *Kyāmkhāṃ rāsā*, 46–47, Alaf Khān represents the ninth ruler and his regnal period is given as VS 1627–1683. Daulat Khān's regnal period is given as VS 1683–VS 1720, which would correspond to either 1626 or 1627 to 1663 or 1664.

mentioned in the inscription commemorating Prāgdās's death. Fatehpur was and has remained a center of the Nāth Yogīs.[40] For Sundardās's time, what the hagiographer Rāghavdās has to say in his *Bhaktamāl* is revealing. According to him, the nawāb paid Sundardās a visit and asked him to produce a visible yogic feat, with which Sundardās complied. It is revealing in two ways: it indicates the ubiquity and authority of yogīs, and the link of the sant yogīs, hardly distinguished from Nāth Yogīs in common perception, with the ruling power whose patronage of the sant is foregrounded by the hagiographer, the authority of the saint being thereby confirmed by royalty.

In the seventeenth century, Fatehpur was also a center of the descendants of Shams Pīr, the Nizārī Ismā'īlī saint. Legend has it that the Nizārī lineage of Fatehpur was established by Tāj-ud-dīn, a contemporary of Alaf Khān (who had been childless and to whom Tāj-ud-dīn had given "the boon of a son," in fact, eventually, five sons![41]). The gift of a son by a religious man is a stock motif of hagiography. If Tāj-ud-dīn was really a contemporary of Alaf Khān he must have come to Fatehpur some decades before Sundardās.

The second of Alaf Khān's five sons, Neyāmat Khān, was the poet whose sobriquet was Jān Kavi. He flourished between 1612 or 1614 and 1664 (VS 1669 or 1671 and 1721).[42] This opens yet another window on the Muslim tradition of Fatehpur, for Jān Kavi was a disciple of Pīr Shaikh Muḥammad Chishtī.[43] Jān Kavi was stupendously productive, and among his works, which include Sufi romances, numerous treatises on *rīti* poetology, lexicography, geography, gemmology, and many other topics, there is also the history of his family, the *Kyāmkhāṃ rāsā*, written in VS 1711/1654. This work is, not only in name but also in style, a *rāso* composition of heroic poetry, populated with Hindu gods and drawing on Hindu mythological motifs. In the opening chapter of this

[40] For the present time, see Bouillier, *Itinérances et vie monastique.*

[41] Khan, *Conversions and Shifting Identities*, 102.

[42] Paraśurām Caturvedī, ed., *Sūfī-kāvya-saṃgrah*, 4th ed. (Prayāg: Hindī Sāhitya Sammelan, 1965), 148–63; for his identity, 148–49. The first work of Jān Kavi is dated VS 1671, that is, two years later than indicated by Caturvedī. Śarmā, Nāhṭā, and Nāhṭā, *Kyāmkhāṃ rāsā*, 3.

[43] Jān Kavi also names four ancestors of Shaikh Muḥammad. Śarmā, Nāhṭā, and Nāhṭā, *Kyāmkhāṃ rāsā*, 4.

history, Jān expresses the unity of Hindus and Muslims, made out of the same clod of earth by God whereby difference is just one of name.[44] To make all men descendants of Adam, God's first human creature, is of course a common Muslim interpretation of the origin of men,[45] and for that matter could be taken by sants to correspond with the unity of men in God because of the identity of their souls with the supreme spirit. In the same opening chapter, as in the rest of Jān Kavi's composition, Indic poetic heritage prevails. This then surely reflects a merging of Islamicate and Hindu traditions, not merely the appreciation of it by the author, but also his being a product of it.

III

Sundardās took stock of the composite culture in which he lived, although in a somewhat discreet fashion. Indeed, the broad religious culture of Sundardās's habitat is reflected in his satirical text *Pañca prahāra* ("Five Strokes"). The text forms the introductory chapter of his *Sarvāṅgayogapradīpikā*. Yet, notably, when it comes to castigating

[44] *Kyāmkhāṃ rāsā*, 12–15. The textreads:
jabahī bhayau karatārako, manuṣa racanako cāi/
taba pahale [jinakau] kīyo, sunahu kathā cita lāi//12//
kahata jāṃna kavi jāniyo, graṃthaniko mata gāṃva/
māṭītaiṃ paidā bhayau, tāteṃ ādama nāṃva//13//
māṃnasa bhaye jahāṃnamaiṃ, te sagare kahi jāṃna/
ādama pāchai ādamī, heṃdū musalamāṃna//14//
yeka piṃḍa ina duhuṃnakau, nāṃ aṃtara rata cāṃma/
pai karatī nāhiṃna milāi, tāteṃ nyāre nāṃva//15//

When the Creator wished to create man,
whom did he make first? Listen attentively to that story! (12)
Jān Kavi says: I know the opinions of the books,
man was made of earth, this is why he is called Adam. (13)
All men on earth are his descendants, says Jān.
After Adam came the scions of Adam (men, *ādmī*), Hindus and Muslims. (14)
One clod of earth for both of them, no difference in blood or skin.
Their tasks, however, do not coincide, therefore their names are different. (15)

[45] *Qur'an*, Sura 38: 75.

the foolish or immoral behavior of religious specialists, he exclusively directs his ire at Hindus. Not a single Muslim is mentioned.[46] The text is one of rich intertextuality, full of motifs and phrases found elsewhere in Sundardās's works.[47] This points to a source of common conventions on which the author drew. The text is thirty-eight stanzas long and ostensibly discusses the "six philosophical systems" and the "sixty-nine heresies," neither of which it really proceeds to do. Probably the way its program is phrased is also part of a convention specific to the genre it represents. Here, I discuss some stanzas. Starting with the "Description of the false views related to ritual," Sundardās first ridicules the orthodox in thirteen stanzas of which the first five are cited here:

> Some perform Vedic sacrifices, such as the Vājapeya, the cow sacrifice, and many other kinds of sacrifices, some rush from sacred place to sacred place, they make the round of the whole earth in a clockwise fashion. (12)
> Some believe in rites that purify and respectable decorum, some perform the six types of rites, the *saṃdhyā, tarpaṇa*, and so forth.[48] (13)
> Some lead the lives of householders of which there is a great variety, day and night clutched in the shackles of wife and children, some opt for the life of a forest hermit, some have moved to the forest with their women. (14)
> Some are *paramahaṃsa saṃnyāsis*, who have abandoned their Vedic school and the sacrificial cord but remain fettered in many ways, some bathe incessantly, in the evening, in the morning, and at noon. (15)
> Some hold all kinds of vows; some fast, diminishing their food as the moon wanes,[49] some pluck leaves and flowers, which they offer in worship believing that there is a difference between the deity and themselves.[50] (16)

[46] For the text, see Śarmā, *Sundar-granthāvalī*, I, 87–94; for an English translation, see Horstmann, "Approaching Sant Satire," in *Indian Satire in the Period of First Modernity*, ed. Monika Horstmann and Heidi Rika Maria Pauwels (Wiesbaden: Harrassowitz, 2012), 95–115.

[47] So, for example, in the *Sahajānanda-aṣṭaka*.

[48] These six are, according to the explanation of Dvārikādās Śāstrī, ed. *ŚrīSundar-granthāvalī*, pt. 2, 2nd ed. (Varanasi: ŚrīDādūdayālu-Śodh-Saṃsthān Ṭrusṭ, 1978), 116, are *saṃdhyā, japa, tarpaṇa, homa, balivaiśvadeva*, and *snāna*.

[49] According to this regimen the intake of food is progressively diminished in proportion to the waning of the moon.

[50] A fatal error in the eyes of monists like Sundardās.

Sundardās continues with a "Description of the false views related to normative texts."[51] Interestingly, what follows is only partly what the subtitle suggests, for in the latter part of that paragraph the author makes fun of poets and would-be poets trying their hand at then current literary forms. In so doing and thereby following a common practice of authors of satire, a lesser poet than Sundardās would have risked making a fool of himself.

> Some have themselves weighed against precious stones, which they distribute along with all sorts of food, garments, and books, some recite Sanskrit texts, they rattle off all the complicated *śloka*s that they know. (25)
> Some study *śāstra*s with logical acumen, for some stuffing in tough sciences means well-being, some are knowledgeable in theories and views, some show off with their study of grammar. (26)
> Some recite poems in the *kavitta* metre, some pen *kuṇḍaliyā*s and *arilla*s, some concoct sequences of *chand*s and *savaiyā*s, the syllables of which they scrape together, some spend their time with music to the lute, flute, cymbals, and drum, some perform mimicry, gesticulate, and sing beguiling songs. (28)

Sundardās goes on to make fun of the virtuosi of fasting and ends by denouncing the monastic garb as a fallacious prop of a religious life. He exasperatedly concludes:

> Some throw magical ashes at people, snatch their belongings, and make away in a wink of the eye, some apply red powder on their bodies, some roam about with a little boy in tow.[52] (47)
> Some swirl a dagger and shout the Narasiṃha or the Bhairav mantra to scare away enemies, some consume *āk* and *dhatūrā*,[53] whereas some stuff red-hot coals into their mouth. (48)
> Some consume opium, poppy leaves, or hashish, the mind of those fools is fluid like a wave. One could go on endlessly talking of such aberrations! Be sensible and clasp the Guru's feet! (49)
> Sundar has observed and considered many views, by the grace of the True Guru you will not get entangled in them. (50)

51 Sundardās, *Pañca prahāra*, stanzas 25–28.

52 The notoriously unholy holy men are known for keeping boys as "disciples." This is also a standard motif in caricatures of ascetics.

53 Both plants, *āk* (*Catotropis gigantea*) and *dhatūra* (*Datura alba*), contain strong narcotics.

The text forms the second part of the first chapter of the *Sarvāṅgayogapradīpikā*, which comprises four chapters altogether. The first part of the first chapter contains the invocation and an overview of the contents of the text. Chapters 2 to 4 treat the various forms of yoga. The satirical *Pañca prahāra* stands in stark contrast to the systematic exposition of yoga which follows. It treats serially the follies pursued by benighted Hindus and Jains alike. Sundardās himself claims a higher knowledge, the knowledge of the sant yogī, and viewed from that perspective, the pandemonium he depicts in his work also requires that in conclusion he expound the valid path to enlightenment.

The didactic method Sundardās used came down to him via the preachers' tradition and had for a long time been especially popular among the Jains, who also expressly theorized about the place of such elements in religious instruction. The serialized format too had ancient antecedents and was one of the common literary forms used in the literature produced by preaching ascetics or monks in general, Jain and Hindu alike.[54] Texts like these were intended to prepare, by entertainment, an audience for the subsequent more serious part of the religious message. The genre is intricately related to Hindu and Jain traditions and is used to redress the false consciousness of followers of those traditions. It is so persistently framed within a Hindu/Jain idiom that the Muslim simply has no role to play. To conclude from the absence of criticism of Muslim misdemeanors that Sundardās took no notice of them because he was not concerned with Muslims, or was deliberately blind to them, is incorrect. In this composition he is just operating within the conventions of an established literary genre,

[54] Sundardās's writings, like those of other sants, and for that matter medieval vernacular poetry in general, are deeply informed by rhetoric strategies which were also popular in classical Sanskrit and Prakrit literature, be it the cliché of the good man and the bad man or the strategies canonical in the genre of the *dharmakathā* of the Jains. See Siegfried Lienhard, *A History of Classical Poetry: Sanskrit, Pali, Prakrit*, vol. 3, fasc. 1 of *A History of Indian Literature*, ed. Jan Gonda (Wiesbaden: Harrassowitz, 1984), 164, for classical Sanskrit poetry, and Ādināth Nemīnāth Upadhye, ed., *Uddyotana Sūri['s]* Kuvalayamālā, vols. 45–46 of *Singhī Jain Granthamālā* (Bombay: Bhāratīya Vidyā Bhavan, 1959–1970), II, 114, 127–28, for Sanskrit and Prakrit literature.

for only thereby would he be able to satisfy the expectations of his audience.

IV

Sundardās responded comprehensively to the Sufi tradition, particularly in two of his compositions which are set in a genuinely Sufi philosophical and terminological register. Whereas these compositions make consistent use of Sufi parlance, other texts of his testify to the ubiquitous presence of the Muslim and especially Sufi tradition in his ambience. A couple of his songs are primarily in Persian, which was quite common in the sant milieu and of which several songs by Dādū offer similar examples.[55] Whereas a natural adaptation to Islamicate culture and aesthetics can be taken for granted with Sundardās and other inhabitants of his region, this should be distinguished from the deliberate artistic and theological effort Sundardās made to express his sant message in Sufi terms in those two compositions. They are given here in the original and in English. Along with two subsequent texts, they form a sequence in Sundardās's works, the final redaction of which he himself authorised, as has been mentioned above.[56]

Text 1: *Pīr-murīd-aṣṭaka*

दोहा	*Dohā:*
सुन्दर षोजत षोजतें पाया मुरसिद पीर। कदम जाइ उसके गहे देष्या अति गम्भीर ॥१॥	While Sundar searched continuously, he found the master, he fell at his feet and clasped them, he saw that which is exceedingly profound. (1)
चामर	*Cāmar:*
औवलि कदम उस्ताद के मैं गहे दोऊ दस्त। उनि मिहर मुझ पर करी ऐसा हवै गया मैं मस्त ॥ जब सुषुन करि मुझ कौं कहया तू बन्दिगी करि षूब। इस राह सीधा जाइगा तब मिलैगा महबूब ॥१॥	At the first step, I clasped both hands of the master. He was kind to me, and at that stage I got intoxicated. When he spoke to me: "Practice intense servitude! Take this straight path, then you will find the Beloved." (1)

[55] Rāga Kāfī, no. 12. Śarmā, *Sundar-granthāvalī*, II, 926–27.

[56] Śarmā, *Sundar-granthāvalī*, I, 281–306.

अब उठि अरज उस्ताद सौं मैं करी ऐसी रौस। तुम मिहर मुझ पर करौ मुरसिद मैं तुम्हारी कौस॥ वह बन्दगी किस रौस करिये मुझै देहु बताइ। वह राह सीधा कौन है जिस राह बन्दा जाइ॥२॥	Then I stood up and asked the master as follows: "Be kind with me, oh Master, I am your bow. Tell me, how one has to practice servitude. What is that straight path on which the servant walks?" (2)
तब कहै पीर मुरीद सौं तूं हिरसरा बुगुजार। यह बन्दगी तब होइगी इस नफ्स कौं गहि मार॥ भी दुई दिल तैं दूर करिये और कुछ न चाह। यह राह तेरा तुझी भीतर चल्या तूं हीं जांइ॥३॥	Then the master said to the disciple: "Let go of all desire! That servitude will arise as you have slain your animal soul. Ban also all duality from your heart, there shall no wish be left. This is your path, inside of you, and you alone can walk it." (3)
तब फिरि कह्या उस्ताद् सौं मैं राह यह बारीक। क्यौं चलै बन्दा बिगरि देषैं सबौं सौं फारीक॥ अब मिहिरि करि उस राह कौं दषिलाइ दीजै पीर। मुझ तलब है उस राह की ज्यौं पिवै प्यास नीर॥४॥	Again I said to the master: "That path is subtle, how can the disciple walk it without seeing, separate from all? Be kind and show me now that path, oh Master! I crave that path like a man thirsting for water." (4)
तब कहै पीर मुरीद सेती बन्दगी है येह। इस राह पहुंचै चुस्तदम करि नांव उसका लेह॥ तूं नांव उसका लेहगा तब जाइगा उस ठौर। जहां अरस ऊपर आप बैठा दुसार नहि और॥५॥	Upon this the master said to the disciple: "Servitude is this: You will reach that road by breathing practice and reciting His name. If you recite His name you will reach the place where He himself sits on the throne, where there is no one else." (5)
तब कहै तालिब सुनौं मुरसिद जहां बैठा आप। वह होइ जैसा कहौ तैसा जिसै माइ न बाप॥ बैठा उठा कहिये तिसै औजूद जिसके होइ। बेचूंन उस कौ कहत हैं अरु बेनमूनै सोइ॥६॥	Then the disciple said: "Listen, oh Master, where He himself sits, what is the place like? Is He like someone who has neither mother nor father? He sits and stands, tell me what kind of existence does He have? People call Him matchless and without precedent." (6)
जब कह्या तालिब सषुन ऐसा पीर पकरी मौन। कौ कहेगा न कह्या न किनहूं अब कहै कहि कौन॥ तब देषि बोर मुरीद की उन पीर मूंदे नैंन। जौ षूब तालिब होइगा तौ समझि लेगा सैन॥७॥	When the disciple had thus spoken the master fell silent. No one has ever told or will tell this to anybody, so how will anyone tell this now? The master gazed at his disciple and then closed his eyes. He who makes a good disciple will understand the sign. (7)

हैरान है हैरान है हैरान निकट न दूर। भी सषुन क्यौं करि कहै तिस कौं सकल है भरपूर॥ सम्बाद पीर मुरीद का यह भेद पावै कोइ। जो कहै सुन्दर सुनै सुन्दर उही सुन्दर होइ॥८॥	There is astonishment, astonishment, astonishment: He is neither near nor far. Moreover, how can one speak of Him who pervades all? Rare are those who will penetrate the mystery of the dialogue of master and disciple. He who speaks is the Beautiful One (Sundar), he who listens is the Beautiful One, he alone becomes the Beautiful One. (8)

Text 2: *Ajab-khyāl-aṣṭaka*

दोहा	*Dohā:*
सिजदा सिरजनहार कौं मुरसिद कौं ताजीम्। सुन्दर तालिब करत है बन्दौं कौ तसलीम॥१॥	Sundar falls at the feet of the Creator, he pays reverence to the master, he bows to the servants of God. (1)
सुन्दर इस औजूद मौं अजब चीज है वाद। तब पावै इस भेद कौं षूब मिलै उस्ताद॥२॥	Sundar, I will speak of a strange thing inside the body. One will penetrate its mystery as soon as one has found a good master. (2)
गीतक	*Gītak:*
उस्ताद सिर पर चुस्तदम कर इश्क अल्लाह लाइये। गुजरान उसकी बंदगी मौं इश्क बिन क्यौं पाइये॥ यह दिल फकीरी दस्तगीरी गस्तगुंज सिनाल है। यौं कहत सुन्दर कब्ज दुन्दर अजब ऐसा ष्याल है॥१॥	The master is on top of your head; by disciplining your breath you will come by the love of Allah. Engage in servitude to Him, how will you gain Him without love? The poverty of the heart is your support, it is an echo reverberating all around, it is a spear. Thus speaks Sundar: Duality subdued, there is that strange sensation. (1)
दोहा	*Dohā:*
सुन्दर रत्ता[57] एक सौं दिल मौं दूजा नेश। इश्क महब्बति बन्दगी सो कहिये दुरवेश॥३॥	Sundar, in love with Him alone, any one else in the heart is a piercing pain.[58] One who has love, compassion, and servitude is called a dervish. (3)

[57] Emendation according to Rameścandra Miśra's edition of Śarmā's work. *Sundar granthāvalī* (New Delhi: Kitābghar, 1992), I, 260.

[58] Or: "there is no one besides in the heart."

छन्द	*Chand:*
दुरवेश दर की षबर जानै दूर दिल की काफिरी। दर दरबन्द षरा दरूनैं उसी बीच मुसाफिरी ॥ है बेतमा इसमाइ हर्दम पाक दिल दर हाल है। यौं कहत सुन्दर कब्ज दुन्दर अजब ऐसा ष्याल है ॥२ ॥	A dervish knows the gate, unbelief is far from his heart. Inside he suffers pain, he is pure inside, just inside of this he travels. He is free of greed, he utters the name [of God], his heart is pure at every breath, he is in the State (*ḥāl*). Thus speaks Sundar: Duality subdued, there is that strange sensation. (4)
दोहा	*Dohā:*
सुन्दर सीनै बीच है वन्दे का चौगांन। पहुंचावै उस हाल कौं इहै गोइ मैदान ॥४ ॥	Sundar, inside the heart there is the servant's polo ground. Here on the polo ground he drives the ball into the State (*ḥāl*). (4)
छन्द	*Chand:*
काब्दस्त इस मैदान मैं चौगांन षेलै षूब है। असवार ऐसा तुरी वैसा प्यार उस महबूब है ॥ इस गोइ कौं लै जै कै पहुंचाइ दे उस हाल है। यौं कहत सुन्दर कब्ज दुन्दर अजब ऐसा ष्याल है ॥३ ॥	Firmly gripping the mallet, he indulges on the field in the polo game. Thus is the horseman, the horse is the like of him, and the love of the Beloved corresponds to this. Seizing the ball, driving it into the goal, he is in that State. Thus speaks Sundar: Duality subdued, there is that strange sensation. (3)
दोहा	*Dohā:*
सुन्दर उसका नांव ले एक उसी की चाह। रब्बु रहीम करीम वह वह कहिये अल्लाह ॥५ ॥	Sundar, utter His name, desire only Him. He is the Lord, the Compassionate, the Noble, He is called Allah. (5)
गीतक	*Gītak:*
अल्लाह षुदाइ करीम् कादिर पाक प्वर्द्दिगार है। सुबिहान तूं सत्तार साहिब साफ सिरजनहार है ॥ मुस्ताक तेरे नांव ऊपर षूब षूबां लाल है। यौ कहत सुन्दर कब्ज दुन्दर अजब ऐसा ष्याल है ॥४ ॥	You are Allah, God, Noble, Forceful, Pure, the Nourisher. Praise be to You, You are the Concealer, Lord, Pure, Creator. I am desirous of Your name, Most Beloved of the beloved. Thus speaks Sundar: Duality subdued, there is that strange sensation. (4)
दोहा	*Dohā:*
सुन्दर इस औजूद मौं इश्क लगाई ऊक। आशिक ठण्डा होइ तब आइ मिलै माशूक ॥६ ॥	Sundar, here inside the body, love is blazing. When the lover will be cold, he will have found the Beloved. (6)

छन्द	*Chand:*
माशूक मौला हक्क ताला तूं जिमी असमान मौं। है आब आतश बाद म्यानै षबरदार जिहान मौं॥ मालिक मलूक मालूम जिस कौ दुरस दिल हर साल है। यौ कहत सुन्दर कब्ज दुन्दर अजब ऐसा ष्याल है॥५॥	Beloved Lord, praise be to the Divine Truth (*ḥaqq*), You are on earth and in heaven. You are water, fire, the wine within, You watch over the world. King of kings, You know those whose heart is always pure. Thus speaks Sundar: Duality subdued, there is that strange sensation. (5)
दोहा	*Dohā:*
सुन्दर जो गाफिल हुवा तौ वह सांई दूर। जो बन्दा हाजिर हुवा तौ हाजरां हजूर॥७॥	Sundar, the sluggish are far from the Lord. The servant who waits upon Him is present in His Presence. (7)
छन्द	*Chand:*
हजार हजूर कहैं गुसैया गाफिलों कौं दूर है। निरसंध इकलस आप वोही तालिबां भरपूर है॥ बारीक सौं बारीक कहिये बड़ा बिसाल है। यौ कहत सुन्दर कब्ज दुन्दर अजब ऐसा ष्याल है॥६॥	Him who is present in His Presence one calls a *gusāī*, he shuns the sluggish. [Between the two] there is no gap, there is only one *rasa*, it is only He who pervades His disciples. He is finer than the finest and vastly expansive. Thus speaks Sundar: Duality subdued, there is that strange sensation. (6)
दोहा	*Dohā:*
सुन्दर सांई हक्क है जहां तहां भरपूर। एक उसी के नूर सौं दीसै सारे नूर॥८॥	Sundar, the Lord is the Divine Truth, He is all-pervading. Only by His light are all other lights visible. (8)
छन्द	*Chand:*
उस नूर तैं सब नूर दीसै तेज तैं सब तेज है। उस जोति सौं सब जोति चमकै हेज सौं सब हेज है॥ अफ्ताब अरु महताब तारे हुकम उसके चाल है। यौ कहत सुन्दर कब्ज दुन्दर अजब ऐसा ष्याल है॥७॥	By His light all lights are visible, all brightness comes from His brightness. All light shines by His light, from His love is all love. The sun and moon and the stars move on His command. Thus speaks Sundar: Duality subdued, there is that strange sensation. (7)
दोहा	*Dohā:*
सुन्दर आलिम इलम सब षूब पढ्या आंषूंन। परि उस कौं क्यौं कहि सकै जो कहिये बेच्यूंन॥९॥	The wise have studied many times all words of wisdom, but how can they speak of Him who is called matchless? (9)

छन्द	*Chand:*
बेच्यूंन उस कौ कहत बुजरग बेनिमून उसै कहैं । अरु औलिया अबिया वै भी गोस कुतब षड़े रहै ॥ को कहि सकै न कह्या न किनहूं सषुन परै निराल है । यौ कहत सुन्दर कब्ज दुन्दर अजब ऐसा ष्याल है ॥८ ॥	They call Him matchless, great, incomparable they call Him, and the *auliyā* and even prophets, saints, and princes stand before Him. Nobody can speak of Him, there are no words for Him, He is beyond all and strange. Thus speaks Sundar: Duality subdued, there is that strange sensation. (8)
दोहा	*Dohā:*
ष्याल अजब उस एक का सुन्दर कह्या न जाइ । सषुन तहां पहुचै नही थक्या उरै ही आइ ॥१० ॥	The strange sensation of the One, oh Sundar, cannot be described. Words do not reach Him, but simply come back here, fatigued.

The two compositions abound with the Perso-Arabic terminology of Sufism. Perhaps Sundardās is just performing a stylistic feat here, using Sufi terms to express his sant message, fond as he was of playing with different language registers.[59] In his *Deśāṭan* ("Travels in the Regions") he uses the stylistic device known from Roḍā's *Rāulavela* (eleventh century?), namely writing in the dialect of a region he refers to or at least mentioning its linguistic oddness.[60] The conscious play with linguistic registers had been a popular literary device since the very beginning of new Indo-Aryan vernacular literature, marked by texts like Roḍā's, not to mention more ancient languages of Indian literature.[61] Thus Sundardās's linguistic playfulness is no novelty.

Is there more to the two octaves beyond the play with style registers? Octaves are basically hymns of praise, chanted in the rhythm of their

[59] There is, e.g., also an octave written by him in Panjabi, which he named "Octave in the Panjabi Language." Śarmā, *Sundar-granthāvalī*, I, 275–76.

[60] For that text, see Monika Horstmann "Als Reiseführer unbrauchbar" (2009): 1–7, http://archiv.ub.uni-heidelberg.de/savifadok/Volltexte/2009, accessed April 6, 2012.

[61] For Roḍā's *Rāulavela*, see the edition, translation, and study by Bhayani. H.C. Bhayani, ed. and trans., *Rāula-vela of Roḍa: A Rare Poem of c. Twelfth Century in Early Indo-Aryan* (Ahmedabad: Parshva Prakashan, 1994).

particular meter. The *Pīr-murīd-aṣṭaka* opens with a *dohā*, the *Ajab-khyāl-aṣṭaka* has *dohā* stanzas alternating with typical octave meters. The *dohā* passages, however, are not recited along with the Sundardās octaves used in Dādūpanthī liturgy. More importantly in our context, the two octaves cited above do not figure in this liturgy. They are, however, by the intention of the author, integral to, and indispensible for, the texts. It is likely that the octaves were originally recited in full and performed also in the homiletic practice where, at least in our time, interspersed *dohā*s and passages of versified praise are a standard feature.[62] Purohit Harinārāyaṇ Śarmā in his commentary on the *Pīr-murīd-aṣṭaka* says: "In this octave there is a description of the four *manzils*, *maqāms*, or states according to Sufi belief. There are shown (1) *šarī'a*, (2) *ṭarīqa*, (3) *ma'rifa*, and (4) *ḥaqīqa* and their symptoms are also given and how the seeker (*ṭālib/jijñāsu*) benefits from these. Those people [the Sufis] call these four stages and the results obtained from them (1) *malakūt*, (2) *jabarūt*, (3) *lāhūt*, and (4) *hāhūt*."[63]

According to this commentary, the octave is specifically keyed to the philosophy of Ibn 'Arabī. It needs, however, to be kept in mind that on the surface, a systematic treatment as suggested by the commentary is less evident in the text, although of course the theme of the text is the spiritual progress of the disciple embarking on the mystical path. The progressive stages are:

Finding the master after long search. (*dohā* 1)
Intoxication upon finding him. The master promises that by becoming a servant the disciple will find the straight path leading to the divine beloved (*maḥbūb*). (*cāmar* 1)
The disciple abandons himself to the master. He becomes the bow in his master's hand. This implies that the master's revealing message is the arrow issuing from it and hitting the target, his disciple's mind.[64] (*cāmar* 2)
The master proceeds to explain that after slaying his animal soul (*nafs*) the disciple will be able to practice servitude and that after doing away with

62 Monika Thiel-Horstmann, "Dādūpanthī Sermons," in *Living Texts from India*, ed. Richard K. Barz and Monika Thiel-Horstmann (Wiesbaden: Otto Harrassowitz, 1989), 141–83.

63 Śarmā, *Sundar-granthāvalī*, I, 285.

64 A common metaphor; see, e.g., Sundardās's *Guru upadeśa jñānāṣṭaka*, *dohā* 3/*gītak* 2. Śarmā, *Sundar-granāvalī*, I, 248.

duality, he will hit the straight path located entirely in his interior and nowhere else. (*cāmar* 3)
The disciple is anxious lest he miss that subtle path, for in the interior there prevails darkness. (*cāmar* 4)
The master tells him of two means which will lead him on to the throne of God, namely breath control and the name of God. (*cāmar* 5)
As the disciple goes on asking about the properties of God residing in the highest heaven, (*cāmar* 6)
the master falls silent, obviously transported to mystical union. He has no words, only his glance communicates to his disciple that he has reached the realm beyond speech. (*cāmar* 7)
The disciple is left with the experience of wonder, for God pervades all. He is the Beautiful One which is why Sundar too is that Beautiful One. (*cāmar* 8)

The spiritual progress described in the composition is less precisely technically Sufi for it also encompasses sant notions. Sundardās rather delineates the common ground of Sufi and sant belief according to which one has to abandon oneself to the master (pīr/guru), leave behind all duality and desire, subdue one's lower impulses and desires (*nafs/man*), practice breath control, and apply himself to the name of God (*ẕikr/nām*). The sants owed the practice of breath control to yoga; Sufis, however, also sympathized with yogic practice.[65] It is likely that Sundardās's yogic proficiency appealed to the local Sufis.

Sundardās displays his command of the Sufi tradition and language, but he does not engage specifically Sufi terminological and ritual details, except for the practice of reciting the name of God in *ẕikr*. In the last line of the first octave there is, however, an indication of the subtle way in which the author weaves together Hindu and Muslim traditions. His own name Sundar, "Beautiful," is used to express the unity of the speaking master, the listening disciple, and God the Beautiful One. This captures in hidden fashion the Muslim idea of God as beautiful. Sundar thus remains on his own ground while reaching out to Muslim traditions, even literally identifying with them by making his own name an epithet of Allāh.

The second octave, *Ajab-khyāl-aṣṭaka*, has a slightly different form. Here, *dohā*s and *gītak*s (a synonym of *chand*) alternate, with two *dohā*s

[65] See Carl W. Ernst, "Situating Sufism and Yoga," *Journal of the Royal Asiatic Society* 15, no. 1 (2005): 15–43.

as opening stanzas. The two types of verses are linked by chiasmus, as for example constituted by the word *ustād* occurring at the end of *dohā* 2 and at the beginning of the following *gītak*. This lays emphasis on the words thus linked by repetition, adding progressive dynamics to the composition. All terms thus emphasized have Sufi conceptual connotations: *ustād* (master), *durveś* (poor), *maidān* (field, of battle or games), *allāh, māśūk* (beloved), *hāzarām hazūr/hazār hazūr* (present in the Presence), *nūr* (light), and *becūn* (matchless). Besides, many other particularly Muslim concepts abound in the hymn, including different names for Allāh, the concept of sluggishness (*ghaflat*), and that of the mystical state (*ḥāl*). By Sundardās's time, these terms had established themselves in the Khaṛī Bolī style of Hindi and in the common parlance of the sants. The distinguishing mark of Sundardās's compositions, however, is the self-conscious, studied, and stringent way in which he construes the devices expressive of the Sufi path.

As mentioned before, these two octaves are followed by two more octaves which are also expressive of the state of mystical union. One is the "Octave of Swinging in Wisdom" (*Jñāna-jhūlanāṣṭaka*, the meter of the composition also being called *jhūlanā*, "swinging"), the other the "Octave of the Bliss of Spontaneous Union" (*Sahajānandāṣṭaka*). Here, too, Sundardās uses Sufi terms, although more sparsely. In the opening stanza of the "Swinging" hymn he locates the master, identical with the Supreme, in the souls (*aravāh*), saying:

उस्ताद के कदम सिर पै धरौं अब झूलना षूब बषानत हौं ।
अरवाह मैं आप विराजत है वह जानका जान है जानत हूं ॥

I will place the master's foot on my head, I am now talking at some length about swinging. He himself resides in the souls, I recognize that He is the Life of life.

Sundardās continues to employ a Khaṛī Bolī Hindi register of speech in the rest of the verses, along with the Perso-Arabic loanwords commonly used in everyday speech. For the *Sahajānandāṣṭaka*, the author dwells on the negative definition of the mystical experience. He declares the difference between Hindu and Turk to be man-made and emphasizes the unity of Rām and Allāh.[66] All of this is basically composed in Dādū's tenor.

[66] The terms Turk and Muslim are often interchangeably used. "Muslim" or variants of this term may, however, also point more specifically to someone who

In the process, Sundardās contrasts Hindu and Muslim religious and ritual terms only to negate their distinction. However, when it comes to positioning himself in a spiritual family, he places Gorakhnāth first, followed by the Nāth mythical heroes Dattātray, Bharatharī, and Gopīcand. These in turn are followed by the sants, enumerated according to their canonical sequence, namely Nāmdev, Kabīr, Pīpā, Sen, Dhanā, Raidās, and finally Dādū.

Reverting to the two above-quoted compositions, we are still left with the quandary of how and what function they might serve in Sundardās's oeuvre. He must have composed them to be performed before an audience, to be chanted separately, or to embellish sermons. Their topic is the common ground shared by sants and Muslims and the path they have to take to attain mystical experience. They appropriate Sufi thought and parlance and thereby reach out to the followers of Sufism who shared the author's habitat. They may form a gesture of reverence to the nominally Muslim Qāimkhānī ruling family among whom Jān Kavi highlighted powerful Sufi inclinations. They are feats of poetic virtuosity. The literary register of the compositions reflects identity only in so far as Sundardās appropriated those features of Sufi thought and practice that would correspond to his own sant "middle way." Put differently, this involved an extraction of the Sufi stance from its Muslim basis. The two Sufi-esque compositions are of course poetry. In his other writings Sundardās did not enter into intellectual debates with the Sufis. Maybe, like other sants, he did not feel challenged to do so. It looks as if the concept of the "middle way" had sealed him off from debate. Instead, aesthetically engaging poetry came to occupy the ground of discourse. Sundardās as a preacher was then talking to the like-minded, to an audience of disciples, not of contestants.

It remains to be explored how much and for how long the two compositions enjoyed popularity in the Dādūpanth and beyond. I have made a sample study by going through the catalogue of the 637 manuscripts kept in the Dādūpanthī headquarters in Narainā.[67] The issue is

---

prides himself on abiding by Muslim norms. Therefore, sant literature often contrasts the false orthodox Muslim with the true orthodox Muslim as seen by the sants, namely someone who has compassion for his fellow creatures.

[67] Brajendrakumār Siṃhal, in collaboration with Gurmukhrāmjī Rāmsnehī, "Sūcīpatra: hastlikhit granthoṃ kā jo dādūdvārā nārāyanā meṃ upalabdh haiṃ," unpublished manuscript, 2004.

vexed because the octaves as separate texts—that is, not just as part of the collected works of Sundardās—were indeed transmitted by collective manuscripts (*guṭkā*), containing variously all of the thirteen octaves written by Sundardās or the first eight or the first five or an unidentified number of them. Of the twenty-one instances I found, the oldest MS (MS 599) is of 1750 (VS 1807), written in Meṛtā and containing all the thirteen octaves. It needs to be remembered that from a point not exactly known, the first five of Sundardās's octaves became part of the Dādūpanthī liturgy. The four octaves discussed are not among these. I found the *Ajab-khyāl-aṣṭaka* transmitted just once as the only text in an undated manuscript (MS 98).

Thus the fate of those octaves in the hands of posterity continues to lie in the dark. Sundardās's designated successor as head of his lineage in Fatehpur, Dayāldās, was interested in poetry, lexicography, and grammar. He was called a great pandit by the hagiographer Rāghavdās.[68] But was he also an ardent disseminator of Sundardās's Sufi-esque compositions? Another disciple of Sundardās, Nārāyaṇdās, is characterized by Rāghavdās as a passionately emotional bhakta. He died young. Sundardās and that disciple are mentioned together on the commemorative slab of Sanganer. Nothing specific is said by Rāghavdās about Sundardās's other three disciples who spread the lineage to Cūrū (Bīkāner, D1) and Rāmgaṛh (Sīkar, D1). Whereas Sundardās's poetry is loved by Dādūpanthīs and his songs of Nāth Yogic inspiration remain popular, I have never heard his Sufi-esque octaves being recited in public worship, and, for that matter, elsewhere, which is of course in no way conclusive. The mystery remains.

BIBLIOGRAPHY

Bandyopadhyay, Pradeep. "The Uses of Kabīr: Missionary Writings and Civilisational Differences." In *Images of Kabīr*, edited by Monika Horstmann, 9–31. New Delhi: Manohar, 2002.

[68] The status and fate of Dayāldās remain unclear. Rāghavdās says that he had received the *ṭīkā* of succession, but he does not figure in the genealogy of Sundardās's spiritual lineage. *Bhaktamāl*, 239 (*manhar chand* 522). Moreover, Rāghavdās completed his hagiography during Sundardās's lifetime. Maybe Dayāldās was the designated successor of Sundardās, but death or some other reason prevented him from becoming the incumbent.

Bhayani, H.C., ed. and trans. *Rāula-vela of Roḍa: A Rare Poem of c. Twelfth Century in Early Indo-Aryan*. Ahmedabad: Parshva Prakashan, 1994.

Bhojak, Amṛtlāl Mohanlāl. "Kavi māvā-māvjī racit vaiṣṇava bhakta-prabodhacopāī." *Sambodhi* 6, nos. 3–4 (1977–1978): 1–5.

Bouillier, Véronique. "Samādhi et dargāh: hindouisme et islam dans la Shekhavati." In *De l'Arabie à l'Himalaya: chemins croisés en hommage à Marc Gaborieau*, edited by Véronique Bouillier and Catherine Servan-Schreiber, 251–72. Paris: Maisonneuve & Larose, 2004.

———. *Itinérances et vie monastique: Les ascètes Nāth Yogīs en Inde contemporaine*. Paris: Editions de la Maison des sciences de l'homme, 2008.

Callewaert, Winand M., ed. and trans. *The Hindī Biography of Dādū Dayāl [Jangopāl's* Dādū-janma-līlā*]*. Delhi: Motilal Banarsidass, 1988.

Caturvedī, Paraśurām, ed. *Sūfī-kāvya-saṃgrah*. 4th edition. Prayāg: Hindī Sāhitya Sammelan, 1965.

Dastūr komvār [transcript of the *taujī* records of the court protocol of Jaipur]. 32 volumes. Bikaner: State Archives of Rajasthan, n.d.

Ernst, Carl W. "Situating Sufism and Yoga." *Journal of the Royal Asiatic Society* 15, no. 1 (2005): 15–43.

Gaborieau, Marc. "Typologie des specialistes religieux chez les musulmans du sous-continent indien." *Archive de sciences sociales des religions* 55, no. 1 (1983): 29–51.

Gold, Daniel. *The Lord as Guru: Hindi Sants in North Indian Tradition*. New York: Oxford University Press, 1987.

Hooja, Rima. *A History of Rajasthan*. New Delhi: Rupa & Co., 2006.

Horstmann, Monika. "Treatises on Dādūpanthī Monastic Discipline." In *Pathways to Literature, Art and Archaeology: Pt. Gopal Narayan Bahura Felicitation Volume*, volume 1, edited by C. Singh and N. Vasishtha, 95–113. Jaipur: Publication Scheme, 1991.

———. "Als Reiseführer unbrauchbar" (2009): 1–7. http://archiv.ub.uni-heidelberg.de/savifadok/Volltexte/2009. Accessed April 6, 2012.

———. "The Test of Words by Kabīr's Disciple Jñānī." In *Gurumālā: Papers in Honour of Shyam Manohar Pandey*, edited by Stefania Cavaliere. *Annali dell'Università degli Studi di Napoli 'L'Orientale'* 68, nos. 1–4 (2008), 2012: 159–73.

Horstmann, Monika and Heidi Rika Maria Pauwels, eds. *Indian Satire in the Period of First Modernity*. Wiesbaden: Harrassowitz, 2012.

Khan, Dominique-Sila. *Conversions and Shifting Identities: Ramdev Pir and the Ismailis in Rajasthan*. New Delhi: Manohar and Centre de Sciences Humaines, 1997.

Lienhard, Siegfried. *A History of Classical Poetry: Sanskrit, Pali, Prakrit*. Volume 3, facsimile 1 of *A History of Indian Literature*, edited by Jan Gonda. Wiesbaden: Harrassowitz, 1984.

Mallison, Françoise. "The Definition of a Vaiṣṇava According to Medieval Gujarātī Devotional Poetry." In *Bhakti in Current Research 1982–85: Proceedings of the Third International Conference on Devotional Literature in the New Indo-Aryan Languages, Noordwijkerhout 1985*, edited by M.K. Gautam and G.H. Schokker, 291–300. Volume 10 of *Kern Institute Miscellanea*. Lucknow, Ghaziabad, Delhi: Indo-European Publications, 2000.

McGregor, Ronald Stuart. *Hindi Literature from Its Beginnings to the Nineteenth Century*. Volume 8, facsimile 6 of *A History of Indian Literature*, edited by Jan Gonda. Wiesbaden: Harrassowitz Verlag, 1984.

Mishra, Ratan Lal. *Epigraphical Studies of Rajasthan Inscriptions*. Delhi: B.R. Publishing Corporation, 1990.

Miśra, Rameścandra, ed. *Sundar granthāvalī*. [New edition of Śarmā VS 1993]. 2 volumes. New Delhi: Kitābghar, 1992.

Rāghavdās. *Bhaktamāl*. Edited by Agaracanda Nāhṭā. Volume 78 of *Rājasthāna purātan granthamālā*. Jodhpur: Rajasthan Pracyavidya Pratishtan, 1965.

Rajjab. *Śrī rajjab vāṇī*. Edited and translated by Svāmī Nārāyaṇdās. Ajmer: Nārāyaṇsiṃh Śekhāvat, 1967.

Śarmā, Daśaratha, Agarcand Nāhṭā, and Bhaṃvarlāl Nāhṭā. *Kyāmkhāṃ rāsā*. 3rd edition. Translated (Hindi) by Ratanlāl Miśra. Jodhpur: Rajasthan Oriental Research Institute, 1996.

Śarmā, Purohit Harinārāyaṇ, ed. *Sundar-granthāvalī*. 2 volumes. Kolkata: Rajasthan Research Society, VS 1993.

Śāstrī, Dvārikādās, ed. *ŚrīSundar-granthāvalī*. Part 2. 2nd ed. Varanasi: ŚrīDādūdayālu-Śodh-Saṃsthān Ṭrusṭ, 1978.

Siṃhal, Brajendrakumār, in collaboration with Gurmukhrāmjī Rāmsnehī. "Sūcīpatra: hastlikhit granthoṃ kā jo dādūdvārā nārāyanā meṃ upalabdh haiṃ." Unpublished manuscript, 2004.

Śukla, Rāmcandra. *Hindī sāhitya kā itihās*. 18th edition. Vārāṇasī: Nāgarīpracāriṇī Sabhā, VS 2035.

Thiel-Horstmann, Monika "The Bhakti Theology of the Dādūpanthī Sundardās." *Indologica Taurinensia* 12 (1984): 263–79.

———. "Dādūpanthī Sermons." In *Living Texts from India*, edited by Richard K. Barz and Monika Thiel-Horstmann, 141–83. Wiesbaden: Harrassowitz, 1989.

Upadhye, Ādināth Nemīnāth, ed. *Uddyotana Sūri['s]* Kuvalayamālā. 2 volumes. Volumes 45–46 of *Singhī Jain Granthamālā*. Bombay: Bhāratīya Vidyā Bhavan, 1959–1970.

Vaudeville, Charlotte. "*Sant Mat*: Santism as the Universal Path to Sanctity." In *The Sants: Studies in a Devotional Tradition of India*, edited by Karine Schomer and W.H. McLeod, 21–40. Berkeley, California and Delhi: Berkeley Religious Studies Series and Motilal Banarsidass, 1987.

9 Hagiography and the "Other" in the Vallabha *Sampradaya**

Vasudha Dalmia

This essay focuses on one early modern bhakti *sampradaya* or devotional community, the Vallabha *sampradaya* or Pushti Marg (way of fulfillment), as it sought to locate itself vis-à-vis other religious formations. These other religious formations would today be regarded as incontrovertibly Hindu, but in the period under question they did not define themselves in terms of their Hinduness, or indeed as even belonging together in any recognizable way. This is not to dispute that those that were text-oriented often drew on the same reservoir of texts or shared many traits. But did shared devotional roots and practices make for the projection of a shared group identity as "Hindu" or even as part of a bhakti movement, particularly when a given community was trying to distinguish itself from competing groups? The rivalries within a given cluster of devotional communities were often bitter. These antagonisms largely derived from similar messages of salvation, competition for support from similar social groups,[1]

* An earlier version of this essay was published with the title "The 'Other' in the World of the Faithful," in *Bhakti in Current Research, 2001–2003: Proceedings of the Ninth International Conference on Early Devotional Literature in New Indo-Aryan Languages, Heidelberg, 23–26 July 2003*, ed. Monika Horstmann (Delhi: Manohar, 2006).

[1] Cf. Richard Burghart, "The Founding of the Ramanandi Sect," *Ethnohistory* 25 (1978): 126.

and efforts to assert dominance over key pilgrimage routes and pilgrimage centers. It was at these sites that both kinds of groups could be encountered—those who were still seeking their path and those who thought they had already found the answers. Both groups could respond to the power of a message and the mode of its conveyance. At established pilgrimage centers there was an additional set of challenges: how to share power with the all-powerful temple deity or, barring that, credibly contest it. We shall see that this is an issue, which is directly addressed below.

Against this competitive backdrop, it was the message itself that distinguished a given *sampradaya* from all the others. Thus, even if conversion "took place along a continuum," between "sought fixities and practised fluidities" and the boundaries between *sampradaya*s were indeed porous, it was precisely the effort to preserve differences and prevent overlapping that propelled the move toward "icy clarities."[2] Transgressions were fiercely and remorselessly punished. In viewing the terms in which the Vallabha *sampradaya*, one of the two major devotional communities centered around Krishna worship, came to define itself in relationship to other groups that comprise Hinduism today, I hope to trace its modes of demarcation. My purpose in this essay is not to insist on the continued validity of these demarcations in the present, but to offer the possibility of mapping more precisely the differences as they existed *before* the nineteenth century. Shandip Saha's article in this volume focuses on the complexity of the Pushti Marg's often-contradictory attitudes toward Muslims.

[2] Thus Sangari's comment on the process we encounter repeatedly in the texts at hand: "Evidently, till the seventeenth century, conversion, conventionally defined as a sudden shift from one belief system to another, took place along a continuum … Conversion was also tied to illumination—the sudden eruption of a new faith through miracles, sight of a holy person, teaching of preceptors, leading to an awakening or immediate transformation. Finally, conversion was often interleaved in individual trajectories of eclectic experimentation, moving from faith to faith though the pathways of intellectual curiosity, spiritual quest, theological attraction, personal friendship and dialogue." Kumkum Sangari, "Tracing Akbar: Hagiographies, Popular Narrative Traditions and the Subject of Conversion," in *Mapping Histories: Essays Presented to Ravinder Kumar*, ed. Neera Chandhoke (Delhi: Tulika, 2000), 93.

DEFINITIONS AND DEMARCATIONS OF NEW MOVEMENTS: THE PUSHTI MARG

The Pushti Marg was established in 1492 by the southern Brahmin Vallabha (1478–1530). It was further expanded and consolidated by his son Vitthalnath (1516–1586), whose period of activity coincided with the expansion and consolidation of the Mughal Empire.

The Vallabha *sampradaya* has attracted much research. Richard Barz's *The Bhakti Sect of Vallabhacarya* (1976) still offers the most accessible English-language account of its theological basis. Since the 1970s a steady spate of monographs have explicated the art, music, and ritual of the *sampradaya*.[3] But we possess relatively little insight into the lifeworlds of the people who were drawn to it.[4] Who were the first devotees and what were their life stories? How were they drawn into Vallabha's fold? I have turned repeatedly to the hagiographical compendia of the *sampradaya* in an effort to glean information on the religious and emotional lives of people represented as ordinary followers, many of whom left all their worldly possessions to follow their teacher.[5]

[3] To name a few, Anne-Marie Gaston, *Krishna's Musicians: Music-Making in the Temples of Nathdvara Rajasthan* (Delhi: Manohar, 1997) on the music of Nathdwara; Norbert Peabody, *Hindu Kingship and Polity in Precolonial India* (Cambridge: Cambridge University Press, 2003) on ritual and political power; and Tryna Lyons, *The Artists of Nathdvara: The Practice of Painting in Rajasthan* (Bloomington: Indiana University Press, in association with Mapin Publishing, Ahmedabad, 2004) on the artists of Nathdwara as they negotiated the transition into the modern era.

[4] Richard Cohen offered some sociological information in "Sectarian Vaishnavism: The Vallabha Sampradaya," in *Identity and Division in Cults and Sects in South Asia*, ed. Peter Gaeffke and David A. Utz, Proceedings of South Asia Seminar, 1980–1981 (Philadelphia: Department of South Asia Regional Studies, University of Pennsylvania, 1984), 69–72.

[5] See Vasudha Dalmia, "Forging Community: The Guru in a Seventeenth Century Vaishnava Hagiography," in *Charisma and Canon: Essays on the Religious History of the Indian Subcontinent*, ed. Vasudha Dalmia, Angelika Malinar, and Martin Christof (Delhi: Oxford University Press, 2001), 129–54, and "Women, Duty and Sanctified Space in a Vaisnava Hagiography of the Seventeenth Century," in *Constructions hagiographiques dans le monde Inde: entre mythe et histoire*, ed. Francoise Mallison, IVe Section—Sciences historiques et

My interest has remained focused on the *Chaurasi Vaishnavan ki Varta*, or the account of the eighty-four Vaishnavas who are considered the first followers of the *sampradaya*, initiated by Vallabha himself, who is referred to as Acharyaji (preceptor). If we go by this first hagiographical compendium, the prime addressees of the Pushti Marg in its initial phase were servant castes and women. There is another crucial compendium, however, comprising tales of the 252 followers credited to Vitthalnath, Vallabha's second son and ultimate successor. This is a later collection, of which manuscripts of the fully formed and commented versions go back only to the late eighteenth and early nineteenth centuries. In the present essay, I focus on the first compendium. To draw information about the lives of the first community as celebrated in a hagiographical compendium is admittedly a risky enterprise. The lives have already been molded to form a pattern, to become exemplary. Yet the self-representation does offer some indication of the people being addressed, since it was to move them to initiation in the *sampradaya* that the tales were cast into a particular form, to be then told and retold to the generations that followed.

According to Hariharnath Tandan, who has to date offered the most comprehensive study of the two compendia,[6] the collections initially comprised the kernel of the tales circulating orally in the *sampradaya*. Krishna Bhatt, one of the eighty-four elect initiated by Vallabha, first wrote these down. Gokulnath, in the third generation of the Vallabha clan, is credited with officially acknowledging the presence and importance of these tales. It is likely that they were in oral circulation by the late sixteenth century. They were later ordered in compendia of 84 and 252 tales respectively, and yet later, in the fourth generation, Gokulnath's nephew and pupil Harirayji further reworked them by folding them into a commentarial frame that located these tales firmly within the now distinct theology of the *sampradaya*. The commentary often tempered the radical content of the tales and softened the rough edges, offering much more biographical information on the life circumstances of the devotees.

---

philologiques—Serie II: Hautes Etudes Orientales (Paris: Ecole Pratique des Hautes Etudes, 2001), 205–19.

[6] Hariharnath Tandan, *Varta Sahitya: Ek Brhat Adhyayan* (Aligarh: Bharat Prakashan Mandir, 1960).

Harirayji is supposed to have completed this commentarial work around 1696, toward the end of his life.[7]

The main *vartas* or *prasangas* (episodes) relate, if taken by themselves, in a somewhat unmediated way—for they are often raw tales of emotion and release—the experience of the ecstasy that followed the devotee's entry into the *sampradaya*. These are preceded by one or another kind of trial prior to the encounter with Acharyaji and the life of intimacy with Thakurji (the lord) thereafter, which, however, Acharyaji mediates. In considering the ideas embedded in the tales and the commentary thereon, we have to bear in mind that the *vartas* are not the site for detailed theological debates; they are, much more, rough and ready models of lives in the devotional mode. The biographical details of the devotee's life, before he/she was received by Acharyaji, are invariably contained in the *Bhava Prakash* or commentary section, rather than the original *varta*. It is here that we are told the jati name of the devotee and informed of the family circumstances and the exact nature of the suffering that first moved the devotee to seek spiritual guidance. It is impossible to know whether these are fictional accounts, added later for effect, or whether they are based on historical facts and figures. As Tandan has pointed out, their primary intent was to depict model lives; it is more than likely that they were subsequently enriched by fantasy, the personal information being added or redacted.[8]

The suffering of which the tales speak is of two kinds. The first is of some sort of loss or deprivation that leaves the devotee with almost no resources to fall back upon. The second ensues when the devotee,

[7] Cf. Richard Barz, *The Bhakti Sect of Vallabhacarya* (Delhi: Munshiram Manoharlal, 1992 [1976]), 102. I have based my study on the edition by Dvarikadas Parikh, *Chaurasi Vaishnavan ki Varta (tin janma ki lila bhavana vali)* (Mathura: Shri Bajrang Pustakalaya, 1971 (Samvat 2027)). Parikh has put the original *varta* or tale in bold print, so that the commentary, which frames the tale and often intersperses it, becomes visible as such. Parikh maintains that his intentions are literary; his claim is that the Brajbhasha prose in which these tales are told is the earliest written prose in Brajbhasha to document living speech. In presenting excerpts from the tales in this essay, I have paraphrased and at times abridged the narrative; the portions in inverted commas, however, are direct translations of the original.

[8] Tandan, *Varta Sahitya*, 66–71.

early in life, is overcome by the kind of *vairagya* or intense detachment that leaves him unfit to lead a normal house-holding life. He invariably wanders from one kind of mendicant to another, one false teacher to another. This continues until he alights upon Acharyaji or one of his followers, who then enlightens the devotee about the falsity of previous teachings. Clearly, there is much scope here for the description of other routes to salvation and those who preach them, even if it is ultimately only to dismantle alternative claims.

How, then, are other religious groups and figures of religious authority described? *Anya* (other) is the most important term used in this regard. *Anyashraya* means to seek refuge in another, *anyamargiya* is a person who follows another *marga*, or path. Vallabha himself did not use these terms; they came into circulation at the instance of his successors and followers. The *vartas* make profuse use of them. Some of the *anya*, as depicted here, will be found to be so outside the pale that they will be roundly condemned and rejected. At other points, it will be more important to establish equations rather than indulge in outright rejection. This will be the case with the great Vaishnava temple deities at the most powerful pilgrimage centers, as we will see below. The treatment of non-Vaishnava temples and gods and goddesses will be more condescending. And in one interesting case, the deity considered alien will simply be replaced.

As for mainstream Brahminical religious authority, we will find that *smarta*[9] ritual will be held up to ridicule and thus disempowered. This will also be the treatment reserved for other religious leaders of the time, particularly Vaishnava leaders. And finally, the punishment for seeking

[9] "*Smarta*" refers to practice based on the *smritis*, or the whole body of codes of law "as handed down memoriter or by tradition (especially the codes of Manu, Yajnavalkya and the 16 succeeding inspired lawgivers ... all these lawgivers being held to be inspired and to have based their precepts on the Veda." Monier Monier-Williams, *A Sanskrit-English Dictionary, Etymologically and Philologically Arranged* (Oxford: Clarendon Press, 1990), 1272. It follows that a "*smarta*" is one who follows these codes. As noted by Frederick M. Smith, in Pushti Marg usage, "*smarta*" does not indicate south Indian *smartas*, who are followers of Shankara *mathas*. "The Hierarchy of Philosophical Systems According to Vallabhacarya," *Journal of Indian Philosophy* 33 (2005): 427.

refuge with leaders of *anya* or other faiths, "folk" or otherwise, will be violent, in some cases leading to death.

DISTANCING FROM *SMARTA* RITES AND RITUALS: *VARNASHRAMA DHARMA* AND *SAMSKARAS*, *VARTAS*

There is no radical detachment from *smarta* Brahminical prescriptions but myriad tales suggest that the Pushti Marg regarded itself as a sharp departure from the dictates of *varnashrama* dharma, from *karmakanda*, or ritual (particularly the life cycle rituals and fasting), and from Shankara's *mayavad*.[10] These are depicted as polarities and are often subjected to extreme polemics. The contentious issue of varna is a good place to begin an evaluation of the ways in which the Pushti Marg sought to distinguish itself.

Among the central questions was not only whether the faith was open to the lower castes but also the subsequent status of lower-caste individuals within the fold. And yet it is not as if the matter was ever explicitly addressed and a definitive stand taken. It is likely that there were many changes after the first period, particularly after the *sampradaya* was firmly established, and there was enough princely patronage to ensure its high status, public visibility, and obvious stability. It is clear, however, that in the first phase, Brahmins did not automatically enjoy higher status, particularly if they were *anyamargiya*. A closer look at a *varta* centrally placed in the compendium would lead us to conclude that although at the end of the tale, the varna hierarchy is not dismantled, it is at least much qualified ideologically, reflecting presumably the lived reality of the early period which forms the mainstay of the tales. The central protagonist of the *varta* is one Vishnudas Chhipa[11] from a village

[10] The principle of "maya," which sees the world as illusory, stands in direct opposition to "*pushti*" (grace), which comes about in the world and within family and community. "*Mayavad*" is the disparaging term used to designate the philosophical-theological edifice erected by Shankara. See Dalmia, "Forging Community," 138; for a brief discussion of the Pushti Marg's conflict-ridden relationship with "*mayavad*," see Smith, "The Hierarchy of Philosophical Systems," 452.

[11] Not only are the Chhipas distinctly low caste, they comprised a mixed community of Hindu and Muslim groups, since many converted to Islam

near Agra. The *varta* consists of three episodes, or *prasangas*, two of which have to do with matters of varna hierarchy.

In the first episode, Acharyaji happens to be passing through the bazaar in Agra, when his eyes fall upon bales of beautifully printed calico cloth. He instructs his follower Krishnadas to purchase these. The seller is a young man, Vishnudas, who sells his father's wares in Agra. Vishnudas asks for fourfold the usual price of the cloth and to his surprise receives it. But he is alarmed once he realizes that the buyer is a close disciple of the powerful Acharya. It seems better not to have to do with such folks; who knows what kind of renunciatory activity could ensue, once their money found entry into the cloth printers' workshop and through its magic power began to affect work there? His efforts to undo the transaction, however, are unsuccessful. He finally asks to see Acharyaji and when he does so, he is moved by some deep inner compulsion to throw himself at the Acharyaji's feet and ask to be accepted into the fold. Acharyaji poses his usual question: You live in the Chhipan (the cloth printers' quarter); will you be able to practice the ways of the Pushti Marg? Vishnudas assures him that he will either persuade his family to adopt them as well, or separate himself from them. Although Acharyaji communicates his teachings to Vishnudas in a remarkably short space of time, he does ask his new disciple to not follow him to Arel (near Prayag, present-day Allahabad), but rather to wait in the Braj area until Vitthalnath, Vallabha's son and successor (called Shri Gusainji in the *vartas*), comes to settle in Gokul. This is where the *varta* text proper sets in. Vishnudas has aged, he is immensely learned, but he has remained unassuming and he waits at Shri Gusainji's door. He soon observes that Shri Gusainji gets a string of Brahmin visitors who engage him in debate. They are invariably defeated, but it means strain for Shri Gusainji.

---

starting around the fourteenth century. "The Chhipas form a distinct caste who employ themselves in printing and stamping chintz or other cotton cloths, and are said to have originally come from Pindarpore in the Deccan. They are Hindus as well as Musalmans … Some of them also work as tailors … They [the Musalman Chhipas] follow the same calling as the Hindu Chhipas, and also comprise several tribes of converted Rajputs who are said long ago, to have adopted the profession of dyers. They form a distinct caste from that of the Rangrez, and do not marry the latter. They are Sunnis." Munshi Hardayal Singh, *The Castes of Marwar* (Jodhpur: Book Treasure, 1993 [1984]), 170.

So, Vishnudas decides to "deal with their arguments himself and send them off" (*prati uttar kari bida kari deun*). Eventually Shri Gusainji notices that he has been thus relieved of work and puts a stop to it, pronouncing that although Vishnudas has knowledge of the shastras, thanks to Shri Acharyaji, the Brahmins who come to his door cannot be allowed to go away empty-handed; he will therefore engage with them himself. Thus Shri Gusainji seems to be restoring the older, more hierarchical balance of power.

But there are contradictions in the attitude of Shri Gusainji himself, for the crowning incident in matters of caste hierarchy takes place when Shri Gusainji has to fulfill a wish expressed by his own Brahmin father-in-law, a Bhatt from Mathura. The Bhatt regularly asks to be allowed to feed the Vaishnavas of the area and Shri Gusainji as regularly asks him to stay out of these matters. Once when Shri Gusainji is himself to dine at his father-in-law's place, he asks Vishnudas to accompany him. He trusts Vishnudas above all other Vaishnavas, when it comes to reacting appropriately in a tricky situation. After Shri Gusainji has eaten at his father-in-law's house, he leaves his leftovers for Vishnudas to partake of (this is considered very auspicious, *mahaprasad*) and departs. The Bhatt tries to serve him fresh food, but Vishnudas declines. He refuses in fact to let the Bhatt touch his food; it would become impure. The Bhatt is angered and follows Shri Gusainji to Gokul to expressly ask him how it was that he, a Brahmin, could pollute a Shudra's food? The answer is clear. It is spelt out at great length in the *Bhava Prakash* that follows: "Do not take from the hands of one that follows another path" (*Anyamargiya ke hath ko sarvatha na lino*)[12] even if he is a high-standing Brahmin and a close relative at that. Even though he is a Shudra, Vishnudas as a Pushti Marg Vaishnava is placed higher in the hierarchy than the Brahmin father-in-law.[13]

12 Parikh, *Chaurasi*, 285.

13 "Vaishnava" here, as elsewhere in the *vartas*, is used as a designation for Pushti Margi Vaishnavas alone. A Gaudiya Vaishnava would be seen as entirely "*anyamargiya*," as also a "*maryada margiya* Vaishnava" (see below). Later Sanskrit Pushti Marg commentaries of Vallabha's doxographic work *Balabodha* have even contended that other Vaishnavas are Shaktas in disguise. On these commentaries, see Smith, "The Hierarchy of Philosophical Systems," 452.

Brahminical authority is also undermined in connection with the performance of life cycle rituals, or the chief *smarta samskaras*, which are so formative a feature of *dvija*, or twice-born identity.[14] However, in the Pushti Marg, which is constituting itself as an autonomous community, there will be little toleration for any kind of *smarta samskaras*. Evidence of this is found scattered through the compendium. There are tales, for instance, which focus upon life cycle rituals such as *chaula* or *mundana* (the tonsure of the head performed in early childhood)[15] and the death rites. Thus, even as the Brahminical performance of these rites is rejected, so too is the merit of performing them at particularly auspicious pilgrimage sites.[16] For instance, the *samskara* of shaving the head in Prayag (which is supposed to be particularly auspicious) is explicitly highlighted as a fruitless exercise. Death rites at auspicious sites are

[14] Cf. Kane: "The samskaras had been treated from very ancient times as necessary for unfolding the latent capacities of man for development and as being outward symbols or signs of the inner change which would fit human beings for corporate life and they also tended to confer a certain status on those who underwent them." P.V. Kane, *History of the Dharmasastra (Ancient and Medieval Religious and Civil Law)* (Pune: Bhandarkar Oriental Research Institute, 1974), I, no. 1, 192.

[15] Cf. P.V. Kane: "First as to the purpose of the samskaras. Manu (11. 27–8) says in the case of dvijatis, the taints (or sins) due to seed and the uterus (i.e., derived from parents) are wiped off by the *homas* (burnt oblations) performed during pregnancy and by *jatakarma* (ceremonies on birth), *caula* (tonsure) and the tying of the girdle of *munja* grass. This (human body) is rendered fit for the attainment of *brahma* by the study of the Veda, by the vrata called *traividya*, by worship (of gods, sages and manes), by generations of sons, by the performance of the five daily sacrifices and by (solemn Vedic) sacrifices." Kane, *History of the Dharmasastra*, II, no. 1, 191.

As Kane further clarifies, there is great divergence about the number of *samskaras*. However, all the *smritis* mention *chaula* or *chudakarma* (197).

[16] As Bhardwaj has shown, life cycle rituals performed at sacred places have particular significance and there has evolved a functional specialization of sacred places, thus Gaya for *shraddha* rituals, but also Kurukshetra and Pehoa "specialize in the performance of death rites for a person whose death occurred accidentally or in bed." Surinder Mohan Bhardwaj, *Hindu Places of Pilgrimage in India (A Study in Cultural Geography)* (Berkeley, Los Angeles: University of California Press, 1973), 150.

treated with similar disdain. Take the story of Prabhudas Bhat, a Khatri from Singhnad. Upon reaching old age he became extremely weak; he also sometimes had no idea where he was. Sensing his imminent death, his relatives take him to Prithodaka *tirtha*, or modern Pehoa, to die. When Prabhudas becomes aware of where his relatives have brought him, however, he insists on being taken back to Singhnad, so that he can take leave of this life in the presence of his *svarupa*.[17] His relatives refuse to heed this plea. But Prabhudas becomes well enough to be taken back to Singhnad. It is there, safe at the feet of his *svarupa*, that he finally takes leave of his body. Subsequently, all the Vaishnavas in Singhnad gather to praise him. He held death at bay for so long in order *not* to die in a *tirtha*.[18]

There is another important episode that speaks to the Pushti Marg's superiority over Brahminical authority. In it, Padmaraval tells Acharyaji, when he seeks refuge with him, that he has little idea of right and wrong. He belongs to the Brahmins of Ujjain, who are *karma-jada smartas*, that is, *smartas* who are duped by the belief that performing certain *samskaras* and sacrifices can actually bear fruit. Reflecting on the pain they had inflicted on him as well as their ineffectiveness, Padmaraval looked to Acharyaji to guide him out of the maze he found himself in.[19]

PILGRIMAGE SITES AND TEMPLE DEITIES

How does this new faith, which claims ancient roots, relate to existing centers of authority—in particular, old and powerful sites of power and the deities housed in the most sacred temples? Not surprisingly, it is Vaishnava centers that play the most prominent role. However, as the tale of Rana Vyas so clearly shows, none of the four main Vaishnava *dhams* (places of pilgrimage) can provide the succor the devotee seeks. In fact, the tale offers an incisive critique of the practices prevalent in these centers. Rana Vyas arrives first in Badrinath, high in the Himalayas, obtains *darshan*, but receives no comfort; it is too cold here, he thinks, and the way here is such that one could well lose one's life. Thereafter, he goes to the Jagannath temple in Puri. Here he does receive some succor,

[17] "*Svarupa*," literally "own form," is a term that identifies the image with the Pushti Marg Thakurji.

[18] Parikh, *Chaurasi*, 140–41.

[19] Parikh, *Chaurasi*, 172.

but he falls ill soon after and it takes him a whole month to recover. So, he takes a southerly direction in order to obtain *darshan* of Shri Ranganathji. But, he reflects, how is it possible to obtain a view of the entire image? If I look at the feet, he notes, I don't see the visage of the deity, and if I look at his visage, I lose sight of his feet. He is too large. And so Rana Vyas heads off to Dvarka. However, when he manages to obtain *darshan* of Ranchorji and is about to touch the feet of the image, the *panda*[20] in charge tells him to pay for the privilege. This Rana Vyas thinks is inappropriate especially since the *brahmacharis* will take the money afterward. Rana Vyas now decides that he must leave Dvarka. Thus the stage is set for his encounter with the true path.[21]

It is noteworthy that Acharyaji does make some concessions for those who have deep faith in the temple deities of these powerful pilgrimage sites. In fact, he often takes the form of the images in the most famous shrines, to provide the devotees with gratification in the mode they deserve. For instance, Acharyaji identifies at times with Jagannathji, the deity residing in Puri, as the two brothers, Narhari Joshi and Jagannath Joshi, who seek out Acharyaji in Puri, find out. In an effort to dispel any doubts about where true power lies, Acharyaji sends them to the temple. When they get to the temple they find Acharyaji standing next to the icon of Jagannath. When they rush back to him to confirm whether he is still at his own place, they find him seated there as well. And thus they recognize the true god.[22] There are many other such tales of Acharyaji merging into Ranchorji of Dvarka or Jagannathji of Puri. On occasion he is even depicted as superseding them.

However, there is little tolerance for a powerful shrine nearer home, namely the famous temple of Keshavdev or Keshavrai in the heart of Braj country. Keshavrai had long been the presiding deity of Mathura. Worship at the temple went back at least to the early medieval period. It was built and destroyed several times, the last time in 1669 on the orders of the Mughal emperor Aurangzeb.[23] Although it is nowhere explicitly clarified in the *vartas*, the Vaishnavas who visit shrines such

[20] The term "*panda*," deriving from "pandit," is used for hereditary Brahmin functionaries at pilgrimage sites.

[21] Parikh, *Chaurasi*, 195–96.

[22] Parikh, *Chaurasi*, 188.

[23] See A.W. Entwistle, *Braj: Centre of Krishna Pilgrimage* (Groningen: Egbert Forsten, 1987) for documentation of the successive temples of Keshavrai.

as Keshavrai's follow ways that are deeply antithetical to the way of Pushti. They are sometimes described as *maryada margiya* Vaishnavas.[24] The fate of such errant devotees is somber, as related in the *varta* of Govinddas Bhalla Kshatri. The introductory *Bhava Prakash* clarifies that Govinddas, who was conscious of being very wealthy, had given up his wife, since she was not a *daivi jiva* or godly being, making a financial settlement for her at Acharyaji's bidding. He had then been accepted into the fold and had followed Acharyaji to Mahavana in the Braj area. However, he was arrogant and unbending, and his service displeased Shrinathji. In fact, it is here, rather abruptly, that the main *varta* sets in: Thakurji communicates to Acharyaji that he is most displeased with Govinddas. To cut a long story short, Acharyaji unceremoniously tells him: *seva chor dehu* (leave off performing *seva*).[25] Govinddas goes to Mathura, but since he has become accustomed to *seva*, he now performs it for Shri Keshavrai, the manifestation of Krishna installed in the temple. But this is *viparita* (contrary) behavior, for this is not Krishna as he is manifested in the Pushti Marg Thakurji, and Govinddas is duly punished.

Thus, there are fine but vital distinctions not only between Vishnu and Krishna but also between the Krishnas of various other *sampradaya*s and the Pushti Marg Krishna. However, these equations need not be belabored as far as Shiva or Mahadev is concerned. Vaishnavas and Shaivas stand high in the competing philosophical and religious systems, as ordered by Vallabha. But they are consigned a position below the highest, which, not surprisingly, is that of Vallabha himself. And here again, as confirmed by the *varta*s, Shiva can only serve as a devotee of Vishnu; he does not possess the power to grant moksha himself.[26] When

[24] "*Maryada*" here means "the bounds or limits of morality and propriety, rule or custom, distinct law or definition." Monier-Williams, *Sanskrit-English Dictionary*, 791. "*Maryada marg*" stands for the path of those who live by the Brahminical or *smarta* code. Thus "*maryada margi*" Vaishnavas are those who have accommodated Vaishnava bhakti within the bounds of the *smarta* code.

[25] Parikh, *Chaurasi*, 101.

[26] See Smith, "The Hierarchy of Philosophical Systems," 427, 442, 445, for further information on the positioning of various philosophical and religious systems in Vallabha's doxography and of the subservient place assigned to Shiva.

a devotee inquires whether there is any difference between Shri Thakurji and Shiva Mahadevji, and which of the two is greater, the answers are simple, as we see in the *varta* of Kaviraj Bhat, Sanodiya Brahmin, resident of Mathura. One day, just as Kaviraj Bhat was reciting his own *kavitta*[27] on Bhuteshwar Mahadev at Vishrant Ghat, Shri Acharyaji arrived there. Because he appeared to be very learned, Kaviraj Bhat threw himself on the ground in obeisance and put a question to him: "Maharaj, is the goddess greater, or Mahadev?" Then Shri Acharyaji said, according to the shastras, Thakurji is the greatest. Kaviraj Bhat asked, "Maharaj, what difference is there between Shri Thakurji and Mahadevji?" Both are called *ishvar.* Shri Acharyaji noted that it has been said in the *Bhagavata Purana* that when Bhagavan assumed the form of Mohini, he was able to cast a spell on Mahadeva. However, even when Mahadeva assumed some other form, he was unable to cast a spell on Shri Thakurji. Therefore, Mahadeva was subservient to Bhagavan and Bhagavan was not subservient to Mahadev; that was the distinction.[28]

According to the *varta*, once he hears this, Kaviraj Bhat's mind is purified and cleansed. Thereafter, he as well as his two brothers are duly initiated by Shri Acharyaji. Whereas the goddess Mohini is not mentioned again, Shiva—as Bisheshwar Maharaj or the powerful Vishvanath of Kashi—is repeatedly shown voluntarily subordinating himself to Thakurji.

Village or "folk" deities are seldom considered worthy foes.[29] However, Vallabha's followers were not averse to replacing even these, as seen in the tale contained in the *Bhava Prakash* or the commentary section leading up to the *varta* of the three friends, Baba Benu (a Sarasvat Brahmin), Krishnadas (a Ghaghari Khatri), and Yadavendradas (a Bania). The ruse

[27] A metrical form of four lines with thirty-one syllables per line.

[28] Parikh, *Chaurasi*, 335.

[29] Cf. Komal Kothari on "folk" gods: "For a moment keep in mind that Krishna, Shiva, or for that matter, Buddha and Mahavir, are not folk gods. When devotees turn to them for personal salvation, they have to embark on a rigorous process of different disciplines—tapasya, sadhana, yoga, or whatever. But so far as folk gods and goddesses are concerned, they can be approached more directly with the faith that they will be able to intervene in the most ordinary problems of everyday life. Once I understood this principle, it became easier for me to decide who is folk god and who isn't." Rustom Bharucha, *Rajasthan, An Oral History: Conversations with Komal Kothari* (Delhi: Penguin, 2003), 119.

adopted is simple. Although a goddess (Devi) is worshipped—since such was the preference of one of the three friends—the mistake consists in not being able to recognize the true form, which was from the beginning that of a *svarupa* of Thakurji. It will take Acharyaji to recognize this and to effect the transformation of the goddess back to the *svarupa*. The three friends will then be initiated as Pushti Margis and the *svarupa* entrusted to them. The village will receive another image—that of a goddess (Devi)—and a Brahmin priest will be appointed to perform the due ritual. But the three friends are *daivi jivas*, or godly beings, destined to be saved. Later, they give the *svarupa* to Krishnadas's two brothers and themselves depart in the direction of Brajbhumi, where they will enter into *lila*. This will then form the main *varta* tale, which depicts their passing into *lila*.[30]

In the welter of deities and sites of religious authority and power, a hierarchy of approval and disapproval, of establishing equations or downgrading and negating, is thus established. Some allowance—by means of merger or uneasy coexistence—is made for the authority radiated by the deities ensconced at the most powerful Vaishnava sites. However, Keshavrai in Mathura, a more immediate rival, is shown little tolerance. Ultimately only one manifestation of Krishna is acceptable, that of Shri Nathji, addressed as Shri Thakurji. Non-Vaishnava deities, particularly the old rival Shiva (as Bisheshwar Maharaj of Kashi), are given short shrift, whereas goddesses, especially folk deities, are entirely sidelined and/or displaced.

CONTEMPORANEOUS VAISHNAVA FIGURES OF AUTHORITY

If it is one thing for Vallabha and his followers to compete with temples and temple icons, it is quite another to compete with Vaishnava religious leaders whose teachings so closely resemble Vallabha's own as to be virtually indistinguishable at the popular level. It is for these charismatic figures that the *vartas* reserve a special kind of rhetorical ire, ranging from outright ridicule to open abuse. The Pushti Marg alone offers a path to the supreme godhead Krishna.

[30] Parikh, *Chaurasi*, 239–41.

The relationship of Vallabha and his followers to the Gaudiya *sampradaya* was particularly fraught. As Barz[31] and Vaudeville[32] have discussed at some length, the Gaudiyas were firmly established in Vrindavan from early on. More significantly, however, they controlled the shrine of Shrinathji at Govardhan from which the Vallabhites derived their legitimation and authority. In time, the Vallabhites succeeded in ousting the Gaudiyas from the shrine, using both violence and chicanery. The *Chaurasi Vaishnavan ki Varta* offers a number of detailed accounts pointing to their tactics.[33]

A particularly vivid tale, woven into the *varta* of Prabhudas Jalota of Simhnad, discredits not only Chaitanya but also his followers Rupa and Sanatana. Rupa and Sanatana apparently grasp and absorb enough of the words of Vallabha and the power that inheres in them to convey them to Chaitanya, who in turn is endowed with enough divine grace to be deeply affected by their power, although he is unable to comprehend the words fully.[34] The *varta* is here invoking the image of Chaitanya, current also in his own *sampradaya*, as particularly prone to fainting in fits of ecstasy and excess emotion. However, in doing so, the *varta* is focusing on one aspect alone of a personality of whom indeed very little is known. Dimock and Stewart describe him thus: "It is clear that he was an ascetic and withdrawn individual, having at the same time an extraordinary personal magnetism. He was almost certainly, especially in the later stages of his life, mad, whether this be interpreted as the divine madness of the holy fool, the random madness of the irresponsible child, or, as A.C. Sena prefers, epilepsy."[35] Before going on to cite the *Bhava*

[31] Barz, *The Bhakti Sect*, 270ff.

[32] Charlotte Vaudeville, "The Govardhan Myth in North India," in *Myths, Saints and Legends in Medieval India*, compiled by Vasudha Dalmia (Delhi: Oxford University Press, 1996).

[33] These primarily occur in the life of Krishnadas. He came to be included in the prestigious group of Ashta Chap (the eight seals or poets, whose poetic works were considered the crowning glory of the liturgical corpus of the *sampradaya*).

[34] Parikh, *Chaurasi*, 134.

[35] Edward C. Dimock, Jr. and Tony K. Stewart, introduction to *Caitanya Caritamrta*, by Krsnadasa Kaviraja, trans. Edward C. Dimock, Jr., ed. Tony K. Stewart, vol. 56 of *Harvard Oriental Series* (Cambridge MA: Department of Sanskrit and Indian Studies, Harvard University, 1999), 23. Dimock and

Prakash comment on these passages, it is perhaps also important to turn to the popular reputation that his followers Rupa and Sanatana enjoyed. Dimock and Stewart offer this summary: "Rupa and Sanatana and their nephew Jiva, were brilliant men, learned in the *sastras* and every conceivable category of learning from esthetics to grammar."[36] Once again, our *vartas* present a one-dimensional image, playing upon the more dominant traits alone, as in Chaitanya's case, or completely reversing them, as with Rupa and Sanatana.[37] The message seems to be that Chaitanya, deeply affected as he is by it, does not yet possess enough divine grace to fully absorb the teaching of Vallabha. And the very erudition of Rupa and Sanatana, textual rather than experiential, debars them from grasping the true meaning of Vallabha's words, which a *maryada margi* could in any case never fully comprehend.

There are further insidious suggestions regarding the true character of Chaitanya's teaching in later passages, which apparently provides cover for, at worst *mlechha* (Muslim), at best syncretic, practices. The *varta* part of the tale of Sundardas and Madhodas, wherein these suggestions are made, is comparatively long. Although the commentarial introductory portion is also long, the *Bhava Prakash* on the whole confines itself to brief comments in the portions *interspersing* the *prasangas*, leaving these to tell their own tale, so to speak. In the introductory portion, we are told that Sundardas and Madhodas are friends. Both are Brahmins: Sundardas was born into a Gangaputra family, Madhodas is a Saraswat Brahmin. But Madhodas's father had placed his faith in a pir (Sufi holy man), and to disguise it, had pretended to be affiliated to Chaitanya. He maintained the pretense of loyalty to Chaitanya even after the birth of a son, whom he named Madhodas. Madhodas's father would place his

---

Stewart also give us some information concerning Chaitanya's visits to the Braj area and presumably his reputation there. Apparently, his first attempts to go to Vrindavan were abortive, since so large a retinue of followers planned to accompany him there that it was not practical to undertake it. When he did set out to go there, it was "in relative secret, and accompanied only by a *brahmana* and that *brahmana*'s servant. While he was in Vrndavana he was in constant ecstasy, and this so frightened his companions that they escorted him away from the place before, in his frenzy, an accident occurred" (21).

[36] Dimock and Stewart, introduction, 24.

[37] Parikh, *Chaurasi*, 135.

food offerings before Thakurji but he would call upon the pir to partake of it. As against this duplicitous behavior, which Madhodas inherits from his father, Sundardas Gangaputra is truly devoted to holy men and would faithfully serve all who came into the village. Once, when Shri Acharyaji comes by the village on his way to Jagannathpuri, Sundardas offers his services to him and after some hesitation, Shri Acharyaji, recognizing him to be a *daivi jiva*, accepts him into this fold. However, and this is where the *varta* sets in, Sundardas also wants Madhodas to give up *anyashraya*, refuge with another,[38] so he asks him to become Shri Acharyaji's follower. But Madhodas protests, saying he can be devoted only to Chaitanya. Even after initiation by Acharyaji, Madhodas cannot transfer his complete allegiance to Thakurji. Through a series of encounters and conversations, it becomes clear that the pir still comes in the guise of a *bhut* (spirit) and gobbles up the food offerings. The upshot is that Shri Acharyaji exorcises the *bhut* by setting him on fire, after trapping him in the act. When Madhodas refuses to believe this has happened, he is physically beaten in the night by followers of Acharyaji who force him into submission. Shri Acharyaji desires to rescue him because Sundardas and Madhodas are true friends and the latter, through no fault of his own, for he has been misguided by his father, has inherited habits that he can unlearn. A further miracle is performed when Shri Acharyaji feeds the whole village *mahaprasad* from that modest portion which is usually reserved for Madhodas and his family. All that is needed, Shri Acharyaji tells the incredulous Madhodas, is firm belief.[39] *Anyashraya* in this tale, then, is an intermingling of belief in the pir with only ostensible belief in Chaitanya, leaving us with the intriguing question whether this is a reference and refutation of the syncretic practices of Bauls and pirs in Bengal which are so closely allied to *sahajiya* devotional practices.[40]

[38] Parikh, *Chaurasi*, 383.

[39] Parikh, *Chaurasi*, 386.

[40] "*Sahaja*" means "easy" or "natural." It is in this sense that the term is applied to systems of belief in which the natural qualities of the senses are to be used rather than suppressed. The historical origins of the belief, as it developed in Bengal, is rooted in the Tantras, and can be said to go back to the eighth or ninth century, to the Buddhist *charya padas*. The "*sahajiya*" tradition as it evolved in Bengal blended with that of the Vaishnavas. "Caitanya, who was considered even by the orthodox to contain Radha and Krsna within his own

Apart from Chaitanya, it is Mirabai, the other vastly popular and beloved devotional figure in the Krishna bhakti movements of the period, although with no affiliation to any sectarian tradition, for whom unqualified derision and rejection are reserved. The first mention, derogatory in the extreme, is in the *varta* of Govind Dube, who goes to the house of Mirabai and spends some days there, conversing about godly matters. When Shri Gusainji hears of this, he sends Mirabai a Sanskrit shloka, the meaning of which the *varta* paraphrases thus: "If you ride once on an elephant, you leave off riding on a donkey, not even if you have to give up your life. So also having tasted of the pollen of his lotus feet, do not take partake of the *rasa* of another." Govind Dube understands that the message is intended for him and he refuses to be persuaded by Mirabai to stay at her side even for a moment. He goes straight to Gusainji, who repeats the injunction so often heard in such context: "Do not speak of your *marga* to *anyamargiya* (followers of alien paths)."[41]

The second mention of Mirabai takes place in the *varta* of Ramdas, a Mewara Brahmin. He sings Shri Acharyaji's kirtan in front of Mirabai's Thakurji. Mirabai then asks him to sing some *vishnu padas* in praise of Shri Thakurji. It is then that Ramdas realizes that he is transgressing by singing verses reserved for the Lord worshipped by his *sampradaya*, Shri Thakurji, to the lord in an alien setting, that is, Mirabai's Thakurji. He abuses her, calling her a prostitute: "*Dari, rand*! Do these *padas* belong to your lord?" And after this, he resolves to never set eyes on her again.[42] The *Bhava Prakash* concludes the tale with the following injunctions: try avoiding an *anyamargiya*; however, if you must be with one for some reason, do not speak of your path lest you suffer subsequent pain. The listener of the tale shares Ramdas's thought processes:

---

body, was a perfect illustration of the Sahajiya principle of unity in seeming duality." The Bauls, itinerant minstrels of the region, Sufi and Vaishnava in their songs and in their appearance, can be said to have *sahajiya*-like appearance, "that of a madman … who goes deliberately against society to prove his independence of it." The above citations are from Edward C. Dimock, Jr., *The Place of the Hidden Moon: Erotic Mysticism in the Vaisnava-sahajiya Cult of Bengal* (Chicago and London: University of Chicago Press, 1989 [1966]), 36, 250.

41 Parikh, *Chaurasi*, 215.

42 Parikh, *Chaurasi*, 269.

I should not stay in this village, if I do so, I may have to set eyes on her face again. I am a Brahmin, Mirabai's *purohita*, house priest, on top of that. And the lure of cash is such a bad thing in this world. It is greed which makes one lose one's dharma. So I should take my departure from this village, along with my family, so that I never have to drink water here again.

ALIEN RELIGIOUS AUTHORITY FIGURES

There are multiple sources of authority in everyday life that take care of domestic problems and offer immediate local relief. Even these are not spared the wrath of Acharyaji, however, who watches over his followers jealously and expressly forbids taking recourse to the remedies they suggest, explicitly designating it as *anyashraya*.

The Dakotia[43] is an important figure in north Indian village life. Connected to the cult of Shani, he also performs astrological functions for lower castes. He becomes the cause of much family distress in the *varta* of Damodardas Harsani, whose wife comes from a rich family. In spite of her high birth, she was very devoted to Acharyaji and performed all *seva* related work herself. Acharyaji once asked Damodardas whether he had any wish that he could fulfill. Damodardas said he had none, whereupon Acharyaji bade him ask his wife. She answered willingly:

[43] Komal Kothari has thus explicated the function of the Dakotias, a caste group which performs different functions in different regions of western India: "One other community with dual functions is the Dakot, who also perform Brahminical ritual functions for low-caste communities in villages all over Rajasthan, while being identified as astrologers (*jvotishis*) for upper-caste families in Gujarat and Maharashtra. Recognized in their respective villages as the chief priests of Shani Maharaj, a potentially vindictive deity who has to be constantly appeased, the Dakots are identified as the horoscope makers of low-caste people. They themselves are involved in the rituals of low-caste groups and eat meat, drink liquor, and are generally treated as low-caste people themselves." Bharucha, *Rajasthan*, 211. Singh has a more straightforward classification: "The Dakot Brahmins belong to the Punch-Gour group, and bear a proportion of 2.45 per cent to the total Brahmin population in Marwar, and in the North-West Provinces are known by the name of Bhadries, or Bhaddalis, so called from following the tenets of Bhaddal, though Sir H.M. Elliot describes them as branch of the Dakot." Singh, *Castes of Marwar*, 84.

their only remaining wish was to have a son. This wish was granted. However, while she was pregnant, a Dakotia came to the village and all the *smarta* women of the village flocked to him to ask him questions. They also asked Damodardas's wife whether she would go with them. Although she chose to stay back, she allowed a young girl to put a question to the Dakotia about the gender of her child. In doing so she implied that she did not simply trust in Acharyaji's power to grant her the son she had asked for. The Dakotia did indeed confirm that she would bear a son, but the mischief was done. When Acharyaji next came by and Damodardas went to pay his respects, Acharyaji forbade him to touch him. Damodardas was innocent and could not understand this reaction. Acharyaji's pronouncement was grim: "You have sought refuge of another" (*anyashraya bhayau hai*). Once the matter was cleared, that Damodardas had not himself sought this advice and the wife only tangentially, Acharyaji relented, but only marginally. The couple would have a son, but he would become a *mlechha*. Whereupon the wife pledged that she would not see the face of her son and that she would send him away to her mother the moment he was born, so that he could be brought up there. And this is precisely what happens. A wet nurse brings him up. Husband and wife lead a life of devotion and depart from life in due course without seeing the son, who does indeed become a Turk.[44]

Another "folk" figure, the Naga Bairagi, is similarly vilified. In fact, any connection to the Naga Bairagis, the ascetic militant groups attached to the Ramanandi *sampradaya* and thus nominally Vaishnava, is considered a sheer loss of time. No further condemnation is needed: they are rogues and child snatchers. The *Bhava Prakash*, which leads to the rather emotion-drenched main *varta* illustrating the consequences of associating with Naga Bairagis, tells us how Gopaldas Jatadhari, a Gaur Brahmin from Prayag, comes to be attached to this group of people and spends his youth with them. As a six-year-old, Gopaldas had gone for the annual Makar Sankranti ritual bath in the river. He began to cry when he lost sight of his father in the crowd. A Naga Bairagi then offered to take him to his father. When the boy consented, the Naga Bairagi took him to his camp, where he took possession of his things. Later, he took the boy along with

44 "Turk" is an ethnic term; in the *vartas*, it is used interchangeably with "*mleccha*" to refer to Muslims.

him to the south. And so Gopaldas came to live in the Bairagi's *jamat* (community), until the latter passed away. Gopaldas had now reached the age of thirty and wanted to visit places of pilgrimage. Accompanying a group of fifty to hundred Nagas, he first went to Dvarka and then Mathura. One evening he encountered Shri Acharyaji performing *sandhya*, evening ritual, on Vishrant Ghat. He stood still watching him. Then Krishnadas Meghan, who had accompanied Acharyaji, asked Gopaldas why he remained standing there and did not join the Naga Bairagis. And Gopaldas answered, "I lost sight of my group (*sang*) many births ago. If Acharyaji will have mercy on me, I will attain the company of devotees and of the lord himself." Tellingly, he does not refer to his father; it is religious affiliation that is uppermost in his mind. And it is as if Acharyaji has known this all along. For he calls out: "Gopaldas, have you come?" Gopaldas throws himself on the floor in obeisance and replies, "Maharaj, take mercy on me, I have come. I have strayed a lot. I have committed many evil deeds in evil company on many paths. I was swept away by the utterly depraved. With your grace I shall cross the ocean of this samsara, cycle of births." He was duly initiated and served faithfully for the duration of his life.[45]

***

It is then important to distinguish between the kind of faith-based "high" religion to which the Pushti Marg aspires in its foundational textual core and the "folk" religion that prevails in everyday life, which it absorbs relatively early in its evolution. In its initial phase, the Pushti Marg created a Sanskrit textual canon, the core of which still invoked the Vedas although the *Bhagavata Purana*, seen as constituting the fifth Veda, is projected as the primary text.[46] However, Vallabha's Sanskrit

45 Parikh, *Chaurasi*, 365.

46 As Frederick M. Smith has pointed out, Vallabha's "family background as well as ideology were preeminently Vedic in spite of his frequent (and ironic) labelling of it as *maryada* or limited." Not surprisingly, Vallabha recognized the *Shruti* texts, the six *Vedangas*, but "most importantly and authoritatively the *Bhagavata Purana*. It is possible that his category designated 'Veda' was larger than this, with the *Bhagavadgita* and *Brahmasutras* as primary, rather than supplementary to the Vedic canon…" "Dark Matter in Vartaland: On

works, and the commentaries thereon by Vitthala and later Pushti Marg commentators, formed a canon that was less than accessible to humbler devotees. The lively Brajbhasha texts that began to emerge in the post-Vallabha period in the form of the orally transmitted *vartas* retained the spoken idiom, even once they came to be ordered by Harirayji, and had a directness and immediacy that had a much wider reach. The folksy idiom has survived even in the printed versions of the Brajbhasha texts available today. These in their turn are used to tell and retell the tales as part of pious domestic ritual. And, as we know, the Brajbhasha songs of the Ashta Chap poets early on formed the mainstay of the elaborate temple service of the *sampradaya* and complemented the *vartas* into which they were also interwoven. They remain a vital part of the ritual life of the temple and house practice even today.

While the Pushti Marg evolved a theological and ritual corpus that adopted high and low texts and practice, it drew demarcating lines in all directions. Thus the Brahminical *smarta* traditions were consistently undermined, if not explicitly denounced. Likewise "folk" traditions lower down the ladder were violently rejected. Muslims could here figure only as the very distant "other."

The most vitriolic diatribe was reserved for the other Vaishnava traditions that hovered so dangerously near the truths proclaimed by the Pushti Marg. They were devalued and discredited, mocked and abused. For faith in the lord remained a mediated act, however direct the access preached. As we have seen, the mediators were less generous about sharing space with like-minded teachers than the followers sometimes were. Thus it is more than likely that in everyday practice, the many Vaishnava denominations were barely distinguishable from each other. The extreme positions taken by the acharyas and gurus, the dire threats and punitive measures articulated by them, would in fact suggest that finer theological differences mattered less at the ground level. The many bhakti traditions of the period, which loosened older ritual bonds on the one hand, while attempting to create new theologically and emotionally bound devotional communities on the other, paved the way for the kind of mergers that could, and indeed would, take place in the colonial period, as Hindu groups consolidated under the pressure of modernity

---

the Enterprise of History in Early Pustimarga Discourse," *The Journal of Hindu Studies* 2, no. 1 (2009): 29.

and new political contingencies. In the closing decades of the nineteenth century Harishchandra of Banaras (1850–1885) and others sought to consolidate all Vaishnava communities of belief, projecting them as the only true religion of the Hindus. And in this equation, the position of the "other" would indeed come to be occupied by the Muslim.[47]

It is worth stressing, then, that the modalities used by early Pushti Marg hagiographies to establish differences diverged entirely from those used by modern-day Hindu nationalists. The self was not primarily defined as "not-other," that is, as against the other, who was demonized for historical wrongs, but rather, for all the violence involved, the claims of one set of beliefs being superior to another were presented as a matter of faith, as offering the *only* path of salvation, and were therefore primarily theological and eschatological. This state of affairs was, however, at all times open to change, especially after the order started to align itself with political power in the princely states of Rajasthan. But in the period under discussion, there was not only no notion of tolerating the somewhat like-minded, there was likely no notion of toleration itself as a virtue, which need, of course, not have precluded relatively unproblematic and even tolerant everyday coexistence with the "othered."[48]

BIBLIOGRAPHY

Barz, Richard. *The Bhakti Sect of Vallabhacarya*. Delhi: Munshiram Manoharlal, 1992 [1976].

Bhardwaj, Surinder Mohan. *Hindu Places of Pilgrimage in India (A Study in Cultural Geography)*. Berkeley, Los Angeles: University of California Press, 1973.

Bharucha, Rustom. *Rajasthan, an Oral History: Conversations with Komal Kothari*. Delhi: Penguin, 2003.

[47] See Vasudha Dalmia, *The Nationalization of Hindu Traditions: Bharatendu Harischandra and Nineteenth Century Banaras* (Delhi: Oxford University Press, 1997), 338–429.

[48] Instructive in this regard is the discussion amongst scholars of religion in early modern Britain. For a review of this literature and for her own very nuanced stance, see Alexandra Walsham, *Charitable Hatred: Tolerance and Intolerance in England, 1500–1700* (Manchester and New York: Manchester University Press, 2006).

Burghart, Richard. "The Founding of the Ramanandi Sect." *Ethnohistory* 25 (1978): 121–39.

Cohen, Richard J. "Sectarian Vaishnavism: The Vallabha Sampradaya." In *Identity and Division in Cults and Sects in South Asia*, edited by Peter Gaeffke and David A. Utz. Proceedings of South Asia Seminar, 1980–1981, 69–72. Philadelphia: Department of South Asia Regional Studies, University of Pennsylvania, 1984.

Dalmia, Vasudha. *The Nationalization of Hindu Traditions: Bharatendu Harischandra and Nineteenth Century Banaras*. Delhi: Oxford University Press, 1997.

_____. "Forging Community: The Guru in a Seventeenth-century Vaishnava Hagiography." In *Charisma and Canon: Essays on the Religious History of the Indian Subcontinent*, edited by Vasudha Dalmia, Angelika Malinar, and Martin Christof, 129–54. Delhi: Oxford University Press, 2001.

_____. "Women, Duty and Sanctified Space in a Vaisnava Hagiography of the Seventeenth Century." In *Constructions hagiographiques dans le monde indien: entre mythe et histoire*, edited by Francoise Mallison, 205–19. IVe Section—Sciences historiques et philologiques—Serie II: Hautes Etudes Orientales. Paris: Ecole Pratique des Hautes Etudes, 2001.

Dimock, Edward C., Jr. *The Place of the Hidden Moon: Erotic Mysticism in the Vaisnava-sahajiya Cult of Bengal.* Chicago and London: University of Chicago Press, 1989 [1966].

Dimock, Edward C., Jr., and Tony K. Stewart. Introduction to *Caitanya Caritamrta*, by Krsnadasa Kaviraja, translated with commentary by Edward C. Dimock, Jr., edited by Tony K. Stewart, 3–143. Volume 56 of *Harvard Oriental Series*. Cambridge MA: Department of Sanskrit and Indian Studies, Harvard University, 1999.

Entwistle, A.W. *Braj: Centre of Krishna Pilgrimage.* Groningen: Egbert Forsten, 1987.

Gaston, Anne-Marie. *Krishna's Musicians: Music-Making in the Temples of Nathdvara Rajasthan,* Delhi: Manohar, 1997.

Kane, P.V. *History of the Dharmasastra (Ancient and Medieval Religious and Civil Law).* 5 volumes. Pune: Bhandarkar Oriental Research Institute, 1974.

Lyons, Tryna. *The Artists of Nathdwara: The Practice of Painting in Rajasthan.* Bloomington: Indiana University Press, in association with Mapin Publishing, Ahmedabad, 2004.

Monier-Williams, Monier. *A Sanskrit-English Dictionary, Etymologically and Philologically Arranged.* Oxford: Clarendon Press, 1990.

Parikh, Dvarikadas, ed. *Chaurasi Vaishnavan ki Varta* (*tin janma ki lila bhavana vali*). Mathura: Shri Bajrang Pustakalaya, 1971 (Samvat 2027).

Peabody, Norbert. *Hindu Kingship and Polity in Precolonial India.* Cambridge: Cambridge University Press, 2003.

Sangari, Kumkum. "Tracing Akbar: Hagiographies, Popular Narrative Traditions and the Subject of Conversion." In *Mapping Histories: Essays Presented to Ravinder Kumar*, edited by Neera Chandhoke, 61–103. Delhi: Tulika, 2000.

Singh, Munshi Hardayal. *The Castes of Marwar.* Jodhpur: Book Treasure, 1993 [1984].

Smith, Frederick M. "The Hierarchy of Philosophical Systems According to Vallabhacarya." *Journal of Indian Philosophy* 33 (2005): 421–53.

_____. "Dark Matter in Vartaland: On the Enterprise of History in Early Pustimarga Discourse." *The Journal of Hindu Studies* 2, no. 1 (2009): 27–47.

Tandan, Hariharnath. *Varta Sahitya: Ek Brhat Adhyayan.* Aligarh: Bharat Prakashan Mandir, 1960.

Vaudeville, Charlotte. "The Govardhan Myth in North India." In *Myths, Saints and Legends in Medieval India*, compiled by Vasudha Dalmia, 72–139. Delhi: Oxford University Press, 1996.

Walsham, Alexandra. *Charitable Hatred: Tolerance and Intolerance in England, 1500–1700.* Manchester and New York: Manchester University Press, 2006.

10 Diatribes against *Śāktas* in Banarasi Bazaars and Rural Rajasthan

*Kabīr and His Rāmānandī Hagiographers**

Heidi Pauwels

One way to rethink the often taken-for-granted understanding of Hindus in opposition to Muslims is to study internal rivalries that figured prominently among what we would now call Hindu groups. With attention primarily focused on the Muslim–Hindu dyad, such animosity is often forgotten or glossed over. In this article, I broadly investigate identity formation by the now arguably mainstream devotional strand in Hinduism, bhakti, in distinction to a Hindu "other." My particular focus is on early bhakti authors of the fifteenth and sixteenth centuries and the pivotal *nirguṇa* bhakta Kabīr.[1] At the heart

* I am grateful to Vasudha Dalmia and Munis Faruqui for inviting me to the 2008 symposium at Berkeley and for their excellent suggestions for improving the paper. A longer version of this essay has meanwhile appeared as "Who are the Enemies of the *Bhaktas*? Testimony about '*Śāktas*' and 'Others' from Kabīr, the Rāmānandīs, Tulsīdās, and Harirām Vyās," *Journal of the American Oriental Society* 130, no. 4 (October–December 2010). This article will focus exclusively on Kabīr.

[1] Kabīr's dates of course have been much debated; see Charlotte Vaudeville, *A Weaver Named Kabīr* (Delhi: Oxford University Press, 1993), 52–55. For a recent critique and discussion of this in connection with the dates of

of this article is a simple question: with whom did Kabīr identify and from whom did he differentiate himself?

Kabīr is well known for poems in which he equates Hindu and Turk, and sees both communities as equally misguided. He rejects all forms of orthodox religion, as well as Sufism and Hindu asceticism. Since he preaches a religion of the heart, many consider Kabīr an apostle of peace. It is easy to project modern sensibilities back onto Kabīr. Yet, if we want to be true to what the historical Kabīr said and avoid conflating the saint with his image, we have to also look at a less politically correct part of his oeuvre: his verse contains frequent diatribes against *śāktas*. Who are these *śāktas*, and why is Kabīr so opposed to them? In the first section, I will look at the corpus attributed to Kabīr, and in the following section, I will highlight the way he is portrayed in the early (that is, sixteenth-century and Rāmānandī) hagiographies and trace the oppositions presented there. To wit, diatribes against *śāktas* seem to be widespread throughout north Indian bhakti texts, although the phenomenon has been little noticed. They can be found in *nirguṇa* as well as *saguṇa* Krishna bhakti.[2] This article offers an attempt at remapping the religious landscape of premodern north India.

It is worth noting at the outset that certain scholars have recently questioned the commonplace understanding of "a bhakti movement" as a largely twentieth-century construct brought into being by both "protestant Orientalists" and "Hindi nationalists."[3] As I see it, there are many "bhaktis" and many bhakti communities, defining themselves in multiple ways, some more inclusive than others.

I think we are justified in understanding Kabīr as an important early exponent of north Indian bhakti. For one, as we will see in the course of this article, Kabīr self-identifies repeatedly as *bhagata* or Vaiṣṇava. Furthermore, he is considered part of at least four bhakti lineages—

Rāmānanda, see Purushottam Agravāl, "In Search of Ramanand: The Guru of Kabir and Others," *Pratilipi* (October 2008): 3–4, http://pratilipi.in/2008/10/in-search-of-ramanand-purushottam-agrawal/, accessed May 7, 2012.

[2] See my paper, "Who Are the Enemies of the *Bhaktas?*"

[3] Well formulated in J.S. Hawley, "Introduction," *International Journal of Hindu Studies* (special issue) 11, no. 3 (2007): 209–25, and with a full treatment expected in his forthcoming work.

as evidenced in the scriptures of the Sikhs,[4] the Dādūpanthīs,[5] the Rāmānandīs,[6] as well as by some Krishna devotees[7]—as early as the sixteenth century. Thus Kabīr's case is indexical for other bhaktis as well. But there are also some elements that are specific to him. One significant factor is his low-caste status that figures prominently in contemporary understandings of the saint. Does his low-caste status have any role to play in his distinguishing himself as a bhakta against *śāktas*? We will have occasion to reflect on this in the course of this article.

First, however, we need to define what exactly is meant by *śākta*.[8] The term is now commonly used to connote two characteristics: (*a*) a religious preference, namely the worship of goddesses—*śakti*—often entailing blood sacrifices alongside the consumption of meat,[9] and

[4] See Pashaura Singh, *The Bhagats of the Guru Granth Sahib: Sikh Self-Definition and the Bhagat Bani* (New York: Oxford University Press, 2003).

[5] See Winand M. Callewaert and Bart Op de Beeck, eds, *Nirguṇ-bhakti Sāgar Devotional Hindī Literature: A Critical Edition of the Pañc-Vāṇī or Five Works of Dādū, Kabīr, Nāmdev, Rāidās, Hardās, with the Hindī Songs of Gorakhnāth and Sundardās, and a Complete Word-index*, 2 vols, South Asia Institute, Heidelberg: South Asian Studies 25 (New Delhi: Manohar, 1991).

[6] See David Lorenzen, *Kabīr Legends and Anata-dās's Kabīr Parachaī* (Albany: State University of New York Press, 1991).

[7] For example, HarirāmVyās. See Heidi Pauwels, *In Praise of Holy Men: Hagiographic Poems by and about Harirām Vyās*, Groningen Oriental Studies 18 (Groningen: Egbert Forsten, 2002).

[8] I am only looking at definitions of the term by outsiders. Self-representation of *śāktas* would be another study, and one fraught with the difficulty of the practice of dissimulation, as several members of the audience of different versions of this paper pointed out to me, quoting from the *Kulārṇavatantra* 11.83: *antaḥ kaulo bahiḥ śaivo janamadhye to vaiṣṇavaḥ* ("internally Kaula, outwardly Śaiva, among people Vaiṣṇava").

[9] Interestingly, its opposite, the Vaiṣṇava, is defined as vegetarian in the seventeenth-century Persian ethnography *Dabistan-i mazahib*: "In Hindostan it is known that whoever abstains from eating meat and hurting living animals is esteemed a Vaishnava without regard to the doctrine beforesaid." David Shea and Anthony Troyer, trans., *The Dabistān, or School of Manners* (Paris: Oriental Translation Fund of Great Britain and Ireland, 1843), III, 262, http://persian.packhum.org/persian/main?url=pf%3Ffile%3D15501050%26ct%3D0, accessed May 7, 2012.

(*b*) particular sexual ritual practices, often perceived by outsiders as sexually loose. Both these elements have an unorthodox, non-Brahminical ring to them and may be associated with low-caste practice. In addition to the specialized meanings, the term *śākta* is sometimes used loosely to refer to "sinners," roughly synonymous with other similar terms such as *vimukha*, "turned away (from God)," or *pākhaṇḍa*, "schismatic, heretic," rather than always referring to a specific group. Still, it is interesting to explore why the particular word *śākta* is used in this way and which group in particular has lent its name to such generalized use. This article seeks to understand the use of the term in the fifteenth and sixteenth centuries, and investigate whether the same connotations applied in Kabir's verse.[10]

I

KABĪR IN THE BANARASI BAZAARS

Kabīr's Diatribes against *Śāktas*

It may come as a surprise to champions of Kabīr as the peacemaker that vitriolic diatribes against *śākta*s can be found in several poems attributed to him. These poems are attested early on. While we cannot confidently claim any poem to be "authentically Kabīr," the closest we can come is to look for poems shared by different branches that have transmitted his work.[11] Several of the verses I quote below seem as close as one can get to the "original" Kabīr in that they are found in at least two of the three major corpora of Kabīr's work: most are found in the Northern recension of the Sikhs (*Goindvāl Pothīs*, *Kartarpur Pothī*, and *Ādi Granth*) and the Western one of the Dādūpanthīs and Nirañjanī Panth (exemplified by the so-called *Kabīr granthāvalī*).[12] In addition, some also appear in

[10] While the term *śākta* is not used, Jaina hagiographical sources from at least the ninth century onward include diatribes against goddess worshippers who are endowed with similar characteristics in the eyes of disapproving Jainas. Anne Monius, personal communication, April 14, 2009.

[11] For a good summary of these recensions, see Vinay Dharwadker, *Kabir: The Weaver's Songs* (New Delhi: Penguin Books India, 2003), 25–58.

[12] See Parśānāth Tivārī, ed., *Kabīra granthāvalī* (Allahabad: Hindi Pariṣad, Prayāg Viśvavidyālay, 1961).

the Eastern recension of the Kabīr Panth, known as the *Bījak*. In terms of genre, abuse of *śākta*s is found in pithy distichs, or *dohā*s, a genre of verse that is a vehicle for sarcasm par excellence, but also in song (*pada*). Let us look at some examples of this rhetoric before venturing into speculation about what Kabīr means by *śākta*.

Kabīr repeatedly warns against keeping company with *śākta*s, whom he characterizes as inherently harmful. An example found in all three recensions:

> I'm dying of bad company, like the plantain cut by the jujube,
> When the jujube moves, the other is cut: sever contact with *śākta*s.[13]

A verse found in two recensions contrasts the *śākta* with the sadhu, and warns against accepting invitations to dine with them:

> Keep the company of saints, if it takes subsisting on chaff!
> Even for feasting on kheer and sugar, do not go near a *śākta*![14]

It is striking how this injunction of shunning is like Brahminical Hinduism's shunning the company of low-castes. However, from another verse it becomes clear that low-caste Vaiṣṇavas are to be embraced, so it is not low-castes as such that are the problem for Kabīr, quite the contrary, and in any case, even Brahmins can be *śākta*, so the rejection of co-dining is not based on caste differences:

> Don't consort with *śākta* Brahmins, but prefer Vaiṣṇava Caṇḍālas,
> Embrace him tightly; it's like meeting God.[15]

[13] *Mārī maruṃ kusaṃga kī, kerā kāṭhaiṃ beri, vā hālai vā cīriai, sākata saṃga niberi* (*Saṃgati kau Aṃga*: *Kabīr granthāvalī*, 24.2; *Gurū Granth Sāhib, saloka* 88, p. 1369; *Bījak*, 242). The text quoted here and below is based on the *Kabīr Granthāvalī* recension, as edited in Callewaert and Op de Beeck, *Nirguṇ-bhakti Sāgar Devotional Hindī Literature*; correspondences are given on the basis of Vaudeville, *A Weaver Named Kabīr*. I provide my own working translations, much indebted to those by Vaudeville, and Linda Hess and Shukdev Singh in *The Bījak of Kabīr* (San Francisco: North Point Press, 1983).

[14] *Sādhu kī saṃgati rahau, jau kī bhūsī khāu, khīra khāṃda bhojana milai, sākata saṃga na jāu* (*Kabīr granthāvalī*, 24.6; *Gurū Granth Sāhib, saloka* 99, p. 1369).

[15] *Sākata bāṃhmana mati milai, baisanauṃ milai caṃḍāla; Aṃkamāla dai bheṭie, māṃnauṃ mile gopāla* (*Sādha Mahimā kau Aṃga*: *Kabīr granthāvalī*, 4.39).

Thus *śākta*s are reviled as corrupting influences of the soul, not of the body. The Western Kabīr recension seems to have been especially fond of the genre of reviling *śākta*s and has three more verses, not attested in the Northern recension of the *Gurū Granth Sāhib*, where *śākta*s are contrasted with bhaktas or sadhus, such as *Kabīr granthāvalī* 25.9 and 4.34 (the latter comparing the *śākta* with a black blanket), and also:

> Better a snippet of sandalwood, than a dense garden of Babuls!
> Better a humble hut of a holy man, than a *śākta*'s rich village![16]

The *Gurū Granth Sāhib* itself has some extra references not attested elsewhere, urging the devout not to associate with *śākta*s, such as in *Gurū Granth Sāhib, saloka* 93,[17] and in *Gurū Granth Sāhib, saloka* 17,[18] which compares associating with them with garlic that makes your breath smell; it also uses the imagery of the black blanket:

> Kabīr [says]: Associate with holy men, profit will double every day.
> [Whereas] the *śākta* is like a black blanket, it won't get white, even washed.[19]

All recensions attest that Kabīr disapproved of accepting donations, or other kinds of sponsorship from *śākta*s, or even of partaking in commercial transactions with them. Kabīr goes as far as to say one should not even speak to them:

> In "Rāma, Rāma, Rāma" immerse yourself, don't speak with a *śākta* even by mistake.
> Would you recite scripture to a dog? Would you sing Hari's praise in front of a *śākta*?
> Why worship a crow with camphor? Why give milk to drink to a poisonous snake?
> Watering the bitter Neem tree with nectar, says Kabīr does not change its nature![20]

[16] *Caṃdana kī kuṭakī bhalī, nāṃ babūra lakharāṃva; Sādhuna kī chaparī bhalī, nāṃ sākata kau baṛa gāṃva* (*Kabīr granthāvalī*, 4.37).

[17] *Gurū Granth Sāhib, saloka* 93, p. 1369.

[18] *Gurū Granth Sāhib, saloka* 17, p. 1365.

[19] *Kabīra saṃgati sādhū kī, dina dina dūnā hetu; Sākata kārī kāṃbarī, dhoe hoi na setu* (*Gurū Granth Sāhib, saloka* 100, p. 1369). See also *saloka* 131, p. 1371.

[20] *Rāṃma Rāṃma Rāṃma rami rahie, sākata setī bhūli na kahie; Kā sunahāṃ kauṃ sumrita sunāeṃ, kā sākata pahiṃ hari guna gāeṃ; Kaüvā kahā kapūra*

In this song, the warning against *śākta*s is built in the refrain itself. Through his lively comparisons, Kabīr makes clear that the *śākta* is irredeemable, and association with him is mistaken. Trying to convert him is fruitless. All well-intended sermons will fall on deaf ears, he says. Furthermore, one should avoid villages where *śākta*s reside, and in the city, one should avoid gatherings where they predominate. Once a *śākta*, always a *śākta*!

What is the discursive field of these poems? The genres of *sākhī* and songs each evoke a different performance context. The songs perhaps best fit with (retrospective) portrayals of Kabīr in art, where he is depicted in front of his hut, singing for his disciples and visitors.[21] The *sākhī* on the other hand seems to best fit the context of the public space, the bazaar or ghats, a context in which Kabīr is firmly placed by his hagiographers.[22] For Kabīr is reputed to have preached in public places in Banares, proclaiming his strong opinions, maybe pointing fingers at the religious group being denounced, which might have been practicing in the same vicinity. Although to some extent the genre of the *sākhī* is formulaic, as many proverbs are remembered in that form,[23] Kabīr's songs and distichs do not sound formulaic but heartfelt and possibly "fired" by a real-life incident.

---

carāeṃ, kā bisahara kauṃ dūdha piāeṃ; Aṃmrita lai lai nīṃba siṃcāi, kahai Kabīra vākī bāṃni na jāī (*Kabīr granthāvalī, pada* 168; *Gurū Granth Sāhib, āsā* 20, p. 481). The song in *Gurū Granth Sāhib* has a few more verses. Interestingly, one can find some very similar songs attributed to Nāmdev: *daha disi rāṃma rahyau bharapūri, saṃtani nerai sākata dūri* ("Rām fills the whole world, but he is close to the Sants and far from the wicked (*śākta*)"). *Nāmdev padāvalī*, 2, in W. M. Callewaert and Mukund Lath, *The Hindī Padāvalī of Nāmdev: A Critical Edition of Nāmdev's Hindi Songs with Translation and Annotation* (Delhi: Motilal Banarsidass, 1989), 143.

21 Compare with the famous seventeenth-century Mughal miniature, purportedly portraying Kabīr, from the Oriental Antiquities Department of British Museum, used on the front cover of Nirmal Dass, *Songs of Kabir from the Adi Granth* (Albany: State University of New York Press, 1991).

22 For example, Priyādās kavitta 270.3: *ṭhāṛhe maṃḍī māṃjha* ("standing in the market"). See Sītārām Śaraṇ "Rūpkalā" Bhagavānprasād, ed., *Gosvāmi nābhājī kṛt śrī bhaktamāl: Śrī priyādāsjī praṇīt ṭikā-kavitta, śrī sītārāmśaraṇ bhagvān prasād rūpkalā viracit bhaktisudhāsvād tilak sahit* (Lucknow: Tejkumār Book Depot, reprint, 1977), 483.

23 See Vaudeville, *A Weaver Named Kabīr*, 225.

It is easy to imagine the poems being created *extempore* after an encounter with a *śākta* for the benefit of his disciples or other onlookers.

We should also reflect on the continued performance of these songs and distichs. The very fact that they were picked up by Dādū-panthīs and Sikhs indicates that the songs touched upon a common sensibility in sixteenth-century devotional milieus.[24] Kabīr was certainly not the only one who felt that *śākta*s were to be shunned.

As an excursus, I want to qualify Kabīr's rejection of *śākta*s, softening the picture that appears from the previous verses, although generally confirming the case. In some poems, Kabīr expressed the thought that even *śākta*s should be given the benefit of the doubt. In the end, when one has attained the highest stages or realization, all dualities should disappear, including the one between bhakta and *śākta*. This is expressed in the following *sākhī*:[25]

[24] Indeed, the Sikh gurus themselves warned against *śākta*s, see, e.g., these lines from poems by Guru Nānak: *sabadi na bhījai sākatā, duramati āvanu jānu* (*Gurū Granth Sāhib, sirirāg sabada* 19, p. 21), and *sākata sacu na bhāvaī, kūḍī kūḍī pāṃi* (*Gurū Granth Sāhib, sirirāg sabada* 21, p. 22). The meaning seems to have broadened, certainly, by the time of the fourth guru who seems to define our term as "Those who do not love the Lord, are *śākta*s, stupid and half-baked men" (*jina kaü prīti nāhī hari setī, te sākata mūḍa nara kāce*) (*Gurū Granth Sāhib, gaurī-purbī* 55, p. 169). Cf. also the longish poem with recurring reference to *śākta*s by the fifth guru (*Gurū Granth Sāhib, gaurī* 7, p. 239).

[25] The same idea is also expressed in a song, attested in both the Western and Northern recensions:

Aba haṃma sakala kusala kari māṃnāṃ, sāṃti bhaī jaba gobiṃda jāṃnāṃ
Tana mahiṃ hotī koṭi upādhi, ulaṭi bhaī sukha sahaja samādhi
Jama taiṃ ulaṭi bhayā rāṃma, dukha binase sukha kiyā bisarāṃma
Bairī ulaṭi bhae haiṃ mītā, sākata ulaṭi sajana bhae cītā
Āpā jāṃni ulaṭi lai āpa, tau nahiṃ byāpai tīnyūṃ tāpa
Aba mana ulaṭi sanātana hūvā, taba jāṃnāṃ jaba jīvata mūvā
Kahai Kabīra sukha sahaja samāvauṃ, āpa na darauṃ na aura parāvauṃ
(Kabīr granthāvalī, 107; Gurū Granth Sāhib, gaurī 17, p. 326)

Now take it that I've found all bliss, I found peace when I got to know God.
The many tricks the body has, have reverted and become the ocean of instant joy.

Kabīr says: no one is a *śākta*, think of everyone as a Vaiṣṇava,
If their mouth does not utter "Rāma," they harm their own body.[26]

This type of poem is mostly only attested in the *Kabīr granthāvalī* subrecension. Another example:

A married *śākta* can be good, if his nature is chaste
A Vaiṣṇava who misbehaves, should be avoided by God's people.[27]

Here Kabīr, true to form, refuses once again to stick by easy labels. Do not judge too rashly, he seems to say: purported devotees who do not show their belief in their actions are worse than *śākta*s. To conclude: even as Kabīr denounces *śākta*s and strictly opposes associating with them or accepting their patronage, he ultimately says that for the accomplished devotee this is a non-issue, because all duality should have been resolved in the one preoccupation with God. The reference to "a married *śākta*" seems to indicate that those to be shunned are the *śākta*s who consort with women outside marriage, which brings us to the next part of this section.

Who Are the *Śāktas* in Kabīr's Poems?

Who exactly are these *śākta* we are urged to avoid? Briefly put, Kabīr's prejudices seem to fit the modern ones: some of his *sākhī*s seem to reinforce the idea that the *śākta* is someone with loose dietary habits and sexual morals. Kabīr goes so far as to compare a *śākta* to a pig,

---

Fear of death has turned into fear of God, sorrow is gone, I rest in bliss
All hatred has turned into friendship, *śākta*s have become good people to my mind.
Knowing the Self, has turned the self around, the three types of sorrow don't apply.
Now has turned and become eternal to my mind, when I realized that, I became dead alive.
Kabīr says: merge with spontaneous bliss, don't fear the self, don't flee anything else.

26 *Kabīra sākata koi nahīṃ, sabai ba isnauṃ jāṃni; Jihi mukhi rāṃma na ūcarai, tāhi tana kī hāṃni* (*Sāragrāhī kau aṃga*: *Kabīr granthāvalī*, 27.4).

27 *Saṃsārī sākata bhalā, kuṃvarā kai bhāi; Durācārī baisnauṃ burā, hari-jana tahāṃ na jāi* (*Upadesa/ citāvanī kau aṃga*: *Kabīr granthāvalī*, 15.73).

indiscriminately eating everything, and his mother to a bitch, indiscriminately sleeping around:

> Better than a *śākta* is a pig: it keeps the village clean
> When the poor *śākta* dies, no one remembers him.[28]
> Better a Vaiṣṇava's she-dog than a *śākta*'s bad mother
> The first will hear Hari's praise, just sitting around, the other rushes to invite sin![29]

There are other hints that *śākta*s are involved in Tantric sexual rites that are evaluated negatively. There is a somewhat obscure song that refers only incidentally to the *śākta* but is useful for our purpose as it hints at the identity of the *śākta*:

> The world is a young bride, beloved by all, wife to all living beings ...
> The holy man flees but she's on his tail, fearing the Guru's word might strike.
> For the *śākta*, her body is another's wife, in our opinion she's a lusty witch.[30]

The poem has some obscure lines, but its main intent is clearly to show up the world of the senses as ephemeral, and demask it as non-essential when compared to God. The holy man stays aloof from the world, but the *śākta*, by contrast, is involved with the world; he sees her in the woman with whom he practices sexual yoga, as the *parāini*. The reference to the *śākta* in this context seems once more to confirm the modern interpretation of the *śākta* as someone engaged in sexual ritual practice, here with a woman who is not one's own wife. Kabīr angrily rhymes the so-called *parāini* with *dāini*, a witch. The broader comparison of the woman with the world of saṃsāra, sustained throughout the poem, projects such sexual practices as thoroughly negative.

[28] *Sākata te sūkara bhalā, rākhai sūcā gāṃuṃ; Sākata bapurā mari gayā, koi na leihai nāṃuṃ* (*Kabīr granthāvalī*, 21.12; *Gurū Granth Sāhib*, *saloka* 143, p. 1372).

[29] *Baisnauṃ kī kūkari bhalī, sākata kī burī māī; Vaha baiṭhī hari jasa sunaiṃ, vaha pāpa bisāhana jāi* (*Sāṃca cāṃṇaka kau aṃga*: *Kabīr granthāvalī*, 21.10; *Gurū Granth Sāhib*, *saloka* 52, p. 1367).

[30] *Eka suhāgini jagata piyārī, sagale jīa jaṃta kī nārī... Saṃta bhāgai vā pāchaiṃ paraiṃ, gura kai sabadani mārahu darai; Sākata kai yahu piṃda parāṃ ini, hamarī dṛṣṭi parai trisi dāṃmini* (*Kabīr granthāvalī*, *pada* 162; *Gurū Granth Sāhib*, *gauṇḍ* 7, p. 871).

An understanding of *śāktas* as goddess worshippers is suggested by a song with a similar theme, of the world or māyā as a woman, which is included also in the *Bījak*:

> You, Sorceress of Raghunāth, have gone off to play the game of hunt:
> Wily, you choose the deer and kill, you don't miss any nearby.
> Silent sage, Muslim and naked ascetic, you've killed, and the yogi, try as he may,
> The Vīraśaiva ascetic in the jungle you've killed, you roam all powerful.
> The Brahmin is killed as he reads his Veda, the priest as he worships,
> Mr. Miśra commenting on scripture is struck down; you roam around madly.
> You carry off *śāktas*, but you are a maidservant of the devotees.
> Kabīrdās: as soon as they're in Rāma's shelter, she has to turn away.[31]

In this poem with the extended metaphor of māyā going out to playfully hunt some game, we get a full list of hypocrites or misguided ascetics in Kabīr's view: he sees all as having fallen victim to māyā. First of all, there are ascetics of all denominations including Hindu (*muni*), Muslim (pir) and Jain ascetics (*digambara*), but also Vīraśaiva ascetics (*jaṅgama*). Further, there are orthodox Brahmins and image worshippers, including the "Mr. Miśras" who write commentaries on scripture, and in that list, also the *śāktas*, who fail to see that it is not the goddess, who is māyā, but her lord, Hari, with whom they should take shelter. Thus the term *śākta* is here brought into clear association with goddess worship.

Sometimes, it seems as if Kabīr is questioning the claim of some Tantric sects that they can guide their adepts to immortality via the use of alchemy. As opposed to the "alchemical solution," the elixir of nectar, he proposes a simpler solution: only the nectar of the name is needed to achieve immortality.[32] So he claims immortality for the sant, while exposing the false claims of the *śākta*:

31 *tū māyā raghunātha kī, khelaṇa caṛhī aheḍaiṃ; Catura cikāre cuṇi cuṇi māre, koī na choḍyā neḍaiṃ; Muniyara pīra digaṃbara māre, jatana karaṃtā jogī; Jaṃgala-mahi ke jaṃgama māre, tūṃ re phirai balivaṃtīṃ; Veda paṛhaṃtā bāṃhana mārā, sevā karaṃtā svāmī; Aratha karaṃtā misara pachāṛyā, tūṃ re phire maimaṃtīṃ; Sākhita [sākata] kai tūṃ haratā karatā, hari bhagatana kai cerī; Dāsa Kabīra rāṃma kai saranai, jyoṃ lāgī tyoṃ pherī (torī)* (*Kabīr granthāvalī, pada* 161 (187); *Bījak*, 12).

32 Similarly in a poem by Kabīr attested only in the *Gurū Granth*: *sākata marahi saṃta sabhi jīvahi, rāma rasāinu rasanā pīvahi* (*Gurū Granth Sāhib, gaüṛī* 13, p. 226).

> I won't die, if the whole world dies, I've found the one who can give life.
> *Śāktas* die, but holy men live, Rāma has them drink their fill of nectar …
> Kabīr says: He has merged my heart with his, I've become immortal, I've reached the ocean of bliss.[33]

What specific communities did Kabīr have in mind when pronouncing his distichs or singing such songs? Might he have had in mind the Tantrically inclined Nāth ascetics, involved in alchemy? The question of Kabīr's attitude toward the Nāths has been discussed by several scholars.[34] The issue is blurred by the problem of contemporary sources for Nāth beliefs. Although Gorakhnāth undoubtedly predated Kabīr, records of *Gorakh-bānī* in Hindi are more recent than manuscripts for Kabīr and may well already have incorporated bhakti elements. Thus it is tricky to determine what came first. This issue is not helped by the fact that Kabīr Panthīs apparently turned hostile to Nāth Yogīs at some later point in history.[35] Several *Bījak* songs (Eastern recension) may find their origin in this later sentiment, so it is not unproblematic to attribute these sentiments to Kabīr. Although once again, there are also some songs of Kabīr in the Western and Northern traditions that seem hostile to Nāths.[36]

A possible clue may be found in an often-quoted song from the *Bījak*[37] in a yet different genre, Rāmainī:

> Never have I seen such yoga, brother! He wanders mindless and heedless,
> proclaiming the way of Mahādeva, he has himself called "great abbot."
> To markets and bazaars he peddles meditation, false *siddha*, lover of māyā.
> When did Dattā(treya) break a fort, when did Śuka join gunmen?
> When did Nārada fire a gun, when did Vyāsa Deva beat the battle drum?

[33] *Haṃma na maraiṃ marihai saṃsārā, haṃmakauṃ milā jiāvanahārī; sākata marahiṃ saṃta jana jīvahiṃ, bhari bhari rāṃma rasāṃina pīvahiṃ…; Kahai Kabīra mana manahiṃ milāvā, amara bhae sukhasāgara pāvā* (*Kabīr granthāvalī, pada* 106; *Gurū Granth Sāhib, gaüṛī* 12.2/13.4, p. 325–26).

[34] Vaudeville, *A Weaver Named Kabīr*, 95–107; Irfan Habib, "Medieval Popular Monotheism and its Humanism: The Historical Setting," *Social Scientist* 21, nos. 3–4 (1993): 84–85; and Mariola Offredi, "Kabīr and Nāthpanth," in *Images of Kabīr*, ed. Monika Horstmann (New Delhi: Manohar, 2002), 127–41.

[35] See Offredi, "Kabīr and Nāthpanth," 127, quoting Bhartwal.

[36] *Kabīr Granthāvalī, pada* 113, which corresponds to *Gurū Granth Sāhib, gaüṛī* 52.

[37] See, e.g., David Lorenzen, "Ascetics in Indian History," *Journal of the American Oriental Society* 98, no. 1 (1978): 61.

They fight dim-witted. Are they ascetics or arrow bearers?
Initiated ascetics, greed firmly in mind, wearing gold, bring shame to [the ascetic's] dress
They collect stallions and mares, acquire villages, and go about as millionaires
Sanaka and his brothers did not travel with pretty women. Put a hand on a black pot, and a stain will stick at some point.[38]

In this poem, Kabīr virulently condemns roaming ascetics engaged in warfare and travelling with female companions. Possibly he is thinking of warrior-ascetics and/or Nātha types, who considered themselves *siddha* but were actually shams.[39] However, this poem occurs only in the *Bījak*, and it has been argued that the reference to gunpowder indicates it is a later composition, post-dating the 1526 Battle of Panipat where firearms presumably were first used.[40] On the other hand, the last line with its reference to the black pot recalls a *dohā* found only in the *Gurū Granth*:

Kabīr says: Don't keep the company of the *śākta*: flee far from him.
If you touch a black vessel, one way or another, you will get stained.[41]

[38] *Aisā joga na dekhā bhāī, bhūlā phirai liye gaphilāī; Mahādeva ko paṃtha calāvai, aiso baṛo mahaṃta kahāvai; Hāṭa bājārai lābai tārī, kaccā siddhahi māyā pyārī; Kaba dattai mānāsī torī, kaba sukadeva topacī jorī; Nārada kaba baṃḍūka calāyā, vyāsa deva kaba baṃba bajāyā; Karahiṃ larāī mati kaṃ maṃdā, ye atīta kī tarakasa baṃdā; Bhaye birakta lobha mana ṭhānā, sonā pahira lajābai bānā; Ghorā ghorā kīnha baṭorā, gāṃva pāya jasa calai karorā; tiya suṃdarī na sohaī sanakādika ke sātha, kabahuṃka dāga lagavaī kārī hāṃḍī hātha* (*Bījak, rāmainī* 69).

[39] Several other poems on hypocrisy have this theme: *Kabīr granthāvalī, pada* 170, which corresponds to the *Bījak, kaharā* 7; the penultimate verse of *Kabīr granthāvalī, pada* 128, which corresponds to *Gurū Granth Sāhib, bhairaū* 11; Vaudeville, *A Weaver Named Kabīr*, 231 and 240 respectively.

[40] Lorenzen, "Ascetics in Indian History," 61, n. 1; but see Iqtidar Alam Khan, "Early Use of Cannon and Musket in India: A.D. 1442–1526," *Journal of the Economic and Social History of the Orient* 24, no. 2 (1981): 146–64, for an argument that there were firearms in India in the second half of the fifteenth century.

[41] *Kabīra sākata saṃgu na kījīai, dūrahi jāīye bhāgi; Bāsanu kāro parsīai, taū kachu lāgai dāgu* (*Gurū Granth Sāhib, saloka* 131, p. 1371). I am grateful to Harpreet Singh, PhD student at Harvard University, for drawing my attention to this poem. Personal communication, May 9, 2009.

In this *dohā*, the reference to the black pot is connected with the appeal to avoid *śākta*s. Thus it may not be too far-fetched to link the poem above with our search for specifics about who these *śākta*s might be.

In general, though, it is a mistake to look for a specific *paramparā* that is the target of Kabīr's anger. His enmity may be less toward a sectarian group and more generically toward people who indulge in *śākta* practices like sacrificing animals. One song found in the *Bījak* links Kabīr's loathing for the killing of animals explicitly with Devi worship and hence is *śākta* in a sense:

> O saints, pandits are expert butchers!
> Killing a goat, wounding a buffalo, no pain touches their heart!
> They bathe, put on a forehead mark, and sit down to worship the goddess all aglow.
> Killing a soul they'll perish in an instant, causing blood-red rivers to flow.
> You may call them very holy, high-caste, foremost in the gathering,
> Everyone begs them for initiation, but, brother, I have to grin.
> Your sin, cut down with recitation, but despicable action they make you display.
> Both (parties) drown, looking at each other, Yama has come to drag them away.
> You may call a slaughterer of cows "Turk," but are they any less?
> Kabīr says, listen, true believers: in this Kali era, Brahmins are a mess.[42]

This poem equates Brahmins slaughtering animals with butchers. It decries the violence involved in animal sacrifice, and links it with goddess worship, Devi puja. While Kabīr does not mention the word *śākta* in this poem, it would make a good fit with what we have been able to glean from the context of poems where he does.

[42] *Saṃto pāṃḍe nipuna kasāī; bakarā māri bhaiṃsā para ghāve, dila meṃ darda na āī; kari asnāna tilaka dai baiṭhe, vidhi se devī pujāī; ātama māri palaka meṃ binase, rudhira ki nadī bahāī; ati punīta ūṃce kula kahiye, sabhā māṃhi adhikāī; inhate dīkṣā saba koī; māṃgai, haṃsi āvai mohiṃ bhāī; pāpa kaṭana ko kathā sunāvai, karma karāvai nīcā; būḍata dou paraspara deṣā, yama lāye haiṃ ṣīṃcā; gāya badhe tehi turkā kahiye, inhate vai kyā choṭe; kahai Kabīra suno ho saṃto, kali meṃ bāhmana ṣoṭe* (*Bījak*, 11).

Similar sentiments, of disgust with animal sacrifice, occur throughout Kabīr's poetry,[43] most notably in a line that all three recensions have in common:

> He may sing "Rāma," instruct others, but without knowing God, he just roams all around.
> His mouth utters Vedic Gāyatrī, his words cross the world of the senses,
> At his feet everyone rushes to fall, but this Brahmin kills living beings!
> Thinks highly of himself, but eats in a low house, filling his belly with low work.
> At eclipse and dark moon, he begs, bowing low. Lamp in hand, he falls in a well.[44]

In short, while it is possible that when he condemns *śākta*s Kabīr has in mind Nāth Yogīs who follow left-handed Tantric practices, he may be more broadly thinking about those who sacrifice animals for goddess worship. He is the ultimate accuser of those who perpetrate animal slaughter.

What can we conclude? Kabīr is virulently opposed to associating with *śākta*s. He is mainly interested in warning of the ill effects of consorting with or accepting the patronage of *śākta*s, and spends very little time describing their actual attributes, or delineating what is so objectionable about them. From the references, however, we see our initial assumption confirmed: *śākta* is a designation for animal sacrificers and meat-eaters, both elements associated with goddess worship. There are some hints that they are suspected of sexual praxes. Kabīr recommends shunning them, in terms similar to those used in Brahminical Hinduism for low-castes. This is striking since he himself is a low-caste. Yet, he is quick to point out that Brahmins can be *śākta* too. There is also a hint that *śākta*s are involved with a search for immortality, perhaps alchemy.

[43] *Kabīr granthāvalī, pada* 191, which corresponds to *Gurū Granth Sāhib, māṛū* 1; *Bījak*, 4 and 10; for opposition to animal slaughter by Muslims, see *Kabīr granthāvalī, sākhī* 21.5; and *pada* 183, which corresponds to *Gurū Granth Sāhib, bibhās* 4; also, *Bījak*, 49.

[44] *Rāmahiṃ gāvai aurahi samujhāvai, hari jānai binu vikala phirai; Jehi muṣa beda gāyatrī ucarai, tāke bacana saṃsāra tarai; Jāke pāṃva jagata uṭhi lāge, so brāmana jīva badha karai; Apane ūṃca nīca ghara bhojana, dhīna karma kari udara bharai; Grahana amāvasa ḍhuki' ḍhuki māṃgai, kara-dīpaka liye kūpa parai* (*Bījak*, 17; *Gurū Granth Sāhib, rāmkalī*; and *Kabīr granthāvalī*, 2.196).

Again, this is something that is unnecessary in Kabīr's worldview, where the name of God is the only secret formula needed to find liberation and immortality.

Kabīr thus understands the *śākta* as the "other" in opposition to "us." For the latter, Kabīr uses the terms sadhu, *santa*, bhakta, *sajana*, and indeed Vaiṣṇava.[45] Interestingly, these terms mean basically "the good," "the righteous." Used alongside these, the term Vaiṣṇava, the devotee of Viṣṇu, acquires the same connotation, coming close to the contemporary interpretation of the Vaiṣṇava as a vegetarian of righteous conduct.

II

KABĪR'S HAGIOGRAPHERS PREACHING IN RURAL RAJASTHAN

Rāmānandīs and Kabīr's *Śākta* Birth

Did Kabīr's hagiographers pick up on the theme of his enmity with *śāktas*? Do they fill out the picture with some concrete examples to enlighten us? I will focus on the earliest hagiographies we have access to, which have of course a bias of their own, as they are Rāmānandī. Although the famous *Bhakt-māl* ("Garland of Devotees") by Nābhādās (ca. 1600) offers little information that would be of help to us, we find a wealth of hagiographical detail in the roughly contemporary late-sixteenth-century *Parcaīs*, or "Introductions," attributed to Anantdās.[46]

The famous Rāmānandī hagiographer, Anantdās, composed his works around 1588.[47] He is said to have lived in Raivās and been a disciple of Vinodīdās who, in turn, was a disciple of Agradās who was also Nābhādās's guru. His *Parcaīs* deal with several of the so-called

[45] Thus the classification of Kabīr among Vaiṣṇava *Vairāgīs*, as given in *Dabistān-i mazāhib*, is not off the mark, contrary to what Habib suggests. "Medieval Popular Monotheism," 84.

[46] See Lorenzen, *Kabīr Legends*; and Winand M. Callewaert and Swapna Sharma, *The Hagiographies of Anantadās: The Bhakti Poets of North India* (Richmond: Curzon Press, 2000).

[47] This is the date of the Nāmdev *Parcaī*. See Callewaert and Sharma, *The Hagiographies of Anantadās*, 31–32.

sants, Nāmdev, Raidās, Pīpā, Dhanā, Tilocan, Aṅgad, as well as Kabīr.[48] Anantdās's main agenda seems to have been to claim these charismatic bhaktas as members of his own sect, the Rāmānanda *sampradāya*.[49] Since the genre he wrote in was narrative, the verse style was linked *caupāī dohā*, rather than isolated *sākhī* or *pada*.

If we focus on the word *śākta*, we find it occurring several times in the *Parcaī*s as a whole and this helps to identify its contemporary use. In the story about Kabīr, though, it occurs only once, in the very first line of the first chapter:

> In Banares lived a weaver,[50] who resorted to the support of Hari's devotees.[51]
> For a long time, he sang among *śākta*s, but now he supports himself by singing Hari's glory.[52]

Thus, at the outset of the story, the contrast is established between, on the one hand, Kabīr's humble birth as a *julāhā* and his associating with *śākta*s, and on the other hand his inclination toward bhakti and his associating with bhaktas and singing praises of the Lord. That fits the pattern of contrast we saw in Kabīr's own works. However, there is a catch. The first chapter is attested only in a few manuscripts and the line in question does not occur in all of them.[53]

[48] For more on the sants, see Heidi Pauwels, "Imagining Religious Communities in the Sixteenth Century: Hariram Vyas and the Haritrayi," *International Journal of Hindu Studies* 13, no. 2 (2009): 143–61.

[49] See Callewaert and Sharma, *The Hagiographies of Anantadās*, 1.

[50] Most manuscripts actually give *Kabīrā* instead of *julāhā*. Callewaert and Sharma, *The Hagiographies of Anantadās*, 55.

[51] One manuscript gives *hari bhagatana kau pahīryā bheṣa* ("He wore the garb of Hari's devotees") as the second half of the line. Callewaert and Sharma, *The Hagiographies of Anantadās*, 55.

[52] *Kāsī basai julāhā eka, hari bhagatana kī pakaṛī ṭeka; bahuta dina sākata maiṃ gaīyā, aba hari kā guṇa le nirabahīyā*. Lorenzen, *Kabīr Legends*, 129.

[53] Lorenzen translates the chapter as if it were unproblematically part of the *Parcaī*, although he points out in a footnote to the text that this chapter is spurious. *Kabīr Legends*, 129. And of course the title of the book makes it clear that this is only one recension of the text, which he calls the Nirañjanī recension. Callewaert disagrees with that characterization, and in his edition and translation points out that only a few manuscripts include the first chapter; the oldest

The story goes on, conspicuously never returning to the issue of Kabīr's *śākta* companions. First, God himself tells Kabīr to become a Vaiṣṇava, otherwise he cannot give Kabīr *darśana*. Key characteristics of the Vaiṣṇava as identified by God in Anantdās's rendition are *tilaka* (forehead mark) and *mālā* (rosary). Kabīr protests, proclaiming himself unfit for receiving such distinction. There is no mention anymore of his being a *śākta*, rather Kabīr objects on grounds of caste (jati), and identifies himself as a *musalamāṃna* in the third verse:

> My caste is Musalman, how can I get prayer beads?[54]

Kabīr's inner voice, again God himself, points him to the eminent way of overcoming this perceived obstacle: to seek initiation from Rāmānanda.[55] One can interpret this as a publicity move for Rāmānanda, proclaiming that outcastes can receive initiation from him.

Thus in the *Kabīr parcaī*, although the word *śākta* shows up right in the beginning, it is immediately dropped. The hagiographer's concern is mainly with caste: Kabīr's being a Muslim is what disqualifies him, not because of religion, but because he is seen as belonging to a low-caste. Further on in the story, though, when the reaction of Kabīr's family to his new "Vaiṣṇava-hood" is described, it is his loss of Islamic identity that is confirmed with reference to key markers of the Islamic faith.[56]

One would be tempted to speculate that the first *caupāī* line with the reference to *śākta* might be the oldest line, for the very reason that it sits uneasily with the rest of the chapter. However, textual attestation is limited to only a few later manuscripts. Could it be, though, that

---

one is dated 1697. Callewaert and Sharma, *The Hagiographies of Anantadās*, 47–48. Most manuscripts do not include the last line, and one of the two that do has a variant: *vrata* for *guṇa*. Callewaert and Sharma, *The Hagiographies of Anantadās*, 55.

[54] *Musalamāṃna hamārī jātī, mālā pāūṃ kaisī bhātī.* (1.3a; Lorenzen, *Kabīr Legends*, 129). This reading is more or less the same in most manuscripts that include this chapter. Callewaert and Sharma, *The Hagiographies of Anantadās*, 55.

[55] *Rāmānanda pai dachyā leha. Kabīr parcaī*, 1.3b; Callewaert and Sharma, *The Hagiographies of Anantadās*, 55.

[56] *Makā madīnā hamārā sājā, kalamāṃ rojā aura nivājā. Kabīr parcaī*, 1.7b; Lorenzen, *Kabīr Legends*, 131; Callewaert and Sharma, *The Hagiographies of Anantadās*, 56.

these manuscripts simply retain an early reference to the *śākta* environment of Kabīr, which is later bypassed in favor of focus on his Muslim identity? The suspicion that the *śākta* reference might be an early one is strengthened by the existence of parallel passages in other *Parcaīs*, which may provide some clues to the meaning of this one line in Kabīr's story. The beginning of the *Parcaī* on the leather worker Raidās is very similar:

> His parents belonged to the caste of Camāra, he landed, born in a house of *śāktas*.
> In a previous birth he had been nothing less than a Brahmin, but he had not given up meat, though day and night he listened to recitations (of sacred scripture).
> For that insult, he was given a low birth, but he managed to remember his previous birth.[57]

The story continues, describing how the baby Raidās refused to drink his mother's milk until his guru Rāmānanda interfered and initiated the whole family. The meaning of *śākta* here seems to be narrowed to one belonging to a low caste who is not initiated by Rāmānanda, and is linked with meat-eating. The reputation of Camārs, that they are meat-eaters, is the reason the infant Raidās cannot have commensality with his own family. Thus for Anantdās the designation *śākta* seems to connote meat-eating (at least as one practice) as well as low caste. What the stories describe is how one can escape this stigma, of belonging to a low caste, as well as being a meat-eater, through conversion by Rāmānanda. And thus the first line of the *Kabīr parcaī* finds an echo in that of Raidās, confirming the suspicion that the reference to *śākta* carries these connotations in the *Parcaīs*.

Animal Slaughterers of All Religions Condemned

That Anantdās was aware of Kabīr's disgust for animal slaughter is confirmed by an incident he relates in the *Kabīr parcaī*. This one occurs in both recensions. Kabīr is portrayed as a staunch opponent of animal

[57] *Jāti caṃmāra pitā ara māī, sāṣita kai ghari janamyo āī; pūraba janama viprahū hotā, māṃsa na chāṛyo nisa diṃna śrotā; tihiṃ aparādhi nīca kuli dīyā, pahlā janma cīnhiṃ tiniṃ līyā. Kabīr parcaī*, 1.2; Callewaert and Sharma, *The Hagiographies of Anantadās*, 336.

slaughter, ironically in a context where both Brahmins and *qāzīs* join forces to have Kabīr put to death: the *qāzīs* on grounds of his apostasy, the Brahmins on grounds of his unauthorized wearing of the symbols of their (caste?) religion.[58] In response, Kabīr calls these would-be defenders of orthodoxy disbelievers themselves. And what is his main reproach? He attacks both religions on grounds of the violence on animals that they proscribe:

> What Holy Book orders cows to be killed? Which called for [killing] goats and chickens?
> May Yama tear the chest of all those who are seen to kill living beings (*ātma*).[59]

The first half of the *caupāī* has been identified as a quote from a *Kabīr ramainī* from the *Bījak* 49.[60] Thus the hagiographer illustrates Kabīr's disgust at the killing of animals by quoting his own words. This same story also has an interesting take on Hindu–Muslim dynamics. For Kabīr is portrayed as having fights with the local *qāzīs* and mullahs as well as the orthodox Brahmins of Banares. He is thus not exactly a precursor of the cow protection movement.

Anantdās builds in the same even-handedness toward Hindu and Muslim opponents when he talks about Kabīr's conflict with the authorities. The best-remembered story in popular memory is his confrontation with the sultan. When Emperor Sikander (Lodi?) comes to town, Anantdās specifies that the ruler turned against Kabīr on the instigation of both Hindus and Muslims (as well as Kabīr's own mother). Kabīr's religion here is seen as apostasy from both Islam and orthodox Hinduism. In the actual accusations, however, it is Brahminical offense to Kabīr that is most elaborated upon.[61] Kabīr is seen as insulting all Brahminical

[58] *Kabīr parcaī*, 8.1–2.

[59] *Kaumna kateba jahi gaū kaṭāī, bakarī mūragī kini phūramāī; Jetā dīsaiṃ ātma ghātī, itana kī jamat oṛai chātī. Kabīr parcaī*, 8.3; Callewaert and Sharma, *The Hagiographies of Anantadās*, 77.

[60] See Lorenzen, *Kabīr Legends*, 76; the whole line is *bakarī muragī kinha phuramāyā, kisake kahe tuma churī calāyā.* Remarkably, this poem has no equivalent in the Rajasthani traditions, but the quote in the *Parcaī* seems to presume knowledge of it, unless of course the *Bījak* verse is based on the Rajasthani hagiography.

[61] *Kabīr parcaī*, 7.2–5.

practices (repetition of the accusation *nindai* at the beginning of lines 2b through 5b, sometimes even at the beginning of half-lines). In his subsequent confrontation with Sikander, what is stressed is that Kabīr refuses to follow court etiquette and submit to the worldly ruler.[62] This conforms to the hagiographical topos of the king meeting with the saint, where the king puts the saint to the test, only to find that the saint's spiritual power is greater than his own worldly one. In this telling, the story is not intended as a confrontation with a Muslim "bigot." Anantdās likewise brings the same topos to play in Kabīr's encounters with the Baghela king, which shows a similar conflict between worldly authority and spiritual authority. While, this story is often forgotten in favor of the confrontation with the Muslim sultan, it is crucial to stress, however, that Anantdās has both the Muslim *bādśāh* and the Hindu king misunderstanding Kabīr, but ending up by falling at his feet and begging him for forgiveness.

Fighting against *Śākta* Stereotyping

Entwined with the story of the Baghela king is an incident that is of interest for our purposes. Kabīr is said to have grown tired of people's admiration, and in order to arouse the disgust of the masses, to have taken up with a prostitute and acted as an alchoholic.[63] This seems to have been an effective way to put people off. The word is not used, but we may well wonder whether we see Kabīr here take on the guise of the *śākta* enemy. The hagiographer reports the sarcastic commentary of the Brahmins and Baniyās, who feel justified in their earlier doubts about Kabīr's sincerity:

> The whole world wants to do bhakti, but how can low-castes get it?
> Kabīr too managed for a few days, but look, now he has taken up with a prostitute.[64]

[62] *Kabīr parcaī*, 7.12.

[63] *Kabīr parcaī*, 4.9–13; Lorenzen, *Kabīr Legends*, 102, 150–151; Callewaert and Sharma, *The Hagiographies of Anantadās*, 67–68.

[64] *Bhagati kīyā cāhai saba koī, nīca jāti taiṃ kaisaiṃ hoī; Dina dasa bhagati-Kabīrai kīnhīṃ, aba deṣau ganikā saṃgi līnhīṃ*. *Kabīr parcaī*, 4.13; Lorenzen, *Kabīr Legends*, 151, and *Kabīr parcaī*, 4.14; Callewaert and Sharma, *The Hagiographies of Anantadās*, 68.

The contrast set up here is between bhakti and low-castes, associating the latter with promiscuity as their "natural" state (and, one could add, addiction to liquor). This high-caste prejudice is what Anantdās holds responsible for the hostility toward Kabīr: not so much that he is a Muslim, but that he is low-caste and hence inherently disqualified for "vegetarian" Vaiṣṇava bhakti. Although the word *śākta* is not used in this context, one suspects that is what the gossipers had in mind.

This story has an obverse, where Kabīr is tested by Hari who sends him an enchanting nymph.[65] When the nymph comes to tempt him, she sings her own praises, pointing out how people strive to make her theirs through pilgrimage and religious penance.[66] The nymph at this point talks very much as if she were the goddess, propitiated by many devotees. Kabīr's response is to point out that he cannot please everyone, and is already exclusively devoted to Hari. Moreover, he calls her "mother" ("I should not take your hand, Mother, my Lord, Rām, would get angry").[67] Defeated, the nymph returns to heaven to report that Kabīr excels even Gorakhnāth as far as sense control is concerned.[68] It is only after her testimony that Hari eventually gives *darśana* to Kabīr. He also offers Kabīr as much as the eight *siddhis* (magic powers) and nine *nidhis* (treasures), with the goddess Kamalā serving at his feet,[69] in short every aspiring yogī's dream. But Kabīr is not interested in any of this. God rewards him by granting him immortality. Thus, the message may well be that while Kabīr himself is immune to *śākta* ways, and does not aspire to *siddhis* and the like, he still one-ups the yoga masters.

The story fits well with Kabīr's own verses quoted above, where he preaches resistance to the temptress māyā, as well as those in which he

[65] *Kabīr parcaī*, 11; Lorenzen, *Kabīr Legends*, 191–97, 118–21 (trans.); Callewaert and Sharma, *The Hagiographies of Anantadās*, 85–89.

[66] *Kabīr parcaī*, 11.5–7.

[67] *Terai hātha na lāṃūṃ māṃī, sāhiba merā rāṃma risāī* (*Kabīr parcaī*, 11.11). This line is not in all manuscripts, but he calls her *māī* also in 11.2a, 11.8b, etc. One should point out, though, that this may also be intended to address her as a woman with whom he cannot have sexual relations. This is clear in another passage that occurs only in some manuscripts in l. 11.4.a. See Callewaert and Sharma, *The Hagiographies of Anantadās*, 86.

[68] *Joga jugati gorakha biṣeṣe* (*Kabīr parcaī*, 12.3).

[69] *Kabīr parcaī*, 12.11.

claims immortality, not thanks to any alchemical concoction, but simply the elixir of God's name. Remarkably, there is a hint of competition with Gorakhnāth here, something we had not been able to pinpoint with any certainty in Kabīr's work.

In addition, Anantdās's story has a defensive ring, similar to the previous story where Kabīr used a *śākta* disguise to put people off. This may bespeak a desire to counter the stigma of *śākta* that apparently automatically attached to the low-caste in the eyes of high-castes. The hagiographer is at pains to establish that, counter to appearances, Kabīr remains ever the pure Vaiṣṇava, untainted by these practices.

The Discursive Field of the Hagiographers

What is going on in these stories? Of course the image of Kabīr that appears is not to be taken at face value, but rather needs to be seen as part of the propaganda machine of the Rāmānandīs. They seek to appropriate successful low-caste gurus for their own sect. Rāmānanda, so the claim goes, can transcend the prevalent caste prejudices. He truly opens up bhakti for low-castes, and thus a path of socially upward mobility.[70] Thus the narratives may have less to do with Kabīr and his message, than with late sixteenth-century Rāmānandīs and the audience they were targeting.[71] They are at pains to establish that, once initiated

[70] This has been convincingly shown by William Pinch, "Reinventing Ramanand: Caste and History in Gangetic India," *Modern Asian Studies* 30, no. 3 (July, 1996): 549–71.

[71] Anantdās's stories were taken up and retold in the eighteenth century in Maharasthra by Mahīpati (1715–1790) in his famous *Bhaktavijaya* (composed in 1762). Mahīpati had his own agenda. A Deśastha Brahmin working as scribe in Tharabad (Ahmedpur district), his grandfather, the saint Bhānudās, was a prominent figure in the circle of devotees of Viṭhoba in Pandharpur. Mahīpati's main political agenda seems to have been to retrospectively link the famous Maratha king Śivājī with the Varkārī bhaktas and turn him into a champion against Muslim enemies. James W. Laine, *Shivaji: Hindu King in Islamic India* (Oxford: Oxford University Press, 2003), 52–62. However, even as he is reinventing Śivājī as a "champion of Hinduism," Hindus never appear as a monolithic block. In the process, Mahīpati is busy delinking Śivājī from the cult of Bhavānī, and thereby opposing the *śākta* and Tantric agents who had featured both at Śivājī's (Niścal Purī) and Sambhājī's courts (Kavi Kailāś).

by Rāmānanda, Kabīr was a true Vaiṣṇava, notwithstanding his *śākta* background. The tone is defensive.

These narratives make sense if we consider their performance context. The hagiographers were mendicants roaming the Rajasthani countryside, supporting themselves with storytelling and *bhajana* singing in the villages they visited. Anantdās's stories about the king-turned-ascetic Pīpā give a clear glimpse into that world.[72] Pīpā, originally a Rajasthani king and a goddess worshipper, is converted to the higher-order Vaiṣṇavism with the consent of the goddess herself, who admits she is only a lower-order deity.[73] After his conversion, he forsakes his kingdom and roams from village to village, on his way to and from places of pilgrimage, singing to enlighten the villagers and turn their hearts toward the true God, that is, Rāma. It is this kind of grassroots preaching that forms the context for the Rāmānandī hagiographer's stories.

However, there was competition for the villagers' and local landlords' attention. This is clear from the stories about the origin of the Rāmānandī institutionalization which seems to have taken place under Anantdās's guru-grandfather, Kṛṣṇadās Payhārī, early in the sixteenth century. This local saint settled in the important site of Galtā near Jaipur

See V.S. Bendrey, *Coronation of Sivaji the Great* (Bombay: P.P.H. Bookstall, 1960). I am grateful to Rosalind O'Hanlon for this information. Personal communication October 23, 2008. We see indeed how Mahīpati takes over Kabīr's anti-*śākta* rhetoric, although he never mentions the word itself in retelling the stories about Kabīr in chapters 5 through 7 of his *Bhaktavijaya*. Justin E. Abbott and Narhar R.Godbole, *Stories of Indian Saints: Translation of Mahipati's Marathi Bhaktavijaya* (Delhi: Motilal Banarsidass, 1982), 78–122.

72 See Callewaert and Sharma, *The Hagiographies of Anantadās*, 141–301.

73 The story of Pīpā too contains references to *śākta*s. In the *Pīpā parcaī* the word *śākta* occurs several times. First it comes up with regard to Sūraj Sen, who was initiated by Pīpā and whose kinmen were *śākta*s (*Pīpā parcaī*, 17.1; ib. 249). The second instance is a reference to a *śākta* village, the inhabitants of which were harsh and unkind to Pīpā (32.14; ib. 270), perhaps illustrating the words of Kabīr about shunning *śākta* villages. There are also some Kabīr-like *dohā*s about *śākta*s: *sāgata prīti kahau kihi kāmāṃ, jadi tadi biraca karai saṃgāmā; sādha saṃgai sabahī mili thāpī, jātaiṃ nrimala hota hai pāpī* (What's the point in associating with a *śākta*, whenever he's displeased, he seeks a fight. The company of a sadhu is positive for all, as it cleanses even a sinner) (34.14; ib. 273). Callewaert and Sharma, *The Hagiographies of Anantadās*, 249, 270, 273.

after ousting a group of Nāth Yogīs.[74] Why was Galtā so desirable? As with all real estate, the answer lies in location, in this case proximity to Amer and major trading routes. Indeed, Kṛṣṇadās managed to get the sponsorship of the local king, Prithvīrāj of Amer, according to the hagiographies. Thus for the Rāmānandī hagiographers of Kabīr, it was the Nāths who were rivals for local sponsorship. They would have reason to include them among those despised by Kabīr, that is, under the umbrella term of *śākta*. The anti-Nāth rhetoric is not very strong yet; there is only a hint at competition with Gorakhnāth in the story of the temptress apsara. The *Kabīr parcaī* has no description of direct confrontation with Nāth Yogīs, while such stories are an important part of the Kabīr Panthī hagiographies and of course in the reverse, stories of Gorakh's victory over Kabīr, as told by the Nāth Yogīs.[75] In any case, we have to interpret the Rāmānandī stories as propaganda in a highly competitive religious market. It is in the Rāmānandī hagiographical tradition that we see a shift from Kabīr's own polemics about *śākta*s, whereby the Nāths have taken clearer shape as rivals and foes, while largely continuing to be addressed as *śākta*s. And here it is also that there is a clear insertion of the Rāmānandīs as the saviors of the lower castes, Kabīr serving as a model, in the forms of both sant and devotee.

***

What can we conclude? We have to problematize our thinking about "Hindu" and "Muslim" in purely binary and oppositional terms. It is clear that these identities did not always take precedence over other identities. Neither Kabīr's poetry, in so far as we can reconstruct it, nor the early narratives about him, highlight antagonism to Islam per se. Ritualistic, orthodox representatives of both groups are what is meant by terms such as "Hindu" and "Turak" and/or "Musalmān." All are denounced. But that is not the main binary in the perception of the authors. As a close study shows, there were other "opponents" of the bhakta, those labeled

[74] Led by a certain Tārānāth, according to later sources; see Monika Horstmann, "The Rāmānandīs of Galtā (Jaipur, Rajasthan)," in *Multiple Histories: Culture and Society in the Study of Rajasthan*, ed. L. Babb, V. Joshi, and M. Meister (Jaipur: Rawat Publications, 2002), 141–97.

[75] See Lorenzen, *Kabīr Legends*, 54–55.

śākta, who came in for truly virulent criticism. Several of Kabīr's poems shared by all three recensions witness antipathy toward and advice to shun *śākta*s. His Rāmānandī hagiographers echo the same point. Here, however, the term *śākta* takes on a decidedly low-caste connotation. Caste figures prominently, and it seems the Rāmānandīs are at pains to defend Kabīr from being called a *śākta*. Let us summarize for each in turn what we have found.

In the urban setting of Banares, Kabīr addresses an audience of onlookers (perhaps overwhelmingly low-caste?) on the ghats and in the market. One of his favorite victims for his diatribes is the *śākta*, associated with a non-vegetarian diet and questionable sexual behavior. *Śākta*s may be high-class Brahmins: they include those who slaughter animals to worship the goddess, even if they are high-born. In addition, there are also poems ascribed to Kabīr that strongly oppose false ascetics, who are for hire in the military labor market and travel with yoginīs, presumably practicing Tantric yoga (these poems are attested only later). Kabīr exposes and opposes these groups in song and in biting, sarcastic distichs. It is in distinction to them that he identifies himself as a Vaiṣṇava or bhakta. For his everyday audience, the stress seems to be on warning them against the company of these animal killers and hypocrites, but when addressing more advanced spiritual seekers, he points out that the truly liberated should transcend even the duality of Vaiṣṇava versus *śākta*.

Kabīr's Rāmānandī hagiographers were preaching in rural Rajasthan, vying for the sponsorship of local landowners with other religious groups, such as the Nāths. Here we see a move to appropriate, for the Rāmānandī *sampradāya*, the apparently very popular low-caste sants and their appeal. It should come as no surprise, then, that caste issues figure prominently. The term *śākta* here connotes meat-eating as well as low caste. Anantdās confirms that Kabīr condemned animal slaughter, an issue that figures more prominently in his hagiography than Hindu–Muslim animosity. Kabīr's Muslim identity seems to have more to do with caste than religion. Most striking in Anantdās's accounts in general is the abhorrence of *śākta*s on grounds of their meat-eating, which is confused and mixed up with the low caste of most of the saints he writes about. According to the hagiographer, though, the problem of commensality with such low-castes can be solved by their conversion to bhakti. That seems to be a major Rāmānandī message: to recommend Rāmānanda as the one guru who can integrate such groups into the Vaiṣṇava mainstream; they no longer need to be stigmatized as *śākta*s, they too can become Vaiṣṇava. In the *Kabīr parcaī*, the hagiographer seems to address a suspicion that Kabīr himself is really a *śākta*. This is the theme of the story where Kabīr takes on the guise of a *śākta*, that is, drinks alcohol and associates with a prostitute, in order to scare away people. High-castes are portayed as gloating over this failure of the low-caste would-be Vaiṣṇava. The story, though, shows that this was just a ruse. Appearances do not count; a bhakta of true devotion can truly become a Vaiṣṇava, no matter what the gossipers say. In turn, one wonders whether it might have been a reason why Kabīr so vehemently opposed *śākta*s: because he himself was under constant suspicion of being one.[76]

The case of Kabīr's diatribes against *śākta*s confirms that we need to rethink the monolithic category of "Hinduism." In the late-fifteenth and sixteenth centuries at least one of the fault lines within this category, that between bhaktas and *śākta*s, figured more prominently than the one we care so much about now, the one between Hindus and Muslims. In the established pilgrimage center of Banares, but also for rural audiences, formal adherence to a great religion was less important than the sincerity of emotion of bhakti. While bhaktas felt a commonality as a category, variously referred to as *bhagata* (bhakta) or Vaiṣṇava, they felt the need to distance themselves from *śākta* practices, as associated with goddess worship via animal sacrifice and Tantric rituals. *Śākta* became a general term to designate non-believers, those who had not been through the transformative experience of bhakti, even if engaged outwardly in bhakti-like practices. Thus, in the fifteenth and sixteenth centuries, at least some "Hindus," namely north Indian bhaktas,[77] working in the

[76] I am grateful to Anne Monius for raising this possibility during the question session of my presentation at Harvard University on April 14, 2009.

[77] Bhaktas and *Śākta*s seem to coexist in more harmony, although still with tension in Bengal, as studied for goddess devotion by Rachel McDermott. *Singing to the Goddess: Poems to Kālī and Umā from Bengal* (New York: Oxford University Press, 2001). For other areas this phenomenon remains to be studied, but I have given already some parallels for Maharashtra. Finally, William Pinch's historical study has shown a strong enmity between Śaiva and Vaiṣṇava monastic orders. *Peasants and Monks in British India* (Berkeley: University of California Press, 1996).

vernacular, felt that another group now designated as "Hindu," namely *śāktas*, figured more prominently as opponents than Muslims.

BIBLIOGRAPHY

Editions

Bhagavānprasād, Sītārām Śaraṇ "Rūpkalā," ed. *Gosvāmi Nābhājī kṛt śrī bhaktamāl: Śrī Priyādāsjī praṇīt ṭikā-kavitta, śrī sītārāmśaraṇ bhagvānprasād rūpkalā viracit bhaktisudhāsvād tilak sahit* (Lucknow: Tejkumār Book Depot, reprint, 1977).

Callewaert, Winand M. and Swapna Sharma, eds. *The Hagiographies of Anantadās: The Bhakti Poets of North India.* Richmond: Curzon Press, 2000.

Callewaert, Winand M. and Bart Op de Beeck, eds. *Nirgu-bhakti Sāgar Devotional Hindī Literature: A Critical Edition of the Pañc-Vāṇī or Five Works of Dādū, Kabīr, Nāmdev, Rāidās, Hardās, with the Hindī Songs of Gorakhnāth and Sundardās, and a Complete Word-index.* 2 volumes. South Asia Institute, Heidelberg: South Asian Studies 25. New Delhi: Manohar, 1991.

Callewaert, Winand M. and Mukund Lath. *The Hindī Padāvalī of Nāmdev: A Critical Edition of Nāmdev's Hindi Songs with Translation and Annotation.* Delhi: Motilal Banarsidass, 1989.

Tivārī, Parśānāth. *Kabīra granthāvalī.* Allahabad: Hindi Pariṣad, Prayāg Viśvavidyālay, 1961.

Secondary Literature

Abbott, Justin E. and Narhar R. Godbole. *Stories of Indian Saints: Translation of Mahipati's Marathi Bhaktavijaya.* 2 volumes. Delhi: Motilal Banarsidass, 1982.

Agrawal, Purushottam. "In Search of Ramanand: The Guru of Kabir and Others." *Pratilipi* (October 2008). http://pratilip.in/2008/10/in-search-of-ramanand-purushottam-agrawal/. Accessed May 7, 2012.

Bendrey, V.S. *Coronation of Sivaji the Great.* Bombay: P.P.H. Bookstall, 1960.

Dharwadker, Vinay. *Kabir: The Weaver's Songs.* New Delhi: Penguin Books India, 2003.

Dass, Nirmal. *Songs of Kabir from the Adi Granth.* Albany: State University of New York Press, 1991.

Habib, Irfan. "Medieval Popular Monotheism and its Humanism: The Historical Setting." *Social Scientist* 21, nos. 3–4 (1993): 78–88.

Hawley, John Stratton. "Introduction." *International Journal of Hindu Studies* (special issue) 11, no. 3 (2007): 209–25.

Hess, Linda and Shukdev Singh. *The Bījak of Kabīr.* San Francisco: North Point Press, 1983.

Horstmann, Monika. "The Rāmānandīs of Galtā (Jaipur, Rajasthan)." In *Multiple Histories: Culture and Society in the Study of Rajasthan*, edited by L. Babb, V. Joshi, and M. Meister, 141–97. Jaipur: Rawat Publications, 2002.

Khan, Iqtidar Alam."Early Use of Cannon and Musket in India: A.D. 1442–1526." *Journal of the Economic and Social History of the Orient* 24, no. 2 (1981): 146–64.

Laine, James W. *Shivaji: Hindu King in Islamic India.* Oxford: Oxford University Press, 2003.

Lorenzen, David. "Ascetics in Indian History." *Journal of the American Oriental Society* 98, no. 1 (1978): 61–75.

———. *Kabīr Legends and Ananta-dās's Kabīr Parachaī.* Albany: State University of New York Press, 1991.

McDermott, Rachel Fell. *Singing to the Goddess: Poems to Kālī and Umā from Bengal.* New York: Oxford University Press, 2001.

Offredi, Mariola. "Kabīr and the Nāthpanth." In *Images of Kabīr*, edited by Monika Horstmann, 127–41. New Delhi: Manohar, 2002.

Pauwels, Heidi. *In Praise of Holy Men: Hagiographic Poems by and about Harirām Vyās.* Groningen Oriental Studies 18. Groningen: Egbert Forsten, 2002.

———. "Imagining Religious Communities in the Sixteenth Century: Hariram Vyas and the Haritrayi." *International Journal of Hindu Studies* 13 no. 2 (2009): 143–61.

———. "Who Are the Enemies of the *Bhaktas*? Testimony about '*Śāktas*' and 'Others' from Kabīr, the Rāmānandīs, Tulsīdās, and HarirāmVyās." *Journal of the American Oriental Society* 130, no. 4 (October–December 2010), 509–40.

———. "Imagining Religious Communities in the Sixteenth Century: Hariram Vyas and the Haritrayi." *International Journal of Hindu Studies* 13, no. 2: 143–61.

Pinch, William. "Reinventing Ramanand: Caste and History in Gangetic India." *Modern Asian Studies* 30, no. 3 (July 1996): 549–71.

———. *Peasants and Monks in British India.* Berkeley: University of California Press, 1996.

Shea, David, and Anthony Troyer, trans. *The Dabistān, or School of Manners.* Paris: Oriental Translation Fund of Great Britain and Ireland, 1843. http://persian.packhum.org/persian/main?url=pf%3Ffile%3D15501050%26ct%3D0. Accessed May 7, 2012.

Singh, Pashaura. *The Bhagats of the Guru Granth Sahib: Sikh Self-Definition and the Bhagat Bani.* New York: Oxford University Press, 2003.

Vaudeville, Charlotte. *A Weaver Named Kabīr.* Delhi: Oxford University Press, 1993.

11 Muslims as Devotees and Outsiders

Attitudes toward Muslims in the Vārtā *Literature of the Vallabha Sampradāya*

Shandip Saha

The collection of hagiographical tales known as the *vārtā*s has been central to the religious life of the Vaiṣṇavite bhakti community known as the Puṣṭi Mārga, founded in sixteenth-century north India by Vallabhacārya (1479–1573).[1] The principal purpose of the *vārtā*s was to shape the religious self-identity of the community by stressing that it should be a closely knit and exclusive fellowship of believers who owed their final allegiance only to Kṛṣṇa and the Community's religious leaders who were known as mahārājas. This paper will focus on images of Muslims in the *vārtā*s and the manner in which these texts advise its audience on how to interact with their Muslim counterparts on a daily basis without compromising their special status as the recipients of Kṛṣṇa's grace. It will be argued that while the *vārtā* literature unequivocally views Muslims as barbarians (*mleccha*s) and outsiders (*yavana*s), the images of Muslims it presents and the advice it gives devotees on how to coexist

[1] Only proper names and terms in both Sanskrit and Hindi have been transliterated in this essay. Geographical locations are identified by their modern place names for which current spelling conventions have been retained.

with their Muslim counterparts are not uniform. This aspect of the *vārtās* was molded, in part, to address the unique social situations of the various caste groupings that made up the devotee base of the community as well reflect the shifting political allegiances of the mahārājas, from the Mughal state to Rājpūt nobility.

A SUMMARY HISTORY OF THE PUṢṬI MĀRGA

The Puṣṭi Mārga was founded toward the end of the fifteenth century. According to Vallabha, a new form of religiosity was needed to replace practices associated with *smārta* Hinduism which Vallabha collectively called the "Path of Rules" (*maryādā mārga*). Vallabha's solution was grounded in Kṛṣṇaite devotionalism in which the individual was to be purified by the divine grace (*puṣṭi*) of the Supreme Lord Kṛṣṇa and then live a householder's life completely devoted to him. Vallabha's community hence came to be known as the Puṣṭi Mārga or the "Path of Grace." A person was initiated by taking the *brahmasambandha mantra*, a sacred formula that cleansed the individual of his impurities and made him fit to enter into a loving relationship with Kṛṣṇa.[2] Vallabha proposed that the bond between the Divine and the devotee was to be maintained through the process of service (*sevā*) which meant the dedication of one's physical labor and material wealth to the Divine through the public worship of Kṛṣṇa's images in sectarian shrines and private prayer in the domestic shrines of individual devotees. *Sevā*, however, was not meant to curry favor with God for specific ends. It was, on the contrary, to be the uninhibited and spontaneous expression of the innate desire to serve Kṛṣṇa and to experience the joy and happiness associated with his boundless grace.[3] Vallabha's message won a following across central and northern India that cut across all four castes of Hindu society, but he found his most

[2] Vallabha states this in verses 2–4 of *Siddhāntarahasyam* which is the fifth of sixteen Sanskrit treatises found in Vallabha's *Ṣoḍaśagranthaḥ*. See James D. Redington, trans., *The Grace of Lord Krishna: The Sixteen Verse Treatises (Soḍaśagranthaḥ) of Vallabha* (Delhi: Sri Satguru Publications, 2000), 64–65.

[3] See Peter Bennett, *The Path of Grace: Social Organisation and Temple Worship in a Vaishnava Sect* (Delhi: Hindustan Publishing Corporation, 1993), 69–72. Also see Vallabha's brief but nonetheless important comment on this in the second verse of *Siddhāntamuktāvalī*. Redington, *The Grace of Lord Krishna*, 26.

receptive audience in Gujarat, primarily among the socially dominant mercantile (Baniā) community and members of the Śūdra community.

The Puṣṭi Mārga experienced one of its greatest periods of growth under the leadership of Vallabha's second son, Viṭṭhalnāth (1515–1585) who took charge of the community in 1543 after the death of his elder brother Gopīnāth (1512–1543). Viṭṭhalnāth primarily focused his expansion efforts in Braj, where he resided with his seven sons and their families. As well as approaching Muslim nobles for aid in securing land grants that offered the Puṣṭi Mārga tax-exempt status, Viṭṭhalnāth also turned to his father's devotees in the Gujarātī mercantile community for financial support and made six trips from Braj to Gujarat between 1543 and 1582. Preaching tours in the region of Kathiawar took him to cities such as Godhara, Ahmedabad, Surat, and Cambay, where he deliberately targeted Hindu elites who were either in the employ of the ruling Muslim administrative structure or came from the Baniā community. Money from the Puṣṭi Mārga's mercantile patrons was primarily channeled toward financing Viṭṭhalnāth's various temple construction projects in Gokul and the maintenance of the community's main shrine at Govardhan where Vallabha had established a temple to an image of Kṛṣṇa known as Śrīnāthjī. Even after Viṭṭhalnāth's death the community continued to receive tax-free land grants (*madad-i māsh*) from the now dominant Mughals. This is attested in imperial documents (*farmāns*) which variously assured that the villages around Govardhan and Gokul would belong exclusively to the Puṣṭi Mārga in perpetuity and that these properties would always be exempt from all forms of taxation and political interference.[4]

When Viṭṭhalnāth died in 1585, the spiritual leadership of the Puṣṭi Mārga was divided equally among his seven sons who inherited the exclusive right to initiate disciples into the community. Viṭṭhalnāth's sons were also given custody over various images of Kṛṣṇa with the principal image of Śrīnāthjī being entrusted to the hands of Viṭṭhalnāth's eldest son and his descendants. This distribution of spiritual authority led to the formation of seven divisions within the Puṣṭi Mārga known

[4] For translations of the *farmāns* received by the Puṣṭi Mārga from its Mughal patrons see Krishnalal Mohanlal Jhaveri, *Imperial Farmans (A.D. 1577 to A.D. 1805) Granted to the Ancestors of His Holiness the Tilakayat Maharaj* (Bombay: New Printing Press, 1928).

as the "Seven Houses," with spiritual leadership of each division being concentrated in the hands of Vallabha's male descendants as traced only through Viṭṭhalnāth. They were now called mahārājas with the special designation of *tilkāyat* being given to the head of the first house who had custody of the Śrīnāthjī image.

Continued Mughal and Gujarātī mercantile patronage of the Puṣṭi Mārga in Braj ensured a particularly significant period of stability and growth for the community for most of the seventeenth century. This period of prosperity, however, was shaken by political unrest in the Braj area caused by the outbreak of the Jāṭ Rebellions in 1669. Vaiṣṇavite communities in the area sought to avoid the continual disruption to their religious activities and the possible destruction of their images by either leaving Braj temporarily or by seeking new sources of patronage in geographical locations where they could be assured greater socioeconomic and political stability. In the case of the Puṣṭi Mārga, the community moved to Rajasthan and established various shrines between 1670 and 1672. The most important of these shrines was in Mewar where the *tilkāyat* and his family settled with the Śrīnāthjī image. Following on the earlier decision by Mahārāṇā Jagat Singh I (r. 1628–52) to be initiated into the third house of the Puṣṭi Mārga,[5] Jagat Singh's son, Rāj Singh I (r. 1653–80) offered the first house of the Puṣṭi Mārga territory over which the reigning *tilkāyat* had complete administrative and economic control. The Śrīnāthjī image was then installed in a new temple and the landholding was given the name of Nathdwara. In time, Nathdwara became a small autonomous kingdom within Mewar with the *tilkāyat*s enjoying the dual status of being revered religious leaders (gurus) and politically influential members of the Mewari nobility (*jāgīrdār*s).[6]

[5] See Kanṭhmaṇi Śāstri, *Kāṁkarolī kā Itihās* (Kāṁkaroli: Vidyā Vibhāg, 1930), 130–31, for the account of Jagat Singh's initiation into the Puṣṭi Mārga. After his initiation into the community, Jagat Singh gave a piece of land in Mewar as a tribute to the mahārāja who initiated him. This piece of land came to be named Kankaroli and became the permanent home to the third house of the Puṣṭi Mārga after it left Braj for Mewar during Rāj Singh's reign.

[6] For reproductions of some of the Mewari *farmāns* given to the Puṣṭi Mārga, see James Tod, *Annals and Antiquities of Rajasthan* (London: Routledge and Sons Ltd., 1914), I, 415–24, 436–39, and 442–43.

THE *VĀRTĀ* LITERATURE AND THE INSTITUTIONAL HISTORY OF THE PUṢṬI MĀRGA

Where does one situate the *vārtā* literature within the larger institutional development of the Puṣṭi Mārga? The production of the *vārtā* literature can be attributed to Viṭṭhalnāth's sons and grandchildren who continued to foster the growth of the community left to them by Vallabha and Viṭṭhalnāth. This third and fourth generations of mahārājas continued to safeguard the community's material interests by seeking Mughal religious patronage and, eventually, Rājpūt patronage once the community migrated from Braj to Rajasthan toward the end of the seventeenth century. The third and fourth generations of mahārājas also focused their efforts on the task of community building by substituting Sanskrit with the more accessible Brajbhāṣā as their principal mode of religious instruction.

The use of Brajbhāṣā in the Puṣṭi Mārga as a vehicle for religious instruction has been attributed to Viṭṭhalnāth's fourth son, Gokulnāth (1551–1640), who regularly instructed his devotees in Brajbhāṣā on matters related to theology and the history of the community. The *Śrī Mahāprabhujī kī Nijvārtā* and the *Gharūvārtā* which form part of the *vārtā* literature are two works which have been associated with Gokulnāth and concern themselves with establishing the divinity of Vallabha and preserving anecdotes about Vallabha and his extended family in Varanasi.[7] Another significant body of Brajbhāṣā literature associated with Gokulnāth is titled *Śrī Gokulnāth ke Caubīs Vacanāmṛta* ("Twenty-Four Nectar Utterances of Gokulnāth"), which are twenty-four short pieces of religious instruction written down by Gokulnāth's devotee, Kalyāṇ Bhaṭṭ.

The *Vacanāmṛta*, in turn, would shape the theological framework for the *Caurāsī Vaiṣṇavan kī Vārtā*.[8] This important collection of stories in the *vārtā* canon is a group of stories gathered by Gokulnāth to amplify themes outlined in his twenty-four utterances, about Vallabha and his eighty-four most exemplary devotees. The *Caurāsī Vaiṣṇavan kī Vārtā*

[7] Gokulnāth, *Śrī Mahāprabhujī kī Nijvārtā, Gharūvārtā, Baiṭhak Caritra* (Indore: Vaiṣṇav Mitr Maṇḍal, 1995).

[8] The edition used here is Harirāy, *Caurāsī Vaiṣṇavan kī Vārtā* (Indore: Vaiṣṇav Mitr Maṇḍal, 1992).

would in turn provide the inspiration for two other collections of literature in the *vārtā* canon. One, attributed to Gokulnāth, but probably compiled by his disciples, is the *Bhāvsindhu kī Vārtā* which retells the lives of certain devotees from the *Caurāsī Vaiṣṇavan kī Vārtā* along with a few devotees said to have been associated with Viṭṭhalnāth.[9] The second is the other major collection of *vārtā* literature attributed to Gokulnāth entitled the *Do Sau Bāvan Vaiṣṇavan kī Vārtā*. These are didactic stories about Viṭṭhalnāth and his 252 exemplary devotees.[10]

These two principal collections of Puṣṭi Mārga hagiography—the *Caurāsī Vaiṣṇavan kī Vārtā* and the *Do Sau Bāvan Vaiṣṇavan kī Vārtā*—seemed to have been revised and finally redacted in the cultural milieu of Rajasthan where Harirāy (1590?–1715), Gokulnāth's nephew, had been residing since 1660. Harirāy made his home in the kingdom of Kota from where he wrote theological texts and made trips to Nathdwara, to advise the *tilkāyat* on the performance of *sevā*, until his death. It was during this period that Harirāy revised the *Caurāsī Vaiṣṇavan kī Vārtā* by adding extensive commentaries to the text while his disciples continued with the task of revising the *Do Sau Bāvan Vaiṣṇavan kī Vārtā* by adding stories related to the establishment of Nathdwara as well as commentaries modeled along those Harirāy had written for the *Caurāsī Vaiṣṇavan kī Vārtā*.[11] The commentaries in both collections expand upon certain parts

[9] Gokulnāth, *Bhāvsindhu kī Vārtā* (Mathura: Śrī Govardhan Granthamālā Kāryālaya, 1972).

[10] The edition used is Harirāy, *Do Sau Bāvan Vaiṣṇavan kī Vārtā* (Indore: Vaiṣṇav Mitr Maṇḍal, 1992). All references from the *Caurāsī Vaiṣṇavan kī Vārtā* and *Do Sau Bāvan Vaiṣṇavan kī Vārtā* are cited by *vārtā* number, the relevant episode number, followed by the page numbers.

[11] The *Caurāsī Vaiṣṇavan kī Vārtā* exists in a commentarial and pre-commentarial form. The earliest extant manuscript for the *Caurāsī Vaiṣṇavan kī Vārtā* has a colophon bearing the date of 1601, and its earliest extant manuscript in a commentarial form has a colophon bearing the date of 1695. The *Do Sau Bāvan Vaiṣṇavan kī Vārtā* contains references to events surrounding Nathdwara which was established in 1672 and a full version of the text in its commentarial form bears the date of 1730. Thus it would seem that the *Do Sau Bāvan Vaiṣṇavan kī Vārtā* was still in the process of being redacted between the late seventeenth and early decades of the eighteenth centuries. For dating concerns see Hariharanāth Ṭaṇḍan's extensive survey of the *vārtā* literature, *Vārtā Sāhitya: Ek Bṛhat Adhyayan* (Aligarh: Bhārat Prakāśan Mandir, 1960), 112–42.

of the main stories and also give advice to devotees on how to carry out their daily lives as recipients of Kṛṣṇa's grace. They are also concerned with legitimizing the claims of the Puṣṭi Mārga mahārājas to be Kṛṣṇa's earthly intermediaries. The two texts would be followed by another text mistakenly attributed to Harirāy entitled the *Śrīnāthjī Prākaṭya kī Vārtā*. This was probably written in the early eighteenth century shortly after the establishment of Nathdwara.[12] The text acted as a type of vernacular *māhātmyam* whose purpose was to extol the sanctity of the newly established pilgrimage site of Nathdwara. The *Śrīnāthjī Prākaṭya kī Vārtā*, however, also had a political dimension to it given its attempts to legitimate the close relationship between the Nathdwara *tilkāyat*s and the Mewar royal house. The text argues that the relationship was divinely ordained by Viṭṭhalnāth and, more importantly, Śrīnāthjī himself.

The history of the *vārtā* literature thus began in Braj in the late sixteenth century and ended in Rajasthan during the mid-eighteenth century. During this period, the membership of the Puṣṭi Mārga came to encompass all four castes of Hindu society and the community came to enjoy great material prosperity due to the financial support they received from their royal patrons and wealthy Gujarātī merchants. Hence the *vārtā* literature, against this larger historical context, should be viewed as the product of a period of stability which allowed the community to turn inward and focus on the task of community building. This was accomplished through the creation of an accessible body of didactic historical writing that could be used to illustrate key theological concepts and to lay out for devotees an ideal vision of a united Puṣṭi

---

Also see Dīndayālu Gupta, *Aṣṭachāp aur Vallabha-Sampradāy* (Prayag: Hindi Sāhitya Sammelan, 1970), I, 129–30; Dhirendra Varma, *La Langue Braj* (Paris: Adrien-Maisonneuve, 1935), 31–32; John Stratton Hawley, *Sūrdās: Poet, Singer, and Saint* (Seattle: University of Washington Press, 1984), 7–8; and Shandip Saha, "A Community of Grace: The Theological and Social World of the Puṣṭi Marga *Vārtā* Literature," *The Bulletin of the School of Oriental and African Studies* 69, no. 2 (2006): 231. For information on Harirāy, see R.G. Shah, *Vallabha Cult and Śrī Harirāyjī (Contribution of Śrī Harirāyji to Vallabha School)* (Delhi: Pratibha Prakashan, 2005), and Prabhudayāl Mītal, *Gosvāmi Harirāy Jī kā Pad-Sāhitya* (Mathura: Sāhitya Sammelan, 1962).

[12] The edition of this text that is currently available is Harirāy, *Śrīnāthjī Prākaṭya kī Vārtā* (Nathdwara: Vidyā Vibhāg, 1988).

Mārga community. This ideal vision emphasized the unique religious identity of the Puṣṭi Mārga as a close-knit, self-sufficient, and very exclusive community, which, as the recipients of Kṛṣṇa's grace, owed final allegiance to Kṛṣṇa and his earthly authorities, the mahārājas.[13]

RELIGIOUS EXCLUSIVITY IN THE *VĀRTĀ* LITERATURE

Given the emphasis placed upon preserving the unique religious identity of the community, it is not surprising that the concept of *anyāśraya* is central to the theology of the Puṣṭi Mārga. *Anyāśraya* means to seek refuge in another individual or set of beliefs that are outside the realm of the Puṣṭi Mārga. The concept is not unique to the *vārtā* literature. Vallabha, although he does not explicitly use the term *anyāśraya*, certainly warns his devotees about the dangers of turning away from the doctrines of the Puṣṭi Mārga. Contact with non-devotees or even practicing any ritual that deviated from Puṣṭi Mārga doctrine—especially the *maryādā mārga*—would compromise the one thing that made the Puṣṭi Mārga unique amongst all other religious communities around them: the fact that they were a closely knit community of spiritual elect who, being infused with divine grace, desired nothing else but to love the form of Lord Kṛṣṇa[14] This theme is built upon in the *Vacanāmṛta* which stresses the importance of the Puṣṭi Mārga as an exclusive group of religious elect who, suffused with the grace of Kṛṣṇa, were to lead lives of humble, selfless devotion to no other deity than Kṛṣṇa. Gokulnāth explicitly uses the term *anyāśraya* in the *Vacanāmṛta* and emphasizes

[13] For a general overview of the theological and social world view of the *vārtā* literature, see Saha, "A Community of Grace." Also see Vasudha Dalmia, "Forging Community: The Guru in a Seventeenth-Century Vaiṣṇava Hagiography," in *Charisma and Canon: Essays on the Religious History of the Indian Subcontinent*, ed. Vasudha Dalmia, Angelika Malinar, and Martin Christof (New Delhi: Oxford University Press, 2001), 129–54; Vasudha Dalmia, "Hagiography and the 'Other' in the Vallabha *Sampraday*," in this volume; and Richard Barz, "The *Caurāsī Vaiṣṇavan kī Vārtā* and the Hagiography of the Puṣṭimārg," in *According to Tradition: Hagiographical Writing in India*, ed. Winand M. Callewaert and Rupert Snell (Wiesbaden: Otto Harrassowitz, 1994), 43–64.

[14] Redington, *The Grace of Lord Krishna*, 44, 47. Vallabha makes this point most emphatically in verses 10–12 and 17–21 of *Puṣṭipravāhamaryādābhedaḥ*, which is the fourth treatise of *Śoḍaśagranthaḥ*.

that should one ever stray from the path set forth by Vallabha, one risks being reborn as a dog or condemned to the depths of hell.[15]

The dangers of *anyāśraya* are reinforced in the *vārtā* literature. *Anyāśraya* does not mean merely to forsake the Puṣṭi Mārga for another religious path; it extends to viewing or keeping an image of Kṛṣṇa that is not a consecrated Puṣṭi Mārga image, going on pilgrimages to sites not associated with Kṛṣṇa or the Puṣṭi Mārga, using goods for *sevā* that have been touched by non-members, and marrying outside the community. For example, a Brahmin woman devotee of Viṭṭhalnāth, famed for the quality of her *sevā* to Kṛṣṇa, is shunned by Viṭṭhalnāth's close disciples because she took gifts from a devotee of the goddess. The woman is told that in accepting the gifts, she has sold the most precious gift that she could have, in the form of her faith, and that is so unpardonable that even Viṭṭhalnāth chooses not to defend her.[16] Shunning seems to be a rather extreme step for what is a seemingly trivial action, but the response of Viṭṭhalnāth and his disciples seems to be a rather common one in the *vārtā* literature to those who have committed an action going against the key beliefs of the community. The dangers of *anyāśraya* is underlined in the commentary accompanying a story found in the *Caurāsī Vaiṣṇavan kī Vārtā* concerning the devotee, Dāmodardās Sambhalvāre: "Thus there is no greater fault than that of *anyāśraya*. Just as the moral conduct of a woman is ruined once she leaves a husband for another man, in the same way, if one shows even the smallest amount of disbelief, then the faith of a Vaiṣṇava is ruined."[17]

Given this strong emphasis on religious exclusivity, how does the *vārta* literature distinguish the Puṣṭi Mārga from the communities around it? Vasudha Dalmia explores this question in her contribution to this volume on the relationship between the Puṣṭi Mārga and both "high" and "low" Hindu religious formations. For the moment, however, it will suffice to say that the devotees in the *vārtā* literature refer to Hindu religious communities around them in terms of sectarian affiliations.

[15] Gokulnāth, *Śrī Gokulnāthjī ke Caubīs Vacanāmṛta*, reprinted in *Gosvāmi Gokulnāth Smṛti Granth*, ed. Bhagavatī Prasād Devapurā (Nathdwara: Nāthdvārā Sāhitya Maṇḍal, 1996), 57–73. For instance, where Gokulnāth stresses the karmic results of straying away from Vallabha's path; see utterances 4 and 6.

[16] *Do Sau Bāvan Vaiṣṇavan kī Vārtā*, I, *vārtā* 38, episode 1, 305–12.

[17] *Caurāsī Vaiṣṇavan kī Vārtā*, *vārtā* 3, episode 5, 37.

A devotee like Viṭṭhalnāth's closest associate, Cācā Harivaṃśa, will refer to himself as a "servant of Viṭṭhalnāth and a member of the 'Vallabhi *sampradāya*,' which was founded by Vallabha to defeat those who follow the *maryādā mārga*."[18] Those who follow the *maryādā mārga* are usually *smārta* Brahmins in the *vārtā*s while the Gauḍīya Vaiṣṇava community who were active in the Braj area during the same time as the Puṣṭi Mārga is referred to in terms of its ethnic background as Bengali.

Muslims are designated as *mleccha*s and *yavana*s in the *vārtā* literature, both terms being used interchangeably for the community. They derive from the longstanding Sanskritic usage for foreign invaders (regardless of religious affiliation) and any group of people, indigenous or otherwise, who fall outside the caste system and hence are viewed as uncivilized or barbaric.[19] Muslims are also occasionally referred to in the *vārtā* literature in terms of their ethnic identity as "Paṭhāns" or "Turks."[20] Crucially, however, no mention is ever made of their religious affiliation. Furthermore, the texts make no mention of Islamic religious beliefs nor do they contain anti-Islamic polemic or stories of Vaiṣṇavas triumphing over their Muslim counterparts in religious debates. This is not surprising given the emphasis placed in the *vārtā* literature upon *anyāśraya*. It is also indicative, however, of how Muslims were never perceived in the *vārtā* literature in terms of religious identity. They were viewed instead in terms of their social identity, and treated as an endogamous community that was assumed to be governed by its own unique set of social customs and rules. Accordingly, religion is but one element. Thus it seems that

18 *Do Sau Bāvan Vaiṣṇavan kī Vārtā*, I, *vārtā* 3, episode 1, 64–65.

19 For discussions about the images of Muslims in Sanskrit texts, see Romila Thapar, "The Image of the Barbarian in Early India," *Comparative Studies in Society and History* 13, no. 4 (1971): 408–36, and B.D. Chattopadhyay, *Representing the 'Other'? Sanskrit Sources and the Muslims 8th–14th Century* (New Delhi: Manohar, 1998).

20 The most notable example in the *vārtā* literature is the famous Hindi poet Raskhān who is said to be a disciple of Viṭṭhalnāth. He is called Raskhān Saiyid Paṭhān in the *vārtā* literature. See *Do Sau Bāvan Vaiṣṇavan kī Vārtā*, III, *vārtā* 244. For a consideration of Raskhān's life and poetry, see Rupert Snell, "Raskhān the Neophyte: Hindu Perspectives on a Muslim Vaishnava," in *Urdu and Muslim Studies in South Asia: Studies in Honour of Ralph Russell*, ed. Christopher Shackle (London: School of Oriental and African Studies, 1988), 29–37.

Muslims are viewed in the *vārtā* literature as being foreigners of Paṭhān or Turkish origin who occupied north India, and whose lifestyle—as opposed to the religion per se—is deemed to be barbaric, uncouth, and contrary to orthodox Vaiṣṇava values.

It is not all that surprising, then, that Muslims in the *vārtā* stories are often portrayed in an unsympathetic light. This is particularly obvious in the *Do Sau Bāvan Vaiṣṇavan kī Vārtā*. It contains the *vārtā* of Govindsvāmī, the poet and singer who was initiated into the Puṣṭi Mārga by Viṭṭhalnāth and is said to be the music teacher of Akbar's legendary Muslim-born court musician Tānsen. According to the *vārtā*, Tānsen entreated Govindsvāmī to take him as his student. Govindsvāmī, however, refused, stating that he could not have any contact with Tānsen because he was a *mlechha*. Tānsen was only able to become Govindsvāmī's student after he renounced his *mleccha* identity and became a member of the Puṣṭi Mārga.[21] Govindsvāmī's dislike for Muslims is highlighted in another *vārtā* as well. This story recounts how a Muslim chances upon Govindsvāmī practicing the morning rāga Bhairav on the banks of the Yamuna and later praises Govindsvāmī's rendition of the rāga. When Govindsvāmī hears this, he is so upset that he vows to never sing the rāga again because any rāga that is praised by a Muslim could never be offered to Śrīnāthjī during *sevā*.[22]

Elsewhere, Govindsvāmī's fellow devotee and poet, Chītsvāmī, echoes a similar disdain for the inferior nature of Muslims. Chītsvāmī is said in the *Do Sau Bāvan Vaiṣṇavan kī Vārtā* to have been the family priest to Akbar's famous Hindu courtier Bīrbal. His *vārtā* details how he visited Bīrbal and sang two poems praising the greatness of Viṭṭhalnāth above all others. Bīrbal is said to have responded by telling the poet that Emperor Akbar might be offended if he heard Chītsvāmī's poems. Chītsvāmī responded by storming out of Bīrbal's home, suggesting that the nobleman had become a *mlechha*. In other words, for Chītsvāmī, Bīrbal's willingness to consider the feelings of the emperor over the evocation of Viṭṭhalnāth's greatness suggested that he had renounced his identity as a Vaiṣṇava and shifted his allegiance to a barbarian emperor.[23]

21 *Do Sau Bāvan Vaiṣṇavan kī Vārtā*, II, *vārtā* 113, episode 1, 152.

22 *Do Sau Bāvan Vaiṣṇavan kī Vārtā*, III, *vārtā* 247, episode 12, 369.

23 *Do Sau Bāvan Vaiṣṇavan kī Vārtā*, III, *vārtā* 244, episode 2, 335–38.

Another, very powerful example of how dismally the *vārtā* literature looks upon Muslims is to be found in the *Caurāsī Vaiṣṇavan kī Vārtā* in the *vārtā* concerning Vallabha's disciple Dāmodardās Sambhalvāre. When Vallabha learns that Dāmodardās's wife has doubted his promise that she will give birth to a son by consulting a low-caste fortune teller (*dākotiyā*), he tells Dāmodardās that his state of grace is compromised by the actions of his wife and then proceeds to curse the child by stating he will grow up to be a *mleccha*. Dāmodardās' wife is so distraught that during her entire pregnancy, she refuses to touch anything to be used in her daily *sevā* to Kṛṣṇa lest it become impure. When Dāmodardās's son is born, he is given to another woman who then raises the child. The outcast child grows up to become what the text calls a "Turk" and proves to be troublesome for Dāmodardās's wife when her husband dies.[24] The wife does not want to give all of her husband's wealth to her impure child and resolves instead to donate it to Vallabha. But Vallabha rejects it, offering two reasons. First, the wealth was rendered impure from the very moment that Dāmodardās' wife conceived the child. Second, he is aware that Dāmodardās's son will attempt to reclaim the wealth as his own. Consequently, all of Dāmodardās' property—including a low-caste maidservant—are thrown into the Yamuna, but not before Vallabha's eldest son, Gopīnāth, chooses to keep some of the wealth for himself.[25] The choice proves to have dire consequences for Gopīnāth. Gopīnāth's decision to partake of wealth that had been tainted by the birth of a Muslim was the reason, according to the *vārtā*, why his lineage came to an abrupt end with the death of his only child, Puruṣottam. In other words, Muslims are considered to be so low that their very birth proves to be detrimental not only for an orthodox devotee like Dāmodardās but even for Vallabha's eldest son and successor.

WARDING OFF THE INFLUENCE OF MUSLIMS IN THE *VĀRTĀ* LITERATURE

If Muslims posed such a threat to the religious identity of the Puṣṭi Mārga how did the latter attempt to protect themselves? For orthodox devotees like Govindsvāmī and Chītsvāmī, the answer was to simply

[24] *Caurāsī Vaiṣṇavan kī Vārtā*, *vārtā* 3, episode 7, 34–36.

[25] *Caurāsī Vaiṣṇavan kī Vārtā*, *vārtā* 3, episode 8, 39–40. This story is contained in the appendix to the *vārtā* of Dāmodardās Sambhalvāre entitled *lauṁḍī kī vārtā*.

isolate themselves from Muslims and avoid them at all costs. This, however, was not quite that easy for the Baniā devotees that made up a large part of the Puṣṭi Mārga's devotee base. Their livelihoods were often dependent upon relationships with Muslim members of the Mughal administration and it was not uncommon for Baniā communities to have to travel and even live in areas such as the Sindh and Afghanistan in order to further their business interests. The *vārtā* literature is very aware of this concern and attempts to address this question by emphasizing that the best way to protect oneself in these situations is to have continual faith in Kṛṣṇa, to be diligent in one's *sevā*, and to create a network of well-knit Vaiṣṇavite communities who can offer religious support to fellow Vaiṣṇavas who live in far-off lands.

This theme is underlined in the story of a devotee named Mādhodās Kṣatrī who made his living in Kabul. Mādhodās concealed his identity by wearing the same clothes as the city locals, but continued with his *sevā* in the privacy of his home. Mādhodās, the story states, was such a dedicated devotee that Kṛṣṇa appeared to him daily during his *sevā*, much to the surprise of another initiate of Viṭṭhalnāth, named Rūpmurārīdās, who visited Kabul for the purpose of business. He became Mādhodās's helpmate in *sevā*.[26] Mādhodās is thus extolled as an ideal Vaiṣṇava because he still maintained his religious identity even in a land of outcastes (*mleccha deś*) and hence is ultimately protected by none other than Kṛṣṇa himself.

The method to ward off the influence of Muslims in the early-eighteenth-century *Śrīnāthjī kī Prākaṭya Vārtā* is, however, quite different from that found in the *Do Sau Bāvan Vaiṣṇavan kī Vārtā*. The *Śrīnāthjī kī Prākaṭya Vārtā* depicts the Mughals as actively trying to persecute the Puṣṭi Mārga as they try to leave Braj for Mewar. The text also describes how certain members of the first house adorn themselves in military attire and set up guards to protect themselves from the Mughals. When Rāj Singh is approached by the *tilkāyat* about possibly sheltering the fleeing religious community, he expresses his fear of military reprisals by the Mughals. The Queen Mother convinces her son that the patronage of the Puṣṭi Mārga is a matter of honor for the kingdom and to protect Mewar and the Puṣṭi Mārga from a possible Mughal attack would be an act of sacrifice for both his country and his faith.[27] Muslims are no longer

[26] *Do Sau Bāvan Vaiṣṇavan kī Vārtā*, I, *vārtā* 8, episode 1, 139–44.

[27] *Śrīnāthjī kī Prākaṭya Vārtā*, 57–61.

viewed as individuals whose presence has the potential to compromise the religious exclusivity of the Puṣṭi Mārga. The Mughals in the *Śrīnāthjī kī Prākaṭya Vārtā* are now equated with Islam and their *mleccha* followers pose a serious threat to all of Vaiṣṇavism and its practitioners.

In the *Śrīnāthjī kī Prākaṭya Vārtā*, Rāj Singh's commitment to protecting his faith is ultimately rewarded with the permanent presence of Śrīnāthjī in Mewar, which is a theme that becomes amplified through folk stories linking three chronologically unrelated events in Mewar's history into a single continuous narrative: Rāj Singh's elopement with Aurangzeb's intended Rājpūt bride, Cārumatī, in 1660, the establishment of Nathdwara in 1672, and Aurangzeb's attack on Mewar in 1679. Aurangzeb's attack upon Mewar is thus a direct result of Rāj Singh's elopement with Cārumatī. Ultimately the fragmented Rājpūt kingdoms are described as coming together to mount a valiant fight against the Mughals under the watchful eye of Śrīnāthjī. The same theme that is found in the *Śrīnāthjī kī Prākaṭya Vārtā* is thus reiterated in these narratives: Rāj Singh's commitment to his duty, his kingdom, and faith in the face of an onslaught of a barbarian religion assures the kingdom of Śrīnāthjī's perpetual protection.[28]

POSITIVE PORTRAYALS OF MUSLIMS IN THE *VĀRTĀ* LITERATURE

It is important to underline that there are instances when Muslims are portrayed in a positive light in the *vārtā* literature. They usually occur in two contexts. The first underlines the salvific power of divine grace and usually involves Muslims renouncing their religious identities and converting to the Puṣṭi Mārga. This is particularly true for an unnamed Muslim woodcutter whose story in the *Do Sau Bāvan Vaiṣṇavan kī Vārtā* seems to be modeled upon the famous story concerning Rāmānanda's initiation of the low-caste weaver, Kabīr. The woodcutter sees Viṭṭhalnāth in Braj, resolves to become his disciple, and goes to Gokul every night to secretly obtain a glimpse of Viṭṭhalnāth. When Viṭṭhalnāth goes to bathe

[28] These tales are recounted in an article written by Surinder Singh Cakra, "Prabhu Śrīnāthjī kī Mevār par Kṛpā," in *Sāhitya Maṇḍal Nāthdvārā Hīrak-Jayanti-Granth*, ed. Bhāgavatī Prasād Devapurā (Nathdwara: Nāthdvārā Sāhityā Maṇḍal, 1996), 223–25.

on the banks of the Yamuna in the middle of the night, he unknowingly steps on the head of the sleeping woodcutter and then utters the *brahmasambandh mantra* three times. When the woodcutter later seeks to have a direct interview with Viṭṭhalnāth on the grounds that he is now his disciple, Viṭṭhalnāth agrees as long as the woodcutter sits at a certain distance from him and his followers. From that point onward, the woodcutter becomes Viṭṭhalnāth's faithful follower and eventually gives up his own body the very moment he hears that Viṭṭhalnāth has passed away.[29]

There is a similar story in the *Do Sau Bāvan Vaiṣṇavan kī Vārtā* concerning a Muslim woman who makes a living as a vegetable seller. When Viṭṭhalnāth happens upon the woman and slakes her thirst with water initially offered to an image of Kṛṣṇa, the woman suddenly recognizes Viṭṭhalnāth to be a manifestation of Kṛṣṇa and resolves to become his follower. She is told, however, by one of Viṭṭhalnāth's personal attendants that becoming Viṭṭhalnāth's devotee will not be easy because she is a Muslim and hence she is trapped in a demonic (*asurī*) body. She is advised to use her savings to purify her body by providing Vaiṣṇavas with only the highest and best food and clothing material so they may donate it to Viṭṭhalnāth for *sevā*. Once she has no longer anything to offer the Vaiṣṇavas, she is advised to enter into a state of separation (*viraha*) where she cares not for her physical well-being, but only to be with Viṭṭhalnāth.[30] After the woman follows this advice, Viṭṭhalnāth eventually hears from the Vaiṣṇavas to whom she sold her goods that the source of his *sevā* materials is on her deathbed and is yearning to see him. Viṭṭhalnāth grants the woman her wish and initiates her into the Puṣṭi Mārga, after which she dies.

The point of the story is to emphasize that Vaiṣṇavas must show mercy to all living beings, but the story also seems to be making another point about the nature of bhakti. At the end of the story, Viṭṭhalnāth personally performs the death rites of his devoted Muslim devotee in the same way that Rāma personally performs the death rites of his vulture devotee, Jaṭāyu, in the Rāmāyaṇa.[31] Thus, the vegetable seller is cast in the same mold as other well-known individuals like Śabrī and Bhuśuṇḍi whose

[29] *Do Sau Bāvan Vaiṣṇavan kī Vārtā*, II, *vārtā* 118, episode 1, 169–71.

[30] *Do Sau Bāvan Vaiṣṇavan kī Vārtā*, I, *vārtā* 69, episode 1, 463–68.

[31] *Do Sau Bāvan Vaiṣṇavan kī Vārtā*, I, *vārtā* 69, episode 1, 469.

impurity or humble status is held up in Purāṇic and bhakti literature as what makes them ideal role models for devotees. In other words, this particular story echoes a sentiment found throughout bhakti literature: it is not the highest of the high who embody the characteristics of the ideal bhakta, but the lowest of the low, whether a low-caste woman, a crow, a vulture, or, in this case, a Muslim.

The second context in which one sees positive depictions of Muslims in the *vārtā* literature is usually in the context of legitimating Muslim support for the Puṣṭi Mārga. The devotee Nārāyandās Dīvān Kāyastha, for example, was employed by a local Muslim governor who was so impressed by the depth of Nārāyandās's *sevā* that he defrayed the costs of maintaining Nārāyandās's household and regularly sent *sevā* material to Viṭṭhalnāth. Nārāyandās's good fortune, according to the commentary, was directly due to the quality of his bhakti. The *vārtā* goes on to explain that the Muslim governor was so receptive to his employee's *sevā* because he was a highly spiritual soul (*daivī jīva)* in his previous life who, for some unknown transgression, was reborn as a *mleccha* who still had the spiritual insight to recognize the strength and value of Nārāyandās's *sevā*.[32]

A somewhat similar explanation is given of the close relationship of Viṭṭhalnāth and Alīkhān, the district ruler (*hākim)* of Mahāban who supplied Viṭṭhalnāth with horses for his journeys across India. The text recounts how Alīkhān's fifteen-year-old daughter, Pīrzādī, used to regularly play with Vaiṣṇavite children when she and her father lived in Delhi. Thus when Alīkhān was sent by the emperor to Braj, he came to revere the sacredness of Braj to the point that he severely punished any individual who picked leaves from its sacred groves. He then built a Kṛṣṇa temple at the request of his daughter so she could have an image of Kṛṣṇa as a playmate. Kṛṣṇa would appear regularly at the temple where the two would play together. When Alīkhān and Pīrzādī wanted to meet Viṭṭhalnāth, however, they were told that this was impossible because he never looked at the faces of *mlecchas*. Finally, Viṭṭhalnāth is said to have initiated the father and daughter into the Puṣṭi Mārga only after Kṛṣṇa appears to Viṭṭhalnāth and orders him to do so. Once Alīkhān is initiated, he immediately renounces his Muslim identity and asks Viṭṭhalnāth what

[32] *Do Sau Bāvan Vaiṣṇavan kī Vārtā*, I, *vārtā* 5, episode 4, 117

crime he committed in his past life that he was born in the body of a *mleccha*. Viṭṭhalnāth then explains to them how Alīkhān and Pīrzādī were high-caste Brahmins who used to worship the Raṅganāth image housed in Śrīraṅgam, but were reborn as Muslims because Alīkhān committed a breach in temple ritual. The commentary for the story then further explains Alīkhān and Pīrzādī's devotion to Kṛṣṇa by positing a more spiritual explanation. Alīkhān and Pīrzādī, according to the commentary, were manifestations of Kṛṣṇa's female attendants (*sakhīs*), Rasataraṅginī and Śubhānanā.[33]

A similar strategy of legitimation is used when explaining why the emperor Akbar had shown such great favor to Viṭṭhalnāth by granting him the Puṣṭi Mārga's first set of land grants in Braj. The *Caurāsī Vaiṣṇavan kī Vārtā* states that Akbar was once a Brahmin who unwittingly swallowed a piece of cow hair while drinking milk. It was this act of ritual impurity that caused him to be reborn as a righteous but still *mleccha* emperor.[34] His status as a righteous *mleccha* is reinforced in the *Do Sau Bāvan Vaiṣṇavan kī Vārtā*, which tells a story in which Akbar supposedly meets with Viṭṭhalnāth in Gokul and asks him what is the easiest way to reach God. Viṭṭhalnāth simply answers: "In the same way you have met me."[35] Viṭṭhalnāth's simple assertion, that the path to the Divine is not a difficult one but is direct and effortless in nature, leaves Akbar so impressed that he acknowledges Viṭṭhalnāth as Kṛṣṇa and lavishes gifts upon him. A humbled Akbar then leaves, marveling at Viṭṭhalnāth's majesty and wisdom.

***

[33] *Do Sau Bāvan Vaiṣṇavan kī Vārtā*, I, *vārtā* 37, episode 2, 302.

[34] *Caurāsī Vaiṣṇavan kī Vārtā*, *vārtā* 81, episode 3, 447. This explanation is found in the *vārtā* of the celebrated bhakti poet, Sūrdās. For a consideration of Akbar's place in hagiographies, see Kumkum Sangari's "Tracing Hagiographies, Popular Narrative Traditions and Conversion," in *Mapping Histories: Essays Presented to Ravinder Kumar*, ed. Neera Chandhoke (New Delhi: Tulika, 2000), 61–103. For Akbar's place in the *vārtā* literature see John Stratton Hawley's essay, "Last Seen with Akbar," in his *Three Bhakti Voices: Mirabai, Surdas, and Kabir in Their Time and Ours* (Delhi: Oxford University Press, 2005), 181–93.

[35] *Do Sau Bāvan Vaiṣṇavan kī Vārtā*, I, *vārtā* 75, episode 1, 503. This is the *vārtā* that deals with Viṭṭhalnāth's supposed connections to Akbar's famed courtier, Bīrbal.

How, then, can we make sense of these conflicting images of Muslims? The *vārtā* literature emphasizes the lowly status of Muslims. According to it, those who commit breaches of religious orthodoxy in previous lives are cursed to become Muslims, albeit Muslims of high status like Alīkhān and Akbar who are regarded as patrons and supporters of the Puṣṭi Mārga. Although the *vārtā* literature seems to be saying that even Muslims are worthy of divine grace, they are never viewed as equal to other Vaiṣṇavas. The woodcutter, for example, is still told to keep a respectable distance from Viṭṭhalnāth and other Vaiṣṇavas even after he is initiated into the Puṣṭi Mārga, and while Akbar and the local governor who supports Nārāyandās's *sevā* are viewed favorably in the *vārtā* literature, they are not considered to be full-fledged, or even honorary, Vaiṣṇavas. They are, instead, deemed to be righteous *mlecchas*. In the *vārtā* literature, a Muslim is a *mleccha* and will always remain one.

Although it is tempting to argue that this attitude toward Muslims is rooted in some sort of fear about the "other," it is important to stress that all religious communities who did not follow the Puṣṭi Mārga are viewed in the *vārtā* literature as having the potential to lead devotees to commit an act of *anyāśraya*. Consequently, all individuals needed to be kept at arm's length regardless of whether or not they were Hindus or Muslims if they did not embrace Vallabha's teachings. One could argue, however, that the difference between the treatment of Hindus and Muslims in the *vārtā* literature is that the depictions of Muslims are rooted in a particularly powerful strain of political, cultural, or racial xenophobia. Even if the Puṣṭi Mārga did discriminate against other Hindus on the grounds of religious affiliation, it certainly did not based on caste affiliations since the community was open to all four castes of Hindu society. Muslims, however, are dismissed as *mleccha*s and *yavana*s on the basis of their ethnicity and the assumption that everything associated with them is uncivilized.

It is difficult to accept such arguments for two reasons. First, the mahārājas overtly declared their political allegiance to the Mughals in order to secure their material well-being and, in doing so, did not stand outside the Mughal social order but placed themselves firmly within it. The stories concerning the Mughals in the *vārtā* literature openly acknowledge the relationship between Mughals and the Puṣṭi Mārga, and in fact attempt to explain the nature of the relationship by deeming the Mughals to be righteous *mlecchas*. Second, the stories in the *Caurāsī Vaiṣṇavan kī Vārtā* and *Do Sau Bāvan Vaiṣṇavan kī Vārtā* concerning the relationship between Muslims and the average Puṣṭi Mārga devotee are not shaped by violent conflict or religious competition. The stories in these two texts tend to reflect the everyday realities of devotees who are struggling to maintain their Vaiṣṇavite identities while trying to coexist with their Muslim counterparts.

The advice given in the *Caurāsī Vaiṣṇavan kī Vārtā* and *Do Sau Bāvan Vaiṣṇavan kī Vārtā* concerning the manner in which devotees should coexist with Muslims, however, was very much shaped by the diverse social composition of the Puṣṭi Mārga in the late seventeenth and early eighteenth centuries when the *vārtā* literature was still being written and redacted. For those who came from orthodox Brahmin communities and were involved daily in the performance of *sevā* in sectarian shrines, the stories surrounding Chītsvāmī, Govindasvāmī, and Dāmodardās Sambhalvāre underline the absolute importance of completely isolating themselves from Muslims in order to preserve their ritual purity. In the case of the members of the Baniā community whose livelihoods were dependent upon their dealings with Mughal officials and traders, the *vārtā* encourages them to fulfill their worldly duties but to constantly protect themselves from the influence of *mlecchas* by regularly performing *sevā* and seeking the spiritual support of Vaiṣṇavas. For the devotees drawn from the Pāṭidār and Kunabī castes of Gujarat, the stories of the Muslim woodcutter and vegetable seller were indicative of how divine grace was accessible even to the lowest rungs of society including barbarians like Muslims. For the Rājpūt patrons of the Puṣṭi Mārga, their *sevā* to Kṛṣṇa was performed by carrying out their kingly duties to protect their faith and kingdoms from what the *Śrīnāthjī Prākaṭya kī Vārtā* portrays as the pernicious onslaught of Islam.

If the *Caurāsī Vaiṣṇavan kī Vārtā* and *Do Sau Bāvan Vaiṣṇavan kī Vārtā* tend to counsel a certain amount of tolerance toward Muslims, how then does one explain the association of Mughals with religious violence in the *Śrīnāthjī kī Prākaṭya Vārtā*? Muslims are not treated as individuals in the *Śrīnāthjī Prākaṭya kī Vārtā* in the way they are in the *Caurāsī Vaiṣṇavan kī Vārtā* and the *Do Sau Bāvan Vaiṣṇavan kī Vārtā*. In the *Do Sau Bāvan Vaiṣṇavan kī Vārtā*, for example, regardless of their status in society Muslims like Akbar or the woodcutter are seen as individuals with whom Vaiṣṇavas dialogue and interact. In the *Śrīnāthjī*

Prākaṭya kī Vārtā, however, Muslims are all collapsed into a single group of marauding *mlecchas* whose goal is to undermine Vaiṣṇavas and those who protect them. This shift in the portrayal of Muslims may be explained by Rājasthānī regional politics. The forced acceptance of Mughal suzerainty in 1614 by the Mewar royal house prompted Jagat Singh I to begin a type of royal propaganda campaign to help reassert Mewar's authority over the Mughals and other Rājpūt states. This entailed rewriting the history of the state to portray its previous rulers as warriors of divine origin who valiantly gave up their lives to protect their land and religion. This history continued to be glorified through painting and architecture. The patronage of the Puṣṭi Mārga was one element of Rāj Singh's efforts to continue his father's attempts to reassert Mewar's role in Rajasthan. The patronage of the Puṣṭi Mārga helped bolster the religious image of the royal house and to revive the state's declining economy by attracting the wealthy merchants of Gujarat who were the Puṣṭi Mārga's principal devotees. The acceptance of Mewari patronage on the part of the Puṣṭi Mārga, on the other hand, seems to have entailed not only asserting the political suzerainty of the Mewar royal house, but also allowing itself to be a vehicle for royal propaganda.[36] Thus the images of Muslims in the *Śrīnāthjī kī Prākaṭya Vārtā* seem so different from those in the *Caurāsī Vaiṣṇavan kī Vārtā* and the *Do Sau Bāvan Vaiṣṇavan kī Vārtā* because the text was shaped by and reflected the political agenda of their Mewari patrons.

Is this shift in the *vārtā* literature, however, symptomatic of a growing communal consciousness on the part of Hindus? The Puṣṭi Mārga only began to define itself as "Hindus" and tried to ally themselves with other Hindu communities in the nineteenth century in response to criticisms of British Orientalists, Hindu reform movements such as the Ārya Samāj, and disaffected devotees who all described the mahārājas and their religious practices as being licentious and morally degenerate. This nineteenth-century quest of the Puṣṭi Mārga for religious legitimacy in the eyes of its Hindu co-religionists underlines an important point about this community. Throughout its history, the Puṣṭi Mārga had been more concerned with defining itself in relationship to other Hindu communities rather than to Muslims. This is perhaps no clearer

[36] See Jennifer Joffee, "Art, Architecture, and Politics in Seventeenth-Century Mewar" (PhD diss., University of Minnesota, 2005), 58–123.

in the *Do Sau Bāvan Vaiṣṇavan kī Vārtā* than when Viṭṭhalnāth's disciple Cācā Harivamṣa refers to himself as a member of a community which was founded specifically to defeat what was called the "*maryādā mārga*" by Vallabha. In other words, it was important that devotees not compromise their journey on the path of devotion by falling back into practices associated with mainstream Hindu religiosity. The Puṣṭi Mārga was founded by Vallabha as an alternative to the *maryādā mārga* and because of his belief that the community's status as the favored recipients of divine grace made it stand apart from its Hindu co-religionists.

The Muslim presence, however, seems to be accepted by the *vārtā* literature with a certain amount of reluctance. No matter how much they are beneath Vaiṣṇavas, the *vārtā* literature also understands that Muslims are an unavoidable presence in society with whom devotees must coexist in ways that are appropriate to their caste status. The mahārājas of the Puṣṭi Mārga seem to have certainly understood this as well. The Mughals represented the ruling political structure and they were willing to express their loyalty to the Mughals as long as it served the community's material interests. The moment Mughal patronage became less certain due to the political instability in Braj, they discarded their Mughal patrons and replaced them with the very Hindu kings with whom the Mughals had battled for years. In short, then, it can be best said that the attitude of the *vārtā* literature to Muslims was not driven so much by religious orthodoxy as by realism and pragmatism.

BIBLIOGRAPHY

Barz, Richard. "The *Caurāsī Vaiṣṇavan kī Vārtā* and the Hagiography of the Puṣṭimārg." In *According to Tradition: Hagiographical Writing in India*, edited by Winand M. Callewaert and Rupert Snell, 43–64. Wiesbaden: Otto Harrassowitz, 1994.

Bennett, Peter. *The Path of Grace: Social Organisation and Temple Worship in a Vaishnava Sect.* Delhi: Hindustan Publishing Corporation, 1993.

Cakra, Surinder Singh. "Prabhu Śrīnāthjī kī Mevār par Kṛpā." In *Sāhitya Maṇḍal Nāthdvārā Hīrak-Jayanti-Granth*, edited by Bhāgavatī Prasād Devapurā, 223–25. Nathdwara: Nāthdvārā Sāhityā Maṇḍal, 1996.

Chattopadhyay, B.D. *Representing the 'Other'? Sanskrit Sources and the Muslims 8th–14th Century.* New Delhi: Manohar, 1998.

Dalmia, Vasudha. "Forging Community: The Guru in a Seventeenth-Century Vaiṣṇava Hagiography." In *Charisma and Canon: Essays on the Religious History of the Indian Subcontinent*, edited by Vasudha Dalmia, Angelika

Malinar, and Martin Christof, 129–54. New Delhi: Oxford University Press, 2001.

Gokulnāth. *Bhāvsindhu kī Vārtā*. Mathura: Śrī Govardhan Granthamālā Kāryālaya, 1972.

———. *Śrī Gokulnāthjī ke Caubīs Vacanāmṛta*. In *Gosvāmi Gokulnāth Smṛti Granth*, edited by Bhagavatī Prasād Devapurā, 57–73. Nathdwara: Nāthdvārā Sāhitya Maṇḍal, 1996.

———. *Śrī Mahāprabhujī kī Nijvārtā, Gharūvārtā, Baiṭhak Caritra*. Indore: Vaiṣṇav Mitr Maṇḍal, 1995.

Gupta, Dīndayālu. *Aṣṭachāp aur Vallabha-Sampradāy*. 2 volumes. Prayag: Hindi Sāhitya Sammelan, 1970.

Harirāy. *Caurāsī Vaiṣṇavan kī Vārtā*. Indore: Vaiṣṇav Mitr Maṇḍal, 1992.

———. *Do Sau Bāvan Vaiṣṇavan kī Vārtā*. 3 volumes. Indore: Vaiṣṇav Mitr Maṇḍal, 1992.

———. *Śrīnāthjī Prākaṭya kī Vārtā*. Nathdwara: Vidyā Vibhāg, 1988.

Hawley, John Stratton. *Sūrdās: Poet, Singer, and Saint*. Seattle: University of Washington Press, 1984.

———. "Last Seen with Akbar." In *Three Bhakti Voices: Mirabai, Surdas, and Kabir in Their Time and Ours*, by John Stratton Hawley, 181–93. Delhi: Oxford University Press, 2005.

Jhaveri, Krishnalal Mohanlal, ed. *Imperial Farmans (A.D. 1577 to A.D. 1805) Granted to the Ancestors of His Holiness the Tilakayat Maharaj*. Bombay: New Printing Press, 1928.

Joffee, Jennifer. "Art, Architecture, and Politics in Seventeenth-Century Mewar." PhD diss., University of Minnesota, 2005.

Mītal, Prabhudayāl. *Gosvāmi Harirāy Jī kā Pad-Sāhitya*. Mathura: Sāhitya Sammelan, 1962.

Redington, James D., trans. *The Grace of Lord Krishna: The Sixteen Verse Treatises (Soḍaśagranthaḥ) of Vallabha*. Delhi: Sri Satguru Publications, 2000.

Saha, Shandip. "A Community of Grace: The Theological and Social World of the Puṣṭi Mārga *Vārtā* Literature." *The Bulletin of the School of Oriental and African Studies* 69, no. 2 (2006): 225–42.

Sangari, Kumkum. "Tracing Hagiographies, Popular Narrative Traditions and Conversion." In *Mapping Histories: Essays Presented to Ravinder Kumar*, edited by Neera Chandhoke, 61–103. New Delhi: Tulika, 2000.

Śāstri, Kanṭhmaṇi. *Kāṁkarolī kā Itihās*. Kāṁkaroli: Vidyā Vibhāg, 1930.

Shah, R.G. *Vallabha Cult and Śrī Harirāyjī (Contribution of Śrī Harirāyji to Vallabha School)*. Delhi: Pratibha Prakashan, 2005.

Snell, Rupert. "Raskhān the Neophyte: Hindu Perspectives on a Muslim Vaishnava." In *Urdu and Muslim Studies in South Asia: Studies in Honour of Ralph Russell*, edited by Christopher Shackle, 29–37. London: School of Oriental and African Studies, 1988.

Ṭaṇḍan, Hariharanāth. *Vārtā Sāhitya: Ek Bṛhat Adhyayan*. Aligarh: Bhārat Prakāśan Mandir, 1960.

Thapar, Romila. "The Image of the Barbarian in Early India." *Comparative Studies in Society and History* 13, no. 4 (1971): 408–36.

Tod, James. *Annals and Antiquities of Rajasthan*. 2 volumes. London: Routledge and Sons Ltd., 1914.

Varma, Dhirendra. *La Langue Braj*. Paris: Adrien-Maisonneuve, 1935.

12 Mahamat Prannath and the Pranami Movement

Hinduism and Islam in a Seventeenth-Century Mercantile Sect

Brendan LaRocque

In 1978 Pyarelal Trivedi, a Pranami sect devotee and scholar, published the Hindi book *The Sun of Dharma and the Removal of Error*, an exposition of Pranami doctrine as well as a staunch defense of the sect's central figure, Mahamat Prannath (1618–1694). According to Trivedi, two individuals named Shyamsundar Tripathi and Trishi Kumar had published a book titled *Nijanand Mimansa*, in which they disparaged the Pranamis while claiming that Prannath's writings "were only based on the ideas of the Quran, that Prannath used Muslim language" and in which they "accuse[d] Shri Prannathji of being a Muslim who tricked Hindus into becoming Muslims." Trivedi goes on to make a blistering and erudite counter-attack on the authors of *Nijanand Mimansa*, arguing,

> For 300 years no one has ever said that the doctrine of Pranami dharma is untrue, that it is non-Vedic, or that it is Muslim. In *Nijanand Mimansa*, Pandit Shyamsundar and Trishi Kumar have attempted to divide Pranamis and Muslims, to divide Pranamis and Hindus, and to divide Hindus and Muslims ... [But] the people have accepted as necessary today the salvation of unity and equality which Prannath delivered 300 years ago.[1]

[1] Pyarelal Trivedi, *Dharmadivakar aur Bhrantinashanam: Nijanand Mimansa ke Mithya Apakshepoka Sampraman Nirakaran* (Panna: Shri Padhyavati Puri

These polemics followed upon the publication, in the mid-1960s, of the major Pranami documents, which the sect's leaders had previously largely kept inaccessible to outsiders.[2] The reason for such secrecy, according to one scholar who has studied the sect's writings, was that "All the Pranamis were afraid that no one should get the wrong understanding and begin calling Prannath a Muslim."[3]

The portrayal of Prannath as a Muslim who undermined Hinduism stands in odd juxtaposition with the studies of Prannath which view him as a staunch defender of Hinduism against the depredations of the Muslim rulers of the Mughal Empire, and as the guru who urged the Bundela Rajput king Maharaja Chhatrasal to rise up against Emperor Aurangzeb in order to protect Hindu dharma. Thus, for example, Bhagwan Das Gupta has written in his *Life and Times of Maharaja Chhatrasal Bundela* that Prannath was "a militant patriot giving moral support to the champions of Hindu India ... The rising fame of Chhatrasal Bundela as the champion of Hindu religion and freedom attracted Prannath to Bundelkhand."[4]

The present essay aims to provide an overview of Prannath's life and teachings in an effort to understand the role and significance of Islamic and Hindu beliefs in his movement as it emerged in the seventeenth century, through an analysis of Pranami ideas and history as presented in the sect's canonical texts. The fact that ideas as religiously dynamic, fluid, and unorthodox as Prannath's found a substantial following in cities and towns across Mughal India can in part be explained by their appearance at a time of extensive social change wrought by imperial rule. The political and economic integration of north India under the Mughals brought varied communities and their respective worldviews into closer

---

Dham Trust, 1978), 3, 209. Unless otherwise noted, all translations from the Hindi/Hindustani are my own.

[2] The secretiveness of the Pranamis concerning Prannath's writings has been widely noted. See W.R. Pogson, *History of the Boondelas* (Delhi: B.R. Publishing Corporation, 1974), 92, fn. 97; Jadunath Sarkar, foreword, in Bhagwan Das Gupta, *Life and Times of Maharaja Chhatrasal Bundela* (New Delhi: Radiant Publishers, 1980); Dominique-Sila Khan, "The Mahdi of Panna: A Short History of the Pranamis," *Indian Journal of Secularism* 6, no. 4 (January–March 2003): 63.

[3] Raj Bala Sidana, *Shri Prananathiji aur Unka Sahitya* (Jamnagar: Sahitya Prakasana Committee, 1969), xi.

[4] Das Gupta, *Life and Times of Maharaja Chhatrasal Bundela*, 96.

and more intense interaction with one another, and many early modern devotional leaders, including Prannath, grappled with the socio-religious implications of this development.[5] Prannath can be considered one of the last important "sant" figures of the precolonial period, holding views that shared significant elements with other devotional movements of the time, specifically in his eclectic engagement with religious traditions, his critique of caste, and his condemnation of ritualistic orthodoxy.[6] At the same time, his effort to transcend established religious identities through a particular combination of Vaishnavite belief with Sufi mysticism and Shia millenarianism marked him out as a unique religious figure. As will be seen below, Prannath was well aware of socio-religious differences between particular Hindu and Muslim groups in Mughal India. However, he came to embrace both Hindu and Islamic scriptures and traditions while himself not identifying as either a Hindu or a Muslim, a view that he encouraged his devotees to also follow by usually referring to them simply as "believers" (*momins*) and "companions" (*saths*). Finally, I will argue that the Pranami movement developed as it did in significant part because of the nature of Prannath and his companions' intense involvement with state authorities during the period of Emperor Aurangzeb's rule (1658–1707), at both the regional and the imperial level.

THE *BITAK* AS AN HISTORICAL SOURCE

The main Pranami sources concerning the life of Mahamat Prannath consist of his own extensive collection of devotional poems called the *Kulzam Swarup*, and his major hagiography, the *Bitak*, written by his lead disciple Lal Das.[7] The *Bitak* tells the story of Prannath's rise to prominence as a

[5] Religious interactions in precolonial South Asia are examined from a variety of perspectives in David Gilmartin and Bruce Lawrence, eds., *Beyond Turk and Hindu: Rethinking Religious Identities in Islamicate South Asia* (Gainesville: University Press of Florida, 2000).

[6] See Karine Schomer, "Introduction: The Sant Tradition in Perspective," in *The Sants: Studies in a Devotional Tradition of India*, ed. Karine Schomer and W.H. McLeod (Delhi: Motilal Banarsidass, 1987), 6.

[7] According to Matabadal Jayasawal, the term "*bitak*," meaning an account of events, while not included in standard Hindi dictionaries, is still used in

religious leader among mercantile communities in Gujarat, his unsuccessful efforts to establish a relationship with Emperor Aurangzeb, followed by his search for patronage in the kingdoms of Rajasthan, and finally his settling in the capital of Maharaja Chhatrasal Bundela's kingdom in Panna, Bundelkhand. Because the *Bitak* serves as the main source, along with Prannath's own writings, for reconstructing this history of Prannath and his movement, it is important to attend to the nature and limitations of this work historiographically.[8] In reading the *Bitak* as a primary source one is confronted with the challenges and issues inherent in the critical analysis of hagiographical literature generally, particularly the inclusion of legendary and supernatural material.[9] However, as a hagiography the *Bitak* is somewhat unusual in the attention it pays to historical accuracy and chronological specificity, a feature that perhaps was developed under the influence of the Sufi biographical (*tazkira*) tradition.[10] But the usefulness of the tales of saints for understanding early modern society and history certainly should not be limited merely to the extraction of

that sense in contemporary Gujarat. See his introduction to Lal Das, *Bitak*, ed. Matabadal Jayaswal and Devkrishna Sharma (Allahabad: Pranami Sahitya Sansthan, 1966), 1, fn. 1. All references in the current essay are to this edition. The text contains a total of seventy-one sections (*prakarans*) and 4308 verses (*chaupais*). The term *bitak* is also evocative of the *Bijak*, the name of the popular compilation of Kabir's poetry. The *Kulzam Swarup* is alternatively referred to as the *Kulzam Sharif*, *Tartam Vani*, and *Shri Tartam Sagar*, among other names. For analyses of the fourteen volumes which make up the *Kulzam Swarup*, see Suchit Narayan Prasad, *Mahamati Prannath Prerit Shri Krishna Pranami Vangmay* (New Delhi: Shri Prannath Mission, 1987), 24–58; also see Naresh Pandya, *Prannath: Sampradaya evam Sahitya* (Jaipur: Panchsila Prakasan, 1973), 59–77.

8 For other primary sources which provide information about Prannath and his movement, see footnotes 28 and 72. I would like to thank Jacqueline Suthren Hirst for her incisive comments which helped me develop and clarify my interpretation of hagiographical works.

9 Cf. Winand M. Callewaert and Rupert Snell, eds, *According to Tradition: Hagiographical Writing in India* (Wiesbaden: Otto Harrassowitz, 1994).

10 See Bruce Lawrence, "The Sant Movement and North Indian Sufis," in *The Sants*, ed. Schomer and McLeod, 371. See Velcheru Narayana Rao, David Shulman, and Sanjay Subrahmanyam, *Textures of Time: Writing History in South India 1600–1800* (New York: Other Press, 2003) for a discussion of the varied ways in which history was written in early modern India.

objective factual descriptions from a given text. The various social roles and purposes that such compositions themselves served, alongside the ideas, observations, and beliefs they express, provide historically significant information about the context in which they were produced.[11] I would argue that prominent among the many purposes served by Mughal-era hagiographies, including the *Bitak*, was to give form to the relationship between devotional groups and the state, as well as promote particular interests in religious and sectarian disputes. In their frequent depictions of interactions between king and saint, always mythologized to some degree, hagiographies simultaneously provided—or denied—legitimacy to rulers and invoked the right to and expectation of protection or patronage from the state. Viewed from this perspective, hagiographies impinged upon what Farhat Hasan, in his study of Mughal Gujarat, has labeled the "moral economy of the state," which "provided the basis of the ideological dominance of the state and a mechanism for the construction of social consent for imperial sovereignty."[12] In its vivid depiction of the Pranamis' ultimately failed effort to come to terms with the Mughal Empire in the person of Aurangzeb, the *Bitak* proclaims the illegitimacy of that state, looking instead to other kingdoms for protection and support, in the end finding the rebel king Chhatrasal. Seen from this perspective, when the *Bitak* depicts attempts at dialogue with the emperor, the verity of specific details for each individual event is of less importance than the fact that the *Bitak* claims such efforts were made at all, and that they were ultimately abandoned. In other words, the text can be viewed as a record of a prominent mercantile sect's rebuffed desire to gain a place in the imperial system, resulting in the community finding another patron in Chhatrasal. The contingencies of history, however, must be inferred from the narrative, which, like all hagiographies, is written in a teleological and retrospective manner. The *Bitak* consequently presents the conflict with Aurangzeb and the alliance with Chhatrasal as inevitable and divinely ordained, while the evolution of Prannath's various religious claims appear in a synchronous, unified narrative.

[11] For an analysis of the roles hagiographies played in community formation, see Heidi R.M. Pauwels, *In Praise of Holy Men: Hagiographic Poems by and about Hariram Vyas* (Netherlands: Egbert Forstern Groningen, 2002).

[12] Farhat Hasan, *State and Locality in Mughal India: Power Relations in Western India, c. 1572–1730* (Cambridge: Cambridge University Press, 2004), 2.

By presenting his teacher's life story and religious views in this way, Lal Das conformed to Prannath's claim to embody a timeless divine reality acting out a preordained destiny.

Lal Das's *Bitak* was presented to Maharaja Chhatrasal at his court in Panna, shortly after Prannath's death in 1694. A critical edition of the original text was published in 1966 by Dr Matabadal Jayasawal and Devkrishna Sharma, based on a close comparison of several available manuscript copies of the work at sites across north India. Altered versions of the *Bitak*, along with other hagiographies containing substantial reinterpretations of Prannath's life, were later produced, and while a careful analysis of the significance of the differences between the various works would be an informative exercise, for purposes of the present article I will base my study on the *Bitak* edition published by Jayasawal and Sharma. Suffice it to say that the later versions of Prannath's hagiography had the effect of de-emphasizing the place of Islam in the original text and projecting a more mainstream Krishna-centered sect.[13]

In the following section I provide an overview of Prannath's life according to the *Bitak*, and interweave a discussion of his own compositions within the context provided by that narrative. Before delving into the story it tells, however, there is one feature of the *Bitak*'s narrative structure that I would like to discuss briefly. As will be seen below, Prannath and Lal Das embraced many of the ideas and terminology of the Nizari Ismaili messianic and prophetic tradition which were widespread in India at the time.[14] In my estimation this initially occurred during Prannath and Lal Das's time in Delhi in 1678–79, and as a result both were subsequently to engage for many years quite intensely, although not exclusively, with the message of Islam, the Prophet Muhammad, and the Quran. Prior to that time, however, I believe

[13] For example, later renditions of the *Bitak* (including the most commonly used version of the text by contemporary Pranamis), replace many of the references to "Islam" with the term "*Nij Dham*," meaning "the true abode," that is, heaven. These and related issues are treated at greater length in my forthcoming book, *The Creation of Social Fabric in Early Modern India: Mahamat Prannath and Community Formation in the Mughal Empire.*

[14] The only scholar I am aware of who has examined the role of Nizari Ismailism in the Pranami tradition is Dominique-Sila Khan, whose "The Mahdi of Panna" contains an insightful discussion of specific Nizari beliefs that appear in Prannath's writings.

(based on evidence I present below) that Prannath was possibly exposed to, but did not explicitly preach Islamic ideas, instead focusing on Hindu scriptures and beliefs. Written in the weeks after Prannath's death in 1694, the *Bitak* tells the story of his life in a retrospective manner which assumes that he was from birth destined to progressively reveal an innate prophetic mission. As a consequence, Lal Das interprets events from the beginning of Prannath's life—indeed, even episodes from the life of Prannath's guru prior to his birth—using language suffused with Nizari Ismaili imagery. For example, those people who accepted the authority of Prannath's leadership from the earliest years are described by Lal Das as having "entered Islam," although Prannath began to write about Islam and the Quran only beginning in 1678. The chronology of Prannath's adaptation of Nizari ideas needs therefore to be kept in mind when reading the *Bitak*'s recollection of past events.

PRANNATH'S LIFE AND TEACHINGS: ORIGINS IN MUGHAL GUJARAT

The Pranami movement arose in Gujarat even as the Mughal Empire was establishing control over the province, and the emergence and subsequent growth of the community across north India needs to be understood in the context of an imperial state that was frequently involved in disputes among regional political and religious leaders.[15] The *Bitak* itself situates its story squarely in the context of the Mughal Empire, opening with a dynastic genealogy of India's rulers, traced back through the Puranic mythological sequence of four cosmic eras (*yugas*), and ending with a list of the Mughal rulers up to Aurangzeb, who is identified as the very embodiment of the final era of moral decline and chaos, Kaliyuga.[16] This genealogy is followed by the life story of Prannath's guru Devchandra (1581–1655) who is considered the founder of the Pranami *sampradaya*, although it is Prannath's personality, ideas, and poetic compositions which have been the central focus for devotees of the Pranami sect. Devchandra was born into a Kayasth business family in the town of Umarkot,

[15] For imperial interactions with local groups in Gujarat, see Hasan, *State and Locality*. Regarding religious disputes, see footnote 36 below.

[16] Lal Das, *Bitak*, Section 1, vss 1–28.

Sind, and the *Bitak* recounts that his religious vocation began when at the age of eleven he left his home and journeyed to Kuchh, Gujarat, where he immersed himself in the teachings of the Radha Vallabha order.[17] A branch of the Vaishnavite devotional community founded by Vallabhacharya and spread by his sons in the sixteenth century, this order gives a prominent role to worship of the goddess Radha alongside Krishna.[18] When Devchandra subsequently assumed the mantle of religious leadership himself, he gave primary emphasis to the worship of Krishna and the teachings of a touchstone text of the bhakti movement, the *Bhagavata Purana*, although he was also well-versed in other traditional Hindu scriptures including other Puranas and the Vedas.

Mahamat Prannath was born in 1618 as Meheraj Thakur in Jamnagar (referred to as "Navatanpuri" in Pranami sources), a city that had recently become the new center of political power and trade in northern Gujarat.[19] His mother was Dhanbai and his father, Keshav Thakur, was of the Lohana Kshatriya caste and served as the chief minister of Jamnagar state.[20] Prannath was introduced by his older brother Govardhan to Guru Devchandra in 1630 and became a lay devotee. Upon reaching adulthood, he served in the Jamnagar state ministry. In 1646 Prannath was ordered by Devchandra to sail to the "Arab" lands—trading ports in the Persian Gulf—to assist with the business operations of several of Devchandra's devotees there.[21] As part of his duties he spent

[17] Lal Das, *Bitak*, Sections 3, passim.

[18] For a history of Vallabhacharya's movement, see Shandip Saha, "The Movement of *Bhakti* along a North–West Axis: Tracing the History of the Pustimarg between the Sixteenth and Nineteenth Centuries," *International Journal of Hindu Studies* 11, no. 3 (December 2007): 299–318. For the worship and mythology of Radha, see the essays collected in John Stratton Hawley and Donna Marie Wulff, eds., *The Divine Consort: Radha and the Goddesses of India* (Boston: Beacon Press, 1986).

[19] See Harald Tambs-Lyche, *Power, Profit and Poetry: Traditional Society in Kathiawar, Western India* (New Delhi: Manohar, 1997), 69ff.

[20] See Shiv Mangal Ram, *Svami Laladas Krit Mahamati Prananath Bitak ka Madhyakalin Bharatiya Itihas ko Yogadan* (New Delhi: Hindi Book Centre, 1996), 59.

[21] Lal Das, *Bitak*, Section 13, vss 1–7.

time visiting Devchandra's followers in Thatta, Basra, Muscat, Bandar Abbas, and Kung (Bandar Kong), remaining in the Persian Gulf region for approximately four years before returning to Gujarat. Additionally, the mercantile pursuits of these devotees meant that they themselves were continually traveling and were able to meet with their guru in various locales.

Devchandra died in 1655, and the *Bitak* notes that at this point in time Prannath accepted Devchandra's biological son, Biharidas, as the legitimate chief devotee and heir of Devchandra, considering himself Biharidas's subordinate. Rivalry was soon to arise, however, between Prannath and Biharidas, as in the view of the *Bitak,* the latter was concerned that Prannath's growing popularity and spiritual accomplishment presented a challenge to his authority.[22] As this conflict played itself out over the next several years, Prannath and Biharidas vied for advantage by appeals to devotees, and became embroiled in intrigue at the various regional courts of Gujarat. The *Bitak* portrays these events through frequent mention of acts of injustice and oppression committed against Prannath and his followers by state officials. In 1657, slander against Prannath reached the ears of the minister (*wazir*) of Jamnagar state, resulting in Prannath's imprisonment in Jamnagar for a year. It is possible, although impossible to document with the currently available evidence, that Prannath was first exposed to Nizari Ismaili ideas when he was imprisoned, possibly alongside Ismaili preachers. It is known that in 1655 the head Nizari missionary, or *da'i*, Ismail Badr al-Din Mulla Raj, had relocated the group's headquarters to Jamnagar from Ahmedabad, and during the entire decade and beyond, Ismaili leaders were regularly imprisoned by Mughal rulers including Aurangzeb.[23]

In any case, it was during these months in jail that Prannath first composed original devotional poetry, namely the works *Ras*, *Prakash*, and *Shatruti*.[24] These poems are in the Vaishnavite tradition, preaching

22 Lal Das, *Bitak*, Sections 27–28, passim.

23 Farhad Daftary, *The Ismai'ilis: Their History and Doctrines* (Cambridge: Cambridge University Press, 1990), 307; Ashgar Ali Engineer, *The Bohras* (New Delhi: Vikas Publishing House, 1980), 123–29.

24 Prannath, *Shri Tartam Sagar (Kulzam Swarup)* (Jamnagar: Shri 5 Navatanpur Dham, 1998), I. This edition contains a translation of the Gujarati original into modern Hindi.

a Krishna-centered bhakti and exhorting devotees to commit themselves more fully to devotional works, with emphasis upon the popular *viraha* theme, describing the longing of the devotee for a remote or absent deity. The illusory nature of earthly life (*maya*) is contrasted with the beatific states awaiting the ardent devotee upon reunion with the Beloved, and the poetry sings the praises of the Braj-Mathura region as the holy land to which Krishna descended as a divine avatar. The importance of the "true spiritual guide" (*satguru*), here in the person of Devchandra, an important theme in sant writings generally, is also stressed. The words of *Prakash* indicate that Prannath had cotton spinners and weavers among his listeners, with several sections of the text exhorting such people to work with diligence and to produce more and higher quality material.[25] *Prakash* emphasizes devotion to Krishna and Devchandra, and invokes the *Bhagavata Purana*. In terms of scriptural references, these works cite the importance of a proper understanding of the *Bhagavata Purana*, as well as the Vedas. Prannath closes the individual sections of his verse with the signature line, or *bhanita*, of "Indravati," the religious nomenclature used for his early compositions.[26] By authoring these works, Prannath was henceforth able to project a degree of creativity and authority that laid the basis for his own position as an autonomous spiritual leader.

Upon release from confinement, Prannath proceeded from city to city in Gujarat, preaching and acquiring followers in Junagadh and Ahmadabad. He also married a Rajput woman named Tejbai Kunwar, who accompanied him throughout his future perambulations. In 1663, at the behest of Biharidas, Prannath assumed a ministerial post in the kingdom of Jamnagar, although after two years he gave up that position to settle in the Portuguese capital of Diu.[27] Here, in 1665, Prannath stayed with a devotee named Jayaram, who was to subsequently author, under the religious name Karunasakhi, a hagiography of Devchandra in which Prannath is mentioned several times. Significantly, the work portrays Devchandra and Prannath as devotees of Krishna, with no mention

[25] Prannath, *Prakash*, in *Shri Tartam Sagar*, I, Sections 25–27, passim (Hindi translation).

[26] For a discussion of *bhanita* in devotionalist poetry, see Charlotte Vaudeville, *A Weaver Named Kabir: Selected Verses With a Detailed Biographical and Historical Introduction* (Oxford: Oxford University Press, 1993), 124–25.

[27] Lal Das, *Bitak*, Sections 16, vss 18–19.

of Islam or the Quran.[28] In Diu Prannath's enemies again floated rumors claiming that he had "slandered the foreigners' god," and fearful of the "very cruel foreigners," he and his followers were compelled to leave the city in 1667, moving on to further travels in Gujarat and the Persian Gulf ports.[29] In 1669 he traveled to the major commercial center of Thatta, Sind, and gave religious discourses to large crowds, debating with sadhus as well as with a follower of Kabir, before departing the city. Prannath later returned for a more extended stay in Thatta, where one Lakshman Das, the future Lal Das, Prannath's hagiographer, heard his religious discourses on various topics, including the story of Krishna at Braj and the meaning of the *Bhagavad Gita* and the *Bhagavata Purana*. Lal Das had previously been a wealthy merchant but had suffered the loss of all of his ships in a sea storm, and after listening to Prannath, he became a committed devotee. Numerous others who heard his sermons also became followers, including several erstwhile members of the Vallabha *sampradaya*, although other Vallabhites, hearing of Prannath's popular discourses, came in order to argue with him. Here, as at many other places in the *Bitak*, the names of new initiates in the sect, both male and female, are provided.[30]

On a trip to Muscat, Prannath stayed at the store of one Mahavji, where many devotees congregated to share information about each other's lives and circumstances, to eat commensally, and to hear his religious discourses.[31] In Muscat a number of men and women, including a rich businessman (*lakhpat*) and a business agent (*kamdar*), "recognized" Prannath's divinity. At the same time, a wealthy trader in Bandar Abbas by the name of Bhairon Seth heard of Prannath's activities and requested that he come there. After Prannath's arrival, Bhairon Seth brought two men

[28] Karunasakhi, *Shri Tartam Sagar Bitak* (Jamnagar: Shri Khijada Mandir Trust, 1982). The exact date of Karunasakhi's composition is not known, but it was obviously after his initial meeting with Prannath in 1665. The content of this text seems to indicate that Prannath was not explicitly preaching about Islam prior to this date.

[29] Lal Das, *Bitak*, Section 20, vss 5–11.

[30] Lal Das, *Bitak*, Section 23, vs. 1–31. For a complete list of the names of Prannath's devotees given in the *Bitak*, see Ram, *Svami Laladas Krit Mahamati Prananath Bitak*, 154–56, 179–86.

[31] Lal Das, *Bitak*, Section 24, vs. 1–50.

from Multan who were disciples (*chelas*) of Guru Nanak and carried with them a book of Kabir's verses, whose meaning Prannath then revealed, which inspired the two to become his devotees.[32] Bhairon Seth also took initiation under Prannath, and was told to give up meat, fish, liquor, and smoking. The *Bitak* next recounts how some Indian women in the port attended Prannath's discourses, but did so without taking the permission of their husbands. When the men tried to stop their wives from going, the women justified their actions by arguing that because Prannath was the first person to give this kind of religious discourse in the Arab port, their husbands should accept him as a blessing. A leading woman of the city also argued with the men, ultimately convincing them to allow their wives to attend the discourses. After remaining a few months in Bandar Abbas, Prannath indicated his desire to return to Gujarat, and his devotees provided him with clothing, ornaments, and money upon his departure.

Hearing of his return in 1671, devotees from various Indian cities gathered to meet with Prannath in Surat, where he spent seventeen months. More encounters with Vallabhites took place, with some continuing to oppose the new preacher, complaining that some of their members continued to attend Prannath's lectures. He acquired here a devotee named Mukand Das, learned in the Sanskrit sciences, who became his life-long companion.[33] Also during this time in Surat, Prannath completed *Kalash*, a Gujarati work that he himself later had translated into Hindustani, in which he proclaims that the world had become ensnared in numerous different paths and religions, and that he possessed the true liberating knowledge which would unite all people.[34]

Matters with Biharidas came to a head in 1673, in a dispute over the legitimate spiritual succession to Devchandra. At issue in the conflict at this point, according to the *Bitak*, was Prannath's insistence that both widows and lower castes (*nich jat*) be allowed to take initiation into the order, against Biharidas's strident objections.[35] Prannath had by this time successfully acquired a large and loyal following, and many or most of the Pranamis supported him in his claim to be the true heir to

[32] Lal Das, *Bitak*, Section 25, vs. 17–18.

[33] See Prasad, *Mahamati Prannath*, 64–66.

[34] Prannath, *Kalash Hindustani*, I (Hindi translation).

[35] Lal Das, *Bitak*, Section 29, vs. 50.

Devchandra. The two religious leaders decided to go their separate ways, and Prannath gathered behind him many devotees in Surat and left Gujarat altogether. Although he was never to return there, he retained devotees in that province as well as in the Persian Gulf; these committed devotees subsequently often traveled to meet him in north India.

DELHI AND EMPEROR AURANGZEB

Following the break with Biharidas, Prannath, along with Lal Das and other devotees, journeyed through Rajasthan to the Mughal capital of Delhi to gain an audience with the emperor and along the way continued to spread his doctrine and acquire new devotees. In these travels, numerous Pranamis who had already established ties with Prannath by traveling to Gujarat, were able to provide the group with support and accommodation. At this point in the *Bitak*'s narrative, Prannath's efforts to reach the emperor emerge as a central theme of the hagiography, with a large number of verses devoted to describing the details of this undertaking. This endeavor is given such primacy, I believe, because it represents an attempt to gain imperial recognition for Prannath's authority which had been disputed by Biharidas. It was in fact a common practice of Mughal rulers to affirm the legitimacy of particular religious leaders, and they often intervened in sectarian disputes to determine the outcome of succession struggles, in Gujarat, Rajasthan, and elsewhere, with religious leaders actively seeking out Mughal emperors to this end.[36]

In Lal Das's depiction, early in their quest during a stay in 1674 in the town of Merta, Rajasthan, one day, Prannath heard a mullah announcing

[36] See Norbert Peabody, *Hindu Kingship and Polity in Precolonial India* (Cambridge: Cambridge University Press, 2003), 70; Engineer, *The Bohras*, 117, 122, 125; Farhad Daftary, *The Ismai'ilis*, 304–07. Phyllis Granoff argues that in the struggles between Jain groups for securing patronage from political authorities, the production of hagiographies was "one tool of sectarian competition." "Svetambara Jains in Northwest India," in Callewaert and Snell, *According to Tradition*, 145. Cf. Derryl L. MacLean, "Real Men and False Men at the Court of Akbar: The Majalis of Shaykh Mustafa Gujarati," in Gilmartin and Lawrence, *Beyond Turk and Hindu*, who argues that the leader of the millenarian Mahdawi order in Gujarat aimed to convince Akbar that his community was politically quiescent and hence not a threat to the Mughal state.

the Arabic call to prayer from the local mosque, causing him to reflect and then identify the God of Islam with that of Hindu tradition:

> The *kalama* came from above: *La illah illallah, Muhammad Rasul Allah.*
> This is the message of Allah.
> "La" means "no" in this saying, "illah" is God (*haq*), the imperishable Supreme Being (*akshar achharatit*). This is the word of the Great One.[37]

The *Bitak* mentions that prior to this time, Prannath had not given discourses on the Quran, and Lal Das now asks that he explain the scripture's meaning. Noting that "Shri Muhammad" had brought the Quran for all people, Prannath provides an explanation, and tells Lal Das that the "Sultan," that is, Aurangzeb, must now be given an invitation to join the true faith (*iman*).[38] A condensed description of Prannath's prophetic mission follows, and then Prannath and his followers set off for Delhi, stopping en route to meet other devotees in Agra and the Braj-Mathura region.

Upon their arrival in Delhi, the group met with other Pranami merchants resident in the Urdu Bazaar area as well as those arriving from Surat, Thatta, and elsewhere. Staying together in the house (*haveli*) of a devotee, they composed a letter containing twenty-two questions concerning the Quran to give to Aurangzeb. One devotee, Ashajit, read the letter and then called into question the entire undertaking, claiming that Aurangzeb "will always be an enemy of Hindus, and [under him] the Sharia is powerful."[39] Despite such doubts, Prannath and his other followers carried on with their efforts to get the message to the emperor. Prannath also continued to deliver sermons, including talks based on the Vedas and Vedanta as well as the Quran, winning over a number of new followers, including one pair of brothers who came to listen on the sly, as they feared an adverse reaction from their elders. An unnamed Sufi who dropped in was filled with envy upon hearing Prannath's "sweet" sermon.[40]

[37] Lal Das, *Bitak*, Section 31, vs. 70–71.

[38] This represents, I would argue, one instance of Lal Das retrospectively viewing an event in Prannath's life through the later acquisition of Nizari ideas. Lal Das, *Bitak*, Section 32, vs. 5.

[39] Lal Das, *Bitak*, Section 32, vs. 39.

[40] Lal Das, *Bitak*, Section 32, vs. 35.

The *Bitak* then describes how Prannath left Delhi to attend the Kumbh Mela in Haridwar, and there is a lengthy description of his debates with numerous sectarian leaders and pandits, with the text including excerpts from various Vedic and Puranic scriptures in Sanskrit. According to Matabadal Jayaswal, however, this section was added to the *Bitak* by someone other than Lal Das, even though Prannath might possibly have traveled to the festival in Haridwar.[41] In any case, Prannath was soon back in Delhi, pursuing his mission to reveal to Aurangzeb the emperor's "true identity" (*asal jat*). Advised that the emperor would not read a Hindi letter, the Pranamis hired a mullah to translate the document into Persian. Around this time, in a dramatic development for his religious views, Prannath acquired a copy of the *Tafsir-i Hussaini*, a highly popular Persian language commentary on the Quran with pronounced Sufi and Shia interpretive strategies.[42] When the mullah translated the book (presumably into Hindustani), Prannath saw his own destiny foretold, interpreting certain Quranic verses as prophesying the sequential incarnations of the divine in the Prophet Muhammad, Lord Krishna, Devchandra, and finally, Prannath himself as Imam Mahdi, the messiah. This revelation brought about a transformative shock, and thereafter Prannath was unable to rise from bed for several days. The *Tafsir-i Hussaini* describes the impending arrival of judgment day (*kayamat*), and many of the ideas and terminology presented in the text appear in Prannath's later works, including the appearance of the Imam with his mystical knowledge (*marifat*), mastery of esoteric exegesis (*batin*) of scripture, and grasp of the ultimate truth (*haq*), the community of true believers (*momins*) and their unbelieving enemies (*kafirs*), stories of the prophets of the Quran, and so on. The *Bitak* itself incorporates these ideas and this terminology.

Subsequent to this change, much of the rest of Prannath's life and work reveals the influence of messianic Shia ideas of the Nizari Ismaili tradition, a set of beliefs which thrived in medieval India, and

[41] Jayaswal, introduction to *Bitak*, 35–36. Jayaswal argues that the interpolated material was added to delineate the Pranami movement as a sect, something that Lal Das and Prannath eschewed.

[42] See Kristin Zahra Sands, "On the Popularity of Husayn Va'iz-i Kashifi's Mavahib-i 'Aliyya: A Persian Commentary on the Quran," *Iranian Studies* 36, no. 4 (December 2003): 469–83.

was particularly strong in Gujarat, Rajasthan, and Sind.[43] The *Bitak* makes one explicit reference to the fact that through the discourses of Prannath, listeners received "the scent of Ismaili."[44] Themes central to Prannath's messianic poetry, including the appearance of Imam Mahdi and the Dajjal, the false messiah in the end-time, the mingling of Vaishnavite and Sufi imagery, and the concern with Judgment Day, are shared with the Nizari Ismaili *ginan* tradition.[45] The temples of the Pranami *sampradaya* in Panna and Ahmedabad are to this day crowned with a *panja*, the open-hand symbol of Shi'ism. Prannath and Lal Das's works adopted the Sufi and Ismaili tendency to treat discourses and texts as consisting of multiple layers of meaning. This is apparent, for example, in Prannath's introduction into his verses of an original self-appellation, "Mahamat," replacing his earlier use of Indravati. In one reading, "Mahamat" can be taken to mean the "supreme religion," combining the prefix "*maha*," meaning great or supreme, with "*mat*," which connotes a religious sect, doctrine, or system of belief. As Prannath's teaching developed so as to incorporate different religious traditions and various scriptures, this name conveyed a religion that would encompass and transcend all major sects and faiths of India.[46] In a second sense, "Mahamat" can be understood as evoking the name Muhammad, the prophet of Islam. This interpretation would resonate with a popular Hadith which circulated in early-modern India, which proclaimed that "The Messenger of God said: 'The earth will be filled with injustice and

[43] See Dominique-Sila Khan, *Conversions and Shifting Identities: Ramdev Pir and the Ismailis in Rajasthan* (New Delhi: Manohar, 1997); Cf. Tazim R. Kassam, *Songs of Wisdom and Circles of Dance: Hymns of the Satpanth Ismaili Muslim Saint, Pir Shams* (Albany: State University of New York Press, 1995).

[44] Lal Das, *Bitak*, Section 15, vs. 9.

[45] Men claiming to be the Mahdi had periodically appeared in Sultanate and Mughal India, with Gujarat being a particularly important center for communities devoted to Mahdi leaders. Saiyid Athar Abbas Rizvi, *Muslim Revivalist Movements in Northern India in the Sixteenth and Seventeenth Centuries* (Agra: Agra University Press, 1965), chs. 2–3.

[46] The term is also similar to the names of two Rajasthani religious groups directly influenced by Nizari Ismailism, namely the Mahadharma and Maha Panth traditions. Khan, *Conversions*, 67.

crime. When it is filled with injustice and crime, God will send a man from me whose name will be my name.'"[47]

In 1678 Prannath traveled to Anup Shahr, a town on the River Ganga, located east of Delhi. Here he had his Gujarati texts *Prakash* and *Kalash* translated into Hindustani, an indication that here too, as in Surat where the texts were originally composed, Prannath was reaching out to a diverse population of spinners and weavers.[48] At this time he also composed his remarkable work *Sanandh*, revealing the transformation that had occurred in his religious thought. The book, which is addressed to "India's Muslims" (*Hind ke Musalman*), begins with some Arabic passages accompanied by Hindustani translations, and has Prannath declare, "Whoever is a true Muslim, I love you very much."[49] He proceeds to contrast his vision of the "true Muslim" and proper Islam with the practices of imperial officials including "Quran-reading *qazis*," intermingling this view with criticism of orthodox Hindu Brahmins as well. On one level, these compositions thematically overlap with the poems of his earlier writings in focusing on the anguished separation of the devotee from the Beloved. However, the language, imagery, and some of the themes have changed, with Arabic and Persian vocabulary, largely absent from his earlier writings, appearing throughout these poems. The Sufi concept for the devotional love of God, *ishq*, is employed in a manner that mirrors the *viraha* motif of Prannath's earlier writings. Devchandra, the *satguru*, is referred to as "Ruh Allah," the "Spirit of Allah," indicating that Prannath now viewed his guru as embodying a mystical Islamic presence. Prannath also introduces into his work the Sufi concepts of *fana* and *baqa*, representing the elimination of the ego in order to dwell in the presence of God, as well as Sufi and Shia cosmological notions based on the belief in four hierarchical levels of existence.

[47] Cited in Rizvi, *Muslim Revivalist Movements*, 69–70. There is a biting historical irony to be noted in that Mahatma Gandhi, whose mother, a Pranami devotee who took her son to a temple of the sect in Porbandar, Gujarat, was called "Muhammad Gandhi" by his Hindu nationalist antagonists as a term of disparagement. Gandhi's mother's Pranami background has often been noted, but has been the subject of little scholarly research.

[48] Prannath, *Shri Tartam Sagar*, II.

[49] Prannath, *Sanandh*, ed. Vimla Mehta and Ranjit Saha (New Delhi: Shri Prannath Mission, 1988), Section 2, vs. 3.

Sanandh retains references to the Vedas and Puranas, but is focused more upon verses from the Quran, aiming to reveal that "Hindus and Muslims are made of a single essence."[50] In contrast to "true Muslims," the tyranny of arrogant state officials acting in the name of Islam (as well as intolerant orthodox Hindus) are denounced in the *Sanandh*:

> The mullahs inform themselves by reading, from this they become conceited
> They tell ordinary people just this, "We read the Quran."
> ...
> They beat, terrify, and throw people down, causing them to weep and wail in grief
> In this way, they change people's identity (*jatan*), [yet] they say, "We are virtuous."
> ...
> They oppress the poor, and no one's allowed to complain
> They circumcise people and feed them meat, [yet] they say, "We are virtuous."
> ...
> They tyrannize on their riding elephants, they go and cause destruction
> They rejoice in playing music, they say, "We are virtuous."
> They make unbelievers into Muslims, these they count as having taken the religion
> They shave their heads and keep a beard; they say, "We are virtuous."
> ...
> They select [a temple] to overthrow, an ancient Hindu one
> They demolish it with force, [yet] they say, "We are virtuous."
> Hindus then demolish mosques, challenging the Muslims
> Thereby showing the splendor of their deity, and they say, "We are virtuous."
> ...
> Whosoever causes anyone sorrow and grief, is not a Muslim
> The Prophet of the Muslims, took the name of compassion.
> None of them understand Islam, nor follow the way of the Prophet
> They understand neither virtue nor devotion, [yet] they say, "We are Muslims."
> ...

[50] Prannath, *Sanandh*, Section 3, vs. 3.

So many tyrants commit acts of oppression, [they] shut their eyes in conceit
They're not afraid of shedding blood, [yet] they say, "We are Muslims."
...
They don't see others' grief, their hearts completely like stone
They aren't ashamed to cause others grief, [yet] they say, "We are Muslims."
Brahmins say "We're the greatest," Muslims say, "We are pure"
[But] both will end as just a handful, one of ash, the other dust.[51]

After returning to Delhi from Anup Shahr, Prannath resumed his attempt to make contact with the emperor, working with twelve of his devotees, namely, Lal Das, Shaikh Badal, Mulla Kayam, Bhim Das, Nagji, Somji, Khimai, Dayaram, Chintamani, Chanchal, Gangaram, and Banarsi. The group composed letters concerning the matter and carried them to the houses of various high-ranking Mughal officials. In trying to rally the sometimes flagging support of his followers, Prannath at one point proclaims, "If you fight with the agents of Aurangzeb, the agents of the Sharia, their folly won't be standing tomorrow."[52] But when Prannath asked Lal Das and Govardhan to seek out a mullah's assistance in contacting the emperor, Govardhan responded by expressing his fear of Muslims, as it was currently "the hour of Aurangzeb," a comment which angered Lal Das and caused an argument between the two.[53]

In the *Bitak*'s representation of their efforts to organize opposition to imperial policy, a number of Prannath's disciples are said to have walked to the Jama Masjid where Aurangzeb went for his Friday prayers, and sung out loud verses from Prannath's *Sanandh*. His followers also affixed a note on a door near the mosque which was picked up by a Mughal officer and delivered to Aurangzeb.[54] The devotees returned to sing again at the Jama Masjid, and finally succeeded in getting the

[51] Prannath, *Sanandh*, Section 40, vss 4, 11, 13, 15–16, 18–19, 24–25, 35, 41–42.

[52] Prannath, *Sanandh*, Section 36, vs. 14.

[53] Lal Das, *Bitak*, Section 37, vs. 6.

[54] The representation of twelve followers carrying forth Prannath's message in Delhi, and the attachment of a document to a door near the main mosque, seem to echo the Biblical story of Christ's twelve apostles, and Martin Luther's posting of his ninety-five theses on the Castle Church door in Wittenburg, respectively. Here Lal Das appears to be employing Christian and Protestant imagery to further promote the universalism of Prannath's religion.

emperor's attention. There they read out some verses to Aurangzeb, who then asked them questions about their claims, but in the end the emperor rebuffed the Pranamis' attempts, and refused to meet with Prannath in person. The Pranamis lament the emperor's refusal to engage in dialogue, comparing the situation to that of the unwillingness of Brahmins to allow Shudras to hear the Vedic Gayatri mantra. They also take the opportunity to reproach him for failing to communicate the message of the Quran to Hindus, and for not listening to what Hindus have to say to him.[55] This grievance, I believe, can be interpreted as a general indictment of the imperial state for its failure at the time to redress subjects' grievances, so that "no one is allowed to complain," in the words of the *Sanandh* verse cited above.

The circumstances of this remonstrance can be identified with some precision, since the period during which Prannath and his companions were in Delhi was a time of documented sociopolitical upheaval in the city. Non-Pranami sources have recorded that in 1679 the capital was riven by protests against Aurangzeb's imposition of the *jizya*, a discriminatory poll tax on non-Muslims; such sources include the Mughal historian Khafi Khan's well-known narration in *Muntakhab al-Lubab*, a chronicle of Aurangzeb's rule. The emperor is in that text reported to have imposed the *jizya* in order to "suppress the infidels, and make clear the distinction between a land of unbelief and the submission to Islam." When the news spread of this order to collect the *jizya*, according to Khafi Khan:

> [A]ll the Hindus of the capital [Delhi] and many of them from the surrounding territories gathered in lakhs [i.e., hundreds of thousands] on the bank of the river below the Jharukah and made a request for its withdrawal, weeping and crying. The Emperor did not pay any heed to their appeals. When the Emperor came out for the Jum'ah prayers, the Hindus crowded in from the gate of the fort to the Jami Masjid in such large number for imploring redress that the passage of the people was blocked. The moneylenders, cloth-merchants and shopkeepers of the camp Urdu Bazar (Army Market) and all the artisans of the city abandoned their work and assembled on the route of the Emperor. In spite of strict orders for arrangements owing to which the hands and feet of many were broken, the Emperor who was riding on an elephant could not

55 Lal Das, *Bitak*, Section 46, vss 6–7.

> reach the mosque. Every moment the number of those unlucky people increased. Then he ordered that the majestic elephants should proceed against them. For some days more, they assembled in the same way and requested remission (of the Jiziyah). At last they submitted to pay the Jiziyah.[56]

Because, according to the *Bitak*, in 1679 Prannath stayed in the Urdu Bazaar, organizing followers, which included merchants and shopkeepers, in opposition to Aurangzeb and the *jizya*, it would appear that Prannath was at the center of the events described by Khafi Khan above. The fact that his protest was conceived in the name of Islam is certainly a remarkable thing. After narrating the tumultuous events in Delhi, the *Bitak* cites verse 97 from the Quran, *Surah al-Qadr*, which contains a description of the "night of power," which Ismailis, like other Muslims, commemorate as the time when the Quran was first revealed to Muhammad. The verse proclaims this night to be "better than 1,000 months," and is discussed at length in *Tafsir-i Hussaini*. Lal Das presents an esoteric interpretation of the material, proclaiming that after Muhammad, the divine became incarnate in Braj (that is, as Krishna), and that 989 years and three months after the first revelation of the Prophet Muhammad, Ruh Allah (Prannath's nomenclature for Devchandra) was to come to fight the Dajjal, the false messiah, a time which, calculated according to the Islamic Hijri calendar, works out to the year of Devchandra's birth, 1581 CE.[57] Thus, in the chronology of the *Bitak*, the advent of Devchandra's spiritual quest at age eleven coincides with the turn of the millennium of the Islamic Hijri calendar, a time which many saw as portending the appearance of the Islamic messiah. The *Bitak* further notes that the battle with the Dajjal would commence exactly 1,000 months after Devchandra's birth (that is, in 1659), implicitly denoting the year of Aurangzeb's coronation, and the struggle which Prannath was to carry forward as the final Imam Mahdi.

[56] Muhammad Hashim Khafi Khan, *Muntakhab al-Lubab*, trans. S. Moinul Haq (Karachi: Pakistan Historical Society, 1975).

[57] Lal Das, *Bitak*, Section 43, vss 13–14. This reference to the Islamic millennium is mentioned numerous times in the *Bitak* and in Prannath's writings.

TRAVELS AND ENCOUNTERS IN RAJASTHAN

Unsuccessful in convincing the emperor about their cause, Prannath and his companions now embarked upon a journey to Rajasthan, searching for a supportive ruler who would become a patron and adherent of the community by recognizing the truth of Prannath's message.[58] Groups of Pranamis converged with Prannath and made efforts to win over local rulers and officials in towns including Amer, Sanganer, Udaipur, Ujjain, Illichpur, Burhanpur, and elsewhere. Among the descriptions of encounters with Rajput rulers, this section of the *Bitak* includes a fascinating and extended account of developments in Udaipur at the time when Aurangzeb carried out his well-known military campaign against Rana Bhao Singh in 1679. Historians have depicted Aurangzeb's demands for submission from the Rana, including the establishment of Islamic courts, converting temples into mosques, and payment of the *jizya*.[59] In the *Bitak*, Aurangzeb is portrayed as saying that the Rana could avoid an attack and would instead be granted five districts (*parganas*) of territory, but only if he accepted the emperor's religion (*din*) and became a Muslim. In the meantime, plots are hatched by the ruler's jealous courtiers, and we read accounts of intrigue and slander, with some telling the Rana that Prannath was a robber in disguise, while others falsely claim that he was actually a Muslim sent by Aurangzeb to make the Rana a Muslim. As it happened, the Rana was unwilling to face the imperial army and instead chose to take flight to the Aravalli hills, issuing orders for the city's residents to do the same. As the population fled, a large number of people joined with the Pranamis while they struggled to make their way to safety. The imperial troops attacked Udaipur and destroyed numerous temples, but due to pressing campaigns in the Deccan, the army ended its siege, allowing Bhao Singh to retain the throne. He was then brought back into imperial service, and was given the post of governor of Aurangabad. Prannath and his followers traveled there in 1680 to continue to appeal to Bhao Singh, although there they were immediately opposed by court Brahmins.

[58] Lal Das, *Bitak*, Section 47, vss 1–100.

[59] Sri Ram Sharma, *Maharana Raj Singh and His Times* (Delhi: Motilal Banarasidass, 1971).

Between 1679 and 1683 Prannath and his companions made repeated efforts to engage with Muslims, orthodox and otherwise, concerning the proper interpretation of Islam and the Quran, often in towns with significant Ismaili populations, including Udaipur, Ujjain, and Burhanpur. The *Bitak* depicts scenes in Udaipur of Pathans, including soldiers and a businessman, coming to hear Prannath's sermons. Several among them initially accepted Prannath's views as correct, while others vehemently opposed his views on Islam. Three Pathans in particular, Mihin Khan, Jahan Muhammad, and Awwal Khan, took an interest in Prannath, coming regularly to hear his sermons, including the *Sanandh*. Mihin Khan accepted Prannath's claims, but the other two Pathans, upon hearing his views about God's incarnation as Krishna, were dismayed and became argumentative. The Pathans' attitude toward Prannath is ultimately depicted in an ambiguous manner. In another episode, occurring in 1680, several Pranamis led by Lal Das traveled to Burhanpur aiming to discuss Prannath's writings on Islam with "Sharia Muslims," including a Muslim judge (*qazi*). Several days of contentious debate ensued, with the judge pronouncing Prannath's claims as false and a distortion of Islam. In response Lal Das angrily declared that such "Shariat people" only hurl slander, and would never accept the true faith.[60]

Prannath's next stop was in the town of Ramnagar, where one Surat Singh heard his discourse, and then brought Devkaran, the minister (*diwan*) and cousin of Maharaja Chhatrasal Bundela, to meet him. Devkaran became Prannath's disciple, and for two years (1682–83), Prannath based himself in Ramnagar, fending off representatives of the local king who, we are told, had been ordered by the Mughals to arrest Prannath. During his stay in Ramnagar, Prannath composed his works *Khulasa* and *Khilawat*. The *Khilawat* emphasizes the need to achieve unity among the true believers, and stresses that Prannath possesses the secret, mystical knowledge of the Quran. The text laments the fact that people have become divided by religion, dress, language, and community, and proffers the recognition of Prannath's message as the key to escaping the illusions of the numerous worlds of existence in order to cross over to the eternal abode. The *Khulasa* continues with the themes discussed in *Khilawat*, deploring divisions between social groups and

[60] Lal Das, *Bitak*, Section 53, vs. 40.

noting, "Everyone lays claim to heaven, whether Hindu or Muslim. These two read the Vedas and the Quran [respectively], but neither can say they recognize [the real heaven]."[61] Quranic tales of the prophets are brought together with descriptions of Krishna's divine play (*lila*) to tell a single story in which the God of Hindus and Muslims brings his message of one truth to them in different forms. But Hindus had since become embroiled in their rituals, and Muslims caught up with the shariah, so that the appearance of Devchandra and Prannath was needed to reveal the essence of love veiled by external rituals.[62] Muslims are told to leave behind the path of shariah, and instead follow the mystical path (*tariqat*) so that they can reach a higher heaven, *malkut*, and ultimately the highest heaven, *lahut*. But it is only the guidance of the true religious guide, the *hadi*—Prannath—that will enable people's souls to cross over to the eternal abode. Prannath notes that while countless *qazi*s have read the Quran, they have failed to understand its inner meaning, while in contrast, although he knows neither the Persian nor Arabic languages, in fact had not even read the Quran earlier, due to God's miracle he is able to open up its secrets.[63] Prannath also observes that his views were being met with opposition from established religious leaders:

> Hindus fight with me, and so do Sharia Muslims
> But I have obtained the Truth of the beloved Ahmad, and I won't forgo the Quran.[64]
> [The Prophet] awakened everyone and showed them the promised land, whether Hindu or Muslim.[65]

In 1683 Devkaran arranged a meeting between Prannath and Maharaja Chhatrasal in the jungle near Mau, Bundelkhand, where the king was awestruck and became Prannath's disciple.[66] This date

[61] Prannath, *Khulasa*, ed. Vimla Mehta and Ranjit Saha (New Delhi: Shri Prannath Mission, 1989), Section 1, vs. 69.

[62] Prannath, *Khulasa*, Section 5, vs. 17, Section 13, vs. 65, Section 17, vs. 23.

[63] Prannath, *Khulasa*, Section 15, vss 2–5.

[64] Prannath, *Khulasa*, Section 1, vs. 100.

[65] Prannath, *Khulasa*, Section 2, vs. 32.

[66] Lal Das, *Bitak*, Section. 60, vs. 27. The meeting of the two is also described in Chhatrasal's court history, *Chattra Prakash*, by Lal Kavi, ed. Mahendra Pratap Singh (New Delhi: Shripatal Prakashan, 1973), 191.

corresponds to the year that Chhatrasal had gone into rebellion against the Mughals, and the *Bitak* notes that the king was at the time preparing to fight a campaign against the Mughal military commander Sher Afghan.[67] Prannath therefore tied a cloth around Chhatrasal's head and blessed him for battle, and the king's subsequent victory was credited to Prannath's intervention. Chhatrasal next invited Prannath to settle in Panna and a consecration ceremony for Chhatrasal was conducted. Prannath declared him to be the sovereign, overshadowing all other "sultans."[68]

Learning of Prannath's claim to esoteric mastery of the Quran, Chhatrasal asked what should be done with the Muslims in his kingdom, suggesting that he might bring them to obey Prannath's command. Questions also arise from those who wonder "why a Hindu is interpreting" Islamic scriptures in this manner. In order to address these matters "*qazi*s, mullahs and pandits" are brought to the capital to discuss matters with the *sant*.[69] Prannath proceeds to question a *qazi* brought in from the town of Mahoba, then displays his superior exegesis of the Quran, whereupon the diwan declares that the *qazi* has been defeated. The *qazi* then accepts Prannath as his preceptor, and upon the diwan's demand, takes an oath to this effect. Following this episode, a number of Hindu pandits are called in to hear Prannath's discussion of the *Bhagavata Purana*, after which they claim that Prannath's interpretation is based on a falsehood. At this, Chhatrasal becomes enraged with the pandits, and announces that henceforth no Bundela shall bow down to them as gurus, and if any person of the Bundela community (jati) dares allow them to tie a strip of cloth to his head, that person will be unable to rise to power. The *Bitak* proclaims that in this way the pandits were all defeated, and "Islam was victorious."[70] Chhatrasal also had Prannath seated on an elephant at the head of the army, and they rode out to a town in northern Bundelkhand where the king ordered "mullahs, *qazi*s, and Saiyids" to gather and hear Prannath's discourse on the Quran and Hadith. Chhatrasal then ordered the assembled group to write a public proclamation acknowledging Prannath's pre-eminent religious authority.

[67] J.N. Sarkar, *Shivaji and His Times* (Calcutta: S.C. Sarkar, 1920), 180.

[68] Lal Das, *Bitak*, Section 58, vs. 60.

[69] Lal Das, *Bitak*, Section 58, vss 85–86.

[70] Lal Das, *Bitak*, Section 58, vss 120–24.

The final sections of the *Bitak* describe the promised holy land that awaits true devotees, and discusses the devotional rites and practices of Prannath's disciples.

Prannath's final works, written in Bundelkhand, are the *Kayamatnama* ("Book of the Day of Judgment"), and *Marphat Sagar* ("The Ocean of Mystical Knowledge").[71] These books continue the appeal to Hindus and Muslims to transcend their separate identities in the name of a higher unity. To this end, the main focus of these works is on Prannath's esoteric interpretation of numerous verses from the Quran as well as collections of Hadith, wherein he deciphers signs of the imminent onset of the end-time. An apocalyptic struggle of good versus evil is linked to the new Islamic millennium, with Prannath citing prophecies of the appearance of the messiah in India who will fight the Dajjal. Although composed by Prannath, several sections of the *Kayamatnama* end with the signature line of "Chhatrasal," indicating the spiritual identification of the king with his guru.

BUNDELKHAND, ROYAL LEGITIMACY, AND THE MUGHALS

In order to understand the meanings which members of devotional sects derived from their leaders' teachings, then, we must carefully attend to the local contexts in which these beliefs were accepted and passed on. While a close examination of the ways in which Prannath's beliefs were received by and assimilated into numerous communities across north India is beyond the scope of this article, an analysis of the relatively well-documented acceptance of Pranami ideas at Chhatrasal's court in Bundelkhand will provide a perspective on how that polity incorporated his views.[72]

[71] The *Kayamatnama* consists of two distinct works, the *Bada Kayamatnama* and the *Chotta Kayamatnama*. Prannath, *Marfat Sagar, Kayamat Nama (Chhota aur Badha)* (New Delhi: Shri Prannath Mission, 1990). Raj Bal Sidana discusses a third, incomplete text written by Prannath in an apocalyptic strain which was not included in the *Kulzam Swarup*, in his *Shri Prannathji*, 145–50.

[72] See, for example, Chattrasal's epistles, Hindi letters no. 67 and 76, *Aitihasik Pramanavali aur Chhatrasal*, ed. Mahendra Pratap Singh (Delhi: National Publishing House, 1975). See also Lal Kavi, *Chhatra Prakash*, 148,

Seventeenth-century Bundelkhand, as with other regions across north India, was being drawn into the larger circuits of power and exchange in the Mughal world. As various groups jostled for power, recognition, and representation, Prannath's teachings and Chhatrasal's associated authority simultaneously drew upon and superseded traditional religious authorities and worldviews of both Hindu and Islamic provenance. This process is concisely encapsulated in the episode depicted in the closing sections of the *Bitak* discussed above. By asserting his mastery of Quranic and Puranic scripture, Prannath, and by extension, Chattrasal, were able to assert their authority over the Muslim and Hindu communities which composed Bundela society, while at the same time displacing the traditional community leaders—"*qazis*, mullahs, and pandits"—who were vested in more socially exclusivist interpretations of those same scriptures.

As noted by Dirk Kolff, Chhatrasal's rise to power occurred at a time when Bundela Rajput rulers frequently alternated between episodes of imperial service and of rebellion, with both Mughals and Bundelas taking advantage of temporary alliances with one another in order to further their respective political and military causes.[73] Bundela leaders, including Chhatrasal, who accepted *mansabdari* positions in imperial service, were able to parlay the power and status they thus acquired into a stronger position in their Bundela homelands. According to Kolff, in a process that began with Akbar (r. 1556–1605), Mughal imperial

---

180, 183–85, 191. The composition in Panna of Braj Bhushan's 1698 *Vritant Muktavali*, ed. Vimla Mehta (Bhivani: Shri Krishna Panami Janakalyan Ashram Trust, 1998) and Hansraj Bakshi's 1748 *Mihiraj Charitra*, ed. Devkrishna Sharma (Jamnagar: Shri Sansthabha, 1969) also attest to the establishment of the Pranami sect there. The longer-term expansion of Prannath's influence is apparent in the subsequent widespread appearance of Pranami temples. For a list of the locations of approximately 100 Pranami temples as of the late 1960s, including sites in Nepal, Bengal, Assam, Punjab, Gujarat, Rajasthan, Madhya Pradesh, and Delhi, see Raj Bala Sidana, *Shri Prannathji*, 363–69. Khan has estimated the number of Pranami adherents to be three million as of 2003. "The Mahdi of Panna," 63.

73 Dirk Kolff, *Naukar, Rajput, and Sepoy: The Ethnohistory of the Military Labour Market in Hindustan, 1450–1850* (Cambridge: Cambridge University Press, 1990). Cf. André Wink's discussion of "fitna," *Land and Sovereignty in India: Agrarian Society and Politics under the Eighteenth-Century Maratha Svarajya* (Cambridge: Cambridge University Press, 1986).

recognition and support allowed the Bundelas, as so-called spurious Rajputs, to acquire a level of legitimacy and power denied them by the traditional Rajput aristocracy of Rajasthan. By granting *mansabs* and by supporting particular Bundela rulers in clan disputes, Mughal rulers were able to obtain the cooperation of otherwise recalcitrant warriors and their followers. At the same time, Mughal interference in Bundela politics encouraged clan factionalism among the Bundelas, preventing as it did any single ruler from becoming too powerful in his own right and thus becoming a threat to imperial control.

Bundela Rajputs had consolidated their control over Bundelkhand in the early sixteenth century, and the major royal genealogies created to legitimize their rule were grounded in the beliefs of Vaishnava bhakti tradition, invoking the authority of the deities Rama and Krishna.[74] Kings were portrayed in these texts as the descendants of the god-king Rama, so that Bundela forms of royal legitimation were shared with other regional kingdoms of north India.[75] In addition to this Vaishnava connection, the Bundelas also partook of trans-regional imperial forms of authority.[76] The widespread prestige of Mughal political idioms meant that regional polities, which had direct and long-standing interactions with imperial forces, made many of these idioms their own. Thus, as with other regional participants in the imperial system, "Bundelkhand became a landscape strewn with an amalgam of kingly features and imperial honours" emanating from Delhi.[77] Moreover, the patronage provided by Mughal emperors to certain favored Bundela kings was recorded in the royal genealogies mentioned above. Finally, Mughal practice influenced regional elements including revenue collection procedures and architectural forms.[78] Alongside this cultural-political

[74] Godard Schokker, "The Legitimation of Kingship in India: Bundelkhand," in *Circumambulations in South Asian History: Essays in Honour of Dirk H.A. Kolff*, eds Jos Gommans and Om Prakash (Leiden: Brill, 2003), 217–31.

[75] Schokker, "The Legitimation of Kingship," 229.

[76] For example, Allison Busch discusses how poets writing in Brajbhasha helped integrate the imperial state with local forms of culture, contributing to the "Mughal politics of pluralism." "Hidden in Plain View: Brajbhasha Poets at the Mughal Court," *Modern Asian Studies* 44, no. 2 (2010): 267–309.

[77] Kolff, *Naukar, Rajput, and Sepoy*, 135.

[78] Catherine B. Asher, *Architecture of Mughal India* (Cambridge: Cambridge University Press, 1992), 162–64.

"inflow" from the imperial center to the provinces, regional state systems were linked outward into trans-regional politics, thereby becoming part of the "wider institutional framework" of empire.[79] In this way, Bundelas were able to make use of their connections with Mughal forces outside of Bundelkhand to buttress their position within their homeland.

In the persons of Maharaja Chhatrasal Bundela and Mahamat Prannath, we can see an illustration of the expanded horizons and interconnected networks which the Mughal imperium made possible. Chhatrasal's career speaks to the military and political sphere, through his service in Mughal campaigns throughout India, while Prannath's experiences reflect economic and religious developments, seen in his travels from Gujarat, to Delhi, Rajasthan, and finally eastern Bundelkhand, at the head of an innovative mercantile *sampradaya*. Bundelkhand itself was undergoing changes that were affecting other erstwhile Mughal provinces, including the increasing involvement of aspiring merchant-supported sects with state politics.[80] Within this broader trend, the specific aspects of Bundela society provided an opening for Prannath's leadership at the Panna court, aided by the relatively weak position of ritual caste hierarchy there. As Ravindra K. Jain remarks, "It is strikingly obvious that [in Bundela kingdoms] we have examples of legitimization of royal authority by founders of sects rather than by brahmin priests," as exemplified by the case of Chhatrasal and Prannath.[81]

While not amenable to anything like precise quantification, the question arises as to how generally influential Prannath's ideas were, taking into account the fact that only a fraction of the population in Bundelkhand (leaving aside for the time being his followers living in other regions) became initiates into the Pranami *sampradaya*. The first point to note is that among Pranamis themselves, the worldview of Prannath and Lal Das was not simply a transferable religious blueprint to be adopted without reflection or adjustment. It can be expected that the socially radical and often agonistic message contained in the *Kulzam Swarup* and the *Bitak* would have led devotees to interpret Prannath's ideals in a way that suited their own social positions and aspirations.

[79] In reference to the Bundelas, see Kolff, *Naukar, Rajput, and Sepoy*, 126.

[80] Peabody, *Hindu Kingship and Polity in Precolonial India*.

[81] Ravindra K. Jain, *Between History and Legend: Status and Power in Bundelkhand* (New Delhi: Oxford University Press, 2002), 47.

This can be seen, for example, in the very distinct paths taken by later hagiographical reworkings of Prannath's story. Hence, whereas one retelling of the *Bitak*, the *Vritant Muktavali*, introduced a strong element of Brahminical caste hierarchy and greatly downplayed Prannath's commitment to Islam, another work, the *Mihiraj Charitra*, repeatedly foregrounded the notion that Prannath strived to unite Hindus and Muslims.[82]

I would also argue that Prannath's influence was not narrowly limited to an exclusive group of sect adherents, but was felt more widely in Bundelkhand. Most important was the official sanction and support given by Chhatrasal to Prannath and his followers, which gave Pranami ideas the imprimatur of a rapidly expanding and prestigious state. To the degree that the state promoted these views from the royal center, all subjects, not just believers or *sampradaya* members, would have been affected by them. This would not necessarily have meant that the king urged his subjects to formally acknowledge Prannath's religious authority, but could take the admittedly more diffuse form of a general dedication to his vision and principles. For example, during the final years of Chhatrasal's life, the Maharaja's son Hriday Shah, who was also a disciple of Prannath, implored others in the Bundela royal family to treat Hindus and Muslims (*Hindu wa Musalman*) resident in their domains on an equal footing, a charge that not unreasonably can be conjectured as having developed from the influence of Prannath's ideology.[83] The sect's impact would have been further magnified with kingly support because, as Ravindra K. Jain has argued, royal authority in early modern Bundelkhand extended well beyond a narrowly conceived political realm, so that "ruling houses had a great deal of influence on the regional *social structure and norms* in the region."[84] Finally, the acquisition of authority by Prannath and Chhatrasal gained further depth and power because it positioned Bundela royal authority within wider fields of discourse on religion and power in Mughal India. It is thus no surprise that when Chhatrasal's legacy was recalled in Bundelkhand in subsequent times, his story became inextricably linked with that of Prannath. This brief analysis of the significance and impact of this movement, however,

82 Braj Bhushan, *Vritant Muktavali*; Hansraj Bakshi, *Mihiraj Charitra*.

83 Singh, *Aitihasik Pramanvali*, Hindi letter no. 8.

84 Jain, *Between History and Legend*, 127–28, emphasis added.

cannot be concluded before addressing one last issue that has shaped the understanding of Prannath's views on religion, namely, the veracity of a widely cited set of verses attributed to Prannath.

INTERPOLATION IN THE *KIRANTAN*

Issues concerning the dating, place of composition, and authenticity of Prannath's collected compositions, including the *Bitak*, have been addressed by scholars who have scrutinized numerous Pranami manuscripts across north India.[85] While there is consensus that the fourteen volumes that make up the *Kulzam Swarup* were put together in complete form in 1694, based on internal evidence it appears that one text, *Kirantan*, contains a small but significant interpolation of several dozen verses. The *Kirantan* is the most frequently cited of Prannath's works, and has had a wider circulation than his other books. It is unique among the compiled works of Prannath in that it contains verses composed in a variety of locales, over a period of many years, and presents material that appears to draw upon themes spanning the entire career of Prannath, with each section corresponding with a particular theme and phase in Prannath's other works. Thus some sections represent the Krishna *viraha* genre, others express Sufi ideas, while yet others seem to have been composed as part of Prannath's Quranic exegesis and apocalyptic Shia Ismaili message. This inclusivity gives the text the appearance of a kind of "compendium" of representative selections from Prannath's oeuvre, although it also gives the work a much less cohesive appearance than that of each of his other texts, in both tone and content. The added material is particularly important to note because the verses in question have been cited repeatedly in modern scholarly studies of Prannath, and ostensibly bear upon his attitude toward Hinduism and Islam.[86] These, then,

[85] In addition to the work on the *Bitak* of Dr Matabadal Jayaswal mentioned above, a thorough discussion and critical assessment of *Kulzam Swarup* manuscripts appears in Sidana, *Sri Prannathji*, 134–70.

[86] Excerpts from section 58 of the *Kirantan* appear, for instance, in Das Gupta, *Maharaja Chhatrasal Bundela*, 97–98; Tanka B. Subba, "The Pranami Dharma in the Darjeeling-Sikkim Himalayas," *Religion and Society* 36, no. I (1989): 63; Prasad, *Mahamati Prannath*, 23; Kamla Sharma, *Dharm Samanvay Udgata Mahamati Prannath* (New Delhi: Shri Prannath Mission, 1993), 24–25.

are verses that purportedly demonstrate that Prannath (along with Maharaja Chhatrasal) was actually promoting a holy war in the name of protecting Hindu dharma against Muslim oppressors:

> Rajas, chiefs, lords, and rulers, will anyone run to rescue the dharma?
> Awake and rise up brave ones, leave this wretched sleep.
> The swords have fallen from the warriors, Hindu dharma is in decline
> Truth-seekers, don't abandon honor, for the Turks are advancing.
> ...
> In the three worlds India (*Bharat*) is supreme, and here Hindu dharma is supreme
> Yet the kings here behave shamefully.
> ...
> The temples and pilgrimage sites of Hardwar have been destroyed; cows are being slaughtered
> Such oppression is everywhere, yet no one takes up the sword.
> There are nobles in the service of the demons, who destroy temples with gunpowder
> They are Hindus in name, but serve in *their* army, this is a calamity for the community.
> ...
> The demons have imposed the *jizya* even on those Hindus who have nothing to eat
> And the poor who cannot pay *jizya* are forced to become Muslims.
> ...
> The year is Vikram Samvat 1735 [1678 CE]
> ...
> When Chhatrasal Bundela heard of all this, he came forward with his sword
> He attracted everyone into his service; and the Lord made him head of the army.[87]

This last verse appears to be a reference to Prannath's conducting of the royal consecration ceremony for Chhatrasal, an event that is recounted in the *Chhatra Prakash* and in the *Bitak*. These verses appear to be apocryphal for several reasons. First, in tone and content they stand in contrast to all the other writings of Prannath, including *Sanandh* which was composed beginning in 1678, the same date cited in the *Kirantan* verses above. The rousing call to the defense of Hindu

[87] Prannath, *Kirantan*, Section 58, vss 1–2, 4, 13–14, 16, 18, 20.

dharma, and the claim that "Hindu dharma is supreme," are not seen elsewhere in his extensive work. As outlined above, by 1678, Prannath was in fact concerned with bringing together both mystical Islamic and devotional Hindu teachings, and was not arguing for the superiority of Hinduism over other religions, including Islam. Furthermore, when Prannath denounced the actions of Aurangzeb and Mughal officials, as he frequently did, he did so by claiming that as Muslims the Mughals were not living up to the high standards of compassion and justice demanded by the Quran and modeled in the behavior of the Prophet Muhammad, not through a call to defend Hinduism. Second, in all of Prannath's compositions which were written after Chattrasal had become his disciple, the justification for Chhatrasal's war against Aurangzeb was expressed in a Shia Ismaili millenarian framework, wherein both Chhatrasal and Prannath were portrayed as fulfilling the end-time prophecy of Muhammad and the Quran. These works do not speak of Chhatrasal as a defender of Hindu dharma. Third, the verses cited above explicitly state that this poem was composed in the year 1678 CE (1735 Vikram Samvat), whereas all sources indicate that Prannath first met Chhatrasal in the year 1683. Apart from this *Kirantan* verse, there is no other mention of Chhatrasal in Prannath's work prior to that date. Finally, the *Kirantan* verses above refer to the imposition of the *jizya*, by Aurangzeb, on Hindus. This tax, however, was imposed only on April 2, 1679, which falls on the Vikram Samvat calendar early in the year 1736, so that the date given in the verses above was before the *jizya* was in fact imposed.[88] While it is impossible to say when exactly these verses were added to the *Kirantan*, they present an image of Prannath that sharply contrasts with the message he articulated in his own lifetime.

***

By formally recognizing Prannath as his preceptor, Chhatrasal brought a religion that claimed to transcend Hindu and Muslim divisions into the center of his royal ideology. This of course does not change

[88] Satish Chandra, "Jizyah and the State in India during the 17th Century," *Journal of the Economic and Social History of the Orient* 12, no. 3 (September 1969): 323.

the fact that in Bundelkhand, as elsewhere in the subcontinent, distinctions between Hindus and Muslims were real and recognized as such, not least by Prannath himself. Prannath's message, however, aimed to reveal that these differences were paradoxically only real in the illusory and temporary, and hence inferior, world of maya. For those who understood Prannath's insight as revelatory of ultimate spiritual truth, these distinctions were misguided and false. Prannath's religious claims were able to account for observable, worldly differences, yet at the same time could deny that these differences existed in a more meaningful, ultimate reality. In putting forth this worldview, Prannath portrayed the transcendence of the boundaries of religious difference as achievable through the pursuit and recognition of universal *haq*, "Truth," but also as connoting a sense of justice. During and after Prannath's lifetime, Pranami adherents adopted and recast his teachings and his story into a variety of different molds, some even at odds with one another, but each of which was forced to grapple with his deeply felt and highly provocative vision of the meanings of Islam and Hinduism, Muslim and Hindu, belief and unbelief. On account of Prannath's explicitly stated understanding of truth as transcending Hindu–Muslim distinctions, it would be misguided to see him as either a crypto-Muslim aiming to convert Hindus, or as an adamant defender of Hinduism against the onslaught of Muslims and Islam. Likewise, Chhatrasal and Prannath's willingness to ally in rebellion against the Mughals was not conceived as a Hindu reaction against an oppressor driven by Islamic imperatives, but rather was framed, in the prophetic mode of the *Bitak*, as an effort to fight an unjust sovereign whose treatment of people had violated codes of conduct inherent in the holy books of all subjects of the Empire.

BIBLIOGRAPHY

Asher, Catherine B. *Architecture of Mughal India*. Cambridge: Cambridge University Press, 1992.

Bakshi, Hansraj. *Mihiraj Charitra*. Edited by Devkrishna Sharma. Jamnagar: Shri Sansthabha, 1969.

Bhushan, Braj. *Vritant Muktavali*. Edited by Vimla Mehta. Bhivani: Shri Krishna Pranami Janakalyan Ashram Trust, 1998.

Busch, Allison. "Hidden in Plain View: Brajbhasha Poets at the Mughal Court." *Modern Asian Studies* 44, no. 2 (2010): 267–309.

Callewaert, Winand M. and Rupert Snell, eds. *According to Tradition: Hagiographical Writing in India*. Wiesbaden: Otto Harrassowitz, 1994.

Chandra, Satish. "Jizyah and the State in India during the 17th Century." *Journal of the Economic and Social History of the Orient* 12, no. 3 (September 1969): 322–40.

Daftary, Farhad. *The Ismai'ilis: Their History and Doctrines*. Cambridge: Cambridge University Press, 1990.

Das, Lal. *Bitak*. Edited by Matabadal Jayaswal and Devkrishna Sharma. Allahabad: Pranami Sahitya Sansthan, 1966.

Das Gupta, Bhagwan. *Life and Times of Maharaja Chhatrasal Bundela*. New Delhi: Radiant Publishers, 1980.

Engineer, Ashgar Ali. *The Bohras*. New Delhi: Vikas Publishing House, 1980.

Gilmartin, David and Bruce Lawrence, eds. *Beyond Turk and Hindu: Rethinking Religious Identities in Islamicate South Asia*. Gainesville: University Press of Florida, 2000.

Granoff, Phyllis. "Svetambara Jains in Northwest India." In *According to Tradition: Hagiographical Writing in India*, edited by Windand M. Callewaert and Rupert Snell, 131–58. Wiesbaden: Otto Harrassowitz, 1994.

Hasan, Farhat. *State and Locality in Mughal India: Power Relations in Western India, c. 1572–1730*. Cambridge: Cambridge University Press, 2004.

Hawley, John Stratton and Donna Marie Wulff, eds. *The Divine Consort: Radha and the Goddesses of India*. Boston: Beacon Press, 1986.

Jain, Ravindra K. *Between History and Legend: Status and Power in Bundelkhand*. New Delhi: Oxford University Press, 2002.

Karunasakhi. *Shri Tartam Sagar Bitak*. Jamnagar: Shri Khijada Mandir Trust Board, 1982.

Kassam, Tazim R. *Songs of Wisdom and Circles of Dance: Hymns of the Satpanth Ismaili Muslim Saint, Pir Shams*. Albany: State University of New York Press, 1995.

Kavi, Lal. *Chattra Prakash*. Edited by Mahendra Pratap Singh. New Delhi: Shripatal Prakashan, 1973.

Khafi Khan, Muhammad Hashim. *Muntakhab al-Lubab*. Translated by S. Moinul Haq. Karachi: Pakistan Historical Society, 1975.

Khan, Dominique-Sila. *Conversions and Shifting Identities: Ramdev Pir and the Ismailis in Rajasthan*. New Delhi: Manohar, 1997.

_____. "The Mahdi of Panna: A Short History of the Prannamis." *Indian Journal of Secularism* 7, no. 1 (January–March 2003): 61–92, and 7, no. 1 (April–June 2003): 46–66.

Kolff, Dirk. *Naukar, Rajput, and Sepoy: The Ethnohistory of the Military Labour Market in Hindustan, 1450–1850*. Cambridge: Cambridge University Press, 1990.

LaRocque, Brendan. *The Creation of Social Fabric in Early Modern India: Mahamat Prannath and Community Formation in the Mughal Empire* (forthcoming).

Lawrence, Bruce. "The Sant Movement and North Indian Sufis." In *The Sants: Studies in a Devotional Tradition of India*, edited by Karine Schomer and W.H. McLeod. Delhi: Motilal Banarsidass, 1987: 359–74.

MacLean, Derryl L. "Real Men and False Men at the Court of Akbar." In *Beyond Turk and Hindu: Rethinking Religious Identities in Islamicate South Asia*, edited by David Gilmartin and Bruce Lawrence, 199–215. Gainesville: University Press of Florida, 2000.

Pandya, Naresh. *Prannath: Sampradaya evam Sahitya*. Jaipur: Panchsila Prakasan, 1973.

Pauwels, Heidi R.M. *In Praise of Holy Men: Hagiographic Poems by and about Hariram Vyas*. Netherlands: Egbert Forstern Groningen, 2002.

Peabody, Norbert. *Hindu Kingship and Polity in Precolonial India*. Cambridge: Cambridge University Press, 2003.

Pogson, W.R. *History of the Boondelas*. Delhi: B.R. Publishing Corporation, 1974.

Prannath, Mahamat. *Kalash Hindustani*. Volume 1. Edited by Amrit Raj Sharma and Ranjit Saha. New Delhi: Shri Prannath Mission, 1987.

_____. *Sanandh*. Edited by Vimla Mehta and Ranjit Saha. New Delhi: Shri Prannath Mission, 1988.

_____. *Khulasa*. Edited by Vimla Mehta and Ranjit Saha. New Delhi: Shri Prannath Mission, 1989.

_____. *Marfat Sagar, Kayamat Nama (Chhota aur Badha)*. New Delhi: Shri Prannath Mission, 1990.

_____. *Khilawat*. Edited by Vimla Mehta and Ranjit Saha. New Delhi: Shri Prannath Mission, 1992.

_____. *Kirantan*. Edited by Ranjit Saha. New Delhi: Shri Prannath Mission, 1993.

_____. *Prakash*. In volume 1 of *Shri Tartam Sagar (Kulzam Swarup)*. Jamnagar: Shri 5 Navatanpur Dham, 1998.

_____. *Ras*. In volume 1 of *Shri Tartam Sagar (Kulzam Swarup)*. Jamnagar: Shri 5 Navatanpur Dham, 1998.

_____. *Shatruti*. In volume 1 of *Shri Tartam Sagar (Kulzam Swarup)*. Jamnagar: Shri 5 Navatanpur Dham, 1998.

_____. *Shri Tartam Sagar (Kulzam Swarup)*. 2 volumes. Jamnagar: Shri 5 Navatanpur Dham, 1998.

Prasad, Suchit Narayan. *Mahamati Prannath Prerit Shri Krishna Pranami Vangmay*. New Delhi: Shri Prannath Mission, 1987.

Ram, Shiv Mangal. *Svami Laladas Krit Mahamati Prananath Bitak ka Madhyakalin Bharatiya Itihas ko Yogadan*. New Delhi: Hindi Book Centre, 1996.

Rizvi, Saiyid Athar Abbas. *Muslim Revivalist Movements in Northern India in the Sixteenth and Seventeenth Centuries*. Agra: Agra University Press, 1965.

Rao, Velcheru Narayana, David Shulman, and Sanjay Subrahmanyam. *Textures of Time: Writing History in South India 1600–1800*. New York: Other Press, 2003.

Saha, Shandip. "The Movement of *Bhakti* along a North–West Axis: Tracing the History of the Pustimarg between the Sixteenth and Nineteenth Centuries." *International Journal of Hindu Studies* 11, no. 3 (December 2007): 299–318.

Sands, Kristin Zahra. "On the Popularity of Husayn Va'iz-i Kashifi's Mavahib-i 'Aliyya: A Persian Commentary on the Quran." *Iranian Studies* 36, no. 4 (December 2003): 469–83.

Sarkar, J.N. *Shivaji and His Times*. Calcutta: S.C. Sarkar, 1920.

Schokker, Godard. "The Legitimation of Kingship in India: Bundelkhand." In *Circumambulations in South Asian History: Essays in Honour of Dirk H.A. Kolff*, edited by Jos Gommans and Om Prakash, 217–31. Leiden: Brill, 2003.

Schomer, Karine. "Introduction: The Sant Tradition in Perspective." In *The Sants: Studies in a Devotional Tradition of India*, edited by Karine Schomer and W.H. McLeod, 1–17. Delhi: Motilal Banarsidass, 1987.

Sharma, Kamla. *Dharm Samanvay Udgata Mahamati Prannath*. New Delhi: Shri Prannath Mission, 1993.

Sharma, Sri Ram. *Maharana Raj Singh and His Times*. Delhi: Motilal Banarsidass, 1971.

Sidana, Raj Bala. *Shri Prananathji aur Unka Sahitya*. Jamnagar: Sahitya Prakasana Committee, 1969.

Singh, Mahendra Pratap, ed. *Aitihasik Pramanavali aur Chhatrasal*. Delhi: National Publishing House, 1975.

Subba, Tanka B. "The Pranami Dharma in the Darjeeling-Sikkim Himalayas." *Religion and Society* 36, no. I (1989): 52–64.

Tambs-Lyche, Harald. *Power, Profit and Poetry: Traditional Society in Kathiawar, Western India*. New Delhi: Manohar, 1997.

Trivedi, Pyarelal. *Dharmadivakar aur Bhrantinashanam: Nijanand Mimansa ke Mithya Apakshepoka Sampraman Nirakaran*. Panna: Shri Padhyavati Puri Dham Trust, 1978.

Vaudeville, Charlotte. *A Weaver Named Kabir: Selected Verses With a Detailed Biographical and Historical Introduction*. Oxford: Oxford University Press, 1993.

Wink, André. *Land and Sovereignty in India: Agrarian Society and Politics under the Eighteenth-Century Maratha Svarajya*. Cambridge: Cambridge University Press, 1986.

Editors and Contributors

EDITORS

Vasudha Dalmia was Chandrika and Ranjan Tandon Professor of Hindu Studies in the Department of Religious Studies at Yale University between 2012 and 2014. Before that she taught at Tuebingen University (Germany) and the University of California-Berkeley where she was the Magistretti Distinguished Professor in the Department of South and Southeast Asian Studies. Her areas of research are religion, literature, and theatre in South Asia, especially in early modern and modern north India.

Munis D. Faruqui is an Associate Professor in the Department of South and Southeast Asian Studies, University of California-Berkeley. He focuses on the Muslim experience in South Asia, especially during the Mughal period.

CONTRIBUTORS

Supriya Gandhi, Department of Religion, Haverford College

Monika Horstmann, South Asia Institute, University of Heidelberg

Brendan LaRocque, Program in Asian Studies, Carleton College

Christopher Minkowski, Faculty of Oriental Studies, University of Oxford

Francesca Orsini, Department of the Languages and Cultures of South Asia, School of Oriental and African Studies

Eva Orthmann, Institute for Oriental and Asian Studies, University of Bonn

Heidi Pauwels, Department of Asian Languages and Literatures, University of Washington-Seattle

Stefano Pellò, Department of Asian and North African Studies, University of Venice

Shandip Saha, Department of Religious Studies, Athabasca University

Ramya Sreenivasan, Department of South Asia Studies, University of Pennsylvania

Index

Abhinanda, 77, 78
Abraham, Prophet, 37, 51
Abu Bakr, 58
Abu'l Fazl, Shaikh, 4–5, 7, 36–37, 166, 174–75
Adam, Prophet, 51–52
Ādi Granth, 293
Advaita Vedanta, xxii, 33, 43, 46–47, 73, 88
Agra, 271, 355
Ahirs, 201, 212–13, 218, 229
Ahmad, Aziz, 32
Ahmadnagar, 106–7
Ahmad, Nizam al-Din, 167, 170, 171, 172, 173, 176
Ahmedabad, 321, 350–51, 357
Ahrar Naqshbandi, Khwaja, 40
A'in-i Akbari, 166
Aitareya, 44
Ajab-khyāl-aṣṭaka, 257–58, 261
Ajmer, 121, 185
Akbar, Emperor, xi, xv–xvi, 4–5, 10, 19, 21, 24, 36, 75, 108, 109, 110, 115, 117, 118, 123–24, 127, 128, 165, 167, 175, 178, 186, 195, 329, 335, 336, 337, 354, 368
Akhlāq-i nāṣirī, 16–17
al-'Ābidīn, Zayn, 74
'Alamgirnama, 31, 67
Alam, Muzaffar, xxiv, 229
al-'Arabi, Ibn, 34–35, 257
al-Biruni, 17–19, 35
al-Dawla, Nawāb Āṣaf, 153, 154
al-Dawla, Nawāb Mukhtār, 154
al-Dawla, Shujā', 140
al-Gardezi, 35
Aligarh Muslim University (India), 161
Alīkhān, 334–35
'Alī, Sayyid Khayrat, 153
al-Ḥaqq, Ẓiyā', 92
al-Jili, 37, 47
Allah, 221, 253, 254, 258, 259, 355, 358
Allahabad, 198, 271, 273, 284
Allahabadi, Shaikh Muhibullah, 38
al-Mulk, Nawāb Burhān, 153
al-Qunawi, 47
al-Qużāt, 'Ayn, 92
al-Shahrastani, 35
Amber, 177, 186
Amer, 240, 242, 314, 363
Amoretti, Biancamaria Scarcia, 135
Amṛtakuṇḍa, 7, 22–23
Ānandaghana, 91, 92
Anantdās, Sant, 305, 310–13

Anīs al-aḥibbā, 156
"Anis," Mohan La'l, 138, 140, 143, 144
Anup Shahr, 360
Anyashraya, 269, 281
Aristotle, 14–15
Ārya Samāj, 338
Āṣafavilāsa, 113
Ashta Chap poets, 286
Aṣṭāvakra Gītā, 96
Atharva veda, 52
Atmavilasa, 39
Aṭvār fī ḥall al-asrār, 78, 96
Aurangzeb, Emperor, xxiii, xxiv, 31, 58, 67, 83, 95, 108, 115, 119, 121, 131, 132, 275, 332, 343–46, 348, 350, 354–56, 360–63, 374
Austin, R.W.J., 47
Awadh, xix, xx, 135–39, 145, 149, 195, 197–201, 213, 227
Awrād-i ghawsiyya, 7, 21
"Azīz," Shabāb Rāy, 139, 146

Bābur, Emperor, 11, 17, 128, 165
Badakhshi, Mulla Shah, 38, 50, 55
Bahadur Shah, Sultan, 165, 168, 169, 170, 171, 172, 173
Bairagi, Naga, 284, 285
Balabhadra, 130–2
Banaras, xiv, xxii, 30, 42, 104–12, 113–19, 122, 124–28, 197, 236, 239, 240, 242, 287, 293–98, 309, 315, 316
Bandar Abbas, 350, 352–3
Bansawi, Abdur Razzaq, 195, 204
"Barahman", Chandra Bhān, 84–86, 88, 142, 143
Barz, Richard, 266, 279
Basra, 350
Bauls, 281
Bayly, C.A., xxiv
Bayrāgī, Bhopat Rāy "Bīgham," 144, 145
Beg, Ulugh, 125
Behl, Aditya, xx, 214, 217, 229
Bengal, xiii, 115, 130, 161, 162, 197, 281, 316, 368
Benu, Baba, 277
Berar, 122
Beyond Turk and Hindu: Rethinking Religious Identities in Islamicate South Asia, ix, x
Bhagavad Gita, 78, 352
Bhagavata Purana, 154, 199, 205–6, 207, 208, 212, 215, 277, 285, 349, 351, 352, 366
Bhaktas, 206, 226, 261, 290, 292, 297, 305, 306, 312, 314, 315, 316, 334
Bhakti Sect of Vallabhacarya, The, 266
Bhaktamāl, 240, 243, 246, 305
Bhaṅgīvibhaṅgīkaraṇa, 126
Bhāradvāja *gotras*, 122
Bhāskara II, 126
Bhatner, 177
Bhat, Prabhudas, 274
Bhatt, Krishna, 267
Bhaṭṭa, Nārāyaṇa, 108, 109–10, 113
Bhaṭṭa, Rāmeśvara, 107
Bhaṭṭa, Śaṅkara, 107
Bhava Prakash, 268, 272, 276, 279–80, 282, 284
Bhāvsindhu kī Vārtā, 324
Bhuteshwar Mahadev, 277
Bible, 51
Biharidas, 350, 354
Bījagaṇita, 123
Bilgrami, Mir 'Abdul Wahid, 40, 198, 230
Bisṭāmī, Bāyazīd, 6
Bitak, 344–50, 352–57, 360–68, 370–73, 375

Bījak songs, 294, 301–2, 309
Brahma *sampradāya*, 244
Brahmasutrabhasya, 39
Brahminical Hinduism, 69, 161, 213, 236, 237, 273, 274, 276, 283, 286, 294, 304, 371
Brahmins, xiii, xvi, xvii, xxii, xxiii, 13, 31, 35–37, 42, 44, 67, 77, 95, 102–32, 198, 199, 200, 202, 218, 227, 229, 240, 270, 274, 275, 277, 278, 280, 282, 283, 284, 294, 300, 303, 304, 308, 309, 310, 312, 315, 327, 328, 335, 337, 358, 360, 361, 363, 370
Bṛhat Saṁhitā, 18
Braj, xxiii, 82, 154, 197, 198, 208, 212, 220, 271, 276, 278, 321, 322, 323, 328, 331–35, 339, 351, 352, 355, 362
Brajbhasha, 154, 164, 166, 174, 179–80, 188, 213, 227, 286, 323, 325
Brhadaranyaka, 44
Bukhari Saiyids, 167
Bundela, Maharaja Chhatrasal, xxiii, 343, 345–47, 364–68, 370–71, 373, 374, 375
Bundelas, 213, 366, 368–71
Bundelkhand, 119–20, 367–72, 375
Burhanpur, 363–64
Burhan, Shaikh, 208
Busch, Allison, 180, 181

Cambay, 321
Cārumatī, 332
Caurāsī Vaiṣṇavan kī Vārtā, 198–99, 267, 279, 323–34, 327, 330, 335, 337–8
Central Asia, xiii
Chahār chaman, 85
Chaitanya, 279–82
Chandra, Satish, 57
Chandogya, 44
Chatterjee, Kumkum, xiii
Chaudhuri, Roma, 48
Chauhans, 162, 175, 178, 180, 181, 184–8
Chauhan, Daulat Khan, 178, 179
Chauhan, Fadan Khan, 177–79
Chauhan, Karamchand, 176, 183, 186
Chauhan, Moterao, 176
Chauhan, Nahir, 162
Chauhan, Qawam Khan, 174
Chauhan, Taj Khan, 166
Chauhan, Usman, 162
Chhatra Prakash, 373
Chhipa, Vishnudas, 270–72
Chishtī, ‘Abd al-Raḥmān, 78–9
Chishtī, Shaikh Salīm ad-Dīn, 19, 97, 246
Chītsvāmī, 329, 330, 337

Dabistān-i maẓāhib, 77–78
Dādūpanthi, 235–42, 244, 257, 260–61, 292, 293, 297
Dalmia, Vasudha, xxi, xxiv, 327
Dāsa, Giridhara, 121
Dasam Skandha, 200, 205
Das, Lakshman, 352
Das, Mukand, 353
Dās, Rāu Jādav, 85
Dās, Sītal, 139, 151
de Bruijn, Thomas, xx
Deccan, xiv, xiii, 46, 213, 271, 363
Delhi, 109, 112, 116, 121, 139, 165, 176, 178, 185, 347, 354–62, 369, 370
Delhi Sultanate, 19
Deol, Jeevan, xx
Deśāan, 256
Devarāta *gotra*, 122–27

Devi, Rukmini, 214
Dhar, 177
Dharmapura, 116
Dharmaśāstra, xxi, 109–10
Dimock, Edward, 279
Diu, 351
Divākara, 124
"Diwana," Sarab Sukh, 138, 140, 142, 143, 146, 147, 156
Doniger, Wendy, 74
Do Sau Bāvan Vaiṣṇavan kī Vārtā, 324, 329, 331–33, 335, 337–39
Dube, Govind, 282
Dunpur, 177
Durgawati, 173
Dwarka, 215, 275, 285

Eaton, Richard, 161
Encyclopedia of Islam, 57
Entwistle, Alan, xix
Etawah, 177

Faruki, Zahiruddin, 32
Faruqui, Munis D., ix, xv–xvi
Farwardīn, 8
Fatehpur, 174, 178, 180, 242, 244, 261
Fātima, 154
Findiriski, Mir 'Abul Qasim, 52
Franke, Heike, 75

Gabriel, Angel, 51
Gadādhara, 123
Gaṇakamaṇḍana, 122
Gandhi, Supriya, xv–xvi, 39
Gangaputra, Sundardas, 281
Ganga, River, 142, 143, 144, 156, 358
Ganges-Brahmaputra delta, 161
Gangohi, Saiyid 'Abdul Quddus, 40
Gaudiya *sampradaya*, 224, 244, 272, 279, 328
Gwalior, 165
Gaya, 142, 143, 148, 156
Gharūvārtā, 323
Ghaws Gwāliyārī, Muḥammad, 7, 20–3, 40
Ginzburg, Carlo, 143
Giridharānanda, 121
Godhara, 321
Goindvāl Pothīs, 293
Gokul, 208, 213, 215, 225, 271, 321, 332, 335
Gokulnāth, 267, 323–24, 326, 327
Gopīnāth, 321
Gorakh-bānī, 301
Gorakhnath, Sant, 95, 225–27, 301, 311–12, 314
Gorakhpanth, 227
Gosth-i Bābā La'l, 85, 94
Govardhan, 65, 66, 321, 360
Govinda, 117
Govindsvāmī, 329, 337
Green, Nile, xiii
Gujarat, 121, 124, 165, 167, 168, 172, 173, 185, 197, 200, 321, 345, 346, 348–54, 357, 370
Gujarat Sultanates, 165
Gul-i ra'nā, 138, 156
Gupta, Bhagwan Das, 343
Guru Arjun, 72
Guru Devchandra, 348–50, 351, 353, 354, 362
Gurū Granth Sāhib, 295
Guru Nānak, 92, 94, 142, 353
Gurusampradāya, 243
Gyān Mālā, 95–96

Ḥadīqa-yi hindī, 153–54
Haft Paykar, 17
Hāfiz, 90

Haider, Najaf, xxiv
Haqā'iq-i Hindī, 40, 198–99, 230
Haq, S. Moinul, 32
Haricharit, 200, 205, 208, 213, 228
Haridwar, 356
Harīhar Sanbādh, 95, 96
Harikatha, 195–96, 197, 199, 200, 201, 205, 207, 227–78
Harirāy, 324–25
Harishchandra, 287
Harivamṣa, Cācā, 339
Harsani, Damodardas, 283, 284
Hārūn, Emperor, 92
Harzer, Edeltraud, 45
Ḥasanāt al-'ārifīn, 71
Hasan, Farhat, 346
Hasrat, B.J., 44
"Hasrat," Sayyid Muḥammad, 150
Hāyanaratna, 130
Ḥazīn, Shah Muḥammad 'Alī, 140
Heck, Paul, 34
Hindāl, Mirzā, 20
"Hindi," Bhagwan Das, xvii, 137–41, 145, 150–56
Hisar, 174
Horāratna, 130
Horstmann, Monika, xix–xx
Huart, Charles, 83–84, 89, 95
Humāyūn, Emperor, xv, 3–24, 115, 128
"*Hunood wa Musalman:* Religion in Mughal India," ix
Husain, Sayyid Abdulrahim, 213
Ḥusayn, 156

Ibn Hazm, 35
"Ikhlas," Kishan Chand, 139, 144
Illichpur, 363
Inden, Ronald, 12
Insan-i kamil, 47, 48, 58, 86
Iran, xiii, 6–7, 11, 150
Iṣfahānī, Abū Ṭālib, 148
Ismaili, xx, xxiii, 237, 246, 347, 348, 350, 356, 357, 362, 372, 374
Īśvaradāsa, 119–21, 131
Ivanow, Vladimir, 85

Jadrūp, 72
"Ja'far," Muḥammad, 150
Jagannātha, 112–13, 275
Jagannath temple, Puri, 274
Jahan Ara, 58
Jahāngiravinodaratnākara, 127
Jahāngīr, Emperor, 72, 75, 112–13, 115, 117, 118, 124, 127, 128, 131
Jains, 69, 188, 235, 237, 239, 250, 293, 300, 354
Jain, Ravindra K., 370–71
Jalota, Prabhudas, 279
Jama Masjid, 360
Jamnagar, 349–50
Janaka, King, 96
Jān-i Jānān, Mīrzā Maẓhar, 150
Jarīr, Ibrāhīm bin, 5
Jatadhari, Gopaldas, 284–85
Jātakapaddhati, 123
Jātakapaddhaty-udāharaṇa, 123
Jaṭāyu, 333
Jawāhir al-khams, 23
Jawāhir al-ulūm, 5–6, 22–23
Jayasawal, Matabadal, 347, 356
Jayasi, Malik Muhammad, xx, 196, 197, 200–1, 203, 205, 208–10, 212–14, 217–19, 221–22, 227–30
Jhunjhunu, 174–75, 177, 178, 186, 245
Jīlānī, 'Abd al-Qādir, 94
Jīu, Krishan, 95
Jivanamukta, 46, 47, 48
Jīvanmukti, 47, 73
Jñāna-jhūlanāṣṭaka, 259

Jodha, Rao, 178, 184
Jog Bāsisht, 73, 75–77, 79, 83, 86–87, 94–96
Junagadh, 351
Jyotiḥśāstra, 130
Jyotirvit Sarasa, 119
Jyotiṣasaukhya, 117

Kabīr granthāvalī, 293, 295
Kabīr Panth, xxii, 197, 294, 301, 314
Kabīr parcaī, 314, 316
Kabīr ramainī, 309
Kabir, Sant, xxii, 71, 75, 195, 204, 208, 222, 237, 260, 290–317, 332, 345, 352–53
Kabul, xiii, 14, 331
Kachhwahas, 177, 179, 186
Kaicker, Abhishek, xxiv
Kalash, 353, 358
Kaliyuga, 348
Kalpi, 153, 177
Kamalākara, 126
Kangra, 178
Kanhāvat, xx, 197, 203, 204–5, 212–13, 215–16, 228–30
Karbalā, 149, 152, 156
Karbalā-yi mu'allā, 149
Kartarpur Pothī, 293
Karunasakhi, 351
Kashi, 116, 277, 278
Kashmir, xiii
Katha, 44
Kathiawar, 321
Kavi, Jan, 166, 174–82, 186–87, 246, 247, 260
Kaviraj, Sudipta, xviii
Kavīndracandrodaya, 82
Kavīndrācārya, 82
Kayamatnama, 367
Kayasthas, xvii, 105
Kāẓim, Mīrzā Muḥammad, 67
Kena, 44
Keśava, 127
Khaṛī Bolī, 259
Khaṇḍelvāl Vaiṣṇava, 239
Khalji, Mahmud, 165
Khan, Akhan (Ikhtiyar Khan), 177
Khān, Alaf, 245
Khan, Alif, 175, 179, 181–82, 187
Khān, Āṣaf, 113, 128, 129, 131, 246
Khan, Awwal, 364
Khan, Fateh, 178, 245
Khān, 'Itibār, 128
Khān, Karīm Dād, 153
Khan, Khafi, 361–62
Khan, Mihin, 364
Khan, Nawab Daulat, 174, 245
Khan, Samas, 177, 178
Khān-i Khānān, Abdur Rahīm, 123, 180
Khatris, xvii
Khatriya, Taj Khan, 166, 175
Khayrābād, 154
Khilawat, 364
Khulasa, 364
Khulāṣat al-khulāṣa, 95
Khusrau, Amir, 35–36
Khusraw, Prince, 72
Khwāndamīr, 5, 7, 10, 14–15
"Khwushgū," Bindrabān Dās, 141
Khyat, 186
Kinra, Rajeev, 32, 92
Kirantan, 372–75
Kishor, Jūgal, 138
Kolff, Dirk, 173, 368
Kota, 324
Krishna bhakti, xii, 196, 197–201, 203, 282, 291, 347
Krishna, Lord, 202, 204, 205, 208, 211–30, 265, 276, 278, 292, 320, 321, 326, 349, 351, 352, 356, 362, 364, 365, 368, 369

Kṛṣṇadevarāya, King, 107
Kshatri, Govinddas Bhalla, 276
Kulzam Swarup, 344, 370, 372
Kumar, Trishi, 342
Kumbh Mela, 356
Kung (Bandar Kong), 350
Kunwar, Tejbai, 351
Kyamkhanis, xx, 166, 174, 175, 177, 178, 179, 180, 181, 183–88, 235, 244, 245, 260
Kyamkhan Rasa, 166, 174–78, 181, 183, 184, 187, 246

Laghu yogavāsiṣṭha, 73–75, 77, 78, 80
La'l Das, Baba, xvi, 39, 69, 71, 83–94, 347, 348, 352, 354–56, 360, 364
LaRocque, Brendan, xxiii
Lawh-i mahfuz, 54
Life and Times of Maharaja Chhatrasal Bundela, 343
Lodi, Sikander, 309–10
Lodi, Bahlul, 178
Lodi dynasty, xiii
Lohana Kshatriya, 349
Lorenzen, David, xix
Lucknow, 85, 136, 137, 138, 140, 142, 147, 148, 152, 153, 156
Lunkaran, Rao, 174, 178

Madhodas, 280–81, 331
Madhumālatī, 229
Madhya Pradesh, 177, 368
Mādhva *sampradāya*, 244
Madīna, 94
Mahābhārat, 95
Maharashtra, 106–7
Mahdi, Imam, 356–57, 362
Majma' al-bahrayn, 40–41, 70, 71, 82
Makar Sankranti, 284
Makhzan al-asrār, 153
Makīn, Mīrzā Fākhir, 140, 141, 148, 153
Maldeo, Rao, 185
Malik, Ẓafar, 107
Malwa, 165, 173
Manāqib-i ghawsiyya, 7
Mandukya, 44
Manjhu, Sikandar, 167, 168, 169, 170, 172, 173, 176
Maratha, xiv
Marphat Sagar, 367
Marwar, 177, 178, 180
Marwari, xx, 164, 188
Mashhad, 149, 150
Mashhad-i muqaddas, 149
Masnavī-yi kajkulāh, 91, 93
Massignon, Louis, 83–84, 89, 95
"Mastāna," Rāy Maykū La'l, 139, 144
Mathura, 210–11, 215, 218, 225, 226, 272, 275–78, 285, 351, 355
Matringe, Denis, xx
Matsya Mahāpurāṇa, 13
Maẓhar al-anwār, 153, 156
Mecca, 94, 148
Meghan, Krishnadas, 285
Merta, 354
Mewar, 165, 171, 322, 331, 332, 338
Middle East, 34
Mihiraj Charitra, 371
Mihr-i żiyā, 153, 155–56
Mīmāṃsā, 109
Minkowski, Christopher, xvi, xvi–xvii, 93
Mirabai, 282, 283
Mir'āt al-ḥaqā'iq, 78
Mir'āt al-makhlūqāt, 79
Mirat-i Sikandari, 167, 168, 172–73
Mir, Farina, xx
Mir, Miyan, 38, 56

"Miskin," Malhār Singh, 139, 142
Miśra, Jagannātha, 74
Mleccha, xxiii, 280, 329–38
Moin, Azfar, xiii
Mokṣopāya, 74, 96
Mount Meru, 18
Muhammad, Jahan, 364
Muhammad, Malik, 211
Muhammad, Prophet, 50, 55, 93, 148, 154, 168, 347, 355–57, 362, 374
Muharram, 150
Muhūrtacintāmaṇi, 117, 118
Muhūrtaratna, 119, 121
Mulla Raj, Ismail Badr al-Din, 350
Multan, 353
Mundaka, 44
Munīśvara, 123–26
Muntakhab al-Lubab, 361
Muscat, 350, 352
Muṣḥafī, Ghulām Hamadānī, 147

Nagari script, xix
Nagaur, 162, 185
Nainsi, Muhata, 184–88
Najaf, 149
Nanddas, 205, 206, 228
Nandigrāma, Gujarat, 124
Nandikeśvara, 121–22
Nārāyaṇa, 123
Nārāyaṇa, Prāṇa, 113
Nārāyandās, Dīvān Kāyastha, 334
Narāyan, Rāja Rām, 152, 156
Narhar, 174
Nasir, Saiyid, 176, 185–86
Nathdwara, xxiii, 322, 324–25, 332
Nath Yogi, xvi, xx, xxii, 69, 227, 237, 242–43, 246, 261, 301, 302, 304, 314
Nawruz, xv, 7, 11–12
Nābhādās, 305
Nādir al-nikāt, 90
Nehru, Jawaharlal, 32
Nibandha, 199
Nicholson, Andrew, xix
Nicomachean Ethics, 15–16
Nijanand Mimansa, 342
Nīlakaṇṭha, 117–18
Niranjan Dev Antarjāmī, 85
Nityānanda, 128–29, 130
Niẓāmī, 156
Noah, Prophet, 175

Orsini, Francesca, xix–xx
Orthmann, Eva, xv–xvi

Pañca prahāra, 250
Paṇḍita, Abhinanda, 73
Paṇḍitarāja, Jagannātha, 108
Panipat, Battle of (1526), 302
Pānipatī, Niẓām, 74, 75
Panna, 357
Parabrahma *sampradāya*, 244
Paramānanda, 128
Paramasivan, Vasudha, xxiv
Pārasīprakāśa, 121
Paraśurāmapratāpa, 107
Parcaīs, 305
Parmananddas, 198
Parshād, Debī, 139
Pauwels, Heidi, xxi, xxii, xxiv
Payhārī, Kṛṣṇadās, 313
Pellò, Stefano, xv, xvii–xviii
Persian Gulf, 352, 354
Phala shruti, 202
Phūl, Shaikh, 20–21
Pingree, David, 102, 114, 126
Pīr-murīd-aṣṭaka, 257
Pīrzādī, 334–35
Pīyūṣadhārā, 117, 118
Prabodhacandronāyak, 145
Prabodhachandrodaya, 39

Prakash, 350–51, 358
Prannami *sampradaya*, xxiii, 342, 357, 370
Prannath, Mahamat, xxiii, xxiv, 342, 343–45, 347–54, 356–58, 358, 360–68, 370–75
Prashna, 44
Praśnottarāvalī, 93
Pratāparāja, Sābāji, 106
Prayogaratna, 109
Prithvīrāj, 314
Punjab, 161, 162, 177, 205, 368
Purabias, 168
Puri, 197, 274, 275, 281
Pushti Marg, 264–74, 276, 278, 285–87, 319–32, 334–39

Qandahar, 14, 57, 85
Qānūn-i humāyūnī, 5, 8, 14
Qatīl, Islam, 149
"Qatīl," Mīrzā Ḥasan, 139, 147, 148, 149, 151
"Qāyim," Shaikh Muḥammad, 145
Qazwīnī, Sharaf Jahān, 140
Qum, 149
Quran, xvi, 51–52, 347–48, 352, 355–56, 359, 362, 364–65, 374
Qureshi, I.H., 32

Raṅganātha, 123, 126
Raghunātha, 118–19
Rai, Medini, 165
Raisen, 165, 168, 169, 172, 173
Rajasthan, xiii, 174, 197, 233, 234, 235, 236–37, 240, 242, 244, 283, 287, 313, 315, 322, 323, 324, 325, 338, 345, 354, 357, 363–67, 369–70
Rāma, Lord, 73, 76–79, 88
Ramadan, Raja, 162
Rāmānanda, 307, 308, 312–13, 315, 332
Rāmānandī, 239, 284, 291, 292, 305, 306, 312–15
Rāmavinoda, 117, 130
Rāmāyaṇa, 73, 333
Ramnagar, 364
Rām, Rāy Dawlat, 139
Rana Kumbha, 165
Rana Sanga, 165
Ranganathji, Shri, 275
Ras, 350
Rasa bhoga, 219–30
Rathor, Dalpat, 179
Rathor, Raja Jaswant Singh, 178, 180
Rathors, 177, 178, 180, 184, 185, 186
Rāulavela, 256
Rawzat al-munajjimīn, 17
Rāy, Harbans, 153
Rāy, Jot, 114–15, 131
Rāy, Paṇḍit, 112–13, 126
Rāy, Pratāp, 106
Rāy, Rāy Jay Singh, 154
Rāy, Vedāṅga, 121
Razzaq, Shah Abdur, 196
Religious Cultures in Early Modern India, x
Rāfi' al-khilāf, 82
Rightly Guided Caliphs of Islam, 58
Rīg Veda, 52, 69
Risala-i haqnuma, 48
Rizā, Imām, 6, 149, 150
Roḍā's *Rāulavela*, 256
Rumi, Jalal al-Din, 35, 90
Rūpmurārīdās, 331

Safina-yi hindī, xvii, xvii–xviii, 138, 141n14, 144, 145, 146–47, 149–52, 156
Sahajānandāṣṭaka, 259
Saha, Shandip, xxiii, 265
Sakīnat al-awliyā', 38, 71, 77
Saksena, Sītā Rām Kāyasth, 82

Salah al-Din, 169, 172
Samarkand, 125
Samarqandī, Qāẓī Muḥammad Fāẓ il, 6
Sama Veda, 52
Sambhalvāre, Dāmodardās, 327, 330, 337
Saṃskṛta-pārasīka-racanā-bheda-kautuka, 121
Saṃvāda, 69
Sana'i, 41
Sanandh, 358–61, 364, 373
Sandilvī, Debī Dās ibn Bāl Chand, 95
Sanganer, 363
Sarasvatī, Kavīndrācārya, 81, 108, 110–12, 120
Śarmā, Harinārāyaṇ, 257
Śarma, Keśava, 119–21
Śarma, Paramānanda, 127–28
Sārtat, 95
Sarvāṅgayogapradīpikā, 247, 250
Sawāniḥ al-nubuwwat, 154
Selak, 154
Sena, A.C., 279
Sen, Lakhman, 173
Śeosingh, Rāo, 245
Seth, Bhairon, 352–53
Shackle, Christopher, xx
"Shafīq," Lachhmī Narāyan, 138, 141
Shāh, Niẓām, 106–7
Shāh, Farrukh, 92
Shāh, Mubarak, 92
Shāh, Ḥaydar, 74
Shah Jahan, Emperor, xv, 30, 57, 59, 84, 93, 111–13, 115, 119, 121, 124, 127, 128, 131
Shah, Jamal, 162
Shāhjahānābād, 140
Shāh, Mubārak, 92
Shāh-nāma, 11
Shāh, Nānak, 92
Shaktas, xxii, 272, 291–317
Shams Pīr, 246
Shani, cult of, 283
Shankaracharya, 33, 39, 43, 44–46, 48–49, 52, 111, 270
Sharma, Devkrishna, 347
Shatruti, 35
Shaṭṭāriyya Ṣūfī order, 6–7, 20–22
Sheikh, Samira, 196, 228
Shekhawat, Raisal, 178–79
Shibli Nomani, 32
Shiva, 181, 187, 206, 214, 223, 276, 277, 278
Shudras, 272, 361
Shujā', Shāh, 115, 130
Shukla, Ramchandra, xii
Shukoh, Dara, xi, xv–xvi, 30–59, 65–97, 111, 112, 131
Shukoh, Sulaiman, 58
Shustari, Qazi Nurullah, xxi
Siddhāntaśiromaṇi, 124
Siddhāntasindhu, 128, 129
Siddhāntasārvabhauma, 124, 125, 126
Siddhāntatattvaviveka, 125, 126
Silhadi, 165, 167–74, 187
Silsilat al-zahab, 153
Simnani, Sayyid Ashraf Jahangir, 208
Sind, 177, 185, 331, 349, 352, 357
Singh, Rana Bhao, 363
Singh, Dīwālī, 151
Singh, Mahārāṇā Jagat, 113, 322, 338
Singh, Raja Mansingh, 240
Singh, Mīrzā Rāja Nidhi, 154
Singh, Nar, 66
Singh, Maharaja Rāj, 322, 331–32
Singh, Surat, 364
Sirhindi, Shaikh Ahmad, xxi
Sirr-i akbar, 30–31, 33, 38, 41–44, 50, 56–58

Sīsodiyā dynasty, 12
Sisodiyas of Mewar, 165
Siyals, 161
Sketches of the Religious Sects of the Hindus, 90
Solanki, Bhuhad, 185
Sreenivasan, Ramya, xviii, xx, 229
Śrī Gokulnāth ke Caubīs Vacanāmṛta, 323
Śrī Mahāprabhujī kī Nijvārtā, 323
Śrīnāthjī Prākaṭya kī Vārtā, 325, 331–32, 337–38
Śrī Vallabhadigvijaya, 198
Stewart, Tony, 279
Subrahmanyam, Sanjay, xiii, xxiv
Sufi, xii, xiii–xv, xx, xxiii, 4, 6, 19–24, 38, 70–72, 74, 80, 84, 88, 91, 94, 97, 147, 197, 198–200, 205, 208, 210, 212–19, 221, 222, 225, 227–30, 234–37, 246, 251, 256–61, 280, 281, 291, 300, 344, 345, 355–58, 372
Ṣūfī, Mullā Muḥammad, 77
Ṣūfī, Shaikh, 78–83, 95, 97
Sultan Mahmud of Gujarat, 185
Sundardas, Sant, xx, 233–39, 249–56, 258, 260–61, 280–81
Sun of Dharma and the Removal of Error, The, 342
Sur, Sher Shah, 21, 185
Sura al-fatir, 53–54
Sura al-isra, 54
Sura al-waqi'ah, 54
Sura al-qadr, 362
Surat, 321, 353–55
Svami, Parmanand, 198

Tabaqat-i Akbari, 167, 170–71, 173
Tabrīzī, Shams al-Dīn, 94
Tafhīm, 17, 19
Tafsir-i Hussaini, 356, 362
Tājikanīlakaṇṭhī, 117
Talbot, Cynthia, 166
Tandan, Hariharnath, 267
Tānsen, 329
Tantric yoga, 315
Ta'rīkh-i humāyūnī, 5–6
Tariqat al-haqiqat, 39, 48
Thatta, 350, 352, 355
Ṭoḍarānanda, 117
Ṭoḍar Mal, Rājā, 108–10, 117
Tripathi, Shyamsundar, 342
Tristhalīsetu, 109
Trivedi, Pyarelal, 342
Tughluq, Emperor Firūz Shāh, 177, 244
Turk, xxiii, 105, 176, 185, 188, 210, 221–22, 259, 284, 291, 303, 314, 328–29, 330, 373

Udaipur, xxiii, 363, 364
Ujjain, 165, 177, 274, 363–64
'Ulama, 53
Umarkot, 348
Upanishadbhasyas, 44
Upanishads, xv, 30, 33, 42, 44, 45, 48–49, 50, 52, 53, 54, 56, 67, 78–79, 81
Urdu Bazaar, 355, 361–62
Uttar Pradesh, 177

Vacanāmṛta, 323, 326
Vaidya, P.L., 110
Vaishnavism, xiii, xx, xxi, xxii, 40, 138, 141, 180, 217, 219, 221, 227, 267, 269, 272, 274, 275, 276, 278, 281, 282, 284, 286, 287, 344, 349, 350, 352, 357, 369
Vaiṣṇava *sampradāyas*, 243, 244, 272, 352
Vallabha, 197, 198, 199–200, 266–69, 271–72, 274–76, 319–23, 326, 327, 328, 330, 336, 339, 349

Vallabha *sampradaya*, xxi, xxiii, 264–87, 279, 319–39, 353
Vālmīki, 73, 76
Varāhamihira, 18, 130
Vasiṣṭha, 88
Vāsudeva, 127
Vaudeville, Charlotte, 279
Vedanta, xvi
Vedantic Hinduism, xvi, 37, 39
Vedas, 51–52, 106
Vedāntin, 122
Veṅkaṭādhvarin, 104
Vijayanagara, 107
Vīraśaiva ascetics, 300
Vishrant Ghat, 285
Vishnu, 43, 204, 221, 276
Viśvaguṇādarśacampū, 104–8
Viśvanātha temple, 108
Viṭṭhalnāth, 198, 266, 267, 271, 272, 282, 286, 321–24, 328, 331, 333–36, 339
Vritant Muktavali, 371

Waliullah, Shah, xxiv
Wilson, Horace Hayman, 90

Yajur Veda, 52
Yavana, 103–6, 108, 112, 126, 319, 328
Yavanajātaka, 130
Yogavāsiṣṭha, xvi, 39, 52, 68–69, 72–74, 77–78, 80–82, 87
Yogavāsiṣṭhasāra, 78
Yoginis, 181
Yogis, 19–24, 162, 207, 208, 218, 219, 220, 221, 222, 226, 227, 235, 237, 241, 242, 243, 246, 250, 261, 300, 301, 304, 311, 314, 315
Yūsuf u zulaykhā, 153, 155

Zīj-i Shāh Jahānī, 128
Zīj-i Ulugh Beg, 125